DISTRIBUTED OPERATING SYSTEMS

Distributed Operating Systems

Andrew S. Tanenbaum

Vrije Universiteit
Amsterdam, The Netherlands

PRENTICE HALL
ENGLEWOOD CLIFFS, N.J. 07632

Library of Congress Cataloging-in-Publication Data

Tanenbaum, Andrew S.
    Distributed operating systems / Andrew S. Tanenbaum.
       p.   cm.
    Includes bibliographical references and index.
    ISBN 0-13-219908-4
    1. Distributed operating systems (Computers)   I. Title.
QA76.76.063T357 1995
005.4'4--dc20   94-27646
                                                                    CIP

Acquisitions Editor: Bill Zobrist
Production Supervisor: Joe Scordato
Cover Designer: DeLuca Design
Buyer: Linda Behrens
Supplements Editor: Alice Dworkin
Interior Designer: Andrew S. Tanenbaum

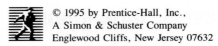

© 1995 by Prentice-Hall, Inc.,
A Simon & Schuster Company
Englewood Cliffs, New Jersey 07632

Printed in the United States of America

10 9 8 7 6 5 4 3 2 1

ISBN 0-13-219908-4

Prentice-Hall International (UK) Limited, *London*
Prentice-Hall of Australia Pty. Limited, *Sydney*
Prentice-Hall of Canada, Inc., *Toronto*
Prentice-Hall Hispanoamericana, S.A., *Mexico*
Prentice-Hall of India Private Limited, *New Delhi*
Prentice-Hall of Japan, Inc., *Tokyo*
Simon & Schuster Asia Pte. Ltd., *Singapore*
Editora Prentice-Hall Do Brazil, Ltda., *Rio de Janeiro*

To Suzanne, Barbara, Marvin, and Little Bram

Contents

PREFACE   **xvi**

1 INTRODUCTION TO DISTRIBUTED SYSTEMS   **1**

1.1 WHAT IS A DISTRIBUTED SYSTEM?   2
1.2 GOALS   3
    1.2.1 Advantages of Distributed Systems over Centralized Systems   3
    1.2.2 Advantages of Distributed Systems over Independent PCs   6
    1.2.3 Disadvantages of Distributed Systems   6
1.3 HARDWARE CONCEPTS   8
    1.3.1 Bus-Based Multiprocessors   10
    1.3.2 Switched Multiprocessors   12
    1.3.3 Bus-Based Multicomputers   13
    1.3.4 Switched Multicomputers   14
1.4 SOFTWARE CONCEPTS   15
    1.4.1 Network Operating Systems   16
    1.4.2 True Distributed Systems   18
    1.4.3 Multiprocessor Timesharing Systems   20
1.5 DESIGN ISSUES   22
    1.5.1 Transparency   22
    1.5.2 Flexibility   25
    1.5.3 Reliability   27
    1.5.4 Performance   28
    1.5.5 Scalability   29
1.6 SUMMARY   31

2 COMMUNICATION IN DISTRIBUTED SYSTEMS   34

2.1 LAYERED PROTOCOLS 35
    2.1.1 The Physical Layer 38
    2.1.2 The Data Link Layer 38
    2.1.3 The Network Layer 40
    2.1.4 The Transport Layer 40
    2.1.5 The Session Layer 41
    2.1.6 The Presentation Layer 41
    2.1.7 The Application Layer 42

2.2 ASYNCHRONOUS TRANSFER MODE NETWORKS 42
    2.2.1 What Is Asynchronous Transfer Mode? 42
    2.2.2 The ATM Physical Layer 44
    2.2.3 The ATM Layer 45
    2.2.4 The ATM Adaptation Layer 46
    2.2.5 ATM Switching 47
    2.2.6 Some Implications of ATM for Distributed Systems 49

2.3 THE CLIENT-SERVER MODEL 50
    2.3.1 Clients and Servers 51
    2.3.2 An Example Client and Server 52
    2.3.3 Addressing 56
    2.3.4 Blocking versus Nonblocking Primitives 58
    2.3.5 Buffered versus Unbuffered Primitives 61
    2.3.6 Reliable versus Unreliable Primitives 63
    2.3.7 Implementing the Client-Server Model 65

2.4 REMOTE PROCEDURE CALL 68
    2.4.1 Basic RPC Operation 68
    2.4.2 Parameter Passing 72
    2.4.3 Dynamic Binding 77
    2.4.4 RPC Semantics in the Presence of Failures 80
    2.4.5 Implementation Issues 84
    2.4.6 Problem Areas 95

2.5 GROUP COMMUNICATION 99
    2.5.1 Introduction to Group Communication 99
    2.5.2 Design Issues 101
    2.5.3 Group Communication in ISIS 110

2.6 SUMMARY 114

3 SYNCHRONIZATION IN DISTRIBUTED SYSTEMS   118

   3.1 CLOCK SYNCHRONIZATION   119
       3.1.1 Logical Clocks   120
       3.1.2 Physical Clocks   124
       3.1.3 Clock Synchronization Algorithms   127
       3.1.4 Use of Synchronized Clocks   132
   3.2 MUTUAL EXCLUSION   134
       3.2.1 A Centralized Algorithm   134
       3.2.2 A Distributed Algorithm   135
       3.2.3 A Token Ring Algorithm   138
       3.2.4 A Comparison of the Three Algorithms   139
   3.3 ELECTION ALGORITHMS   140
       3.3.1 The Bully Algorithm   141
       3.3.2 A Ring Algorithm   143
   3.4 ATOMIC TRANSACTIONS   144
       3.4.1 Introduction to Atomic Transactions   144
       3.4.2 The Transaction Model   145
       3.4.3 Implementation   150
       3.4.4 Concurrency Control   154
   3.5 DEADLOCKS IN DISTRIBUTED SYSTEMS   158
       3.5.1 Distributed Deadlock Detection   159
       3.5.2 Distributed Deadlock Prevention   163
   3.6 SUMMARY   165

4 PROCESSES AND PROCESSORS IN DISTRIBUTED SYSTEMS   169

   4.1 THREADS   169
       4.1.1 Introduction to Threads   170
       4.1.2 Thread Usage   171
       4.1.3 Design Issues for Threads Packages   174
       4.1.4 Implementing a Threads Package   178
       4.1.5 Threads and RPC   184
   4.2 SYSTEM MODELS   186
       4.2.1 The Workstation Model   186
       4.2.2 Using Idle Workstations   189
       4.2.3 The Processor Pool Model   193
       4.2.4 A Hybrid Model   197
   4.3 PROCESSOR ALLOCATION   197
       4.3.1 Allocation Models   197

4.3.2 Design Issues for Processor Allocation Algorithms   199

4.3.3 Implementation Issues for Processor Allocation Algorithms   201

4.3.4 Example Processor Allocation Algorithms   203

4.4 SCHEDULING IN DISTRIBUTED SYSTEMS   210

4.5 FAULT TOLERANCE   212

4.5.1 Component Faults   212

4.5.2 System Failures   213

4.5.3 Synchronous versus Asynchronous Systems 214

4.5.4 Use of Redundancy   214

4.5.5 Fault Tolerance Using Active Replication   215

4.5.6 Fault Tolerance Using Primary-Backup   217

4.5.7 Agreement in Faulty Systems   219

4.6 REAL-TIME DISTRIBUTED SYSTEMS   223

4.6.1 What Is a Real-Time System?   223

4.6.2 Design Issues   226

4.6.3 Real-Time Communication   230

4.6.4 Real-Time Scheduling   234

4.7 SUMMARY   240

5   DISTRIBUTED FILE SYSTEMS   **245**

5.1 DISTRIBUTED FILE SYSTEM DESIGN   246

5.1.1 The File Service Interface   246

5.1.2 The Directory Server Interface   248

5.1.3 Semantics of File Sharing   253

5.2 DISTRIBUTED FILE SYSTEM IMPLEMENTATION   256

5.2.1 File Usage   256

5.2.2 System Structure   258

5.2.3 Caching   262

5.2.4 Replication   268

5.2.5 An Example: Sun's Network File System   272

5.2.6 Lessons Learned   278

5.3 TRENDS IN DISTRIBUTED FILE SYSTEMS   279

5.3.1 New Hardware   280

5.3.2 Scalability   282

5.3.3 Wide Area Networking   283

5.3.4 Mobile Users   284

5.3.5 Fault Tolerance   284

5.3.6 Multimedia   285

5.4 SUMMARY   285

6 DISTRIBUTED SHARED MEMORY   289

6.1 INTRODUCTION 290
6.2 WHAT IS SHARED MEMORY? 292
    6.2.1 On-Chip Memory 293
    6.2.2 Bus-Based Multiprocessors 293
    6.2.3 Ring-Based Multiprocessors 298
    6.2.4 Switched Multiprocessors 301
    6.2.5 NUMA Multiprocessors 308
    6.2.6 Comparison of Shared Memory Systems 312
6.3 CONSISTENCY MODELS 315
    6.3.1 Strict Consistency 315
    6.3.2 Sequential Consistency 317
    6.3.3 Causal Consistency 321
    6.3.4 PRAM Consistency and Processor Consistency 322
    6.3.5 Weak Consistency 325
    6.3.6 Release Consistency 327
    6.3.7 Entry Consistency 330
    6.3.8 Summary of Consistency Models 331
6.4 PAGE-BASED DISTRIBUTED SHARED MEMORY 333
    6.4.1 Basic Design 334
    6.4.2 Replication 334
    6.4.3 Granularity 336
    6.4.4 Achieving Sequential Consistency 337
    6.4.5 Finding the Owner 339
    6.4.6 Finding the Copies 342
    6.4.7 Page Replacement 343
    6.4.8 Synchronization 344
6.5 SHARED-VARIABLE DISTRIBUTED SHARED MEMORY 345
    6.5.1 Munin 346
    6.5.2 Midway 353
6.6 OBJECT-BASED DISTRIBUTED SHARED MEMORY 356
    6.6.1 Objects 356
    6.6.2 Linda 358
    6.6.3 Orca 365
6.7 COMPARISON 371
6.8 SUMMARY 372

7 **CASE STUDY 1: AMOEBA** **376**

7.1 INTRODUCTION TO AMOEBA 376
    7.1.1 History of Amoeba 376
    7.1.2 Research Goals 377
    7.1.3 The Amoeba System Architecture 378
    7.1.4 The Amoeba Microkernel 380
    7.1.5 The Amoeba Servers 382
7.2 OBJECTS AND CAPABILITIES IN AMOEBA 384
    7.2.1 Capabilities 384
    7.2.2 Object Protection 385
    7.2.3 Standard Operations 387
7.3 PROCESS MANAGEMENT IN AMOEBA 388
    7.3.1 Processes 388
    7.3.2 Threads 391
7.4 MEMORY MANAGEMENT IN AMOEBA 392
    7.4.1 Segments 392
    7.4.2 Mapped Segments 393
7.5 COMMUNICATION IN AMOEBA 393
    7.5.1 Remote Procedure Call 394
    7.5.2 Group Communication in Amoeba 398
    7.5.3 The Fast Local Internet Protocol 407
7.6 THE AMOEBA SERVERS 415
    7.6.1 The Bullet Server 415
    7.6.2 The Directory Server 420
    7.6.3 The Replication Server 425
    7.6.4 The Run Server 425
    7.6.5 The Boot Server 427
    7.6.6 The TCP/IP Server 427
    7.6.7 Other Servers 428
7.7 SUMMARY 428

8 **CASE STUDY 2: MACH** **431**

8.1 INTRODUCTION TO MACH 431
    8.1.1 History of Mach 431
    8.1.2 Goals of Mach 433
    8.1.3 The Mach Microkernel 433
    8.1.4 The Mach BSD UNIX Server 435

8.2 PROCESS MANAGEMENT IN MACH 436
    8.2.1 Processes 436
    8.2.2 Threads 439
    8.2.3 Scheduling 442
8.3 MEMORY MANAGEMENT IN MACH 445
    8.3.1 Virtual Memory 446
    8.3.2 Memory Sharing 449
    8.3.3 External Memory Managers 452
    8.3.4 Distributed Shared Memory in Mach 456
8.4 COMMUNICATION IN MACH 457
    8.4.1 Ports 457
    8.4.2 Sending and Receiving Messages 464
    8.4.3 The Network Message Server 469
8.5 UNIX EMULATION IN MACH 471
8.6 SUMMARY 472

9 CASE STUDY 3: CHORUS   **475**

9.1 INTRODUCTION TO CHORUS 475
    9.1.1 History of Chorus 476
    9.1.2 Goals of Chorus 477
    9.1.3 System Structure 478
    9.1.4 Kernel Abstractions 479
    9.1.5 Kernel Structure 481
    9.1.6 The UNIX Subsystem 483
    9.1.7 The Object-Oriented Subsystem 483
9.2 PROCESS MANAGEMENT IN CHORUS 483
    9.2.1 Processes 484
    9.2.2 Threads 485
    9.2.3 Scheduling 486
    9.2.4 Traps, Exceptions, and Interrupts 487
    9.2.5 Kernel Calls for Process Management 488
9.3 MEMORY MANAGEMENT IN CHORUS 490
    9.3.1 Regions and Segments 490
    9.3.2 Mappers 491
    9.3.3 Distributed Shared Memory 492
    9.3.4 Kernel Calls for Memory Management 493

9.4 COMMUNICATON IN CHORUS 495
   9.4.1 Messages 495
   9.4.2 Ports 495
   9.4.3 Communication Operations 496
   9.4.4 Kernel Calls for Communication 498
9.5 UNIX EMULATION IN CHORUS 499
   9.5.1 Structure of a UNIX Process 500
   9.5.2 Extensions to UNIX 500
   9.5.3 Implementation of UNIX on Chorus 501
9.6 COOL: AN OBJECT-ORIENTED SUBSYSTEM 507
   9.6.1 The COOL Architecture 507
   9.6.2 The COOL Base Layer 507
   9.6.3 The COOL Generic Runtime System 509
   9.6.4 The Language Runtime System 509
   9.6.5 Implementation of COOL 510
9.7 COMPARISON OF AMOEBA, MACH, AND CHORUS 510
   9.7.1 Philosophy 511
   9.7.2 Objects 512
   9.7.3 Processes 513
   9.7.4 Memory Model 514
   9.7.5 Communication 515
   9.7.6 Servers 516
9.8 SUMMARY 517

10 CASE STUDY 4: DCE   **520**
10.1 INTRODUCTION TO DCE 520
   10.1.1 History of DCE 520
   10.1.2 Goals of DCE 521
   10.1.3 DCE Components 522
   10.1.4 Cells 525
10.2 THREADS 527
   10.2.1 Introduction to DCE Threads 527
   10.2.2 Scheduling 529
   10.2.3 Synchronization 530
   10.2.4 Thread Calls 531
10.3 REMOTE PROCEDURE CALL 535
   10.3.1 Goals of DCE RPC 535
   10.3.2 Writing a Client and a Server 536
   10.3.3 Binding a Client to a Server 538
   10.3.4 Performing an RPC 539

10.4 TIME SERVICE   540
    10.4.1 DTS Time Model   541
    10.4.2 DTS Implementation   543
10.5 DIRECTORY SERVICE   544
    10.5.1 Names   546
    10.5.2 The Cell Directory Service   547
    10.5.3 The Global Directory Service   549
10.6 SECURITY SERVICE   554
    10.6.1 Security Model   555
    10.6.2 Security Components   557
    10.6.3 Tickets and Authenticators   558
    10.6.4 Authenticated RPC   559
    10.6.5 ACLs   562
10.7 DISTRIBUTED FILE SYSTEM   564
    10.7.1 DFS Interface   565
    10.7.2 DFS Components in the Server Kernel   566
    10.7.3 DFS Components in the Client Kernel   569
    10.7.4 DFS Components in User Space   571
10.8 SUMMARY   573

11 BIBLIOGRAPHY AND SUGGESTED READINGS   **577**

11.1 SUGGESTED READINGS   577
11.2 ALPHABETICAL BIBLIOGRAPHY   584

INDEX   **603**

Preface

With the publication of *Distributed Operating Systems* I have now completed my trilogy on operating systems. The three volumes of this trilogy are:

- *Operating Systems: Design and Implementation*
- *Distributed Operating Systems*
- *Modern Operating Systems*

The three volumes are not completely independent, however. For schools having a two-course sequence in operating systems (or an undergraduate course plus a graduate course), one possible choice is to use *Operating Systems: Design and Implementation* in the first course and *Distributed Operating Systems* in the second one.

The former book treats the standard principles of single-processor systems, including processes, synchronization, I/O, deadlocks, memory management, file systems, security, and so on. It also illustrates these principles in great detail through the use of MINIX, a UNIX-clone whose source listing is given in an appendix. MINIX is available on diskette from Prentice Hall for the IBM PC (8088 and up), Atari, Amiga, Macintosh, and SPARC processors.

The latter book (this one), covers distributed operating systems in detail, including communication, synchronization, processes, file systems, and memory management, but this time in the context of distributed systems. Four examples of distributed systems are given in great detail: Amoeba, Mach, Chorus, and DCE. Amoeba is available for free to universities for educational use. It runs on the Intel 386/486, SPARC, and Sun 3 processors. For information on how to obtain Amoeba please FTP the file *amoeba/Intro.ps.Z* from *ftp.cs.vu.nl* or contact the author by electronic mail at *ast@cs.vu.nl*. Potential users should be forewarned that Amoeba is considerably more complex than MINIX: the documentation alone (available by FTP), runs to well over 1000 pages and the system requires at least five large machines and an Ethernet to run well.

By studying these two books in sequence and using both MINIX and Amoeba, students will obtain a thorough knowledge of the principles and practice of both single-processor and distributed operating systems. Now that the trilogy is completed, I plan to revise MINIX and the book describing it.

For universities or computer professionals with less time available, *Modern Operating Systems* can be thought of as a condensed version of the other two books. It provides an introduction to the principles of both single-processor and distributed operating systems, but without the detailed example of MINIX. It also omits many of the advanced topics present in this book, including an introduction to ATM, fault-tolerant distributed systems, real time distributed systems, distributed shared memory, Chorus, DCE, and other topics. In all, about 230 pages of material on distributed systems present in this book have been omitted from *Modern Operating Systems*.

Many people have helped me with this book. I would especially like to thank the following people for reading portions of the manuscript and giving me many useful suggestions for improvement: Irina Athanasiu, Henri Bal, Saniya Ben Hassen, David Black, John Carter, Randall Dean, Wiebren de Jonge, John Dugas, Dick Grune, Anoop Gupta, Frans Kaashoek, Marcus Koebler, Hermann Kopetz, Ed Lazowska, Dan Lenoski, Kai Li, Marc Maathuis, David Mosberger, Douglas Orr, Craig Partridge, Carlton Pu, Marc Rozier, Rich Salz, Mike Schroeder, Karsten Schwan, Greg Sharp, Dennis Shasha, Sol Shatz, Jennifer Steiner, Chuck Thacker, John Turek, Walt Tuvell, Leendert van Doorn, Robbert van Renesse, Kees Verstoep, Ellen Zegura, Willy Zwaenpoel, and the anonymous reviewers. My editor, Bill Zobrist, put up with my attempts to get everything perfect with nary a whimper.

Despite all this help, no doubt some errors remain. That seems to be inevitable, no matter how many people read the manuscript. People who wish to report errors should contact me by electronic mail.

Finally, I would like to thank Suzanne again. After eight books, she knows the implications of another one, but her patience and love are boundless. I also want to thank Barbara and Marvin for using their computers and leaving mine alone (except for the printer). Teaching them how to use PC word processing programs has made me appreciate *troff* more than ever. Finally, I would like to thank Little Bram for being quiet while I was writing.

Andrew S. Tanenbaum

1

Introduction to Distributed Systems

Computer systems are undergoing a revolution. From 1945, when the modern computer era began, until about 1985, computers were large and expensive. Even minicomputers normally cost tens of thousands of dollars each. As a result, most organizations had only a handful of computers, and for lack of a way to connect them, these operated independently from one another.

Starting in the mid-1980s, however, two advances in technology began to change that situation. The first was the development of powerful microprocessors. Initially, these were 8-bit machines, but soon 16-, 32-, and even 64-bit CPUs became common. Many of these had the computing power of a decent-sized mainframe (i.e., large) computer, but for a fraction of the price.

The amount of improvement that has occurred in computer technology in the past half century is truly staggering and totally unprecedented in other industries. From a machine that cost 10 million dollars and executed 1 instruction per second, we have come to machines that cost 1000 dollars and execute 10 million instructions per second, a price/performance gain of 10^{11}. If cars had improved at this rate in the same time period, a Rolls Royce would now cost 10 dollars and get a billion miles per gallon. (Unfortunately, it would probably also have a 200-page manual telling how to open the door.)

The second development was the invention of high-speed computer networks. The **local area networks** or **LANs** allow dozens, or even hundreds, of machines within a building to be connected in such a way that small amounts of information can be transferred between machines in a millisecond or so. Larger amounts of data can be moved between machines at rates of 10 to 100 million bits/sec and sometimes more. The **wide area networks** or **WANs** allow millions of machines all over the earth to be connected at speeds varying from 64 Kbps (kilobits per second) to gigabits per second for some advanced experimental networks.

The result of these technologies is that it is now not only feasible, but easy, to put together computing systems composed of large numbers of CPUs connected by a high-speed network. They are usually called **distributed systems,** in contrast to the previous **centralized systems** (or **single-processor systems**) consisting of a single CPU, its memory, peripherals, and some terminals.

There is only one fly in the ointment: software. Distributed systems need radically different software than centralized systems do. In particular, the necessary operating systems are only beginning to emerge. The first few steps have been taken, but there is still a long way to go. Nevertheless, enough is already known about these distributed operating systems that we can present the basic ideas. The rest of this book is devoted to studying concepts, implementation, and examples of distributed operating systems.

1.1. WHAT IS A DISTRIBUTED SYSTEM?

Various definitions of distributed systems have been given in the literature, none of them satisfactory and none of them in agreement with any of the others. For our purposes it is sufficient to give a loose characterization:

> *A distributed system is a collection of independent computers*
> *that appear to the users of the system as a single computer.*

This definition has two aspects. The first one deals with hardware: the machines are autonomous. The second one deals with software: the users think of the system as a single computer. Both are essential. We will come back to these points later in this chapter, after going over some background material on both the hardware and the software.

Rather than going further with definitions, it is probably more helpful to give several examples of distributed systems. As a first example, consider a network of workstations in a university or company department. In addition to each user's personal workstation, there might be a pool of processors in the machine room that are not assigned to specific users but are allocated dynamically as needed. Such a system might have a single file system, with all files accessible from all machines in the same way and using the same path name. Furthermore, when a user typed a command, the system could look for the best place to execute that command, possibly on the user's own workstation, possibly on an idle workstation belonging to someone else, and possibly on one of the unassigned processors in the machine room. If the system as a whole looked and acted like a classical single-processor timesharing system, it would qualify as a distributed system.

As a second example, consider a factory full of robots, each containing a powerful computer for handling vision, planning, communication, and other tasks. When a robot on the assembly line notices that a part it is supposed to install is defective, it asks another robot in the parts department to bring it a replacement. If all the robots act like peripheral devices attached to the same central computer and the system can be programmed that way, it too counts as a distributed system.

As a final example, think about a large bank with hundreds of branch offices all over the world. Each office has a master computer to store local accounts and handle local transactions. In addition, each computer has the ability to talk to all other branch computers and with a central computer at headquarters. If transactions can be done without regard to where a customer or account is, and the users do not notice any difference between this system and the old centralized mainframe that it replaced, it too would be considered a distributed system.

1.2. GOALS

Just because it is possible to build distributed systems does not necessarily mean that it is a good idea. After all, with current technology it is possible to put four floppy disk drives on a personal computer. It is just that doing so would be pointless. In this section we will discuss the motivation and goals of typical distributed systems and look at their advantages and disadvantages compared to traditional centralized systems.

1.2.1. Advantages of Distributed Systems over Centralized Systems

The real driving force behind the trend toward decentralization is economics. A quarter of a century ago, computer pundit and gadfly Herb Grosch stated what later came to be known as Grosch's law: The computing power of a CPU is proportional to the square of its price. By paying twice as much, you could get four times the performance. This observation fit the mainframe technology of its time quite well, and led most organizations to buy the largest single machine they could afford.

With microprocessor technology, Grosch's law no longer holds. For a few hundred dollars you can get a CPU chip that can execute more instructions per second than one of the largest 1980s mainframes. If you are willing to pay twice as much, you get the same CPU, but running at a somewhat higher clock speed.

As a result, the most cost-effective solution is frequently to harness a large number of cheap CPUs together in a system. Thus the leading reason for the trend toward distributed systems is that these systems potentially have a much better price/performance ratio than a single large centralized system would have. In effect, a distributed system gives more bang for the buck.

A slight variation on this theme is the observation that a collection of microprocessors cannot only give a better price/performance ratio than a single mainframe, but may yield an absolute performance that no mainframe can achieve at any price. For example, with current technology it is possible to build a system from 10,000 modern CPU chips, each of which runs at 50 MIPS (Millions of Instructions Per Second), for a total performance of 500,000 MIPS. For a single processor (i.e., CPU) to achieve this, it would have to execute an instruction in 0.002 nsec (2 picosec). No existing machine even comes close to this, and both theoretical and engineering considerations make it unlikely that any machine ever will. Theoretically, Einstein's theory of relativity dictates that nothing can travel faster than light, which can cover only 0.6 mm in 2 picosec. Practically, a computer of that speed fully contained in a 0.6-mm cube would generate so much heat that it would melt instantly. Thus whether the goal is normal performance at low cost or extremely high performance at greater cost, distributed systems have much to offer.

As an aside, some authors make a distinction between *distributed systems*, which are designed to allow many users to work together, and *parallel systems*, whose only goal is to achieve maximum speedup on a single problem, as our 500,000-MIPS machine might. We believe that this distinction is difficult to maintain because the design spectrum is really a continuum. We prefer to use the term "distributed system" in the broadest sense to denote any system in which multiple interconnected CPUs work together.

A next reason for building a distributed system is that some applications are inherently distributed. A supermarket chain might have many stores, each of which gets goods delivered locally (possibly from local farms), makes local sales, and makes local decisions about which vegetables are so old or rotten that they must be thrown out. It therefore makes sense to keep track of inventory at each store on a local computer rather than centrally at corporate headquarters. After all, most queries and updates will be done locally. Nevertheless, from time to time, top management may want to find out how many rutabagas it currently owns. One way to accomplish this goal is to make the complete system look like a single computer to the application programs, but implement decentrally, with one computer per store as we have described. This would then be a commercial distributed system.

Another inherently distributed system is what is often called **computer-supported cooperative work**, in which a group of people, located far from each other, are working together, for example, to produce a joint report. Given the long term trends in the computer industry, one can easily imagine a whole new area, **computer-supported cooperative games**, in which players at different locations play against each other in real time. One can imagine electronic hide-and-seek in a big multidimensional maze, and even electronic dogfights with each player using a local flight simulator to try to shoot down the other players, with each player's screen showing the view out of the player's plane, including other planes that fly within visual range.

Another potential advantage of a distributed system over a centralized system is higher reliability. By distributing the workload over many machines, a single chip failure will bring down at most one machine, leaving the rest intact. Ideally, if 5 percent of the machines are down at any moment, the system should be able to continue to work with a 5 percent loss in performance. For critical applications, such as control of nuclear reactors or aircraft, using a distributed system to achieve high reliability may be the dominant consideration.

Finally, incremental growth is also potentially a big plus. Often, a company will buy a mainframe with the intention of doing all its work on it. If the company prospers and the workload grows, at a certain point the mainframe will no longer be adequate. The only solutions are either to replace the mainframe with a larger one (if it exists) or to add a second mainframe. Both of these can wreak major havoc on the company's operations. In contrast, with a distributed system, it may be possible simply to add more processors to the system, thus allowing it to expand gradually as the need arises. These advantages are summarized in Fig. 1-1.

Item	Description
Economics	Microprocessors offer a better price/performance than mainframes
Speed	A distributed system may have more total computing power than a mainframe
Inherent distribution	Some applications involve spatially separated machines
Reliability	If one machine crashes, the system as a whole can still survive
Incremental growth	Computing power can be added in small increments

Fig. 1-1. Advantages of distributed systems over centralized systems.

In the long term, the main driving force will be the existence of large numbers of personal computers and the need for people to work together and share information in a convenient way without being bothered by geography or the physical distribution of people, data, and machines.

1.2.2. Advantages of Distributed Systems over Independent PCs

Given that microprocessors are a cost-effective way to do business, why not just give everyone his† own PC and let people work independently? For one thing, many users need to share data. For example, airline reservation clerks need access to the master data base of flights and existing reservations. Giving each clerk his own private copy of the entire data base would not work, since nobody would know which seats the other clerks had already sold. Shared data are absolutely essential to this and many other applications, so the machines must be interconnected. Interconnecting the machines leads to a distributed system.

Sharing often involves more than just data. Expensive peripherals, such as color laser printers, phototypesetters, and massive archival storage devices (e.g., optical jukeboxes), are also candidates.

A third reason to connect a group of isolated computers into a distributed system is to achieve enhanced person-to-person communication. For many people, electronic mail has numerous attractions over paper mail, telephone, and FAX. It is much faster than paper mail, does not require both parties to be available at the same time as does the telephone, and unlike FAX, produces documents that can be edited, rearranged, stored in the computer, and manipulated with text processing programs.

Finally, a distributed system is potentially more flexible than giving each user an isolated personal computer. Although one model is to give each person a personal computer and connect them all with a LAN, this is not the only possibility. Another one is to have a mixture of personal and shared computers, perhaps of different sizes, and let jobs run on the most appropriate one, rather than always on the owner's machine. In this way, the workload can be spread over the computers more effectively, and the loss of a few machines may be compensated for by letting people run their jobs elsewhere. Figure 1-2 summarizes these points.

1.2.3. Disadvantages of Distributed Systems

Although distributed systems have their strengths, they also have their weaknesses. In this section, we will point out a few of them. We have already hinted at the worst problem: software. With the current state-of-the-art, we do not have much experience in designing, implementing, and using distributed software. What kinds of operating systems, programming languages, and applications are appropriate for these systems? How much should the users know

---

† Please read "his" as "his or hers" throughout this book.

Item	Description
Data sharing	Allow many users access to a common data base
Device sharing	Allow many users to share expensive peripherals like color printers
Communication	Make human-to-human communication easier, for example, by electronic mail
Flexibility	Spread the workload over the available machines in the most cost effective way

Fig. 1-2. Advantages of distributed systems over isolated (personal) computers.

about the distribution? How much should the system do and how much should the users do? The experts differ (not that this is unusual with experts, but when it comes to distributed systems, they are barely on speaking terms). As more research is done, this problem will diminish, but for the moment it should not be underestimated.

A second potential problem is due to the communication network. It can lose messages, which requires special software to be able to recover, and it can become overloaded. When the network saturates, it must either be replaced or a second one must be added. In both cases, some portion of one or more buildings may have to be rewired at great expense, or network interface boards may have to be replaced (e.g., by fiber optics). Once the system comes to depend on the network, its loss or saturation can negate most of the advantages the distributed system was built to achieve.

Finally, the easy sharing of data, which we described above as an advantage, may turn out to be a two-edged sword. If people can conveniently access data all over the system, they may equally be able to conveniently access data that they have no business looking at. In other words, security is often a problem. For data that must be kept secret at all costs, it is often preferable to have a dedicated, isolated personal computer that has no network connections to any other machines, and is kept in a locked room with a secure safe in which all the floppy disks are stored. The disadvantages of distributed systems are summarized in Fig. 1-3.

Despite these potential problems, many people feel that the advantages outweigh the disadvantages, and it is expected that distributed systems will become increasingly important in the coming years. In fact, it is likely that within a few years, most organizations will connect most of their computers into large distributed systems to provide better, cheaper, and more convenient service for the users. An isolated computer in a medium-sized or large business or other organization will probably not even exist in ten years.

Item	Description
Software	Little software exists at present for distributed systems
Networking	The network can saturate or cause other problems
Security.	Easy access also applies to secret data

Fig. 1-3. Disadvantages of distributed systems.

1.3. HARDWARE CONCEPTS

Even though all distributed systems consist of multiple CPUs, there are several different ways the hardware can be organized, especially in terms of how they are interconnected and how they communicate. In this section we will take a brief look at distributed system hardware, in particular, how the machines are connected together. In the next section we will examine some of the software issues related to distributed systems.

Various classification schemes for multiple CPU computer systems have been proposed over the years, but none of them have really caught on and been widely adopted. Probably the most frequently cited taxonomy is Flynn's (1972), although it is fairly rudimentary. Flynn picked two characteristics that he considered essential: the number of instruction streams and the number of data streams. A computer with a single instruction stream and a single data stream is called SISD. All traditional uniprocessor computers (i.e., those having only one CPU) fall in this category, from personal computers to large mainframes.

The next category is SIMD, single instruction stream, multiple data stream. This type refers to array processors with one instruction unit that fetches an instruction, and then commands many data units to carry it out in parallel, each with its own data. These machines are useful for computations that repeat the same calculation on many sets of data, for example, adding up all the elements of 64 independent vectors. Some supercomputers are SIMD.

The next category is MISD, multiple instruction stream, single data stream. No known computers fit this model. Finally, comes MIMD, which essentially means a group of independent computers, each with its own program counter, program, and data. All distributed systems are MIMD, so this classification system is not tremendously useful for our purposes.

Although Flynn stopped here, we will go further. In Fig. 1-4, we divide all MIMD computers into two groups: those that have shared memory, usually called **multiprocessors**, and those that do not, sometimes called **multicomputers**. The essential difference is this: in a multiprocessor, there is a single virtual address space that is shared by all CPUs. If any CPU writes, for example, the value 44 to address 1000, any other CPU subsequently reading from *its* address 1000 will get the value 44. All the machines share the same memory.

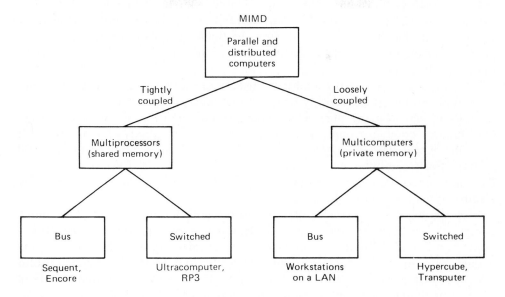

Fig. 1-4. A taxonomy of parallel and distributed computer systems.

In contrast, in a multicomputer, every machine has its own private memory. If one CPU writes the value 44 to address 1000, when another CPU reads address 1000 it will get whatever value was there before. The write of 44 does not affect *its* memory at all. A common example of a multicomputer is a collection of personal computers connected by a network.

Each of these categories can be further divided based on the architecture of the interconnection network. In Fig. 1-4 we describe these two categories as **bus** and **switched**. By bus we mean that there is a single network, backplane, bus, cable, or other medium that connects all the machines. Cable television uses a scheme like this: the cable company runs a wire down the street, and all the subscribers have taps running to it from their television sets.

Switched systems do not have a single backbone like cable television. Instead, there are individual wires from machine to machine, with many different wiring patterns in use. Messages move along the wires, with an explicit switching decision made at each step to route the message along one of the outgoing wires. The worldwide public telephone system is organized in this way.

Another dimension to our taxonomy is that in some systems the machines are **tightly coupled** and in others they are **loosely coupled**. In a tightly-coupled system, the delay experienced when a message is sent from one computer to another is short, and the data rate is high; that is, the number of bits per second that can be transferred is large. In a loosely-coupled system, the opposite is true: the intermachine message delay is large and the data rate is low. For example, two CPU chips on the same printed circuit board and connected by wires etched onto the board are likely to be tightly coupled, whereas two computers connected by a 2400 bit/sec modem over the telephone system are certain to be loosely coupled.

Tightly-coupled systems tend to be used more as parallel systems (working on a single problem) and loosely-coupled ones tend to be used as distributed systems (working on many unrelated problems), although this is not always true. One famous counterexample is a project in which hundreds of computers all over the world worked together trying to factor a huge number (about 100 digits). Each computer was assigned a different range of divisors to try, and they all worked on the problem in their spare time, reporting the results back by electronic mail when they finished.

On the whole, multiprocessors tend to be more tightly coupled than multi-computers, because they can exchange data at memory speeds, but some fiber-optic based multicomputers can also work at memory speeds. Despite the vagueness of the terms "tightly coupled" and "loosely coupled," they are useful concepts, just as saying "Jack is fat and Jill is thin" conveys information about girth even though one can get into a fair amount of discussion about the concepts of "fatness" and "thinness."

In the following four sections, we will look at the four categories of Fig. 1-4 in more detail, namely bus multiprocessors, switched multiprocessors, bus multicomputers, and switched multicomputers. Although these topics are not directly related to our main concern, distributed operating systems, they will shed some light on the subject because as we shall see, different categories of machines use different kinds of operating systems.

1.3.1. Bus-Based Multiprocessors

Bus-based multiprocessors consist of some number of CPUs all connected to a common bus, along with a memory module. A simple configuration is to have a high-speed backplane or motherboard into which CPU and memory cards can be inserted. A typical bus has 32 or 64 address lines, 32 or 64 data lines, and perhaps 32 or more control lines, all of which operate in parallel. To read a word of memory, a CPU puts the address of the word it wants on the bus address lines, then puts a signal on the appropriate control lines to indicate that it wants to read. The memory responds by putting the value of the word on the data lines to allow the requesting CPU to read it in. Writes work in a similar way.

Since there is only one memory, if CPU *A* writes a word to memory and then CPU *B* reads that word back a microsecond later, *B* will get the value just written. A memory that has this property is said to be **coherent**. Coherence plays an important role in distributed operating systems in a variety of ways that we will study later.

The problem with this scheme is that with as few as 4 or 5 CPUs, the bus will usually be overloaded and performance will drop drastically. The solution is to add a high-speed **cache memory** between the CPU and the bus, as shown in Fig. 1-5. The cache holds the most recently accessed words. All memory requests go through the cache. If the word requested is in the cache, the cache itself responds to the CPU, and no bus request is made. If the cache is large enough, the probability of success, called the **hit rate**, will be high, and the amount of bus traffic per CPU will drop dramatically, allowing many more CPUs in the system. Cache sizes of 64K to 1M are common, which often gives a hit rate of 90 percent or more.

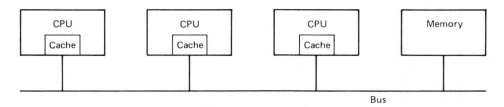

Fig. 1-5. A bus-based multiprocessor.

However, the introduction of caches also brings a serious problem with it. Suppose that two CPUs, *A* and *B*, each read the same word into their respective caches. Then *A* overwrites the word. When *B* next reads that word, it gets the old value from its cache, not the value *A* just wrote. The memory is now incoherent, and the system is difficult to program.

Many researchers have studied this problem, and various solutions are known. Below we will sketch one of them. Suppose that the cache memories are designed so that whenever a word is written to the cache, it is written through to memory as well. Such a cache is, not surprisingly, called a **write-through cache.** In this design, cache hits for reads do not cause bus traffic, but cache misses for reads, and all writes, hits and misses, cause bus traffic.

In addition, all caches constantly monitor the bus. Whenever a cache sees a write occurring to a memory address present in its cache, it either removes that entry from its cache, or updates the cache entry with the new value. Such a cache is called a **snoopy cache** (or sometimes, a **snooping cache**) because it is always "snooping" (eavesdropping) on the bus. A design consisting of snoopy write-through caches is coherent and is invisible to the programmer. Nearly all bus-based multiprocessors use either this architecture or one closely related to it.

Using it, it is possible to put about 32 or possibly 64 CPUs on a single bus. For more about bus-based multiprocessors, see Lilja (1993).

1.3.2. Switched Multiprocessors

To build a multiprocessor with more than 64 processors, a different method is needed to connect the CPUs with the memory. One possibility is to divide the memory up into modules and connect them to the CPUs with a **crossbar switch**, as shown in Fig. 1-6(a). Each CPU and each memory has a connection coming out of it, as shown. At every intersection is a tiny electronic **crosspoint switch** that can be opened and closed in hardware. When a CPU wants to access a particular memory, the crosspoint switch connecting them is closed momentarily, to allow the access to take place. The virtue of the crossbar switch is that many CPUs can be accessing memory at the same time, although if two CPUs try to access the same memory simultaneously, one of them will have to wait.

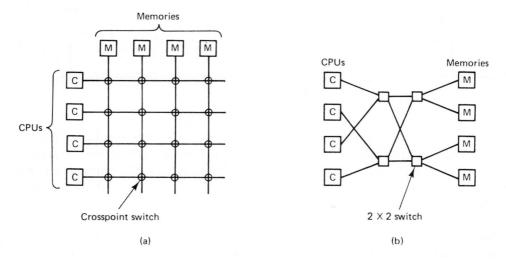

Fig. 1-6. (a) A crossbar switch. (b) An omega switching network.

The downside of the crossbar switch is that with n CPUs and n memories, n^2 crosspoint switches are needed. For large n, this number can be prohibitive. As a result, people have looked for, and found, alternative switching networks that require fewer switches. The **omega network** of Fig. 1-6(b) is one example. This network contains four 2×2 switches, each having two inputs and two outputs. Each switch can route either input to either output. A careful look at the figure will show that with proper settings of the switches, every CPU can access every memory. These switches can be set in nanoseconds or less.

In the general case, with n CPUs and n memories, the omega network requires $\log_2 n$ switching stages, each containing $n/2$ switches, for a total of $(n \log_2 n)/2$ switches. Although for large n this is much better than n^2, it is still substantial.

Furthermore, there is another problem: delay. For example, for $n = 1024$, there are 10 switching stages from the CPU to the memory, and another 10 for the word requested to come back. Suppose that the CPU is a modern RISC chip running at 100 MIPS; that is, the instruction execution time is 10 nsec. If a memory request is to traverse a total of 20 switching stages (10 outbound and 10 back) in 10 nsec, the switching time must be 500 picosec (0.5 nsec). The complete multiprocessor will need 5120 500-picosec switches. This is not going to be cheap.

People have attempted to reduce the cost by going to hierarchical systems. Some memory is associated with each CPU. Each CPU can access its own local memory quickly, but accessing anybody else's memory is slower. This design gives rise to what is known as a **NUMA (NonUniform Memory Access)** machine. Although NUMA machines have better average access times than machines based on omega networks, they have the new complication that the placement of the programs and data becomes critical in order to make most access go to the local memory.

To summarize, bus-based multiprocessors, even with snoopy caches, are limited by the amount of bus capacity to about 64 CPUs at most. To go beyond that requires a switching network, such as a crossbar switch, an omega switching network, or something similar. Large crossbar switches are very expensive, and large omega networks are both expensive and slow. NUMA machines require complex algorithms for good software placement. The conclusion is clear: building a large, tightly-coupled, shared memory multiprocessor is possible, but is difficult and expensive.

1.3.3. Bus-Based Multicomputers

On the other hand, building a multicomputer (i.e., no shared memory) is easy. Each CPU has a direct connection to its own local memory. The only problem left is how the CPUs communicate with each other. Clearly, some interconnection scheme is needed here, too, but since it is only for CPU-to-CPU communication, the volume of traffic will be several orders of magnitude lower than when the interconnection network is also used for CPU-to-memory traffic.

In Fig. 1-7 we see a bus-based multicomputer. It looks topologically similar to the bus-based multiprocessor, but since there will be much less traffic over it, it need not be a high-speed backplane bus. In fact, it can be a much lower speed LAN (typically, 10–100 Mbps, compared to 300 Mbps and up for a backplane bus). Thus Fig. 1-7 is more often a collection of workstations on a LAN than a collection of CPU cards inserted into a fast bus (although the latter configuration is definitely a possible design).

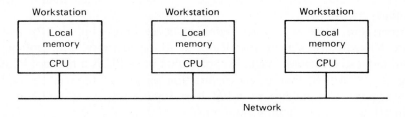

Fig. 1-7. A multicomputer consisting of workstations on a LAN.

1.3.4. Switched Multicomputers

Our last category consists of switched multicomputers. Various interconnection networks have been proposed and built, but all have the property that each CPU has direct and exclusive access to its own, private memory. Figure 1-8 shows two popular topologies, a grid and a hypercube. Grids are easy to understand and lay out on printed circuit boards. They are best suited to problems that have an inherent two-dimensional nature, such as graph theory or vision (e.g., robot eyes or analyzing photographs).

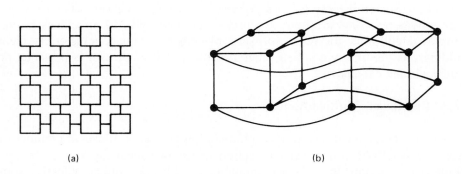

(a)   (b)

Fig. 1-8. (a) Grid. (b) Hypercube.

A **hypercube** is an *n*-dimensional cube. The hypercube of Fig. 1-8(b) is four-dimensional. It can be thought of as two ordinary cubes, each with 8 vertices and 12 edges. Each vertex is a CPU. Each edge is a connection between two CPUs. The corresponding vertices in each of the two cubes are connected.

To expand the hypercube to five dimensions, we would add another set of two interconnected cubes to the figure, connect the corresponding edges in the two halves, and so on. For an *n*-dimensional hypercube, each CPU has *n* connections to other CPUs. Thus the complexity of the wiring increases only logarithmically with the size. Since only nearest neighbors are connected, many messages have to make several hops to reach their destination. However, the longest possible path also grows logarithmically with the size, in contrast to the grid, where it grows as the square root of the number of CPUs. Hypercubes with 1024 CPUs have been commercially available for several years, and hypercubes with as many as 16,384 CPUs are starting to become available.

1.4. SOFTWARE CONCEPTS

Although the hardware is important, the software is even more important. The image that a system presents to its users, and how they think about the system, is largely determined by the operating system software, not the hardware. In this section we will introduce the various types of operating systems for the multiprocessors and multicomputers we have just studied, and discuss which kind of software goes with which kind of hardware.

Operating systems cannot be put into nice, neat pigeonholes like hardware. By nature software is vague and amorphous. Still, it is more-or-less possible to distinguish two kinds of operating systems for multiple CPU systems: loosely coupled and tightly coupled. As we shall see, loosely and tightly-coupled software is roughly analogous to loosely and tightly-coupled hardware.

Loosely-coupled software allows machines and users of a distributed system to be fundamentally independent of one another, but still to interact to a limited degree where that is necessary. Consider a group of personal computers, each of which has its own CPU, its own memory, its own hard disk, and its own operating system, but which share some resources, such as laser printers and data bases, over a LAN. This system is loosely coupled, since the individual machines are clearly distinguishable, each with its own job to do. If the network should go down for some reason, the individual machines can still continue to run to a considerable degree, although some functionality may be lost (e.g., the ability to print files).

To show how difficult it is to make definitions in this area, now consider the same system as above, but without the network. To print a file, the user writes the file on a floppy disk, carries it to the machine with the printer, reads it in, and then prints it. Is this still a distributed system, only now even more loosely coupled? It's hard to say. From a fundamental point of view, there is not really any theoretical difference between communicating over a LAN and communicating by carrying floppy disks around. At most one can say that the delay and data rate are worse in the second example.

At the other extreme we might find a multiprocessor dedicated to running a single chess program in parallel. Each CPU is assigned a board to evaluate, and it spends its time examining that board and all the boards that can be generated from it. When the evaluation is finished, the CPU reports back the results and is given a new board to work on. The software for this system, both the application program and the operating system required to support it, is clearly much more tightly coupled than in our previous example.

We have now seen four kinds of distributed hardware and two kinds of distributed software. In theory, there should be eight combinations of hardware and software. In fact, only four are worth distinguishing, because to the user, the interconnection technology is not visible. For most purposes, a multiprocessor is a multiprocessor, whether it uses a bus with snoopy caches or uses an omega network. In the following sections we will look at some of the most common combinations of hardware and software.

1.4.1. Network Operating Systems

Let us start with loosely-coupled software on loosely-coupled hardware, since this is probably the most common combination at many organizations. A typical example is a network of workstations connected by a LAN. In this model, each user has a workstation for his exclusive use. It may or may not have a hard disk. It definitely has its own operating system. All commands are normally run locally, right on the workstation.

However, it is sometimes possible for a user to log into another workstation remotely by using a command such as

```
rlogin machine
```

The effect of this command is to turn the user's own workstation into a remote terminal logged into the remote machine. Commands typed on the keyboard are sent to the remote machine, and output from the remote machine is displayed on the screen. To switch to a different remote machine, it is necessary first to log out, then to use the *rlogin* command to connect to another machine. At any instant, only one machine can be used, and the selection of the machine is entirely manual.

Networks of workstations often also have a remote copy command to copy files from one machine to another. For example, a command like

```
rcp machine1:file1 machine2:file2
```

might copy the file *file1* from *machine1* to *machine2* and give it the name *file2* there. Again here, the movement of files is explicit and requires the user to be completely aware of where all files are located and where all commands are being executed.

While better than nothing, this form of communication is extremely primitive and has led system designers to search for more convenient forms of communication and information sharing. One approach is to provide a shared, global file system accessible from all the workstations. The file system is supported by one or more machines called **file servers**. The file servers accept requests from user programs running on the other (nonserver) machines, called **clients**, to read and write files. Each incoming request is examined and executed, and the reply is sent back, as illustrated in Fig. 1-9.

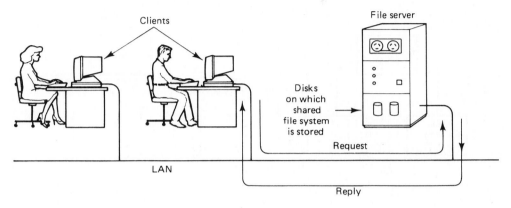

Fig. 1-9. Two clients and a server in a network operating system.

File servers generally maintain hierarchical file systems, each with a root directory containing subdirectories and files. Workstations can import or mount these file systems, augmenting their local file systems with those located on the servers. For example, in Fig. 1-10, two file servers are shown. One has a directory called *games*, while the other has a directory called *work*. These directories each contain several files. Both of the clients shown have mounted both of the servers, but they have mounted them in different places in their respective file systems. Client 1 has mounted them in its root directory, and can access them as */games* and */work*, respectively. Client 2, like client 1, has mounted *games* in its root directory, but regarding the reading of mail and news as a kind of game, has created a directory */games/work* and mounted *work* there. Consequently, it can access *news* using the path */games/work/news* rather than */work/news*.

While it does not matter where a client mounts a server in its directory hierarchy, it is important to notice that different clients can have a different view of the file system. The name of a file depends on where it is being accessed from, and how that machine has set up its file system. Because each workstation operates relatively independently of the others, there is no guarantee that they all present the same directory hierarchy to their programs.

The operating system that is used in this kind of environment must manage the individual workstations and file servers and take care of the communication

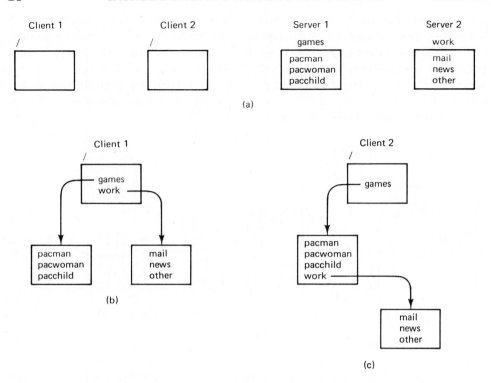

Fig. 1-10. Different clients may mount the servers in different places.

between them. It is possible that the machines all run the same operating system, but this is not required. If the clients and servers run on different systems, as a bare minimum they must agree on the format and meaning of all the messages that they may potentially exchange. In a situation like this, where each machine has a high degree of autonomy and there are few system-wide requirements, people usually speak of a **network operating system**.

1.4.2. True Distributed Systems

Network operating systems are loosely-coupled software on loosely-coupled hardware. Other than the shared file system, it is quite apparent to the users that such a system consists of numerous computers. Each can run its own operating system and do whatever its owner wants. There is essentially no coordination at all, except for the rule that client-server traffic must obey the system's protocols.

The next evolutionary step beyond this is tightly-coupled software on the same loosely-coupled (i.e., multicomputer) hardware. The goal of such a system is to create the illusion in the minds of the users that the entire network of computers is a single timesharing system, rather than a collection of distinct machines. Some authors refer to this property as the **single-system image**. Others put it slightly differently, saying that a distributed system is one that runs on a collection of networked machines but acts like a **virtual uniprocessor**. No matter how it is expressed, the essential idea is that the users should not have to be aware of the existence of multiple CPUs in the system. No current system fulfills this requirement entirely, but a number of candidates are on the horizon. These will be discussed later in the book.

What are some characteristics of a distributed system? To start with, there must be a single, global interprocess communication mechanism so that any process can talk to any other process. It will not do to have different mechanisms on different machines or different mechanisms for local communication and remote communication. There must also be a global protection scheme. Mixing access control lists, the UNIX® protection bits, and capabilities will not give a single system image.

Process management must also be the same everywhere. How processes are created, destroyed, started, and stopped must not vary from machine to machine. In short, the idea behind network operating systems, namely that any machine can do whatever it wants to as long as it obeys the standard protocols when engaging in client-server communication, is not enough. Not only must there be a single set of system calls available on all machines, but these calls must be designed so that they make sense in a distributed environment.

The file system must look the same everywhere, too. Having file names restricted to 11 characters in some locations and being unrestricted in others is undesirable. Also, every file should be visible at every location, subject to protection and security constraints, of course.

As a logical consequence of having the same system call interface everywhere, it is normal that identical kernels run on all the CPUs in the system. Doing so makes it easier to coordinate activities that must be global. For example, when a process has to be started up, all the kernels have to cooperate in finding the best place to execute it. In addition, a global file system is needed.

Nevertheless, each kernel can have considerable control over its own local resources. For example, since there is no shared memory, it is logical to allow each kernel to manage its own memory. For example, if swapping or paging is used, the kernel on each CPU is the logical place to determine what to swap or page. There is no reason to centralize this authority. Similarly, if multiple processes are running on some CPU, it makes sense to do the scheduling right there, too.

A considerable body of knowledge is now available about designing and implementing distributed operating systems. Rather than going into these issues here, we will first finish off our survey of the different combinations of hardware and software, and come back to them in Sec. 1.5.

1.4.3. Multiprocessor Timesharing Systems

The last combination we wish to discuss is tightly-coupled software on tightly-coupled hardware. While various special-purpose machines exist in this category (such as dedicated data base machines), the most common general-purpose examples are multiprocessors that are operated as a UNIX timesharing system, but with multiple CPUs instead of one CPU. To the outside world, a multiprocessor with 32 30-MIPS CPUs acts very much like a single 960-MIPS CPU (this is the single-system image discussed above). Except that implementing it on a multiprocessor makes life much easier, since the entire design can be centralized.

The key characteristic of this class of system is the existence of a single run queue: a list of all the processes in the system that are logically unblocked and ready to run. The run queue is a data structure kept in the shared memory. As an example, consider the system of Fig. 1-11, which has three CPUs and five processes that are ready to run. All five processes are located in the shared memory, and three of them are currently executing: process *A* on CPU 1, process *B* on CPU 2, and process *C* on CPU 3. The other two processes, *D* and *E*, are also in memory, waiting their turn.

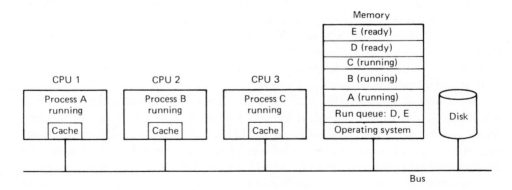

Fig. 1-11. A multiprocessor with a single run queue.

Now suppose that process *B* blocks waiting for I/O or its quantum runs out. Either way, CPU 2 must suspend it, and find another process to run. CPU 2 will normally begin executing operating system code (located in the shared memory). After having saved all of *B*'s registers, it will enter a critical region to run the scheduler to look for another process to run. It is essential that the scheduler be run as a critical region to prevent two CPUs from choosing the same process to run next. The necessary mutual exclusion can be achieved by using monitors, semaphores, or any other standard construction used in singleprocessor systems.

Once CPU 2 has gained exclusive access to the run queue, it can remove the first entry, D, exit from the critical region, and begin executing D. Initially, execution will be slow, since CPU 2's cache is full of words belonging to that part of the shared memory containing process B, but after a little while, these will have been purged and the cache will be full of D's code and data, so execution will speed up.

Because none of the CPUs have local memory and all programs are stored in the global shared memory, it does not matter on which CPU a process runs. If a long-running process is scheduled many times before it completes, on the average, it will spend about the same amount of time running on each CPU. The only factor that has any effect at all on CPU choice is the slight gain in performance when a process starts up on a CPU that is currently caching part of its address space. In other words, if all CPUs are idle, waiting for I/O, and one process becomes ready, it is slightly preferable to allocate it to the CPU it was last using, assuming that no other process has used that CPU since (Vaswani and Zahorjan, 1991).

As an aside, if a process blocks for I/O on a multiprocessor, the operating system has the choice of suspending it or just letting it do busy waiting. If most I/O is completed in less time than it takes to do a process switch, busy waiting is preferable. Some systems let the process keep its processor for a few milliseconds, in the hope that the I/O will complete soon, but if that does not occur before the timer runs out, a process switch is made (Karlin et al., 1991). If most critical regions are short, this approachcan avoid many expensive process switches.

An area in which this kind of multiprocessor differs appreciably from a network or distributed system is in the organization of the file system. The operating system normally contains a traditional file system, including a single, unified block cache. When any process executes a system call, a trap is made to the operating system, which carries it out, using semaphores, monitors, or something equivalent, to lock out other CPUs while critical sections are being executed or central tables are being accessed. In this way, when a WRITE system call is done, the central block cache is locked, the new data entered into the cache, and the lock released. Any subsequent READ call will see the new data, just as on a single-processor system. On the whole, the file system is hardly different from a single-processor file system. In fact, on some multiprocessors, one of the CPUs is dedicated to running the operating system; the other ones run user programs. This situation is undesirable, however, as the operating system machine is often a bottleneck. This point is discussed in detail by Boykin and Langerman (1990).

It should be clear that the methods used on the multiprocessor to achieve the appearance of a virtual uniprocessor are not applicable to machines that do not have shared memory. Centralized run queues and block only caches work when all CPUs have access to them with very low delay. Although these data structures could be simulated on a network of machines, the communication costs make this approach prohibitively expensive.

Figure 1-12 shows some of the differences between the three kinds of systems we have examined above.

Item	Network operating system	Distributed operating system	Multiprocessor operating system
Does it look like a virtual uniprocessor?	No	Yes	Yes
Do all have to run the same operating system?	No	Yes	Yes
How many copies of the operating system are there?	N	N	1
How is communication achieved?	Shared files	Messages	Shared memory
Are agreed upon network protocols required?	Yes	Yes	No
Is there a single run queue?	No	No	Yes
Does file sharing have well-defined semantics?	Usually no	Yes	Yes

Fig. 1-12. Comparison of three different ways of organizing n CPUs.

1.5. DESIGN ISSUES

In the preceding sections we have looked at distributed systems and related topics from both the hardware and software points of view. In the remainder of this chapter we will briefly look at some of the key design issues that people contemplating building a distributed operating system must deal with. We will come back to them in more detail later in the book.

1.5.1. Transparency

Probably the single most important issue is how to achieve the single-system image. In other words, how do the system designers fool everyone into thinking that the collection of machines is simply an old-fashioned timesharing system? A system that realizes this goal is often said to be **transparent**.

Transparency can be achieved at two different levels. Easiest to do is to hide the distribution from the users. For example, when a UNIX user types *make* to recompile a large number of files in a directory, he need not be told that all the compilations are proceeding in parallel on different machines and are using a variety of file servers to do it. To him, the only thing that is unusual is that the performance of the system is halfway decent for a change. In terms of commands issued from the terminal and results displayed on the terminal, the distributed system can be made to look just like a single-processor system.

At a lower level, it is also possible, but harder, to make the system look transparent to programs. In other words, the system call interface can be designed so that the existence of multiple processors is not visible. Pulling the wool over the programmer's eyes is harder than pulling the wool over the terminal user's eyes, however.

What does transparency really mean? It is one of those slippery concepts that sounds reasonable but is more subtle than it at first appears. As an example, imagine a distributed system consisting of workstations each running some standard operating system. Normally, system services (e.g., reading files) are obtained by issuing a system call that traps to the kernel. In such a system, remote files should be accessed the same way. A system in which remote files are accessed by explicitly setting up a network connection to a remote server and then sending messages to it is not transparent because remote services are then being accessed differently than local ones. The programmer can tell that multiple machines are involved, and this is not allowed.

The concept of transparency can be applied to several aspects of a distributed system, as shown in Fig. 1-13. **Location transparency** refers to the fact that in a true distributed system, users cannot tell where hardware and software resources such as CPUs, printers, files, and data bases are located. The name of the resource must not secretly encode the location of the resource, so names like *machine1:prog.c* or */machine1/prog.c* are not acceptable.

Kind	Meaning
Location transparency	The users cannot tell where resources are located
Migration transparency	Resources can move at will without changing their names
Replication transparency	The users cannot tell how many copies exist
Concurrency transparency	Multiple users can share resources automatically
Parallelism transparency	Activities can happen in parallel without users knowing

Fig. 1-13. Different kinds of transparency in a distributed system.

Migration transparency means that resources must be free to move from one location to another without having their names change. In the example of

Fig. 1-10 we saw how server directories could be mounted in arbitrary places in the clients' directory hierarchy. Since a path like */work/news* does not reveal the location of the server, it is location transparent. However, now suppose that the folks running the servers decide that reading network news really falls in the category "games" rather than in the category "work." Accordingly, they move *news* from server 2 to server 1. The next time client 1 boots and mounts the servers in his customary way, he will notice that */work/news* no longer exists. Instead, there is a new entry, */games/news*. Thus the mere fact that a file or directory has migrated from one server to another has forced it to acquire a new name because the system of remote mounts is not migration transparent.

If a distributed system has **replication transparency**, the operating system is free to make additional copies of files and other resources on its own without the users noticing. Clearly, in the previous example, automatic replication is impossible because the names and locations are so closely tied together. To see how replication transparency might be achievable, consider a collection of *n* servers logically connected to form a ring. Each server maintains the entire directory tree structure but holds only a subset of the files themselves. To read a file, a client sends a message containing the full path name to any of the servers. That server checks to see if it has the file. If so, it returns the data requested. If not, it forwards the request to the next server in the ring, which then repeats the algorithm. In this system, the servers can decide by themselves to replicate any file on any or all servers, without the users having to know about it. Such a scheme is replication transparent because it allows the system to make copies of heavily used files without the users even being aware that this is happening.

Distributed systems usually have multiple, independent users. What should the system do when two or more users try to access the same resource at the same time? For example, what happens if two users try to update the same file at the same time? If the system is **concurrency transparent**, the users will not notice the existence of other users. One mechanism for achieving this form of transparency would be for the system to lock a resource automatically once someone had started to use it, unlocking it only when the access was finished. In this manner, all resources would only be accessed sequentially, never concurrently.

Finally, we come to the hardest one, **parallelism transparency**. In principle, a distributed system is supposed to appear to the users as a traditional, uniprocessor timesharing system. What happens if a programmer knows that his distributed system has 1000 CPUs and he wants to use a substantial fraction of them for a chess program that evaluates boards in parallel? The theoretical answer is that together the compiler, runtime system, and operating system should be able to figure out how to take advantage of this potential parallelism without the programmer even knowing it. Unfortunately, the current state-of-the-art is nowhere near allowing this to happen. Programmers who actually want to use multiple CPUs for a single problem will have to program this explicitly, at least for the foreseeable future. Parallelism transparency can be regarded as the holy grail for distributed systems designers. When that has been achieved, the work will have been completed, and it will be time to move on to new fields.

All this notwithstanding, there are times when users do *not* want complete transparency. For example, when a user asks to print a document, he often prefers to have the output appear on the local printer, not one 1000 km away, even if the distant printer is fast, inexpensive, can handle color and smell, and is currently idle.

1.5.2. Flexibility

The second key design issue is flexibility. It is important that the system be flexible because we are just beginning to learn about how to build distributed systems. It is likely that this process will incur many false starts and considerable backtracking. Design decisions that now seem reasonable may later prove to be wrong. The best way to avoid problems is thus to keep one's options open.

Flexibility, along with transparency, is like parenthood and apple pie: who could possibly be against them? It is hard to imagine anyone arguing in favor of an inflexible system. However, things are not as simple as they seem. There are two schools of thought concerning the structure of distributed systems. One school maintains that each machine should run a traditional kernel that provides most services itself. The other maintains that the kernel should provide as little as possible, with the bulk of the operating system services available from user-level servers. These two models, known as the monolithic kernel and microkernel, respectively, are illustrated in Fig. 1-14.

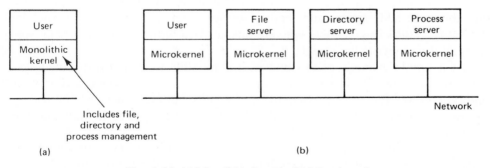

Fig. 1-14. (a) Monolithic kernel. (b) Microkernel.

The monolithic kernel is basically today's centralized operating system augmented with networking facilities and the integration of remote services. Most system calls are made by trapping to the kernel, having the work performed there, and having the kernel return the desired result to the user process. With this approach, most machines have disks and manage their own local file systems. Many distributed systems that are extensions or imitations of UNIX use this approach because UNIX itself has a large, monolithic kernel.

If the monolithic kernel is the reigning champion, the microkernel is the up-and-coming challenger. Most distributed systems that have been designed from scratch use this method. The microkernel is more flexible because it does almost nothing. It basically provides just four minimal services:

1. An interprocess communication mechanism.

2. Some memory management.

3. A small amount of low-level process management and scheduling.

4. Low-level input/output.

In particular, unlike the monolithic kernel, it does not provide the file system, directory system, full process management, or much system call handling. The services that the microkernel does provide are included because they are difficult or expensive to provide anywhere else. The goal is to keep it small.

All the other operating system services are generally implemented as user-level servers. To look up a name, read a file, or obtain some other service, the user sends a message to the appropriate server, which then does the work and returns the result. The advantage of this method is that it is highly modular: there is a well-defined interface to each service (the set of messages the server understands), and every service is equally accessible to every client, independent of location. In addition, it is easy to implement, install, and debug new services, since adding or changing a service does not require stopping the system and booting a new kernel, as is the case with a monolithic kernel. It is precisely this ability to add, delete, and modify services that gives the microkernel its flexibility. Furthermore, users who are not satisfied with any of the official services are free to write their own.

As a simple example of this power, it is possible to have a distributed system with multiple file servers, one supporting MS-DOS file service and another supporting UNIX file service. Individual programs can use either or both, if they choose. In contrast, with a monolithic kernel, the file system is built into the kernel, and users have no choice but to use it.

The only potential advantage of the monolithic kernel is performance. Trapping to the kernel and doing everything there may well be faster than sending messages to remote servers. However, a detailed comparison of two distributed operating systems, one with a monolithic kernel (Sprite), and one with a microkernel (Amoeba), has shown that in practice this advantage is nonexistent

(Douglis et al., 1991). Other factors tend to dominate, and the small amount of time required to send a message and get a reply (typically, about 1 msec) is usually negligible. As a consequence, it is likely that microkernel systems will gradually come to dominate the distributed systems scheme, and monolithic kernels will eventually vanish or evolve into microkernels. Perhaps future editions of Silberschatz and Galvin's book on operating systems (1994) will feature hummingbirds and swifts on the cover instead of stegasauruses and triceratopses.

1.5.3. Reliability

One of the original goals of building distributed systems was to make them more reliable than single-processor systems. The idea is that if a machine goes down, some other machine takes over the job. In other words, theoretically the overall system reliability could be the Boolean OR of the component reliabilities. For example, with four file servers, each with a 0.95 chance of being up at any instant, the probability of all four being down simultaneously is $0.05^4 = 0.000006$, so the probability of at least one being available is 0.999994, far better than that of any individual server.

That is the theory. The practice is that to function at all, current distributed systems count on a number of specific servers being up. As a result, some of them have an availability more closely related to the Boolean AND of the components than to the Boolean OR. In a widely-quoted remark, Leslie Lamport once defined a distributed system as "one on which I cannot get any work done because some machine I have never heard of has crashed." While this remark was (presumably) made somewhat tongue-in-cheek, there is clearly room for improvement here.

It is important to distinguish various aspects of reliability. **Availability**, as we have just seen, refers to the fraction of time that the system is usable. Lamport's system apparently did not score well in that regard. Availability can be enhanced by a design that does not require the simultaneous functioning of a substantial number of critical components. Another tool for improving availability is redundancy: key pieces of hardware and software should be replicated, so that if one of them fails the others will be able to take up the slack.

A highly reliable system must be highly available, but that is not enough. Data entrusted to the system must not be lost or garbled in any way, and if files are stored redundantly on multiple servers, all the copies must be kept consistent. In general, the more copies that are kept, the better the availability, but the greater the chance that they will be inconsistent, especially if updates are frequent. The designers of all distributed systems must keep this dilemma in mind all the time.

Another aspect of overall reliability is security. Files and other resources must be protected from unauthorized usage. Although the same issue occurs in single-processor systems, in distributed systems it is more severe. In a single-processor system, the user logs in and is authenticated. From then on, the system knows who the user is and can check whether each attempted access is legal. In a distributed system, when a message comes in to a server asking for something, the server has no simple way of determining who it is from. No name or identification field in the message can be trusted, since the sender may be lying. At the very least, considerable care is required here.

Still another issue relating to reliability is **fault tolerance**. Suppose that a server crashes and then quickly reboots. What happens? Does the server crash bring users down with it? If the server has tables containing important information about ongoing activities, recovery will be difficult at best.

In general, distributed systems can be designed to mask failures, that is, to hide them from the users. If a file service or other service is actually constructed from a group of closely cooperating servers, it should be possible to construct it in such a way that users do not notice the loss of one or two servers, other than some performance degradation. Of course, the trick is to arrange this cooperation so that it does not add substantial overhead to the system in the normal case, when everything is functioning correctly.

1.5.4. Performance

Always lurking in the background is the issue of performance. Building a transparent, flexible, reliable distributed system will not win you any prizes if it is as slow as molasses. In particular, when running a particular application on a distributed system, it should not be appreciably worse than running the same application on a single processor. Unfortunately, achieving this is easier said than done.

Various performance metrics can be used. Response time is one, but so are throughput (number of jobs per hour), system utilization, and amount of network capacity consumed. Furthermore, the results of any benchmark are often highly dependent on the nature of the benchmark. A benchmark that involves a large number of independent highly CPU-bound computations may give radically different results from a benchmark that consists of scanning a single large file for some pattern.

The performance problem is compounded by the fact that communication, which is essential in a distributed system (and absent in a single-processor system) is typically quite slow. Sending a message and getting a reply over a LAN takes about 1 msec. Most of this time is due to unavoidable protocol handling on both ends, rather than the time the bits spend on the wire. Thus to optimize performance, one often has to minimize the number of messages. The difficulty with this strategy is that the best way to gain performance is to have many activities running in parallel on different processors, but doing so requires sending many messages. (Another solution is to do all the work on one machine, but that is hardly appropriate in a distributed system.)

One possible way out is to pay considerable attention to the **grain size** of all computations. Starting up a small computation remotely, such as adding two integers, is rarely worth it, because the communication overhead dwarfs the extra CPU cycles gained. On the other hand, starting up a long compute-bound job remotely may be worth the trouble. In general, jobs that involve a large number of small computations, especially ones that interact highly with one another, may cause trouble on a distributed system with relatively slow communication. Such jobs are said to exhibit **fine-grained parallelism**. On the other hand, jobs that involve large computations, low interaction rates, and little data, that is, **coarse-grained parallelism**, may be a better fit.

Fault tolerance also exacts its price. Good reliability is often best achieved by having several servers closely cooperating on a single request. For example, when a request comes in to a server, it could immediately send a copy of the message to one of its colleagues so that if it crashes before finishing, the colleague can take over. Naturally, when it is done, it must inform the colleague that the work has been completed, which takes another message. Thus we have at least two extra messages, which in the normal case cost time and network capacity and produce no tangible gain.

1.5.5. Scalability

Most current distributed systems are designed to work with a few hundred CPUs. It is possible that future systems will be orders of magnitude larger, and solutions that work well for 200 machines will fail miserably for 200,000,000. Consider the following. The French PTT (Post, Telephone and Telegraph administration) is in the process of installing a terminal in every household and business in France. The terminal, known as a **minitel**, will allow online access to a data base containing all the telephone numbers in France, thus eliminating the need for printing and distributing expensive telephone books. It will also vastly reduce the need for information operators who do nothing but give out telephone numbers all day. It has been calculated that the system will pay for itself within a few years. If the system works in France, other countries will inevitably adopt similar systems.

Once all the terminals are in place, the possibility of also using them for electronic mail (especially in conjunction with printers) is clearly present. Since postal services lose a huge amount of money in every country in the world, and telephone services are enormously profitable, there are great incentives to having electronic mail replace paper mail.

Next comes interactive access to all kinds of data bases and services, from electronic banking to reserving places in planes, trains, hotels, theaters, and restaurants, to name just a few. Before long, we have a distributed system with tens of millions of users. The question is: Will the methods we are currently developing scale to such large systems?

Although little is known about such huge distributed systems, one guiding principle is clear: avoid centralized components, tables, and algorithms (see Fig. 1-15). Having a single mail server for 50 million users would not be a good idea. Even if it had enough CPU and storage capacity, the network capacity into and out of it would surely be a problem. Furthermore, the system would not tolerate faults well. A single power outage could bring the entire system down. Finally, most mail is local. Having a message sent by a user in Marseille to another user two blocks away pass through a machine in Paris is not the way to go.

Concept	Example
Centralized components	A single mail server for all users
Centralized tables	A single on-line telephone book
Centralized algorithms	Doing routing based on complete information

Fig. 1-15. Potential bottlenecks that designers should try to avoid in very large distributed systems.

Centralized tables are almost as bad as centralized components. How should one keep track of the telephone numbers and addresses of 50 million people? Suppose that each data record could be fit into 50 characters. A single 2.5-gigabyte disk would provide enough storage. But here again, having a single data base would undoubtedly saturate all the communication lines into and out of it. It would also be vulnerable to failures (a single speck of dust could cause a head crash and bring down the entire directory service). Furthermore, here too, valuable network capacity would be wasted shipping queries far away for processing.

Finally, centralized algorithms are also a bad idea. In a large distributed system, an enormous number of messages have to be routed over many lines. From a theoretical point of view, the optimal way to do this is collect complete information about the load on all machines and lines, and then run a graph theory algorithm to compute all the optimal routes. This information can then be spread around the system to improve the routing.

The trouble is that collecting and transporting all the input and output information would again be a bad idea for the reasons discussed above. In fact, any algorithm that operates by collecting information from all sites, sends it to a single machine for processing, and then distributes the results must be avoided.

Only decentralized algorithms should be used. These algorithms generally have the following characteristics, which distinguish them from centralized algorithms:

1. No machine has complete information about the system state.
2. Machines make decisions based only on local information.
3. Failure of one machine does not ruin the algorithm.
4. There is no implicit assumption that a global clock exists.

The first three follow from what we have said so far. The last is perhaps less obvious, but also important. Any algorithm that starts out with: "At precisely 12:00:00 all machines shall note the size of their output queue" will fail because it is impossible to get all the clocks exactly synchronized. Algorithms should take into account the lack of exact clock synchronization. The larger the system, the larger the uncertainty. On a single LAN, with considerable effort it may be possible to get all clocks synchronized down to a few milliseconds, but doing this nationally is tricky. We will discuss distributed clock synchronization in Chap. 3.

1.6. SUMMARY

Distributed systems consist of autonomous CPUs that work together to make the complete system look like a single computer. They have a number of potential selling points, including good price/performance ratios, the ability to match distributed applications well, potentially high reliability, and incremental growth as the workload grows. They also have some disadvantages, such as more complex software, potential communication bottlenecks, and weak security. Nevertheless, there is considerable interest worldwide in building and installing them.

Modern computer systems often have multiple CPUs. These can be organized as multiprocessors (with shared memory) or as multicomputers (without shared memory). Both types can be bus-based or switched. The former tend to be tightly coupled, while the latter tend to be loosely coupled.

The software for multiple CPU systems can be divided into three rough classes. Network operating systems allow users at independent workstations to communicate via a shared file system but otherwise leave each user as the master of his own workstation. Distributed operating systems turn the entire collection of hardware and software into a single integrated system, much like a traditional timesharing system. Shared-memory multiprocessors also offer a single system image, but do so by centralizing everything, so there really is only a single system. Shared-memory multiprocessors are not distributed systems.

Distributed systems have to be designed carefully, since there are many pitfalls for the unwary. A key issue is transparency—hiding all the distribution from the users and even from the application programs. Another issue is flexibility. Since the field is only now in its infancy, the design should be made with the idea of making future changes easy. In this respect, microkernels are superior to monolithic kernels. Other important issues are reliability, performance, and scalability.

PROBLEMS

1. The price/performance ratio of computers has improved by something like 11 orders of magnitude since the first commercial mainframes came out in the early 1950s. The text shows what a similar gain would have meant in the automobile industry. Give another example of what such a large gain means.

2. Name two advantages and two disadvantages of distributed systems over centralized ones.

3. What is the difference between a multiprocessor and a multicomputer?

4. The terms *loosely-coupled system* and *tightly-coupled system* are often used to described distributed computer systems. What is the different between them?

5. What is the different between an MIMD computer and an SIMD computer?

6. A bus-based multiprocessor uses snoopy caches to achieve a coherent memory. Will semaphores work on this machine?

7. Crossbar switches allow a large number of memory requests to be processed at once, giving excellent performance. Why are they rarely used in practice?

8. A multicomputer with 256 CPUs is organized as a 16×16 grid. What is the worst-case delay (in hops) that a message might have to take?

9. Now consider a 256-CPU hypercube. What is the worst-case delay here, again in hops?

10. A multiprocessor has 4096 50-MIPS CPUs connected to memory by an omega network. How fast do the switches have to be to allow a request to

go to memory and back in one instruction time?

11. What is meant by a *single-system image*?

12. What is the main difference between a distributed operating system and a network operating system?

13. What are the primary tasks of a microkernel?

14. Name two advantages of a microkernel over a monolithic kernel.

15. Concurrency transparency is a desirable goal for distributed systems. Do centralized systems have this property automatically?

16. Explain in your own words the concept of parallelism transparency.

17. An experimental file server is up 3/4 of the time and down 1/4 of the time, due to bugs. How many times does this file server have to be replicated to give an availability of at least 99 percent?

18. Suppose that you have a large source program consisting of m files to compile. The compilation is to take place on a system with n processors, where $n \gg m$. The best you can hope for is an m-fold speedup over a single processor. What factors might cause the speedup to be less than this maximum?

2

Communication in Distributed Systems

The single most important difference between a distributed system and a uniprocessor system is the interprocess communication. In a uniprocessor system, most interprocess communication implicitly assumes the existence of shared memory. A typical example is the producer-consumer problem, in which one process writes into a shared buffer and another process reads from it. Even that most basic form of synchronization, the semaphore, requires that one word (the semaphore variable itself) is shared. In a distributed system there is no shared memory whatsoever, so the entire nature of interprocess communication must be completely rethought from scratch. In this chapter we will discuss numerous issues, examples, and problems associated with interprocess communication in distributed operating systems.

We will start out by discussing the rules that communicating processes must adhere to, known as protocols. For wide-area distributed systems these protocols often take the form of multiple layers, each with its own goals and rules. Two sets of layers, OSI and ATM, will be examined. Then we will look at the client-server model in some detail. After that, it is time to find out how messages are exchanged and the many options available to system designers.

One particular option, remote procedure call, is important enough to warrant its own section. Remote procedure call is really a nicer way of packaging message passing, to make it more like conventional programming and easier to use. Nevertheless, it has its own peculiarities and issues, which we will also look at.

We will conclude the chapter by studying how groups of processes can communicate, instead of just two processes. A detailed example of group communication, ISIS, will be discussed.

2.1. LAYERED PROTOCOLS

Due to the absence of shared memory, all communication in distributed systems is based on message passing. When process A wants to communicate with process B, it first builds a message in its own address space. Then it executes a system call that causes the operating system to fetch the message and send it over the network to B. Although this basic idea sounds simple enough, in order to prevent chaos, A and B have to agree on the meaning of the bits being sent. If A sends a brilliant new novel written in French and encoded in IBM's EBCDIC character code, and B expects the inventory of a supermarket written in English and encoded in ASCII, communication will be less than optimal.

Many different agreements are needed. How many volts should be used to signal a 0-bit, and how many volts for a 1-bit? How does the receiver know which is the last bit of the message? How can it detect if a message has been damaged or lost, and what should it do if it finds out? How long are numbers, strings, and other data items, and how are they represented? In short, agreements are needed at a variety of levels, varying from the low-level details of bit transmission to the high-level details of how information is to be expressed.

To make it easier to deal with the numerous levels and issues involved in communication, the International Standards Organization (ISO) has developed a reference model that clearly identifies the various levels involved, gives them standard names, and points out which level should do which job. This model is called the **Open Systems Interconnection Reference Model** (Day and Zimmerman, 1983), usually abbreviated as **ISO OSI** or sometimes just the **OSI model**. Although we do not intend to give a full description of this model and all of its implications here, a short introduction will be helpful. For more details, see (Tanenbaum, 1988).

To start with, the OSI model is designed to allow open systems to communicate. An **open system** is one that is prepared to communicate with any other open system by using standard rules that govern the format, contents, and meaning of the messages sent and received. These rules are formalized in what are called **protocols**. Basically, a protocol is an agreement between the communicating parties on how communication is to proceed. When a woman is introduced to a man, she may choose to stick out her hand. He, in turn, may decide either to shake it or kiss it, depending, for example, whether she is an American lawyer at a business meeting or a European princess at a formal ball. Violating the protocol will make communication more difficult, if not impossible.

At a more technological level, many companies make memory boards for the IBM PC. When the CPU wants to read a word from memory, it puts the address and certain control signals on the bus. The memory board is expected to see these signals and respond by putting the word requested on the bus within a certain time interval. If the memory board observes the required bus protocol, it will work correctly, otherwise it will not.

Similarly, to allow a group of computers to communicate over a network, they must all agree on the protocols to be used. The OSI model distinguishes between two general types of protocols. With **connection-oriented** protocols, before exchanging data, the sender and receiver first explicitly establish a connection, and possibly negotiate the protocol they will use. When they are done, they must release (terminate) the connection. The telephone is a connection-oriented communication system. With **connectionless** protocols, no setup in advance is needed. The sender just transmits the first message when it is ready. Dropping a letter in a mailbox is an example of connectionless communication. With computers, both connection-oriented and connectionless communication are common.

In the OSI model, communication is divided up into seven levels or layers, as shown in Fig. 2-1. Each layer deals with one specific aspect of the communication. In this way, the problem can be divided up into manageable pieces, each of which can be solved independent of the others. Each layer provides an **interface** to the one above it. The interface consists of a set of operations that together define the service the layer is prepared to offer its users.

In the OSI model, when process A on machine 1 wants to communicate with process B on machine 2, it builds a message and passes the message to the application layer on its machine. This layer might be a library procedure, for example, but it could also be implemented in some other way (e.g., inside the operating system, on an external coprocessor chip, etc.). The application layer software then adds a **header** to the front of the message and passes the resulting message across the layer 6/7 interface to the presentation layer. The presentation layer in turn adds its own header and passes the result down to the session layer, and so on. Some layers add not only a header to the front, but also a trailer to the end. When it hits bottom, the physical layer actually transmits the message, which by now might look as shown in Fig. 2-2.

When the message arrives at machine 2, it is passed upward, with each layer stripping off and examining its own header. Finally, the message arrives at the receiver, process B, which may reply to it using the reverse path. The information in the layer n header is used for the layer n protocol.

As an example of why layered protocols are important, consider communication between two companies, Zippy Airlines and its caterer, Mushy Meals, Inc. Every month, the head of passenger service at Zippy asks her secretary to contact the sales manager's secretary at Mushy to order 100,000 boxes of rubber

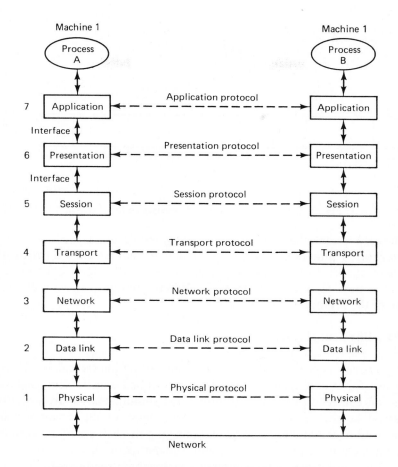

Fig. 2-1. Layers, interfaces, and protocols in the OSI model.

chicken. Traditionally, the orders have gone via the post office. However, as the postal service deteriorates, at some point the two secretaries decide to abandon it and communicate by FAX. They can do this without bothering their bosses, since their protocol deals with the physical transmission of the orders, not their contents.

Similarly, the head of passenger service can decide to drop the rubber chicken and go for Mushy's new special, prime rib of goat, without that decision affecting the secretaries. The thing to notice is that we have two layers here, the bosses and the secretaries. Each layer has its own protocol (subjects of discussion and technology) that can be changed independently of the other one. It is precisely this independence that makes layered protocols attractive. Each one can be changed as technology improves, without the other ones being affected.

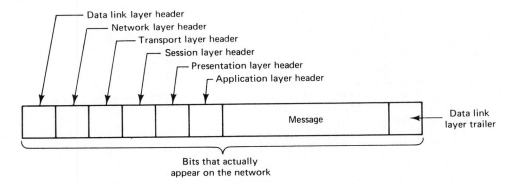

Fig. 2-2. A typical message as it appears on the network.

In the OSI model, there are not two layers, but seven, as we saw in Fig. 2-1. The collection of protocols used in a particular system is called a **protocol suite** or **protocol stack**. In the following sections, we will briefly examine each of the layers in turn, starting at the bottom. Where appropriate, we will also point out some of the protocols used in each layer.

2.1.1. The Physical Layer

The physical layer is concerned with transmitting the 0s and 1s. How many volts to use for 0 and 1, how many bits per second can be sent, and whether transmission can take place in both directions simultaneously are key issues in the physical layer. In addition, the size and shape of the network connector (plug), as well as the number of pins and meaning of each are of concern here.

The physical layer protocol deals with standardizing the electrical, mechanical, and signaling interfaces so that when one machine sends a 0 bit it is actually received as a 0 bit and not a 1 bit. Many physical layer standards have been developed (for different media), for example, the RS-232-C standard for serial communication lines.

2.1.2. The Data Link Layer

The physical layer just sends bits. As long as no errors occur, all is well. However, real communication networks are subject to errors, so some mechanism is needed to detect and correct them. This mechanism is the main task of the data link layer. What it does is to group the bits into units, sometimes called **frames**, and see that each frame is correctly received.

The data link layer does its work by putting a special bit pattern on the start and end of each frame, to mark them, as well as computing a **checksum** by adding up all the bytes in the frame in a certain way. The data link layer appends the checksum to the frame. When the frame arrives, the receiver recomputes the checksum from the data and compares the result to the checksum following the frame. If they agree, the frame is considered correct and is accepted. It they disagree, the receiver asks the sender to retransmit it. Frames are assigned sequence numbers (in the header), so everyone can tell which is which.

In Fig. 2-3 we see a (slightly pathological) example of *A* trying to send two messages, 0 and 1, to *B*. At time 0, data message 0 is sent, but when it arrives, at time 1, noise on the transmission line has caused it to be damaged, so the checksum is wrong. *B* notices this, and at time 2 asks for a retransmission using a control message. Unfortunately, at the same time, *A* is sending data message 1. When *A* gets the request for retransmission, it resends 0. However, when *B* gets message 1, instead of the requested message 0, it sends control message 1 to *A* complaining that it wants 0, not 1. When *A* sees this, it shrugs its shoulders and sends message 0 for the third time.

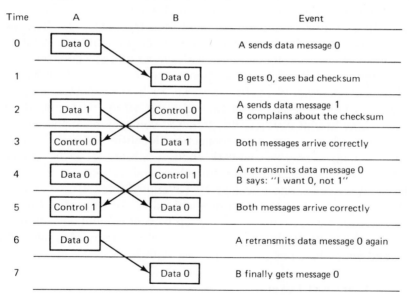

Fig. 2-3. Discussion between a receiver and a sender in the data link layer.

The point here is not so much whether the protocol of Fig. 2-3 is a great one (it is not), but rather to illustrate that in each layer there is a need for discussion between the sender and the receiver. Typical messages are "Please retransmit message *n*," "I already retransmitted it," "No you did not," "Yes I did," "All right, have it your way, but send it again," and so forth. This discussion takes place in the header field, where various requests and responses are defined, and parameters (such as frame numbers) can be supplied.

2.1.3. The Network Layer

On a LAN, there is usually no need for the sender to locate the receiver. It just puts the message out on the network and the receiver takes it off. A wide-area network, however, consists of a large number of machines, each with some number of lines to other machines, rather like a large-scale map showing major cities and roads connecting them. For a message to get from the sender to the receiver it may have to make a number of hops, at each one choosing an outgoing line to use. The question of how to choose the best path is called **routing**, and is the primary task of the network layer.

The problem is complicated by the fact that the shortest route is not always the best route. What really matters is the amount of delay on a given route, which, in turn, is related to the amount of traffic and the number of messages queued up for transmission over the various lines. The delay can thus change over the course of time. Some routing algorithms try to adapt to changing loads, whereas others are content to make decisions based on long-term averages.

Two network-layer protocols are in widespread use, one connection-oriented and one connectionless. The connection-oriented one is called **X.25**, and is favored by the operators of public networks, such as telephone companies and the European PTTs. The X.25 user first sends a *Call Request* to the destination, which can either accept or reject the proposed connection. If the connection is accepted, the caller is given a connection identifier to use in subsequent requests. In many cases, the network chooses a route from the sender to the receiver during this setup, and uses it for subsequent traffic.

The connectionless one is called **IP** (Internet Protocol) and is part of the DoD (U.S. Department of Defense) protocol suite. An IP **packet** (the technical term for a message in the network layer) can be sent without any setup. Each IP packet is routed to its destination independent of all others. No internal path is selected and remembered as is often the case with X.25.

2.1.4. The Transport Layer

Packets can be lost on the way from the sender to the receiver. Although some applications can handle their own error recovery, others prefer a reliable connection. The job of the transport layer is to provide this service. The idea is that the session layer should be able to deliver a message to the transport layer with the expectation that it will be delivered without loss.

Upon receiving a message from the session layer, the transport layer breaks it into pieces small enough for each to fit in a single packet, assigns each one a sequence number, and then sends them all. The discussion in the transport layer header concerns which packets have been sent, which have been received, how many more the receiver has room to accept, and similar topics.

Reliable transport connections (which by definition are connection-oriented) can be built on top of either X.25 or IP. In the former case all the packets will arrive in the correct sequence (if they arrive at all), but in the latter case it is possible for one packet to take a different route and arrive earlier than the packet sent before it. It is up to the transport layer software to put everything back in order to maintain the illusion that a transport connection is like a big tube—you put messages into it and they come out undamaged and in the same order in which they went in.

The official ISO transport protocol has five variants, known as **TP0** through **TP4**. The differences relate to error handling and the ability to send several transport connections over a single X.25 connection. The choice of which one to use depends on the properties of the underlying network layer.

The DoD transport protocol is called **TCP (Transmission Control Protocol**) and is described in detail in (Comer, 1991). It is similar to TP4. The combination TCP/IP is widely used at universities and on most UNIX systems. The DoD protocol suite also supports a connectionless transport protocol called **UDP** (Universal Datagram Protocol), which is essentially just IP with some minor additions. User programs that do not need a connection-oriented protocol normally use UDP.

2.1.5. The Session Layer

The session layer is essentially an enhanced version of the transport layer. It provides dialog control, to keep track of which party is currently talking, and it provides synchronization facilities. The latter are useful to allow users to insert checkpoints into long transfers, so that in the event of a crash it is only necessary to go back to the last checkpoint, rather than all the way back to the beginning. In practice, few applications are interested in the session layer and it is rarely supported. It is not even present in the DoD protocol suite.

2.1.6. The Presentation Layer

Unlike the lower layers, which are concerned with getting the bits from the sender to the receiver reliably and efficiently, the presentation layer is concerned with the meaning of the bits. Most messages do not consist of random bit strings, but more structured information such as people's names, addresses, amounts of money, and so on. In the presentation layer it is possible to define records containing fields like these and then have the sender notify the receiver that a message contains a particular record in a certain format. This makes it easier for machines with different internal representations to communicate.

2.1.7. The Application Layer

The application layer is really just a collection of miscellaneous protocols for common activities such as electronic mail, file transfer, and connecting remote terminals to computers over a network. The best known of these are the X.400 electronic mail protocol and the X.500 directory server. Neither this layer nor the two layers directly under it will be of interest to us in this book.

2.2. ASYNCHRONOUS TRANSFER MODE NETWORKS

The OSI world sketched in the previous section was developed in the 1970s and implemented (to some extent) in the 1980s. New developments in the 1990s are overtaking OSI, certainly in the technology-driven lower layers. In this section we will touch just briefly on some of these advances in networking, since future distributed systems will very likely be built on them, and it is important for operating system designers to be aware of them. For a more complete treatment of the state-of-the-art in network technology, see (Kleinrock, 1992; and Partridge, 1993, 1994).

In the past quarter century, computers have improved in performance by *many* orders of magnitude. Networks have not. When the ARPANET, the predecessor to the Internet, was inaugurated in 1969, it used 56 Kbps communication lines between the nodes. This was state-of-the-art communication then. In the late 1970s and early 1980s, many of these lines were replaced by T1 lines running at 1.5 Mbps. Eventually, the main backbone evolved into a T3 network at 45 Mbps, but most lines on the Internet are still T1 or slower.

New developments are suddenly about to make 155 Mbps the low-end standard, with major trunks running at 1 gigabit/sec and up (Catlett, 1992; Cheung, 1992; and Lyles and Swinehart, 1992). This rapid change will have an enormous impact on distributed systems, making possible all kinds of applications that were previously unthinkable, but it also brings new challenges. It is this new technology that we will describe below.

2.2.1. What Is Asynchronous Transfer Mode?

In the late 1980s, the world's telephone companies finally began to realize that there was more to telecommunications than transmitting voice in 4 KHz analog channels. It is true that data networks, such as X.25, existed for years, but they were clearly stepchildren and frequently ran at 56 or 64 Kbps. Systems like the Internet were regarded as academic curiosities, akin to a two-headed cow in a circus sideshow. Analog voice was where the action (and money) was.

When the telephone companies decided to build networks for the 21st Century, they faced a dilemma: voice traffic is smooth, needing a low, but constant bandwidth, whereas data traffic is bursty, usually needing no bandwidth (when there is no traffic), but sometimes needing a great deal for very short periods of time. Neither traditional circuit switching (used in the Public Switched Telephone Network) nor packet switching (used in the Internet) was suitable for both kinds of traffic.

After much study, a hybrid form using fixed-size blocks over virtual circuits was chosen as a compromise that gave reasonably good performance for both types of traffic. This scheme, called **ATM** (**Asynchronous Transfer Mode**) has become an international standard and is likely to play a major role in future distributed systems, both local-area ones and wide-area ones. For tutorials on ATM, see (Le Boudec, 1992; Minzer, 1989; and Newman, 1994).

The ATM model is that a sender first establishes a connection (i.e., a virtual circuit) to the receiver or receivers. During connection establishment, a route is determined from the sender to the receiver(s) and routing information is stored in the switches along the way. Using this connection, packets can be sent, but they are chopped up by the hardware into small, fixed-sized units called **cells**. The cells for a given virtual circuit all follow the path stored in the switches. When the connection is no longer needed, it is released and the routing information purged from the switches.

This scheme has a number of advantages over traditional packet and circuit switching. The most important one is that a single network can now be used to transport an arbitrary mix of voice, data, broadcast television, videotapes, radio, and other information efficiently, replacing what were previously separate networks (telephone, X.25, cable TV, etc.). New services, such as video conferencing for businesses, will also use it. In all cases, what the network sees is cells; it does not care what is in them. This integration represents an enormous cost saving and simplification that will make it possible for each home and business to have a single wire (or fiber) coming in for all its communication and information needs. It will also make possible new applications, such as video-on-demand, teleconferencing, and access to thousands of remote data bases.

Cell switching lends itself well to multicasting (one cell going to many destinations), a technique needed for transmitting broadcast television to thousands of houses at the same time. Conventional circuit switching, as used in the telephone system, cannot handle this. Broadcast media, such as cable TV can, but they cannot handle point-to-point traffic without wasting bandwidth (effectively broadcasting every message). The advantage of cell switching is that it can handle both point-to-point and multicasting efficiently.

Fixed-size cells allow rapid switching, something much harder to achieve with current store-and-forward packet switches. They also eliminate the danger of a small packet being delayed because a big one is hogging a needed line. With cell switching, after each cell is transmitted , a new one can be sent, even a new one belonging to a different packet.

ATM has its own protocol hierarchy, as shown in Fig. 2-4. The physical layer has the same functionality as layer 1 in the OSI model. The ATM layer deals with cells and cell transport, including routing, so it covers OSI layer 2 and part of layer 3. However, unlike OSI layer 2, the ATM layer does not recover lost or damaged cells. The adaptation layer handles breaking packets into cells and reassembling them at the other end, which does not appear explicitly in the OSI model until layer 4. The service offered by the adaptation layer is not a perfectly reliable end-to-end service, so transport connections must be implemented in the upper layers, for example, by using ATM cells to carry TCP/IP traffic.

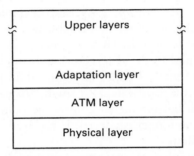

Fig. 2-4. The ATM reference model.

In the following sections, we will examine the lowest three layers of Fig. 2-4 in turn, starting at the bottom and working our way up.

2.2.2. The ATM Physical Layer

An ATM adaptor board plugged into a computer can put out a stream of cells onto a wire or fiber. The transmission stream must be continuous. When there are no data to be sent, empty cells are transmitted, which means that in the physical layer, ATM is really synchronous, not asynchronous. Within a virtual circuit, however, it is asynchronous.

Alternatively, the adaptor board can use **SONET (Synchronous Optical NETwork**) in the physical layer, putting its cells into the payload portion of SONET frames. The virtue of this approach is compatibility with the internal transmission system of AT&T and other carriers that use SONET. In Europe, a system called **SDH (Synchronous Digital Hierarchy**) that is closely patterned after SONET is available in some countries.

In SONET, the basic unit (analogous to a 193-bit T1 frame) is a 9×90 array of bytes called a **frame**. Of these 810 bytes, 36 bytes are overhead, leaving 774 bytes of payload. One frame is transmitted every 125 μsec, to match the telephone system's standard sampling rate of 8000 samples/sec, so the gross data rate (including overhead) is 51.840 Mbps and the net data rate (excluding overhead) is 49.536 Mbps.

These parameters were chosen after five years of tortuous negotiation between U.S., European, Japanese, and other telephone companies in order to handle the U.S. T3 data stream (44.736 Mbps) and the standards used by other countries. The computer industry did not play a significant role here (a 9×90 array with 36 bytes of overhead is not something a computer scientist is likely to propose).

The basic 51.840-Mbps channel is called **OC-1**. It is possible to send a group of n OC-1 frames as a group, which is designated OC-n when it is used for n independent OC-1 channels and OC-nc (for concatenated) when used for a single high-speed channel. Standards have been established for OC-3, OC-12, OC-48, and OC-192. The most important of these for ATM are OC-3c, at 155.520 Mbps and OC-12c, at 622.080 Mbps, because computers can probably produce data at these rates in the near future. For long-haul transmission within the telephone system, OC-12 and OC-48 are the most widely used at present.

OC-3c SONET adaptors for computers are now available to allow a computer to output SONET frames directly. OC-12c is expected shortly. Since even OC-1 is overkill for a telephone, it is unlikely that many audio telephones will ever speak ATM or SONET directly (ISDN will be used instead), but for videophones ATM and SONET are ideal.

2.2.3. The ATM Layer

When ATM was being developed, two factions developed within the standards committee. The Europeans wanted 32-byte cells because these had a small enough delay that echo suppressors would not be needed in most European countries. The Americans, who already had echo suppressors, wanted 64-byte cells due to their greater efficiency for data traffic.

The end result was a 48-byte cell, which no one really liked. It is too big for voice and too small for data. To make it even worse, a 5-byte header was added, giving a 53-byte cell containing a 48-byte data field. Note that a 53-byte cell is not a good match for a 774-byte SONET payload, so ATM cells will span SONET frames. Two separate levels of synchronization are thus needed: one to detect the start of a SONET frame, and one to detect the start of the first full ATM cell within the SONET payload. However, a standard for packing ATM cells into SONET frames exists, and the entire layer can be done in hardware.

The layout of a cell header from a computer to the first ATM switch is shown in Fig. 2-5. Unfortunately, the layout of a cell header between two ATM switches is different, with the *GFC* field being replaced by four more bits for the VPI field. In the view of many, this is unfortunate, since it introduces an unnecessary distinction between computer-to-switch and switch-to-switch cells and hence adaptor hardware. Both kinds of cells have 48-byte payloads directly following the header.

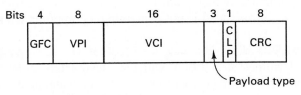

GFC = Generic flow control
VPI = Virtual path idenifier
VCI = Virtual channel identifier
CLP = Cell loss priority
CRC = Cyclic redundancy checksum

Fig. 2-5. User-to-network cell header layout.

The *GFC* may some day be used for flow control, if an agreement on how to do it can be achieved. The *VPI* and *VCI* fields together identify which path and virtual circuit a cell belongs to. Routing tables along the way use this information for routing. These fields are modified at each hop along the path. The purpose of the *VPI* field is to group together a collection of virtual circuits for the same destination and make it possible for a carrier to reroute all of them without having to examine the *VCI* field.

The *Payload type* field distinguishes data cells from control cells, and further identifies several kinds of control cells. The *CLP* field can be used to mark some cells as less important than others, so if congestion occurs, the least important ones will be the ones dropped. Finally, there is a 1-byte checksum over the header (but not the data).

2.2.4. The ATM Adaptation Layer

At 155 Mbps, a cell can arrive every 3 μsec. Few, if any, current CPUs can handle in excess of 300,000 interrupts/sec. Thus a mechanism is needed to allow a computer to send a packet and to have the ATM hardware break it into cells, transmit the cells, and then have them reassembled at the other end, generating one interrupt per packet, not per cell. This disassembly/reassembly is the job of the adaptation layer. It is expected that most host adaptor boards will run the adaptation layer on the board and give one interrupt per incoming packet, not one per incoming cell.

Unfortunately, here too, the standards writers did not get it quite right. Originally adaptation layers were defined for four classes of traffic:

1. Constant bit rate traffic (for audio and video).

2. Variable bit rate traffic but with bounded delay.

3. Connection-oriented data traffic.

4. Connectionless data traffic.

Quickly it was discovered that classes 3 and 4 were essentially the same, so they were merged into a new class, 3/4. At that point the computer industry woke up from a short nap and noticed that none of the adaptation layers were suitable for data traffic, so they drafted AAL 5, for computer-to-computer traffic (Suzuki, 1994). Its nickname, **SEAL (Simple and Efficient Adaptation Layer)**, hints at what its designers thought of the other three AAL layers. (In all fairness, it should be pointed out that getting people from two industries with very different traditions, telephony and computers, to agree to a standard at all was a nontrivial achievement.)

Let us focus on SEAL, due to its simplicity. It uses only one bit in the ATM header, one of the bits in the *Payload type* field. This bit is normally 0, but is set to 1 in the last cell of a packet. The last cell contains a trailer in the final 8 bytes. In most cases there will be some padding (with zeros) between the end of the packet and the start of the trailer. With SEAL, the destination just assembles incoming cells for each virtual circuit until it finds one with the end-of-packet bit set. Then it extracts and processes the trailer.

The trailer has four fields. The first two are each 1 byte long and are not used. Then comes a 2-byte field giving the packet length, and a 4-byte checksum over the packet, padding, and trailer.

2.2.5. ATM Switching

ATM networks are built up of copper or optical cables and switches. Figure 2-6(a) illustrates a network with four switches. Cells originating at any of the eight computers attached to the system can be switched to any of the other computers by traversing one or more switches. Each of these switches has four ports, each used for both input and output.

The inside of a generic switch is illustrated in Fig. 2-6(b). It has input lines and output lines and a parallel **switching fabric** that connects them. Because a cell has to be switched in 3 μsec (at OC-3), and as many cells as there are input lines can arrive at once, parallel switching is essential.

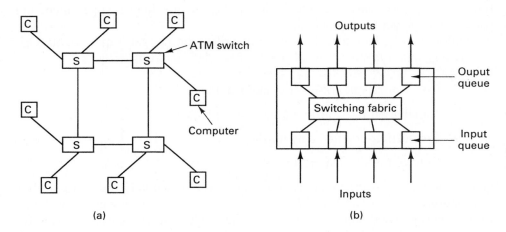

Fig. 2-6. (a) An ATM switching network. (b) Inside one switch.

When a cell arrives, its VPI and VCI fields are examined. Based on these and information stored in the switch when the virtual circuit was established, the cell is routed to the correct output port. Although the standard allows cells to be dropped, it requires that those delivered must be delivered in order.

A problem arises when two cells arrive at the same time on different input lines and need to go to the same output port. Just throwing one of them away is allowed by the standard, but if your switch drops more than 1 cell in 10^{12}, you are unlikely to sell many switches. An alternative scheme is to pick one of them at random and forward it, holding the other cell until later. In the next round, this algorithm is applied again. If two ports each have streams of cells for the same destination, substantial input queues will build up, blocking other cells behind them that want to go to output ports that are free. This problem is known as **head-of-line blocking**.

A different switch design copies the cell into a queue associated with the output buffer and lets it wait there, instead of keeping it in the input buffer. This approach eliminates head-of-line blocking and gives better performance. It is also possible for a switch to have a pool of buffers that can be used for both input and output buffering. Still another possibility is to buffer on the input side, but allow the second or third cell in line to be switched, even if the first one cannot be.

Many other switch designs have been proposed and tried. These include time division switches using shared memory, buses or rings, as well as space division switches with one or more paths between each input and each output.

Some of these switches are discussed in (Ahmadi and Denzel, 1989; Anderson et al., 1993; Gopal et al., 1992; Pattavina, 1993; Rooholamini et al., 1994; and Zegura, 1993).

2.2.6. Some Implications of ATM for Distributed Systems

The availability of ATM networks at 155 Mbps, 622 Mbps, and potentially at 2.5 Gbps has some major implications for the design of distributed systems. For the most part, the effects are due primarily to the enormously high bandwidth suddenly available, rather than due to specific properties of ATM networks. The effects are most pronounced on wide-area distributed systems.

To start with, consider sending a 1-Mbit file across the United States and waiting for an acknowledgement that it has arrived correctly. The speed of light in copper wire or fiber optics is about 2/3 the speed of light in vacuum, so it takes a bit about 15 msec to go across the US one way. At 64 Kbps, it takes about 15.6 sec to pump the bits out, so the additional 30 msec round-trip delay does not add much. At 622 Mbps, it takes 1/622 of a second, or about 1.6 msec, to push the whole file out the door. In the best case, the reply can come back after 31.6 msec, during which time the line was idle for 30 msec, or 95 percent of the total. As speeds go up, the time-to-reply asymptotically approaches 30 msec, and the fraction of the available virtual circuit bandwidth that can be used approaches 0. For messages shorter than 1 Mbps, which are common in distributed systems, it is even worse. The conclusion is: For high-speed wide-area distributed systems, new protocols and system architectures will be needed to deal with the latency in many applications, especially interactive ones.

Another problem is flow control. Suppose that we have a truly large file, say a videotape consisting of 10 GB. The sender begins transmitting at 622 Mbps, and the data begin to roll in at the receiver. The receiver may not happen to have a 10 GB buffer handy, so it sends back a cell saying: STOP. By the time the STOP cell has gotten back to the sender, 30 msec later, almost 20 Mbits of data are under way. If most of these are lost due to inadequate buffer space, they will have to be transmitted again. Using a traditional sliding window protocol gets us back to the situation we just had, namely, if the sender is allowed to send only 1 Mbit and then has to wait for an acknowledgement, the virtual circuit is 95 percent idle. Alternatively, a large amount of buffering capacity can be put in the switches and adaptor boards, but at increased cost. Still another possibility is rate control, in which the sender and receiver agree in advance how many bits/sec the sender may transmit. Flow control and congestion control in ATM networks are discussed in (Eckberg, 1992; Hong and Suda, 1991; and Trajkovic and Golestani, 1992). A bibliography with over 250 references to performance in ATM networks is given in (Nikolaidis and Onvural, 1992).

A different approach to dealing with the now-huge 30 msec latency is to send some bits, then stop the sending process and run something else while waiting for the reply. The trouble with this strategy is that computers are becoming so inexpensive, that for many applications, each process has its own computer, so there is nothing else to run. Wasting the CPU time is not important, since it is cheap, but it is clear that going from 64 Kbps to 622 Mbps has not bought a 10,000-fold gain in performance, even in communication-limited applications.

The effect of the transcontinental delay can show up in various ways. For example, if some application program in New York has to make 20 sequential requests from a server in California to get an answer, the 600-msec delay will be noticeable to the user, as people find delays above 200 msec annoying.

Alternatively, we could move the computation itself to the machine in California and let each user keystroke be sent as a separate cell across the country and come back to be displayed. Doing this will add 60 msec to each keystroke, which no one will notice. However, this reasoning quickly leads us to abandoning the idea of a distributed system and putting all the computing in one place, with remote users. In effect, we have built a big centralized timesharing system with just the users distributed.

One observation that does relate to specific properties of ATM is the fact that switches are permitted to drop cells if they get congested. Dropping even one cell probably means waiting for a timeout and having the whole packet be retransmitted. For services that need a uniform rate, such as playing music, this could be a problem. (Oddly enough, the ear is far more sensitive than the eye to irregular delivery.)

As a consequence of these and other problems, while high-speed networks in general and ATM in particular introduce new opportunities, taking advantage of them will not be simple. Considerable research will be needed before we know how to deal with them effectively.

2.3. THE CLIENT-SERVER MODEL

While ATM networks are going to be important in the future, for the moment they are too expensive for most applications, so let us go back to more conventional networking. At first glance, layered protocols along the OSI lines look like a fine way to organize a distributed system. In effect, a sender sets up a connection (a bit pipe) with the receiver, and then pumps the bits in, which arrive without error, in order, at the receiver. What could be wrong with this?

Plenty. To start with, look at Fig. 2-2. The existence of all those headers generates a considerable amount of overhead. Every time a message is sent it must be processed by about half a dozen layers, each one generating and adding a header on the way down or removing and examining a header on the way up. All of this work takes time. On wide-area networks, where the number of bits/sec that can be sent is typically fairly low (often as little as 64K bits/sec), this overhead is not serious. The limiting factor is the capacity of the lines, and even with all the header manipulation, the CPUs are fast enough to keep the lines running at full speed. Thus a wide-area distributed system can probably use the OSI or TCP/IP protocols without any loss in (the already meager) performance. Aith ATM, even here serious problems may arise.

However, for a LAN-based distributed system, the protocol overhead is often substantial. So much CPU time is wasted running protocols that the effective throughput over the LAN is often only a fraction of what the LAN can do. As a consequence, most LAN-based distributed systems do not use layered protocols at all, or if they do, they use only a subset of the entire protocol stack.

In addition, the OSI model addresses only a small aspect of the problem— getting the bits from the sender to the receiver (and in the upper layers, what they mean). It does not say anything about how the distributed system should be structured. Something more is needed.

2.3.1. Clients and Servers

This something is often the client-server model that we introduced in the preceding chapter. The idea behind this model is to structure the operating system as a group of cooperating processes, called **servers**, that offer services to the users, called **clients**. The client and server machines normally all run the same microkernel, with both the clients and servers running as user processes, as we saw earlier. A machine may run a single process, or it may run multiple clients, multiple servers, or a mixture of the two.

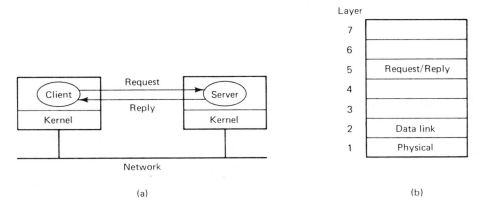

Fig. 2-7. The client-server model. Although all message passing is actually done by the kernels, this simplified form of drawing will be used when there is no ambiguity.

To avoid the considerable overhead of the connection-oriented protocols such as OSI or TCP/IP, the client server model is usually based on a simple, connectionless **request/reply protocol**. The client sends a request message to the server asking for some service (e.g., read a block of a file). The server does the work and returns the data requested or an error code indicating why the work could not be performed, as depicted in Fig. 2-7(a).

The primary advantage of Fig. 2-7(a) is the simplicity. The client sends a request and gets an answer. No connection has to be established before use or torn down afterward. The reply message serves as the acknowledgement to the request.

From the simplicity comes another advantage: efficiency. The protocol stack is shorter and thus more efficient. Assuming that all the machines are identical, only three levels of protocol are needed, as shown in Fig. 2-7(b). The physical and data link protocols take care of getting the packets from client to server and back. These are always handled by the hardware, for example, an Ethernet or token ring chip. No routing is needed and no connections are established, so layers 3 and 4 are not needed. Layer 5 is the request/reply protocol. It defines the set of legal requests and the set of legal replies to these requests. There is no session management because there are no sessions. The upper layers are not needed either.

Due to this simple structure, the communication services provided by the (micro)kernel can, for example, be reduced to two system calls, one for sending messages and one for receiving them. These system calls can be invoked through library procedures, say, *send(dest, &mptr)* and *receive(addr, &mptr)*. The former sends the message pointed to by *mptr* to a process identified by *dest* and causes the caller to be blocked until the message has been sent. The latter causes the caller to be blocked until a message arrives. When one does, the message is copied to the buffer pointed to by *mptr* and the caller is unblocked. The *addr* parameter specifies the address to which the receiver is listening. Many variants of these two procedures and their parameters are possible. We will discuss some of these later in this chapter.

2.3.2. An Example Client and Server

To provide more insight into how clients and servers work, in this section we will present an outline of a client and a file server in C. Both the client and the server need to share some definitions, so we will collect these into a file called *header.h*, which is shown in Fig. 2-8. Both the client and server include these using the

```
#include <header.h>
```

statement. This statement has the effect of causing a preprocessor to literally insert the entire contents of *header.h* into the source program just before the compiler starts compiling the program.

```
/* Definitions needed by clients and servers. */
#define MAX_PATH      255       /* maximum length of a file name */
#define BUF_SIZE      1024      /* how much data to transfer at once */
#define FILE_SERVER   243       /* file server's network address */

/* Definitions of the allowed operations. */
#define CREATE        1         /* create a new file */
#define READ          2         /* read a piece of a file and return it */
#define WRITE         3         /* write a piece of a file */
#define DELETE        4         /* delete an existing file */

/* Error codes. */
#define OK            0         /* operation performed correctly */
#define E_BAD_OPCODE  -1        /* unknown operation requested */
#define E_BAD_PARAM   -2        /* error in a parameter */
#define E_IO          -3        /* disk error or other I/O error */

/* Definition of the message format. */
struct message {
  long source;                  /* sender's identity */
  long dest;                    /* receiver's identity */
  long opcode;                  /* which operation: CREATE, READ, etc. */
  long count;                   /* how many bytes to transfer */
  long offset;                  /* where in file to start reading or writing */
  long extra1;                  /* extra field */
  long extra2;                  /* extra field */
  long result;                  /* result of the operation reported here */
  char name[MAX_PATH];          /* name of the file being operated on */
  char data[BUF_SIZE];          /* data to be read or written */
};
```

Fig. 2-8. The *header.h* file used by the client and server.

Let us first take a look at *header.h*. It starts out by defining two constants, *MAX_PATH* and *BUF_SIZE*, that determine the size of two arrays needed in the message. The former tells how many characters a file name (i.e., a path name like */usr/ast/books/opsys/chapter1.t*) may contain. The latter fixes the amount of data that may be read or written in one operation by setting the buffer size. The next constant, *FILE_SERVER*, provides the network address of the file server so that clients can send messages to it.

The second group of constants defines the operation numbers. These are needed to ensure that the client and server agree on which code will represent a READ, which code will represent a WRITE, and so on. We have only shown four here, but in a real system there would normally be more.

Every reply contains a result code. If the operation succeeds, the result code often contains useful information (such as the number of bytes actually read). If there is no value to be returned (such as when a file is created), the value *OK* is used. If the operation is unsuccessful for some reason, the result code tells why, using codes such as *E_BAD_OPCODE*, *E_BAD_PARAM*, and so on.

Finally, we come to the most important part of *header.h*, the definition of the message itself. In our example it is a structure with 10 fields. All requests from the client to the server use this format, as do all replies. In a real system, one would probably not have a fixed format message (because not all the fields are needed in all cases), but it makes the explanation simpler here. The *source* and *dest* fields identify the sender and receiver, respectively. The *opcode* field is one of the operations defined above, that is, *CREATE*, *READ*, *WRITE*, or *DELETE*. The *count* and *offset* fields are used for parameters, and two other fields, *extra1* and *extra2*, are defined to provide space for additional parameters in case the server is expanded in the future. The *result* field is not used for client-to-server requests but holds the result value for server-to-client replies. Finally, we have two arrays. The first, *name*, holds the name of the file being accessed. The second, *data*, holds the data sent back on a reply to READ or the data sent to the server on a WRITE.

Let us now look at the code, as outlined in Fig. 2-9. In (a) we have the server; in (b) we have the client. The server is straightforward. The main loop starts out by calling *receive* to get a request message. The first parameter identifies the caller by giving its address, and the second parameter points to a message buffer where the incoming message can be stored. The library procedure *receive* traps to the kernel to suspend the server until a message arrives. When one comes in, the server continues and dispatches on the opcode type. For each opcode, a different procedure is called. The incoming message and a buffer for the outgoing message are given as parameters. The procedure examines the incoming message, *m1*, and builds the reply in *m2*. It also returns a function value that is sent back in the *result* field. After the *send* has completed, the server goes back to the top of the loop to execute *receive* and wait for the next incoming message.

In Fig. 2-9(b) we have a procedure that copies a file using the server. Its body consists of a loop that reads one block from the source file and writes it to the destination file. The loop is repeated until the source file has been copied completely, as indicated by a zero or negative return code from the read.

The first part of the loop is concerned with building a message for the READ operation and sending it to the server. After the reply has been received, the second part of the loop is entered, which takes the data just received and sends it back to the server in the form of a WRITE to the destination file. The programs of Fig. 2-9 are just sketches of the code. Many details have been omitted. For example, the *do_xxx* procedures (the ones that actually do the work) are not shown, and no error checking is done. Still, the general idea of how a client and a server interact should be clear. In the following sections we will look at some of the issues that relate to clients and servers in more detail.

```
#include <header.h>
void main(void)
{
  struct message m1, m2;          /* incoming and outgoing messages */
  int r;                          /* result code */

  while (1) {                     /* server runs forever */
        receive(FILE_SERVER,&m1); /* block waiting for a message */
        switch(m1.opcode) {       /* dispatch on type of request */
                case CREATE:    r = do_create(&m1, &m2);      break;
                case READ:      r = do_read(&m1, &m2);        break;
                case WRITE:     r = do_write(&m1, &m2);       break;
                case DELETE:    r = do_delete(&m1, &m2);      break;
                default:        r = E_BAD_OPCODE;
        }
        m2.result = r;            /* return result to client */
        send(m1.source, &m2);     /* send reply */
  }
}
                                (a)
#include <header.h>
int copy(char *src, char *dst)    /* procedure to copy file using the server */
{
  struct message m1;              /* message buffer */
  long position;                  /* current file position */
  long client = 110;              /* client's address */

  initialize();                   /* prepare for execution */
  position = 0;
  do {
        /* Get a block of data from the source file. */
        m1.opcode = READ;         /* operation is a read */
        m1.offset = position;     /* current position in the file */
        m1. count = BUF_SIZE;     /* how many bytes to read */
        strcpy(&m1.name, src);    /* copy name of file to be read to message */
        send(FILE_SERVER, &m1);   /* send the message to the file server */
        receive(client, &m1);     /* block waiting for the reply */

        /* Write the data just received to the destination file. */
        m1.opcode = WRITE;        /* operation is a write */
        m1.offset = position;     /* current position in the file */
        m1. count = m1.result;    /* how many bytes to write */
        strcpy(&m1.name, dst);    /* copy name of file to be written to buf */
        send(FILE_SERVER, &m1);   /* send the message to the file server */
        receive(client, &m1);     /* block waiting for the reply */
        position += m1.result;    /* m1.result is number of bytes written */
  } while (m1.result > 0);        /* iterate until done */
  return(m1.result >= 0 ? OK : m1.result);       /* return OK or error code */
}
                                (b)
```

Fig. 2-9. (a) A sample server. (b) A client procedure using that server to copy
a file.

2.3.3. Addressing

In order for a client to send a message to a server, it must know the server's address. In the example of the preceding section, the server's address was simply hardwired into *header.h* as a constant. While this strategy might work in an especially simple system, usually a more sophisticated form of addressing is needed. In this section we will describe some issues concerning addressing.

In our example, the file server has been assigned a numerical address (243), but we have not really specified what this means. In particular, does it refer to a specific machine, or to a specific process? If it refers to a specific machine, the sending kernel can extract it from the message structure and use it as the hardware address for sending the packet to the server. All the sending kernel has to do then is build a frame using the 243 as the data link address and put the frame out on the LAN. The server's interface board will see the frame, recognize 243 as its own address, and accept it.

If there is only one process running on the destination machine, the kernel will know what to do with the incoming message—give it to the one and only process running there. However, what happens if there are several processes running on the destination machine? Which one gets the message? The kernel has no way of knowing. Consequently, a scheme that uses network addresses to identify processes means that only one process can run on each machine. While this limitation is not fatal, it is sometimes a serious restriction.

An alternative addressing system sends messages to processes rather than to machines. Although this method eliminates all ambiguity about who the real recipient is, it does introduce the problem of how processes are identified. One common scheme is to use two part names, specifying both a machine and a process number. Thus 243.4 or 4@243 or something similar designates process 4 on machine 243. The machine number is used by the kernel to get the message correctly delivered to the proper machine, and the process number is used by the kernel on that machine to determine which process the message is intended for. A nice feature of this approach is that every machine can number its processes starting at 0. No global coordination is needed because there is never any ambiguity between process 0 on machine 243 and process 0 on machine 199. The former is 243.0 and the latter is 199.0. This scheme is illustrated in Fig. 2-10(a).

A slight variation on this addressing scheme uses *machine.local-id* instead of *machine.process*. The *local-id* field is normally a randomly chosen 16-bit or 32-bit integer (or the next one in sequence). One process, typically a server, starts up by making a system call to tell the kernel that it wants to listen to *local-id*. Later, when a message comes in addressed to *machine.local_id*, the kernel knows which process to give the message to. Most communication in Berkeley UNIX, for example, uses this method, with 32-bit Internet addresses used for specifying machines and 16-bit numbers for the *local-id* fields.

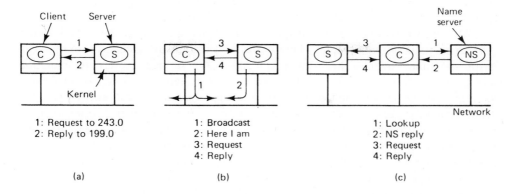

Fig. 2-10. (a) Machine.process addressing. (b) Process addressing with broadcasting. (c) Address lookup via a name server.

Nevertheless, *machine.process* addressing is far from ideal. Specifically, it is not transparent since the user is obviously aware of where the server is located, and transparency is one of the main goals of building a distributed system. To see why this matters, suppose that the file server normally runs on machine 243, but one day that machine is down. Machine 176 is available, but programs previously compiled using *header.h* all have the number 243 built into them, so they will not work if the server is unavailable. Clearly, this situation is undesirable.

An alternative approach is to assign each process a unique address that does not contain an embedded machine number. One way to achieve this goal is to have a centralized process address allocator that simply maintains a counter. Upon receiving a request for an address, it simply returns the current value of the counter and then increments it by one. The disadvantage of this scheme is that centralized components like this do not scale to large systems and thus should be avoided.

Yet another method for assigning process identifiers is to let each process pick its own identifier from a large, sparse address space, such as the space of 64-bit binary integers. The probability of two processes picking the same number is tiny, and the system scales well. However, here, too, there is a problem: How does the sending kernel know what machine to send the message to? On a LAN that supports broadcasting, the sender can broadcast a special **locate packet** containing the address of the destination process. Because it is a broadcast packet, it will be received by all machines on the network. All the kernels check to see if the address is theirs, and if so, send back a **here I am** message giving their network address (machine number). The sending kernel then uses this address, and furthermore, caches it, to avoid broadcasting the next time the server is needed. This method is shown in Fig. 2-10(b).

Although this scheme is transparent, even with caching, the broadcasting puts extra load on the system. This extra load can be avoided by providing an extra machine to map high-level (i.e., ASCII) service names to machine addresses, as shown in Fig. 2-10(c). When this system is employed, processes such as servers are referred to by ASCII strings, and it is these strings that are embedded in programs, not binary machine or process numbers. Every time a client runs, on the first attempt to use a server, the client sends a query message to a special mapping server, often called a **name server**, asking it for the machine number where the server is currently located. Once this address has been obtained, the request can be sent directly. As in the previous case, addresses can be cached.

In summary, we have the following methods for addressing processes:

1. Hardwire *machine.number* into client code.

2. Let processes pick random addresses; locate them by broadcasting.

3. Put ASCII server names in clients; look them up at run time.

Each of these has problems. The first one is not transparent, the second one generates extra load on the system, and the third one requires a centralized component, the name server. Of course, the name server can be replicated, but doing so introduces the problems associated with keeping them consistent.

A completely different approach is to use special hardware. Let processes pick random addresses. However, instead of locating them by broadcasting, the network interface chips have to be designed to allow processes to store process addresses in them. Frames would then use process addresses instead of machine addresses. As each frame came by, the network interface chip would simply examine the frame to see if the destination process was on its machine. If so, the frame would be accepted; otherwise, it would not be.

2.3.4. Blocking versus Nonblocking Primitives

The message-passing primitives we have described so far are what are called **blocking primitives** (sometimes called **synchronous primitives**). When a process calls *send* it specifies a destination and a buffer to send to that destination. While the message is being sent, the sending process is blocked (i.e., suspended). The instruction following the call to *send* is not executed until the message has been completely sent, as shown in Fig. 2-11(a). Similarly, a call to *receive* does not return control until a message has actually been received and put in the message buffer pointed to by the parameter. The process remains suspended in *receive* until a message arrives, even if it takes hours. In some systems, the receiver can specify from whom it wishes to receive, in which case it remains blocked until a message from that sender arrives.

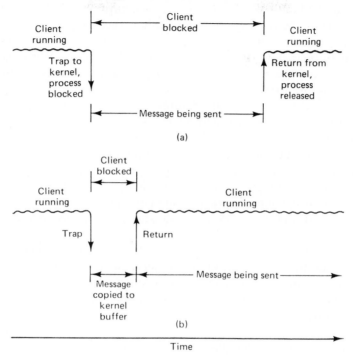

Fig. 2-11. (a) A blocking send primitive. (b) A nonblocking send primitive.

An alternative to blocking primitives are **nonblocking primitives** (sometimes called **asynchronous primitives**). If *send* is nonblocking, it returns control to the caller immediately, before the message is sent. The advantage of this scheme is that the sending process can continue computing in parallel with the message transmission, instead of having the CPU go idle (assuming no other process is runnable). The choice between blocking and nonblocking primitives is normally made by the system designers (i.e., either one primitive is available or the other), although in a few systems both are available and users can choose their favorite.

However, the performance advantage offered by nonblocking primitives is offset by a serious disadvantage: the sender cannot modify the message buffer until the message has been sent. The consequences of the process overwriting the message during transmission are too horrible to contemplate. Worse yet, the sending process has no idea of when the transmission is done, so it never knows when it is safe to reuse the buffer. It can hardly avoid touching it forever.

There are two possible ways out. The first solution is to have the kernel copy the message to an internal kernel buffer and then allow the process to continue, as shown in Fig. 2-11(b). From the sender's point of view, this scheme is the same as a blocking call: as soon as it gets control back, it is free to reuse the buffer. Of course, the message will not yet have been sent, but the sender is not hindered by this fact. The disadvantage of this method is that every outgoing message has to be copied from user space to kernel space. With many network interfaces, the message will have to be copied to a hardware transmission buffer later anyway, so the first copy is essentially wasted. The extra copy can reduce the performance of the system considerably.

The second solution is to interrupt the sender when the message has been sent to inform it that the buffer is once again available. No copy is required here, which saves time, but user-level interrupts make programming tricky, difficult, and subject to race conditions, which makes them irreproducible. Most experts agree that although this method is highly efficient and allows the most parallelism, the disadvantages greatly outweigh the advantages: programs based on interrupts are difficult to write correctly and nearly impossible to debug when they are wrong.

Sometimes the interrupt can be disguised by starting up a new thread of control (to discussed in Chap. 4) within the sender's address space. Although this is somewhat cleaner than a raw interrupt, it is still far more complicated than synchronous communication. If only a single thread of control is available, the choices come down to:

1. Blocking send (CPU idle during message transmission).

2. Nonblocking send with copy (CPU time wasted for the extra copy).

3. Nonblocking send with interrupt (makes programming difficult).

Under normal conditions, the first choice is the best. It does not maximize the parallelism, but is simple to understand and simple to implement. It also does not require any kernel buffers to manage. Furthermore, as can be seen from comparing Fig. 2-11(a) to Fig. 2-11(b), the message will usually be out the door faster if no copy is required. On the other hand, if overlapping processing and transmission are essential for some application, a nonblocking send with copying is the best choice.

For the record, we would like to point out that some authors use a different criterion to distinguish synchronous from asynchronous primitives (Andrews, 1991). In our view, the essential difference between a synchronous primitive and an asynchronous one is whether the sender can reuse the message buffer immediately after getting control back without fear of messing up the *send*. When the message actually gets to the receiver is irrelevant.

In the alternative view, a synchronous primitive is one in which the sender is blocked until the receiver has accepted the message and the acknowledgement has gotten back to the sender. Everything else is asynchronous in this view. There is complete agreement that if the sender gets control back before the message has been copied or sent, the primitive is asynchronous. Similarly, everyone agrees that when the sender is blocked until the receiver has acknowledged the message, we have a synchronous primitive.

The disagreement comes on whether the intermediate cases (message copied or copied and sent, but not acknowledged) counts as one or the other. Operating systems designers tend to prefer our way, since their concern is with buffer management and message transmission. Programming language designers tend to prefer the alternative definition, because that is what counts at the language level.

Just as *send* can be blocking or nonblocking, so can *receive*. A nonblocking *receive* just tells the kernel where the buffer is, and returns control almost immediately. Again here, how does the caller know when the operation has completed? One way is to provide an explicit *wait* primitive that allows the receiver to block when it wants to. Alternatively (or in addition to *wait*), the designers may provide a *test* primitive to allow the receiver to poll the kernel to check on the status. A variant on this idea is a *conditional_receive*, which either gets a message or signals failure, but in any event returns immediately, or within some timeout interval. Finally, here too, interrupts can be used to signal completion. For the most part, a blocking version of *receive* is much simpler and greatly preferred.

If multiple threads of control are present within a single address space, the arrival of a message can cause a thread to be created spontaneously. We will come back to this issue after we have looked at threads in Chap. 4.

An issue closely related to blocking versus nonblocking calls is that of timeouts. In a system in which *send* calls block, if there is no reply, the sender will block forever. To prevent this situation, in some systems the caller may specify a time interval within which it expects a reply. If none arrives in that interval, the *send* call terminates with an error status.

2.3.5. Buffered versus Unbuffered Primitives

Just as system designers have a choice between blocking and nonblocking primitives, they also have a choice between buffered and unbuffered primitives. The primitives we have described so far are essentially **unbuffered primitives**. What this means is that an address refers to a specific process, as in Fig. 2-9. A call *receive*(*addr*, &*m*) tells the kernel of the machine on which it is running that the calling process is listening to address *addr* and is prepared to receive one message sent to that address. A single message buffer, pointed to by *m*, is provided to hold the incoming message. When the message comes in, the receiving kernel copies it to the buffer and unblocks the receiving process. The use of an address to refer to a specific process is illustrated in Fig. 2-12(a).

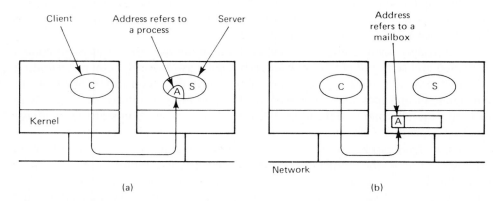

Fig. 2-12. (a) Unbuffered message passing. (b) Buffered message passing.

This scheme works fine as long as the server calls *receive* before the client calls *send*. The call to *receive* is the mechanism that tells the server's kernel which address the server is using and where to put the incoming message. The problem arises when the *send* is done before the *receive*. How does the server's kernel know which of its processes (if any) is using the address in the newly arrived message, and how does it know where to copy the message? The answer is simple: it does not.

One implementation strategy is to just discard the message, let the client time out, and hope the server has called *receive* before the client retransmits. This approach is easy to implement, but with bad luck, the client (or more likely, the client's kernel) may have to try several times before succeeding. Worse yet, if enough consecutive attempts fail, the client's kernel may give up, falsely concluding that the server has crashed or that the address is invalid.

In a similar vein, suppose that two or more clients are using the server of Fig. 2-9(a). After the server has accepted a message from one of them, it is no longer listening to its address until it has finished its work and gone back to the top of the loop to call *receive* again. If it takes a while to do the work, the other clients may make multiple attempts to send to it, and some of them may give up, depending on the values of their retransmission timers and how impatient they are.

The second approach to dealing with this problem is to have the receiving kernel keep incoming messages around for a little while, just in case an appropriate *receive* is done shortly. Whenever an "unwanted" message arrives, a timer is started. If the timer expires before a suitable *receive* happens, the message is discarded.

Although this method reduces the chance that a message will have to be thrown away, it introduces the problem of storing and managing prematurely arriving messages. Buffers are needed and have to be allocated, freed, and generally managed. A conceptually simple way of dealing with this buffer management is to define a new data structure called a **mailbox**. A process that is interested in receiving messages tells the kernel to create a mailbox for it, and specifies an address to look for in network packets. Henceforth, all incoming messages with that address are put in the mailbox. The call to *receive* now just removes one message from the mailbox, or blocks (assuming blocking primitives) if none is present. In this way, the kernel knows what to do with incoming messages and has a place to put them. This technique is frequently referred to as a **buffered primitive**, and is illustrated in Fig. 2-12(b).

At first glance, mailboxes appear to eliminate the race conditions caused by messages being discarded and clients giving up. However, mailboxes are finite and can fill up. When a message arrives for a mailbox that is full, the kernel once again is confronted with the choice of either keeping it around for a while, hoping that at least one message will be extracted from the mailbox in time, or discarding it. These are precisely the same choices we had in the unbuffered case. Although we have perhaps reduced the probability of trouble, we have not eliminated it, and have not even managed to change its nature.

In some systems, another option is available: do not let a process send a message if there is no room to store it at the destination. To make this scheme work, the sender must block until an acknowledgement comes back saying that the message has been received. If the mailbox is full, the sender can be backed up and retroactively suspended as though the scheduler had decided to suspend it just *before* it tried to send the message. When space becomes available in the mailbox, the sender is allowed to try again.

2.3.6. Reliable versus Unreliable Primitives

So far we have tacitly assumed that when a client sends a message, the server will receive it. As usual, reality is more complicated than our abstract model. Messages can get lost, which affects the semantics of the message passing model. Suppose that blocking primitives are being used. When a client sends a message, it is suspended until the message has been sent. However, when it is restarted, there is no guarantee that the message has been delivered. The message might have been lost.

Three different approaches to this problem are possible. The first one is just to redefine the semantics of *send* to be unreliable. The system gives no guarantee about messages being delivered. Implementing reliable communication is entirely up to the users. The post office works this way. When you drop a letter in a letterbox, the post office does its best (more or less) to deliver it, but it promises nothing.

The second approach is to require the kernel on the receiving machine to send an acknowledgement back to the kernel on the sending machine. Only when this acknowledgement is received will the sending kernel free the user (client) process. The acknowledgement goes from kernel to kernel; neither the client nor the server ever sees an acknowledgement. Just as the request from client to server is acknowledged by the server's kernel, the reply from the server back to the client is acknowledged by the client's kernel. Thus a request and reply now take four messages, as shown in Fig. 2-13(a).

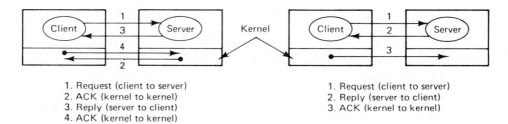

1. Request (client to server)
2. ACK (kernel to kernel)
3. Reply (server to client)
4. ACK (kernel to kernel)

1. Request (client to server)
2. Reply (server to client)
3. ACK (kernel to kernel)

Fig. 2-13. (a) Individually acknowledged messages. (b) Reply being used as the acknowledgement of the request. Note that the ACKs are handled entirely within the kernels.

The third approach is to take advantage of the fact that client-server communication is structured as a request from the client to the server followed by a reply from the server to the client. In this method, the client is blocked after sending a message. The server's kernel does not send back an acknowledgement. Instead, the reply itself acts as the acknowledgement. Thus the sender remains blocked until the reply comes in. If it takes too long, the sending kernel can resend the request to guard against the possibility of a lost message. This approach is shown in Fig. 2-13(b).

Although the reply functions as an acknowledgement for the request, there is no acknowledgement for the reply. Whether this omission is serious or not depends on the nature of the request. If, for example, the client asks the server to read a block of a file and the reply is lost, the client will just repeat the request and the server will send the block again. No damage is done and little time is lost.

On the other hand, if the request requires extensive computation on the part of the server, it would be a pity to discard the answer before the server is sure that the client has received the reply. For this reason, an acknowledgement from the client's kernel to the server's kernel is sometimes used. Until this packet is received, the server's *send* does not complete and the server remains blocked (assuming blocking primitives are used). In any event, if the reply is lost and the request is retransmitted, the server's kernel can see that the request is an old one and just send the reply again without waking up the server. Thus in some systems the reply is acknowledged and in others it is not [see Fig. 2-13(b)].

A compromise between Fig. 2-13(a) and Fig. 2-13(b) that often works goes like this. When a request arrives at the server's kernel, a timer is started. If the server sends the reply quickly enough (i.e., before the timer expires), the reply functions as the acknowledgement. If the timer goes off, a separate acknowledgement is sent. Thus in most cases, only two messages are needed, but when a complicated request is being carried out, a third one is used.

2.3.7. Implementing the Client-Server Model

In the preceding sections we have looked at four design issues, addressing, blocking, buffering, and reliability, each with several options. The major alternatives are summarized in Fig. 2-14. For each item we have listed three possibilities. Simple arithmetic shows that there are $3^4 = 81$ combinations. Not all of them are equally good. Nevertheless, just in this one area (message passing), the system designers have a considerable amount of leeway in choosing a set (or multiple sets) of communication primitives.

Item	Option 1	Option 2	Option 3
Addressing	Machine number	Sparse process addresses	ASCII names looked up via server
Blocking	Blocking primitives	Nonblocking with copy to kernel	Nonblocking with interrupt
Buffering	Unbuffered, discarding unexpected messages	Unbuffered, temporarily keeping unexpected messages	Mailboxes
Reliability	Unreliable	Request–Ack–Reply Ack	Request–Reply–Ack

Fig. 2-14. Four design issues for the communication primitives and some of the principal choices available.

While the details of how message passing is implemented depend to some extent on which choices are made, it is still possible to make some general comments about the implementation, protocols, and software. To start with, virtually all networks have a maximum packet size, typically a few thousand bytes at most. Messages larger than this must be split up into multiple packets and sent separately. Some of these packets may be lost or garbled, and they may even arrive in the wrong order. To deal with this problem, it is usually sufficient to assign a message number to each message, and put it in each packet belonging to the message, along with a sequence number giving the order of the packets.

However, an issue that still must be resolved is the use of acknowledgements. One strategy is to acknowledge each individual packet. Another one is to acknowledge only entire messages. The former has the advantage that if a packet is lost, only that packet has to be retransmitted, but it has the disadvantage of requiring more packets on the network. The latter has the advantage of fewer packets, but the disadvantage of a more complicated recovery when a packet is lost (because a client timeout requires retransmitting the entire message). The choice depends largely on the loss rate of the network being used.

Another interesting issue is the underlying protocol used in client-server communication. Figure 2-15 shows six packet types that are commonly used to implement client-server protocols. The first one is the REQ packet, used to send a request message from a client to a server. (For simplicity, for the rest of this section we will assume that each message fits in a single packet.) The next one is the REP packet that carries results back from the server to the client. Then comes the ACK packet, which is used in reliable protocols to confirm the correct receipt of a previous packet.

Code	Packet type	From	To	Description
REQ	Request	Client	Server	The client wants service
REP	Reply	Server	Client	Reply from the server to the client
ACK	Ack	Either	Other	The previous packet arrived
AYA	Are you alive?	Client	Server	Probe to see if the server has crashed
IAA	I am alive	Server	Client	The server has not crashed
TA	Try again	Server	Client	The server has no room
AU	Address unknown	Server	Client	No process is using this address

Fig. 2-15. Packet types used in client-server protocols.

The next four packet types are not essential, but often useful. Consider the situation in which a request has been sent successfully from the client to the server and the acknowledgement has been received. At this point the client's kernel knows that the server is working on the request. But what happens if no answer is forthcoming within a reasonable time? Is the request really that complicated, or has the server crashed? To be able to distinguish these two cases, the AYA packet is sometimes provided, so the client can ask the server what is going on. If the answer is IAA, the client's kernel knows that all is well and just continues to wait. Even better is a REP packet, of course. If the AYA does not generate any response, the client's kernel waits a short interval and tries again. If this procedure fails more than a specified number of times, the client's kernel normally gives up and reports failure back to the user. The AYA and IAA packets can also be used even in a protocol in which REQ packets are not acknowledged. They allow the client to check on the server's status.

Finally, we come to the last two packet types, which are useful in case a REQ packet cannot be accepted. There are two reasons why this might happen, and it is important for the client's kernel to be able to distinguish them. One reason is that the mailbox to which the request is addressed is full. By sending this packet back to the client's kernel, the server's kernel can indicate that the address is valid, and the request should be repeated later. The other reason is that the address does not belong to any process or mailbox. Repeating it later will not help.

This situation can also arise when buffering is not used and the server is not currently blocked in a *receive* call. Since having the server's kernel forget that the address even exists in between calls to *receive* can lead to problems, in some systems a server can make a call whose only function is to register a certain address with the kernel. In that way, at least the kernel can tell the difference between an address to which no one is currently listening, and one that is simply wrong. It can then send TA in the former case and AU in the latter.

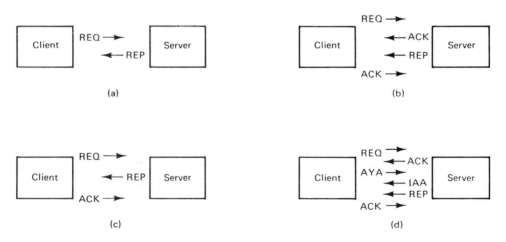

Fig. 2-16. Some examples of packet exchanges for client-server communication.

Many packet sequences are possible. A few common ones are shown in Fig. 2-16. In Fig. 2-16(a), we have the straight request/reply, with no acknowledgement. In Fig. 2-16(b), we have a protocol in which each message is acknowledged individually. In Fig. 2-16(c), we see the reply acting as the acknowledgement, reducing the sequence to three packets. Finally, in Fig. 2-16(d), we see a nervous client checking to see if the server is still there.

2.4. REMOTE PROCEDURE CALL

Although the client-server model provides a convenient way to structure a distributed operating system, it suffers from one incurable flaw: the basic paradigm around which all communication is built is input/output. The procedures *send* and *receive* are fundamentally engaged in doing I/O. Since I/O is not one of the key concepts of centralized systems, making it the basis for distributed computing has struck many workers in the field as a mistake. Their goal is to make distributed computing look like centralized computing. Building everything around I/O is not the way to do it.

This problem has long been known, but little was done about it until a paper by Birrell and Nelson (1984) introduced a completely different way of attacking the problem. Although the idea is refreshingly simple (once someone has thought of it), the implications are often subtle. In this section we will examine the concept, its implementation, its strengths, and its weaknesses.

In a nutshell, what Birrell and Nelson suggested was allowing programs to call procedures located on other machines. When a process on machine *A* calls a procedure on machine *B*, the calling process on *A* is suspended, and execution of the called procedure takes place on *B*. Information can be transported from the caller to the callee in the parameters and can come back in the procedure result. No message passing or I/O at all is visible to the programmer. This method is known as **remote procedure call**, or often just **RPC**.

While the basic idea sounds simple and elegant, subtle problems exist. To start with, because the calling and called procedures run on different machines, they execute in different address spaces, which causes complications. Parameters and results also have to be passed, which can be complicated, especially if the machines are not identical. Finally, both machines can crash, and each of the possible failures causes different problems. Still, most of these can be dealt with, and RPC is a widely-used technique that underlies many distributed operating systems.

2.4.1. Basic RPC Operation

To understand how RPC works, it is important first to fully understand how a conventional (i.e., single machine) procedure call works. Consider a call like

```
count = read(fd, buf, nbytes);
```

where *fd* is an integer, *buf* is an array of characters, and *nbytes* is another integer. If the call is made from the main program, the stack will be as shown in Fig. 2-17(a) before the call. To make the call, the caller pushes the parameters onto the stack in order, last one first, as shown in Fig. 2-17(b). (The reason that C compilers push the parameters in reverse order has to do with *printf*—by doing so, *printf* can always locate its first parameter, the format string.) After *read* has finished running, it puts the return value in a register, removes the return address, and transfers control back to the caller. The caller then removes the parameters from the stack, returning it to the original state, as shown in Fig. 2-17(c).

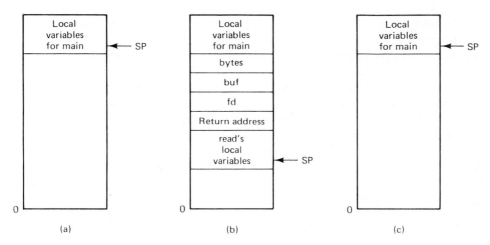

Fig. 2-17. (a) The stack before the call to *read*. (b) The stack while the called procedure is active. (c) The stack after the return to the caller.

Several things are worth noting. For one, in C, parameters can be **call-by-value** or **call-by-reference**. A value parameter, such as *fd* or *nbytes*, is simply copied to the stack as shown in Fig. 2-17(b). To the called procedure, a value parameter is just an initialized local variable. The called procedure may modify it, but such changes do not affect the original value at the calling side.

A reference parameter in C is a pointer to a variable (i.e., the address of the variable), rather than the value of the variable. In the call to *read*, the second parameter is a reference parameter because arrays are always passed by reference in C. What is actually pushed onto the stack is the address of the character array. If the called procedure uses this parameter to store something into the character array, it *does* modify the array in the calling procedure. The difference between call-by-value and call-by-reference is quite important for RPC, as we shall see.

One other parameter passing mechanism also exists, although it is not used in C. It is called **call-by-copy/restore**. It consists of having the variable copied to the stack by the caller, as in call-by-value, and then copied back after the call, overwriting the caller's original value. Under most conditions, this achieves the same effect as call-by-reference, but in some situations, such as the same parameter being present multiple times in the parameter list, the semantics are different.

The decision of which parameter passing mechanism to use is normally made by the language designers and is a fixed property of the language. Sometimes it depends on the data type being passed. In C, for example, integers and other scalar types are always passed by value, whereas arrays are always passed by reference, as we have seen. In contrast, Pascal programmers can choose which mechanism they want for each parameter. The default is call-by-value, but programmers can force call-by-reference by inserting the keyword **var** before specific parameters. Some Ada® compilers use copy/restore for **in out** parameters, but others use call-by-reference. The language definition permits either choice, which makes the semantics a bit fuzzy.

The idea behind RPC is to make a remote procedure call look as much as possible like a local one. In other words, we want RPC to be transparent—the calling procedure should not be aware that the called procedure is executing on a different machine, or vice versa. Suppose that a program needs to read some data from a file. The programmer puts a call to *read* in the code to get the data. In a traditional (single-processor) system, the *read* routine is extracted from the library by the linker and inserted into the object program. It is a short procedure, usually written in assembly language, that puts the parameters in registers and then issues a READ system call by trapping to the kernel. In essence, the *read* procedure is a kind of interface between the user code and the operating system.

Even though *read* issues a kernel trap, it is called in the usual way, by pushing the parameters onto the stack, as shown in Fig. 2-17. Thus the programmer does not know that *read* is actually doing something fishy.

RPC achieves its transparency in an analogous way. When *read* is actually a remote procedure (e.g., one that will run on the file server's machine), a different version of *read,* called a **client stub**, is put into the library. Like the original one, it too, is called using the calling sequence of Fig. 2-17. Also like the original one, it too, traps to the kernel. Only unlike the original one, it does not put the parameters in registers and ask the kernel to give it data. Instead, it packs the parameters into a message and asks the kernel to send the message to the server as illustrated in Fig. 2-18. Following the call to *send*, the client stub calls *receive*, blocking itself until the reply comes back.

When the message arrives at the server, the kernel passes it up to a **server stub** that is bound with the actual server. Typically the server stub will have called *receive* and be blocked waiting for incoming messages. The server stub

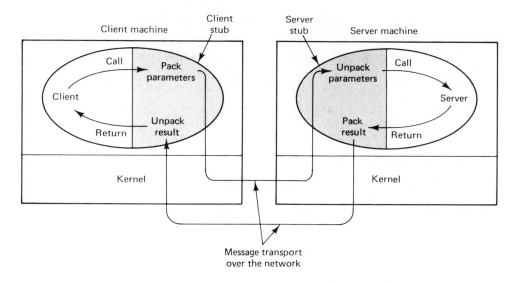

Fig. 2-18. Calls and messages in an RPC. Each ellipse represents a single process, with the shaded portion being the stub.

unpacks the parameters from the message and then calls the server procedure in the usual way (i.e., as in Fig. 2-17). From the server's point of view, it is as though it is being called directly by the client—the parameters and return address are all on the stack where they belong and nothing seems unusual. The server performs its work and then returns the result to the caller in the usual way. For example, in the case of *read*, the server will fill the buffer, pointed to by the second parameter, with the data. This buffer will be internal to the server stub.

When the server stub gets control back after the call has completed, it packs the result (the buffer) in a message and calls *send* to return it to the client. Then it goes back to the top of its own loop to call *receive*, waiting for the next message.

When the message gets back to the client machine, the kernel sees that it is addressed to the client process (to the stub part of that process, but the kernel does not know that). The message is copied to the waiting buffer and the client process unblocked. The client stub inspects the message, unpacks the result, copies it to its caller, and returns in the usual way. When the caller gets control following the call to *read*, all it knows is that its data are available. It has no idea that the work was done remotely instead of by the local kernel.

This blissful ignorance on the part of the client is the beauty of the whole scheme. As far as it is concerned, remote services are accessed by making ordinary (i.e., local) procedure calls, not by calling *send* and *receive* as in Fig. 2-9.

All the details of the message passing are hidden away in the two library procedures, just as the details of actually making system call traps are hidden away in traditional libraries.

To summarize, a remote procedure call occurs in the following steps:

1. The client procedure calls the client stub in the normal way.

2. The client stub builds a message and traps to the kernel.

3. The kernel sends the message to the remote kernel.

4. The remote kernel gives the message to the server stub.

5. The server stub unpacks the parameters and calls the server.

6. The server does the work and returns the result to the stub.

7. The server stub packs it in a message and traps to the kernel.

8. The remote kernel sends the message to the client's kernel.

9. The client's kernel gives the message to the client stub.

10. The stub unpacks the result and returns to the client.

The net effect of all these steps is to convert the local call by the client procedure to the client stub to a local call to the server procedure without either client or server being aware of the intermediate steps.

2.4.2. Parameter Passing

The function of the client stub is to take its parameters, pack them into a message, and send it to the server stub. While this sounds straightforward, it is not quite as simple as it at first appears. In this section we will look at some of the issues concerned with parameter passing in RPC systems. Packing parameters into a message is called **parameter marshaling**.

As the simplest possible example, consider a remote procedure, $sum(i, j)$, that takes two integer parameters and returns their arithmetic sum. (As a practical matter, one would not normally make such a simple procedure remote due to the overhead, but as an example it will do.) The call to sum, with parameters 4 and 7, is shown in the left-hand portion of the client process in Fig. 2-19. The client stub takes its two parameters and puts them in a message as indicated. It also puts the name or number of the procedure to be called in the message because the server might support several different calls, and it has to be told which one is required.

When the message arrives at the server, the stub examines the message to see which procedure is needed, and then makes the appropriate call. If the

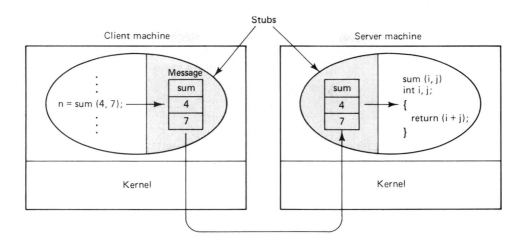

Fig. 2-19. Computing *sum*(4, 7) remotely.

server also supports the remote procedures *difference*, *product*, and *quotient*, the server stub might have a switch statement in it, to select the procedure to be called, depending on the first field of the message. The actual call from the stub to the server looks much like the original client call, except that the parameters are variables initialized from the incoming message, rather than constants.

When the server has finished, the server stub gains control again. It takes the result, provided by the server, and packs it into a message. This message is sent back to the client stub, which unpacks it and returns the value to the client procedure (not shown in the figure).

As long as the client and server machines are identical and all the parameters and results are scalar types, such as integers, characters, and Booleans, this model works fine. However, in a large distributed system, it is common that multiple machine types are present. Each machine often has its own representation for numbers, characters, and other data items. For example, IBM mainframes use the EBCDIC character code, whereas IBM personal computers use ASCII. As a consequence, it is not possible to pass a character parameter from an IBM PC client to an IBM mainframe server using the simple scheme of Fig. 2-19: the server will interpret the character incorrectly.

Similar problems can occur with the representation of integers (1s complement versus 2s complement), and especially with floating-point numbers. In addition, an even more annoying problem exists because some machines, such as the Intel 486, number their bytes from right to left, whereas others, such as the Sun SPARC, number them the other way. The Intel format is called **little**

endian and the SPARC format is called **big endian**, after the politicians in *Gulliver's Travels* who went to war over which end of an egg to break (Cohen, 1981). As an example, consider a server with two parameters, an integer and a four-character string. Each parameter requires one 32-bit word. Figure 2-20(a) shows what the parameter portion of a message built by a client stub on an Intel 486 might look like. The first word contains the integer parameter, 5 in this case, and the second contains the string "JILL".

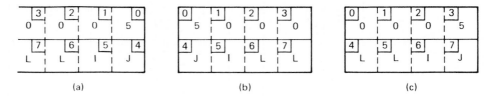

Fig. 2-20. (a) The original message on the 486. (b) The message after receipt on the SPARC. (c) The message after being inverted. The little numbers in boxes indicate the address of each byte.

Since messages are transferred byte for byte (actually, bit for bit) over the network, the first byte sent is the first byte to arrive. In Fig. 2-20(b) we show what the message of Fig. 2-20(a) would look like if received by a SPARC, which numbers its bytes with byte 0 at the left (high-order byte) instead of at the right (low-order byte) as do all the Intel chips. When the server stub reads the parameters at addresses 0 and 4, respectively, it will find an integer equal to 83,886,080 (5×2^{24}) and a string "JILL".

One obvious, but unfortunately incorrect, approach is to invert the bytes of each word after they are received, leading to Fig. 2-20(c). Now the integer is 5 and the string is "LLIJ". The problem here is that integers are reversed by the different byte ordering, but strings are not. Without additional information about what is a string and what is an integer, there is no way to repair the damage.

Fortunately, this information is implicitly available. Remember that the items in the message correspond to the procedure identifier and parameters. Both the client and server know what the types of the parameters are. Thus a message corresponding to a remote procedure with n parameters will have $n + 1$ fields, one identifying the procedure and one for each of the n parameters. Once a standard has been agreed upon for representing each of the basic data types, given a parameter list and a message, it is possible to deduce which bytes belong to which parameter, and thus to solve the problem.

As a simple example, consider the procedure of Fig. 2-21(a). It has three parameters, a character, a floating-point number, and an array of five integers. We might decide to transmit a character in the rightmost byte of a word (leaving the next 3 bytes empty), a float as a whole word, and an array as a group of words equal to the array length, preceded by a word giving the length, as shown in Fig. 2-21(b). Thus given these rules, the client stub for *foobar* knows that it must use the format of Fig. 2-21(b), and the server stub knows that incoming messages for *foobar* will have the format of Fig. 2-21(b). Having the type information for the parameters makes it possible to make any necessary conversions.

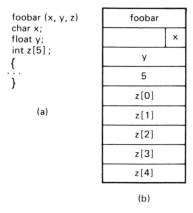

Fig. 2-21. (a) A procedure. (b) The corresponding message.

Even with this additional information, there are still some issues open. In particular, how should information be represented in the messages? One way is to devise a network standard or **canonical form** for integers, characters, Booleans, floating-point numbers, and so on, and require all senders to convert their internal representation to this form while marshaling. For example, suppose that it is decided to use two's complement for integers, ASCII for characters, 0 (false) and 1 (true) for Booleans, and IEEE format for floating-point numbers, with everything stored in little endian. For any list of integers, characters, Booleans, and floating-point numbers, the exact pattern required is now deterministic down to the last bit. As a result, the server stub no longer has to worry about which byte ordering the client has because the order of the bits in the message is now fixed, independent of the client's hardware.

The problem with this method is that it is sometimes inefficient. Suppose that a big endian client is talking to a big endian server. According to the rules, the client must convert everything to little endian in the message, and the server must convert it back again when it arrives. Although this is unambiguous, it requires two conversions when in fact none were necessary. This observation gives rise to a second approach: the client uses its own native format and indicates in the first byte of the message which format this is. Thus a little endian client builds a little endian message and a big endian client builds a big endian message. As soon as a message comes in, the server stub examines the first byte to see what the client is. If it is the same as the server, no conversion is needed. Otherwise, the server stub converts everything. Although we have only discussed converting from one endian to the other, conversions between one's and two's complement, EBCDIC to ASCII, and so on, can be handled in the same way. The trick is knowing what the message layout is and what the client is. Once these are known, the rest is easy (provided that everyone can convert from everyone else's format).

Now we come to the question of where the stub procedures come from. In many RPC-based systems, they are generated automatically. As we have seen, given a specification of the server procedure and the encoding rules, the message format is uniquely determined. Thus it is possible to have a compiler read the server specification and generate a client stub that packs its parameters into the officially approved message format. Similarly, the compiler can also produce a server stub that unpacks them and calls the server. Having both stub procedures generated from a single formal specification of the server not only makes life easier for the programmers, but reduces the chance of error and makes the system transparent with respect to differences in internal representation of data items.

Finally, we come to our last and most difficult problem: How are pointers passed? The answer is: only with the greatest of difficulty, if at all. Remember that a pointer is meaningful only within the address space of the process in which it is being used. Getting back to our *read* example discussed earlier, if the second parameter (the address of the buffer) happens to be 1000 on the client, one cannot just pass the number 1000 to the server and expect it to work. Address 1000 on the server might be in the middle of the program text.

One solution is just to forbid pointers and reference parameters in general. However, these are so important that this solution is highly undesirable. In fact, it is not necessary either. In the *read* example, the client stub knows that the second parameter points to an array of characters. Suppose, for the moment, that it also knows how big the array is. One strategy then becomes apparent: copy the array into the message and send it to the server. The server stub can then call the server with a pointer to this array, even though this pointer has a different numerical value than the second parameter of *read* has. Changes the server makes using the pointer (e.g., storing data into it) directly affect the message buffer inside the server stub. When the server finishes, the original message can be sent back to the client stub, which then copies it back to the client. In effect, call-by-reference has been replaced by copy/restore. Although this is not always identical, it frequently is good enough.

One optimization makes this mechanism twice as efficient. If the stubs know whether the buffer is an input parameter or an output parameter to the server, one of the copies can be eliminated. If the array is input to the server (e.g., in a call to *write*) it need not be copied back. If it is output, it need not be sent over in the first place. The way to tell them is in the formal specification of the server procedure. Thus associated with every remote procedure is a formal specification of the procedure, written in some kind of specification language, telling what the parameters are, which are input and which are output (or both), and what their (maximum) sizes are. It is from this formal specification that the stubs are generated by a special stub compiler.

As a final comment, it is worth noting that although we can now handle pointers to simple arrays and structures, we still cannot handle the most general case of a pointer to an arbitrary data structure such as a complex graph. Some systems attempt to deal with this case by actually passing the pointer to the server stub and generating special code in the server procedure for using pointers.

Normally, a pointer is followed (dereferenced) by putting it in a register and indirecting through the register. When this special technique is used, a pointer is dereferenced by sending a message back to the client stub asking it to fetch and send the item being pointed to (reads) or store a value at the address pointed to (writes). While this method works, it is often highly inefficient. Imagine having the file server store the bytes in the buffer by sending back each one in a separate message. Still, it is better than nothing, and some systems use it.

2.4.3. Dynamic Binding

An issue that we have glossed over so far is how the client locates the server. One method is just to hardwire the network address of the server into the client. The trouble with this approach is that it is extremely inflexible. If the server moves or if the server is replicated or if the interface changes, numerous programs will have to be found and recompiled. To avoid all these problems, some distributed systems use what is called **dynamic binding** to match up clients and servers. In this section we will describe the ideas behind dynamic binding.

The starting point for dynamic binding is the server's formal specification. As an example, consider the server of Fig. 2-9(a), specified in Fig. 2-22. The specification tells the name of the server (*file_server*), the version number (3.1), and a list of procedures provided by the server (*read*, *write*, *create*, and *delete*).

For each procedure, the types of the parameters are given. Each parameter is specified as being an *in* parameter, an *out* parameter, or an *in out* parameter. The direction is relative to the server. An *in* parameter, such as the file name, *name*, is sent from the client to the server. This one is used to tell the server which file to read from, write to, create, or delete. Similarly, *bytes* tells the server how many bytes to transfer and *position* tells where in the file to begin

```
#include <header.h>

specification of file_server, version 3.1:

    long read(in char name[MAX_PATH], out char buf[BUF_SIZE],
              in long bytes, in long position);

    long write(in char name[MAX_PATH], in char buf[BUF_SIZE],
               in long bytes, in long position);

    int create(in char[MAX_PATH], in int mode);

    int delete(in char[MAX_PATH]);

end;
```

Fig. 2-22. A specification of the stateless server of Fig. 2-9.

reading or writing. An *out* parameter such as *buf* in *read*, is sent from the server to the client. *Buf* is the place where the file server puts the data that the client has requested. An *in out* parameter, of which there are none in this example, would be sent from the client to the server, modified there, and then sent back to the client (copy/restore). Copy/restore is typically used for pointer parameters in cases where the server both reads and modifies the data structure being pointed to. The directions are crucial, so the client stub knows which parameters to send to the server, and the server stub knows which ones to send back.

As we pointed out earlier, this particular example is a stateless server. For a UNIX-like server, one would have additional procedures *open* and *close*, and different parameters for *read* and *write*. The concept of RPC itself is neutral, permitting the system designers to build any kind of servers they desire.

The primary use of the formal specification of Fig. 2-22 is as input to the stub generator, which produces both the client stub and the server stub. Both are then put into the appropriate libraries. When a user (client) program calls any of the procedures defined by this specification, the corresponding client stub procedure is linked into its binary. Similarly, when the server is compiled, the server stubs are linked with it too.

When the server begins executing, the call to *initialize* outside the main loop [see Fig. 2-9(a)] **exports** the server interface. What this means is that the server sends a message to a program called a **binder**, to make its existence known. This process is referred to as **registering** the server. To register, the server gives the binder its name, its version number, a unique identifier, typically 32 bits long, and a **handle** used to locate it. The handle is system dependent, and might be an Ethernet address, an IP address, an X.500 address, a sparse process identifier, or something else. In addition, other information, for example, concerning authentication, might also be supplied. A server can also deregister with the binder when it is no longer prepared to offer service. The binder interface is shown in Fig. 2-23.

Call	Input	Output
Register	Name, version, handle, unique id	
Deregister	Name, version, unique id	
Lookup	Name, version	Handle, unique id

Fig. 2-23. The binder interface.

Given this background, now consider how the client locates the server. When the client calls one of the remote procedures for the first time, say, *read*, the client stub sees that it is not yet bound to a server, so it sends a message to the binder asking to **import** version 3.1 of the *file_server* interface. The binder checks to see if one or more servers have already exported an interface with this name and version number. If no currently running server is willing to support this interface, the *read* call fails. By including the version number in the matching process, the binder can ensure that clients using obsolete interfaces will fail to locate a server rather than locate one and get unpredictable results due to incorrect parameters.

On the other hand, if a suitable server exists, the binder gives its handle and unique identifier to the client stub. The client stub uses the handle as the address to send the request message to. The message contains the parameters and the unique identifier, which the server's kernel uses to direct the incoming message to the correct server in the event that several servers are running on that machine.

This method of exporting and importing interfaces is highly flexible. For example, it can handle multiple servers that support the same interface. The binder can spread the clients randomly over the servers to even the load if it wants to. It can also poll the servers periodically, automatically deregistering any server that fails to respond, to achieve a degree of fault tolerance. Furthermore, it can also assist in authentication. A server could specify, for example, that it only wished to be used by a specific list of users, in which case the binder would refuse to tell users not on the list about it. The binder can also verify that both client and server are using the same version of the interface.

However, this form of dynamic binding also has its disadvantages. The extra overhead of exporting and importing interfaces costs time. Since many client processes are short lived and each process has to start all over again, the effect may be significant. Also, in a large distributed system, the binder may become a bottleneck, so multiple binders are needed. Consequently, whenever an interface is registered or deregistered, a substantial number of messages will be needed to keep all the binders synchronized and up to date, creating even more overhead.

2.4.4. RPC Semantics in the Presence of Failures

The goal of RPC is to hide communication by making remote procedure calls look just like local ones. With a few exceptions, such as the inability to handle global variables and the subtle differences introduced by using copy/restore for pointer parameters instead of call-by-reference, so far we have come fairly close. Indeed, as long as both client and server are functioning perfectly, RPC does its job remarkably well. The problem comes in when errors occur. It is then that the differences between local and remote calls are not always easy to mask. In this section we will examine some of the possible errors and what can be done about them.

To structure our discussion, let us distinguish between five different classes of failures that can occur in RPC systems, as follows:

1. The client is unable to locate the server.

2. The request message from the client to the server is lost.

3. The reply message from the server to the client is lost.

4. The server crashes after receiving a request.

5. The client crashes after sending a request.

Each of these categories poses different problems and requires different solutions.

Client Cannot Locate the Server

To start with, it can happen that the client cannot locate a suitable server. The server might be down, for example. Alternatively, suppose that the client is compiled using a particular version of the client stub, and the binary is not used for a considerable period of time. In the meantime, the server evolves and a new version of the interface is installed and new stubs are generated and put into use. When the client is finally run, the binder will be unable to match it up with a server and will report failure. While this mechanism is used to protect the client from accidentally trying to talk to a server that may not agree with it in terms of what parameters are required or what it is supposed to do, the problem remains of how this failure should be dealt with.

With the server of Fig. 2-9(a), each of the procedures returns a value, with the code −1 conventionally used to indicate failure. For such procedures, just returning −1 will clearly tell the caller that something is amiss. In UNIX, a global variable, *errno*, is also assigned a value indicating the error type. In such a system, adding a new error type "Cannot locate server" is simple.

The trouble is, this solution is not general enough. Consider the *sum* procedure of Fig. 2-19. Here −1 is a perfectly legal value to be returned, for example, the result of adding 7 to −8. Another error-reporting mechanism is needed.

One possible candidate is to have the error raise an **exception**. In some languages (e.g., Ada), programmers can write special procedures that are invoked upon specific errors, such as division by zero. In C, signal handlers can be used for this purpose. In other words, we could define a new signal type *SIG-NOSERVER*, and allow it to be handled in the same way as other signals.

This approach, too, has drawbacks. To start with, not every language has exceptions or signals. To name one, Pascal does not. Another point is that having to write an exception or signal handler destroys the transparency we have been trying to achieve. Suppose that you are a programmer and your boss tells you to write the *sum* procedure. You smile and tell her it will be written, tested, and documented in five minutes. Then she mentions that you also have to write an exception handler as well, just in case the procedure is not there today. At this point it is pretty hard to maintain the illusion that remote procedures are no different from local ones, since writing an exception handler for "Cannot locate server" would be a rather unusual request in a single-processor system.

Lost Request Messages

The second item on the list is dealing with lost request messages. This is the easiest one to deal with: just have the kernel start a timer when sending the request. If the timer expires before a reply or acknowledgement comes back, the kernel sends the message again. If the message was truly lost, the server will not be able to tell the difference between the retransmission and the original, and everything will work fine. Unless, of course, so many request messages are lost that the kernel gives up and falsely concludes that the server is down, in which case we are back to "Cannot locate server."

Lost Reply Messages

Lost replies are considerably more difficult to deal with. The obvious solution is just to rely on the timer again. If no reply is forthcoming within a reasonable period, just send the request once more. The trouble with this solution is that the client's kernel is not really sure why there was no answer. Did the request or reply get lost, or is the server merely slow? It may make a difference.

In particular, some operations can safely be repeated as often as necessary with no damage being done. A request such as asking for the first 1024 bytes of a file has no side effects and can be executed as often as necessary without any harm being done. A request that has this property is said to be **idempotent**.

Now consider a request to a banking server asking to transfer a million dollars from one account to another. If the request arrives and is carried out, but the reply is lost, the client will not know this and will retransmit the message. The bank server will interpret this request as a new one, and will carry it out too. Two million dollars will be transferred. Heaven forbid that the reply is lost 10 times. Transferring money is not idempotent.

One way of solving this problem is to try to structure all requests in an idempotent way. In practice, however, many requests (e.g., transferring money) are inherently nonidempotent, so something else is needed. Another method is to have the client's kernel assign each request a sequence number. By having each server's kernel keep track of the most recently received sequence number from each client's kernel that is using it, the server's kernel can tell the difference between an original request and a retransmission and can refuse to carry out any request a second time. An additional safeguard is to have a bit in the message header that is used to distinguish initial requests from retransmissions (the idea being that it is always safe to perform an original request; retransmissions may require more care).

Server Crashes

The next failure on the list is a server crash. It too relates to idempotency, but unfortunately it cannot be solved using sequence numbers. The normal sequence of events at a server is shown in Fig. 2-24(a). A request arrives, is carried out, and a reply is sent. Now consider Fig. 2-24(b). A request arrives and is carried out, just as before, but the server crashes before it can send the reply. Finally, look at Fig. 2-24(c). Again a request arrives, but this time the server crashes before it can even be carried out.

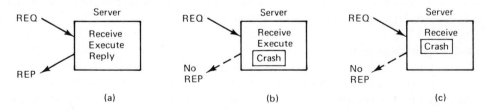

Fig. 2-24. (a) Normal case. (b) Crash after execution. (c) Crash before execution.

The annoying part of Fig. 2-24 is that the correct treatment differs for (b) and (c). In (b) the system has to report failure back to the client (e.g., raise an exception), whereas in (c) it can just retransmit the request. The problem is that the client's kernel cannot tell which is which. All it knows is that its timer has expired.

Three schools of thought exist on what to do here. One philosophy is to wait until the server reboots (or rebinds to a new server) and try the operation again. The idea is to keep trying until a reply has been received, then give it to the client. This technique is called **at least once semantics** and guarantees that the RPC has been carried out at least one time, but possibly more.

The second philosophy gives up immediately and reports back failure. This way is called **at most once semantics** and guarantees that the RPC has been carried out at most one time, but possibly none at all.

The third philosophy is to guarantee nothing. When a server crashes, the client gets no help and no promises. The RPC may have been carried out anywhere from 0 to a large number of times. The main virtue of this scheme is that it is easy to implement.

None of these are terribly attractive. What one would like is **exactly once semantics**, but as can be seen fairly easily, there is no way to arrange this in general. Imagine that the remote operation consists of printing some text, and is accomplished by loading the printer buffer and then setting a single bit in some control register to start the printer. The crash can occur a microsecond before setting the bit, or a microsecond afterward. The recovery procedure depends entirely on which it is, but there is no way for the client to discover it.

In short, the possibility of server crashes radically changes the nature of RPC and clearly distinguishes single-processor systems from distributed systems. In the former case, a server crash also implies a client crash, so recovery is neither possible nor necessary. In the latter it is both possible and necessary to take some action.

Client Crashes

The final item on the list of failures is the client crash. What happens if a client sends a request to a server to do some work and crashes before the server replies? At this point a computation is active and no parent is waiting for the result. Such an unwanted computation is called an **orphan**.

Orphans can cause a variety of problems. As a bare minimum, they waste CPU cycles. They can also lock files or otherwise tie up valuable resources. Finally, if the client reboots and does the RPC again, but the reply from the orphan comes back immediately afterward, confusion can result.

What can be done about orphans? Nelson (1981) proposed four solutions. In solution 1, before a client stub sends an RPC message, it makes a log entry telling what it is about to do. The log is kept on disk or some other medium that survives crashes. After a reboot, the log is checked and the orphan is explicitly killed off. This solution is called **extermination**.

The disadvantage of this scheme is the horrendous expense of writing a disk record for every RPC. Furthermore, it may not even work, since orphans themselves may do RPCs, thus creating **grandorphans** or further descendants that are impossible to locate. Finally, the network may be partitioned, due to a failed gateway, making it impossible to kill them, even if they can be located. All in all, this is not a promising approach.

In solution 2, called **reincarnation**, all these problems can be solved without the need to write disk records. The way it works is to divide time up into sequentially numbered epochs. When a client reboots, it broadcasts a message to all machines declaring the start of a new epoch. When such a broadcast comes in, all remote computations are killed. Of course, if the network is partitioned, some orphans may survive. However, when they report back, their replies will contain an obsolete epoch number, making them easy to detect.

Solution 3 is a variant on this idea, but less Draconian. It is called **gentle reincarnation**. When an epoch broadcast comes in, each machine checks to see if it has any remote computations, and if so, tries to locate their owner. Only if the owner cannot be found is the computation killed.

Finally, we have solution 4, **expiration**, in which each RPC is given a standard amount of time, T, to do the job. If it cannot finish, it must explicitly ask for another quantum, which is a nuisance. On the other hand, if after a crash the server waits a time T before rebooting, all orphans are sure to be gone. The problem to be solved here is choosing a reasonable value of T in the face of RPCs with wildly differing requirements.

In practice, none of these methods are desirable. Worse yet, killing an orphan may have unforeseen consequences. For example, suppose that an orphan has obtained locks on one or more files or data base records. If the orphan is suddenly killed, these locks may remain forever. Also, an orphan may have already made entries in various remote queues to start up other processes at some future time, so even killing the orphan may not remove all traces of it. Orphan elimination is discussed in more detail by Panzieri and Shrivastava (1988).

2.4.5. Implementation Issues

The success or failure of a distributed system often hinges on its performance. The system performance, in turn, is critically dependent on the speed of communication. The communication speed, more often than not, stands or falls with its implementation, rather than with its abstract principles. In this section we will look at some of the implementation issues for RPC systems, with a special emphasis on the performance and where the time is spent.

RPC Protocols

The first issue is the choice of the RPC protocol. Theoretically, any old protocol will do as long as it gets the bits from the client's kernel to the server's kernel, but practically there are several major decisions to be made here, and the choices made can have a major impact on the performance. The first decision is between a connection-oriented protocol and a connectionless protocol. With a connection-oriented protocol, at the time the client is bound to the server, a connection is established between them. All traffic, in both directions, uses this connection.

The advantage of having a connection is that communication becomes much easier. When a kernel sends a message, it does not have to worry about it getting lost, nor does it have to deal with acknowledgements. All that is handled at a lower level, by the software that supports the connection. When operating over a wide-area network, this advantage is often too strong to resist.

The disadvantage, especially over a LAN, is the performance loss. All that extra software gets in the way. Besides, the main advantage (no lost packets) is hardly needed on a LAN, since LANs are so reliable. As a consequence, most distributed operating systems that are intended for use in a single building or campus use connectionless protocols.

The second major choice is whether to use a standard general-purpose protocol or one specifically designed for RPC. Since there are no standards in this area, using a custom RPC protocol often means designing your own (or borrowing a friend's). System designers are split about evenly on this one.

Some distributed systems use IP (or UDP, which is built on IP) as the basic protocol. This choice has several things going for it:

1. The protocol is already designed, saving considerable work.

2. Many implementations are available, again saving work.

3. These packets can be sent and received by nearly all UNIX systems.

4. IP and UDP packets are supported by many existing networks.

In short, IP and UDP are easy to use and fit in well with existing UNIX systems and networks such as the Internet. This makes it straightforward to write clients and servers that run on UNIX systems, which certainly aids in getting code running quickly and in testing it.

As usual, the downside is the performance. IP was not designed as an end-user protocol. It was designed as a base upon which reliable TCP connections could be established over recalcitrant internetworks. For example, it can deal with gateways that fragment packets into little pieces so they can pass through networks with a tiny maximum packet size. Although this feature is never needed in a LAN-based distributed system, the IP packet header fields dealing with fragmentation have to be filled in by the sender and verified by the receiver to make them legal IP packets. IP packets have in total 13 header fields, of which three are useful: the source and destination addresses and the packet length. The other 10 just come along for the ride, and one of them, the header checksum, is time consuming to compute. To make matters worse, UDP has another checksum, covering the data as well.

The alternative is to use a specialized RPC protocol that, unlike IP, does not attempt to deal with packets that have been bouncing around the network for a few minutes and then suddenly materialize out of thin air at an inconvenient moment. Of course, the protocol has to be invented, implemented, tested, and embedded in existing systems, so it is considerably more work. Furthermore, the rest of the world tends not to jump with joy at the birth of yet another new protocol. In the long run, the development and widespread acceptance of a high-performance RPC protocol is definitely the way to go, but we are not there yet.

One last protocol-related issue is packet and message length. Doing an RPC has a large, fixed overhead, independent of the amount of data sent. Thus reading a 64K file in a single 64K RPC is vastly more efficient than reading it in 64 1K RPCs. It is therefore important that the protocol and network allow large transmissions. Some RPC systems are limited to small sizes (e.g., Sun Microsystem's limit is 8K). In addition, many networks cannot handle large packets (Ethernet's limit is 1536 bytes), so a single RPC will have to be split over multiple packets, causing extra overhead.

Acknowledgements

When large RPCs have to be broken up into many small packets as just described, a new issue arises: Should individual packets be acknowledged or not? Suppose, for example, that a client wants to write a 4K block of data to a file server, but the system cannot handle packets larger than 1K. One strategy, known as a **stop-and-wait protocol**, is for the client to send packet 0 with the first 1K, then wait for an acknowledgement from the server, as illustrated in Fig. 2-25(b). Then the client sends the second 1K, waits for another acknowledgement, and so on.

The alternative, often called a **blast protocol**, is simply for the client to send all the packets as fast as it can. With this method, the server acknowledges the entire message when *all* the packets have been received, not one by one. The blast protocol is illustrated in Fig. 2-25(c).

These protocols have quite different properties. With stop-and-wait, if a packet is damaged or lost, the client fails to receive an acknowledgement on

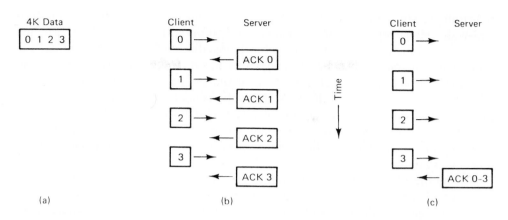

Fig. 2-25. (a) A 4K message. (b) A stop-and-wait protocol. (c) A blast protocol.

time, so it retransmits the one bad packet. With the blast protocol, the server is faced with a decision when, say, packet 1 is lost but packet 2 subsequently arrives correctly. It can abandon everything and do nothing, waiting for the client to time out and retransmit the entire message. Or alternatively, it can buffer packet 2 (along with 0), hope that 3 comes in correctly, and then specifically ask the client to send it packet 1. This technique is called **selective repeat**.

Both stop-and-wait and abandoning everything when an error occurs are easy to implement. Selective repeat requires more administration, but uses less network bandwidth. On highly reliable LANs, lost packets are so rare that selective repeat is usually more trouble than it is worth, but on wide-area networks it is frequently a good idea.

However, error control aside, there is another consideration that is actually more important: **flow control**. Many network interface chips are able to send consecutive packets with almost no gap between them, but they are not always able to receive an unlimited number of back-to-back packets due to finite buffer capacity on chip. With some designs, a chip cannot even accept two back-to-back packets because after receiving the first one, the chip is temporarily disabled during the packet-arrived interrupt, so it misses the start of the second one. When a packet arrives and the receiver is unable to accept it, an **overrun error** occurs and the incoming packet is lost. In practice, overrun errors are a much more serious problem than packets lost due to noise or other forms of damage.

The two approaches of Fig. 2-25 are quite different with respect to overrun errors. With stop-and-wait, overrun errors are impossible, because the second packet is not sent until the receiver has explicitly indicated that it is ready for it. (Of course, with multiple senders, overrun errors are still possible.)

With the blast protocol, receiver overrun is a possibility, which is unfortunate, since the blast protocol is clearly much more efficient than stop-and-wait. However, there are also ways of dealing with overrun. If, on the one hand, the problem is caused by the chip being disabled temporarily while it is processing an interrupt, a smart sender can insert a delay between packets to give the receiver just enough time to generate the packet-arrived interrupt and reset itself. If the required delay is short, the sender can just loop (busy waiting); if it is long, it can set up a timer interrupt and go do something else while waiting. If it is in between (a few hundred microseconds), which it often is, probably the best solution is busy waiting and just accepting the wasted time as a necessary evil.

If, on the other hand, the overrun is caused by the finite buffer capacity of the network chip, say n packets, the sender can send n packets, followed by a substantial gap (or the protocol can be defined to require an acknowledgement after every n packets).

It should be clear that minimizing acknowledgement packets and getting good performance may be dependent on the timing properties of the network chip, so the protocol may have to be tuned to the hardware being used. A custom-designed RPC protocol can take issues like flow control into account more easily than a general-purpose protocol, which is why specialized RPC protocols usually outperform systems based on IP or UDP by a wide margin.

Before leaving the subject of acknowledgements, there is one other sticky point that is worth looking at. In Fig. 2-16(c) the protocol consists of a request, a reply, and an acknowledgement. The last one is needed to tell the server that it can discard the reply as it has arrived safely. Now suppose that the acknowledgement is lost in transit (unlikely, but not impossible). The server will not discard the reply. Worse yet, as far as the client is concerned, the protocol is finished. No timers are running and no packets are expected.

We could change the protocol to have acknowledgements themselves acknowledged, but this adds extra complexity and overhead for very little potential gain. In practice, the server can start a timer when sending the reply, and discard the reply when either the acknowledgement arrives or the timer expires. Also, a new request from the same client can be interpreted as a sign that the reply arrived, otherwise the client would not be issuing the next request.

Critical Path

Since the RPC code is so crucial to the performance of the system, let us take a closer look at what actually happens when a client performs an RPC with a remote server. The sequence of instructions that is executed on every RPC is called the **critical path**, and is depicted in Fig. 2-26. It starts when the client calls the client stub, proceeds through the trap to the kernel, the message transmission, the interrupt on the server side, the server stub, and finally arrives at the server, which does the work and sends the reply back the other way.

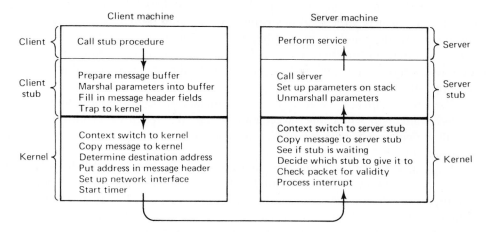

Fig. 2-26. Critical path from client to server.

Let us examine these steps a bit more carefully now. After the client stub has been called, its first job is to acquire a buffer into which it can assemble the outgoing message. In some systems, the client stub has a single fixed buffer that it fills in from scratch on every call. In other systems, a pool of partially filled in buffers is maintained, and an appropriate one for the server required is obtained. This method is especially appropriate when the underlying packet format has a substantial number of fields that must be filled in, but which do not change from call to call.

Next, the parameters are converted to the appropriate format and inserted into the message buffer, along with the rest of the header fields, if any. At this point the message is ready for transmission, so a trap to the kernel is issued.

When it gets control, the kernel switches context, saving the CPU registers and memory map, and setting up a new memory map that it will use while running in kernel mode. Since the kernel and user contexts are generally disjoint, the kernel must now explicitly copy the message into its address space so it can access it, fill in the destination address (and possibly other header fields), and have it copied to the network interface. At this point the client's critical path ends, as additional work done from here on does not add to the total RPC time: nothing the kernel does now affects how long it takes for the packet to arrive at the server. After starting the retransmission timer, the kernel can either enter a busy waiting loop to wait for the reply, or call the scheduler to look for another process to run. The former speeds up the processing of the reply, but effectively means that no multiprogramming can take place.

On the server side, the bits will come in and be put either in an on-board buffer or in memory by the receiving hardware. When all of them arrive, the receiver will generate an interrupt. The interrupt handler then examines the packet to see if it is valid, and determines which stub to give it to. If no stub is waiting for it, the handler must either buffer it or discard it. Assuming that a stub is waiting, the message is copied to the stub. Finally, a context switch is done, restoring the registers and memory map to the values they had at the time the stub called *receive*.

The server can now be restarted. It unmarshals the parameters and sets up an environment in which the server call be called. When everything is ready, the call is made. After the server has run, the path back to the client is similar to the forward path, but the other way.

A question that all implementers are keenly interested in is: "Where is most of the time spent on the critical path?" Once that is known, work can begin on speeding it up. Schroeder and Burrows (1990) have provided us with a glimpse by analyzing in detail the critical path of the RPC on the DEC Firefly multiprocessor workstation. The results of their work are expressed in Fig. 2-27 as histograms with 14 bars, each bar corresponding to one of the steps from client to server (the reverse path is not shown, but is roughly analogous). Figure 2-27(a) gives results for a null RPC (no data), and Fig. 2-27(b) gives it for an array parameter with 1440 bytes. Although the fixed overhead is the same in both cases, considerably more time is needed for marshaling parameters and moving messages around in the second case.

For the null RPC, the dominant costs are the context switch to the server stub when a packet arrives, the interrupt service routine, and moving the packet to the network interface for transmission. For the 1440-byte RPC, the picture changes considerably, with the Ethernet transmission time now being the largest single component, with the time for moving the packet into and out of the interface coming in close behind.

Although Fig. 2-27 yields valuable insight into where the time is going, a few words of caution are necessary for interpreting these data. First, the Firefly is a multiprocessor, with five VAX CPUs. When the same measurements are run with only one CPU, the RPC time doubles, indicating that substantial parallel processing is taking place here, something that will not be true of most other machines.

Second, the Firefly uses UDP, and its operating system manages a pool of UDP buffers, which client stubs use to avoid having to fill in the entire UDP header every time.

Third, the kernel and user share the same address space, eliminating the need for context switches and for copying between kernel and user spaces, a great timesaver. Page table protection bits prevent the user from reading or writing parts of the kernel other than the shared buffers and certain other parts

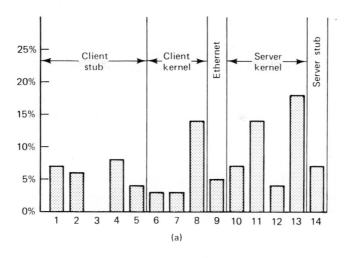

(a)

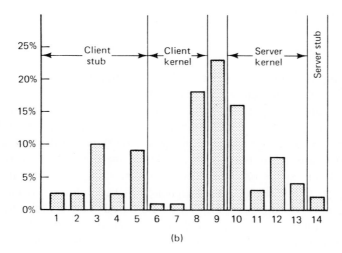

(b)

1. Call stub
2. Get message buffer
3. Marshal parameters
4. Fill in headers
5. Compute UDP checksum
6. Trap to kernel
7. Queue packet for transmission

8. Move packet to controller over the QBus
9. Ethernet transmission time
10. Get packet from controller
11. Interrupt service routine
12. Compute UDP checksum
13. Context switch to user space
14. Server stub code

(c)

Fig. 2-27. Breakdown of the RPC critical path. (a) For a null RPC. (b) For an RPC with a 1440-byte array parameter. (c) The 14 steps in the RPC from client to server.

intended for user access. This design cleverly exploits particular features of the VAX architecture that facilitate sharing between kernel space and user space, but is not applicable to all computers.

Fourth and last, the entire RPC system has been carefully coded in assembly language and hand optimized. This last point is probably the reason that the various components in Fig. 2-27 are as uniform as they are. No doubt when the measurements were first made, they were more skewed, prompting the authors to attack the most time consuming parts until they no longer stuck out.

Schroeder and Burrows give some advice to future designers based on their experience. To start with, they recommend avoiding weird hardware (only one of the Firefly's five processors has access to the Ethernet, so packets have to be copied there before being sent, and getting them there is unpleasant). They also regret having based their system on UDP. The overhead, especially from the checksum, was not worth the cost. In retrospect, they believe a simple custom RPC protocol would have been better. Finally, using busy waiting instead of having the server stub go to sleep would have largely eliminated the single largest time sink in Fig. 2-27(a).

Copying

An issue that frequently dominates RPC execution times is copying. On the Firefly this effect does not show up because the buffers are mapped into both the kernel and user address spaces, but in most other systems the kernel and user address spaces are disjoint. The number of times a message must be copied varies from one to about eight, depending on the hardware, software, and type of call. In the best case, the network chip can DMA the message directly out of the client stub's address space onto the network (copy 1), depositing it in the server kernel's memory in real time (i.e., the packet-arrived interrupt occurs within a few microseconds of the last bit being DMA'ed out of the client stub's memory). Then the kernel inspects the packet and maps the page containing it into the server's address space. If this type of mapping is not possible, the kernel copies the packet to the server stub (copy 2).

In the worst case, the kernel copies the message from the client stub into a kernel buffer for subsequent transmission, either because it is not convenient to transmit directly from user space or the network is currently busy (copy 1). Later, the kernel copies the message, in software, to a hardware buffer on the network interface board (copy 2). At this point, the hardware is started, causing the packet to be moved over the network to the interface board on the destination machine (copy 3). When the packet-arrived interrupt occurs on the server's machine, the kernel copies it to a kernel buffer, probably because it cannot tell where to put it until it has examined it, which is not possible until it has extracted it from the hardware buffer (copy 4). Finally, the message has to be copied to the server stub (copy 5). In addition, if the call has a large array passed as a value parameter, the array has to be copied onto the client's stack for the call stub, from the stack to the message buffer during marshaling within the client stub, and from the incoming message in the server stub to the server's stack preceding the call to the server, for three more copies, or eight in all.

Suppose that it takes an average of 500 nsec to copy a 32-bit word; then with eight copies, each word needs 4 microsec, giving a maximum data rate of about 1 Mbyte/sec, no matter how fast the network itself is. In practice, achieving even 1/10 of this would be pretty good.

One hardware feature that greatly helps eliminate unnecessary copying is **scatter-gather**. A network chip that can do scatter-gather can be set up to assemble a packet by concatenating two or more memory buffers. The advantage of this method is that the kernel can build the packet header in kernel space, leaving the user data in the client stub, with the hardware pulling them together as the packet goes out the door. Being able to gather up a packet from multiple sources eliminates copying. Similarly, being able to scatter the header and body of an incoming packet into different buffers also helps on the receiving end.

In general, eliminating copying is easier on the sending side than on the receiving side. With cooperative hardware, a reusable packet header inside the kernel and a data buffer in user space can be put out onto the network with no internal copying on the sending side. When it comes in at the receiver, however, even a very intelligent network chip will not know which server it should be given to, so the best the hardware can do is dump it into a kernel buffer and let the kernel figure out what to do with it.

In operating systems using virtual memory, a trick is available to avoid the copy to the stub. If the kernel packet buffer happens to occupy an entire page, beginning on a page boundary, and the server stub's receive buffer also happens to be an entire page, also starting on a page boundary, the kernel can change the memory map to map the packet buffer into the server's address space, simultaneously giving the server stub's buffer to the kernel. When the server stub starts running, its buffer will contain the packet, and this will have been achieved without copying.

Whether going to all this trouble is a good idea is a close call. Again assuming that it takes 500 nsec to copy a 32-bit word, copying a 1K packet takes 128 microsec. If the memory map can be updated in less time, mapping is faster than copying, otherwise it is not. This method also requires careful buffer control, making sure that all buffers are aligned properly with respect to page boundaries. If a buffer starts at a page boundary, the user process gets to see the entire packet, including the low-level headers, something that most systems try to hide in the name of portability.

Alternatively, if the buffers are aligned so that the header is at the end of one page and the data are at the start of the next, the data can be mapped without the header. This approach is cleaner and more portable, but costs two pages per buffer: one mostly empty except for a few bytes of header at the end, and one for the data.

Finally, many packets are only a few hundred bytes, in which case it is doubtful that mapping will beat copying. Still, it is an interesting idea that is certainly worth thinking about.

Timer Management

All protocols consist of exchanging messages over some communication medium. In virtually all systems, messages can occasionally be lost, due either to noise or receiver overrun. Consequently, most protocols set a timer whenever a message is sent and an answer (reply or acknowledgement) is expected. If the reply is not forthcoming within the expected time, the timer expires and the original message is retransmitted. This process is repeated until the sender gets bored and gives up.

The amount of machine time that goes into managing the timers should not be underestimated. Setting a timer requires building a data structure specifying when the timer is to expire and what is to be done when that happens. The data structure is then inserted into a list consisting of the other pending timers. Usually, the list is kept sorted on time, with the next timeout at the head of the list and the most distant one at the end, as shown in Fig. 2-28.

When an acknowledgement or reply arrives before the timer expires, the timeout entry must be located and removed from the list. In practice, very few timers actually expire, so most of the work of entering and removing a timer from the list is wasted effort. Furthermore, timers need not be especially accurate. The timeout value chosen is usually a wild guess in the first place ("a few seconds sounds about right"). Besides, using a poor value does not affect the correctness of the protocol, only the performance. Too low a value will cause timers to expire too often, resulting in unnecessary retransmissions. Too high a value will cause a needlessly long delay in the event that a packet is actually lost.

The combination of these factors suggests that a different way of handling the timers might be more efficient. Most systems maintain a process table, with one entry containing all the information about each process in the system. While an RPC is being carried out, the kernel has a pointer to the current process table entry in a local variable. Instead of storing timeouts in a sorted linked list, each process table entry has a field for holding its timeout, if any, as shown in Fig. 2-28(b). Setting a timer for an RPC now consists of adding the length of the timeout to the current time and storing in the process table. Turning a timer off consists of merely storing a zero in the timer field. Thus the actions of setting and clearing timers are now reduced to a few machine instructions each.

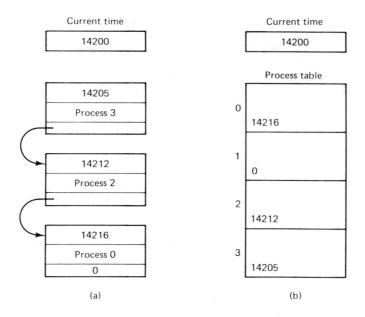

Fig. 2-28. (a) Timeouts in a sorted list. (b) Timeouts in the process table.

To make this method work, periodically (say, once per second), the kernel scans the entire process table, checking each timer value against the current time. Any nonzero value that is less than or equal to the current time corresponds to an expired timer, which is then processed and reset. For a system that sends, for example, 100 packets/sec, the work of scanning the process table once per second is only a fraction of the work of searching and updating a linked list 200 times a second. Algorithms that operate by periodically making a sequential pass through a table like this are called **sweep algorithms**.

2.4.6. Problem Areas

Remote procedure call using the client-server model is widely used as the basis for distributed operating systems. It is a simple abstraction that makes dealing with the complexity inherent in a distributed system more manageable than pure message passing. Nevertheless, there are a few problem areas that still have to be resolved. In this section we will discuss some of them.

Ideally, RPC should be transparent. That is, the programmer should not have to know which library procedures are local and which are remote. He should also be able to write procedures without regard to whether they will be executed locally or remote. Even stricter, the introduction of RPC into a system that was previously run on a single CPU should not be accompanied by a set of new rules prohibiting constructions that were previously legal, or requiring constructions that were previously optional. Under this stringent criterion, few, if any, current distributed systems can be said to be completely transparent. Thus the holy grail of transparency will remain a research topic for the foreseeable future.

As an example, consider the problem of global variables. In single CPU systems these are legal, even for library procedures. For example, in UNIX, there is a global variable *errno*. After an incorrect system call, *errno* contains a code telling what went wrong. The existence of *errno* is public information, since the official UNIX standard, POSIX, requires it to be visible in one of the mandatory header files, *errno.h*. Thus it is not permitted for an implementation to hide it from the programmers.

Now suppose that a programmer writes two procedures that both directly access *errno*. One of these is run locally; the other is run remote. Since the compiler does not (and may not) know which variables and procedures are located where, no matter where *errno* is stored, one of the procedures will fail to access it correctly. The problem is that allowing local procedures unconstrained access to remote global variables, and vice versa, cannot be implemented, yet prohibiting this access violates the transparency principle (that programs should not have to act differently due to RPC).

A second problem is weakly-typed languages, like C. In a strongly-typed language, like Pascal, the compiler, and thus the stub procedure, knows everything there is to know about all the parameters. This knowledge allows the stub to marshal the parameters without difficulty. In C, however, it is perfectly legal to write a procedure that computes the inner product of two vectors (arrays), without specifying how large either one is. Each could be terminated by a special value known only to the calling and called procedure. Under these circumstances, it is essentially impossible for the client stub to marshal the parameters: it has no way of determining how large they are.

The usual solution is to force the programmer to define the maximum size when writing the formal definition of the server, but suppose that the programmer wants the procedure to work with any size input? He can put an arbitrary limit in the specification, say, 1 million, but that means that the client stub will have to pass 1 million elements even when the actually array size is 100 elements. Furthermore, the call will fail when the actual array is 1,000,001 elements or the total memory can only hold 200,000 elements.

A similar problem occurs when passing a pointer to a complex graph as a parameter. On a single CPU system, doing so works fine, but with RPC, the client stub has no way to find the entire graph.

Still another problem occurs because it is not always possible to deduce the types of the parameters, not even from a formal specification or the code itself. An example is *printf*, which may have any number of parameters (at least one), and they can be an arbitrary mixture of integers, shorts, longs, characters, strings, floating point numbers of various lengths, and other types. Trying to call *printf* as a remote procedure would be practically impossible because C is so permissive. However, a rule saying that RPC can be used provided that you do not program in C would violate transparency.

The problems described above deal with transparency, but there is another class of difficulties that is even more fundamental. Consider the implementation of the UNIX command

```
sort <f1 >f2
```

Since *sort* knows it is reading standard input and writing standard output, it can act as a client for both input and output, performing RPCs with the file server to read *f1* as well as performing RPCs with the file server to write *f2*. Similarly, in the command

```
grep rat <f3 >f4
```

the *grep* program acts as a client to read the file *f3*, extracting only those lines containing the string "rat" and writing them to *f4*.

Now consider the UNIX pipeline

```
grep rat < f5 | sort >f6
```

As we have just seen, both *grep* and *sort* act as a client for both standard input and standard output. This behavior has to be compiled into the code to make the first two examples work. But how do they interact? Does *grep* act as a client doing writes to the server *sort*, or does *sort* act as the client doing reads from the server *grep*? Either way, one of them has to act as a server (i.e., passive), but as we have just seen, both have been programmed as clients (active). The difficulty here is that the client-server model really is not suitable at all.

In general, there is a problem with all pipelines of the form

```
p1 <f1 | p2 | p3 > f2
```

One approach to avoiding the client-client interface we just saw is to make the entire pipeline **read driven**, as illustrated in Fig. 2-29(b). The program *p1* acts as the (active) client and issues a read request to the file server to get *f1*. The program *p2*, also acting as a client, issues a read request to *p1* and the program *p3* issues a read request to *p2*. So far, so good. The trouble is that the file server does not act as a client issuing read requests to *p3* to collect the final output. Thus a read-driven pipeline does not work.

In Fig. 2-29(c) we see the write-driven approach. It has the mirror-image problem. Here *p1* acts as a client, doing writes to *p2*, which also acts as a client,

(a)   p1 < f1 | p2 | p3 > f2

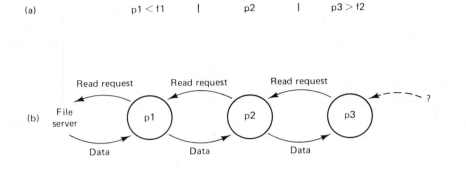

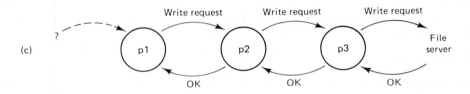

Fig. 2-29. (a) A pipeline. (b) The read-driven approach. (c) The write-driven approach.

doing writes to *p3*, which also acts as a client, writing to the file server, but there is no client issuing calls to *p1* asking it to accept the input file.

While ad hoc solutions can be found, it should be clear that the client-server model inherent in RPC is not a good fit to this kind of communication pattern. As an aside, one possible ad hoc solution is to implement pipes as dual servers, responding to both write requests from the left and read requests from the right. Alternatively, pipes can be implemented with temporary files that are always read from, or written to, the file server. Doing so generates unnecessary overhead, however.

A similar problem occurs when the shell wants to get input from the user. Normally, it sends read requests to the terminal server, which simply collects keystrokes and waits until the shell asks for them. But what happens when the user hits the interrupt key (DEL, CTRL-C, break, etc.)? If the terminal server just passively puts the interrupt character in the buffer waiting until the shell asks for it, it will be impossible for the user to break off the current program. On the other hand, how can the terminal server act as a client and make an RPC to the shell, which is not expecting to act as a server? Clearly, this role reversal causes trouble, just as the role ambiguity does in the pipeline. In fact, any time an unexpected message has to be sent, there is a potential problem. While the client-server model is frequently a good fit, it is not perfect.

2.5. GROUP COMMUNICATION

An underlying assumption intrinsic to RPC is that communication involves only *two* parties, the client and the server. Sometimes there are circumstances in which communication involves multiple processes, not just two. For example, consider a group of file servers cooperating to offer a single, fault-tolerant file service. In such a system, it might be desirable for a client to send a message to all the servers, to make sure that the request could be carried out even if one of them crashed. RPC cannot handle communication from one sender to many receivers, other than by performing separate RPCs with each one. In this section we will discuss alternative communication mechanisms in which a message can be sent to multiple receivers in one operation.

2.5.1. Introduction to Group Communication

A group is a collection of processes that act together in some system or user-specified way. The key property that all groups have is that when a message is sent to the group itself, all members of the group receive it. It is a form of **one-to-many** communication (one sender, many receivers), and is contrasted with **point-to-point** communication in Fig. 2-30.

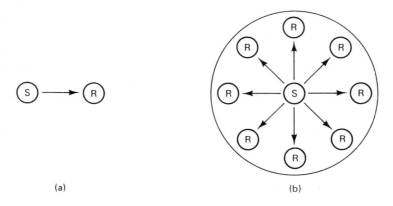

(a)   (b)

Fig. 2-30. (a) Point-to-point communication is from one sender to one receiver. (b) One-to-many communication is from one sender to multiple receivers.

Groups are dynamic. New groups can be created and old groups can be destroyed. A process can join a group or leave one. A process can be a member of several groups at the same time. Consequently, mechanisms are needed for managing groups and group membership.

Groups are roughly analogous to social organizations. A person might be a member of a book club, a tennis club, and an environmental organization. On a particular day, he might receive mailings (messages) announcing a new birthday cake cookbook from the book club, the annual Mother's Day tennis tournament from the tennis club, and the start of a campaign to save the Southern groundhog from the environmental organization. At any moment, he is free to leave any or all of these groups, and possibly join other groups.

Although in this book we will study only operating system (i.e., process) groups, it is worth mentioning that other groups are also commonly encountered in computer systems. For example, on the USENET computer network, there are hundreds of news groups, each about a specific subject. When a person sends a message to a particular news group, all members of the group receive it, even if there are tens of thousands of them. These higher-level groups usually have looser rules about who is a member, what the exact semantics of message delivery are, and so on, than do operating system groups. In most cases, this looseness is not a problem.

The purpose of introducing groups is to allow processes to deal with collections of processes as a single abstraction. Thus a process can send a message to a group of servers without having to know how many there are or where they are, which may change from one call to the next.

How group communication is implemented depends to a large extent on the hardware. On some networks, it is possible to create a special network address (for example, indicated by setting one of the high-order bits to 1), to which multiple machines can listen. When a packet is sent to one of these addresses, it is automatically delivered to all machines listening to the address. This technique is called **multicasting**. Implementing groups using multicast is straightforward: just assign each group a different multicast address.

Networks that do not have multicasting sometimes still have **broadcasting**, which means that packets containing a certain address (e.g., 0) are delivered to all machines. Broadcasting can also be used to implement groups, but it is less efficient. Each machine receives each broadcast, so its software must check to see if the packet is intended for it. If not, the packet is discarded, but some time is wasted processing the interrupt. Nevertheless, it still takes only one packet to reach all the members of a group.

Finally, if neither multicasting nor broadcasting is available, group communication can still be implemented by having the sender transmit separate packets to each of the members of the group. For a group with n members, n packets are required, instead of one packet when either multicasting or broadcasting is used. Although less efficient, this implementation is still workable, especially if most groups are small. The sending of a message from a single sender to a single receiver is sometimes called **unicasting** (point-to-point transmission), to distinguish it from multicasting and broadcasting.

2.5.2. Design Issues

Group communication has many of the same design possibilities as regular message passing, such as buffered versus unbuffered, blocking versus nonblocking, and so forth. However, there are also a large number of additional choices that must be made because sending to a group is inherently different from sending to a single process. Furthermore, groups can be organized in various ways internally. They can also be addressed in novel ways not relevant in point-to-point communication. In this section we will look at some of the most important design issues and point out the various alternatives.

Closed Groups versus Open Groups

Systems that support group communication can be divided into two categories depending on who can send to whom. Some systems support **closed groups**, in which only the members of the group can send to the group. Outsiders cannot send messages to the group as a whole, although they may be able to send messages to individual members. In contrast, other systems support **open groups**, which do not have this property. When open groups are used, any process in the system can send to any group. The difference between closed and open groups is shown in Fig. 2-31.

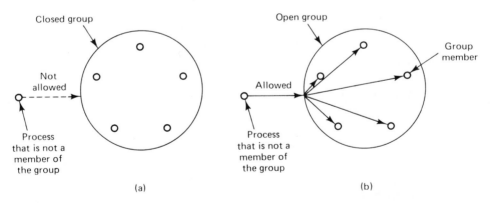

Fig. 2-31. (a) Outsiders may not send to a closed group. (b) Outsiders may send to an open group.

The decision as to whether a system supports closed or open groups usually relates to the reason groups are being supported in the first place. Closed groups are typically used for parallel processing. For example, a collection of processes working together to play a game of chess might form a closed group. They have their own goal and do not interact with the outside world.

On the other hand, when the idea of groups is to support replicated servers, it is important that processes that are not members (clients) can send to the group. In addition, the members of the group may also need to use group communication, for example to decide who should carry out a particular request. The distinction between closed and open groups is often made for implementation reasons.

Peer Groups versus Hierarchical Groups

The distinction between closed and open groups relates to who can communicate with the group. Another important distinction has to do with the internal structure of the group. In some groups, all the processes are equal. No one is boss and all decisions are made collectively. In other groups, some kind of hierarchy exists. For example, one process is the coordinator and all the others are workers. In this model, when a request for work is generated, either by an external client or by one of the workers, it is sent to the coordinator. The coordinator then decides which worker is best suited to carry it out, and forwards it there. More complex hierarchies are also possible, of course. These communication patterns are illustrated in Fig. 2-32.

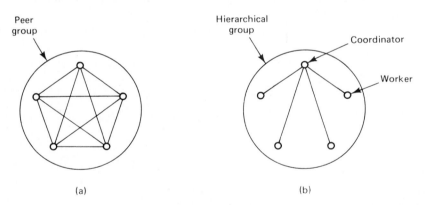

Fig. 2-32. (a) Communication in a peer group. (b) Communication in a simple hierarchical group.

Each of these organizations has its own advantages and disadvantages. The peer group is symmetric and has no single point of failure. If one of the processes crashes, the group simply becomes smaller, but can otherwise continue. A disadvantage is that decision making is more complicated. To decide anything, a vote has to be taken, incurring some delay and overhead.

The hierarchical group has the opposite properties. Loss of the coordinator brings the entire group to a grinding halt, but as long as it is running, it can make decisions without bothering everyone else. For example, a hierarchical group might be appropriate for a parallel chess program. The coordinator takes the current board, generates all the legal moves from it, and farms them out to the workers for evaluation. During this evaluation, new boards are generated and sent back to the coordinator to have them evaluated. When a worker is idle, it asks the coordinator for a new board to work on. In this manner, the coordinator controls the search strategy and prunes the game tree (e.g., using the alpha-beta search method), but leaves the actual evaluation to the workers.

Group Membership

When group communication is present, some method is needed for creating and deleting groups, as well as for allowing processes to join and leave groups. One possible approach is to have a **group server** to which all these requests can be sent. The group server can then maintain a complete data base of all the groups and their exact membership. This method is straightforward, efficient, and easy to implement. Unfortunately, it shares with all centralized techniques a major disadvantage: a single point of failure. If the group server crashes, group management ceases to exist. Probably most or all groups will have to be reconstructed from scratch, possibly terminating whatever work was going on.

The opposite approach is to manage group membership in a distributed way. In an open group, an outsider can send a message to all group members announcing its presence. In a closed group, something similar is needed (in effect, even closed groups have to be open with respect to joining). To leave a group, a member just sends a goodbye message to everyone.

So far, all of this is straightforward. However, there are two issues associated with group membership that are a bit trickier. First, if a member crashes, it effectively leaves the group. The trouble is, there is no polite announcement of this fact as there is when a process leaves voluntarily. The other members have to discover this experimentally by noticing that the crashed member no longer responds to anything. Once it is certain that the crashed member is really down, it can be removed from the group.

The other knotty issue is that leaving and joining have to be synchronous with messages being sent. In other words, starting at the instant that a process has joined a group, it must receive all messages sent to that group. Similarly, as soon as a process has left a group, it must not receive any more messages from the group, and the other members must not receive any more messages from it. One way of making sure that a join or leave is integrated into the message stream at the right place is to convert this operation into a message sent to the whole group.

One final issue relating to group membership is what to do if so many machines go down that the group can no longer function at all. Some protocol is needed to rebuild the group. Invariably, some process will have to take the initiative to start the ball rolling, but what happens if two or three try at the same time? The protocol will have to be able to withstand this.

Group Addressing

In order to send a message to a group, a process must have some way of specifying which group it means. In other words, groups need to be addressed, just as processes do. One way is to give each group a unique address, much like a process address. If the network supports multicast, the group address can be associated with a multicast address, so that every message sent to the group address can be multicast. In this way, the message will be sent to all those machines that need it, and no others.

If the hardware supports broadcast but not multicast, the message can be broadcast. Every kernel will then get it and extract from it the group address. If none of the processes on the machine is a member of the group, the broadcast is simply discarded. Otherwise, it is passed to all group members.

Finally, if neither multicast nor broadcast is supported, the kernel on the sending machine will have to have a list of machines that have processes belonging to the group. The kernel then sends each one a point-to-point message. These three implementation methods are shown in Fig. 2-33. The thing to notice is that in all three cases, a process just sends a message to a group address and it is delivered to all the members. How that happens is up to the operating system. The sender is not aware of the size of the group or whether communication is implemented by multicasting, broadcasting, or unicasting.

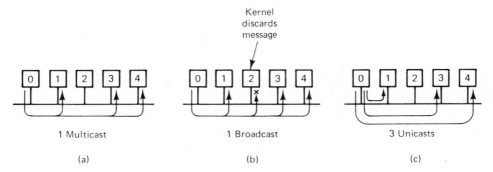

Fig. 2-33. Process 0 sending to a group consisting of processes 1, 3, and 4. (a) Multicast implementation. (b) Broadcast implementation. (c) Unicast implementation.

A second method of group addressing is to require the sender to provide an explicit list of all destinations (e.g., IP addresses). When this method is used, the parameter in the call to *send* that specifies the destination is a pointer to a list of addresses. This method has the serious drawback that it forces user processes (i.e., the group members) to be aware of precisely who is a member of which group. In other words, it is not transparent. Furthermore, whenever group membership changes, the user processes must update their membership lists. In Fig. 2-33, this administration can easily be done by the kernels to hide it from the user processes.

Group communication also allows a third, and quite novel method of addressing as well, which we will call **predicate addressing**. With this system, each message is sent to all members of the group (or possibly the entire system) using one of the methods described above, but with a new twist. Each message contains a predicate (Boolean expression) to be evaluated. The predicate can involve the receiver's machine number, its local variables, or other factors. If the predicate evaluates to TRUE, the message is accepted. If it evaluates to FALSE, the message is discarded. Using this scheme it is possible, for example, to send a message to only those machines that have at least 4M of free memory and which are willing to take on a new process.

Send and Receive Primitives

Ideally, point-to-point and group communication should be merged into a single set of primitives. However, if RPC is the usual user communication mechanism, rather than raw *send* and *receive*, it is hard to merge RPC and group communication. Sending a message to a group cannot be modeled as a procedure call. The primary difficulty is that with RPC, the client sends one message to the server and gets back one answer. With group communication there are potentially *n* different replies. How can a procedure call deal with *n* replies? Consequently, a common approach is to abandon the (two-way) request/reply model underlying RPC and go back to explicit calls for sending and receiving (one-way model).

The library procedures that processes call to invoke group communication may be the same as for point-to-point communication or they may be different. If the system is based on RPC, user processes never call *send* and *receive* directly anyway, so there is less incentive to merge the point-to-point and group primitives. If user programs directly call *send* and *receive* themselves, there is something to be said for doing group communication with these existing primitives instead of inventing a new set.

Suppose, for the moment, that we wish to merge the two forms of communication. To send a message, one of the parameters of *send* indicates the destination. If it is a process address, a single message is sent to that one process. If it is a group address (or a pointer to a list of destinations), a message is sent to all members of the group. A second parameter to *send* points to the message.

The call can be buffered or unbuffered, blocking or nonblocking, reliable or not reliable, for both the point-to-point and group cases. Generally, these choices are made by the system designers and are fixed, rather than being selectable on a per message basis. Introducing group communication does not change this.

Similarly, *receive* indicates a willingness to accept a message, and possibly blocks until one is available. If the two forms of communication are merged, *receive* completes when either a point-to-point message or a group message arrives. However, since these two forms of communication are frequently used for different purposes, some systems introduce new library procedures, say, *group_send* and *group_receive*, so a process can indicate whether it wants a point-to-point or a group message.

In the design just described, communication is one-way. Replies are independent messages in their own right and are not associated with previous requests. Sometimes this association is desirable, to try to achieve more of the RPC flavor. In this case, after sending a message, a process is required to call *getreply* repeatedly to collect all the replies, one at a time.

Atomicity

A characteristic of group communication that we have alluded to several times is the all-or-nothing property. Most group communication systems are designed so that when a message is sent to a group, it will either arrive correctly at all members of the group, or at none of them. Situations in which some members receive a message and others do not are not permitted. The property of all-or-nothing delivery is called **atomicity** or **atomic broadcast**.

Atomicity is desirable because it makes programming distributed systems much easier. When any process sends a message to the group, it does not have to worry about what to do if some of them do not get it. For example, in a replicated distributed data base system, suppose that a process sends a message to all the data base machines to create a new record in the data base, and later sends a second message to update it. If some of the members miss the message creating the record, they will not be able to perform the update and the data base will become inconsistent. Life is just a lot simpler if the system guarantees that every message is delivered to all the members of the group, or if that is not possible, that it is not delivered to any, and that failure is reported back to the sender so it can take appropriate action to recover.

Implementing atomic broadcast is not quite as simple as it looks. The method of Fig. 2-33 fails because receiver overrun is possible at one or more machines. The only way to be sure that every destination receives every message is to require them to send back an acknowledgement upon message receipt. As long as machines never crash, this method will do.

However, many distributed systems aim at fault tolerance, so for them it is essential that atomicity also holds even in the presence of machine failures. In this light, all the methods of Fig. 2-33 are inadequate because some of the initial messages might not arrive due to receiver overrun, followed by the sender's crashing. Under these circumstances, some members of the group will have received the message and others will not have, precisely the situation that is unacceptable. Worse yet, the group members that have not received the message do not even know they are missing anything, so they cannot ask for a retransmission. Finally, with the sender now down, even if they did know, there is no one to provide the message.

Nevertheless, there is hope. Here is a simple algorithm that demonstrates that atomic broadcast is at least possible. The sender starts out by sending a message to all members of the group. Timers are set and retransmissions sent where necessary. When a process receives a message, if it has not yet seen this particular message, it, too, sends the message to all members of the group (again with timers and retransmissions if necessary). If it has already seen the message, this step is not necessary and the message is discarded. No matter how many machines crash or how many packets are lost, eventually all the surviving processes will get the message. Later we will describe more efficient algorithms for ensuring atomicity.

Message Ordering

To make group communication easy to understand and use, two properties are required. The first one is atomic broadcast, as discussed above. It ensures that a message sent to the group arrives at either all members or at none of them. The second property concerns message ordering. To see what the issue is here, consider Fig. 2-34, in which we have five machines, each with one process. Processes 0, 1, 3, and 4 belong to the same group. Processes 0 and 4 want to send a message to the group simultaneously. Assume that multicasting and broadcasting are not available, so that each process has to send three separate (unicast) messages. Process 0 sends to 1, 3, and 4; process 4 sends to 0, 1, and 3. These six messages are shown interleaved in time in Fig. 2-34(a).

The trouble is that when two processes are contending for access to a LAN, the order in which the messages are sent is nondeterministic. In Fig. 2-34(a) we see that (by accident), process 0 has won the first round and sends to process 1. Then process 4 wins three rounds in a row and sends to processes 0, 1, and 3. Finally, process 0 gets to send to 3 and 4. The order of these six messages is shown in different ways in the two parts of Fig. 2-34.

Now consider the situation as viewed by processes 1 and 3 as shown in Fig. 2-34(b). Process 1 first receives a message from 0, then immediately

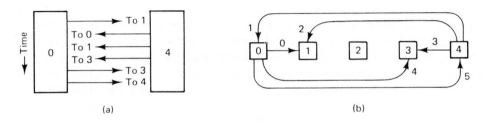

Fig. 2-34. (a) The three messages sent by processes 0 and 4 are interleaved in time. (b) Graphical representation of the six messages, showing the arrival order.

afterward it receives one from 4. Process 3 does not receive anything initially, then it receives messages from 4 and 0, in that order. Thus the two messages arrive in a different order. If processes 0 and 4 are both trying to update the same record in a data base, 1 and 3 end up with different final values. Needless to say, this situation is just as bad as one in which a (true hardware multicast) message sent to the group arrives at some members and not at others (atomicity failure). Thus to make programming reasonable, a system has to have well-defined semantics with respect to the order in which messages are delivered.

The best guarantee is to have all messages delivered instantaneously and in the order in which they were sent. If process 0 sends message *A* and then slightly later, process 4 sends message *B*, the system should first deliver *A* to all members of the group, and then deliver *B* to all members of the group. That way, all recipients get all messages in exactly the same order. This delivery pattern is something that programmers can understand and base their software on. We will call this **global time ordering**, since it delivers all messages in the exact order in which they were sent (conveniently ignoring the fact that according to Einstein's special theory of relativity there is no such thing as absolute global time).

Absolute time ordering is not always easy to implement, so some systems offer various watered-down variations. One of these is **consistent time ordering**, in which if two messages, say *A* and *B*, are sent close together in time, the system picks one of them as being "first" and delivers it to all group members, followed by the other. It may happen that the one chosen as first was not really first, but since no one knows this, the argument goes, system behavior should not depend on it. In effect, messages are guaranteed to arrive at all group members in the same order, but that order may not be the real order in which they were sent.

Even weaker time orderings have been used. We will study one of these, based on the idea of causality, when we come to ISIS later in this chapter.

Overlapping Groups

As we mentioned earlier, a process can be a member of multiple groups at the same time. This fact can lead to a new kind of inconsistency. To see the problem, look at Fig. 2-35, which shows two groups, 1 and 2. Processes *A*, *B*, and *C* are members of group 1. Processes *B*, *C*, and *D* are members of group 2.

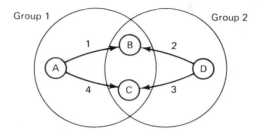

Fig. 2-35. Four processes, *A*, *B*, *C*, and *D*, and four messages. Processes *B* and *C* get the messages from *A* and *D* in a different order.

Now suppose that processes *A* and *D* each decide simultaneously to send a message to their respective groups, and that the system uses global time ordering within each group. As in our previous example, unicasting is used. The message order is shown in Fig. 2-35 by the numbers 1 through 4. Again we have the situation where two processes, in this case *B* and *C*, receive messages in a different order. *B* first gets a message from *A* followed by a message from *D*. *C* gets them in the opposite order.

The culprit here is that although there is a global time ordering within each group, there is not necessarily any coordination among multiple groups. Some systems support well-defined time ordering among overlapping groups and others do not. (If the groups are disjoint, the issue does not arise.) Implementing time ordering among different groups is frequently difficult to do, so the question arises as to whether it is worth it.

Scalability

Our final design issue is scalability. Many algorithms work fine as long as all the groups only have a few members, but what happens when there are tens, hundreds, or even thousands of members per group? Or thousands of groups? Also, what happens when the system is so large that it no longer fits on a single LAN, so multiple LANs and gateways are required? And what happens when the groups are spread over several continents?

The presence of gateways can affect many properties of the implementation. To start with, multicasting becomes more complicated. Consider, for example, the internetwork shown in Fig. 2-36. It consists of four LANs and four gateways, to provide protection against the failure of any gateway.

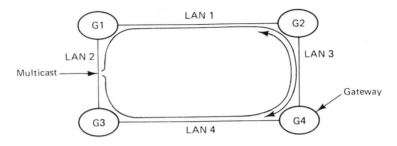

Fig. 2-36. Multicasting in an internetwork causes trouble.

Imagine that one of the machines on LAN 2 issues a multicast. When the multicast packet arrives at gateways *G1* and *G3*, what should they do? If they discard it, most of the machines will never see it, destroying its value as a multicast. If, however, the algorithm is just to have gateways forward all multicasts, then the packet will be copied to LAN 1 and LAN 4, and shortly thereafter to LAN 3 twice. Worse yet, gateway *G2* will see *G4*'s multicast and copy it to LAN 2, and vice versa. Clearly, a more sophisticated algorithm involving keeping track of previous packets is required to avoid exponential growth in the number of packets multicast.

Another problem with an internetwork is that some methods of group communication take advantage of the fact that only one packet can be on a LAN at any instant. In effect, the order of packet transmission defines an absolute global time order, which as we have seen, is frequently crucial. With gateways and multiple networks, it is possible for two packets to be "on the wire" simultaneously, thus destroying this useful property.

Finally, some algorithms may not scale well due to their computational complexity, their use of centralized components, or other factors.

2.5.3. Group Communication in ISIS

As an example of group communication, let us look at the ISIS system developed at Cornell (Birman, 1993; Birman and Joseph, 1987a, 1987b; and Birman and Van Renesse, 1994). ISIS is a toolkit for building distributed applications, for example, coordinating stock trading among all the brokers at a Wall Street securities firm. ISIS is not a complete operating system but rather, a set of programs that can run on top of UNIX or other existing operating systems. It is interesting to study because it has been widely described in the literature and has been used for numerous real applications. In Chap. 7 we will study group communication in Amoeba, which takes a quite different approach.

The key idea in ISIS is **synchrony** and the key communication primitives are different forms of atomic broadcast. Before looking at how ISIS does atomic broadcast, it is necessary first to examine the various forms of synchrony it distinguishes. A **synchronous system** is one in which events happen strictly sequentially, with each event (e.g., a broadcast) taking essentially zero time to complete. For example, if process *A* sends a message to processes *B*, *C*, and *D*, as shown in Fig. 2-37(a), the message arrives instantaneously at all the destinations. Similarly, a subsequent message from *D* to the others also takes zero time to be delivered everywhere. As viewed by an outside observer, the system consists of discrete events, none of which ever overlap the others. This property makes it easy to understand system behavior.

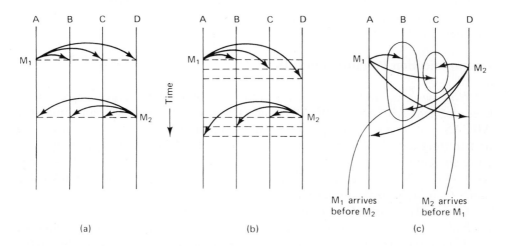

Fig. 2-37. (a) A synchronous system. (b) Loose synchrony. (c) Virtual synchrony.

Synchronous systems are impossible to build, so we need to investigate other types of systems, with weaker requirements on time. A **loosely synchronous system** is one like that of Fig. 2-37(b), in which events take a finite amount of time but all events appear in the same order to all parties. In particular, all processes receive all messages in the same order. Earlier, we discussed essentially the same idea under the name consistent time ordering.

Such systems are possible to build, but for some applications even weaker semantics are acceptable, and the hope is to be able to capitalize on these weak semantics to gain performance. Fig. 2-37(c) shows a **virtually synchronous system**, one in which the ordering constraint has been relaxed, but in such a way that under carefully selected circumstances, it does not matter.

Let us look at these circumstances. In a distributed system, two events are said to be **causally related** if the nature or behavior of the second one might have been influenced in any way by the first one. Thus if A sends a message to B, which inspects it and then sends a new message to C, the second message is causally related to the first one, since its contents might have been derived in part from the first one. Whether this actually happened is irrelevant. The relation holds if there *might* have been an influence.

Two events that are unrelated are said to be **concurrent**. If A sends a message to B, and about the same time, C sends a message to D, these events are concurrent because neither can influence the other. What virtual synchrony really means is that if two messages are causally related, all processes *must* receive them in the same (correct) order. If, however, they are concurrent, no guarantees are made, and the system is free to deliver them in a different order to different processes if this is easier. Thus when it matters, messages are always delivered in the same order, but when it does not matter, they may or may not be.

Communication Primitives in ISIS

Now we come to the broadcast primitives used in ISIS. Three of them have been defined: ABCAST, CBCAST, and GBCAST, all with different semantics. ABCAST provides loosely synchronous communication and is used for transmitting data to the members of a group. CBCAST provides virtually synchronous communication and is also used for sending data. GBCAST is somewhat like ABCAST, except that it is used for managing group membership rather than for sending ordinary data.

Originally, ABCAST used a form of two-phase commit protocol that worked like this. The sender, A, assigned a timestamp (actually just a sequence number) to the message and sent it to all the group members (by explicitly naming them all). Each one picked its own timestamp, larger than any other timestamp number it had sent or received, and sent it back to A. When all of these arrived, A chose the largest one and sent a *Commit* message to all the members again containing it. Committed messages were delivered to the application programs in order of the timestamps. It can be shown that this protocol guarantees that all messages will be delivered to all processes in the same order.

It can also be shown that this protocol is complex and expensive. For this reason, the ISIS designers invented the CBCAST primitive, which guarantees ordered delivery only for messages that are causally related. (The ABCAST protocol just described has subsequently been replaced, but even the new one is much slower than CBCAST.) The CBCAST protocol works as follows. If a group has n members, each process maintains a vector with n components, one per group member. The ith component of this vector is the number of the last message received in sequence from process i. The vectors are managed by the runtime system, not the user processes themselves, and are initialized to zero, as shown at the top of Fig. 2-38.

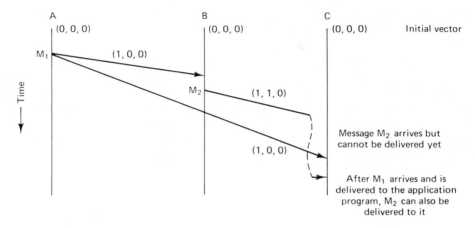

Fig. 2-38. Messages can be delivered only when all causally earlier messages have already been delivered.

When a process has a message to send, it increments its own slot in its vector, and sends the vector as part of the message. When M_1 in Fig. 2-38 gets to B, a check is made to see if it depends on anything that B has not yet seen. The first component of the vector is one higher than B's own first component, which is expected (and required) for a message from A, and the others are the same, so the message is accepted and passed to the group member running on B. If any other component of the incoming vector had been larger than the corresponding component of B's vector, the message could not have been delivered yet.

Now B sends a message of its own, M_2, to C, which arrives before M_1. From the vector, C sees that B had already received one message from A before M_2 was sent, and since it has not yet received anything from A, M_2 is buffered until a message from A arrives. Under no conditions may it be delivered before A's message.

The general algorithm for deciding whether to pass an incoming message to the user process or delay it can now be stated. Let V_i be the ith component of the vector in the incoming message, and L_i be the ith component of the vector stored in the receiver's memory. Suppose that the message was sent by j. The first condition for acceptance is $V_j = L_j + 1$. This simply states that this is the next message in sequence from j, that is, no messages have been missed. (Messages from the same sender are always causally related.) The second condition for acceptance is $V_i \leq L_i$ for all $i \neq j$. This condition simply states that the sender has not seen any message that the receiver has missed. If an incoming message passes both tests, the runtime system can pass it to the user process without delay. Otherwise, it must wait.

In Fig. 2-39 we show a more detailed example of the vector mechanism. Here process 0 has sent a message containing the vector (4, 6, 8, 2, 1, 5) to the other five members of its group. Process 1 has seen the same messages as process 0 except for message 7 just sent by process 1 itself, so the incoming message passes the test, is accepted, and can be passed up to the user process. Process 2 has missed message 6 sent by process 1, so the incoming message must be delayed. Process 3 has seen everything the sender has seen, and in addition message 7 from process 1, which apparently has not yet gotten to process 0, so the message is accepted. Process 4 missed the previous message from 0 itself. This omission is serious, so the new message will have to wait. Finally, process 5 is also slightly ahead of 0, so the message can be accepted immediately.

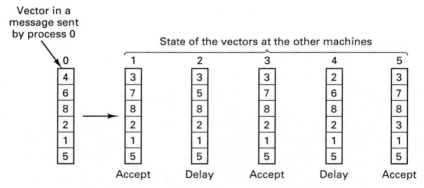

Fig. 2-39. Examples of the vectors used by CBCAST.

ISIS also provides fault tolerance and support for message ordering for overlapping groups using CBCAST. The algorithms used are somewhat complicated, though. For details, see (Birman et al., 1991).

2.6. SUMMARY

The key difference between a centralized operating system and a distributed one is the importance of communication in the latter. Various approaches to communication in distributed systems have been proposed and implemented. For relatively slow, wide-area distributed systems, connection-oriented layered protocols such as OSI and TCP/IP are sometimes used because the main problem to be overcome is how to transport the bits reliably over poor physical lines.

For LAN-based distributed systems, layered protocols are rarely used. Instead, a much simpler model is usually adopted, in which the client sends a message to the server and the server sends back a reply to the client. By eliminating most of the layers, much higher performance can be achieved. Many of the design issues in these message-passing systems concern the communication primitives: blocking versus nonblocking, buffered versus unbuffered, reliable versus unreliable, and so on.

The problem with the basic client-server model is that conceptually interprocess communication is handled as I/O. To present a better abstraction, remote procedure call is widely used. With RPC, a client running on one machine calls a procedure running on another machine. The runtime system, embodied in stub procedures, handles collecting parameters, building messages, and the interface with the kernel to actually move the bits.

Although RPC is a step forward above raw message passing, it has its own problems. The correct server has to be located. Pointers and complex data structures are hard to pass. Global variables are difficult to use. The exact semantics of RPC are tricky because clients and servers can fail independently of one another. Finally, implementing RPC efficiently is not straightforward and requires careful thought.

RPC is limited to those situations where a single client wants to talk to a single server. When a collection of processes, for example, replicated file servers, need to communicate with each other as a group, something else is needed. Systems such as ISIS provide a new abstraction for this purpose: group communication. ISIS offers a variety of primitives, the most important of which is CBCAST. CBCAST offers weakened communication semantics based on causality and implemented by including sequence number vectors in each message to allow the receiver to see whether the message should be delivered immediately or delayed until some prior messages have arrived.

PROBLEMS

1. In many layered protocols, each layer has its own header. Surely it would be more efficient to have a single header at the front of each message with all the control in it than all these separate headers. Why is this not done?

2. What is meant by an *open system*? Why are some systems not open?

3. What is the difference between a connection-oriented and connectionless communication protocol?

4. An ATM system is transmitting cells at the OC-3 rate. Each packet is 48 bytes long, and thus fits into a cell. An interrupt takes 1 μsec. What fraction of the CPU is devoted to interrupt handling? Now repeat this problem for 1024-byte packets.

5. What is the probability that a totally garbled ATM header will be accepted as being correct?

6. Suggest a simple modification to Fig. 2-9 that reduces network traffic.

7. If the communication primitives in a client-server system are nonblocking, a call to *send* will complete before the message has actually been sent. To reduce overhead, some systems do not copy the data to the kernel, but transmit it directly from user space. For such a system, devise two ways in which the sender can be told that the transmission has been completed and the buffer can be reused.

8. In many communication systems, calls to *send* set a timer to guard against hanging the client forever if the server crashes. Suppose that a fault-tolerant system is implemented using multiple processors for all clients and all servers, so the probability of a client or server crashing is effectively zero. Do you think it is safe to get rid of timeouts in this system?

9. When buffered communication is used, a primitive is normally available for user processes to create mailboxes. In the text it was not specified whether this primitive must specify the size of the mailbox. Give an argument each way.

10. In all the examples in this chapter, a server can only listen to a single address. In practice, it is sometimes convenient for a server to listen to multiple addresses at the same time, for example, if the same process performs a set of closely related services that have been assigned separate addresses. Invent a scheme by which this goal can be accomplished.

11. Consider a procedure *incr* with two integer parameters. The procedure adds one to each parameter. Now suppose that it is called with the same variable twice, for example, as *incr(i, i)*. If i is initially 0, what value will it have afterward if call-by-reference is used? How about if copy/restore is used?

12. Pascal has a construction called a record variant, in which a field of a record can hold any one of several alternatives. At run time, there is no sure-fire way to tell which one is in there. Does this feature of Pascal have any implications for remote procedure call? Explain your answer.

13. The usual sequence of steps in an RPC involves trapping to the kernel to have the message sent from the client to the server. Suppose that a special

co-processor chip for doing network I/O exists and that this chip is directly addressable from user space. Would it be worth having? What steps would an RPC consist of in that case?

14. The SPARC chip uses a 32-bit word in big endian format. If a SPARC sends the integer 2 to a 486, which is little endian, what numerical value does the 486 see?

15. One way to handle parameter conversion in RPC systems is to have each machine send parameters in its native representation, with the other one doing the translation, if need be. In the text it was suggested that the native system could be indicated by a code in the first byte. However, since locating the first byte in the first word is precisely the problem, can this work, or is the book wrong?

16. In Fig. 2-23 the *deregister* call to the binder has the unique identifier as one of the parameters. Is this really necessary? After all, the name and version are also provided, which uniquely identifies the service.

17. Reading the first block of a file from a remote file server is an idempotent operation. What about writing the first block?

18. For each of the following applications, do you think at least once semantics or at most once semantics is best? Discuss.

    (a) Reading and writing files from a file server.
    (b) Compiling a program.
    (c) Remote banking.

19. Suppose that the time to do a null RPC (i.e., 0 data bytes) is 1.0 msec, with an additional 1.5 msec for every 1K of data. How long does it take to read 32K from the file server in a single 32K RPC? How about as 32 1K RPCs?

20. How can atomic broadcast be used to manage group membership?

21. When a computation runs for a long time, it is sometimes wise to make checkpoints periodically, that is, to save the state of the process on disk in case it crashes. In that way, the process can be restarted from the checkpoint instead of from the beginning. Try to devise a way of checkpointing a computation that consists of multiple processes running in parallel.

22. Imagine that in a particular distributed system all the machines are redundant multiprocessors, so that the possibility of a machine crashing is so low that it can be ignored. Devise a simple method for implementing global time-ordered atomic broadcast using only unicasting. (*Hint*: Arrange the machines in a logical ring.)

3

Synchronization in Distributed Systems

In Chap. 2, we saw how processes in a distributed system communicate with one another. The methods used include layered protocols, request/reply message passing (including RPC), and group communication. While communication is important, it is not the entire story. Closely related is how processes cooperate and synchronize with one another. For example, how are critical regions implemented in a distributed system, and how are resources allocated? In this chapter we will study these and other issues related to interprocess cooperation and synchronization in distributed systems.

In single CPU systems, critical regions, mutual exclusion, and other synchronization problems are generally solved using methods such as semaphores and monitors. These methods are not well suited to use in distributed systems because they invariably rely (implicitly) on the existence of shared memory. For example, two processes that are interacting using a semaphore must both be able to access the semaphore. If they are running on the same machine, they can share the semaphore by having it stored in the kernel, and execute system calls to access it. If, however, they are running on different machines, this method no longer works, and other techniques are needed. Even seemingly simple matters, such as determining whether event A happened before or after event B, require careful thought.

We will start out by looking at time and how it can be measured, because time plays a major role in some synchronization methods. Then we will look at mutual exclusion and election algorithms. After that we will study a high-level synchronization technique called atomic transactions. Finally, we will look at deadlock in distributed systems.

3.1. CLOCK SYNCHRONIZATION

Synchronization in distributed systems is more complicated than in centralized ones because the former have to use distributed algorithms. It is usually not possible (or desirable) to collect all the information about the system in one place, and then let some process examine it and make a decision as is done in the centralized case. In general, distributed algorithms have the following properties:

1. The relevant information is scattered among multiple machines.

2. Processes make decisions based only on local information.

3. A single point of failure in the system should be avoided.

4. No common clock or other precise global time source exists.

The first three points all say that it is unacceptable to collect all the information in a single place for processing. For example, to do resource allocation (assigning I/O devices in a deadlock-free way), it is generally not acceptable to send all the requests to a single manager process, which examines them all and grants or denies requests based on information in its tables. In a large system, such a solution puts a heavy burden on that one process.

Furthermore, having a single point of failure like this makes the system unreliable. Ideally, a distributed system should be more reliable than the individual machines. If one goes down, the rest should be able to continue to function. Having the failure of one machine (e.g., the resource allocator) bring a large number of other machines (its customers) to a grinding halt is the last thing we want. Achieving synchronization without centralization requires doing things in a different way from traditional operating systems.

The last point in the list is also crucial. In a centralized system, time is unambiguous. When a process wants to know the time, it makes a system call and the kernel tells it. If process *A* asks for the time, and then a little later process *B* asks for the time, the value that *B* gets will be higher than (or possibly equal to) the value *A* got. It will certainly not be lower. In a distributed system, achieving agreement on time is not trivial.

Just think, for a moment, about the implications of the lack of global time on the UNIX *make* program, as a single example. Normally, in UNIX, large programs are split up into multiple source files, so that a change to one source file only requires one file to be recompiled, not all the files. If a program consists of 100 files, not having to recompile everything because one file has been changed greatly increases the speed at which programmers can work.

The way *make* normally works is simple. When the programmer has finished changing all the source files, he starts *make*, which examines the times at which all the source and object files were last modified. If the source file *input.c* has time 2151 and the corresponding object file *input.o* has time 2150, *make* knows that *input.c* has been changed since *input.o* was created, and thus *input.c* must be recompiled. On the other hand, if *output.c* has time 2144 and *output.o* has time 2145, no compilation is needed here. Thus *make* goes through all the source files to find out which ones need to be recompiled and calls the compiler to recompile them.

Now imagine what could happen in a distributed system in which there is no global agreement on time. Suppose that *output.o* has time 2144 as above, and shortly thereafter *output.c* is modified but is assigned time 2143 because the clock on its machine is slightly slow, as shown in Fig. 3-1. *Make* will not call the compiler. The resulting executable binary program will then contain a mixture of object files from the old sources and the new sources. It will probably not work, and the programmer will go crazy trying to understand what is wrong with the code.

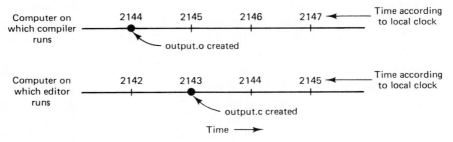

Fig. 3-1. When each machine has its own clock, an event that occurred after another event may nevertheless be assigned an earlier time.

Since time is so basic to the way people think, and the effect of not having all the clocks synchronized can be so dramatic, as we have just seen, it is fitting that we begin our study of synchronization with the simple question: Is it possible to synchronize all the clocks in a distributed system?

3.1.1. Logical Clocks

Nearly all computers have a circuit for keeping track of time. Despite the widespread use of the word "clock" to refer to these devices, they are not actually clocks in the usual sense. **Timer** is perhaps a better word. A computer timer is usually a precisely machined quartz crystal. When kept under tension, quartz crystals oscillate at a well-defined frequency that depends on the kind of crystal, how it is cut, and the amount of tension. Associated with each crystal are two registers, a **counter** and a **holding register**. Each oscillation of the crystal decrements the counter by one. When the counter gets to zero, an interrupt is generated and the counter is reloaded from the holding register. In this way, it is possible to program a timer to generate an interrupt 60 times a second, or at any other desired frequency. Each interrupt is called one **clock tick**.

When the system is booted initially, it usually asks the operator to enter the date and time, which is then converted to the number of ticks after some known starting date and stored in memory. At every clock tick, the interrupt service procedure adds one to the time stored in memory. In this way, the (software) clock is kept up to date.

With a single computer and a single clock, it does not matter much if this clock is off by a small amount. Since all processes on the machine use the same clock, they will still be internally consistent. For example, if the file *input.c* has time 2151 and file *input.o* has time 2150, *make* will recompile the source file, even if the clock is off by 2 and the true times are 2153 and 2152, respectively. All that really matters are the relative times.

As soon as multiple CPUs are introduced, each with its own clock, the situation changes. Although the frequency at which a crystal oscillator runs is usually fairly stable, it is impossible to guarantee that the crystals in different computers all run at exactly the same frequency. In practice, when a system has n computers, all n crystals will run at slightly different rates, causing the (software) clocks gradually to get out of sync and give different values when read out. This difference in time values is called **clock skew**. As a consequence of this clock skew, programs that expect the time associated with a file, object, process, or message to be correct and independent of the machine on which it was generated (i.e., which clock it used) can fail, as we saw in the *make* example above.

This brings us back to our original question, whether it is possible to synchronize all the clocks to produce a single, unambiguous time standard. In a classic paper, Lamport (1978) showed that clock synchronization is possible and presented an algorithm for achieving it. He extended his work in (Lamport, 1990).

Lamport pointed out that clock synchronization need not be absolute. If two processes do not interact, it is not necessary that their clocks be synchronized because the lack of synchronization would not be observable and thus could not cause problems. Furthermore, he pointed out that what usually matters is not that all processes agree on exactly what time it is, but rather, that they agree on the order in which events occur. In the *make* example above, what counts is whether *input.c* is older or newer than *input.o*, not their absolute creation times.

For many purposes, it is sufficient that all machines agree on the same time. It is not essential that this time also agree with the real time as announced on the radio every hour. For running *make*, for example, it is adequate that all machines agree that it is 10:00, even if it is really 10:02. Thus for a certain class of algorithms, it is the internal consistency of the clocks that matters, not whether they are particularly close to the real time. For these algorithms, it is conventional to speak of the clocks as **logical clocks**.

When the additional constraint is present that the clocks must not only be the same, but also must not deviate from the real time by more than a certain amount, the clocks are called **physical clocks**. In this section we will discuss Lamport's algorithm, which synchronizes logical clocks. In the following sections we will introduce the concept of physical time and show how physical clocks can be synchronized.

To synchronize logical clocks, Lamport defined a relation called **happens-before**. The expression $a \rightarrow b$ is read "*a* happens before *b*" and means that all processes agree that first event *a* occurs, then afterward, event *b* occurs. The happens-before relation can be observed directly in two situations:

1. If *a* and *b* are events in the same process, and *a* occurs before *b*, then $a \rightarrow b$ is true.

2. If *a* is the event of a message being sent by one process, and *b* is the event of the message being received by another process, then $a \rightarrow b$ is also true. A message cannot be received before it is sent, or even at the same time it is sent, since it takes a finite amount of time to arrive.

Happens-before is a transitive relation, so if $a \rightarrow b$ and $b \rightarrow c$, then $a \rightarrow c$. If two events, *x* and *y*, happen in different processes that do not exchange messages (not even indirectly via third parties), then $x \rightarrow y$ is not true, but neither is $y \rightarrow x$. These events are said to be **concurrent**, which simply means that nothing can be said (or need be said) about when they happened or which is first.

What we need is a way of measuring time such that for every event, *a*, we can assign it a time value $C(a)$ on which all processes agree. These time values must have the property that if $a \rightarrow b$, then $C(a) < C(b)$. To rephrase the conditions we stated earlier, if *a* and *b* are two events within the same process and *a* occurs before *b*, then $C(a) < C(b)$. Similarly, if *a* is the sending of a message by one process and *b* is the reception of that message by another process, then $C(a)$ and $C(b)$ must be assigned in such a way that everyone agrees on the values of $C(a)$ and $C(b)$ with $C(a) < C(b)$. In addition, the clock time, *C*, must always go forward (increasing), never backward (decreasing). Corrections to time can be made by adding a positive value, never by subtracting one.

Now let us look at the algorithm Lamport proposed for assigning times to events. Consider the three processes depicted in Fig. 3-2(a). The processes run on different machines, each with its own clock, running at its own speed. As can be seen from the figure, when the clock has ticked 6 times in process 0, it has ticked 8 times in process 1 and 10 times in process 2. Each clock runs at a constant rate, but the rates are different due to differences in the crystals.

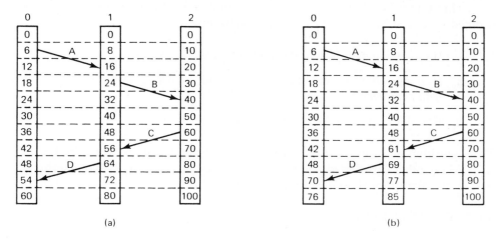

Fig. 3-2. (a) Three processes, each with its own clock. The clocks run at different rates. (b) Lamport's algorithm corrects the clocks.

At time 6, process 0 sends message *A* to process 1. How long this message takes to arrive depends on whose clock you believe. In any event, the clock in process 1 reads 16 when it arrives. If the message carries the starting time, 6, in it, process 1 will conclude that it took 10 ticks to make the journey. This value is certainly possible. According to this reasoning, message *B* from 1 to 2 takes 16 ticks, again a plausible value.

Now comes the fun part. Message *C* from 2 to 1 leaves at 60 and arrives at 56. Similarly, message *D* from 1 to 0 leaves at 64 and arrives at 54. These values are clearly impossible. It is this situation that must be prevented.

Lamport's solution follows directly from the happened-before relation. Since *C* left at 60, it must arrive at 61 or later. Therefore, each message carries the sending time, according to the sender's clock. When a message arrives and the receiver's clock shows a value prior to the time the message was sent, the receiver fast forwards its clock to be one more than the sending time. In Fig. 3-2(b) we see that *C* now arrives at 61. Similarly, *D* arrives at 70.

With one small addition, this algorithm meets our requirements for global time. The addition is that between every two events, the clock must tick at least once. If a process sends or receives two messages in quick succession, it must advance its clock by (at least) one tick in between them.

In some situations, an additional requirement is desirable: no two events ever occur at exactly the same time. To achieve this goal, we can attach the number of the process in which the event occurs to the low-order end of the time, separated by a decimal point. Thus if events happen in processes 1 and 2, both with time 40, the former becomes 40.1 and the latter becomes 40.2.

Using this method, we now have a way to assign time to all events in a distributed system subject to the following conditions:

1. If a happens before b in the same process, $C(a) < C(b)$.

2. If a and b represent the sending and receiving of a message, $C(a) < C(b)$.

3. For all events a and b, $C(a) \neq C(b)$.

This algorithm gives us a way to provide a total ordering of all events in the system. Many other distributed algorithms need such an ordering to avoid ambiguities, so the algorithm is widely cited in the literature.

3.1.2. Physical Clocks

Although Lamport's algorithm gives an unambiguous event ordering, the time values assigned to events are not necessarily close to the actual times at which they occur. In some systems (e.g., real-time systems), the actual clock time is important. For these systems external physical clocks are required. For reasons of efficiency and redundancy, multiple physical clocks are generally considered desirable, which yields two problems: (1) How do we synchronize them with real-world clocks, and (2) How do we synchronize the clocks with each other?

Before answering these questions, let us digress slightly to see how time is actually measured. It is not nearly as simple as one might think, especially when high accuracy is required. Since the invention of mechanical clocks in the 17th century, time has been measured astronomically. Every day, the sun appears to rise on the eastern horizon, climbs to a maximum height in the sky, and sinks in the west. The event of the sun's reaching its highest apparent point in the sky is called the **transit of the sun**. This event occurs at about noon each day. The interval between two consecutive transits of the sun is called the **solar day**. Since there are 24 hours in a day, each containing 3600 seconds, the **solar second** is defined as exactly 1/86400th of a solar day. The geometry of the mean solar day calculation is shown in Fig. 3-3.

In the 1940s, it was established that the period of the earth's rotation is not constant. The earth is slowing down due to tidal friction and atmospheric drag. Based on studies of growth patterns in ancient coral, geologists now believe that

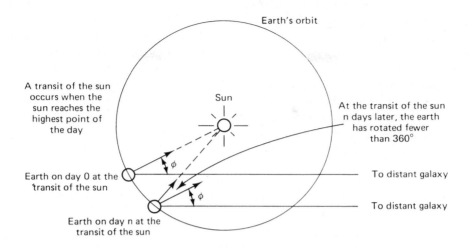

Fig. 3-3. Computation of the mean solar day.

300 million years ago there were about 400 days per year. The length of the year, that is, the time for one trip around the sun, is not thought to have changed; the day has simply become longer. In addition to this long-term trend, short-term variations in the length of the day also occur, probably caused by turbulence deep in the earth's core of molten iron. These revelations led astronomers to compute the length of the day by measuring a large number of days and taking the average before dividing by 86,400. The resulting quantity was called the **mean solar second**.

With the invention of the atomic clock in 1948, it became possible to measure time much more accurately, and independent of the wiggling and wobbling of the earth, by counting transitions of the cesium 133 atom. The physicists took over the job of timekeeping from the astronomers, and defined the second to be the time it takes the cesium 133 atom to make exactly 9,192,631,770 transitions. The choice of 9,192,631,770 was made to make the atomic second equal to the mean solar second in the year of its introduction. Currently, about 50 laboratories around the world have cesium 133 clocks. Periodically, each laboratory tells the Bureau International de l'Heure (BIH) in Paris how many times its clock has ticked. The BIH averages these to produce **International Atomic Time**, which is abbreviated **TAI**. Thus TAI is just the mean number of ticks of the cesium 133 clocks since midnight on Jan. 1, 1958 (the beginning of time) divided by 9,192,631,770.

Although TAI is highly stable and available to anyone who wants to go to the trouble of buying a cesium clock, there is a serious problem with it; 86,400 TAI seconds is now about 3 msec less than a mean solar day (because the mean solar day is getting longer all the time). Using TAI for keeping time would mean that over the course of the years, noon would get earlier and earlier, until it would eventually occur in the wee hours of the morning. People might notice this and we could have the same kind of situation as occurred in 1582 when Pope Gregory XIII decreed that 10 days be omitted from the calendar. This event caused riots in the streets because landlords demanded a full month's rent and bankers a full month's interest, while employers refused to pay workers for the 10 days they did not work, to mention only a few of the conflicts. The Protestant countries, as a matter of principle, refused to have anything to do with papal decrees and did not accept the Gregorian calendar for 170 years.

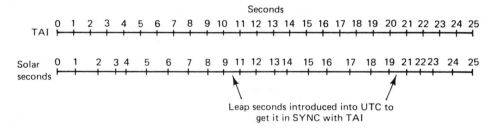

Fig. 3-4. TAI seconds are of constant length, unlike solar seconds. Leap seconds are introduced when necessary to keep in phase with the sun.

BIH solves the problem by introducing **leap seconds** whenever the discrepancy between TAI and solar time grows to 800 msec. The use of leap seconds is illustrated in Fig. 3-4. This correction gives rise to a time system based on constant TAI seconds but which stays in phase with the apparent motion of the sun. It is called **Universal Coordinated Time**, but is abbreviated as **UTC**. UTC is the basis of all modern civil timekeeping. It has essentially replaced the old standard, Greenwich Mean Time, which is astronomical time.

Most electric power companies base the timing of their 60-Hz or 50-Hz clocks on UTC, so when BIH announces a leap second, the power companies raise their frequency to 61 Hz or 51 Hz for 60 or 50 sec, to advance all the clocks in their distribution area. Since 1 sec is a noticeable interval for a computer, an operating system that needs to keep accurate time over a period of years must have special software to account for leap seconds as they are announced (unless they use the power line for time, which is usually too crude). The total number of leap seconds introduced into UTC so far is about 30.

To provide UTC to people who need precise time, the National Institute of Standard Time (NIST) operates a shortwave radio station with call letters WWV from Fort Collins, Colorado. WWV broadcasts a short pulse at the start of each UTC second. The accuracy of WWV itself is about ±1 msec, but due to random atmospheric fluctuations that can affect the length of the signal path, in practice the accuracy is no better than ±10 msec. In England, the station MSF, operating from Rugby, Warwickshire, provides a similar service, as do stations in several other countries.

Several earth satellites also offer a UTC service. The Geostationary Environment Operational Satellite can provide UTC accurately to 0.5 msec, and some other satellites do even better.

Using either shortwave radio or satellite services requires an accurate knowledge of the relative position of the sender and receiver, in order to compensate for the signal propagation delay. Radio receivers for WWV, GEOS, and the other UTC sources are commercially available. The cost varies from a few thousand dollars each to tens of thousands of dollars each, being more for the better sources. UTC can also be obtained more cheaply, but less accurately, by telephone from NIST in Fort Collins, but here too, a correction must be made for the signal path and modem speed. This correction introduces some uncertainty, making it difficult to obtain the time with extremely high accuracy.

3.1.3. Clock Synchronization Algorithms

If one machine has a WWV receiver, the goal becomes keeping all the other machines synchronized to it. If no machines have WWV receivers, each machine keeps track of its own time, and the goal is to keep all the machines together as well as possible. Many algorithms have been proposed for doing this synchronization (e.g., Cristian, 1989; Drummond and Babaoglu, 1993; and Kopetz and Ochsenreiter, 1987). A survey is given in (Ramanathan et al., 1990b).

All the algorithms have the same underlying model of the system, which we will now describe. Each machine is assumed to have a timer that causes an interrupt H times a second. When this timer goes off, the interrupt handler adds 1 to a software clock that keeps track of the number of ticks (interrupts) since some agreed-upon time in the past. Let us call the value of this clock C. More specifically, when the UTC time is t, the value of the clock on machine p is $C_p(t)$. In a perfect world, we would have $C_p(t) = t$ for all p and all t. In other words, dC/dt ideally should be 1.

Real timers do not interrupt exactly H times a second. Theoretically, a timer with $H = 60$ should generate 216,000 ticks per hour. In practice, the relative error obtainable with modern timer chips is about 10^{-5}, meaning that a particular machine can get a value in the range 215,998 to 216,002 ticks per hour. More precisely, if there exists some constant ρ such that

$$1 - \rho \leq \frac{dC}{dt} \leq 1 + \rho$$

the timer can be said to be working within its specification. The constant ρ is specified by the manufacturer and is known as the **maximum drift rate**. Slow, perfect, and fast clocks are shown in Fig. 3-5.

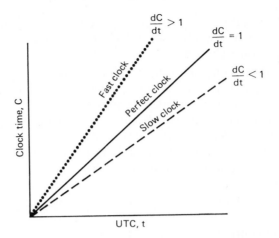

Fig. 3-5. Not all clocks tick precisely at the correct rate.

If two clocks are drifting from UTC in the opposite direction, at a time Δt after they were synchronized, they may be as much as $2\rho \, \Delta t$ apart. If the operating system designers want to guarantee that no two clocks ever differ by more than δ, clocks must be resynchronized (in software) at least every $\delta/2\rho$ seconds. The various algorithms differ in precisely how this resynchronization is done.

Cristian's Algorithm

Let us start with an algorithm that is well suited to systems in which one machine has a WWV receiver and the goal is to have all the other machines stay synchronized with it. Let us call the machine with the WWV receiver a **time server**. Our algorithm is based on the work of Cristian (1989) and prior work. Periodically, certainly no more than every $\delta/2\rho$ seconds, each machine sends a message to the time server asking it for the current time. That machine responds as fast as it can with a message containing its current time, C_{UTC}, as shown in Fig. 3-6.

As a first approximation, when the sender gets the reply, it can just set its clock to C_{UTC}. However, this algorithm has two problems, one major and one minor. The major problem is that time must never run backward. If the sender's clock is fast, C_{UTC} will be smaller than the sender's current value of C. Just taking over C_{UTC} could cause serious problems, such as an object file compiled just after the clock change having a time earlier than the source which was modified just before the clock change.

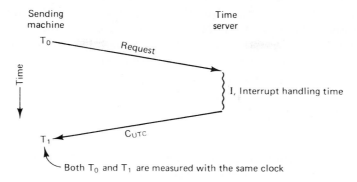

Fig. 3-6. Getting the current time from a time server.

Such a change must be introduced gradually. One way is as follows. Suppose that the timer is set to generate 100 interrupts per second. Normally, each interrupt would add 10 msec to the time. When slowing down, the interrupt routine adds only 9 msec each time, until the correction has been made. Similarly, the clock can be advanced gradually by adding 11 msec at each interrupt instead of jumping it forward all at once.

The minor problem is that it takes a nonzero amount of time for the time server's reply to get back to the sender. Worse yet, this delay may be large and vary with the network load. Cristian's way of dealing with it is to attempt to measure it. It is simple enough for the sender to record accurately the interval between sending the request to the time server and the arrival of the reply. Both the starting time, T_0, and the ending time, T_1, are measured using the same clock, so the interval will be relatively accurate, even if the sender's clock is off from UTC by a substantial amount.

In the absence of any other information, the best estimate of the message propagation time is $(T_1 - T_0)/2$. When the reply comes in, the value in the message can be increased by this amount to give an estimate of the server's current time. If the theoretical minimum propagation time is known, other properties of the time estimate can be calculated.

This estimate can be improved if it is known approximately how long it takes the time server to handle the interrupt and process the incoming message. Let us call the interrupt handling time I. Then the amount of the interval from T_0 to T_1 that was devoted to message propagation is $T_1 - T_0 - I$, so the best estimate of the one-way propagation time is half this. Systems do exist in which messages from A to B systematically take a different route than messages from B to A, and thus have a different propagation time, but we will not consider such systems here.

To improve the accuracy, Cristian suggested making not one measurement, but a series of them. Any measurements in which $T_1 - T_0$ exceeds some threshold value are discarded as being victims of network congestion and thus unreliable. The estimates derived from the remaining probes can then be averaged to get a better value. Alternatively, the message that came back fastest can be taken to be the most accurate since it presumably encountered the least traffic underway and thus is the most representative of the pure propagation time.

The Berkeley Algorithm

In Cristian's algorithm, the time server is passive. Other machines ask it for the time periodically. All it does is respond to their queries. In Berkeley UNIX, exactly the opposite approach is taken (Gusella and Zatti, 1989). Here the time server (actually, a time daemon) is active, polling every machine periodically to ask what time it is there. Based on the answers, it computes an average time and tells all the other machines to advance their clocks to the new time or slow their clocks down until some specified reduction has been achieved. This method is suitable for a system in which no machine has a WWV receiver. The time daemon's time must be set manually by the operator periodically. The method is illustrated in Fig. 3-7.

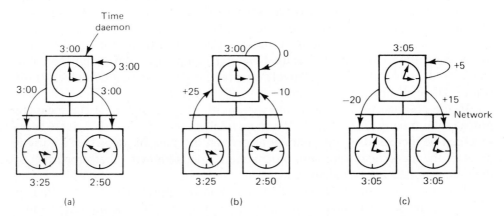

Fig. 3-7. (a) The time daemon asks all the other machines for their clock values. (b) The machines answer. (c) The time daemon tells everyone how to adjust their clock.

In Fig. 3-7(a), at 3:00, the time daemon tells the other machines its time and asks for theirs. In Fig. 3-7(b), they respond with how far ahead or behind the time daemon they are. Armed with these numbers, the time daemon computes the average and tells each machine how to adjust its clock [see Fig. 3-7(c)].

Averaging Algorithms

Both of the methods described above are highly centralized, with the usual disadvantages. Decentralized algorithms are also known. One class of decentralized clock synchronization algorithms works by dividing time into fixed-length resynchronization intervals. The ith interval starts at $T_0 + iR$ and runs until $T_0 + (i +1)R$, where T_0 is an agreed upon moment in the past, and R is a system parameter. At the beginning of each interval, every machine broadcasts the current time according to its clock. Because the clocks on different machines do not run at exactly the same speed, these broadcasts will not happen precisely simultaneously.

After a machine broadcasts its time, it starts a local timer to collect all other broadcasts that arrive during some interval S. When all the broadcasts arrive, an algorithm is run to compute a new time from them. The simplest algorithm is just to average the values from all the other machines. A slight variation on this theme is first to discard the m highest and m lowest values, and average the rest. Discarding the extreme values can be regarded as self defense against up to m faulty clocks sending out nonsense.

Another variation is to try to correct each message by adding to it an estimate of the propagation time from the source. This estimate can be made from the known topology of the network, or by timing how long it takes for probe messages to be echoed.

Additional clock synchronization algorithms are discussed in the literature (e.g., Lundelius-Welch and Lynch, 1988; Ramanathan et al., 1990a; and Srikanth and Toueg, 1987).

Multiple External Time Sources

For systems in which extremely accurate synchronization with UTC is required, it is possible to equip the system with multiple receivers for WWV, GEOS, or other UTC sources. However, due to inherent inaccuracy in the time source itself as well as fluctuations in the signal path, the best the operating system can do is establish a range (time interval) in which UTC falls. In general, the various time sources will produce different ranges, which requires the machines attached to them to come to agreement.

To reach this agreement, each processor with a UTC source can broadcast its range periodically, say, at the precise start of each UTC minute. None of the processors will get the time packets instantaneously. Worse yet, the delay between transmission and reception depends on the cable distance and number of gateways that the packets have to traverse, which is different for each (UTC source, processor) pair. Other factors can also play a role, such as delays due to collisions when multiple machines try to transmit on an Ethernet at the same instant. Furthermore, if a processor is busy handling a previous packet, it may not even look at the time packet for a considerable number of milliseconds, introducing additional uncertainty into the time. In Chap. 10 we will examine how clocks are synchronized in OSF's DCE.

3.1.4. Use of Synchronized Clocks

Only quite recently has the necessary hardware and software for synchronizing clocks on a wide scale (e.g., over the entire Internet) become easily available. With this new technology, it is possible to keep millions of clocks synchronized to within a few milliseconds of UTC. New algorithms that utilize synchronized clocks are just starting to appear. Below we summarize two of the examples discussed by Liskov (1993).

At-Most-Once Message Delivery

Our first example concerns how to enforce at-most-once message delivery to a server, even in the face of crashes. The traditional approach is for each message to bear a unique message number, and have each server store all the numbers of the messages it has seen so it can detect new messages from retransmissions. The problem with this algorithm is that if a server crashes and reboots, it loses its table of message numbers. Also, for how long should message numbers be saved?

Using time, the algorithm can be modified as follows. Now, every message carries a connection identifier (chosen by the sender) and a timestamp. For each connection, the server records in a table the most recent timestamp it has seen. If any incoming message for a connection is lower than the timestamp stored for that connection, the message is rejected as a duplicate.

To make it possible to remove old timestamps, each server continuously maintains a global variable

$$G = CurrentTime - MaxLifetime - MaxClockSkew$$

where *MaxLifetime* is the maximum time a message can live and *MaxClockSkew* is how far from UTC the clock might be at worst. Any timestamp older than G can safely be removed from the table because all messages that old have died out already. If an incoming message has an unknown connection identifier, it is accepted if its timestamp is more recent than G and rejected if its timestamp is older than G because anything that old surely is a duplicate. In effect, G is a summary of the message numbers of all old messages. Every ΔT, the current time is written to disk.

When a server crashes and then reboots, it reloads G from the time stored on disk and increments it by the update period, ΔT. Any incoming message with a timestamp older than G is rejected as a duplicate. As a consequence, every message that might have been accepted before the crash is rejected. Some new messages may be incorrectly rejected, but under all conditions the algorithm maintains at-most-once semantics.

Clock-Based Cache Consistency

Our second example concerns cache consistency in a distributed file system. For performance reasons, it is desirable for clients to be able to cache files locally. However, caching introduces potential inconsistency if two clients modify the same file at the same time. The usual solution is to distinguish between caching a file for reading and caching a file for writing. The disadvantage of this scheme is that if a client has a file cached for reading, before another client can get a copy for writing, the server has to first ask the reading client to invalidate its copy, even if the copy was made hours ago. This extra overhead can be eliminated using synchronized clocks.

The basic idea is that when a client wants a file, it is given a **lease** on it that specifies how long the copy is valid (Gray and Cheriton, 1989). When the lease is about to expire, the client can ask for it to be renewed. If a lease expires, the cached copy may no longer be used. In this way when a client needs to read a file once, it can ask for it. When the lease expires, it just times out; there is no need to explicitly send a message telling the server that it has been purged from the cache.

If a lease has expired and the file (still cached) is needed again shortly thereafter, the client can ask the server if the copy it has (identified by a time-stamp) is still the current one. If so, a new lease is generated, but the file need not be retransmitted.

If one or more clients have a file cached for reading and then another client wants to write on the file, the server has to ask the readers to prematurely terminate their leases. If one or more of them has crashed, the server can just wait until the dead server's lease times out. In the traditional algorithm, where permission-to-cache must be returned explicitly from the client to the server, a problem occurs if the server asks the client or clients to return the file (i.e., discard it from its cache) and there is no response. The server cannot tell if the client is dead or merely slow. With the timer-based algorithm, the server can just wait and let the lease expire.

In addition to these two algorithms, Liskov (1993) also describes how synchronized clocks can be used to time out tickets used in distributed system authentication, and handle commitment in atomic transactions. As timer synchronization gets better, no doubt new applications for it will be found.

3.2. MUTUAL EXCLUSION

Systems involving multiple processes are often most easily programmed using critical regions. When a process has to read or update certain shared data structures, it first enters a critical region to achieve mutual exclusion and ensure that no other process will use the shared data structures at the same time. In single-processor systems, critical regions are protected using semaphores, monitors, and similar constructs. We will now look at a few examples of how critical regions and mutual exclusion can be implemented in distributed systems. For a taxonomy and bibliography of other methods, see (Raynal, 1991). Other work is discussed in (Agrawal and El Abbadi, 1991; Chandy et al., 1983; and Sanders, 1987).

3.2.1. A Centralized Algorithm

The most straightforward way to achieve mutual exclusion in a distributed system is to simulate how it is done in a one-processor system. One process is elected as the coordinator (e.g., the one running on the machine with the highest network address). Whenever a process wants to enter a critical region, it sends a request message to the coordinator stating which critical region it wants to enter and asking for permission. If no other process is currently in that critical region, the coordinator sends back a reply granting permission, as shown in Fig. 3-8(a). When the reply arrives, the requesting process enters the critical region.

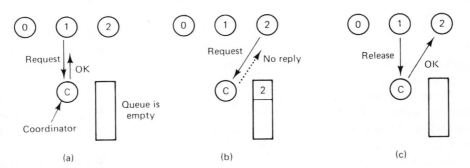

Fig. 3-8. (a) Process 1 asks the coordinator for permission to enter a critical region. Permission is granted. (b) Process 2 then asks permission to enter the same critical region. The coordinator does not reply. (c) When process 1 exits the critical region, it tells the coordinator, which then replies to 2.

Now suppose that another process, 2 in Fig. 3-8(b), asks for permission to enter the same critical region. The coordinator knows that a different process is already in the critical region, so it cannot grant permission. The exact method used to deny permission is system dependent. In Fig. 3-8(b), the coordinator just refrains from replying, thus blocking process 2, which is waiting for a reply. Alternatively, it could send a reply saying "permission denied." Either way, it queues the request from 2 for the time being.

When process 1 exits the critical region, it sends a message to the coordinator releasing its exclusive access, as shown in Fig. 3-8(c). The coordinator takes the first item off the queue of deferred requests and sends that process a grant message. If the process was still blocked (i.e., this is the first message to it), it unblocks and enters the critical region. If an explicit message has already been sent denying permission, the process will have to poll for incoming traffic, or block later. Either way, when it sees the grant, it can enter the critical region.

It is easy to see that the algorithm guarantees mutual exclusion: the coordinator only lets one process at a time into each critical region. It is also fair, since requests are granted in the order in which they are received. No process ever waits forever (no starvation). The scheme is easy to implement, too, and requires only three messages per use of a critical region (request, grant, release). It can also be used for more general resource allocation rather than just managing critical regions.

The centralized approach also has shortcomings. The coordinator is a single point of failure, so if it crashes, the entire system may go down. If processes normally block after making a request, they cannot distinguish a dead coordinator from "permission denied" since in both cases no message comes back. In addition, in a large system, a single coordinator can become a performance bottleneck.

3.2.2. A Distributed Algorithm

Having a single point of failure is frequently unacceptable, so researchers have looked for distributed mutual exclusion algorithms. Lamport's 1978 paper on clock synchronization presented the first one. Ricart and Agrawala (1981) made it more efficient. In this section we will describe their method.

Ricart and Agrawala's algorithm requires that there be a total ordering of all events in the system. That is, for any pair of events, such as messages, it must be unambiguous which one happened first. Lamport's algorithm presented in Sec. 3.1.1 is one way to achieve this ordering and can be used to provide timestamps for distributed mutual exclusion.

The algorithm works as follows. When a process wants to enter a critical region, it builds a message containing the name of the critical region it wants to enter, its process number, and the current time. It then sends the message to all other processes, conceptually including itself. The sending of messages is assumed to be reliable; that is, every message is acknowledged. Reliable group communication if available, can be used instead of individual messages.

When a process receives a request message from another process, the action it takes depends on its state with respect to the critical region named in the message. Three cases have to be distinguished:

1. If the receiver is not in the critical region and does not want to enter it, it sends back an *OK* message to the sender.

2. If the receiver is already in the critical region, it does not reply. Instead, it queues the request.

3. If the receiver wants to enter the critical region but has not yet done so, it compares the timestamp in the incoming message with the one contained in the message that it has sent everyone. The lowest one wins. If the incoming message is lower, the receiver sends back an *OK* message. If its own message has a lower timestamp, the receiver queues the incoming request and sends nothing.

After sending out requests asking permission to enter a critical region, a process sits back and waits until everyone else has given permission. As soon as all the permissions are in, it may enter the critical region. When it exits the critical region, it sends *OK* messages to all processes on its queue and deletes them all from the queue.

Let us try to understand why the algorithm works. If there is no conflict, it clearly works. However, suppose that two processes try to enter the same critical region simultaneously, as shown in Fig. 3-9(a).

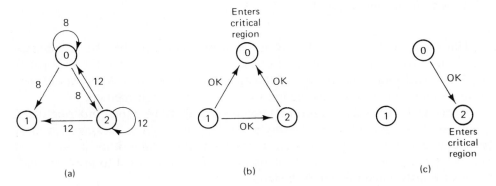

Fig. 3-9. (a) Two processes want to enter the same critical region at the same moment. (b) Process 0 has the lowest timestamp, so it wins. (c) When process 0 is done, it sends an *OK* also, so 2 can now enter the critical region.

Process 0 sends everyone a request with timestamp 8, while at the same time, process 2 sends everyone a request with timestamp 12. Process 1 is not interested in entering the critical region, so it sends *OK* to both senders. Processes 0 and 2 both see the conflict and compare timestamps. Process 2 sees that it has lost, so it grants permission to 0 by sending *OK*. Process 0 now queues the request from 2 for later processing and enters the critical region, as shown in Fig. 3-9(b). When it is finished, it removes the request from 2 from its queue and sends an *OK* message to process 2, allowing the latter to enter its critical region, as shown in Fig. 3-9(c). The algorithm works because in the case of a conflict, the lowest timestamp wins and everyone agrees on the ordering of the timestamps.

Note that the situation in Fig. 3-9 would have been essentially different if process 2 had sent its message earlier in time so that process 0 had gotten it and granted permission before making its own request. In this case, 2 would have noticed that it itself was in a critical region at the time of the request, and queued it instead of sending a reply.

As with the centralized algorithm discussed above, mutual exclusion is guaranteed without deadlock or starvation. The number of messages required per entry is now $2(n - 1)$, where the total number of processes in the system is n. Best of all, no single point of failure exists.

Unfortunately, the single point of failure has been replaced by n points of failure. If any process crashes, it will fail to respond to requests. This silence will be interpreted (incorrectly) as denial of permission, thus blocking all subsequent attempts by all processes to enter all critical regions. Since the probability of one of the n processes failing is n times as large as a single coordinator failing, we have managed to replace a poor algorithm with one that is n times worse and requires much more network traffic to boot.

The algorithm can be patched up by the same trick that we proposed earlier. When a request comes in, the receiver always sends a reply, either granting or denying permission. Whenever either a request or a reply is lost, the sender times out and keeps trying until either a reply comes back or the sender concludes that the destination is dead. After a request is denied, the sender should block waiting for a subsequent *OK* message.

Another problem with this algorithm is that either a group communication primitive must be used, or each process must maintain the group membership list itself, including processes entering the group, leaving the group, and crashing. The method works best with small groups of processes that never change their group memberships.

Finally, recall that one of the problems with the centralized algorithm is that making it handle all requests can lead to a bottleneck. In the distributed algorithm, *all* processes are involved in *all* decisions concerning entry into critical regions. If one process is unable to handle the load, it is unlikely that forcing everyone to do exactly the same thing in parallel is going to help much.

Various minor improvements are possible to this algorithm. For example, getting permission from everyone to enter a critical region is really overkill. All that is needed is a method to prevent two processes from entering the critical region at the same time. The algorithm can be modified to allow a process to enter a critical region when it has collected permission from a simple majority of the other processes, rather than from all of them. Of course, in this variation, after a process has granted permission to one process to enter a critical region, it cannot grant the same permission to another process until the first one has released that permission. Other improvements are also possible (e.g., Maekawa et al., 1987).

Nevertheless, this algorithm is slower, more complicated, more expensive, and less robust that the original centralized one. Why bother studying it under these conditions? For one thing, it shows that a distributed algorithm is at least possible, something that was not obvious when we started. Also, by pointing out the shortcomings, we may stimulate future theoreticians to try to produce algorithms that are actually useful. Finally, like eating spinach and learning Latin in high school, some things are said to be good for you in some abstract way.

3.2.3. A Token Ring Algorithm

A completely different approach to achieving mutual exclusion in a distributed system is illustrated in Fig. 3-10. Here we have a bus network, as shown in Fig. 3-10(a), (e.g., Ethernet), with no inherent ordering of the processes. In software, a logical ring is constructed in which each process is assigned a position in the ring, as shown in Fig. 3-10(b). The ring positions may be allocated in numerical order of network addresses or some other means. It does not matter what the ordering is. All that matters is that each process knows who is next in line after itself.

When the ring is initialized, process 0 is given a **token**. The token circulates around the ring. It is passed from process k to process $k +1$ (modulo the ring size) in point-to-point messages. When a process acquires the token from its neighbor, it checks to see if it is attempting to enter a critical region. If so, the process enters the region, does all the work it needs to, and leaves the region. After it has exited, it passes the token along the ring. It is not permitted to enter a second critical region using the same token.

If a process is handed the token by its neighbor and is not interested in entering a critical region, it just passes it along. As a consequence, when no processes want to enter any critical regions, the token just circulates at high speed around the ring.

The correctness of this algorithm is evident. Only one process has the token at any instant, so only one process can be in a critical region. Since the token circulates among the processes in a well-defined order, starvation cannot occur. Once a process decides it wants to enter a critical region, at worst it will have to

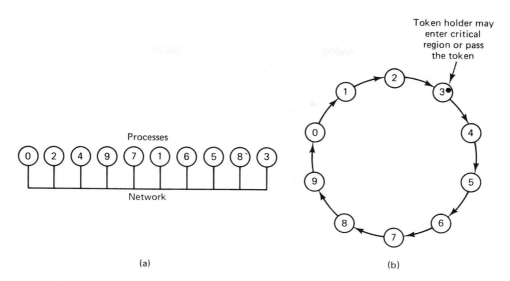

Fig. 3-10. (a) An unordered group of processes on a network. (b) A logical ring constructed in software.

wait for every other process to enter and leave one critical region.

As usual, this algorithm has problems too. If the token is ever lost, it must be regenerated. In fact, detecting that it is lost is difficult, since the amount of time between successive appearances of the token on the network is unbounded. The fact that the token has not been spotted for an hour does not mean that it has been lost; somebody may still be using it.

The algorithm also runs into trouble if a process crashes, but recovery is easier than in the other cases. If we require a process receiving the token to acknowledge receipt, a dead process will be detected when its neighbor tries to give it the token and fails. At that point the dead process can be removed from the group, and the token holder can throw the token over the head of the dead process to the next member down the line, or the one after that, if necessary. Of course, doing so requires that everyone maintains the current ring configuration.

3.2.4. A Comparison of the Three Algorithms

A brief comparison of the three mutual exclusion algorithms we have looked at is instructive. In Fig. 3-11 we have listed the algorithms and three key properties: the number of messages required for a process to enter and exit a critical region, the delay before entry can occur (assuming messages are passed sequentially over a LAN), and some problems associated with each algorithm.

The centralized algorithm is simplest and also most efficient. It requires

Algorithm	Messages per entry/exit	Delay before entry (in message times)	Problems
Centralized	3	2	Coordinator crash
Distributed	$2(n-1)$	$2(n-1)$	Crash of any process
Token ring	1 to ∞	0 to $n-1$	Lost token, process crash

Fig. 3-11. A comparison of three mutual exclusion algorithms.

only three messages to enter and leave a critical region: a request and a grant to enter, and a release to exit. The distributed algorithm requires $n-1$ request messages, one to each of the other processes, and an additional $n-1$ grant messages, for a total of $2(n-1)$. With the token ring algorithm, the number is variable. If every process constantly wants to enter a critical region, then each token pass will result in one entry and exit, for an average of one message per critical region entered. At the other extreme, the token may sometimes circulate for hours without anyone being interested in it. In this case, the number of messages per entry into a critical region is unbounded.

The delay from the moment a process needs to enter a critical region until its actual entry also varies for the three algorithms. When critical regions are short and rarely used, the dominant factor in the delay is the actual mechanism for entering a critical region. When they are long and frequently used, the dominant factor is waiting for everyone else to take their turn. In Fig. 3-11 we show the former case. It takes only two message times to enter a critical region in the centralized case, but $2(n-1)$ message times in the distributed case, assuming that the network can handle only one message at a time. For the token ring, the time varies from 0 (token just arrived) to $n-1$ (token just departed).

Finally, all three algorithms suffer badly in the event of crashes. Special measures and additional complexity must be introduced to avoid having a crash bring down the entire system. It is slightly ironic that the distributed algorithms are even more sensitive to crashes than the centralized one. In a fault-tolerant system, none of these would be suitable, but if crashes are very infrequent, they are all acceptable.

3.3. ELECTION ALGORITHMS

Many distributed algorithms require one process to act as coordinator, initiator, sequencer, or otherwise perform some special role. We have already seen several examples, such as the coordinator in the centralized mutual exclusion algorithm. In general, it does not matter which process takes on this special responsibility, but one of them has to do it. In this section we will look at algorithms for electing a coordinator (using this as a generic name for the special process).

If all processes are exactly the same, with no distinguishing characteristics, there is no way to select one of them to be special. Consequently, we will assume that each process has a unique number, for example its network address (for simplicity, we will assume one process per machine). In general, election algorithms attempt to locate the process with the highest process number and designate it as coordinator. The algorithms differ in the way they do the location.

Furthermore, we also assume that every process knows the process number of every other process. What the processes do not know is which ones are currently up and which ones are currently down. The goal of an election algorithm is to ensure that when an election starts, it concludes with all processes agreeing on who the new coordinator is to be. Various algorithms are known, for example, (Fredrickson and Lynch, 1987; Garcia-Molina, 1982; and Singh and Kurose, 1994).

3.3.1. The Bully Algorithm

As a first example, consider the **bully algorithm** devised by Garcia-Molina (1982). When a process notices that the coordinator is no longer responding to requests, it initiates an election. A process, P, holds an election as follows:

1. P sends an *ELECTION* message to all processes with higher numbers.

2. If no one responds, P wins the election and becomes coordinator.

3. If one of the higher-ups answers, it takes over. P's job is done.

At any moment, a process can get an *ELECTION* message from one of its lower-numbered colleagues. When such a message arrives, the receiver sends an *OK* message back to the sender to indicate that he is alive and will take over. The receiver then holds an election, unless it is already holding one. Eventually, all processes give up but one, and that one is the new coordinator. It announces its victory by sending all processes a message telling them that starting immediately it is the new coordinator.

If a process that was previously down comes back up, it holds an election. If it happens to be the highest-numbered process currently running, it will win the election and take over the coordinator's job. Thus the biggest guy in town always wins, hence the name "bully algorithm."

In Fig. 3-12 we see an example of how the bully algorithm works. The group consists of eight processes, numbered from 0 to 7. Previously process 7 was the coordinator, but it has just crashed. Process 4 is the first one to notice this, so it sends *ELECTION* messages to all the processes higher than it, namely 5, 6, and 7, as shown in Fig. 3-12(a). Processes 5 and 6 both respond with *OK*, as shown in Fig. 3-12(b). Upon getting the first of these responses, 4 knows that its job is over. It knows that one of these bigwigs will take over and become coordinator. It just sits back and waits to see who the winner will be (although at this point it can make a pretty good guess).

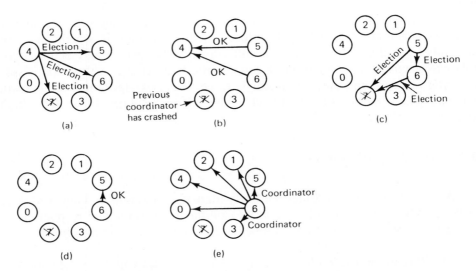

Fig. 3-12. The bully election algorithm. (a) Process 4 holds an election. (b) Processes 5 and 6 respond, telling 4 to stop. (c) Now 5 and 6 each hold an election. (d) Process 6 tells 5 to stop. (e) Process 6 wins and tells everyone.

In Fig. 3-13(c), both 5 and 6 hold elections, each one only sending messages to those processes higher than itself. In Fig. 3-13(d) process 6 tells 5 that it will take over. At this point 6 knows that 7 is dead and that it (6) is the winner. If there is state information to be collected from disk or elsewhere to pick up where the old coordinator left off, 6 must now do what is needed. When it is ready to take over, 6 announces this by sending a *COORDINATOR* message to all running processes. When 4 gets this message, it can now continue with the operation it was trying to do when it discovered that 7 was dead, but using 6 as the coordinator this time. In this way the failure of 7 is handled and the work can continue.

If process 7 is ever restarted, it will just send all the others a *COORDINATOR* message and bully them into submission.

3.3.2. A Ring Algorithm

Another election algorithm is based on the use of a ring, but without a token. We assume that the processes are physically or logically ordered, so that each process knows who its successor is. When any process notices that the coordinator is not functioning, it builds an *ELECTION* message containing its own process number and sends the message to its successor. If the successor is down, the sender skips over the successor and goes to the next member along the ring, or the one after that, until a running process is located. At each step, the sender adds its own process number to the list in the message.

Eventually, the message gets back to the process that started it all. That process recognizes this event when it receives an incoming message containing its own process number. At that point, the message type is changed to *COORDINATOR* and circulated once again, this time to inform everyone else who the coordinator is (the list member with the highest number) and who the members of the new ring are. When this message has circulated once, it is removed and everyone goes back to work.

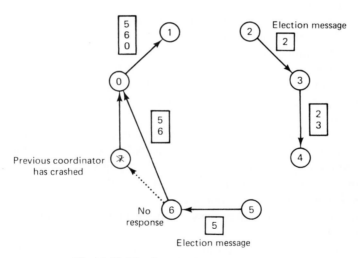

Fig. 3-13. Election algorithm using a ring.

In Fig. 3-13 we see what happens if two processes, 2 and 5, discover simultaneously that the previous coordinator, process 7, has crashed. Each of these builds an *ELECTION* message and starts circulating it. Eventually, both messages will go all the way around, and both 2 and 5 will convert them into *COORDINATOR* messages, with exactly the same members and in the same order. When both have gone around again, both will be removed. It does no harm to have extra messages circulating; at most it wastes a little bandwidth.

3.4. ATOMIC TRANSACTIONS

All the synchronization techniques we have studied so far are essentially low level, like semaphores. They require the programmer to be intimately involved with all the details of mutual exclusion, critical region management, deadlock prevention, and crash recovery. What we would really like is a much higher-level abstraction, one that hides these technical issues and allows the programmer to concentrate on the algorithms and how the processes work together in parallel. Such an abstraction exists and is widely used in distributed systems. We will call it an **atomic transaction**, or simply **transaction**. The term **atomic action** is also widely used. In this section we will examine the use, design, and implementation of atomic transactions.

3.4.1. Introduction to Atomic Transactions

The original model of the atomic transaction comes from the world of business. Suppose that the International Dingbat Corporation needs a batch of widgets. They approach a potential supplier, U.S. Widget, known far and wide for the quality of its widgets, for a quote on 100,000 10-cm purple widgets for June delivery. U.S. Widget makes a bid on 100,000 4-inch mauve widgets to be delivered in December. International Dingbat agrees to the price, but dislikes mauve, wants them by July, and insists on 10 cm for its international customers. U.S. Widget replies by offering 3 15/16 inch lavender widgets in October. After much further negotiation, they finally agree on 3 959/1024 inch violet widgets for delivery on August 15.

Up until this point, both parties are free to terminate the discussion, in which case the world returns to the state it was in before they started talking. However, once both companies have signed a contract, they are both legally bound to complete the sale, come what may. Thus until both parties have signed on the dotted line, either one can back out and it is as if nothing ever happened, but at the moment they both sign, they pass the point of no return and the transaction must be carried out.

The computer model is similar. One process announces that it wants to begin a transaction with one or more other processes. They can negotiate various options, create and delete objects, and perform operations for a while. Then the initiator announces that it wants all the others to commit themselves to the work done so far. If all of them agree, the results are made permanent. If one or more processes refuse (or crash before agreement), the situation reverts to exactly the state it had before the transaction began, with all side effects on objects, files, data bases, and so on, magically wiped out. This all-or-nothing property eases the programmer's job.

The use of transactions in computer systems goes back to the 1960s. Before there were disks and online data bases, all files were kept on magnetic tape. Imagine a supermarket with an automated inventory system. Every day after closing, a computer run was made with two input tapes. The first one contained the complete inventory as of opening time that morning. The second one contained a list of the day's updates: products sold to customers and products delivered by suppliers. The computer read both input tapes and produced a new master inventory tape, as shown in Fig. 3-14.

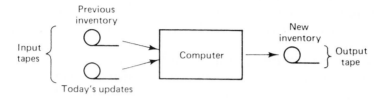

Fig. 3-14. Updating a master tape is fault tolerant.

The great beauty of this scheme (although the people who had to live with it did not realize that) is that if a run failed for any reason, all the tapes could be rewound and the job restarted with no harm done. Primitive as it was, the old magnetic tape system had the all-or-nothing property of an atomic transaction.

Now look at a modern banking application that updates an online data base in place. The customer calls up the bank using a PC with a modem with the intention of withdrawing money from one account and depositing it in another. The operation is performed in two steps:

1. Withdraw(amount, account1).

2. Deposit(amount, account2).

If the telephone connection is broken after the first one but before the second one, the first account will have been debited but the second one will not have been credited. The money vanishes into thin air.

Being able to group these two operations in an atomic transaction would solve the problem. Either both would be completed, or neither would be completed. The key is rolling back to the initial state if the transaction fails to complete. What we really want is a way to rewind the data base as we could the magnetic tapes. This ability is what the atomic transaction has to offer.

3.4.2. The Transaction Model

We will now develop a more precise model of what a transaction is and what its properties are. The system is assumed to consist of some number of independent processes, each of which can fail at random. Communication is normally unreliable in that messages can be lost, but lower levels can use a timeout and retransmission protocol to recover from lost messages. Thus for this discussion we can assume that communication errors are handled transparently by underlying software.

Stable Storage

Storage comes in three categories. First we have ordinary RAM memory, which is wiped out when the power fails or a machine crashes. Next we have disk storage, which survives CPU failures but which can be lost in disk head crashes.

Finally, we have **stable storage**, which is designed to survive anything except major calamities such as floods and earthquakes. Stable storage can be implemented with a pair of ordinary disks, as shown in Fig. 3-15(a). Each block on drive 2 is an exact copy of the corresponding block on drive 1. When a block is updated, first the block on drive 1 is updated and verified, then the same block on drive 2 is done.

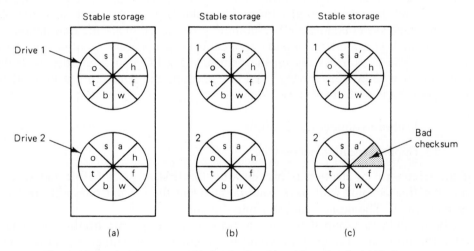

Fig. 3-15. (a) Stable storage. (b) Crash after drive 1 is updated. (c) Bad spot.

Suppose that the system crashes after drive 1 is updated but before drive 2 is updated, as shown in Fig. 3-15(b). Upon recovery, the disk can be compared block for block. Whenever two corresponding blocks differ, it can be assumed that drive 1 is the correct one (because drive 1 is always updated before drive 2), so the new block is copied from drive 1 to drive 2. When the recovery process is complete, both drives will again be identical.

Another potential problem is the spontaneous decay of a block. Dust particles or general wear and tear can give a previously valid block a sudden checksum error, without cause or warning, as shown in Fig. 3-15(c). When such an error is detected, the bad block can be regenerated from the corresponding block on the other drive.

As a consequence of its implementation, stable storage is well suited to applications that require a high degree of fault tolerance, such as atomic transactions. When data are written to stable storage and then read back to check that they have been written correctly, the chance of them subsequently being lost is extremely small.

Transaction Primitives

Programming using transactions requires special primitives that must either be supplied by the operating system or by the language runtime system. Examples are:

1. BEGIN_TRANSACTION: Mark the start of a transaction.

2. END_TRANSACTION: Terminate the transaction and try to commit.

3. ABORT_TRANSACTION: Kill the transaction; restore the old values.

4. READ: Read data from a file (or other object).

5. WRITE: Write data to a file (or other object).

The exact list of primitives depends on what kinds of objects are being used in the transaction. In a mail system, there might be primitives to send, receive, and forward mail. In an accounting system, they might be quite different. READ and WRITE are typical examples, however. Ordinary statements, procedure calls, and so on, are also allowed inside a transaction.

BEGIN_TRANSACTION and END_TRANSACTION are used to delimit the scope of a transaction. The operations between them form the body of the transaction. Either all of them are executed or none are executed. These may be system calls, library procedures, or bracketing statements in a language, depending on the implementation.

Consider, for example, the process of reserving a seat from White Plains, New York, to Malindi, Kenya, in an airline reservation system. One route is White Plains to JFK, JFK to Nairobi, and Nairobi to Malindi. In Fig. 3-16(a) we see reservations for these three separate flights being made as three actions. Now suppose that the first two flights have been reserved but the third one is booked solid. The transaction is aborted and the results of the first two bookings are undone—the airline data base is restored to the value it had before the transaction started [see Fig. 3-16(b)]. It is as though nothing happened.

```
BEGIN_TRANSACTION                    BEGIN_TRANSACTION
    reserve WP-JFK;                      reserve WP-JFK;
    reserve JFK-Nairobi;                 reserve JFK-Nairobi;
    reserve Nairobi-Malindi;             Nairobi-Malindi full ⇒ ABORT_TRANSACTION;
END_TRANSACTION

        (a)                                      (b)
```

Fig. 3-16. (a) Transaction to reserve three flights commits. (b) Transaction aborts when third flight is unavailable.

Properties of Transactions

Transactions have four essential properties. Transactions are:

1. Atomic: To the outside world, the transaction happens indivisibly.

2. Consistent: The transaction does not violate system invariants.

3. Isolated: Concurrent transactions do not interfere with each other.

4. Durable: Once a transaction commits, the changes are permanent.

These properties are often referred to by their initial letters, **ACID**.

The first key property exhibited by all transactions is that they are **atomic**. This property ensures that each transaction either happens completely, or not at all, and if it happens, it happens in a single indivisible, instantaneous action. While a transaction is in progress, other processes (whether or not they are themselves involved in transactions) cannot see any of the intermediate states.

Suppose, for example, that some file is 10 bytes long when a transaction starts to append to it. If other processes read the file while the transaction is in progress, they see only the original 10 bytes, no matter how many bytes the transaction has appended. If the transaction commits successfully, the file grows instantaneously to its new size at the moment of commitment, with no intermediate states, no matter how many operations it took to get it there.

The second property says that they are **consistent**. What this means is that if the system has certain invariants that must always hold, if they held before the transaction, they will hold afterward too. For example, in a banking system, a key invariant is the law of conservation of money. After any internal transfer, the amount of money in the bank must be the same as it was before the transfer, but for a brief moment during the transaction, this invariant may be violated. The violation is not visible outside the transaction, however.

The third property says that transactions are **isolated** or **serializable**. What it means is that if two or more transactions are running at the same time, to each of them and to other processes, the final result looks as though all transactions ran sequentially in some (system dependent) order.

In Fig. 3-17(a)-(c) we have three transactions that are executed simultaneously by three separate processes. If they were to be run sequentially, the final value of x would be 1, 2, or 3, depending which one ran last (x could be a shared variable, a file, or some other kind of object). In Fig. 3-17(d) we see various orders, called **schedules**, in which they might be interleaved. Schedule 1 is actually serialized. In other words, the transactions run strictly sequentially, so it meets the serializability condition by definition. Schedule 2 is not serialized, but is still legal because it results in a value for x that could have been achieved by running the transactions strictly sequentially. The third one is illegal since it sets x to 5, something that no sequential order of the transactions could produce. It is up to the system to ensure that individual operations are interleaved correctly. By allowing the system the freedom to choose any ordering of the operations it wants to—provided that it gets the answer right—we eliminate the need for programmers to do their own mutual exclusion, thus simplifying the programming.

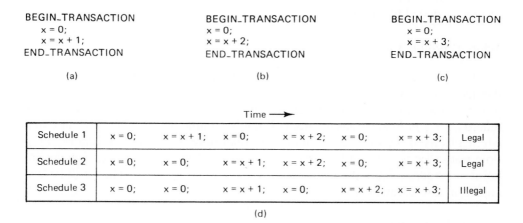

Fig. **3-17.** (a)–(c) Three transactions. (d) Possible schedules.

The fourth property says that transactions are **durable**. It refers to the fact that once a transaction commits, no matter what happens, the transaction goes forward and the results become permanent. No failure after the commit can undo the results or cause them to be lost.

Nested Transactions

Transactions may contain subtransactions, often called **nested transactions**. The top-level transaction may fork off children that run in parallel with one another, on different processors, to gain performance or simplify programming.

Each of these children may execute one or more subtransactions, or fork off its own children.

Subtransactions give rise to a subtle, but important, problem. Imagine that a transaction starts several subtransactions in parallel, and one of these commits, making its results visible to the parent transaction. After further computation, the parent aborts, restoring the entire system to the state it had before the top-level transaction started. Consequently, the results of the subtransaction that committed must nevertheless be undone. Thus the permanence referred to above applies only to top-level transactions.

Since transactions can be nested arbitrarily deeply, considerable administration is needed to get everything right. The semantics are clear, however. When any transaction or subtransaction starts, it is conceptually given a private copy of all objects in the entire system for it to manipulate as it wishes. If it aborts, its private universe just vanishes, as if it had never existed. If it commits, its private universe replaces the parent's universe. Thus if a subtransaction commits and then later a new subtransaction is started, the second one sees the results produced by the first one.

3.4.3. Implementation

Transactions sound like a great idea, but how are they implemented? That is the question we will tackle in this section. It should be clear by now that if each process executing a transaction just updates the objects it uses (files, data base records, etc.) in place, transactions will not be atomic and changes will not vanish magically if the transaction aborts. Furthermore, the results of running multiple transactions will not be serializable either. Clearly, some other implementation method is required. Two methods are commonly used. They will be discussed in turn below.

Private Workspace

Conceptually, when a process starts a transaction, it is given a private workspace containing all the files (and other objects) to which it has access. Until the transaction either commits or aborts, all of its reads and writes go to the private workspace, rather than the "real" one, by which we mean the normal file system. This observation leads directly to the first implementation method: actually giving a process a private workspace at the instant it begins a transaction.

The problem with this technique is that the cost of copying everything to a private workspace is prohibitive, but various optimizations make it feasible. The first optimization is based on the realization that when a process reads a file but does not modify it, there is no need for a private copy. It can just use the real one (unless it has been changed since the transaction started). Consequently, when a process starts a transaction, it is sufficient to create a private workspace for it that is empty except for a pointer back to its parent's workspace. When the transaction is at the top level, the parent's workspace is the "real" file system. When the process opens a file for reading, the back pointers are followed until the file is located in the parent's (or further ancestor's) workspace.

When a file is opened for writing, it can be located in the same way as for reading, except that now it is first copied to the private workspace. However, a second optimization removes most of the copying, even here. Instead of copying the entire file, only the file's index is copied into the private workspace. The index is the block of data associated with each file telling where its disk blocks are. In UNIX, the index is the i-node. Using the private index, the file can be read in the usual way, since the disk addresses it contains are for the original disk blocks. However, when a file block is first modified, a copy of the block is made and the address of the copy inserted into the index, as shown in Fig. 3-18. The block can then be updated without affecting the original. Appended blocks are handled this way too. The new blocks are sometimes called **shadow blocks**.

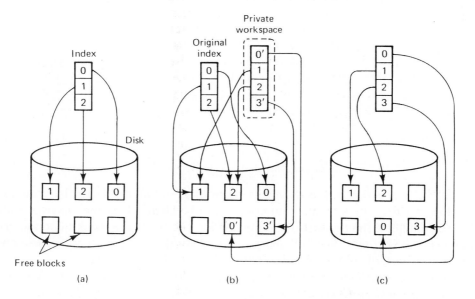

Fig. 3-18. (a) The file index and disk blocks for a three-block file. (b) The situation after a transaction has modified block 0 and appended block 3. (c) After committing.

As can be seen from Fig. 3-18(b), the process running the transaction sees the modified file, but all other processes continue to see the original file. In a more complex transaction, the private workspace might contain a large number of files instead of just one. If the transaction aborts, the private workspace is simply deleted and all the private blocks that it points to are put back on the free list. If the transaction commits, the private indices are moved into the parent's workspace atomically, as shown in Fig. 3-18(c). The blocks that are no longer reachable are put onto the free list.

Writeahead Log

The other common method of implementing transactions is the **writeahead log**, sometimes called an **intentions list**. With this method, files are actually modified in place, but before any block is changed, a record is written to the writeahead log on stable storage telling which transaction is making the change, which file and block is being changed, and what the old and new values are. Only after the log has been written successfully is the change made to the file.

Figure 3-19 gives an example of how the log works. In Fig. 3-19(a) we have a simple transaction that uses two shared variables (or other objects), x and y, both initialized to 0. For each of the three statements inside the transaction, a log record is written before executing the statement, giving the old and new values, separated by a slash.

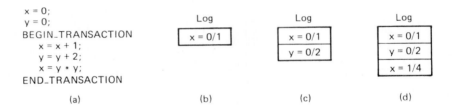

Fig. 3-19. (a) A transaction. (b)–(d) The log before each statement is executed.

If the transaction succeeds and is committed, a commit record is written to the log, but the data structures do not have to be changed, as they have already been updated. If the transaction aborts, the log can be used to back up to the original state. Starting at the end and going backward, each log record is read and the change described in it undone. This action is called a **rollback**.

The log can also be used for recovering from crashes. Suppose that the process doing the transaction crashes just after having written the last log record of Fig. 3-19(d), but before changing x. After the failed machine is rebooted, the log is checked to see if any transactions were in progress at the time of the crash. When the last record is read and the current value of x is seen to be 1, it is clear that the crash occurred *before* the update was made, so x is set to 4. If, on the other hand, x is 4 at the time of recovery, it is equally clear that the crash occurred *after* the update, so nothing need be changed. Using the log, it is possible to go forward (do the transaction) or go backward (undo the transaction).

Two-Phase Commit Protocol

As we have pointed out repeatedly, the action of committing a transaction must be done atomically, that is, instantaneously and indivisibly. In a distributed system, the commit may require the cooperation of multiple processes on different machines, each of which holds some of the variables, files, and data bases, and other objects changed by the transaction. In this section we will study a protocol for achieving atomic commit in a distributed system.

The protocol we will look at is called the **two-phase commit protocol** (Gray, 1978). Although it is not the only such protocol, it is probably the most widely used. The basic idea is illustrated in Fig. 3-20. One of the processes involved functions as the coordinator. Usually, this is the one executing the transaction. The commit protocol begins when the coordinator writes a log entry saying that it is starting the commit protocol, followed by sending each of the other processes involved (the subordinates) a message telling them to prepare to commit.

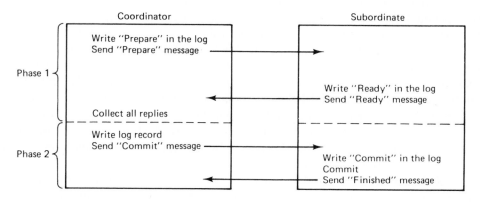

Fig. 3-20. The two-phase commit protocol when it succeeds.

When a subordinate gets the message it checks to see if it is ready to commit, makes a log entry, and sends back its decision. When the coordinator has received all the responses, it knows whether to commit or abort. If all the processes are prepared to commit, the transaction is committed. If one or more are unable to commit (or do not respond), the transaction is aborted. Either way, the coordinator writes a log entry and then sends a message to each subordinate informing it of the decision. It is this write to the log that actually commits the transaction and makes it go forward no matter what happens afterward.

Due to the use of the log on stable storage, this protocol is highly resilient in the face of (multiple) crashes. If the coordinator crashes after having written the initial log record, upon recovery it can just continue where it left off, repeating the initial message if need be. If it crashes after having written the result of the vote to the log, upon recovery it can just reinform all the subordinates of the result. If a subordinate crashes before having replied to the first message, the coordinator will keep sending it messages, until it gives up. If it crashes later, it can see from the log where it was, and thus what it must do.

3.4.4. Concurrency Control

When multiple transactions are executing simultaneously in different processes (on different processors), some mechanism is needed to keep them out of each other's way. That mechanism is called a **concurrency control algorithm**. In this section we will study three different ones.

Locking

The oldest and most widely used concurrency control algorithm is **locking**. In the simplest form, when a process needs to read or write a file (or other object) as part of a transaction, it first locks the file. Locking can be done using a single centralized lock manager, or with a local lock manager on each machine for managing local files. In both cases the lock manager maintains a list of locked files, and rejects all attempts to lock files that are already locked by another process. Since well-behaved processes do not attempt to access a file before it has been locked, setting a lock on a file keeps everyone else away from it and thus ensures that it will not change during the lifetime of the transaction. Locks are normally acquired and released by the transaction system and do not require action by the programmer.

This basic scheme is overly restrictive and can be improved by distinguishing read locks from write locks. If a read lock is set on a file, other read locks are permitted. Read locks are set to make sure that the file does not change (i.e., exclude all writers), but there is no reason to forbid other transactions from reading the file. In contrast, when a file is locked for writing, no other locks of any kind are permitted. Thus read locks are shared, but write locks must be exclusive.

For simplicity, we have assumed that the unit of locking is the entire file. In practice, it might be a smaller item, such as an individual record or page, or a larger item, such as an entire data base. The issue of how large an item to lock is called the **granularity of locking**. The finer the granularity, the more precise the lock can be, and the more parallelism can be achieved (e.g., by not blocking a process that wants to use the end of a file just because some other process is using the beginning). On the other hand, fine-grained locking requires more locks, is more expensive, and is more likely to lead to deadlocks.

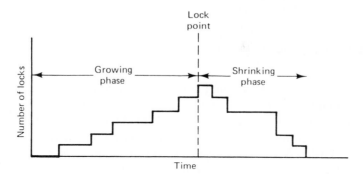

Fig. 3-21. Two-phase locking.

Acquiring and releasing locks precisely at the moment they are needed or no longer needed can lead to inconsistency and deadlocks. Instead, most transactions that are implemented by locking use what is called **two-phase locking**. In two-phase locking, which is illustrated in Fig. 3-21, the process first acquires all the locks it needs during the **growing phase**, then releases them during the **shrinking phase**. If the process refrains from updating any files until it reaches the shrinking phase, failure to acquire some lock can be dealt with simply by releasing all locks, waiting a little while, and starting all over. Furthermore, it can be proven (Eswaran et al., 1976) that if all transactions use two-phase locking, all schedules formed by interleaving them are serializable. This is why two-phase locking is widely used.

In many systems, the shrinking phase does not take place until the transaction has finished running and has either committed or aborted. This policy, called **strict two-phase locking**, has two main advantages. First, a transaction always reads a value written by a committed transaction; therefore, one never has to abort a transaction because its calculations were based on a file it should not have seen. Second, all lock acquisitions and releases can be handled by the system without the transaction being aware of them: locks are acquired whenever a file is to be accessed and released when the transaction has finished. This policy eliminates **cascaded aborts**: having to undo a committed transaction because it saw a file it should not have seen.

Locking, even two-phase locking, can lead to deadlocks. If two processes each try to acquire the same pair of locks but in the opposite order, a deadlock may result. The usual techniques apply here, such as acquiring all locks in some canonical order to prevent hold-and-wait cycles. Also possible is deadlock detection by maintaining an explicit graph of which process has which locks and wants which locks, and checking the graph for cycles. Finally, when it is known in advance that a lock will never be held longer than T sec, a timeout scheme can be used: if a lock remains continuously under the same ownership for longer than T sec, there must be a deadlock.

Optimistic Concurrency Control

A second approach to handling multiple transactions at the same time is **optimistic concurrency control** (Kung and Robinson, 1981). The idea behind this technique is surprisingly simple: just go ahead and do whatever you want to, without paying attention to what anybody else is doing. If there is a problem, worry about it later. (Many politicians use this algorithm, too.) In practice, conflicts are relatively rare, so most of the time it works all right.

Although conflicts may be rare, they are not impossible, so some way is needed to handle them. What optimistic concurrency control does is keep track of which files have been read and written. At the point of committing, it checks all other transactions to see if any of its files have been changed since the transaction started. If so, the transaction is aborted. If not, it is committed.

Optimistic concurrency control fits best with the implementation based on private workspaces. That way, each transaction changes its files privately, without interference from the others. At the end, the new files are either committed or released.

The big advantages of optimistic concurrency control are that it is deadlock free and allows maximum parallelism because no process ever has to wait for a lock. The disadvantage is that sometimes it may fail, in which case the transaction has to be run all over again. Under conditions of heavy load, the probability of failure may go up substantially, making optimistic concurrency control a poor choice.

Timestamps

A completely different approach to concurrency control is to assign each transaction a timestamp at the moment it does BEGIN_TRANSACTION (Reed, 1983). Using Lamport's algorithm, we can ensure that the timestamps are unique, which is important here. Every file in the system has a read timestamp and a write timestamp associated with it, telling which committed transaction last read and wrote it, respectively. If transactions are short and widely spaced in time, it will normally occur that when a process tries to access a file, the file's read and write timestamps will be lower (older) than the current transaction's timestamp. This ordering means that the transactions are being processed in the proper order, so everything is all right.

When the ordering is incorrect, it means that a transaction that started later than the current one has managed to get in there, access the file, and commit. This situation means that the current transaction is too late, so it is aborted. In a sense, this mechanism is also optimistic, like that of Kung and Robinson, although the details are quite different. In Kung and Robinson's method, we are hoping that concurrent transactions do not use the same files. In the timestamp method, we do not mind if concurrent transactions use the same files, as long as the lower numbered transaction always goes first.

It is easiest to explain the timestamp method by means of an example. Imagine that there are three transactions, alpha, beta, and gamma. Alpha ran a long time ago, and used every file needed by beta and gamma, so all their files have read and write timestamps set to alpha's timestamp. Beta and gamma start concurrently, with beta having a lower timestamp than gamma (but higher than alpha, of course).

Let us first consider beta writing a file. Call its timestamp, T, and the read and write timestamps of the file to be written T_{RD} and T_{WR}, respectively. Unless gamma has snuck in already and committed, both T_{RD} and T_{WR} will be alpha's timestamp, and thus less than T. In Fig. 3-22(a) and (b) we see that T is larger than both T_{RD} and T_{WR} (gamma has not already committed), so the write is accepted and done tentatively. It will become permanent when beta commits. Beta's timestamp is now recorded in the file as a tentative write.

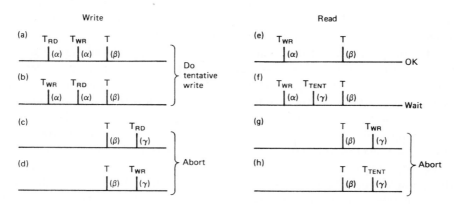

Fig. 3-22. Concurrency control using timestamps.

In Fig. 3-22(c) and (d) beta is out of luck. Gamma has either read (c) or written (d) the file and committed. Beta's transaction is aborted. However, it can apply for a new timestamp and start all over again.

Now look at reads. In Fig. 3-22(e), there is no conflict, so the read can happen immediately. In Fig. 3-22(f), some interloper has gotten in there and is trying to write the file. The interloper's timestamp is lower than beta's, so beta simply waits until the interloper commits, at which time it can read the new file and continue.

In Fig. 3-22(g), gamma has changed the file and already committed. Again beta must abort. In Fig. 3-22(h), gamma is in the process of changing the file, although it has not committed yet. Still, beta is too late and must abort.

Timestamping has different properties than locking. When a transaction encounters a larger (later) timestamp, it aborts, whereas under the same circumstances with locking it would either wait or be able to proceed immediately. On the other hand, it is deadlock free, which is a big plus.

All in all, transactions offer many advantages and thus are a promising technique for building reliable distributed systems. Their chief problem is their great implementation complexity, which yields low performance. These problems are being worked on, and perhaps in due course they will be solved.

3.5. DEADLOCKS IN DISTRIBUTED SYSTEMS

Deadlocks in distributed systems are similar to deadlocks in single-processor systems, only worse. They are harder to avoid, prevent, or even detect, and harder to cure when tracked down because all the relevant information is scattered over many machines. In some systems, such as distributed data base systems, they can be extremely serious, so it is important to understand how they differ from ordinary deadlocks and what can be done about them.

Some people make a distinction between two kinds of distributed deadlocks: communication deadlocks and resource deadlocks. A communication deadlock occurs, for example, when process A is trying to send a message to process B, which in turn is trying to send one to process C, which is trying to send one to A. There are various scenarios in which this situation leads to deadlock, such as no buffers being available. A resource deadlock occurs when processes are fighting over exclusive access to I/O devices, files, locks, or other resources.

We will not make that distinction here, since communication channels, buffers, and so on, are also resources and can be modeled as resource deadlocks because processes can request them and release them. Furthermore, circular communication patterns of the type just described are quite rare in most systems. In client-server systems, for example, a client might send a message (or perform an RPC) with a file server, which might send a message to a disk server. However, it is unlikely that the disk server, acting as a client, would send a message to the original client, expecting it to act like a server. Thus the circular wait condition is unlikely to occur as a result of communication alone.

Various strategies are used to handle deadlocks. Four of the best-known ones are listed and discussed below.

1. The ostrich algorithm (ignore the problem).

2. Detection (let deadlocks occur, detect them, and try to recover).

3. Prevention (statically make deadlocks structurally impossible).

4. Avoidance (avoid deadlocks by allocating resources carefully).

All four are potentially applicable to distributed systems. The ostrich algorithm is as good and as popular in distributed systems as it is in single-processor systems. In distributed systems used for programming, office automation, process control, and many other applications, no system-wide deadlock mechanism is present, although individual applications, such as distributed data bases, can implement their own if they need one.

Deadlock detection and recovery is also popular, primarily because prevention and avoidance are so difficult. We will discuss several algorithms for deadlock detection below.

Deadlock prevention is also possible, although more difficult than in single-processor systems. However, in the presence of atomic transactions, some new options become available. Two algorithms are discussed below.

Finally, deadlock avoidance is never used in distributed systems. It is not even used in single-processor systems, so why should it be used in the more difficult case of distributed systems? The problem is that the banker's algorithm and similar algorithms need to know (in advance) how much of each resource every process will eventually need. This information is rarely, if ever, available. Thus our discussion of deadlocks in distributed systems will focus on just two of the techniques: deadlock detection and deadlock prevention.

3.5.1. Distributed Deadlock Detection

Finding general methods for preventing or avoiding distributed deadlocks appears to be quite difficult, so many researchers have tried to deal with the simpler problem of just detecting deadlocks, rather than trying to inhibit their occurrence.

However, the presence of atomic transactions in some distributed systems makes a major conceptual difference. When a deadlock is detected in a conventional operating system, the way to resolve it is to kill off one or more processes. Doing so invariably leads to one or more unhappy users. When a deadlock is detected in a system based on atomic transactions, it is resolved by aborting one or more transactions. But as we have seen in detail above, transactions have been designed to withstand being aborted. When a transaction is aborted because it contributes to a deadlock, the system is first restored to the state it had before the transaction began, at which point the transaction can start again. With a little bit of luck, it will succeed the second time. Thus the difference is that the consequences of killing off a process are much less severe when transactions are used than when they are not used.

Centralized Deadlock Detection

As a first attempt, we can use a centralized deadlock detection algorithm and try to imitate the nondistributed algorithm. Although each machine maintains the resource graph for its own processes and resources, a central coordinator maintains the resource graph for the entire system (the union of all the individual graphs). When the coordinator detects a cycle, it kills off one process to break the deadlock.

Unlike the centralized case, where all the information is automatically available in the right place, in a distributed system it has to be sent there explicitly. Each machine maintains the graph for its own processes and resources. Several possibilities exist for getting it there. First, whenever an arc is added or deleted from the resource graph, a message can be sent to the coordinator providing the update. Second, periodically, every process can send a list of arcs added or deleted since the previous update. This method requires fewer messages than the first one. Third, the coordinator can ask for information when it needs it.

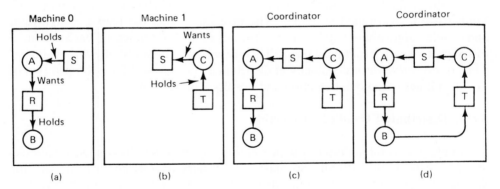

Fig. 3-23. (a) Initial resource graph for machine 0. (b) Initial resource graph for machine 1. (c) The coordinator's view of the world. (d) The situation after the delayed message.

Unfortunately, none of these methods work well. Consider a system with processes *A* and *B* running on machine 0, and process *C* running on machine 1. Three resources exist: *R*, *S*, and *T*. Initially, the situation is as shown in Fig. 3-23(a) and (b): *A* holds *S* but wants *R*, which it cannot have because *B* is using it;

C has T and wants S, too. The coordinator's view of the world is shown in Fig. 3-23(c). This configuration is safe. As soon as B finishes, A can get R and finish, releasing S for C.

After a while, B releases R and asks for T, a perfectly legal and safe swap. Machine 0 sends a message to the coordinator announcing the release of R, and machine 1 sends a message to the coordinator announcing the fact that B is now waiting for its resource, T. Unfortunately, the message from machine 1 arrives first, leading the coordinator to construct the graph of Fig. 3-23(d). The coordinator incorrectly concludes that a deadlock exists and kills some process. Such a situation is called a **false deadlock**. Many deadlock algorithms in distributed systems produce false deadlocks like this due to incomplete or delayed information.

One possible way out might be to use Lamport's algorithm to provide global time. Since the message from machine 1 to the coordinator is triggered by the request from machine 0, the message from machine 1 to the coordinator will indeed have a later timestamp than the message from machine 0 to the coordinator. When the coordinator gets the message from machine 1 that leads it to suspect deadlock, it could send a message to every machine in the system saying: "I just received a message with timestamp T which leads to deadlock. If anyone has a message for me with an earlier timestamp, please send it immediately." When every machine has replied, positively or negatively, the coordinator will see that the arc from R to B has vanished, so the system is still safe. Although this method eliminates the false deadlock, it requires global time and is expensive. Furthermore, other situations exist where eliminating false deadlock is much harder.

Distributed Deadlock Detection

Many distributed deadlock detection algorithms have been published. Surveys of the subject are given in Knapp (1987) and Singhal (1989). Let us examine a typical one here, the Chandy-Misra-Haas algorithm (Chandy et al., 1983). In this algorithm, processes are allowed to request multiple resources (e.g., locks) at once, instead of one at a time. By allowing multiple requests simultaneously, the growing phase of a transaction can be speeded up considerably. The consequence of this change to the model is that a process may now wait on two or more resources simultaneously.

In Fig. 3-24, we present a modified resource graph, where only the processes are shown. Each arc passes through a resource, as usual, but for simplicity the resources have been omitted from the figure. Notice that process 3 on machine 1 is waiting for two resources, one held by process 4 and one held by process 5.

Some of the processes are waiting for local resources, such as process 1, but

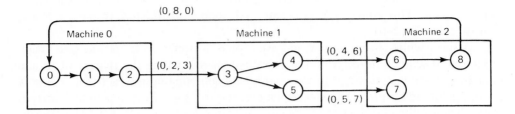

Fig. 3-24. The Chandy-Misra-Haas distributed deadlock detection algorithm.

others, such are process 2, are waiting for resources that are located on a different machine. It is precisely these cross-machine arcs that make looking for cycles difficult. The Chandy-Misra-Haas algorithm is invoked when a process has to wait for some resource, for example, process 0 blocking on process 1. At that point a special **probe** message is generated and sent to the process (or processes) holding the needed resources. The message consists of three numbers: the process that just blocked, the process sending the message, and the process to whom it is being sent. The initial message from 0 to 1 contains the triple (0, 0, 1).

When the message arrives, the recipient checks to see if it itself is waiting for any processes. If so, the message is updated, keeping the first field but replacing the second field by its own process number and the third one by the number of the process it is waiting for. The message is then sent to the process on which it is blocked. If it is blocked on multiple processes, all of them are sent (different) messages. This algorithm is followed whether the resource is local or remote. In Fig. 3-24 we see the remote messages labeled (0, 2, 3), (0, 4, 6), (0, 5, 7), and (0, 8, 0). If a message goes all the way around and comes back to the original sender, that is, the process listed in the first field, a cycle exists and the system is deadlocked.

There are various ways in which the deadlock can be broken. One way is to have the process that initiated the probe commit suicide. However, this method has problems if several processes invoke the algorithm simultaneously. In Fig. 3-24, for example, imagine that both 0 and 6 block at the same moment, and both initiate probes. Each would eventually discover the deadlock, and each would kill itself. This is overkill. Getting rid of one of them is enough.

An alternative algorithm is to have each process add its identity to the end of the probe message so that when it returned to the initial sender, the complete cycle would be listed. The sender can then see which process has the highest number, and kill that one or send it a message asking it to kill itself. Either way, if multiple processes discover the same cycle at the same time, they will all choose the same victim.

There are few areas of computer science in which theory and practice diverge as much as in distributed deadlock detection algorithms. Discovering yet another deadlock detection algorithm is the goal of many a researcher. Unfortunately, these models often have little relation to reality. For example, some of the algorithms require processes to send probes when they are blocked. However, sending a probe when you are blocked is not entirely trivial.

Many of the papers contain elaborate analyses of the performance of the new algorithm, pointing out, for example, that while the new one requires two traversals of the cycle, it uses shorter messages, as if these factors balanced out somehow. The authors would no doubt be surprised to learn that a typical "short" message (20 bytes) on a LAN takes about 1 msec, and a typical "long" message (100 bytes) on the same LAN takes perhaps 1.1 msec. It would also no doubt come as a shock to these people to realize that experimental measurements have shown that 90 percent of all deadlock cycles involve exactly two processes (Gray et al., 1981).

Worst of all, a large fraction of all the published algorithms in this area are just plain wrong, including those proven to be correct. Knapp (1987) and Singhal (1989) point out some examples. It often occurs that shortly after an algorithm is invented, proven correct, and then published, somebody finds a counterexample. Thus we have an active research area in which the model of the problem does not correspond well to reality, the solutions found are generally impractical, the performance analyses given are meaningless, and the proven results are frequently incorrect. To end on a positive note, this is an area that offers great opportunities for improvement.

3.5.2. Distributed Deadlock Prevention

Deadlock prevention consists of carefully designing the system so that deadlocks are structurally impossible. Various techniques include allowing processes to hold only one resource at a time, requiring processes to request all their resources initially, and making processes release all resources when asking for a new one. All of these are cumbersome in practice. A method that sometimes works is to order all the resources and require processes to acquire them in strictly increasing order. This approach means that a process can never hold a high resource and ask for a low one, thus making cycles impossible.

However, in a distributed system with global time and atomic transactions, two other practical algorithms are possible. Both are based on the idea of assigning each transaction a global timestamp at the moment it starts. As in many timestamp-based algorithms, in these two it is essential that no two transactions are ever assigned exactly the same timestamp. As we have seen, Lamport's algorithm guarantees uniqueness (effectively by using process numbers to break ties).

The idea behind the algorithm is that when one process is about to block waiting for a resource that another process is using, a check is made to see which has a larger timestamp (i.e., is younger). We can then allow the wait only if the waiting process has a lower timestamp (is older) than the process waited for. In this manner, following any chain of waiting processes, the timestamps always increase, so cycles are impossible. Alternatively, we can allow processes to wait only if the waiting process has a higher timestamp (is younger) than the process waited for, in which case the timestamps decrease along the chain.

Although both methods prevent deadlocks, it is wiser to give priority to older processes. They have run longer, so the system has a larger investment in them, and they are likely to hold more resources. Also, a young process that is killed off will eventually age until it is the oldest one in the system, so this choice eliminates starvation. As we have pointed out before, killing a transaction is relatively harmless, since by definition it can be restarted safely later.

To make this algorithm clearer, consider the situation of Fig. 3-25. In (a), an old process wants a resource held by a young process. In (b), a young process wants a resource held by an old process. In one case we should allow the process to wait; in the other we should kill it. Suppose that we label (a) *dies* and (b) *wait*. Then we are killing off an old process trying to use a resource held by a young process, which is inefficient. Thus we must label it the other way, as shown in the figure. Under these conditions, the arrows always point in the direction of increasing transaction numbers, making cycles impossible. This algorithm is called **wait-die**.

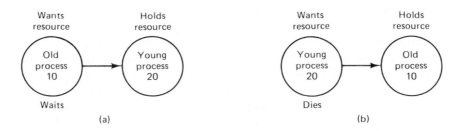

Fig. 3-25. The wait-die deadlock prevention algorithm.

Once we are assuming the existence of transactions, we can do something that had previously been forbidden: take resources away from running processes. In effect we are saying that when a conflict arises, instead of killing the process making the request, we can kill the resource owner. Without transactions, killing a process might have severe consequences, since the process might have modified files, for example. With transactions, these effects will vanish magically when the transaction dies.

Now consider the situation of Fig. 3-26, where we are going to allow preemption. Given that our system believes in ancestor worship, as we discussed above, we do not want a young whippersnapper preempting a venerable old sage, so Fig. 3-26(a) and not Fig. 3-26(b) is labeled *preempt*. We can now safely label Fig. 3-26(b) *wait*. This algorithm is known as **wound-wait**, because one transaction is supposedly wounded (it is actually killed) and the other waits. It is unlikely that this algorithm will make it to the Nomenclature Hall of Fame.

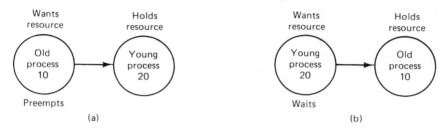

Fig. 3-26. The wound-wait deadlock prevention algorithm.

If an old process wants a resource held by a young one, the old process preempts the young one, whose transaction is then killed, as depicted in Fig. 3-26(a). The young one probably starts up again immediately, and tries to acquire the resource, leading to Fig. 3-26(b), forcing it to wait. Contrast this algorithm with wait-die. There, if an oldtimer wants a resource held by a young squirt, the oldtimer waits politely. However, if the young one wants a resource held by the old one, the young one is killed. It will undoubtedly start up again and be killed again. This cycle may go on many times before the old one releases the resource. Wound-wait does not have this nasty property.

3.6. SUMMARY

This chapter is about synchronization in distributed systems. We started out by giving Lamport's algorithm for synchronizing clocks without reference to external time sources, and later saw how useful this algorithm is. We also saw how physical clocks can be used for synchronization when real time is important.

Next we looked at mutual exclusion in distributed systems and studied three algorithms. The centralized algorithm kept all the information at a single site. The distributed algorithm ran the computation at all sites in parallel. The token ring algorithm passed control around the ring. Each has its strengths and weaknesses.

Many distributed algorithms require a coordinator, so we looked at two ways of electing a coordinator, the bully algorithm and another ring algorithm.

Although all of the foregoing are interesting and important, they are all low-level concepts. Transactions are a high-level concept that makes it easier for the programmer to handle mutual exclusion, locking, fault tolerance, and deadlocks in a distributed system. We looked at the transaction model, how transactions are implemented, and three concurrency control schemes: locking, optimistic concurrency control, and timestamps.

Finally, we revisited the problem of deadlocks and saw some algorithms for detecting and preventing them in distributed systems.

PROBLEMS

1. Add a new message to Fig. 3-2(b) that is concurrent with message *A*, that is, it neither happens before *A* nor happens after *A*.

2. Name at least three sources of delay that can be introduced between WWV broadcasting the time and the processors in a distributed system setting their internal clocks.

3. Consider the behavior of two machines in a distributed system. Both have clocks that are supposed to tick 1000 times per millisecond. One of them actually does, but the other ticks only 990 times per millisecond. If UTC updates come in once a minute, what is the maximum clock skew that will occur?

4. In the approach to cache consistency using leases, is it really essential that the clocks are synchronized? If not, what is it that is required?

5. In the centralized approach to mutual exclusion (Fig. 3-8), upon receiving a message from a processing releasing its exclusive access to the critical region it was using, the coordinator normally grants permission to the first process on the queue. Give another possible algorithm for the coordinator.

6. Consider Fig. 3-8 again. Suppose that the coordinator crashes. Does this always bring the system down? If not, under what circumstances does this happen? Is there any way to avoid the problem and make the system able to tolerate coordinator crashes?

7. Ricart and Agrawala's algorithm has the problem that if a process has crashed and does not reply to a request from another process to enter a critical region, the lack of response will be interpreted as denial of permission. We suggested that all requests be answered immediately, to make it easy to detect crashed processes. Are there any circumstances where even this method is insufficient? Discuss.

8. A distributed system may have multiple, independent critical regions. Imagine that process 0 wants to enter critical region *A* and process 1 wants to enter critical region *B*. Can Ricart and Agrawala's algorithm lead to deadlocks? Explain your answer.

9. In Fig. 3-12 a small optimization is possible. What is it?

10. Suppose that two processes detect the demise of the coordinator simultaneously and both decide to hold an election using the bully algorithm. What happens?

11. In Fig. 3-13 we have two *ELECTION* messages circulating simultaneously. While it does no harm to have two of them, it would be more elegant if one could be killed off. Devise an algorithm for doing this without affecting the operation of the basic election algorithm.

12. In Fig. 3-14 we saw a way to update an inventory list atomically using magnetic tape. Since a tape can easily be simulated on disk (as a file), why do you think this method is not used any more?

13. For some ultrasensitive applications it is conceivable that stable storage implemented with two disks is not reliable enough. Can the idea be extended to three disks? If so, how would it work? If not, why not?

14. In Fig. 3-17(d) three schedules are shown, two legal and one illegal. For the same transactions, give a complete list of all values that *x* might have at the end, and state which are legal and which are illegal.

15. When a private workspace is used to implement transactions, it may happen that a large number of file indices must be copied back to the parent's workspace. How can this be done without introducing race conditions?

16. In the writeahead log, both the old and new values are stored in the log entries. Is it not adequate just to store the new value? What good is the old one?

17. In Fig. 3-20, at what instant is the point-of-no-return reached? That is, when is the atomic commit actually performed?

18. Give the full algorithm for whether an attempt to lock a file should succeed or fail. Consider both read and write locks, and the possibility that the file was unlocked, read locked, or write locked.

19. Systems that use locking for concurrency control usually distinguish read locks from write locks. What should happen if a process has already acquired a read lock and now wants to change it into a write lock? What about changing a write lock into a read lock?

20. Is optimistic concurrency control more or less restrictive than using time-stamps? Why?

21. Does using timestamping for concurrency control ensure serializability? Discuss.

22. We have repeatedly said that when a transaction is aborted, the world is restored to its previous state, as though the transaction had never happened. We lied. Give an example where resetting the world is impossible.

23. The centralized deadlock detection algorithm described in the text initially gave a false deadlock, but was later patched up using global time. Suppose that it has been decided not to maintain global time (too expensive). Devise an alternative way to fix the bug in the algorithm.

24. A process with transaction timestamp 50 needs a resource held by a process with transaction timestamp 100. What happens in:

   (a) Wait-die?
   (b) Wound-wait?

4

Processes and Processors in Distributed Systems

In the preceding two chapters, we have looked at two related topics, communication and synchronization in distributed systems. In this chapter we will switch to a different subject: processes. Although processes are also an important concept in uniprocessor systems, in this chapter we will emphasize aspects of process management that are usually not studied in the context of classical operating systems. In particular, we will look at how the existence of multiple processors is dealt with.

In many distributed systems, it is possible to have multiple threads of control within a process. This ability provides some important advantages, but also introduces various problems. We will study these issues first. Then we come to the subject of how the processors and processes are organized and see that several different models are possible. Then we will look at processor allocation and scheduling in distributed systems. Finally, we consider two special kinds of distributed systems, fault-tolerant systems and real-time systems.

4.1. THREADS

In most traditional operating systems, each process has an address space and a single thread of control. In fact, that is almost the definition of a process. Nevertheless, there are frequently situations in which it is desirable to have

169

multiple threads of control sharing one address space but running in quasi-parallel, as though they were separate processes (except for the shared address space). In this section we will discuss these situations and their implications.

4.1.1. Introduction to Threads

Consider, for example, a file server that occasionally has to block waiting for the disk. If the server had multiple threads of control, a second thread could run while the first one was sleeping. The net result would be a higher throughput and better performance. It is not possible to achieve this goal by creating two independent server processes because they must share a common buffer cache, which requires them to be in the same address space. Thus a new mechanism is needed, one that historically was not found in single-processor operating systems.

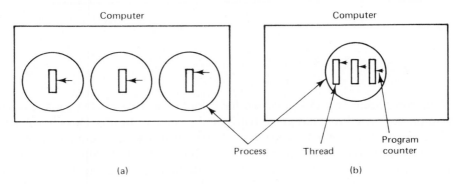

Fig. 4-1. (a) Three processes with one thread each. (b) One process with three threads.

In Fig. 4-1(a) we see a machine with three processes. Each process has its own program counter, its own stack, its own register set, and its own address space. The processes have nothing to do with each other, except that they may be able to communicate through the system's interprocess communication primitives, such as semaphores, monitors, or messages. In Fig. 4-1(b) we see another machine, with one process. Only this process contains multiple threads of control, usually just called **threads**, or sometimes **lightweight processes**. In many respects, threads are like little mini-processes. Each thread runs strictly sequentially and has its own program counter and stack to keep track of where it is. Threads share the CPU just as processes do: first one thread runs, then another does (timesharing). Only on a multiprocessor do they actually run in parallel. Threads can create child threads and can block waiting for system calls to complete, just like regular processes. While one thread is blocked, another thread in the same process can run, in exactly the same way that when one process blocks, another process in the same machine can run. The analogy: thread is to process as process is to machine, holds in many ways.

Different threads in a process are not quite as independent as different processes, however. All threads have exactly the same address space, which means that they also share the same global variables. Since every thread can access every virtual address, one thread can read, write, or even completely wipe out another thread's stack. There is no protection between threads because (1) it is impossible, and (2) it should not be necessary. Unlike different processes, which may be from different users and which may be hostile to one another, a process is always owned by a single user, who has presumably created multiple threads so that they can cooperate, not fight. In addition to sharing an address space, all the threads share the same set of open files, child processes, timers, and signals, etc. as shown in Fig. 4-2. Thus the organization of Fig. 4-1(a) would be used when the three processes are essentially unrelated, whereas Fig. 4-1(b) would be appropriate when the three threads are actually part of the same job and are actively and closely cooperating with each other.

Per thread items	Per process items
Program counter Stack Register set Child threads State	Address space Global variables Open files Child processes Timers Signals Semaphores Accounting information

Fig. 4-2. Per thread and per process concepts.

Like traditional processes (i.e., processes with only one thread), threads can be in any one of several states: running, blocked, ready, or terminated. A running thread currently has the CPU and is active. A blocked thread is waiting for another thread to unblock it (e.g., on a semaphore). A ready thread is scheduled to run, and will as soon as its turn comes up. Finally, a terminated thread is one that has exited, but which has not yet been collected by its parent (in UNIX terms, the parent thread has not yet done a WAIT).

4.1.2. Thread Usage

Threads were invented to allow parallelism to be combined with sequential execution and blocking system calls. Consider our file server example again. One possible organization is shown in Fig. 4-3(a). Here one thread, the

dispatcher, reads incoming requests for work from the system mailbox. After examining the request, it chooses an idle (i.e., blocked) **worker thread** and hands it the request, possibly by writing a pointer to the message into a special word associated with each thread. The dispatcher then wakes up the sleeping worker (e.g., by doing an UP on the semaphore on which it is sleeping).

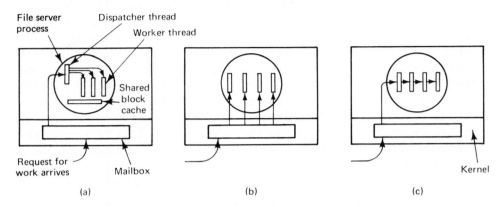

Fig. 4-3. Three organizations of threads in a process. (a) Dispatcher/worker model. (b) Team model. (c) Pipeline model.

When the worker wakes up, it checks to see if the request can be satisfied from the shared block cache, to which all threads have access. If not, it sends a message to the disk to get the needed block (assuming it is a READ) and goes to sleep awaiting completion of the disk operation. The scheduler will now be invoked and another thread will be started, possibly the dispatcher, in order to acquire more work, or possibly another worker that is now ready to run.

Consider how the file server could be written in the absence of threads. One possibility is to have it operate as a single thread. The main loop of the file server gets a request, examines it, and carries it out to completion before getting the next one. While waiting for the disk, the server is idle and does not process any other requests. If the file server is running on a dedicated machine, as is commonly the case, the CPU is simply idle while the file server is waiting for the disk. The net result is that many fewer requests/sec can be processed. Thus threads gain considerable performance, but each thread is programmed sequentially, in the usual way.

So far we have seen two possible designs: a multithreaded file server and a single-threaded file server. Suppose that threads are not available but the system designers find the performance loss due to single threading unacceptable. A third possibility is to run the server as a big finite-state machine. When a request comes in, the one and only thread examines it. If it can be satisfied from the cache, fine, but if not, a message must be sent to the disk.

However, instead of blocking, it records the state of the current request in a table and then goes and gets the next message. The next message may either be a request for new work or a reply from the disk about a previous operation. If it is new work, that work is started. If it is a reply from the disk, the relevant information is fetched from the table and the reply processed. Since it is not permitted to send a message and block waiting for a reply here, RPC cannot be used. The primitives must be nonblocking calls to *send* and *receive*.

In this design, the "sequential process" model that we had in the first two cases is lost. The state of the computation must be explicitly saved and restored in the table for every message sent and received. In effect, we are simulating the threads and their stacks the hard way. The process is being operated as a finite-state machine that gets an event and then reacts to it, depending on what is in it.

It should now be clear what threads have to offer. They make it possible to retain the idea of sequential processes that make blocking system calls (e.g., RPC to talk to the disk) and still achieve parallelism. Blocking system calls make programming easier and parallelism improves performance. The single-threaded server retains the ease of blocking system calls, but gives up performance. The finite-state machine approach achieves high performance through parallelism, but uses nonblocking calls and thus is hard to program. These models are summarized in Fig. 4-4.

Model	Characteristics
Threads	Parallelism, blocking system calls
Single-thread process	No parallelism, blocking system calls
Finite-state machine	Parallelism, nonblocking system calls

Fig. 4-4. Three ways to construct a server.

The dispatcher structure of Fig. 4-3(a) is not the only way to organize a multithreaded process. The **team** model of Fig. 4-3(b) is also a possibility. Here all the threads are equals, and each gets and processes its own requests. There is no dispatcher. Sometimes work comes in that a thread cannot handle, especially if each thread is specialized to handle a particular kind of work. In this case, a job queue can be maintained, with pending work kept in the job queue. With this organization, a thread should check the job queue before looking in the system mailbox.

Threads can also be organized in the **pipeline** model of Fig. 4-3(c). In this model, the first thread generates some data and passes them on to the next thread for processing. The data continue from thread to thread, with processing going on at each step. Although this is not appropriate for file servers, for other problems, such as the producer-consumer, it may be a good choice. Pipelining is widely used in many areas of computer systems, from the internal structure of RISC CPUs to UNIX command lines.

Threads are frequently also useful for clients. For example, if a client wants a file to be replicated on multiple servers, it can have one thread talk to each server. Another use for client threads is to handle signals, such as interrupts from the keyboard (DEL or BREAK). Instead of letting the signal interrupt the process, one thread is dedicated full time to waiting for signals. Normally, it is blocked, but when a signal comes in, it wakes up and processes the signal. Thus using threads can eliminate the need for user-level interrupts.

Another argument for threads has nothing to do with RPC or communication. Some applications are easier to program using parallel processes, the producer-consumer problem for example. Whether the producer and consumer actually run in parallel is secondary. They are programmed that way because it makes the software design simpler. Since they must share a common buffer, having them in separate processes will not do. Threads fit the bill exactly here.

Finally, although we are not explicitly discussing the subject here, in a multiprocessor system, it is actually possible for the threads in a single address space to run in parallel, on different CPUs. This is, in fact, one of the major ways in which sharing is done on such systems. On the other hand, a properly designed program that uses threads should work equally well on a single CPU that timeshares the threads or on a true multiprocessor, so the software issues are pretty much the same either way.

4.1.3. Design Issues for Threads Packages

A set of primitives (e.g., library calls) available to the user relating to threads is called a **threads package**. In this section we will consider some of the issues concerned with the architecture and functionality of threads packages. In the next section we will consider how threads packages can be implemented.

The first issue we will look at is thread management. Two alternatives are possible here, static threads and dynamic threads. With a static design, the choice of how many threads there will be is made when the program is written or when it is compiled. Each thread is allocated a fixed stack. This approach is simple, but inflexible.

A more general approach is to allow threads to be created and destroyed on-the-fly during execution. The thread creation call usually specifies the thread's main program (as a pointer to a procedure) and a stack size, and may specify other parameters as well, for example, a scheduling priority. The call usually returns a thread identifier to be used in subsequent calls involving the thread. In this model, a process starts out with one (implicit) thread, but can create one or more threads as needed, and these can exit when finished.

Threads can be terminated in one of two ways. A thread can exit voluntarily when it finishes its job, or it can be killed from outside. In this respect, threads are like processes. In many situations, such as the file servers of Fig. 4-3, the threads are created immediately after the process starts up and are never killed.

Since threads share a common memory, they can, and usually do, use it for holding data that are shared among multiple threads, such as the buffers in a producer-consumer system. Access to shared data is usually programmed using critical regions, to prevent multiple threads from trying to access the same data at the same time. Critical regions are most easily implemented using semaphores, monitors, and similar constructions. One technique that is commonly used in threads packages is the **mutex**, which is a kind of watered-down semaphore. A mutex is always in one of two states, unlocked or locked. Two operations are defined on mutexes. The first one, LOCK, attempts to lock the mutex. If the mutex is unlocked, the LOCK succeeds and the mutex becomes locked in a single atomic action. If two threads try to lock the same mutex at exactly the same instant, an event that is possible only on a multiprocessor, on which different threads run on different CPUs, one of them wins and the other loses. A thread that attempts to lock a mutex that is already locked is blocked.

The UNLOCK operation unlocks a mutex. If one or more threads are waiting on the mutex, exactly one of them is released. The rest continue to wait.

Another operation that is sometimes provided is TRYLOCK, which attempts to lock a mutex. If the mutex is unlocked, TRYLOCK returns a status code indicating success. If, however, the mutex is locked, TRYLOCK does not block the thread. Instead, it returns a status code indicating failure.

Mutexes are like binary semaphores (i.e., semaphores that may only have the values 0 or 1). They are not like counting semaphores. Limiting them in this way makes them easier to implement.

Another synchronization feature that is sometimes available in threads packages is the **condition variable**, which is similar to the condition variable used for synchronization in monitors. Each condition variable is normally associated with a mutex at the time it is created. The difference between mutexes and condition variables is that mutexes are used for short-term locking, mostly for guarding the entry to critical regions. Condition variables are used for long-term waiting until a resource becomes available.

The following situation occurs all the time. A thread locks a mutex to gain entry to a critical region. Once inside the critical region, it examines system tables and discovers that some resource it needs is busy. If it simply locks a second mutex (associated with the resource), the outer mutex will remain locked and the thread holding the resource will not be able to enter the critical region to free it. Deadlock results. Unlocking the outer mutex lets other threads into the critical region, causing chaos, so this solution is not acceptable.

One solution is to use condition variables to acquire the resource, as shown in Fig. 4-5(a). Here, waiting on the condition variable is defined to perform the wait and unlock the mutex atomically. Later, when the thread holding the resource frees it, as shown in Fig. 4-5(b), it calls *wakeup*, which is defined to wakeup either exactly one thread or all the threads waiting on the specified condition variable. The use of WHILE instead of IF in Fig. 4-5(a) guards against the case that the thread is awakened but that someone else seizes the resource before the thread runs.

```
lock mutex;                             lock mutex;
    check data structures;                  mark resource as free;
    while (resource busy)               unlock mutex;
        wait (condition variable);      wakeup (condition variable);
    mark resource as busy;
unlock mutex;

         (a)                                       (b)
```

Fig. 4-5. Use of mutexes and condition variables.

The need for the ability to wake up all the threads, rather than just one, is demonstrated in the reader-writer problem. When a writer finishes, it may choose to wake up pending writers or pending readers. If it chooses readers, it should wake them all up, not just one. Providing primitives for waking up exactly one thread and for waking up all the threads provides the needed flexibility.

The code of a thread normally consists of multiple procedures, just like a process. These may have local variables, global variables, and procedure parameters. Local variables and parameters do not cause any trouble, but variables that are global to a thread but not global to the entire program do.

As an example, consider the *errno* variable maintained by UNIX. When a process (or a thread) makes a system call that fails, the error code is put into *errno*. In Fig. 4-6, thread 1 executes the system call ACCESS to find out if it has permission to access a certain file. The operating system returns the answer in the global variable *errno*. After control has returned to thread 1, but before it has a chance to read *errno*, the scheduler decides that thread 1 has had enough CPU time for the moment and decides to switch to thread 2. Thread 2 executes an OPEN call that fails, which causes *errno* to be overwritten and thread 1's access code to be lost forever. When thread 1 starts up later, it will read the wrong value and behave incorrectly.

Various solutions to this problem are possible. One is to prohibit global variables altogether. However worthy this ideal may be, it conflicts with much existing software, such as UNIX. Another is to assign each thread its own private global variables, as shown in Fig. 4-7. In this way, each thread has its own private copy of *errno* and other global variables, so conflicts are avoided. In effect, this decision creates a new scoping level, variables visible to all the

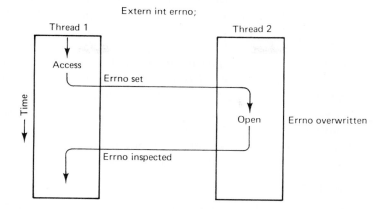

Fig. 4-6. Conflicts between threads over the use of a global variable.

procedures of a thread, in addition to the existing scoping levels of variables visible only to one procedure and variables visible everywhere in the program.

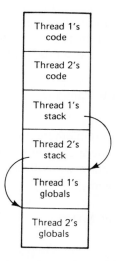

Fig. 4-7. Threads can have private global variables.

Accessing the private global variables is a bit tricky, however, since most programming languages have a way of expressing local variables and global variables, but not intermediate forms. It is possible to allocate a chunk of memory for the globals and pass it to each procedure in the thread, as an extra parameter. While hardly an elegant solution, it works.

Alternatively, new library procedures can be introduced to create, set, and read these thread-wide global variables. The first call might look like this:

```
create_global("bufptr");
```

It allocates storage for a pointer called *bufptr* on the heap or in a special storage area reserved for the calling thread. No matter where the storage is allocated, only the calling thread has access to the global variable. If another thread creates a global variable with the same name, it gets a different storage location that does not conflict with the existing one.

Two calls are needed to access global variables: one for writing them and the other for reading them. For writing, something like

```
set_global("bufptr", &buf);
```

will do. It stores the value of a pointer in the storage location previously created by the call to *create_global*. To read a global variable, the call might look like

```
bufptr = read_global("bufptr");
```

This call returns the address stored in the global variable, so the data value can be accessed.

Our last design issue relating to threads is scheduling. Threads can be scheduled using various scheduling algorithms, including priority, round robin, and others. Threads packages often provide calls to give the user the ability to specify the scheduling algorithm and set the priorities, if any.

4.1.4. Implementing a Threads Package

There are two main ways to implement a threads package: in user space and in the kernel. The choice is moderately controversial, and a hybrid implementation is also possible. In this section we will describe these methods, along with their advantages and disadvantages.

Implementing Threads in User Space

The first method is to put the threads package entirely in user space. The kernel knows nothing about them. As far as the kernel is concerned, it is managing ordinary, single-threaded processes. The first, and most obvious, advantage is that a user-level threads package can be implemented on an operating system that does not support threads. For example, UNIX originally did not support threads, but various user-space threads packages were written for it.

All of these implementations have the same general structure, which is illustrated in Fig. 4-8(a). The threads run on top of a runtime system, which is a collection of procedures that manage threads. When a thread executes a system call, goes to sleep, performs an operation on a semaphore or mutex, or otherwise does something that may cause it to be suspended, it calls a runtime system procedure. This procedure checks to see if the thread must be suspended. If so, it stores the thread's registers (i.e., its own) in a table, looks for an unblocked thread to run, and reloads the machine registers with the new thread's saved values. As soon as the stack pointer and program counter have been switched, the new thread comes to life again automatically. If the machine has an instruction to store all the registers and another one to load them all, the entire thread switch can be done in a handful of instructions. Doing thread switching like this is at least an order of magnitude faster than trapping to the kernel, and is a strong argument in favor of user-level threads packages.

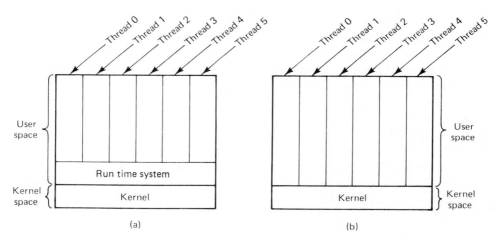

Fig. 4-8. (a) A user-level threads package. (b) A threads packaged managed by the kernel.

User-level threads also have other advantages. They allow each process to have its own customized scheduling algorithm. For some applications, for example, those with a garbage collector thread, not having to worry about a thread being stopped at an inconvenient moment is a plus. They also scale better, since kernel threads invariably require some table space and stack space in the kernel, which can be a problem if there are a very large number of threads.

Despite their better performance, user-level threads packages have some major problems. First among these is the problem of how blocking system calls are implemented. Suppose that a thread reads from an empty pipe or does something else that will block. Letting the thread actually make the system call is unacceptable, since this will stop all the threads. One of the main goals of having threads in the first place was to allow each one to use blocking calls, but to prevent one blocked thread from affecting the others. With blocking system calls, this goal cannot be achieved.

The system calls could all be changed to be nonblocking (e.g., a read on a empty pipe could just fail), but requiring changes to the operating system is unattractive. Besides, one of the arguments for user-level threads was precisely that they could run with *existing* operating systems. In addition, changing the semantics of READ will require changes to many user programs.

Another alternative is possible in the event that it is possible to tell in advance if a call will block. In some versions of UNIX, a call SELECT exists, which allows the caller to tell whether a pipe is empty, and so on. When this call is present, the library procedure *read* can be replaced with a new one that first does a SELECT call and then only does the READ call if it is safe (i.e., will not block). If the READ call will block, the call is not made. Instead, another thread is run. The next time the runtime system gets control, it can check again to see if the READ is now safe. This approach requires rewriting parts of the system call library, is inefficient and inelegant, but there is little choice. The code placed around the system call to do the checking is called a **jacket**.

Somewhat analogous to the problem of blocking system calls is the problem of page faults. If a thread causes a page fault, the kernel, not even knowing about the existence of threads, naturally blocks the entire process until the needed page has been fetched, even though other threads might be runnable.

Another problem with user-level thread packages is that if a thread starts running, no other thread in that process will ever run unless the first thread voluntarily gives up the CPU. Within a single process, there are no clock interrupts, making round-robin scheduling impossible. Unless a thread enters the runtime system of its own free will, the scheduler will never get a chance.

An area in which the absence of clock interrupts is crucial is synchronization. It is common in distributed applications for one thread to initiate an activity to which another thread must respond and then just sit in a tight loop testing whether the response has happened. This situation is called a **spin lock** or **busy waiting**. This approach is especially attractive when the response is expected quickly and the cost of using semaphores is high. If threads are rescheduled automatically every few milliseconds based on clock interrupts, this approach works fine. However, if threads run until they block, this approach is a recipe for deadlock.

One possible solution to the problem of threads running forever is to have the runtime system request a clock signal (interrupt) once a second to give it control, but this too is crude and messy to program. Periodic clock interrupts at a higher frequency are not always possible, and even if they are, the total overhead may be substantial. Furthermore, a thread might also need a clock interrupt, interfering with the runtime system's use of the clock.

Another, and probably most devastating argument against user-level threads is that programmers generally want threads in applications where the threads block often, as, for example, in a multithreaded file server. These threads are constantly making system calls. Once a trap has occurred to the kernel to carry out the system call, it is hardly any more work for the kernel to switch threads if the old one has blocked, and having the kernel do this eliminates the need for constantly checking to see if system calls are safe. For applications that are essentially entirely CPU bound and rarely block, what is the point of having threads at all? No one would seriously propose to compute the first n prime numbers or play chess using threads because there is nothing to be gained by doing it that way.

Implementing Threads in the Kernel

Now let us consider having the kernel know about and manage the threads. No runtime system is needed, as shown in Fig. 4-8(b). Instead, when a thread wants to create a new thread or destroy an existing thread, it makes a kernel call, which then does the creation or destruction.

To manage all the threads, the kernel has one table per process with one entry per thread. Each entry holds the thread's registers, state, priority, and other information. The information is the same as with user-level threads, but it is now in the kernel instead of in user space (inside the runtime system). This information is also the same information that traditional kernels maintain about each of their single-threaded processes, that is, the process state.

All calls that might block a thread, such as interthread synchronization using semaphores, are implemented as system calls, at considerably greater cost than a call to a runtime system procedure. When a thread blocks, the kernel, at its option, can run either another thread from the same process (if one is ready), or a thread from a different process. With user-level threads, the runtime system keeps running threads from its own process until the kernel takes the CPU away from it (or there are no ready threads left to run).

Due to the relatively greater cost of creating and destroying threads in the kernel, some systems take an environmentally correct approach and recycle their threads. When a thread is destroyed, it is marked as not runnable, but its kernel data structures are not otherwise affected. Later, when a new thread must be created, an old thread is reactivated, saving some overhead. Thread recycling is also possible for user-level threads, but since the thread management overhead is much smaller, there is less incentive to do this.

Kernel threads do not require any new, nonblocking system calls, nor do they lead to deadlocks when spin locks are used. In addition, if one thread in a process causes a page fault, the kernel can easily run another thread while waiting for the required page to be brought in from the disk (or network). Their main disadvantage is that the cost of a system call is substantial, so if thread operations (creation, deletion, synchronization, etc.) are common, much more overhead will be incurred.

In addition to the various problems specific to user threads and those specific to kernel threads, there are some other problems that occur with both of them. For example, many library procedures are not reentrant. For example, sending a message over the network may well be programmed to assemble the message in a fixed buffer first, then to trap to the kernel to send it. What happens if one thread has assembled its message in the buffer, then a clock interrupt forces a switch to a second thread that immediately overwrites the buffer with its own message? Similarly, after a system call completes, a thread switch may occur before the previous thread has had a chance to read out the error status (*errno*, as discussed above). Also, memory allocation procedures, such as the UNIX *malloc*, fiddle with crucial tables without bothering to set up and use protected critical regions, because they were written for single-threaded environments where that was not necessary. Fixing all these problems properly effectively means rewriting the entire library.

A different solution is to provide each procedure with a jacket that locks a global semaphore or mutex when the procedure is started. In this way, only one thread may be active in the library at once. Effectively, the entire library becomes a big monitor.

Signals also present difficulties. Suppose that one thread wants to catch a particular signal (say, the user hitting the DEL key), and another thread wants this signal to terminate the process. This situation can arise if one or more threads run standard library procedures and others are user-written. Clearly, these wishes are incompatible. In general, signals are difficult enough to manage in a single-threaded environment. Going to a multithreaded environment does not make them any easier to handle. Signals are typically a per-process concept, not a per-thread concept, especially if the kernel is not even aware of the existence of the threads.

Scheduler Activations

Various researchers have attempted to combine the advantage of user threads (good performance) with the advantage of kernel threads (not having to use a lot of tricks to make things work). Below we will describe one such approach devised by Anderson et al. (1991), called **scheduler activations**. Related work is discussed by Edler et al. (1988) and Scott et al. (1990).

The goals of the scheduler activation work are to mimic the functionality of kernel threads, but with the better performance and greater flexibility usually associated with threads packages implemented in user space. In particular, user threads should not have to be make special nonblocking system calls or check in advance if it is safe to make certain system calls. Nevertheless, when a thread blocks on a system call or on a page fault, it should be possible to run other threads within the same process, if any are ready.

Efficiency is achieved by avoiding unnecessary transitions between user and kernel space. If a thread blocks on a local semaphore, for example, there is no reason to involve the kernel. The user-space runtime system can block the synchronizing thread and schedule a new one by itself.

When scheduler activations are used, the kernel assigns a certain number of virtual processors to each process and lets the (user-space) runtime system allocate threads to processors. This mechanism can also be used on a multiprocessor where the virtual processors may be real CPUs. The number of virtual processors allocated to a process is initially one, but the process can ask for more and can also return processors it no longer needs. The kernel can take back virtual processors already allocated to assign them to other, more needy, processes.

The basic idea that makes this scheme work is that when the kernel knows that a thread has blocked (e.g., by its having executed a blocking system call or caused a page fault), the kernel notifies the process' runtime system, passing as parameters on the stack the number of the thread in question and a description of the event that occurred. The notification happens by having the kernel activate the runtime system at a known starting address, roughly analogous to a signal in UNIX. This mechanism is called an **upcall**.

Once activated like this, the runtime system can reschedule its threads, typically by marking the current thread as blocked and taking another thread from the ready list, setting up its registers, and restarting it. Later, when the kernel learns that the original thread can run again (e.g., the pipe it was trying to read from now contains data, or the page it faulted over has been brought in from disk), it makes another upcall to the runtime system to inform it of this event. The runtime system, at its own discretion, can either restart the blocked thread immediately, or put it on the ready list to be run later.

When a hardware interrupt occurs while a user thread is running, the interrupted CPU switches into kernel mode. If the interrupt is caused by an event not of interest to the interrupted process, such as completion of another process' I/O, when the interrupt handler has finished, it puts the interrupted thread back in the state it was in before the interrupt. If, however, the process is interested in the interrupt, such as the arrival of a page needed by one of the process' threads, the interrupted thread is not restarted. Instead, the interrupted thread is suspended and the runtime system started on that virtual CPU, with the state of the interrupted thread on the stack. It is then up to the runtime system to decide which thread to schedule on that CPU: the interrupted one, the newly ready one, or some third choice.

Although scheduler activations solve the problem of how to pass control to an unblocked thread in a process one of whose threads has just blocked, it creates a new problem. The new problem is that an interrupted thread might have been executing a semaphore operation at the time it was suspended, in which case it would probably be holding a lock on the ready list. If the runtime system started by the upcall then tries to acquire this lock itself, in order to put a newly ready thread on the list, it will fail to acquire the lock and a deadlock will ensue. The problem can be solved by keeping track of when threads are or are not in critical regions, but the solution is complicated and hardly elegant.

Another objection to scheduler activations is the fundamental reliance on upcalls, a concept that violates the structure inherent in any layered system. Normally, layer n offers certain services that layer $n + 1$ can call on, but layer n may not call procedures in layer $n + 1$.

4.1.5. Threads and RPC

It is common for distributed systems to use both RPC and threads. Since threads were invented as a cheap alternative to standard (heavyweight) processes, it is natural that researchers would take a closer look at RPC in this context, to see if it could be made more lightweight as well. In this section we will discuss some interesting work in this area.

Bershad et al. (1990) have observed that even in a distributed system, a substantial number of RPCs are to processes on the same machine as the caller (e.g., to the window manager). Obviously, this result depends on the system, but it is common enough to be worth considering. They have proposed a new scheme that makes it possible for a thread in one process to call a thread in another process on the same machine much more efficiently than the usual way.

The idea works like this. When a server thread, S, starts up, it exports its interface by telling the kernel about it. The interface defines which procedures are callable, what their parameters are, and so on. When a client thread C starts up, it imports the interface from the kernel and is given a special identifier to use for the call. The kernel now knows that C is going to call S later, and creates special data structures to prepare for the call.

One of these data structures is an argument stack that is shared by both C and S and is mapped read/write into both of their address spaces. To call the server, C pushes the arguments onto the shared stack, using the normal procedure passing conventions, and then traps to the kernel, putting the special identifier in a register. The kernel sees this and knows that the call is local. (If it had been remote, the kernel would have treated the call in the normal manner for remote calls.) It then changes the client's memory map to put the client in the server's address space and starts the client thread executing the server's procedure. The call is made in such a way that the arguments are already in place, so no copying or marshaling is needed. The net result is that local RPCs can be done much faster this way.

Another technique to speed up RPCs is based on the observation that when a server thread blocks waiting for a new request, it really does not have any important context information. For example, it rarely has any local variables, and there is typically nothing important in its registers. Therefore, when a thread has finished carrying out a request, it simply vanishes and its stack and context information are discarded.

When a new message comes in to the server's machine, the kernel creates a new thread on-the-fly to service the request. Furthermore, it maps the message into the server's address space, and sets up the new thread's stack to access the message. This scheme is sometimes called **implicit receive** and it is in contrast to a conventional thread making a system call to receive a message. The thread that is created spontaneously to handle an incoming RPC is occasionally referred to as a **pop-up thread**. The idea is illustrated in Fig. 4-9.

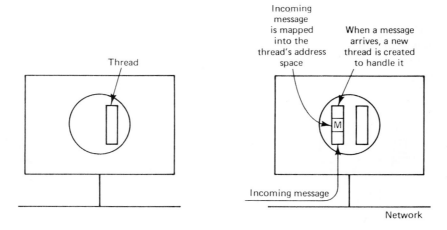

Fig. 4-9. Creating a thread when a message arrives.

The method has several major advantages over conventional RPC. First, threads do not have to block waiting for new work. Thus no context has to be saved. Second, creating a new thread is cheaper than restoring an existing one, since no context has to be restored. Finally, time is saved by not having to copy incoming messages to a buffer within a server thread. Various other techniques can also be used to reduce the overhead. All in all, a substantial gain in speed is possible.

Threads are an ongoing research topic. Some other results are presented in (Marsh et al., 1991; and Draves et al., 1991).

4.2. SYSTEM MODELS

Processes run on processors. In a traditional system, there is only one processor, so the question of how the processor should be used does not come up. In a distributed system, with multiple processors, it is a major design issue. The processors in a distributed system can be organized in several ways. In this section we will look at two of the principal ones, the workstation model and the processor pool model, and a hybrid form encompassing features of each one. These models are rooted in fundamentally different philosophies of what a distributed system is all about.

4.2.1. The Workstation Model

The workstation model is straightforward: the system consists of workstations (high-end personal computers) scattered throughout a building or campus and connected by a high-speed LAN, as shown in Fig. 4-10. Some of the workstations may be in offices, and thus implicitly dedicated to a single user, whereas others may be in public areas and have several different users during the course of a day. In both cases, at any instant of time, a workstation either has a single user logged into it, and thus has an "owner" (however temporary), or it is idle.

Fig. 4-10. A network of personal workstations, each with a local file system.

In some systems the workstations have local disks and in others they do not. The latter are universally called **diskless workstations**, but the former are variously known as **diskful workstations**, or **disky workstations**, or even stranger names. If the workstations are diskless, the file system must be implemented by one or more remote file servers. Requests to read and write files are sent to a file server, which performs the work and sends back the replies.

Diskless workstations are popular at universities and companies for several reasons, not the least of which is price. Having a large number of workstations equipped with small, slow disks is typically much more expensive than having one or two file servers equipped with huge, fast disks and accessed over the LAN.

A second reason that diskless workstations are popular is their ease of maintenance. When a new release of some program, say a compiler, comes out, the system administrators can easily install it on a small number of file servers in the machine room. Installing it on dozens or hundreds of machines all over a building or campus is another matter entirely. Backup and hardware maintenance is also simpler with one centrally located 5-gigabyte disk than with fifty 100-megabyte disks scattered over the building.

Another point against disks is that they have fans and make noise. Many people find this noise objectionable and do not want it in their office.

Finally, diskless workstations provide symmetry and flexibility. A user can walk up to any workstation in the system and log in. Since all his files are on the file server, one diskless workstation is as good as another. In contrast, when all the files are stored on local disks, using someone else's workstation means that you have easy access to *his* files, but getting to your own requires extra effort, and is certainly different from using your own workstation.

When the workstations have private disks, these disks can be used in one of at least four ways:

1. Paging and temporary files.

2. Paging, temporary files, and system binaries.

3. Paging, temporary files, system binaries, and file caching.

4. Complete local file system.

The first design is based on the observation that while it may be convenient to keep all the user files on the central file servers (to simplify backup and maintenance, etc.) disks are also needed for paging (or swapping) and for temporary files. In this model, the local disks are used only for paging and files that are temporary, unshared, and can be discarded at the end of the login session. For example, most compilers consist of multiple passes, each of which creates a temporary file read by the next pass. When the file has been read once, it is discarded. Local disks are ideal for storing such files.

The second model is a variant of the first one in which the local disks also hold the binary (executable) programs, such as the compilers, text editors, and electronic mail handlers. When one of these programs is invoked, it is fetched from the local disk instead of from a file server, further reducing the network load. Since these programs rarely change, they can be installed on all the local disks and kept there for long periods of time. When a new release of some system program is available, it is essentially broadcast to all machines. However, if that machine happens to be down when the program is sent, it will miss the program and continue to run the old version. Thus some administration is needed to keep track of who has which version of which program.

A third approach to using local disks is to use them as explicit caches (in addition to using them for paging, temporaries, and binaries). In this mode of operation, users can download files from the file servers to their own disks, read and write them locally, and then upload the modified ones at the end of the login session. The goal of this architecture is to keep long-term storage centralized, but reduce network load by keeping files local while they are being used. A disadvantage is keeping the caches consistent. What happens if two users download the same file and then each modifies it in different ways? This problem is not easy to solve, and we will discuss it in detail later in the book.

Fourth, each machine can have its own self-contained file system, with the possibility of mounting or otherwise accessing other machines' file systems. The idea here is that each machine is basically self-contained and that contact with the outside world is limited. This organization provides a uniform and guaranteed response time for the user and puts little load on the network. The disadvantage is that sharing is more difficult, and the resulting system is much closer to a network operating system than to a true transparent distributed operating system.

The one diskless and four diskful models we have discussed are summarized in Fig. 4-11. The progression from top to bottom in the figure is from complete dependence on the file servers to complete independence from them.

The advantages of the workstation model are manifold and clear. The model is certainly easy to understand. Users have a fixed amount of dedicated computing power, and thus guaranteed response time. Sophisticated graphics programs can be very fast, since they can have direct access to the screen. Each user has a large degree of autonomy and can allocate his workstation's resources as he sees fit. Local disks add to this independence, and make it possible to continue working to a lesser or greater degree even in the face of file server crashes.

However, the model also has two problems. First, as processor chips continue to get cheaper, it will soon become economically feasible to give each user first 10 and later 100 CPUs. Having 100 workstations in your office makes it hard to see out the window. Second, much of the time users are not using their workstations, which are idle, while other users may need extra computing capacity and cannot get it. From a system-wide perspective, allocating resources in such a way that some users have resources they do not need while other users need these resources badly is inefficient.

The first problem can be addressed by making each workstation a personal multiprocessor. For example, each window on the screen can have a dedicated CPU to run its programs. Preliminary evidence from some early personal multiprocessors such as the DEC Firefly, suggest, however, that the mean number of CPUs utilized is rarely more than one, since users rarely have more than one

Disk usage	Advantages	Disadvantages
(Diskless)	Low cost, easy hardware and software maintenance, symmetry and flexibility	Heavy network usage; file servers may become bottlenecks
Paging, scratch files	Reduces network load over diskless case	Higher cost due to large number of disks needed
Paging, scratch files, binaries	Reduces network load even more	Higher cost; additional complexity of updating the binaries
Paging, scratch files, binaries, file caching	Still lower network load; reduces load on file servers as well	Higher cost; cache consistency problems
Full local file system	Hardly any network load; eliminates need for file servers	Loss of transparency

Dependence on file servers

Fig. 4-11. Disk usage on workstations.

active process at once. Again, this is an inefficient use of resources, but as CPUs get cheaper nd cheaper as the technology improves, wasting them will become less of a sin.

4.2.2. Using Idle Workstations

The second problem, idle workstations, has been the subject of considerable research, primarily because many universities have a substantial number of personal workstations, some of which are idle (an idle workstation is the devil's playground?). Measurements show that even at peak periods in the middle of the day, often as many as 30 percent of the workstations are idle at any given moment. In the evening, even more are idle. A variety of schemes have been proposed for using idle or otherwise underutilized workstations (Litzkow et al., 1988; Nichols, 1987; and Theimer et al., 1985). We will describe the general principles behind this work in this section.

The earliest attempt to allow idle workstations to be utilized was the *rsh* program that comes with Berkeley UNIX. This program is called by

```
rsh machine command
```

in which the first argument names a machine and the second names a command to run on it. What *rsh* does is run the specified command on the specified machine. Although widely used, this program has several serious flaws. First, the user must tell which machine to use, putting the full burden of keeping track of idle machines on the user. Second, the program executes in the environment of the remote machine, which is usually different from the local environment. Finally, if someone should log into an idle machine on which a remote process is running, the process continues to run and the newly logged-in user either has to accept the lower performance or find another machine.

The research on idle workstations has centered on solving these problems. The key issues are:

1. How is an idle workstation found?

2. How can a remote process be run transparently?

3. What happens if the machine's owner comes back?

Let us consider these three issues, one at a time.

How is an idle workstation found? To start with, what is an idle workstation? At first glance, it might appear that a workstation with no one logged in at the console is an idle workstation, but with modern computer systems things are not always that simple. In many systems, even with no one logged in there may be dozens of processes running, such as clock daemons, mail daemons, news daemons, and all manner of other daemons. On the other hand, a user who logs in when arriving at his desk in the morning, but otherwise does not touch the computer for hours, hardly puts any additional load on it. Different systems make different decisions as to what "idle" means, but typically, if no one has touched the keyboard or mouse for several minutes and no user-initiated processes are running, the workstation can be said to be idle. Consequently, there may be substantial differences in load between one idle workstation and another, due, for example, to the volume of mail coming into the first one but not the second.

The algorithms used to locate idle workstations can be divided into two categories: server driven and client driven. In the former, when a workstation goes idle, and thus becomes a potential compute server, it announces its availability. It can do this by entering its name, network address, and properties in a registry file (or data base), for example. Later, when a user wants to execute a command on an idle workstation, he types something like

```
remote command
```

and the *remote* program looks in the registry to find a suitable idle workstation. For reliability reasons, it is also possible to have multiple copies of the registry.

An alternative way for the newly idle workstation to announce the fact that it has become unemployed is to put a broadcast message onto the network. All other workstations then record this fact. In effect, each machine maintains its own private copy of the registry. The advantage of doing it this way is less overhead in finding an idle workstation and greater redundancy. The disadvantage is requiring all machines to do the work of maintaining the registry.

Whether there is one registry or many, there is a potential danger of race conditions occurring. If two users invoke the *remote* command simultaneously, and both of them discover that the same machine is idle, they may both try to start up processes there at the same time. To detect and avoid this situation, the *remote* program can check with the idle workstation, which, if still free, removes itself from the registry and gives the go-ahead sign. At this point, the caller can send over its environment and start the remote process, as shown in Fig. 4-12.

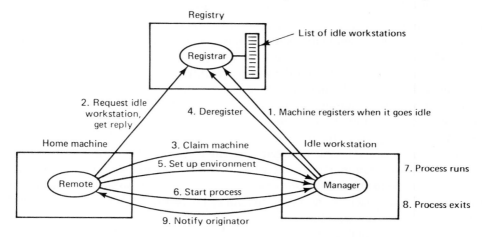

Fig. 4-12. A registry-based algorithm for finding and using idle workstations.

The other way to locate idle workstations is to use a client-driven approach. When *remote* is invoked, it broadcasts a request saying what program it wants to run, how much memory it needs, whether or not floating point is needed, and so on. These details are not needed if all the workstations are identical, but if the system is heterogeneous and not every program can run on every workstation, they are essential. When the replies come back, *remote* picks one and sets it up. One nice twist is to have "idle" workstations delay their responses slightly, with the delay being proportional to the current load. In this way, the reply from the least heavily loaded machine will come back first and be selected.

Finding a workstation is only the first step. Now the process has to be run there. Moving the code is easy. The trick is to set up the remote process so that it sees the same environment it would have locally, on the **home workstation**, and thus carries out the same computation it would have locally.

To start with, it needs the same view of the file system, the same working directory, and the same environment variables (shell variables), if any. After these have been set up, the program can begin running. The trouble starts when the first system call, say a READ, is executed. What should the kernel do? The answer depends very much on the system architecture. If the system is diskless, with all the files located on file servers, the kernel can just send the request to the appropriate file server, the same way the home machine would have done had the process been running there. On the other hand, if the system has local disks, each with a complete file system, the request has to be forwarded back to the home machine for execution.

Some system calls must be forwarded back to the home machine no matter what, even if all the machines are diskless. For example, reads from the keyboard and writes to the screen can never be carried out on the remote machine. However, other system calls must be done remotely under all conditions. For example, the UNIX system calls SBRK (adjust the size of the data segment), NICE (set CPU scheduling priority), and PROFIL (enable profiling of the program counter) cannot be executed on the home machine. In addition, all system calls that query the state of the machine have to be done on the machine on which the process is actually running. These include asking for the machine's name and network address, asking how much free memory it has, and so on.

System calls involving time are a problem because the clocks on different machines may not be synchronized. In Chap. 3, we saw how hard it is to achieve synchronization. Using the time on the remote machine may cause programs that depend on time, like *make*, to give incorrect results. Forwarding all time-related calls back to the home machine, however, introduces delay, which also causes problems with time.

To complicate matters further, certain special cases of calls which normally might have to be forwarded back, such as creating and writing to a temporary file, can be done much more efficiently on the remote machine. In addition, mouse tracking and signal propagation have to be thought out carefully as well. Programs that write directly to hardware devices, such as the screen's frame buffer, diskette, or magnetic tape, cannot be run remotely at all. All in all, making programs run on remote machines as though they were running on their home machines is possible, but it is a complex and tricky business.

The final question on our original list is what to do if the machine's owner comes back (i.e., somebody logs in or a previously inactive user touches the keyboard or mouse). The easiest thing is to do nothing, but this tends to defeat the idea of "personal" workstations. If other people can run programs on your workstation at the same time that you are trying to use it, there goes your guaranteed response.

Another possibility is to kill off the intruding process. The simplest way is to do this abruptly and without warning. The disadvantage of this strategy is that all work will be lost and the file system may be left in a chaotic state. A better way is to give the process fair warning, by sending it a signal to allow it to detect impending doom, and shut down gracefully (write edit buffers to the disk, close files, and so on). If it has not exited within a few seconds, it is then terminated. Of course, the program must be written to expect and handle this signal, something most existing programs definitely are not.

A completely different approach is to migrate the process to another machine, either back to the home machine or to yet another idle workstation. Migration is rarely done in practice because the actual mechanism is complicated. The hard part is not moving the user code and data, but finding and gathering up all the kernel data structures relating to the process that is leaving. For example, it may have open files, running timers, queued incoming messages, and other bits and pieces of information scattered around the kernel. These must all be carefully removed from the source machine and successfully reinstalled on the destination machine. There are no theoretical problems here, but the practical engineering difficulties are substantial. For more information, see (Artsy and Finkel, 1989; Douglis and Ousterhout, 1991; and Zayas, 1987).

In both cases, when the process is gone, it should leave the machine in the same state in which it found it, to avoid disturbing the owner. Among other items, this requirement means that not only must the process go, but also all its children and their children. In addition, mailboxes, network connections, and other system-wide data structures must be deleted, and some provision must be made to ignore RPC replies and other messages that arrive for the process after it is gone. If there is a local disk, temporary files must be deleted, and if possible, any files that had to be removed from its cache restored.

4.2.3. The Processor Pool Model

Although using idle workstations adds a little computing power to the system, it does not address a more fundamental issue: What happens when it is feasible to provide 10 or 100 times as many CPUs as there are active users? One solution, as we saw, is to give everyone a personal multiprocessor. However this is a somewhat inefficient design.

An alternative approach is to construct a **processor pool**, a rack full of CPUs in the machine room, which can be dynamically allocated to users on demand. The processor pool approach is illustrated in Fig. 4-13. Instead of giving users personal workstations, in this model they are given high-performance graphics terminals, such as X terminals (although small workstations can also be used as terminals). This idea is based on the observation that what many users really want is a high-quality graphical interface and good performance. Conceptually, it is much closer to traditional timesharing than to the personal computer model, although it is built with modern technology (low-cost microprocessors).

The motivation for the processor pool idea comes from taking the diskless workstation idea a step further. If the file system can be centralized in a small

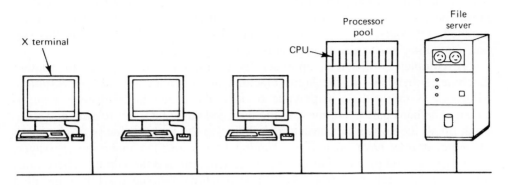

Fig. 4-13. A system based on the processor pool model.

number of file servers to gain economies of scale, it should be possible to do the same thing for compute servers. By putting all the CPUs in a big rack in the machine room, power supply and other packaging costs can be reduced, giving more computing power for a given amount of money. Furthermore, it permits the use of cheaper X terminals (or even ordinary ASCII terminals), and decouples the number of users from the number of workstations. The model also allows for easy incremental growth. If the computing load increases by 10 percent, you can just buy 10 percent more processors and put them in the pool.

In effect, we are converting all the computing power into "idle workstations" that can be accessed dynamically. Users can be assigned as many CPUs as they need for short periods, after which they are returned to the pool so that other users can have them. There is no concept of ownership here: all the processors belong equally to everyone.

The biggest argument for centralizing the computing power in a processor pool comes from queueing theory. A queueing system is a situation in which users generate random requests for work from a server. When the server is busy, the users queue for service and are processed in turn. Common examples of queueing systems are bakeries, airport check-in counters, supermarket check-out counters, and numerous others. The bare basics are depicted in Fig. 4-14.

Queueing systems are useful because it is possible to model them analytically. Let us call the total input rate λ requests per second, from all the users combined. Let us call the rate at which the server can process requests μ. For stable operation, we must have $\mu > \lambda$. If the server can handle 100 requests/sec, but the users continuously generate 110 requests/sec, the queue will grow without bound. (Small intervals in which the input rate exceeds the service rate are acceptable, provided that the mean input rate is lower than the service rate and there is enough buffer space.)

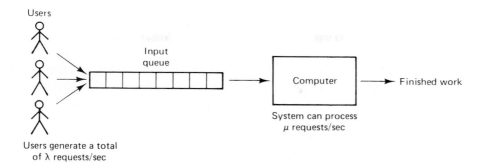

Fig. 4-14. A basic queueing system.

It can be proven (Kleinrock, 1974) that the mean time between issuing a request and getting a complete response, T, is related to λ and μ by the formula

$$T = \frac{1}{\mu - \lambda}$$

As an example, consider a file server that is capable of handling as many as 50 requests/sec but which only gets 40 requests/sec. The mean response time will be 1/10 sec or 100 msec. Note that when λ goes to 0 (no load), the response time of the file server does not go to 0, but to 1/50 sec or 20 msec. The reason is obvious once it is pointed out. If the file server can process only 50 requests/sec, it must take 20 msec to process a single request, even in the absence of any competition, so the response time, which includes the processing time, can never go below 20 msec.

Suppose that we have n personal multiprocessors, each with some number of CPUs, and each one forms a separate queueing system with request arrival rate λ and CPU processing rate μ. The mean response time, T, will be as given above. Now consider what happens if we scoop up all the CPUs and place them in a single processor pool. Instead of having n small queueing systems running in parallel, we now have one large one, with an input rate $n\lambda$ and a service rate $n\mu$. Let us call the mean response time of this combined system T_1. From the formula above we find

$$T_1 = \frac{1}{n\mu - n\lambda} = T/n$$

This surprising result says that by replacing n small resources by one big one that is n times more powerful, we can reduce the average response time n-fold.

This result is extremely general and applies to a large variety of systems. It is one of the main reasons that airlines prefer to fly a 300-seat 747 once every 5 hours to a 10-seat business jet every 10 minutes. The effect arises because dividing the processing power into small servers (e.g., personal workstations), each with one user, is a poor match to a workload of randomly arriving requests. Much of the time, a few servers are busy, even overloaded, but most are idle. It is this wasted time that is eliminated in the processor pool model, and the reason why it gives better overall performance. The concept of using idle workstations is a weak attempt at recapturing the wasted cycles, but it is complicated and has many problems, as we have seen.

In fact, this queueing theory result is one of the main arguments against having distributed systems at all. Given a choice between one centralized 1000-MIPS CPU and 100 private, dedicated, 10-MIPS CPUs, the mean response time of the former will be 100 times better, because no cycles are ever wasted. The machine goes idle only when no user has any work to do. This fact argues in favor of concentrating the computing power as much as possible.

However, mean response time is not everything. There are also arguments in favor of distributed computing, such as cost. If a single 1000-MIPS CPU is much more expensive than 100 10-MIPS CPUs, the price/performance ratio of the latter may be much better. It may not even be possible to build such a large machine at any price. Reliability and fault tolerance are also factors.

Also, personal workstations have a uniform response, independent of what other people are doing (except when the network or file servers are jammed). For some users, a low variance in response time may be perceived as more important than the mean response time itself. Consider, for example, editing on a private workstation on which asking for the next page to be displayed always takes 500 msec. Now consider editing on a large, centralized, shared computer on which asking for the next page takes 5 msec 95 percent of the time and 5 sec one time in 20. Even though the mean here is twice as good as on the workstation, the users may consider the performance intolerable. On the other hand, to the user with a huge simulation to run, the big computer may win hands down.

So far we have tacitly assumed that a pool of n processors is effectively the same thing as a single processor that is n times as fast as a single processor. In reality, this assumption is justified only if all requests can be split up in such a way as to allow them to run on all the processors in parallel. If a job can be split into, say, only 5 parts, then the processor pool model has an effective service time only 5 times better than that of a single processor, not n times better.

Still, the processor pool model is a much cleaner way of getting extra computing power than looking around for idle workstations and sneaking over there while nobody is looking. By starting out with the assumption that no processor belongs to anyone, we get a design based on the concept of requesting machines from the pool, using them, and putting them back when done. There is also no need to forward anything back to a "home" machine because there are none.

There is also no danger of the owner coming back, because there are no owners.

In the end, it all comes down to the nature of the workload. If all people are doing is simple editing and occasionally sending an electronic mail message or two, having a personal workstation is probably enough. If, on the other hand, the users are engaged in a large software development project, frequently running *make* on large directories, or are trying to invert massive sparse matrices, or do major simulations or run big artificial intelligence or VLSI routing programs, constantly hunting for substantial numbers of idle workstations will be no fun at all. In all these situations, the processor pool idea is fundamentally much simpler and more attractive.

4.2.4. A Hybrid Model

A possible compromise is to provide each user with a personal workstation and to have a processor pool in addition. Although this solution is more expensive than either a pure workstation model or a pure processor pool model, it combines the advantages of both of the others.

Interactive work can be done on workstations, giving guaranteed response. Idle workstations, however, are not utilized, making for a simpler system design. They are just left unused. Instead, all noninteractive processes run on the processor pool, as does all heavy computing in general. This model provides fast interactive response, an efficient use of resources, and a simple design.

4.3. PROCESSOR ALLOCATION

By definition, a distributed system consists of multiple processors. These may be organized as a collection of personal workstations, a public processor pool, or some hybrid form. In all cases, some algorithm is needed for deciding which process should be run on which machine. For the workstation model, the question is when to run a process locally and when to look for an idle workstation. For the processor pool model, a decision must be made for every new process. In this section we will study the algorithms used to determine which process is assigned to which processor. We will follow tradition and refer to this subject as "processor allocation" rather than "process allocation," although a good case can be made for the latter.

4.3.1. Allocation Models

Before looking at specific algorithms, or even at design principles, it is worthwhile saying something about the underlying model, assumptions, and goals of the work on processor allocation. Nearly all work in this area assumes that all the machines are identical, or at least code-compatible, differing at most by speed. An occasional paper assumes that the system consists of several disjoint processor pools, each of which is homogeneous. These assumptions are usually valid, and make the problem much simpler, but leave unanswered for the time being such questions as whether a command to start up the text formatter should be started up on a 486, SPARC, or MIPS CPU, assuming that binaries for all of them are available.

Almost all published models assume that the system is fully interconnected, that is, every processor can communicate with every other processor. We will assume this as well. This assumption does not mean that every machine has a wire to every other machine, just that transport connections can be established between every pair. That messages may have to be routed hop by hop over a sequence of machines is of interest only to the lower layers. Some networks support broadcasting or multicasting, and some algorithms use these facilities.

New work is generated when a running process decides to fork or otherwise create a subprocess. In some cases the forking process is the command interpreter (shell) that is starting up a new job in response to a command from the user. In others, a user process itself creates one or more children, for example, in order to gain performance by having all the children run in parallel.

Processor allocation strategies can be divided into two broad classes. In the first, which we shall call **nonmigratory**, when a process is created, a decision is made about where to put it. Once placed on a machine, the process stays there until it terminates. It may not move, no matter how badly overloaded its machine becomes and no matter how many other machines are idle. In contrast, with **migratory** allocation algorithms, a process can be moved even if it has already started execution. While migratory strategies allow better load balancing, they are more complex and have a major impact on system design.

Implicit in an algorithm that assigns processes to processors is that we are trying to optimize something. If this were not the case, we could just make the assignments at random or in numerical order. Precisely what it is that is being optimized, however, varies from one system to another. One possible goal is to maximize **CPU utilization**, that is, maximize the number of CPU cycles actually executed on behalf of user jobs per hour of real time. Maximizing CPU utilization is another way of saying that CPU idle time is to be avoided at all costs. When in doubt, make sure that every CPU has something to do.

Another worthy objective is minimizing mean **response time**. Consider, for example, the two processors and two processes of Fig. 4-15. Processor 1 runs at 10 MIPS; processor 2 runs at 100 MIPS, but has a waiting list of backlogged processes that will take 5 sec to finish off. Process A has 100 million instructions and process B has 300 million. The response times for each process on each processor (including the wait time) are shown in the figure. If we assign A to processor 1 and B to processor 2, the mean response time will be $(10 + 8)/2$

or 9 sec. If we assign them the other way around, the mean response time will be (30 + 6)/2 or 18 sec. Clearly, the former is a better assignment in terms of minimizing mean response time.

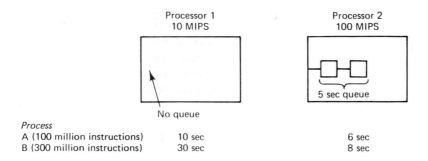

Process	Processor 1 10 MIPS No queue	Processor 2 100 MIPS 5 sec queue
A (100 million instructions)	10 sec	6 sec
B (300 million instructions)	30 sec	8 sec

Fig. 4-15. Response times of two processes on two processors.

A variation of minimizing the response time is minimizing the **response ratio**. The response ratio is defined as the amount of time it takes to run a process on some machine, divided by how long it would take on some unloaded benchmark processor. For many users, response ratio is a more useful metric than response time since it takes into account the fact that big jobs are supposed to take longer than small ones. To see this point, which is better, a 1-sec job that takes 5 sec or a 1-min job that takes 70 sec? Using response time, the former is better, but using response ratio, the latter is much better because $5/1 \gg 70/60$.

4.3.2. Design Issues for Processor Allocation Algorithms

A large number of processor allocation algorithms have been proposed over the years. In this section we will look at some of the key choices involved in these algorithms and point out the various trade-offs. The major decisions the designers must make can be summed up in five issues:

1. Deterministic versus heuristic algorithms.

2. Centralized versus distributed algorithms.

3. Optimal versus suboptimal algorithms.

4. Local versus global algorithms.

5. Sender-initiated versus receiver-initiated algorithms.

Other decisions also come up, but these are the main ones that have been studied extensively in the literature. Let us look at each of these in turn.

Deterministic algorithms are appropriate when everything about process behavior is known in advance. Imagine that you have a complete list of all processes, their computing requirements, their file requirements, their communication requirements, and so on. Armed with this information, it is possible to make a perfect assignment. In theory, one could try all possible assignments and take the best one.

In few, if any, systems, is total knowledge available in advance, but sometimes a reasonable approximation is obtainable. For example, in banking, insurance, or airline reservations, today's work is just like yesterday's. The airlines have a pretty good idea of how many people want to fly from New York to Chicago on a Monday morning in early Spring, so the nature of the workload can be accurately characterized, at least statistically, making it possible to consider deterministic allocation algorithms.

At the other extreme are systems where the load is completely unpredictable. Requests for work depend on who's doing what, and can change dramatically from hour to hour, or even from minute to minute. Processor allocation in such systems cannot be done in a deterministic, mathematical way, but of necessity uses ad hoc techniques called **heuristics**.

The second design issue is centralized versus distributed. This theme has occurred repeatedly throughout the book. Collecting all the information in one place allows a better decision to be made, but is less robust and can put a heavy load on the central machine. Decentralized algorithms are usually preferable, but some centralized algorithms have been proposed for lack of suitable decentralized alternatives.

The third issue is related to the first two: Are we trying to find the best allocation, or merely an acceptable one? Optimal solutions can be obtained in both centralized and decentralized systems, but are invariably more expensive than suboptimal ones. They involve collecting more information and processing it more thoroughly. In practice, most actual distributed systems settle for heuristic, distributed, suboptimal solutions because it is hard to obtain optimal ones.

The fourth issue relates to what is often called **transfer policy**. When a process is about to be created, a decision has to be made whether or not it can be run on the machine where it is being generated. If that machine is too busy, the new process must be transferred somewhere else. The choice here is whether or not to base the transfer decision entirely on local information. One school of thought advocates a simple (local) algorithm: if the machine's load is below some threshold, keep the new process; otherwise, try to get rid of it. Another school says that this heuristic is too crude. Better to collect (global) information about the load elsewhere before deciding whether or not the local machine is too busy for another process. Each school has its points. Local algorithms are simple, but may be far from optimal, whereas global ones may only give a slightly better result at much higher cost.

The last issue in our list deals with **location policy**. Once the transfer policy has decided to get rid of a process, the location policy has to figure out where to send it. Clearly, the location policy cannot be local. It needs information about the load elsewhere to make an intelligent decision. This information can be disseminated in two ways, however. In one method, the senders start the information exchange. In another, it is the receivers that take the initiative.

As a simple example, look at Fig. 4-16(a). Here an overloaded machine sends out requests for help to other machines, in hopes of offloading its new process on some other machine. The sender takes the initiative in locating more CPU cycles in this example. In contrast, in Fig. 4-16(b), a machine that is idle or underloaded announces to other machines that it has little to do and is prepared to take on extra work. Its goal is to locate a machine that is willing to give it some work to do.

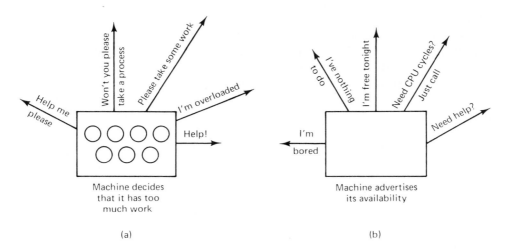

Fig. 4-16. (a) A sender looking for an idle machine. (b) A receiver looking for work to do.

For both the sender-initiated and receiver-initiated cases, various algorithms have different strategies for whom to probe, how long to continue probing, and what to do with the results. Nevertheless, the difference between the two approaches should be clear by now.

4.3.3. Implementation Issues for Processor Allocation Algorithms

The points raised in the preceding section are all clear-cut theoretical issues about which one can have endless wonderful debates. In this section we will look at some other issues that are more related to the nitty-gritty details of implementing processor allocation algorithms than to the great principles behind them.

To start with, virtually all the algorithms assume that machines know their own load, so they can tell if they are underloaded or overloaded, and can tell other machines about their state. Measuring load is not as simple as it first appears. One approach is simply to count the number of processes on each machine and use that number as the load. However, as we have pointed out before, even on an idle system there may be many processes running, including mail and news daemons, window managers, and other processes. Thus the process count says almost nothing about the current load.

The next step is to count only processes that are running or ready. After all, every running or runnable process puts some load on the machine, even if it is a background process. However, many of these daemons wake up periodically, check to see if anything interesting has happened, and if not, go back to sleep. Most put only a small load on the system.

A more direct measurement, although it is more work to capture, is the fraction of time the CPU is busy. Clearly, a machine with a 20 percent CPU utilization is more heavily loaded than one with a 10 percent CPU utilization, whether it is running user or daemon programs. One way to measure the CPU utilization is to set up a timer and let it interrupt the machine periodically. At each interrupt, the state of the CPU is observed. In this way, the fraction of time spent in the idle loop can be observed.

A problem with timer interrupts is that when the kernel is executing critical code, it will often disable all interrupts, including the timer interrupt. Thus if the timer goes off while the kernel is active, the interrupt will be delayed until the kernel finishes. If the kernel was in the process of blocking the last active processes, the timer will not go off until the kernel has finished—and entered the idle loop. This effect will tend to underestimate the true CPU usage.

Another implementation issue is how overhead is dealt with. Many theoretical processor allocation algorithms ignore the overhead of collecting measurements and moving processes around. If an algorithm discovers that by moving a newly created process to a distant machine it can improve system performance by 10 percent, it may be better to do nothing, since the cost of moving the process may eat up all the gain. A proper algorithm should take into account the CPU time, memory usage, and network bandwidth consumed by the processor allocation algorithm itself. Few do, mostly because it is not easy.

Our next implementation consideration is complexity. Virtually all researchers measure the quality of their algorithms by looking at analytical, simulation, or experimental measures of CPU utilization, network usage, and response time. Seldom is the complexity of the software considered, despite the obvious implications for system performance, correctness, and robustness. It rarely happens that someone publishes a new algorithm, demonstrates how good its performance is, and then concludes that the algorithm is not worth using because its performance is only slightly better than existing algorithms but is much more complicated to implement (or slower to run).

In this vein, a study by Eager et al. (1986) sheds light on the subject of pursuing complex, optimal algorithms. They studied three algorithms. In all cases, each machine measures its own load and decides for itself whether it is underloaded. Whenever a new process is created, the creating machine checks to see if it is overloaded. If so, it seeks out a remote machine on which to start the new process. The three algorithms differ in how the candidate machine is located.

Algorithm 1 picks a machine at random and just sends the new process there. If the receiving machine itself is overloaded, it, too, picks a random machine and sends the process off. This process is repeated until either somebody is willing to take it, or a hop counter is exceeded, in which case no more forwarding is permitted.

Algorithm 2 picks a machine at random and sends it a probe asking if it is underloaded or overloaded. If the machine admits to being underloaded, it gets the new process; otherwise, a new probe is tried. This loop is repeated until a suitable machine is found or the probe limit is exceeded, in which case it stays where it is created.

Algorithm 3 probes k machines to determine their exact loads. The process is then sent to the machine with the smallest load.

Intuitively, if we ignore all the overhead of the probes and process transfers, one would expect algorithm 3 to have the best performance, and indeed it does. But the gain in performance of algorithm 3 over algorithm 2 is small, even though the complexity and amount of additional work required are larger. Eager et al. concluded that if using a simple algorithm gives you most of the gain of a much more expensive and complicated one, it is better to use the simple one.

Our final point here is that stability is also an issue that crops up. Different machines run their algorithms asynchronously from one another, so the system is rarely in equilibrium. It is possible to get into situations where neither A nor B has quite up-to-date information, and each thinks the other has a lighter load, resulting in some poor process being shuttled back and forth a repeatedly. The problem is that most algorithms that exchange information can be shown to be correct after all the information has been exchanged and everything has settled down, but little can be said about their operation while tables are still being updated. It is in these nonequilibrium situations that problems often arise.

4.3.4. Example Processor Allocation Algorithms

To provide insight into how processor allocation can really be accomplished, in this section we will discuss several different algorithms. These have been selected to cover a broad range of possibilities, but there are others as well.

A Graph-Theoretic Deterministic Algorithm

A widely-studied class of algorithm is for systems consisting of processes with known CPU and memory requirements, and a known matrix giving the average amount of traffic between each pair of processes. If the number of CPUs, k, is smaller than the number of processes, several processes will have to be assigned to each CPU. The idea is to perform this assignment such as to minimize network traffic.

The system can be represented as a weighted graph, with each node being a process and each arc representing the flow of messages between two processes. Mathematically, the problem then reduces to finding a way to partition (i.e., cut) the graph into k disjoint subgraphs, subject to certain constraints (e.g., total CPU and memory requirements below some limits for each subgraph). For each solution that meets the constraints, arcs that are entirely within a single subgraph represent intramachine communication and can be ignored. Arcs that go from one subgraph to another represent network traffic. The goal is then to find the partitioning that minimizes the network traffic while meeting all the constraints. Figure 4-17 shows two ways of partitioning the same graph, yielding two different network loads.

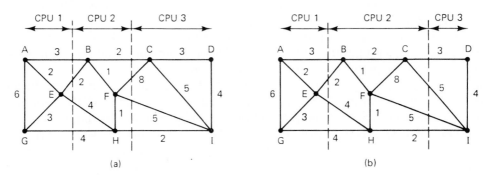

Fig. 4-17. Two ways of allocating nine processes to three processors.

In Fig. 4-17(a), we have partitioned the graph with processes A, E, and G on one processor, processes B, F, and H on a second, and processes C, D, and I on the third. The total network traffic is the sum of the arcs intersected by the dotted cut lines, or 30 units. In Fig. 4-17(b) we have a different partitioning that has only 28 units of network traffic. Assuming that it meets all the memory and CPU constraints, this is a better choice because it requires less communication.

Intuitively, what we are doing is looking for clusters that are tightly coupled (high intracluster traffic flow) but which interact little with other clusters (low intercluster traffic flow). Some of the many papers discussing the problem are (Chow and Abraham, 1982; Stone and Bokhari, 1978; and Lo, 1984).

A Centralized Algorithm

Graph-theoretic algorithms of the kind we have just discussed are of limited applicability since they require complete information in advance, so let us turn to a heuristic algorithm that does not require any advance information. This algorithm, called **up-down** (Mutka and Livny, 1987), is centralized in the sense that a coordinator maintains a **usage table** with one entry per personal workstation (i.e., per user), initially zero. When significant events happen, messages are sent to the coordinator to update the table. Allocation decisions are based on the table. These decisions are made when scheduling events happen: a processor is being requested, a processor has become free, or the clock has ticked.

The unusual thing about this algorithm, and the reason that it is centralized, is that instead of trying to maximize CPU utilization, it is concerned with giving each workstation owner a fair share of the computing power. Whereas other algorithms will happily let one user take over all the machines if he promises to keep them all busy (i.e., achieve a high CPU utilization), this algorithm is designed to prevent precisely that.

When a process is to be created, and the machine it is created on decides that the process should be run elsewhere, it asks the usage table coordinator to allocate it a processor. If there is one available and no one else wants it, the request is granted. If no processors are free, the request is temporarily denied and a note is made of the request.

When a workstation owner is running processes on other people's machines, it accumulates penalty points, a fixed number per second, as shown in Fig. 4-18. These points are added to its usage table entry. When it has unsatisfied requests pending, penalty points are subtracted from its usage table entry. When no requests are pending and no processors are being used, the usage table entry is moved a certain number of points closer to zero, until it gets there. In this way, the score goes up and down, hence the name of the algorithm.

Usage table entries can be positive, zero, or negative. A positive score indicates that the workstation is a net user of system resources, whereas a negative score means that it needs resources. A zero score is neutral.

The heuristic used for processor allocation can now be given. When a processor becomes free, the pending request whose owner has the lowest score wins. As a consequence, a user who is occupying no processors and who has had a request pending for a long time will always beat someone who is using many processors. This property is the intention of the algorithm, to allocate capacity fairly.

In practice this means that if one user has a fairly continuous load on the system, and another user comes along and wants to start a process, the light user will be favored over the heavy one. Simulation studies (Mutka and Livny, 1987) show that the algorithm works as expected under a variety of load conditions.

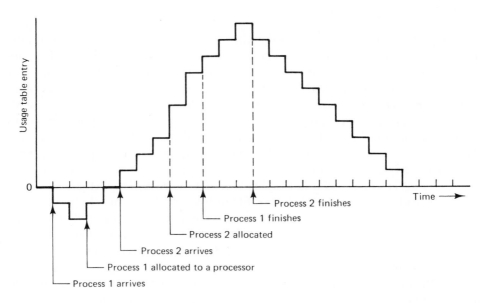

Fig. 4-18. Operation of the up-down algorithm.

A Hierarchical Algorithm

Centralized algorithms, such as up-down, do not scale well to large systems. The central node soon becomes a bottleneck, not to mention a single point of failure. These problems can be attacked by using a hierarchical algorithm instead of a centralized one. Hierarchical algorithms retain much of the simplicity of centralized ones, but scale better.

One approach that has been proposed for keeping tabs on a collection of processors is to organize them in a logical hierarchy independent of the physical structure of the network, as in MICROS (Wittie and van Tilborg, 1980). This approach organizes the machines like people in corporate, military, academic, and other real-world hierarchies. Some of the machines are workers and others are managers.

For each group of k workers, one manager machine (the "department head") is assigned the task of keeping track of who is busy and who is idle. If the system is large, there will be an unwieldy number of department heads, so some machines will function as "deans," each riding herd on some number of department heads. If there are many deans, they too can be organized hierarchically, with a "big cheese" keeping tabs on a collection of deans. This hierarchy can be extended ad infinitum, with the number of levels needed growing logarithmically with the number of workers. Since each processor need only maintain communication with one superior and a few subordinates, the information stream is manageable.

An obvious question is: What happens when a department head, or worse yet, a big cheese, stops functioning (crashes)? One answer is to promote one of the direct subordinates of the faulty manager to fill in for the boss. The choice of which can be made by the subordinates themselves, by the deceased's peers, or in a more autocratic system, by the sick manager's boss.

To avoid having a single (vulnerable) manager at the top of the tree, one can truncate the tree at the top and have a committee as the ultimate authority, as shown in Fig. 4-19. When a member of the ruling committee malfunctions, the remaining members promote someone one level down as replacement.

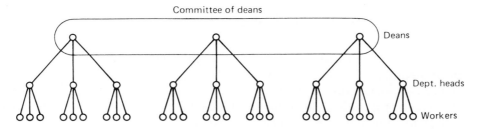

Fig. 4-19. A processor hierarchy can be modeled as an organizational hierarchy.

While this scheme is not really distributed, it is feasible, and in practice works well. In particular, the system is self-repairing and can survive occasional crashes of both workers and managers without any long-term effects.

In MICROS, the processors are monoprogrammed, so if a job requiring S processes suddenly appears, the system must allocate S processors for it. Jobs can be created at any level of the hierarchy. The strategy used is for each manager to keep track of approximately how many workers below it are available (possibly several levels below it). If it thinks that a sufficient number are available, it reserves some number R of them, where $R \geq S$, because the estimate of available workers may not be exact and some machines may be down.

If the manager receiving the request thinks that it has too few processors available, it passes the request upward in the tree to its boss. If the boss cannot handle it either, the request continues propagating upward until it reaches a level that has enough available workers at its disposal. At that point, the manager splits the request into parts and parcels them out among the managers below it, which then do the same thing until the wave of allocation requests hits bottom. At the bottom level, the processors are marked as "busy" and the actual number of processors allocated is reported back up the tree.

To make this strategy work well, R must be large enough that the probability is high that enough workers will be found to handle the entire job. Otherwise the request will have to move up one level in the tree and start all over, wasting considerable time and computing power. On the other hand, if R is too large, too many processors will be allocated, wasting computing capacity until word gets back to the top and they can be released.

The whole situation is greatly complicated by the fact that requests for processors can be generated randomly anywhere in the system, so at any instant, multiple requests are likely to be in various stages of the allocation algorithm, potentially giving rise to out-of-date estimates of available workers, race conditions, deadlocks, and more. In Van Tilborg and Wittie (1981) a mathematical analysis of the problem is given and various other aspects not described here are covered in detail.

A Sender-Initiated Distributed Heuristic Algorithm

The algorithms described above are all centralized or semicentralized. Distributed algorithms also exist. Typical of these are the ones described by Eager et al. (1986). As mentioned above, in the most cost-effective algorithm they studied, when a process is created, the machine on which it originates sends probe messages to a randomly-chosen machine, asking if its load is below some threshold value. If so, the process is sent there. If not, another machine is chosen for probing. Probing does not go on forever. If no suitable host is found within N probes, the algorithm terminates and the process runs on the originating machine.

An analytical queueing model of this algorithm has been constructed and investigated. Using this model, it was established that the algorithm behaves well and is stable under a wide range of parameters, including different threshold values, transfer costs, and probe limits.

Nevertheless, it should be observed that under conditions of heavy load, all machines will constantly send probes to other machines in a futile attempt to find one that is willing to accept more work. Few processes will be off-loaded, but considerable overhead may be incurred in the attempt to do so.

A Receiver-Initiated Distributed Heuristic Algorithm

A complementary algorithm to the one given above, which is initiated by an overloaded sender, is one initiated by an underloaded receiver. With this algorithm, whenever a process finishes, the system checks to see if it has enough work. If not, it picks some machine at random and asks it for work. If that machine has nothing to offer, a second, and then a third machine is asked. If no work is found with N probes, the receiver temporarily stops asking, does any work it has queued up, and tries again when the next process finishes. If no work is available, the machine goes idle. After some fixed time interval, it begins probing again.

An advantage of this algorithm is that it does not put extra load on the system at critical times. The sender-initiated algorithm makes large numbers of probes precisely when the system can least tolerate it—when it is heavily loaded. With the receiver-initiated algorithm, when the system is heavily loaded, the chance of a machine having insufficient work is small, but when this does happen, it will be easy to find work to take over. Of course, when there is little work to do, the receiver-initiated algorithm, creates considerable probe traffic as all the unemployed machines desperately hunt for work. However, it is far better to have the overhead go up when the system is underloaded than when it is overloaded.

It is also possible to combine both of these algorithms and have machines try to get rid of work when they have too much, and try to acquire work when they do not have enough. Furthermore, machines can perhaps improve on random polling by keeping a history of past probes to determine if any machines are chronically underloaded or overloaded. One of these can be tried first, depending on whether the initiator is trying to get rid of work or acquire it.

A Bidding Algorithm

Another class of algorithms tries to turn the computer system into a miniature economy, with buyers and sellers of services and prices set by supply and demand (Ferguson et al., 1988). The key players in the economy are the processes, which must buy CPU time to get their work done, and processors, which auction their cycles off to the highest bidder.

Each processor advertises its approximate price by putting it in a publicly readable file. This price is not guaranteed, but gives an indication of what the service is worth (actually, it is the price that the last customer paid). Different processors may have different prices, depending on their speed, memory size, presence of floating-point hardware, and other features. An indication of the service provided, such as expected response time, can also be published.

When a process wants to start up a child process, it goes around and checks out who is currently offering the service that it needs. It then determines the set of processors whose services it can afford. From this set, it computes the best candidate, where "best" may mean cheapest, fastest, or best price/performance, depending on the application. It then generates a bid and sends the bid to its first choice. The bid may be higher or lower than the advertised price.

Processors collect all the bids sent to them, and make a choice, presumably by picking the highest one. The winners and losers are informed, and the winning process is executed. The published price of the server is then updated to reflect the new going rate.

Although Ferguson et al. do not go into the details, such an economic model raises all kinds of interesting questions, among them the following. Where do processes get money to bid? Do they get regular salaries? Does everyone get the same monthly salary, or do deans get more than professors, who in turn get more than students? If new users are introduced into the system without a corresponding increase in resources, do prices get bid up (inflation)? Can processors form cartels to gouge users? Are users' unions allowed? Is disk space also chargeable? How about laser printer output? The list goes on and on.

4.4. SCHEDULING IN DISTRIBUTED SYSTEMS

There is not really a lot to say about scheduling in a distributed system. Normally, each processor does its own local scheduling (assuming that it has multiple processes running on it), without regard to what the other processors are doing. Usually, this approach works fine. However, when a group of related, heavily interacting processes are all running on different processors, independent scheduling is not always the most efficient way.

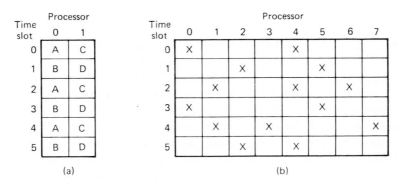

Fig. 4-20. (a) Two jobs running out of phase with each other. (b) Scheduling matrix for eight processors, each with six time slots. The Xs indicated allocated slots.

The basic difficulty can be illustrated by an example in which processes A and B run on one processor and processes C and D run on another. Each processor is timeshared in, say, 100-msec time slices, with A and C running in the even slices and B and D running in the odd ones, as shown in Fig. 4-20(a). Suppose that A sends many messages or makes many remote procedure calls to D. During time slice 0, A starts up and immediately calls D, which unfortunate is not running because it is now C's turn. After 100 msec, process switching takes place, and D gets A's message, carries out the work, and quickly replies. Because B is now running, it will be another 100 msec before A gets the reply and can proceed. The net result is one message exchange every 200 msec. What is needed is a way to ensure that processes that communicate frequently run simultaneously.

Although it is difficult to determine dynamically the interprocess communication patterns, in many cases, a group of related processes will be started off together. For example, it is usually a good bet that the filters in a UNIX pipeline will communicate with each other more than they will with other, previously started processes. Let us assume that processes are created in groups and that intragroup communication is much more prevalent than intergroup communication. Let us assume further that a sufficiently large number of processors is available to handle the largest group, and that each processor is multiprogrammed with N process slots (N-way multiprogramming).

Ousterhout (1982) proposed several algorithms based on a concept he calls **co-scheduling**, which takes interprocess communication patterns into account while scheduling to ensure that all members of a group run at the same time. The first algorithm uses a conceptual matrix in which each column is the process table for one processor, as shown in Fig. 4-20(b). Thus, column 4 consists of all the processes that run on processor 4. Row 3 is the collection of all processes that are in slot 3 of some processor, starting with the process in slot 3 of processor 0, then the process in slot 3 of processor 1, and so on. The gist of his idea is to have each processor use a round-robin scheduling algorithm with all processors first running the process in slot 0 for a fixed period, then all processors running the process in slot 1 for a fixed period, and so on. A broadcast message could be used to tell each processor when to do process switching, to keep the time slices synchronized.

By putting all the members of a process group in the same slot number, but on different processors, one has the advantage of N-fold parallelism, with a guarantee that all the processes will be run at the same time, to maximize communication throughput. Thus in Fig. 4-20(b), four processes that must communicate should be put into slot 3, on processors 1, 2, 3, and 4 for optimum performance. This scheduling technique can be combined with the hierarchical model of process management used in MICROS by having each department head maintain the matrix for its workers, assigning processes to slots in the matrix and broadcasting time signals.

Ousterhout also described several variations to this basic method to improve performance. One of these breaks the matrix into rows and concatenates the rows to form one long row. With k processors, any k consecutive slots belong to different processors. To allocate a new process group to slots, one lays a window k slots wide over the long row such that the leftmost slot is empty but the slot just outside the left edge of the window is full. If sufficient empty slots are present in the window, the processes are assigned to the empty slots; otherwise, the window is slid to the right and the algorithm repeated. Scheduling is done by starting the window at the left edge and moving rightward by about one window's worth per time slice, taking care not to split groups over windows. Ousterhout's paper discusses these and other methods in more detail and gives some performance results.

4.5. FAULT TOLERANCE

A system is said to fail when it does not meet its specification. In some cases, such as a supermarket's distributed ordering system, a failure may result in some store running out of canned beans. In other cases, such in a distributed air traffic control system, a failure may be catastrophic. As computers and distributed systems become widely used in safety-critical missions, the need to prevent failures becomes correspondingly greater. In this section we will examine some issues concerning system failures and how they can be avoided. Additional introductory material can be found in (Cristian, 1991; and Nelson, 1990). Gantenbein (1992) has compiled a bibliography on the subject.

4.5.1. Component Faults

Computer systems can fail due to a fault in some component, such as a processor, memory, I/O device, cable, or software. A **fault** is a malfunction, possibly caused by a design error, a manufacturing error, a programming error, physical damage, deterioration in the course of time, harsh environmental conditions (it snowed on the computer), unexpected inputs, operator error, rodents eating part of it, and many other causes. Not all faults lead (immediately) to system failures, but some do.

Faults are generally classified as transient, intermittent, or permanent. **Transient faults** occur once and then disappear. If the operation is repeated, the fault goes away. A bird flying through the beam of a microwave transmitter may cause lost bits on some network (not to mention a roasted bird). If the transmission times out and is retried, it will probably work the second time.

An **intermittent fault** occurs, then vanishes of its own accord, then reappears, and so on. A loose contact on a connector will often cause an intermittent fault. Intermittent faults cause a great deal of aggravation because they are difficult to diagnose. Typically, whenever the fault doctor shows up, the system works perfectly.

A **permanent fault** is one that continues to exist until the faulty component is repaired. Burnt-out chips, software bugs, and disk head crashes often cause permanent faults.

The goal of designing and building fault-tolerant systems is to ensure that the system as a whole continues to function correctly, even in the presence of faults. This aim is quite different from simply engineering the individual components to be highly reliable, but allowing (even expecting) the system to fail if one of the components does so.

Faults and failures can occur at all levels: transistors, chips, boards, processors, operating systems, user programs, and so on. Traditional work in the area of fault tolerance has been concerned mostly with the statistical analysis of electronic component faults. Very briefly, if some component has a probability p of malfunctioning in a given second of time, the probability of it *not* failing for k consecutive seconds and then failing is $p(1 - p)^k$. The expected time to failure is then given by the formula

$$\text{mean time to failure} = \sum_{k=1}^{\infty} kp(1 - p)^{k-1}$$

Using the well-known equation for an infinite sum starting at $k=1$: $\sum \alpha^k = \alpha/(1 - \alpha)$, substituting $\alpha = 1 - p$, differentiating both sides of the resulting equation with respect to p, and multiplying through by $-p$ we see that

$$\text{mean time to failure} = 1/p$$

For example, if the probably of a crash is 10^{-6} per second, the mean time to failure is 10^6 sec or about 11.6 days.

4.5.2. System Failures

In a critical distributed system, often we are interested in making the *system* be able to survive component (in particular, processor) faults, rather than just making these unlikely. System reliability is especially important in a distributed system due to the large number of components present, hence the greater chance of one of them being faulty.

For the rest of this section, we will discuss processor faults or crashes, but this should be understood to mean equally well process faults or crashes (e.g., due to software bugs). Two types of processor faults can be distinguished:

1. Fail-silent faults.

2. Byzantine faults.

With **fail-silent faults**, a faulty processor just stops and does not respond to subsequent input or produce further output, except perhaps to announce that it is no longer functioning. These are also called **fail-stop faults**. With **Byzantine faults**, a faulty processor continues to run, issuing wrong answers to questions, and possibly working together maliciously with other faulty processors to give the impression that they are all working correctly when they are not. Undetected software bugs often exhibit Byzantine faults. Clearly, dealing with Byzantine faults is going to be much more difficult than dealing with fail-silent ones.

The term "Byzantine" refers to the Byzantine Empire, a time (330-1453) and place (the Balkans and modern Turkey) in which endless conspiracies, intrigue, and untruthfulness were alleged to be common in ruling circles. Byzantine faults were first analyzed by Pease et al. (1980) and Lamport et al. (1982). Some researchers also consider combinations of these faults with communication line faults, but since standard protocols can recover from line errors in predictable ways, we will examine only processor faults.

4.5.3. Synchronous versus Asynchronous Systems

As we have just seen, component faults can be transient, intermittent, or permanent, and system failures can be fail-silent or Byzantine. A third orthogonal axis deals with performance in a certain abstract sense. Suppose that we have a system in which if one processor sends a message to another, it is guaranteed to get a reply within a time T known in advance. Failure to get a reply means that the receiving system has crashed. The time T includes sufficient time to deal with lost messages (by sending them up to n times).

In the context of research on fault tolerance, a system that has the property of always responding to a message within a known finite bound if it is working is said to be **synchronous**. A system not having this property is said to be **asynchronous**. While this terminology is unfortunately, since it conflicts with more traditional uses of the terms, it is widely used among workers in fault tolerance.

It should be intuitively clear that asynchronous systems are going to be harder to deal with than synchronous ones. If a processor can send a message and know that the absence of a reply within T sec means that the intended recipient has failed, it can take corrective action. If there is no upper limit to how long the response might take, even determining whether there has been a failure is going to be a problem.

4.5.4. Use of Redundancy

The general approach to fault tolerance is to use redundancy. Three kinds are possible: information redundancy, time redundancy, and physical redundancy. With information redundancy, extra bits are added to allow recovery from garbled bits. For example, a Hamming code can be added to transmitted data to recover from noise on the transmission line.

With time redundancy, an action is performed, and then, if need be, it is performed again. Using the atomic transactions described in Chap. 3 is an example of this approach. If a transaction aborts, it can be redone with no harm. Time redundancy is especially helpful when the faults are transient or intermittent.

With physical redundancy, extra equipment is added to make it possible for the system as a whole to tolerate the loss or malfunctioning of some components. For example, extra processors can be added to the system so that if a few of them crash, the system can still function correctly.

There are two ways to organize these extra processors: active replication and primary backup. Consider the case of a server. When active replication is used, all the processors are used all the time as servers (in parallel) in order to hide faults completely. In contrast, the primary backup scheme just uses one processor as a server, replacing it with a backup if it fails.

We will discuss these two strategies below. For both of them, the issues are:

1. The degree of replication required.

2. The average and worst-case performance in the absence of faults.

3. The average and worst-case performance when a fault occurs.

Theoretical analyses of many fault-tolerant systems can be done in these terms. For more information, see (Schneider, 1990; and Budhiraja et al., 1993).

4.5.5. Fault Tolerance Using Active Replication

Active replication is a well-known technique for providing fault tolerance using physical redundancy. It is used in biology (mammals have two eyes, two ears, two lungs, etc.), aircraft (747s have four engines but can fly on three), and sports (multiple referees in case one misses an event). Some authors refer to active replication as the **state machine approach**.

It has also been used for fault tolerance in electronic circuits for years. Consider, for example, the circuit of Fig. 4-21(a). Here signals pass through devices A, B, and C, in sequence. If one of them is faulty, the final result will probably be wrong.

In Fig. 4-21(b), each device is replicated three times. Following each stage in the circuit is a triplicated voter. Each voter is a circuit that has three inputs and one output. If two or three of the inputs are the same, the output is equal to that input. If all three inputs are different, the output is undefined. This kind of design is known as **TMR (Triple Modular Redundancy)**.

Suppose element A_2 fails. Each of the voters, V_1, V_2, and V_3 gets two good

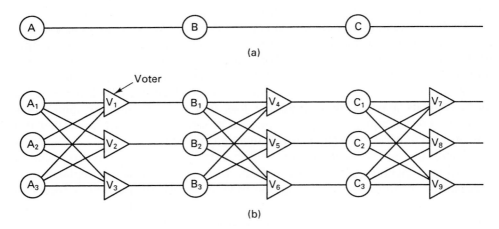

Fig. 4-21. Triple modular redundancy.

(identical) inputs and one rogue input, and each of them outputs the correct value to the second stage. In essence, the effect of A_2 failing is completed masked, so that the inputs to B_1, B_2, and B_3 are exactly the same as they would have been had no fault occurred.

Now consider what happens if B_3 and C_1 are also faulty, in addition to A_2. These effects are also masked, so the three final outputs are still correct.

At first it may not be obvious why three voters are needed at each stage. After all, one voter could also detect and pass though the majority view. However, a voter is also a component and can also be faulty. Suppose, for example, that V_1 malfunctions. The input to B_1 will then be wrong, but as long as everything else works, B_2 and B_3 will produce the same output and V_4, V_5, and V_6 will all produce the correct result into stage three. A fault in V_1 is effectively no different than a fault in B_1. In both cases B_1 produces incorrect output, but in both cases it is voted down later.

Although not all fault-tolerant distributed operating systems use TMR, the technique is very general, and should give a clear feeling for what a fault-tolerant system is, as opposed to a system whose individual components are highly reliable but whose organization is not fault tolerant. Of course, TMR can be applied recursively, for example, to make a chip highly reliable by using TMR inside it, unknown to the designers who use the chip.

Getting back to fault tolerance in general and active replication in particular, in many systems, servers act like big finite-state machines: they accept requests and produce replies. Read requests do not change the state of the server, but write requests do. If each client request is sent to each server, and they all are received and processed in the same order, then after processing each one, all nonfaulty servers will be in exactly the same state and will give the same replies. The client or voter can combine all the results to mask faults.

An important issue is how much replication is needed. The answer depends on the amount of fault tolerance desired. A system is said to be **k fault tolerant** if it can survive faults in k components and still meet its specifications. If the components, say processors, fail silently, then having $k + 1$ of them is enough to provide k fault tolerance. If k of them simply stop, then the answer from the other one can be used.

On the other hand, if the processors exhibit Byzantine failures, continuing to run when sick and sending out erroneous or random replies, a minimum of $2k + 1$ processors are needed to achieve k fault tolerance. In the worst case, the k failing processors could accidentally (or even intentionally) generate the same reply. However, the remaining $k + 1$ will also produce the same answer, so the client or voter can just believe the majority.

Of course, in theory it is fine to say that a system is k fault tolerant and just let the $k + 1$ identical replies outvote the k identical replies, but in practice it is hard to imagine circumstances in which one can say with certainty that k processors can fail but $k + 1$ processors cannot fail. Thus even in a fault-tolerant system some kind of statistical analysis may be needed.

An implicit precondition for this finite state machine model to be relevant is that all requests arrive at all servers in the same order, sometimes called the **atomic broadcast problem**. Actually, this condition can be relaxed slightly, since reads do not matter and some writes may commute, but the general problem remains. One way to make sure that all requests are processed in the same order at all servers is to number them globally. Various protocols have been devised to accomplish this goal. For example, all requests could first be sent to a global number server to get a serial number, but then provision would have to be made for the failure of this server (e.g., by making it internally fault tolerant).

Another possibility is to use Lamport's logical clocks, as described in Chap. 3. If each message sent to a server is tagged with a timestamp, and servers process all requests in timestamp order, all requests will be processed in the same order at all servers. The trouble with this method is that when a server receives a request, it does not know whether any earlier requests are currently under way. In fact, most timestamp solutions suffer from this problem. In short, active replication is not a trivial matter. Schneider (1990) discusses the problems and solutions in some detail.

4.5.6. Fault Tolerance Using Primary Backup

The essential idea of the primary-backup method is that at any one instant, one server is the primary and does all the work. If the primary fails, the backup takes over. Ideally, the cutover should take place in a clean way and be noticed only by the client operating system, not by the application programs. Like active replication, this scheme is widely used in the world. Some examples are government (the Vice President), aviation (co-pilots), automobiles (spare tires), and diesel-powered electrical generators in hospital operating rooms.

Primary-backup fault tolerance has two major advantages over active replication. First, it is simpler during normal operation since messages go to just one server (the primary) and not to a whole group. The problems associated with ordering these messages also disappear. Second, in practice it requires fewer machines, because at any instant one primary and one backup is needed (although when a backup is put into service as a primary, a new backup is needed instantly). On the downside, it works poorly in the presence of Byzantine failures in which the primary erroneously claims to be working perfectly. Also, recovery from a primary failure can be complex and time consuming.

As an example of the primary-backup solution, consider the simple protocol of Fig. 4-22 in which a write operation is depicted. The client sends a message to the primary, which does the work and then sends an update message to the backup. When the backup gets the message, it does the work and then sends an acknowledgement back to the primary. When the acknowledgement arrives, the primary sends the reply to the client.

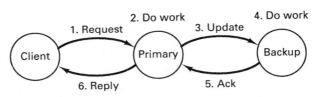

Fig. 4-22. A simple primary-backup protocol on a write operation.

Now let us consider the effect of a primary crash at various moments during an RPC. If the primary crashes before doing the work (step 2), no harm is done. The client will time out and retry. If it tries often enough, it will eventually get the backup and the work will be done exactly once. If the primary crashes after doing the work but before sending the update, when the backup takes over and the request comes in again, the work will be done a second time. If the work has side effects, this could be a problem. If the primary crashes after step 4 but before step 6, the work may end up being done three times, once by the primary, once by the backup as a result of step 3, and once after the backup becomes the primary. If requests carry identifiers, it may be possible to ensure that the work is done only twice, but getting it done exactly once is difficult to impossible.

One theoretical and practical problem with the primary-backup approach is when to cut over from the primary to the backup. In the protocol above, the backup could send: "Are you alive?" messages periodically to the primary. If the primary fails to respond within a certain time, the backup would take over.

However, what happens if the primary has not crashed, but is merely slow (i.e., we have an asynchronous system)? There is no way to distinguish between a slow primary and one that has gone down. Yet there is a need to make sure that when the backup takes over, the primary really stops trying to act like the primary. Ideally the backup and primary should have a protocol to discuss this, but it is hard to negotiate with the dead. The best solution is a hardware mechanism in which the backup can forcibly stop or reboot the primary. Note that all primary-backup schemes require agreement, which is tricky to achieve, whereas active replication does not always require an agreement protocol (e.g., TMR).

A variant of the approach of Fig. 4-22 uses a dual-ported disk shared between the primary and secondary. In this configuration, when the primary gets a request, it writes the request to disk before doing any work and also writes the results to disk. No messages to or from the backup are needed. If the primary crashes, the backup can see the state of the world by reading the disk. The disadvantage of this scheme is that there is only one disk, so if that fails, everything is lost. Of course, at the cost of extra equipment and performance, the disk could also be replicated and all writes could be done to both disks.

4.5.7. Agreement in Faulty Systems

In many distributed systems there is a need to have processes agree on something. Examples are electing a coordinator, deciding whether to commit a transaction or not, dividing up tasks among workers, synchronization, and so on. When the communication and processors are all perfect, reaching such agreement is often straightforward, but when they are not, problems arise. In this section we will look at some of the problems and their solutions (or lack thereof).

The general goal of distributed agreement algorithms is to have all the non-faulty processors reach consensus on some issue, and do that within a finite number of steps. Different cases are possible depending on system parameters, including:

1. Are messages delivered reliably all the time?

2. Can processes crash, and if so, fail-silent or Byzantine?

3. Is the system synchronous or asynchronous?

Before considering the case of faulty processors, let us look at the "easy" case of perfect processors but communication lines that can lose messages. There is a famous problem, known as the **two-army problem**, which illustrates the difficulty of getting even two perfect processors to reach agreement about 1 bit of information. The red army, with 5000 troops, is encamped in a valley. Two blue armies, each 3000 strong, are encamped on the surrounding hillsides overlooking the valley. If the two blue armies can coordinate their attacks on the red army, they will be victorious. However, if either one attacks by itself it will be slaughtered. The goal of the blue armies is to reach agreement about attacking. The catch is that they can only communicate using an unreliable channel: sending a messenger who is subject to capture by the red army.

Suppose that the commander of blue army 1, General Alexander, sends a message to the commander of blue army 2, General Bonaparte, reading: "I have a plan—let's attack at dawn tomorrow." The messenger gets through and Bonaparte sends him back with a note saying: "Splendid idea, Alex. See you at dawn tomorrow." The messenger gets back to his base safely, delivers his messages, and Alexander tells his troops to prepare for battle at dawn.

However, later that day, Alexander realizes that Bonaparte does not know if the messenger got back safely and not knowing this, may not dare to attack. Consequently, Alexander tells the messenger to go tell Bonaparte that his (Bonaparte's) message arrived and that the battle is set.

Once again the messenger gets through and delivers the acknowledgement. But now Bonaparte worries that Alexander does not know if the acknowledgement got through. He reasons that if Bonaparte thinks that the messenger was captured, he will not be sure about his (Alexander's) plans, and may not risk the attack, so he sends the messenger back again.

Even if the messenger makes it through every time, it is easy to show that Alexander and Bonaparte will never reach agreement, no matter how many acknowledgements they send. Assume that there is some protocol that terminates in a finite number of steps. Remove any extra steps at the end to get the minimum protocol that works. Some message is now the last one and it is essential to the agreement (because this is the minimum protocol). If this message fails to arrive, the war is off.

However, the sender of the last message does not know if the last message arrived. If it did not, the protocol did not complete and the other general will not attack. Thus the sender of the last message cannot know if the war is scheduled or not, and hence cannot safely commit his troops. Since the receiver of the last message knows the sender cannot be sure, he will not risk certain death either, and there is no agreement. Even with nonfaulty processors (generals), agreement between even two processes is not possible in the face of unreliable communication.

Now let us assume that the communication is perfect but the processors are not. The classical problem here also occurs in a military setting and is called the **Byzantine generals problem**. In this problem the red army is still encamped in the valley, but n blue generals all head armies on the nearby hills. Communication is done pairwise by telephone and is perfect, but m of the generals are traitors (faulty) and are actively trying to prevent the loyal generals from reaching agreement by feeding them incorrect and contradictory information (to model malfunctioning processors). The question is now whether the loyal generals can still reach agreement.

For the sake of generality, we will define agreement in a slightly different way here. Each general is assumed to know how many troops he has. The goal of the problem is for the generals to exchange troop strengths, so that at the end of the algorithm, each general has a vector of length n corresponding to all the armies. If general i is loyal, then element i is his troop strength; otherwise, it is undefined.

A recursive algorithm was devised by Lamport et al. (1982) that solves this problem under certain conditions. In Fig. 4-23 we illustrate the working of the algorithm for the case of $n = 4$ and $m = 1$. For these parameters, the algorithm operates in four steps. In step one, every general sends a (reliable) message to every other general announcing his truth strength. Loyal generals tell the truth; traitors may tell every other general a different lie. In Fig. 4-23(a) we see that general 1 reports 1K troops, general 2 reports 2K troops, general 3 lies to everyone, giving x, y, and z, respectively, and general 4 reports 4K troops. In step 2, the results of the announcements of step 1 are collected together in the form of the vectors of Fig. 4-23(b).

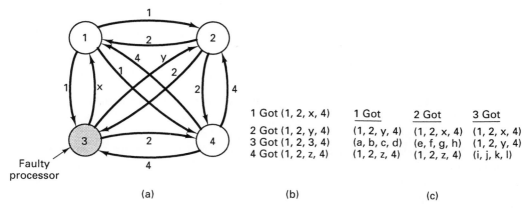

Fig. 4-23. The Byzantine generals problem for 3 loyal generals and 1 traitor. (a) The generals announce their troop strengths (in units of 1K). (b) The vectors that each general assembles based on (a). (c) The vectors that each general receives in step 2.

Step 3 consists of every general passing his vector from Fig. 4-23(b) to every other general. Here, too, general 3 lies through his teeth, inventing 12 new values, a through l. The results of step 3 are shown in Fig. 4-23(c). Finally, in step 4, each general examines the ith element of each of the newly received vectors. If any value has a majority, that value is put into the result vector. If no value has a majority, the corresponding element of the result vector is marked UNKNOWN. From Fig. 4-23(c) we see that generals 1, 2, and 4 all come to agreement on

(1, 2, UNKNOWN, 4)

which is the correct result. The traitor was not able to gum up the works.

Now let us revisit this problem for $m = 3$ and $n = 1$, that is, only two loyal generals and one traitor, as illustrated in Fig. 4-24. Here we see that in Fig. 4-24(c) neither of the loyal generals sees a majority for element 1, element 2, or element 3, so all of them are marked UNKNOWN. The algorithm has failed to produce agreement.

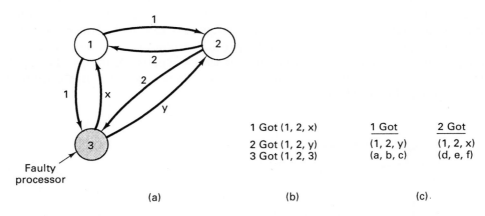

Faulty processor

1 Got (1, 2, x)	1 Got	2 Got
2 Got (1, 2, y)	(1, 2, y)	(1, 2, x)
3 Got (1, 2, 3)	(a, b, c)	(d, e, f)

(a)　　　　　(b)　　　　　(c)

Fig. 4-24. The same as Fig. 4-23, except now with 2 loyal generals and one traitor.

In their paper, Lamport et al. (1982) proved that in a system with m faulty processors, agreement can be achieved only if $2m + 1$ correctly functioning processors are present, for a total of $3m + 1$. Put in slightly different terms, agreement is possible only if *more* than two-thirds of the processors are working properly.

Worse yet, Fischer et al. (1985) proved that in a distributed system with asynchronous processors and unbounded transmission delays, no agreement is possible if even one processor is faulty (even if that one processor fails silently). The problem with asynchronous systems is that arbitrarily slow processors are indistinguishable from dead ones. Many other theoretical results are known about when agreement is possible and when it is not. Surveys of these results are given by Barborak et al. (1993) and Turek and Shasha (1992).

4.6. REAL-TIME DISTRIBUTED SYSTEMS

Fault-tolerant systems are not the only kind of specialized distributed systems. The real-time systems form another category. Sometimes these two are combined to give fault-tolerant real-time systems. In this section we will examine various aspects of real-time distributed systems. For additional material, see for example, (Burns and Wellings, 1990; Klein et al., 1994; and Shin, 1991).

4.6.1. What Is a Real-Time System?

For most programs, correctness depends only on the logical sequence of instructions executed, not when they are executed. If a C program correctly computes the double-precision floating-point square root function on a 200-MHz engineering workstation, it will also compute the function correctly on a 4.77-MHz 8088-based personal computer, only slower.

In contrast, **real-time programs** (and systems) interact with the external world in a way that involves time. When a stimulus appears, the system must respond to it in a certain way and before a certain deadline. If it delivers the correct answer, but after the deadline, the system is regarded as having failed. *When* the answer is produced is as important as *which* answer is produced.

Consider a simple example. An audio compact disk player consists of a CPU that takes the bits arriving from the disk and processes them to generate music. Suppose that the CPU is just barely fast enough to do the job. Now imagine that a competitor decides to build a cheaper player using a CPU running at one-third the speed. If it buffers all the incoming bits and plays them back at one-third the expected speed, people will wince at the sound, and if it only plays every third note, the audience will not be wildly ecstatic either. Unlike the earlier square root example, time is inherently part of the specification of correctness here.

Many other applications involving the external world are also inherently real time. Examples include computers embedded in television sets and video recorders, computers controlling aircraft ailerons and other parts (so called fly-by-wire), automobile subsystems controlled by computers (drive-by-wire?), military computers controlling guided antitank missiles (shoot-by-wire?), computerized air traffic control systems, scientific experiments ranging from particle accelerators to psychology lab mice with electrodes in their brains, automated factories, telephone switches, robots, medical intensive care units, CAT scanners, automatic stock trading systems, and numerous others.

Many real-time applications and systems are highly structured, much more so than general-purpose distributed systems. Typically, an external device (possibly a clock) generates a stimulus for the computer, which must then perform certain actions before a deadline. When the required work has been completed, the system becomes idle until the next stimulus arrives.

Frequently, the stimulii are **periodic**, with a stimulus occurring regularly every ΔT seconds, such as a computer in a TV set or VCR getting a new frame every 1/60 of a second. Sometimes stimulii are **aperiodic**, meaning that they are recurrent, but not regular, as in the arrival of an aircraft in a air traffic controller's air space. Finally, some stimulii are **sporadic** (unexpected), such as a device overheating.

Even in a largely periodic system, a complication is that there may be many types of events, such as video input, audio input, and motor drive management, each with its own period and required actions. Figure 4-25 depicts a situation with three periodic event streams, A, B, and C, plus one sporadic event, X.

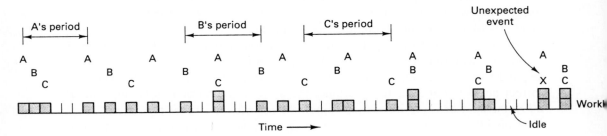

Fig. 4-25. Superposition of three event streams plus one sporadic event.

Despite the fact that the CPU may have to deal with multiple event streams, it is not acceptable for it to say: It is true that I missed event B, but it is not my fault—I was still working on A when B happened. While it is not hard to manage two or three input streams with priority interrupts, as applications get larger and more complex (e.g., automated factory assembly lines with thousands of robots), it will become more and more difficult for one machine to meet all the deadlines and other real-time constraints.

Consequently, some designers are experimenting with the idea of putting a dedicated microprocessor in front of each real-time device to accept output from it whenever it has something to say, and give it input at whatever speed it requires. Of course, this does not make the real-time character go away, but instead gives rise to a distributed real-time system, with its own unique characteristics and challenges (e.g., real-time communication).

Distributed real-time systems can often be structured as illustrated in Fig. 4-26. Here we see a collection of computers connected by a network. Some of these are connected to external devices that produce or accept data or expect to be controlled in real time. The computers may be tiny microcontrollers built into the devices, or stand-alone machines. In both cases they usually have sensors for receiving signals from the devices and/or actuators for sending signals to them. The sensors and actuators may be digital or analog.

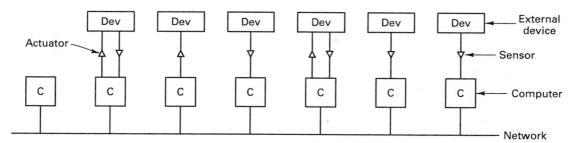

Fig. 4-26. A distributed real-time computer system.

Real-time systems are generally split into two types depending on how serious their deadlines are and the consequences of missing one. These are:

1. Soft real-time systems.

2. Hard real-time systems.

Soft real-time means that missing an occasional deadline is all right. For example, a telephone switch might be permitted to lose or misroute one call in 10^5 under overload conditions and still be within specification. In contrast, even a single missed deadline in a **hard real-time** system is unacceptable, as this might lead to loss of life or an environmental catastrophe. In practice, there are also intermediate systems where missing a deadline means you have to kill off the current activity, but the consequence is not fatal. For example, if a soda bottle on a conveyor belt has passed by the nozzle, there is no point in continuing to squirt soda at it, but the results are not fatal. Also, in some real-time systems, some subsystems are hard real time whereas others are soft real time.

Real-time systems have been around for decades, so there is a considerable amount of folk wisdom accumulated about them, most of it wrong. Stankovic (1988) has pointed out some of these myths, the worst of which are summarized here.

Myth 1: Real-time systems are about writing device drivers in assembly code.

This was perhaps true in the 1970s for real-time systems consisting of a few instruments attached to a minicomputer, but current real-time systems are too complicated to trust to assembly language and writing the device drivers is the least of a real-time system designer's worries.

Myth 2: Real-time computing is fast computing.

Not necessarily. A computer-controlled telescope may have to track stars or galaxies in real time, but the apparent rotation of the heavens is only 15 degrees of arc per hour of time, not especially fast. Here accuracy is what counts.

Myth 3: Fast computers will make real-time system obsolete.

No. They just encourage people to build real-time systems that were previously beyond the state-of-the-art. Cardiologists would love to have an MRI scanner that shows a beating heart inside an exercising patient in real time. When they get that, they will ask for it in three dimensions, in full color, and with the possibility of zooming in and out. Furthermore, making systems faster by using multiple processors introduces new communication, synchronization, and scheduling problems that have to be solved.

4.6.2. Design Issues

Real-time distributed systems have some unique design issues. In this section we will examine some of the most important ones.

Clock Synchronization

The first issue is the maintenance of time itself. With multiple computers, each having its own local clock, keeping the clocks in synchrony is a key issue. We examined this point in Chap. 3, so we will not repeat that discussion here.

Event-Triggered versus Time-Triggered Systems

In an **event-triggered real-time system**, when a significant event in the outside world happens, it is detected by some sensor, which then causes the attached CPU to get an interrupt. Event-triggered systems are thus interrupt driven. Most real-time systems work this way. For soft real-time systems with lots of computing power to spare, this approach is simple, works well, and is still widely used. Even for more complex systems, it works well if the compiler can analyze the program and know all there is to know about the system behavior once an event happens, even if it cannot tell when the event will happen.

The main problem with event-triggered systems is that they can fail under conditions of heavy load, that is, when many events are happening at once. Consider, for example, what happens when a pipe ruptures in a computer-controlled nuclear reactor. Temperature alarms, pressure alarms, radioactivity alarms, and other alarms will all go off at once, causing massive interrupts. This **event shower** may overwhelm the computing system and bring it down, potentially causing problems far more serious than the rupture of a single pipe.

An alternative design that does not suffer from this problem is the **time-triggered real-time system**. In this kind of system, a clock interrupt occurs every ΔT milliseconds. At each clock tick (selected) sensors are sampled and (certain) actuators are driven. No interrupts occur other than clock ticks.

In the ruptured pipe example given above, the system would become aware of the problem at the first clock tick after the event, but the interrupt load would not change on account of the problem, so the system would not become overloaded. Being able to operate normally in times of crisis increases the chances of dealing successfully with the crisis.

It goes without saying that ΔT must be chosen with extreme care. If it is too small, the system will get many clock interrupts and waste too much time fielding them. If it is too large, serious events may not be noticed until it is too late. Also, the decision about which sensors to check on every clock tick, and which to check on every other clock tick, and so on, is critical. Finally, some events may be shorter than a clock tick, so they must be saved to avoid losing them. They can be preserved electrically by latch circuits or by microprocessors embedded in the external devices.

As an example of the difference between these two approaches, consider the design of an elevator controller in a 100-story building. Suppose that the elevator is sitting peacefully on the 60th floor waiting for customers. Then someone pushes the call button on the first floor. Just 100 msec later, someone else pushes the call button on the 100th floor. In an event-triggered system, the first call generates an interrupt, which causes the elevator to take off downward. The second call comes in after the decision to go down has already been made, so it is noted for future reference, but the elevator continues on down.

Now consider a time-triggered elevator controller that samples every 500 msec. If both calls fall within one sampling period, the controller will have to make a decision, for example, using the nearest-customer-first rule, in which case it will go up.

In summary, event-triggered designs give faster response at low load but more overhead and chance of failure at high load. Time-trigger designs have the opposite properties and are furthermore only suitable in a relatively static environment in which a great deal is known about system behavior in advance. Which one is better depends on the application. In any event, we note that there is much lively controversy over this subject in real-time circles.

Predictability

One of the most important properties of any real-time system is that its behavior be predictable. Ideally, it should be clear at design time that the system can meet all of its deadlines, even at peak load. Statistical analyses of behavior assuming independent events are often misleading because there may be unsuspected correlations between events, as between the temperature, pressure, and radioactivity alarms in the ruptured pipe example above.

Most distributed system designers are used to thinking in terms of independent users accessing shared files at random or numerous travel agents accessing a shared airline data base at unpredictable times. Fortunately, this kind of chance behavior rarely holds in a real-time system. More often, it is known that when event E is detected, process X should be run, followed by processes Y and Z, in either order or in parallel. Furthermore, it is often known (or should be known) what the worst-case behavior of these processes is. For example, if it is known that X needs 50 msec, Y and Z need 60 msec each, and process startup takes 5 msec, then it can be guaranteed in advance that the system can flawlessly handle five periodic type E events per second in the absence of any other work. This kind of reasoning and modeling leads to a deterministic rather than a stochastic system.

Fault Tolerance

Many real-time systems control safety-critical devices in vehicles, hospitals, and power plants, so fault tolerance is frequently an issue. Active replication is sometimes used, but only if it can be done without extensive (and thus time-consuming) protocols to get everyone to agree on everything all the time. Primary-backup schemes are less popular because deadlines may be missed during cutover after the primary fails. A hybrid approach is to follow the leader, in which one machine makes all the decisions, but the others just do what it says to do without discussion, ready to take over at a moment's notice.

In a safety-critical system, it is especially important that the system be able to handle the worst-case scenario. It is not enough to say that the probability of three components failing at once is so low that it can be ignored. Failures are not always independent. For example, during a sudden electric power failure, everyone grabs the telephone, possibly causing the phone system to overload, even though it has its own independent power generation system. Furthermore, the peak load on the system often occurs precisely at the moment when the maximum number of components have failed because much of the traffic is related to reporting the failures. Consequently, fault-tolerant real-time systems must be able to cope with the maximum number of faults and the maximum load at the same time.

Some real-time systems have the property that they can be stopped cold when a serious failure occurs. For instance, when a railroad signaling system unexpectedly blacks out, it may be possible for the control system to tell every train to stop immediately. If the system design always spaces trains far enough apart and all trains start braking more-or-less simultaneously, it will be possible to avert disaster and the system can recover gradually when the power comes back on. A system that can halt operation like this without danger is said to be **fail-safe**.

Language Support

While many real-time systems and applications are programmed in general-purpose languages such as C, specialized real-time languages can potentially be of great assistance. For example, in such a language, it should be easy to express the work as a collection of short tasks (e.g., lightweight processes or threads) that can be scheduled independently, subject to user-defined precedence and mutual exclusion constraints.

The language should be designed so that the maximum execution time of every task can be computed at compile time. This requirement means that the language cannot support general **while** loops. Iteration must be done using **for** loops with constant parameters. Recursion cannot be tolerated either (it is beginning to look like FORTRAN has a use after all). Even these restrictions may not be enough to make it possible to calculate the execution time of each task in advance since cache misses, page faults, and cycle stealing by DMA channels all affect performance, but they are a start.

Real-time languages need a way to deal with time itself. To start with, a special variable, *clock*, should be available, containing the current time in ticks. However, one has to be careful about the unit that time is expressed in. The finer the resolution, the faster *clock* will overflow. If it is a 32-bit integer, for example, the range for various resolutions is shown in Fig. 4-27. Ideally, the clock should be 64 bits wide and have a 1 nsec resolution.

Clock resolution	Range
1 nsec	4 seconds
1 μsec	72 minutes
1 msec	50 days
1 sec	136 years

Fig. 4-27. Range of a 32-bit clock before overflowing for various resolutions.

The language should have a way to express minimum and maximum delays. In Ada®, for example, there is a delay statement that specifies a minimum value that a process must be suspended. However, the actual delay may be more by an unbounded amount. There is no way to give an upper bound or a time interval in which the delay is required to fall.

There should also be a way to express what to do if an expected event does not occur within a certain interval. For example, if a process blocks on a semaphore for more than a certain time, it should be possible to time out and be released. Similarly, if a message is sent, but no reply is forthcoming fast enough, the sender should be able to specify that it is to be deblocked after k msec.

Finally, since periodic events play such a big role in real-time systems, it would be useful to have a statement of the form

```
every (25 msec) { ... }
```

that causes the statements within the curly brackets to be executed every 25 msec. Better yet, if a task contains several such statements, the compiler should be able to compute what percentage of the CPU time is required by each one, and from these data compute the minimum number of machines needed to run the entire program and how to assign processes to machines.

4.6.3. Real-Time Communication

Communication in real-time distributed systems is different from communication in other distributed systems. While high performance is always welcome, predictability and determinism are the real keys to success. In this section we will look at some real-time communication issues, for both LANs and WANs. Finally, we will examine one example system in some detail to show how it differs from conventional (i.e., non-real-time) distributed systems. Alternative approaches are described in (Malcolm and Zhao, 1994; and Ramanathan and Shin, 1992)

Achieving predictability in a distributed system means that communication between processors must also be predictable. LAN protocols that are inherently stochastic, such as Ethernet, are unacceptable because they do not provide a known upper bound on transmission time. A machine wanting to send a packet on an Ethernet may collide with one or more other machines. All machines then wait a random time and then try again, but these transmissions may also collide, and so on. Consequently, it is not possible to give a worst-case bound on packet transmission in advance.

As a contrast to Ethernet, consider a token ring LAN. Whenever a processor has a packet to send, it waits for the circulating token to pass by, then it captures the token, sends its packet, and puts the token back on the ring so that the next machine downstream gets the opportunity to seize it. Assuming that each of the k machines on the ring is allowed to send at most one n-byte packet per token capture, it can be guaranteed that an urgent packet arriving anywhere in the system can always be transmitted within kn byte times. This is the kind of upper bound that a real-time distributed system needs.

Token rings can also handle traffic consisting of multiple priority classes. The goal here is to ensure that if a high-priority packet is waiting for transmission, it will be sent before any low-priority packets that its neighbors may have. For example, it is possible to add a reservation field to each packet, which can be increased by any processor as the packet goes by. When the packet has gone all the way around, the reservation field indicates the priority class of the next packet. When the current sender is finished transmitting, it regenerates a token bearing this priority class. Only processors with a pending packet of this class may capture it, and then only to send one packet. Of course, this scheme means that the upper bound of *kn* byte times now applies only to packets of the highest priority class.

An alternative to a token ring is the **TDMA (Time Division Multiple Access)** protocol shown in Fig. 4-28. Here traffic is organized in fixed-size frames, each of which contains *n* slots. Each slot is assigned to one processor, which may use it to transmit a packet when its time comes. In this way collisions are avoided, the delay is bounded, and each processor gets a guaranteed fraction of the bandwidth, depending on how many slots per frame it has been assigned.

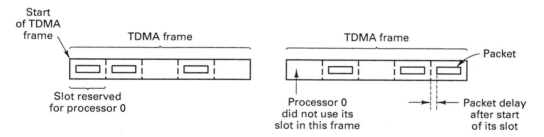

Fig. 4-28. TDMA (Time Division Multiple Access) frames.

Real-time distributed systems operating over wide-area networks have the same need for predictability as those confined to a room or building. The communication in these systems is invariably connection oriented. Often, there is the ability to establish **real-time connections** between distant machines. When such a connection is established, the quality of service is negotiated in advance between the network users and the network provider. This quality may involve a guaranteed maximum delay, maximum jitter (variance of packet delivery times), minimum bandwidth, and other parameters. To make good on its guarantees, the network may have to reserve memory buffers, table entries, CPU cycles, link capacity, and other resources for this connection throughout its lifetime. The user is likely to be charged for these resources, whether or not they are used, since they are not available to other connections.

A potential problem with wide-area real-time distributed systems is their relatively high packet loss rates. Standard protocols deal with packet loss by setting a timer when each packet is transmitted. If the timer goes off before the acknowledgement is received, the packet is sent again. In real-time systems, this kind of unbounded transmission delay is rarely acceptable.

One easy solution is for the sender *always* to transmit each packet two (or more) times, preferably over independent connections if that option is available. Although this scheme wastes at least half the bandwidth, if one packet in, say, 10^5 is lost, only one time in 10^{10} will both copies be lost. If a packet takes a millisecond, this works out to one lost packet every four months. With three transmissions, one packet is lost every 30,000 years. The net effect of multiple transmissions of every packet right from the start is a low and bounded delay virtually all the time.

The Time-Triggered Protocol

On account of the constraints on real-time distributed systems, their protocols are often quite unusual. In this section we will examine one such protocol, **TTP (Time-Triggered Protocol)** (Kopetz and Grunsteidl, 1994), which is as different from the Ethernet protocol as a Victorian drawing room is from a Wild West saloon. TTP is used in the MARS real-time system (Kopetz et al., 1989) and is intertwined with it in many ways, so we will refer to properties of MARS where necessary.

A node in MARS consists of at least one CPU, but often two or three work together to present the image of a single fault-tolerant, fail-silent node to the outside world. The nodes in MARS are connected by two reliable and independent TDMA broadcast networks. All packets are sent on both networks in parallel. The expected loss rate is one packet every 30 million years.

MARS is a time-triggered system, so clock synchronization is critical. Time is discrete, with clock ticks generally occurring every microsecond. TTP assumes that all the clocks are synchronized with a precision on the order of tens of microseconds. This precision is possible because the protocol itself provides continuous clock synchronization and has been designed to allow it to be done in hardware to extremely high precision.

All nodes in MARS are aware of the programs being run on all the other nodes. In particular, all nodes know when a packet is to be sent by another node and can detect its presence or absence easily. Since packets are assumed not to be lost (see above), the absence of a packet at a moment when one is expected means that the sending node has crashed.

For example, suppose that some exceptional event is detected and a packet is broadcast to tell everyone else about it. Node 6 is expected to make some computation and then broadcast a reply after 2 msec in slot 15 of the TDMA frame. If the message is not forthcoming in the expected slot, the other nodes assume that node 6 has gone down, and take whatever steps are necessary to recover from its failure. This tight bound and instant consensus eliminate the need for time-consuming agreement protocols and allow the system to be both fault tolerant and operate in real time.

Every node maintains the global state of the system. These states are required to be identical everywhere. It is a serious (and detectable) error if someone is out of step with the rest. The global state consists of three components:

1.   The current mode.

2.   The global time.

3.   A bit map giving the current system membership.

The mode is defined by the application and has to do with which phase the system is in. For example, in a space application, the countdown, launch, flight, and landing might all be separate modes. Each mode has its own set of processes and the order in which they run, list of participating nodes, TDMA slot assignments, message names and formats, and legal successor modes.

The second field in the global state is the global time. Its granularity is application defined, but in any event must be coarse enough that all nodes agree on it. The third field keeps track of which nodes are up and which are down.

Unlike the OSI and Internet protocol suites, the TTP protocol consists of a single layer that handles end-to-end data transport, clock synchronization, and membership management. A typical packet format is illustrated in Fig. 4-29. It consists of a start-of-packet field, a control field, a data field, and a CRC field.

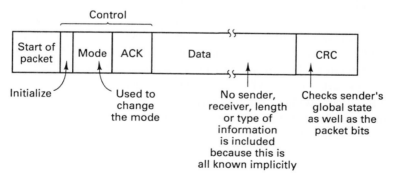

Fig. 4-29. A typical TTP packet.

The control field contains a bit used to initialize the system (more about which later), a subfield for changing the current mode, and a subfield for acknowledging the packets sent by the preceding node (according to the current membership list). The purpose of this field is to let the previous node know that it is functioning correctly and its packets are getting onto the network as they should be. If an expected acknowledgement is lacking, all nodes mark the expected sender as down and expunge it from the membership bit maps in their current state. The rejected node is expected to go along with being excommunicated without protest.

The data field contains whatever data are required. The CRC field is quite unusual, as it provides a checksum over not only the packet contents, but over the sender's global state as well. This means that if a sender has an incorrect global state, the CRC of any packets it sends will not agree with the values the receivers compute using their states. The next sender will not acknowledge the packet, and all nodes, including the one with the bad state, mark it as down in their membership bit maps.

Periodically, a packet with the initialization bit is broadcast. This packet also contains the current global state. Any node that is marked as not being a member, but which is supposed to be a member in this mode, can now join as a passive member. If a node is supposed to be a member, it has a TDMA slot assigned, so there is no problem of when to respond (in its own TDMA slot). Once its packet has been acknowledged, all the other nodes mark it as being active (operational) again.

A final interesting aspect of the protocol is the way it handles clock synchronization. Because each node knows the time when TDMA frames start and the position of its slot within the frame, it knows exactly when to begin its packet. This scheme avoids collisions. However, it also contains valuable timing information. If a packet begins n microseconds before or after it is supposed to, each other node can detect this tardiness and use it as an estimate of the skew between its clock and the sender's clock. By monitoring the starting position of every packet, a node might learn, for example, that every other node appears to be starting its transmissions 10 microseconds too late. In this case it can reasonably conclude that its own clock is actually 10 microseconds fast and make the necessary correction. By keeping a running average of the earliness or lateness of all other packets, each node can adjust its clock continuously to keep it in sync with the others without running any special clock management protocol.

In summary, the unusual properties of TTP are the detection of lost packets by the receivers, not the senders, the automatic membership protocol, the CRC on the packet plus global state, and the way that clock synchronization is done.

4.6.4. Real-Time Scheduling

Real-time systems are frequently programmed as a collection of short tasks (processes or threads), each with a well-defined function and a well-bounded execution time. The response to a given stimulus may require multiple tasks to be run, generally with constraints on their execution order. In addition, a decision has to be made about which tasks to run on which processors. In this section we will deal with some of the issues concerning task scheduling in real-time systems.

Real-time scheduling algorithms can be characterized by the following parameters:

1. Hard real time versus soft real time.

2. Preemptive versus nonpreemptive scheduling.

3. Dynamic versus static.

4. Centralized versus decentralized.

Hard real-time algorithms must guarantee that all deadlines are met. Soft real-time algorithms can live with a best efforts approach. The most important case is hard real time.

Preemptive scheduling allows a task to be suspended temporarily when a higher-priority task arrives, resuming it later when no higher-priority tasks are available to run. Nonpreemptive scheduling runs each task to completion. Once a task is started, it continues to hold its processor until it is done. Both kinds of scheduling strategies are used.

Dynamic algorithms make their scheduling decisions during execution. When an event is detected, a dynamic preemptive algorithm decides on the spot whether to run the (first) task associated with the event or to continue running the current task. A dynamic nonpreemptive algorithm just notes that another task is runnable. When the current task finishes, a choice among the now-ready tasks is made.

With static algorithms, in contrast, the scheduling decisions, whether preemptive or not, are made in advance, before execution. When an event occurs, the runtime scheduler just looks in a table to see what to do.

Finally, scheduling can be centralized, with one machine collecting all the information and making all the decisions, or it can be decentralized, with each processor making its own decisions. In the centralized case, the assignment of tasks to processors can be made at the same time. In the decentralized case, assigning tasks to processors is distinct from deciding which of the tasks assigned to a given processor to run next.

A key question that all real-time system designers face is whether or not it is even possible to meet all the constraints. If a system has one processor and it gets 60 interrupts/sec, each requiring 50 msec of work, the designers have a Big Problem on their hands.

Suppose that a periodic real-time distributed system has m tasks and N processors to run them on. Let C_i be the CPU time needed by task i, and let P_i be its period, that is, the time between consecutive interrupts. To be feasible, the utilization of the system, μ, must be related to N by the equation

$$\mu = \sum_{i=1}^{m} \frac{C_i}{P_i} \leq N$$

For example, if a task is started every 20 msec and runs for 10 msec each time, it uses up 0.5 CPUs. Five such tasks would need three CPUs to do the job. A set of tasks that meets the foregoing requirement is said to be **schedulable**. Note that the equation above really gives a lower bound on the number of CPUs needed, since it ignores task switching time, message transport, and other sources of overhead, and assumes that optimal scheduling is possible.

In the following two sections we will look at dynamic and static scheduling, respectively, of sets of periodic tasks. For additional information, see (Ramamritham et al., 1990; and Schwan and Zhou, 1992).

Dynamic Scheduling

Let us look first at a few of the better-known dynamic scheduling algorithms—algorithms that decide during program execution which task to run next. The classic algorithm is the **rate monotonic algorithm** (Liu and Layland, 1973). It was designed for preemptively scheduling periodic tasks with no ordering or mutual exclusion constraints on a single processor. It works like this. In advance, each task is assigned a priority equal to its execution frequency. For example, a task run every 20 msec is assigned priority 50 and a task run every 100 msec is assigned priority 10. At run time, the scheduler always selects the highest priority task to run, preempting the current task if need be. Liu and Layland proved that this algorithm is optimal. They also proved that any set of tasks meeting the utilization condition

$$\mu = \sum_{i=1}^{m} \frac{C_i}{P_i} \leq m(2^{1/m} - 1)$$

is schedulable using the rate monotonic algorithm. The right-hand side converges to ln 2 (about 0.693) as $m \rightarrow \infty$. In practice, this limit is overly pessimistic; a set of tasks with μ as high as 0.88 can usually be scheduled.

A second popular preemptive dynamic algorithm is **earliest deadline first**. Whenever an event is detected, the scheduler adds it to the list of waiting tasks. This list is always keep sorted by deadline, closest deadline first. (For a periodic task, the deadline is the next occurrence.) The scheduler then just chooses the first task on the list, the one closest to its deadline. Like the rate monotonic algorithm, it produces optimal results, even for task sets with $\mu = 1$.

A third preemptive dynamic algorithm first computes for each task the amount of time it has to spare, called the **laxity** (slack). For a task that must finish in 200 msec but has another 150 msec to run, the laxity is 50 msec. This algorithm, called **least laxity**, chooses the task with the least laxity, that is, the one with the least breathing room.

None of the algorithms above are provably optimal in a distributed system, but they can be used as heuristics. Also, none of them takes into account order or mutex constraints, even on a uniprocessor, which makes them less useful in practice than they are in theory. Consequently, many practical systems use static scheduling when enough information is available. Not only can static algorithms take side constraints into account, but they have very low overhead at run time.

Static Scheduling

Static scheduling is done before the system starts operating. The input consists of a list of all the tasks and the times that each must run. The goal is to find an assignment of tasks to processors and for each processor, a static schedule giving the order in which the tasks are to be run. In theory, the scheduling algorithm can run an exhaustive search to find the optimal solution, but the search time is exponential in the number of tasks (Ullman, 1976), so heuristics of the type described above are generally used. Rather than simply give some additional heuristics here, we will go into one example in detail, to show the interplay of scheduling and communication in a real-time distributed system with nonpreemptive static scheduling (Kopetz et al., 1989).

Let us assume that every time a certain event is detected, task 1 is started on processor *A*, as shown in Fig. 4-30. This task, in turn, starts up additional tasks, both locally and on a second processor, *B*. For simplicity, we will assume that the assignment of tasks to processors is dictated by external considerations (which task needs access to which I/O device) and is not a parameter here. All tasks take 1 unit of CPU time.

Task 1 starts up tasks 2 and 3 on its machine, as well as task 7 on processor *B*. Each of these three tasks starts up another task, and so on, as illustrated. The arrows indicate messages being sent between tasks. In this simple example, it is perhaps easiest to think of $X \rightarrow Y$ as meaning that Y cannot start until a message from X has arrived. Some tasks, such as 8, require two messages before they may start. The cycle is completed when task 10 has run and generated the expected response to the initial stimulus.

After task 1 has completed, tasks 2 and 3 are both runnable. The scheduler has a choice of which one to schedule next. Suppose that it decides to schedule task 2 next. It then has a choice between tasks 3 and 4 as the successor to task 2. If it chooses task 3, it then has a choice between tasks 4 and 5 next. However, if

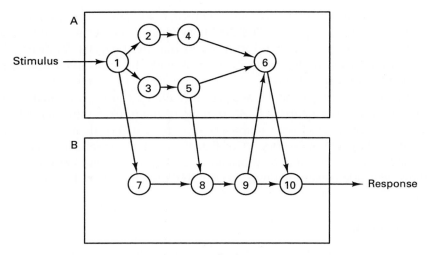

Fig. 4-30. Ten real-time tasks to be executed on two processors.

it chooses 4 instead of 3, it must run 3 following 4, because 6 is not enabled yet, and will not be until both 5 and 9 have run.

Meanwhile, activity is also occurring in parallel on processor *B*. As soon as task 1 has initiated it, task 7 can start on *B*, at the same time as either 2 or 3. When both 5 and 7 have finished, task 8 can be started, and so on. Note that task 6 requires input from 4, 5, and 9 to start, and produces output for 10.

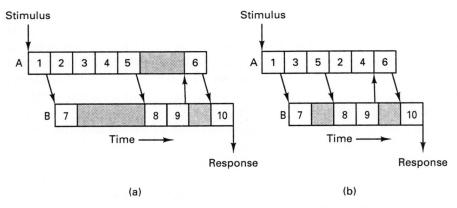

(a)   (b)

Fig. 4-31. Two possible schedules for the tasks of Fig. 4-30.

Two potential schedules are given in Fig. 4-31(a) and (b). Messages between tasks on different processors are depicted as arrows here; messages between tasks on the same machine are handled internally and are not shown. Of the two schedules illustrated, the one in Fig. 4-31(b) is a better choice because it allows task 5 to run early, thus making it possible for task 8 to start earlier. If task 5 is delayed significantly, as in Fig. 4-31(a), then tasks 8 and 9 are delayed, which also means that 6 and eventually 10 are delayed, too.

It is important to realize that with static scheduling, the decision of whether to use one of these schedules, or one of several alternatives is made by the scheduler *in advance*, before the system starts running. It analyzes the graph of Fig. 4-30, also using as input information about the running times of all the tasks, and then applies some heuristic to find a good schedule. Once a schedule has been selected, the choices made are incorporated into tables so that at run time a simple dispatcher can carry out the schedule with little overhead.

Now let us consider the problem of scheduling the same tasks again, but this time taking communication into account. We will use TDMA communication, with eight slots per TDMA frame. In this example, a TDMA slot is equal to one-fourth of a task execution time. We will arbitrarily assign slot 1 to processor *A* and slot 5 to processor *B*. The assignment of TDMA slots to processors is up to the static scheduler and may differ between program phases.

In Fig. 4-32 we show both schedules of Fig. 4-31, but now taking the use of TDMA slots into account. A task may not send a message until a slot owned by its processor comes up. Thus, task 5 may not send to task 8 until the first slot of the next TDMA frame occurs in rotation, requiring a delay in starting task 8 in Fig. 4-32(a) that was not present before.

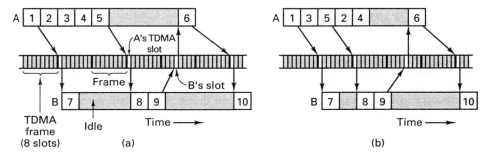

Fig. 4-32. Two schedules, including processing and communication.

The important thing to notice about this example is that the runtime behavior is completely deterministic, and known even before the program starts executing. As long as communication and processor errors do not occur, the system will always meet its real-time deadlines. Processor failures can be masked by having each node consist of two or more CPUs actively tracking each other. Some extra time may have to be statically allocated to each task interval to allow for recovery, if need be. Lost or garbled packets can be handled by having every one sent twice initially, either on disjoint networks or on one network by making the TDMA slots two packets wide.

It should be clear by now that real-time systems do not try to squeeze the last drop of performance out of the hardware, but rather use extra resources to make sure that the real-time constraints are met under all conditions. However, the relatively low use of the communication bandwidth in our example is not typical. It is a consequence of this example using only two processors with modest communication requirements. Practical real-time systems have many processors and extensive communication.

A Comparison of Dynamic versus Static Scheduling

The choice of dynamic or static scheduling is an important one and has far-reaching consequences for the system. Static scheduling is a good fit with a time-triggered design, and dynamic scheduling is a good fit for an event-triggered design. Static scheduling must be carefully planned in advance, with considerable effort going into choosing the various parameters. Dynamic scheduling does not require as much advance work, since scheduling decisions are made on-the-fly, during execution.

Dynamic scheduling can potentially make better use of resources than static scheduling. In the latter, the system must frequently be overdimensioned to have so much capacity that it can handle even the most unlikely cases. However, in a hard real-time system, wasting resources is often the price that must be paid to guarantee that all deadlines will be met.

On the other hand, given enough computing power, an optimal or nearly optimal schedule can be derived in advance for a static system. For an application such as reactor control, it may well be worth investing months of CPU time to find the best schedule. A dynamic system cannot afford the luxury of a complex scheduling calculation during execution, so to be safe, may have to be heavily overdimensioned as well, and even then, there is no guarantee that it will meet its specifications. Instead, extensive testing is required.

As a final thought, it should be pointed out that our discussion has simplified matters considerably. For example, tasks may need access to shared variables, so these have to be reserved in advance. Often there are scheduling constraints, which we have ignored. Finally, some systems do advance planning during run-time, making them hybrids between static and dynamic.

4.7. SUMMARY

Although threads are not an inherent feature of distributed operating systems, most of them have a threads package, so we have studied them in this chapter. A thread is a kind of lightweight process that shares an address space with one or more other threads. Each thread has its own program counter and stack and is scheduled independently of the other threads. When a thread makes a blocking system call, the other threads in the same address space are not affected. Threads packages can be implemented in either user space or by the kernel, but there are problems to be solved either way. The use of lightweight threads has led to some interesting results in lightweight RPC as well. Pop-up threads are also an important technique.

Two models of organizing the processors are commonly used: the workstation model and the processor pool model. In the former, each user has his own workstation, sometimes with the ability to run processes on idle workstations. In the latter, the entire computing facility is a shared resource. Processors are then allocated dynamically to users as needed and returned to the pool when the work is done. Hybrid models are also possible.

Given a collection of processors, some algorithm is needed for assigning processes to processors. Such algorithms can be deterministic or heuristic, centralized or distributed, optimal or suboptimal, local or global, and sender-initiated or receiver-initiated.

Although processes are normally scheduled independently, using co-scheduling, to make sure that processes that must communicate are running at the same time, performance can be improved.

Fault tolerance is important in many distributed systems. It can be achieved using triple modular redundancy, active replication, or primary-backup replication. The two-army problem cannot be solved in the presence of unreliable communication, but the Byzantine generals problem can be solved if more than two-thirds of the processors are nonfaulty.

Finally, real-time distributed systems are also important. They come in two varieties: soft real time and hard real time. Event-triggered systems are interrupt driven, whereas time-triggered systems sample the external devices at fixed intervals. Real-time communication must use predictable protocols, such as token rings or TDMA. Both dynamic and static scheduling of tasks is possible. Dynamic scheduling happens at run time; static scheduling happens in advance.

PROBLEMS

1. In this problem you are to compare reading a file using a single-threaded file server and a multithreaded server. It takes 15 msec to get a request for work, dispatch it, and do the rest of the necessary processing, assuming that the data needed are in the block cache. If a disk operation is needed, as is the case one-third of the time, an additional 75 msec is required, during which time the thread sleeps. How many requests/sec can the server handle if it is single threaded? If it is multithreaded?

2. In Fig. 4-3 the register set is listed as a per-thread rather than a per-process item. Why? After all, the machine has only one set of registers.

3. In the text, we described a multithreaded file server, showing why it is better than a single-threaded server and a finite-state machine server. Are there any circumstances in which a single-threaded server might be better? Give an example.

4. In the discussion on global variables in threads, we used a procedure *create_global* to allocate storage for a pointer to the variable, rather than the variable itself. Is this essential, or could the procedures work with the values themselves just as well?

5. Consider a system in which threads are implemented entirely in user space, with the runtime system getting a clock interrupt once a second. Suppose that a clock interrupt occurs while some thread is executing in the runtime system. What problem might occur? Can you suggest a way to solve it?

6. Suppose that an operating system does not have anything like the SELECT system call to see in advance if it is safe to read from a file, pipe, or device, but it does allow alarm clocks to be set that interrupt blocked system calls. Is it possible to implement a threads package in user space under these conditions? Discuss.

7. In a certain workstation-based system, the workstations have local disks that hold the system binaries. When a new binary is released, it is sent to each workstation. However, some workstations may be down (or switched off) when this happens. Devise an algorithm that allows the updating to be done automatically, even though workstations are occasionally down.

8. Can you think of any other kinds of files that can safely be stored on user workstations of the type described in the preceding problem?

9. Would the scheme of Bershad et al. to make local RPCs go faster also work in a system with only one thread per process? How about with Peregrine?

10. When two users examine the registry in Fig. 4-12 simultaneously, they may accidentally pick the same idle workstation. How can the algorithm be subtly changed to prevent this race?

11. Imagine that a process is running remotely on a previously idle workstation, which, like all the workstations, is diskless. For each of the following UNIX system calls, tell whether it has to be forwarded back to the home machine:

   (a) READ (get data from a file).
   (b) IOCTL (change the mode of the controlling terminal).
   (c) GETPID (return the process id).

12. Compute the response ratios for Fig. 4-15 using processor 1 as the benchmark processor. Which assignment minimizes the average response ratio?

13. In the discussion of processor allocation algorithms, we pointed out that one choice is between centralized and distributed and another is between optimal and suboptimal. Devise two optimal location algorithms, one centralized and one decentralized.

14. In Fig. 4-17 we see two different allocation schemes, with different amounts of network traffic. Are there any other allocations that are better still? Assume that no machine may run more than four processes.

15. The up-down algorithm described in the text is a centralized algorithm design to allocate processors fairly. Invent a centralized algorithm whose goal is not fairness but distributing the load uniformly.

16. When a certain distributed system is overloaded, it makes m attempts to find an idle workstation to offload work to. The probability of a workstation having k jobs is given by the Poisson formula

$$P(k) = \frac{\lambda^k e^{-\lambda}}{k!}$$

where λ is the mean number of jobs per workstation. What is the probability that an overloaded workstation finds an idle one (i.e., one with $k = 0$) in m attempts? Evaluate your answer numerically for $m = 3$ and values of λ from 1 to 4.

17. Using the data of Fig. 4-20, what is the longest UNIX pipeline that can be co-scheduled?

18. Can the model of triple modular redundancy described in the text handle Byzantine failures?

19. How many failed elements (devices plus voters) can Fig. 4-21 handle? Given an example of the worst case that can be masked.

20. Does TMR generalize to five elements per group instead of three? If so, what properties does it have?

21. Eloise lives at the Plaza Hotel. Her favorite activity is standing in the main lobby pushing the elevator. She can do this over and hour, for hours on end. The Plaza is installing a new elevator system. They can choose between a time-triggered system and an event-triggered system. Which one should they choose? Discuss.

22. A real-time system has periodic processes with the following computational requirements and periods:

    P1: 20 msec every 40 msec
    P2: 60 msec every 500 msec
    P3: 5 msec every 20 msec
    P4: 15 msec every 100 msec

    Is this system schedulable on one CPU?

23. Is it possible to determine the priorities that the rate monotonic algorithm would assign to the processes in the preceding problem? If so, what are they? If not, what information is lacking?

24. A network consists of two parallel wires: the forward link, on which packets travel from left to right, and the reverse link, on which they travel from right to left. A generator at the head of each wire generates a continuous stream of packet frames, each holding an empty/full bit (initially empty). All the computers are located between the two wires, attached to both. To send a packet, a computer determines which wire to use (depending on whether the destination is to the left or right of it), waits for an empty frame, puts a packet in it, and marks the frame as full. Does this network satisfy the requirements for a real-time system? Explain.

25. The assignment of processes to slots in Fig. 4-32 is arbitrary. Other assignments are also possible. Find an alternative assignment that improves the performance of the second example.

5

Distributed File Systems

A key component of any distributed system is the file system. As in single processor systems, in distributed systems the job of the file system is to store programs and data and make them available as needed. Many aspects of distributed file systems are similar to conventional file systems, so we will not repeat that material here. Instead, we will concentrate on those aspects of distributed file systems that are different from centralized ones.

To start with, in a distributed system, it is important to distinguish between the concepts of the file service and the file server. The **file service** is the specification of what the file system offers to its clients. It describes the primitives available, what parameters they take, and what actions they perform. To the clients, the file service defines precisely what service they can count on, but says nothing about how it is implemented. In effect, the file service specifies the file system's interface to the clients.

A **file server**, in contrast, is a process that runs on some machine and helps implement the file service. A system may have one file server or several. In particular, they should not know how many file servers there are and what the location or function of each one is. All they know is that when they call the procedures specified in the file service, the required work is performed somehow, and the required results are returned. In fact, the clients should not even know that the file service is distributed. Ideally, it should look the same as a normal single-processor file system.

Since a file server is normally just a user process (or sometimes a kernel process) running on some machine, a system may contain multiple file servers, each offering a different file service. For example, a distributed system may have two servers that offer UNIX file service and MS-DOS file service, respectively, with each user process using the one appropriate for it. In that way, it is possible to have a terminal with multiple windows, with UNIX programs running in some windows and MS-DOS programs running in other windows, with no conflicts. Whether the servers offer specific file services, such as UNIX or MS-DOS, or more general file services is up to the system designers. The type and number of file services available may even change as the system evolves.

5.1. DISTRIBUTED FILE SYSTEM DESIGN

A distributed file system typically has two reasonably distinct components: the true file service and the directory service. The former is concerned with the operations on individual files, such as reading, writing, and appending, whereas the latter is concerned with creating and managing directories, adding and deleting files from directories, and so on. In this section we will discuss the true file service interface; in the next one we will discuss the directory service interface.

5.1.1. The File Service Interface

For any file service, whether for a single processor or for a distributed system, the most fundamental issue is: What is a file? In many systems, such as UNIX and MS-DOS, a file is an uninterpreted sequence of bytes. The meaning and structure of the information in the files is entirely up to the application programs; the operating system is not interested.

On mainframes, however, many types of files exist, each with different properties. A file can be structured as a sequence of records, for example, with operating system calls to read or write a particular record. The record can usually be specified by giving either its record number (i.e., position within the file) or the value of some field. In the latter case, the operating system either maintains the file as a B-tree or other suitable data structure, or uses hash tables to locate records quickly. Since most distributed systems are intended for UNIX or MS-DOS environments, most file servers support the notion of a file as a sequence of bytes rather than as a sequence of keyed records.

A files can have **attributes**, which are pieces of information about the file but which are not part of the file itself. Typical attributes are the owner, size, creation date, and access permissions. The file service usually provides primitives to read and write some of the attributes. For example, it may be possible to change the access permissions but not the size (other than by appending data to the file). In a few advanced systems, it may be possible to create and manipulate user-defined attributes in addition to the standard ones.

Another important aspect of the file model is whether files can be modified after they have been created. Normally, they can be, but in some distributed systems, the only file operations are CREATE and READ. Once a file has been created, it cannot be changed. Such a file is said to be **immutable**. Having files be immutable makes it much easier to support file caching and replication because it eliminates all the problems associated with having to update all copies of a file whenever it changes.

Protection in distributed systems uses essentially the same techniques as in single-processor systems: capabilities and access control lists. With capabilities, each user has a kind of ticket, called a **capability**, for each object to which it has access. The capability specifies which kinds of accesses are permitted (e.g., reading is allowed but writing is not).

All **access control list** schemes associate with each file a list of users who may access the file and how. The UNIX scheme, with bits for controlling reading, writing, and executing each file separately for the owner, the owner's group, and everyone else is a simplified access control list.

File services can be split into two types, depending on whether they support an upload/download model or a remote access model. In the **upload/download model**, shown in Fig. 5-1(a), the file service provides only two major operations: read file and write file. The former operation transfers an entire file from one of the file servers to the requesting client. The latter operation transfers an entire file the other way, from client to server. Thus the conceptual model is moving whole files in either direction. The files can be stored in memory or on a local disk, as needed.

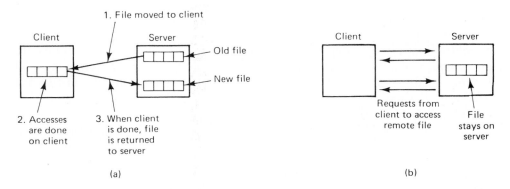

Fig. 5-1. (a) The upload/download model. (b) The remote access model.

The advantage of the upload/download model is its conceptual simplicity. Application programs fetch the files they need, then use them locally. Any modified files or newly created files are written back when the program finishes. No complicated file service interface has to be mastered to use this model. Furthermore, whole file transfer is highly efficient. However, enough storage must be available on the client to store all the files required. Furthermore, if only a fraction of a file is needed, moving the entire file is wasteful.

The other kind of file service is the **remote access model**, as illustrated in Fig. 5-1(b). In this model, the file service provides a large number of operations for opening and closing files, reading and writing parts of files, moving around within files (LSEEK), examining and changing file attributes, and so on. Whereas in the upload/download model, the file service merely provides physical storage and transfer, here the file system runs on the servers, not on the clients. It has the advantage of not requiring much space on the clients, as well as eliminating the need to pull in entire files when only small pieces are needed.

5.1.2. The Directory Server Interface

The other part of the file service is the directory service, which provides operations for creating and deleting directories, naming and renaming files, and moving them from one directory to another. The nature of the directory service does not depend on whether individual files are transferred in their entirety or accessed remotely.

The directory service defines some alphabet and syntax for composing file (and directory) names. File names can typically be from 1 to some maximum number of letters, numbers, and certain special characters. Some systems divide file names into two parts, usually separated by a period, such as *prog.c* for a C program or *man.txt* for a text file. The second part of the name, called the **file extension**, identifies the file type. Other systems use an explicit attribute for this purpose, instead of tacking an extension onto the name.

All distributed systems allow directories to contain subdirectories, to make it possible for users to group related files together. Accordingly, operations are provided for creating and deleting directories as well as entering, removing, and looking up files in them. Normally, each subdirectory contains all the files for one project, such as a large program or document (e.g., a book). When the (sub)directory is listed, only the relevant files are shown; unrelated files are in other (sub)directories and do not clutter the listing. Subdirectories can contain their own subdirectories, and so on, leading to a tree of directories, often called a **hierarchical file system**. Figure 5-2(a) illustrates a tree with five directories

In some systems, it is possible to create links or pointers to an arbitrary directory. These can be put in any directory, making it possible to build not only trees, but arbitrary directory graphs, which are more powerful. The distinction between trees and graphs is especially important in a distributed system.

The nature of the difficulty can be seen by looking at the directory graph of

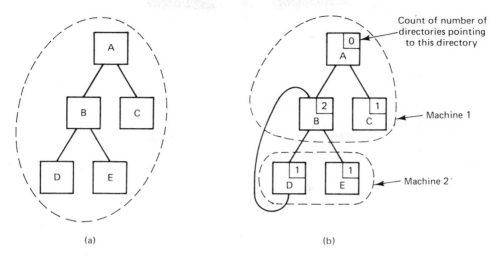

Fig. 5-2. (a) A directory tree contained on one machine. (b) A directory graph on two machines.

Fig. 5-2(b). In this figure, directory D has a link to directory B. The problem occurs when the link from A to B is removed. In a tree-structured hierarchy, a link to a directory can be removed only when the directory pointed to is empty. In a graph, it is allowed to remove a link to a directory as long as at least one other link exists. By keeping a reference count, shown in the upper right-hand corner of each directory in Fig. 5-2(b), it can be determined when the link being removed is the last one.

After the link from A to B is removed, B's reference count is reduced from 2 to 1, which on paper is fine. However, B is now unreachable from the root of the file system (A). The three directories, B, D, and E, and all their files are effectively orphans.

This problem exists in centralized systems as well, but it is more serious in distributed ones. If everything is on one machine, it is possible, albeit somewhat expensive, to discover orphaned directories, because all the information is in one place. All file activity can be stopped and the graph traversed starting at the root, marking all reachable directories. At the end of this process, all unmarked directories are known to be unreachable. In a distributed system, multiple machines are involved and all activity cannot be stopped, so getting a "snapshot" is difficult, if not impossible.

A key issue in the design of any distributed file system is whether or not all machines (and processes) should have exactly the same view of the directory hierarchy. As an example of what we mean by this remark, consider Fig. 5-3. In Fig. 5-3(a) we show two file servers, each holding three directories and some files. In Fig. 5-3(b) we have a system in which all clients (and other machines) have the same view of the distributed file system. If the path /D/E/x is valid on one machine, it is valid on all of them.

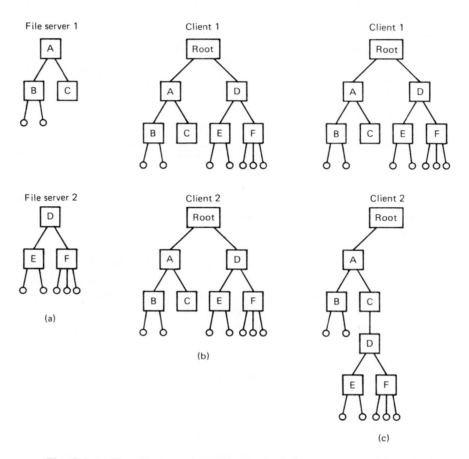

Fig. 5-3. (a) Two file servers. The squares are directories and the circles are files. (b) A system in which all clients have the same view of the file system. (c) A system in which different clients may have different views of the file system.

In contrast, in Fig. 5-3(c), different machines can have different views of the file system. To repeat the preceding example, the path /D/E/x might well be valid on client 1 but not on client 2. In systems that manage multiple file servers by remote mounting, Fig. 5-3(c) is the norm. It is flexible and straightforward to implement, but it has the disadvantage of not making the entire system behave like a single old-fashioned timesharing system. In a timesharing system, the file system looks the same to any process [i.e., the model of Fig. 5-3(b)]. This property makes a system easier to program and understand.

A closely related question is whether or not there is a global root directory, which all machines recognize as the root. One way to have a global root directory is to have this root contain one entry for each server and nothing else. Under these circumstances, paths take the form */server/path*, which has its own disadvantages, but at least is the same everywhere in the system.

Naming Transparency

The principal problem with this form of naming is that it is not fully transparent. Two forms of transparency are relevant in this context and are worth distinguishing. The first one, **location transparency**, means that the path name gives no hint as to where the file (or other object) is located. A path like */server1/dir1/dir2/x* tells everyone that *x* is located on server 1, but it does not tell where that server is located. The server is free to move anywhere it wants to in the network without the path name having to be changed. Thus this system has location transparency.

However, suppose that file *x* is extremely large and space is tight on server 1. Furthermore, suppose that there is plenty of room on server 2. The system might well like to move *x* to server 2 automatically. Unfortunately, when the first component of all path names is the server, the system cannot move the file to the other server automatically, even if *dir1* and *dir2* exist on both servers. The problem is that moving the file automatically changes its path name from */server1/dir1/dir2/x* to */server2/dir1/dir2/x*. Programs that have the former string built into them will cease to work if the path changes. A system in which files can be moved without their names changing is said to have **location independence**. A distributed system that embeds machine or server names in path names clearly is not location independent. One based on remote mounting is not either, since it is not possible to move a file from one file group (the unit of mounting) to another and still be able to use the old path name. Location independence is not easy to achieve, but it is a desirable property to have in a distributed system.

To summarize what we have said earlier, there are three common approaches to file and directory naming in a distributed system:

1. Machine + path naming, such as */machine/path* or *machine:path*.

2. Mounting remote file systems onto the local file hierarchy.

3. A single name space that looks the same on all machines.

The first two are easy to implement, especially as a way to connect up existing systems that were not designed for distributed use. The latter is difficult and requires careful design, but it is needed if the goal of making the distributed system act like a single computer is to be achieved.

Two-Level Naming

Most distributed systems use some form of two-level naming. Files (and other objects) have **symbolic names** such as *prog.c*, for use by people, but they can also have internal, **binary names** for use by the system itself. What directories in fact really do is provide a mapping between these two naming levels. It is convenient for people and programs to use symbolic (ASCII) names, but for use within the system itself, these names are too long and cumbersome. Thus when a user opens a file or otherwise references a symbolic name, the system immediately looks up the symbolic name in the appropriate directory to get the binary name that will be used to locate the file. Sometimes the binary names are visible to the users and sometimes they are not.

The nature of the binary name varies considerably from system to system. In a system consisting of multiple file servers, each of which is self-contained (i.e., does not hold any references to directories or files on other file servers), the binary name can just be a local i-node number, as in UNIX.

A more general naming scheme is to have the binary name indicate both a server and a specific file on that server. This approach allows a directory on one server to hold a file on a different server. An alternative way to do the same thing that is sometimes preferred is to use a **symbolic link**. A symbolic link is a directory entry that maps onto a (server, file name) string, which can be looked up on the server named to find the binary name. The symbolic link itself is just a path name.

Yet another idea is to use capabilities as the binary names. In this method, looking up an ASCII name yields a capability, which can take one of many forms. For example, it can contain a physical or logical machine number or network address of the appropriate server, as well as a number indicating which specific file is required. A physical address can be used to send a message to the server without further interpretation. A logical address can be located either by broadcasting or by looking it up on a name server.

One last twist that is sometimes present in a distributed system but rarely in a centralized one is the possibility of looking up an ASCII name and getting not *one* but *several* binary names (i-nodes, capabilities, or something else). These would typically represent the original file and all its backups. Armed with multiple binary names, it is then possible to try to locate one of the corresponding files, and if that one is unavailable for any reason, to try one of the others. This method provides a degree of fault tolerance through redundancy.

5.1.3. Semantics of File Sharing

When two or more users share the same file, it is necessary to define the semantics of reading and writing precisely to avoid problems. In single-processor systems that permit processes to share files, such as UNIX, the semantics normally state that when a READ operation follows a WRITE operation, the READ returns the value just written, as shown in Fig. 5-4(a). Similarly, when two WRITEs happen in quick succession, followed by a READ, the value read is the value stored by the last write. In effect, the system enforces an absolute time ordering on all operations and always returns the most recent value. We will refer to this model as **UNIX semantics**. This model is easy to understand and straightforward to implement.

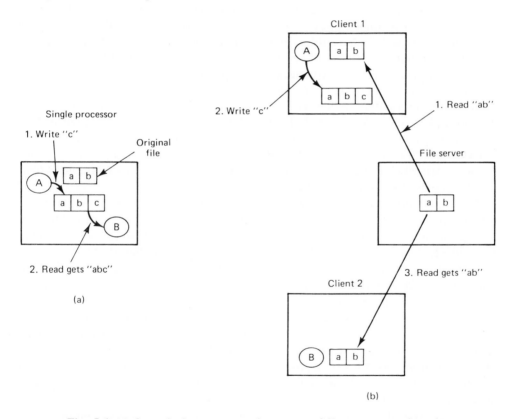

Fig. 5-4. (a) On a single processor, when a READ follows a WRITE, the value returned by the READ is the value just written. (b) In a distributed system with caching, obsolete values may be returned.

In a distributed system, UNIX semantics can be achieved easily as long as there is only one file server and clients do not cache files. All READs and WRITEs go directly to the file server, which processes them strictly sequentially. This approach gives UNIX semantics (except for the minor problem that network delays may cause a READ that occurred a microsecond after a WRITE to arrive at the server first and thus get the old value).

In practice, however, the performance of a distributed system in which all file requests must go to a single server is frequently poor. This problem is often solved by allowing clients to maintain local copies of heavily used files in their private caches. Although we will discuss the details of file caching below, for the moment it is sufficient to point out that if a client locally modifies a cached file and shortly thereafter another client reads the file from the server, the second client will get an obsolete file, as illustrated in Fig. 5-4(b).

One way out of this difficulty is to propagate all changes to cached files back to the server immediately. Although conceptually simple, this approach is inefficient. An alternative solution is to relax the semantics of file sharing. Instead of requiring a READ to see the effects of all previous WRITEs, one can have a new rule that says: "Changes to an open file are initially visible only to the process (or possibly machine) that modified the file. Only when the file is closed are the changes made visible to other processes (or machines)." The adoption of such a rule does not change what happens in Fig. 5-4(b), but it does redefine the actual behavior (*B* getting the original value of the file) as being the correct one. When *A* closes the file, it sends a copy to the server, so that subsequent READs get the new value, as required. This rule is widely implemented and is known as **session semantics**.

Using session semantics raises the question of what happens if two or more clients are simultaneously caching and modifying the same file. One solution is to say that as each file is closed in turn, its value is sent back to the server, so the final result depends on who closes last. A less pleasant, but slightly easier to implement alternative is to say that the final result is one of the candidates, but leave the choice of which one unspecified.

One final difficulty with using caching and session semantics is that it violates another aspect of the UNIX semantics in addition to not having all READs return the value most recently written. In UNIX, associated with each open file is a pointer that indicates the current position in the file. READs take data starting at this position and WRITEs deposit data there. This pointer is shared between the process that opened the file and all its children. With session semantics, when the children run on different machines, this sharing cannot be achieved.

To see what the consequences of having to abandon shared file pointers are, consider a command like

```
run >out
```

where *run* is a shell script that executes two programs, *a* and *b*, one after another. If both programs produce output, it is expected that the output produced by *b* will directly follow the output from *a* within *out*. The way this is achieved is that when *b* starts up, it inherits the file pointer from *a*, which is shared by the shell and both processes. In this way, the first byte that *b* writes directly follows the last byte written by *a*. With session semantics and no shared file pointers, a completely different mechanism is needed to make shell scripts and similar constructions that use shared file pointers work. Since no general-purpose solution to this problem is known, each system must deal with it in an ad hoc way.

A completely different approach to the semantics of file sharing in a distributed system is to make all files immutable. There is thus no way to open a file for writing. In effect, the only operations on files are CREATE and READ.

What is possible is to create an entirely new file and enter it into the directory system under the name of a previous existing file, which now becomes inaccessible (at least under that name). Thus although it becomes impossible to modify the file *x*, it remains possible to replace *x* by a new file atomically. In other words, although *files* cannot be updated, *directories* can be. Once we have decided that files cannot be changed at all, the problem of how to deal with two processes, one of which is writing on a file and the other of which is reading it, simply disappears.

What does remain is the problem of what happens when two processes try to replace the same file at the same time. As with session semantics, the best solution here seems to be to allow one of the new files to replace the old one, either the last one or nondeterministically.

A somewhat stickier problem is what to do if a file is replaced while another process is busy reading it. One solution is to somehow arrange for the reader to continue using the old file, even if it is no longer in any directory, analogous to the way UNIX allows a process that has a file open to continue using it, even after it has been deleted from all directories. Another solution is to detect that the file has changed and make subsequent attempts to read from it fail.

A fourth way to deal with shared files in a distributed system is to use atomic transactions, as we discussed in detail in Chap. 3. To summarize briefly, to access a file or a group of files, a process first executes some type of BEGIN TRANSACTION primitive to signal that what follows must be executed indivisibly. Then come system calls to read and write one or more files. When the work has been completed, an END TRANSACTION primitive is executed. The key property of this method is that the system guarantees that all the calls contained within the transaction will be carried out in order, without any interference from other, concurrent transactions. If two or more transactions start up at the same time, the system ensures that the final result is the same as if they were all run in some (undefined) sequential order.

The classical example of where transactions make programming much easier is in a banking system. Imagine that a certain bank account contains 100 dollars, and that two processes are each trying to add 50 dollars to it. In an unconstrained system, each process might simultaneously read the file containing the current balance (100), individually compute the new balance (150), and successively overwrite the file with this new value. The final result could either be 150 or 200, depending on the precise timing of the reading and writing. By grouping all the operations into a transaction, interleaving cannot occur and the final result will always be 200.

In Fig. 5-5 we summarize the four approaches we have discussed for dealing with shared files in a distributed system.

Method	Comment
UNIX semantics	Every operation on a file is instantly visible to all processes
Session semantics	No changes are visible to other processes until the file is closed
Immutable files	No updates are possible; simplifies sharing and replication
Transactions	All changes have the all-or-nothing property

Fig. 5-5. Four ways of dealing with the shared files in a distributed system.

5.2. DISTRIBUTED FILE SYSTEM IMPLEMENTATION

In the preceding section, we have described various aspects of distributed file systems from the user's perspective, that is, how they appear to the user. In this section we will see how these systems are implemented. We will start out by presenting some experimental information about file usage. Then we will go on to look at system structure, the implementation of caching, replication in distributed systems, and concurrency control. We will conclude with a short discussion of some lessons that have been learned from experience.

5.2.1. File Usage

Before implementing any system, distributed or otherwise, it is useful to have a good idea of how it will be used, to make sure that the most commonly executed operations will be efficient. To this end, Satyanarayanan (1981) made a study of file usage patterns. We will present his major results below.

However, first, a few words of warning about these and similar measurements are in order. Some of the measurements are static, meaning that they represent a snapshot of the system at a certain instant. Static measurements are made by examining the disk to see what is on it. These measurements include the distribution of file sizes, the distribution of file types, and the amount of storage occupied by files of various types and sizes. Other measurements are dynamic, made by modifying the file system to record all operations to a log for subsequent analysis. These data yield information about the relative frequency of various operations, the number of files open at any moment, and the amount of sharing that takes place. By combining the static and dynamic measurements, even though they are fundamentally different, we can get a better picture of how the file system is used.

One problem that always occurs with measurements of any existing system is knowing how typical the observed user population is. Satyanarayanan's measurements were made at a university. Do they also apply to industrial research labs? To office automation projects? To banking systems? No one really knows for sure until these systems, too, are instrumented and measured.

Another problem inherent in making measurements is watching out for artifacts of the system being measured. As a simple example, when looking at the distribution of file names in an MS-DOS system, one could quickly conclude that file names are never more than eight characters (plus an optional three-character extension). However, it would be a mistake to draw the conclusion that eight characters are therefore enough, since nobody ever uses more than eight characters. Since MS-DOS does not allow more than eight characters in a file name, it is impossible to tell what users would do if they were not constrained to eight-character file names.

Finally, Satyanarayanan's measurements were made on more-or-less traditional UNIX systems. Whether or not they can be transferred or extrapolated to distributed systems is not really known.

This being said, the most important conclusions are listed in Fig. 5-6. From these observations, one can draw certain conclusions. To start with, most files are under 10K, which agrees with the results of Mullender and Tanenbaum (1984) made under different circumstances. This observation suggests that it may be feasible to transfer entire files rather than disk blocks between server and client. Since whole file transfer is typically simpler and more efficient, this idea is worth considering. Of course, some files are large, so provision has to be made for them too. Still, a good guideline is to optimize for the normal case and treat the abnormal case specially.

An interesting observation is that most files have short lifetimes. A common pattern is to create a file, read it (probably once), and then delete it. A typical usage might be a compiler that creates temporary files for transmitting information between its passes. The implication here is that it is probably a good

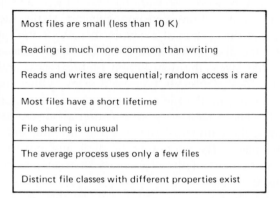

Most files are small (less than 10 K)
Reading is much more common than writing
Reads and writes are sequential; random access is rare
Most files have a short lifetime
File sharing is unusual
The average process uses only a few files
Distinct file classes with different properties exist

Fig. 5-6. Observed file system properties.

idea to create the file on the client and keep it there until it is deleted. Doing so may eliminate a considerable amount of unnecessary client-server traffic.

The fact that few files are shared argues for client caching. As we have seen already, caching makes the semantics more complicated, but if files are rarely shared, it may well be best to do client caching and accept the consequences of session semantics in return for the better performance.

Finally, the clear existence of distinct file classes suggests that perhaps different mechanisms should be used to handle the different classes. System binaries need to be widespread but hardly ever change, so they should probably be widely replicated, even if this means that an occasional update is complex. Compiler and other temporary files are short, unshared, and disappear quickly, so they should be kept locally wherever possible. Electronic mailboxes are frequently updated but rarely shared, so replication is not likely to gain anything. Ordinary data files may be shared, so they may need still other handling.

5.2.2. System Structure

In this section we will look at some of the ways that file servers and directory servers are organized internally, with special attention to alternative approaches. Let us start with a very simple question: Are clients and servers different? Surprisingly enough, there is no agreement on this matter.

In some systems, there is no distinction between clients and servers. All machines run the same basic software, so any machine wanting to offer file service to the public is free to do so. Offering file service is just a matter of exporting the names of selected directories so that other machines can access them.

In other systems, the file server and directory server are just user programs, so a system can be configured to run client and server software on the same machines or not, as it wishes. Finally, at the other extreme, are systems in which clients and servers are fundamentally different machines, in terms of either hardware or software. The servers may even run a different version of the operating system from the clients. While separation of function may seem a bit cleaner, there is no fundamental reason to prefer one approach over the others.

A second implementation issue on which systems differ is how the file and directory service is structured. One organization is to combine the two into a single server that handles all the directory and file calls itself. Another possibility, however, is to keep them separate. In the latter case, opening a file requires going to the directory server to map its symbolic name onto its binary name (e.g., machine + i-node) and then going to the file server with the binary name to read or write the file.

Arguing in favor of the split is that the two functions are really unrelated, so keeping them separate is more flexible. For example, one could implement an MS-DOS directory server and a UNIX directory server, both of which use the same file server for physical storage. Separation of function is also likely to produce simpler software. Weighing against this is that having two servers requires more communication.

Let us consider the case of separate directory and file servers for the moment. In the normal case, the client sends a symbolic name to the directory server, which then returns the binary name that the file server understands. However, it is possible for a directory hierarchy to be partitioned among multiple servers, as illustrated in Fig. 5-7. Suppose, for example, that we have a system in which the current directory, on server 1, contains an entry, a, for another directory on server 2. Similarly, this directory contains an entry, b, for a directory on server 3. This third directory contains an entry for a file c, along with its binary name.

To look up $a/b/c$, the client sends a message to server 1, which manages its current directory. The server finds a, but sees that the binary name refers to another server. It now has a choice. It can either tell the client which server holds b and have the client look up b/c there itself, as shown in Fig. 5-7(a), or it can forward the remainder of the request to server 2 itself and not reply at all, as shown in Fig. 5-7(b). The former scheme requires the client to be aware of which server holds which directory, and requires more messages. The latter method is more efficient, but cannot be handled using normal RPC since the process to which the client sends the message is not the one that sends the reply.

Looking up path names all the time, especially if multiple directory servers are involved, can be expensive. Some systems attempt to improve their performance by maintaining a cache of hints, that is, recently looked up names and the results of these lookups. When a file is opened, the cache is checked to see if the path name is there. If so, the directory-by-directory lookup is skipped and the binary address is taken from the cache. If not, it is looked up.

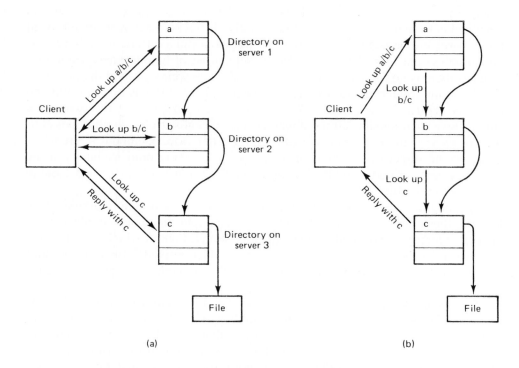

Fig. 5-7. (a) Iterative lookup of *a/b/c*. (b) Automatic lookup.

For name caching to work, it is essential that when an obsolete binary name is used inadvertently, the client is somehow informed so it can fall back on the directory-by-directory lookup to find the file and update the cache. Furthermore, to make hint caching worthwhile in the first place, the hints have to be right most of the time. When these conditions are fulfilled, caching hints can be a powerful technique that is applicable in many distributed operating systems.

The final structural issue that we will consider here is whether or not file, directory, and other servers should maintain state information about clients. This issue is moderately controversial, with two competing schools of thought in existence.

One school thinks that servers should be **stateless**. In other words, when a client sends a request to a server, the server carries out the request, sends the reply, and then removes from its internal tables all information about the request. Between requests, no client-specific information is kept on the server. The other school of thought maintains that it is all right for servers to maintain state information about clients between requests. After all, centralized operating systems maintain state information about active processes, so why should this traditional behavior suddenly become unacceptable?

To better understand the difference, consider a file server that has commands to open, read, write, and close files. After a file has been opened, the server must maintain information about which client has which file open. Typically, when a file is opened, the client is given a file descriptor or other number which is used in subsequent calls to identify the file. When a request comes in, the server uses the file descriptor to determine which file is needed. The table mapping the file descriptors onto the files themselves is state information.

With a stateless server, each request must be self-contained. It must contain the full file name and the offset within the file, in order to allow the server to do the work. This information increases message length.

Another way to look at state information is to consider what happens if a server crashes and all its tables are lost forever. When the server is rebooted, it no longer knows which clients have which files open. Subsequent attempts to read and write open files will then fail, and recovery, if possible at all, will be entirely up to the clients. As a consequence, stateless servers tend to be more fault tolerant than those that maintain state, which is one of the arguments in favor of the former.

Advantages of stateless servers	Advantages of stateful servers
Fault tolerance	Shorter request messages
No OPEN/CLOSE calls needed	Better performance
No server space wasted on tables	Readahead possible
No limits on number of open files	Idempotency easier
No problems if a client crashes	File locking possible

Fig. 5-8. A comparison of stateless and stateful servers.

The arguments both ways are summarized in Fig. 5-8. Stateless servers are inherently more fault tolerant, as we just mentioned. OPEN and CLOSE calls are not needed, which reduces the number of messages, especially for the common case in which the entire file is read in a single blow. No server space is wasted on tables. When tables are used, if too many clients have too many files open at once, the tables can fill up and new files cannot be opened. Finally, with a stateful server, if a client crashes when a file is open, the server is in a bind. If it does nothing, its tables will eventually fill up with junk. If it times out inactive open files, a client that happens to wait too long between requests will be refused service, and correct programs will fail to function correctly. Statelessness eliminates these problems.

Stateful servers also have things going for them. Since READ and WRITE messages do not have to contain file names, they can be shorter, thus using less network bandwidth. Better performance is frequently possible since information about open files (in UNIX terms, the i-nodes) can be kept in main memory until the files are closed. Blocks can be read in advance to reduce delay, since most files are read sequentially. If a client ever times out and sends the same request twice, for example, APPEND, it is much easier to detect this with state (by having a sequence number in each message). Achieving idempotency in the face of unreliable communication with stateless operation takes more thought and effort. Finally, file locking is impossible to do in a truly stateless system, since the only effect setting a lock has is to enter state into the system. In stateless systems, file locking has to be done by a special lock server.

5.2.3. Caching

In a client-server system, each with main memory and a disk, there are four potential places to store files, or parts of files: the server's disk, the server's main memory, the client's disk (if available), or the client's main memory, as illustrated in Fig. 5-9. These different storage locations all have different properties, as we shall see.

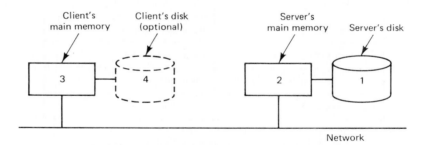

Fig. 5-9. Four places to store files or parts of files.

The most straightforward place to store all files is on the server's disk. There is generally plenty of space there and the files are then accessible to all clients. Furthermore, with only one copy of each file, no consistency problems arise.

The problem with using the server's disk is performance. Before a client can read a file, the file must be transferred from the server's disk to the server's main memory, and then again over the network to the client's main memory. Both transfers take time.

A considerable performance gain can be achieved by **caching** (i.e., holding) the most recently used files in the server's main memory. A client reading a file that happens to be in the server's cache eliminates the disk transfer, although the network transfer still has to be done. Since main memory is invariably smaller than the disk, some algorithm is needed to determine which files or parts of files should be kept in the cache.

This algorithm has two problems to solve. First, what is the unit the cache manages? It can be either whole files or disk blocks. If entire files are cached, they can be stored contiguously on the disk (or at least in very large chunks), allowing high-speed transfers between memory and disk and generally good performance. Disk block caching, however, uses cache and disk space more efficiently.

Second, the algorithm must decide what to do when the cache fills up and something must be evicted. Any of the standard caching algorithms can be used here, but because cache references are so infrequent compared to memory references, an exact implementation of LRU using linked lists is generally feasible. When something has to be evicted, the oldest one is chosen. If an up-to-date copy exists on disk, the cache copy is just discarded. Otherwise, the disk is first updated.

Having a cache in the server's main memory is easy to do and totally transparent to the clients. Since the server can keep its memory and disk copies synchronized, from the clients' point of view, there is only one copy of each file, so no consistency problems arise.

Although server caching eliminates a disk transfer on each access, it still has a network access. The only way to get rid of the network access is to do caching on the client side, which is where all the problems come in. The trade-off between using the client's main memory or its disk is one of space versus performance. The disk holds more but is slower. When faced with a choice between having a cache in the server's main memory versus the client's disk, the former is usually somewhat faster, and it is always much simpler. Of course, if large amounts of data are being used, a client disk cache may be better. In any event, most systems that do client caching do it in the client's main memory, so we will concentrate on that.

If the designers decide to put the cache in the client's main memory, three options are open as to precisely where to put it. The simplest is to cache files directly inside each user process' own address space, as shown in Fig. 5-10(b). Typically, the cache is managed by the system call library. As files are opened, closed, read, and written, the library simply keeps the most heavily used ones around, so that when a file is reused, it may already be available. When the process exits, all modified files are written back to the server. Although this scheme has an extremely low overhead, it is effective only if individual processes open and close files repeatedly. A data base manager process might fit this description, but in the usual program development environment, most processes read each file only once, so caching within the library wins nothing.

The second place to put the cache is in the kernel, as shown in Fig. 5-10(c).

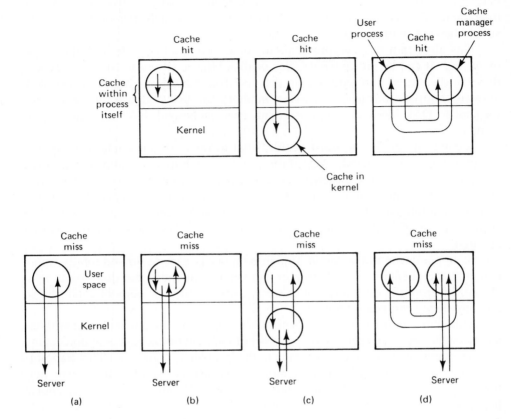

Fig. 5-10. Various ways of doing caching in client memory. (a) No caching. (b) Caching within each process. (c) Caching in the kernel. (d) The cache manager as a user process.

The disadvantage here is that a kernel call is needed in all cases, even on a cache hit, but the fact that the cache survives the process more than compensates. For example, suppose that a two-pass compiler runs as two processes. Pass one writes an intermediate file read by pass two. In Fig. 5-10(c), after the pass one process terminates, the intermediate file will probably be in the cache, so no server calls will have to be made when the pass two process reads it in.

The third place for the cache is in a separate user-level cache manager process, as shown in Fig. 5-10(d). The advantage of a user-level cache manager is that it keeps the (micro)kernel free of file system code, is easier to program because it is completely isolated, and is more flexible.

On the other hand, when the kernel manages the cache, it can dynamically decide how much memory to reserve for programs and how much for the cache.

With a user-level cache manager running on a machine with virtual memory, it is conceivable that the kernel could decide to page out some or all of the cache to a disk, so that a so-called "cache hit" requires one or more pages to be brought in. Needless to say, this defeats the idea of client caching completely. However, if it is possible for the cache manager to allocate and lock in memory some number of pages, this ironic situation can be avoided.

When evaluating whether caching is worth the trouble at all, it is important to note that in Fig. 5-10(a), it takes exactly one RPC to make a file request, no matter what. In both Fig. 5-10(c) and Fig. 5-10(d) it takes either one or two, depending on whether or not the request can be satisfied out of the cache. Thus the mean number of RPCs is always greater when caching is used. In a situation in which RPCs are fast and network transfers are slow (fast CPUs, slow networks), caching can give a big gain in performance. If, however, network transfers are very fast (e.g., with high-speed fiber optic networks), the network transfer time will matter less, so the extra RPCs may eat up a substantial fraction of the gain. Thus the performance gain provided by caching depends to some extent on the CPU and network technology available, and of course, on the applications.

Cache Consistency

As usual in computer science, you never get something for nothing. Client caching introduces inconsistency into the system. If two clients simultaneously read the same file and then both modify it, several problems occur. For one, when a third process reads the file from the server, it will get the original version, not one of the two new ones. This problem can be defined away by adopting session semantics (officially stating that the effects of modifying a file are not supposed to be visible globally until the file is closed). In other words, this "incorrect" behavior is simply declared to be the "correct" behavior. Of course, if the user expects UNIX semantics, the trick does not work.

Another problem, unfortunately, that cannot be defined away at all is that when the two files are written back to the server, the one written last will overwrite the other one. The moral of the story is that client caching has to be thought out fairly carefully. Below we will discuss some of the problems and proposed solutions.

One way to solve the consistency problem is to use the **write-through algorithm.** When a cache entry (file or block) is modified, the new value is kept in the cache, but is also sent immediately to the server. As a consequence, when another process reads the file, it gets the most recent value.

However, the following problem arises. Suppose that a client process on machine *A* reads a file, *f*. The client terminates but the machine keeps *f* in its cache. Later, a client on machine *B* reads the same file, modifies it, and writes it through to the server. Finally, a new client process is started up on machine *A*. The first thing it does is open and read *f*, which is taken from the cache. Unfortunately, the value there is now obsolete.

A possible way out is to require the cache manager to check with the server before providing any client with a file from the cache. This check could be done by comparing the time of last modification of the cached version with the server's version. If they are the same, the cache is up-to-date. If not, the current version must be fetched from the server. Instead of using dates, version numbers or checksums can also be used. Although going to the server to verify dates, version numbers, or checksums takes an RPC, the amount of data exchanged is small. Still, it takes some time.

Another trouble with the write-through algorithm is that although it helps on reads, the network traffic for writes is the same as if there were no caching at all. Many system designers find this unacceptable, and cheat: instead of going to the server the instant the write is done, the client just makes a note that a file has been updated. Once every 30 seconds or so, all the file updates are gathered together and sent to the server all at once. A single bulk write is usually more efficient than many small ones.

Besides, many programs create scratch files, write them, read them back, and then delete them, all in quick succession. In the event that this entire sequence happens before it is time to send all modified files back to the server, the now-deleted file does not have to be written back at all. Not having to use the file server at all for temporary files can be a major performance gain.

Of course, delaying the writes muddies the semantics, because when another process reads the file, what it gets depends on the timing. Thus postponing the writes is a trade-off between better performance and cleaner semantics (which translates into easier programming).

The next step in this direction is to adopt session semantics and write a file back to the server only after it has been closed. This algorithm is called **write-on-close**. Better yet, wait 30 seconds after the close to see if the file is going to be deleted. As we saw earlier, going this route means that if two cached files are written back in succession, the second one overwrites the first one. The only solution to this problem is to note that it is not nearly as bad as it first appears. In a single CPU system, it is possible for two processes to open and read a file, modify it within their respective address spaces, and then write it back. Consequently, write-on-close with session semantics is not that much worse than what can happen on a single CPU system.

A completely different approach to consistency is to use a centralized control algorithm. When a file is opened, the machine opening it sends a message to the file server to announce this fact. The file server keeps track of who has which file open, and whether it is open for reading, writing, or both. If a file is open for reading, there is no problem with letting other processes open it for reading, but opening it for writing must be avoided. Similarly, if some process has a file open for writing, all other accesses must be prevented. When a file is closed, this event must be reported, so the server can update its tables telling which client has which file open. The modified file can also be shipped back to the server at this point.

When a client tries to open a file and the file is already open elsewhere in the system, the new request can either be denied or queued. Alternatively, the server can send an **unsolicited message** to all clients having the file open, telling them to remove that file from their caches and disable caching just for that one file. In this way, multiple readers and writers can run simultaneously, with the results being no better and no worse than would be achieved on a single CPU system.

Although sending unsolicited messages is clearly possible, it is inelegant, since it reverses the client and server roles. Normally, servers do not spontaneously send messages to clients or initiate RPCs with them. If the clients are multithreaded, one thread can be permanently allocated to waiting for server requests, but if they are not, the unsolicited message must cause an interrupt.

Even with these precautions, one must be careful. In particular, if a machine opens, caches, and then closes a file, upon opening it again the cache manager must still check to see if the cache is valid. After all, some other process might have subsequently opened, modified, and closed the file. Many variations of this centralized control algorithm are possible, with differing semantics. For example, servers can keep track of cached files, rather than open files. All these methods have a single point of failure and none of them scale well to large systems.

Method	Comments
Write through	Works, but does not affect write traffic
Delayed write	Better performance but possibly ambiguous semantics
Write on close	Matches session semantics
Centralized control	UNIX semantics, but not robust and scales poorly

Fig. 5-11. Four algorithms for managing a client file cache.

The four cache management algorithms discussed above are summarized in Fig. 5-11. To summarize the subject of caching as a whole, server caching is easy to do and almost always worth the trouble, independent of whether client caching is present or not. Server caching has no effect on the file system semantics seen by the clients. Client caching, in contrast, offers better performance at the price of increased complexity and possibly fuzzier semantics. Whether it is worth doing or not depends on how the designers feel about performance, complexity, and ease of programming.

Earlier in this chapter, when we were discussing the semantics of distributed file systems, we pointed out that one of the design options is immutable files. One of the great attractions of an immutable file is the ability to cache it on machine *A* without having to worry about the possibility that machine *B* will change it. Changes are not permitted. Of course, a new file may have been created and bound to the same symbolic name as the cached file, but this can be checked for whenever a cached file is reopened. This model has the same RPC overhead discussed above, but the semantics are less fuzzy.

5.2.4. Replication

Distributed file systems often provide file replication as a service to their clients. In other words, multiple copies of selected files are maintained, with each copy on a separate file server. The reasons for offering such a service vary, but among the major reasons are:

1. To increase reliability by having independent backups of each file. If one server goes down, or is even lost permanently, no data are lost. For many applications, this property is extremely desirable.

2. To allow file access to occur even if one file server is down. The motto here is: The show must go on. A server crash should not bring the entire system down until the server can be rebooted.

3. To split the workload over multiple servers. As the system grows in size, having all the files on one server can become a performance bottleneck. By having files replicated on two or more servers, the least heavily loaded one can be used.

The first two relate to improving reliability and availability; the third concerns performance. All are important.

A key issue relating to replication is transparency (as usual). To what extent are the users aware that some files are replicated? Do they play any role in the replication process, or is it handled entirely automatically? At one extreme, the users are fully aware of the replication process and can even control it. At the other, the system does everything behind their backs. In the latter case, we say that the system is **replication transparent**.

Figure 5-12 shows three ways replication can be done. The first way, shown in Fig. 5-12(a), is for the programmer to control the entire process. When a process makes a file, it does so on one specific server. Then it can make additional copies on other servers, if desired. If the directory server permits multiple copies of a file, the network addresses of all copies can then be associated with the file name, as shown at the bottom of Fig. 5-12(a), so that when the name is looked up, all copies will be found. When the file is subsequently opened, the copies can be tried sequentially in some order, until an available one is found.

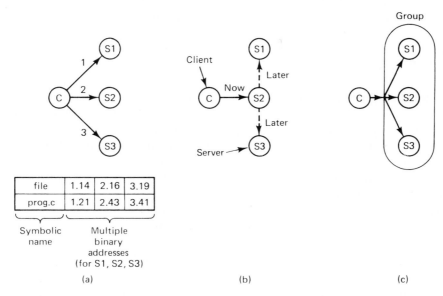

file	1.14	2.16	3.19
prog.c	1.21	2.43	3.41

Symbolic   Multiple
name   binary
              addresses
              (for S1, S2, S3)

(a)   (b)   (c)

Fig. 5-12. (a) Explicit file replication. (b) Lazy file replication. (c) File replication using a group.

To make the concept of explicit replication more familiar, consider how it can be done in a system based on remote mounting in UNIX. Suppose that a programmer's home directory is */machine1/usr/ast*. After creating a file, for example the file, */machine1/usr/ast/xyz*, the programmer, process, or library can use the *cp* command (or equivalent) to make copies in */machine2/usr/ast/xyz* and */machine3/usr/ast/xyz*. Programs can be written to accept strings like */usr/ast/xyz* as arguments, and successively try to open the copies until one succeeds. While this scheme can be made to work, it is a lot of trouble. For this reason, a distributed system should do better.

In Fig. 5-12(b) we see an alternative approach, **lazy replication**. Here, only one copy of each file is created, on some server. Later, the server itself makes replicas on other servers automatically, without the programmer's knowledge. The system must be smart enough to be able to retrieve any of these copies if need be. When making copies in the background like this, it is important to pay attention to the possibility that the file might change before the copies can be made.

Our final method is to use group communication, as shown in Fig. 5-13(c).

In this scheme, all WRITE system calls are simultaneously transmitted to all the servers, so extra copies are made at the same time the original is made. There are two principal differences between lazy replication and using a group. First, with lazy replication, one server is addressed rather than a group. Second, lazy replication happens in the background, when the server has some free time, whereas when group communication is used, all copies are made at the same time.

Update Protocols

Above we looked at the problem of how replicated files can be created. Now let us see how existing ones can be modified. Just sending an update message to each copy in sequence is not a good idea because if the process doing the update crashes partway through, some copies will be changed and others not. As a result, some future reads may get the old value and others may get the new value, hardly a desirable situation. We will now look at two well-known algorithms that solve this problem.

The first algorithm is called **primary copy replication**. When it is used, one server is designated as the primary. All the others are secondaries. When a replicated file is to be updated, the change is sent to the primary server, which makes the change locally and then sends commands to the secondaries, ordering them to change, too. Reads can be done from any copy, primary or secondary.

To guard against the situation that the primary crashes before it has had a chance to instruct all the secondaries, the update should be written to stable storage prior to changing the primary copy. In this way, when a server reboots after a crash, a check can be made to see if any updates were in progress at the time of the crash. If so, they can still be carried out. Sooner or later, all the secondaries will be updated.

Although the method is straightforward, it has the disadvantage that if the primary is down, no updates can be performed. To get around this asymmetry, Gifford (1979) proposed a more robust method, known as **voting**. The basic idea is to require clients to request and acquire the permission of multiple servers before either reading or writing a replicated file.

As a simple example of how the algorithm works, suppose that a file is replicated on N servers. We could make a rule stating that to update a file, a client must first contact at least half the servers plus 1 (a majority) and get them to agree to do the update. Once they have agreed, the file is changed and a new version number is associated with the new file. The version number is used to identify the version of the file and is the same for all the newly updated files.

To read a replicated file, a client must also contact at least half the servers plus 1 and ask them to send the version numbers associated with the file. If all the version numbers agree, this must be the most recent version because an attempt to update only the remaining servers would fail because there are not enough of them.

For example, if there are five servers and a client determines that three of them have version 8, it is impossible that the other two have version 9. After all, any successful update from version 8 to version 9 requires getting three servers to agree to it, not just two.

Gifford's scheme is actually somewhat more general than this. In it, to read a file of which N replicas exist, a client needs to assemble a **read quorum**, an arbitrary collection of any N_r servers, or more. Similarly, to modify a file, a **write quorum** of at least N_w servers is required. The values of N_r and N_w are subject to the constraint that $N_r + N_w > N$. Only after the appropriate number of servers has agreed to participate can a file be read or written.

To see how this algorithm works, consider Fig. 5-13(a), which has $N_r = 3$ and $N_w = 10$. Imagine that the most recent write quorum consisted of the 10 servers C through L. All of these get the new version and the new version number. Any subsequent read quorum of three servers will have to contain at least one member of this set. When the client looks at the version numbers, it will know which is most recent and take that one.

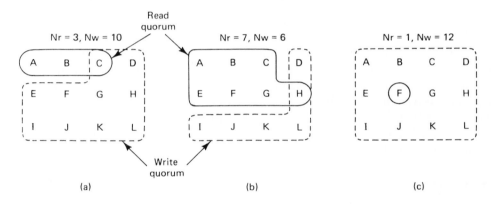

Fig. 5-13. Three examples of the voting algorithm.

In Fig. 5-13(b) and (c), we see two more examples. The latter is especially interesting because it sets N_r to 1, making it possible to read a replicated file by finding any copy and using it. The price paid, however, is that write updates need to acquire all copies.

An interesting variation on voting is **voting with ghosts** (Van Renesse and Tanenbaum, 1988). In most applications, reads are much more common than writes, so N_r is typically a small number and N_w is nearly N. This choice means that if a few servers are down, it may be impossible to obtain a write quorum.

Voting with ghosts solves this problem by creating a dummy server, with no storage, for each real server that is down. A ghost is not permitted in a read quorum (it does not have any files, after all), but it may join a write quorum, in which case it just throws away the file written to it. A write succeeds only if at least one server is real.

When a failed server is rebooted, it must obtain a read quorum to locate the most recent version, which it then copies to itself before starting normal operation. The algorithm works because it has the same property as the basic voting scheme, namely, N_r and N_w are chosen so that acquiring a read quorum and a write quorum at the same time is impossible. The only difference here is that dead machines are allowed in a write quorum, subject to the condition that when they come back up they immediately obtain the current version before going into service.

Other replication algorithms are described in (Bernstein and Goodman, 1984; Brereton, 1986; Pu et al., 1986; and Purdin et al., 1987).

5.2.5. An Example: Sun's Network File System

In this section we will examine an example network file system, Sun Microsystem's **Network File System**, universally known as **NFS**. NFS was originally designed and implemented by Sun Microsystems for use on its UNIX-based workstations. Other manufacturers now support it as well, for both UNIX and other operating systems (including MS-DOS). NFS supports heterogeneous systems, for example, MS-DOS clients making use of UNIX servers. It is not even required that all the machines use the same hardware. It is common to find MS-DOS clients running on Intel 386 CPUs getting service from UNIX file servers running on Motorola 68030 or Sun SPARC CPUs.

Three aspects of NFS are of interest: the architecture, the protocol, and the implementation. Let us look at these in turn.

NFS Architecture

The basic idea behind NFS is to allow an arbitrary collection of clients and servers to share a common file system. In most cases, all the clients and servers are on the same LAN, but this is not required. It is possible to run NFS over a wide-area network. For simplicity we will speak of clients and servers as though they were on distinct machines, but in fact, NFS allows every machine to be both a client and a server at the same time.

Each NFS server exports one or more of its directories for access by remote clients. When a directory is made available, so are all of its subdirectories, so in fact, entire directory trees are normally exported as a unit. The list of directories a server exports is maintained in the /etc/exports file, so these directories can be exported automatically whenever the server is booted.

Clients access exported directories by mounting them. When a client mounts a (remote) directory, it becomes part of its directory hierarchy, as shown in Fig. 5-13. Many Sun workstations are diskless. If it so desires, a diskless client can mount a remote file system on its root directory, resulting in a file system that is supported entirely on a remote server. Those workstations that do have local disks can mount remote directories anywhere they wish on top of their local directory hierarchy, resulting in a file system that is partly local and partly remote. To programs running on the client machine, there is (almost) no difference between a file located on a remote file server and a file located on the local disk.

Thus the basic architectural characteristic of NFS is that servers export directories and clients mount them remotely. If two or more clients mount the same directory at the same time, they can communicate by sharing files in their common directories. A program on one client can create a file, and a program on a different one can read the file. Once the mounts have been done, nothing special has to be done to achieve sharing. The shared files are just there in the directory hierarchy of multiple machines and can be read and written the usual way. This simplicity is one of the great attractions of NFS.

NFS Protocols

Since one of the goals of NFS is to support a heterogeneous system, with clients and servers possibly running different operating systems on different hardware, it is essential that the interface between the clients and servers be well defined. Only then is it possible for anyone to be able to write a new client implementation and expect it to work correctly with existing servers, and vice versa.

NFS accomplishes this goal by defining two client-server protocols. A **protocol** is a set of requests sent by clients to servers, along with the corresponding replies sent by the servers back to the clients. (Protocols are an important topic in distributed systems; we will come back to them later in more detail.) As long as a server recognizes and can handle all the requests in the protocols, it need not know anything at all about its clients. Similarly, clients can treat servers as "black boxes" that accept and process a specific set of requests. How they do it is their own business.

The first NFS protocol handles mounting. A client can send a path name to a server and request permission to mount that directory somewhere in its directory hierarchy. The place where it is to be mounted is not contained in the message, as the server does not care where it is to be mounted. If the path name is legal and the directory specified has been exported, the server returns a **file handle** to the client. The file handle contains fields uniquely identifying the file system type, the disk, the i-node number of the directory, and security information. Subsequent calls to read and write files in the mounted directory use the file handle.

Many clients are configured to mount certain remote directories without manual intervention. Typically, these clients contain a file called /etc/rc, which is a shell script containing the remote mount commands. This shell script is executed automatically when the client is booted.

Alternatively, Sun's version of UNIX also supports **automounting**. This feature allows a set of remote directories to be associated with a local directory. None of these remote directories are mounted (or their servers even contacted) when the client is booted. Instead, the first time a remote file is opened, the operating system sends a message to each of the servers. The first one to reply wins, and its directory is mounted.

Automounting has two principal advantages over static mounting via the /etc/rc file. First, if one of the NFS servers named in /etc/rc happens to be down, it is impossible to bring the client up, at least not without some difficulty, delay, and quite a few error messages. If the user does not even need that server at the moment, all that work is wasted. Second, by allowing the client to try a set of servers in parallel, a degree of fault tolerance can be achieved (because only one of them need to be up), and the performance can be improved (by choosing the first one to reply—presumably the least heavily loaded).

On the other hand, it is tacitly assumed that all the file systems specified as alternatives for the automount are identical. Since NFS provides no support for file or directory replication, it is up to the user to arrange for all the file systems to be the same. Consequently, automounting is most often used for read-only file systems containing system binaries and other files that rarely change.

The second NFS protocol is for directory and file access. Clients can send messages to servers to manipulate directories and to read and write files. In addition, they can also access file attributes, such as file mode, size, and time of last modification. Most UNIX system calls are supported by NFS, with the perhaps surprising exception of OPEN and CLOSE.

The omission of OPEN and CLOSE is not an accident. It is fully intentional. It is not necessary to open a file before reading it, nor to close it when done. Instead, to read a file, a client sends the server a message containing the file name, with a request to look it up and return a file handle, which is a structure that identifies the file. Unlike an OPEN call, this LOOKUP operation does not copy any information into internal system tables. The READ call contains the file handle of the file to read, the offset in the file to begin reading, and the number of bytes desired. Each such message is self-contained. The advantage of this scheme is that the server does not have to remember anything about open connections in between calls to it. Thus if a server crashes and then recovers, no information about open files is lost, because there is none. A server like this that does not maintain state information about open files is said to be **stateless**.

In contrast, in UNIX System V, the **Remote File System** (**RFS**) requires a file to be opened before it can be read or written. The server then makes a table entry keeping track of the fact that the file is open, and where the reader currently is, so each request need not carry an offset. The disadvantage of this scheme is that if a server crashes and then quickly reboots, all open connections are lost, and client programs fail. NFS does not have this property.

Unfortunately, the NFS method makes it difficult to achieve the exact UNIX file semantics. For example, in UNIX a file can be opened and locked so that other processes cannot access it. When the file is closed, the locks are released. In a stateless server such as NFS, locks cannot be associated with open files, because the server does not know which files are open. NFS therefore needs a separate, additional mechanism to handle locking.

NFS uses the UNIX protection mechanism, with the *rwx* bits for the owner, group, and others. Originally, each request message simply contained the user and group ids of the caller, which the NFS server used to validate the access. In effect, it trusted the clients not to cheat. Several years' experience abundantly demonstrated that such an assumption was—how shall we put it?—naive. Currently, public key cryptography can be used to establish a secure key for validating the client and server on each request and reply. When this option is enabled, a malicious client cannot impersonate another client because it does not know that client's secret key. As an aside, cryptography is used only to authenticate the parties. The data themselves are never encrypted.

All the keys used for the authentication, as well as other information are maintained by the **NIS** (**Network Information Service**). The NIS was formerly known as the **yellow pages**. Its function is to store (key, value) pairs. When a key is provided, it returns the corresponding value. Not only does it handle encryption keys, but it also stores the mapping of user names to (encrypted) passwords, as well as the mapping of machine names to network addresses, and other items.

The network information servers are replicated using a master/slave arrangement. To read their data, a process can use either the master or any of the copies (slaves). However, all changes must be made only to the master, which then propagates them to the slaves. There is a short interval after an update in which the data base is inconsistent.

NFS Implementation

Although the implementation of the client and server code is independent of the NFS protocols, it is interesting to take a quick peek at Sun's implementation. It consists of three layers, as shown in Fig. 5-14. The top layer is the system call layer. This handles calls like OPEN, READ, and CLOSE. After parsing the call and checking the parameters, it invokes the second layer, the virtual file system (VFS) layer.

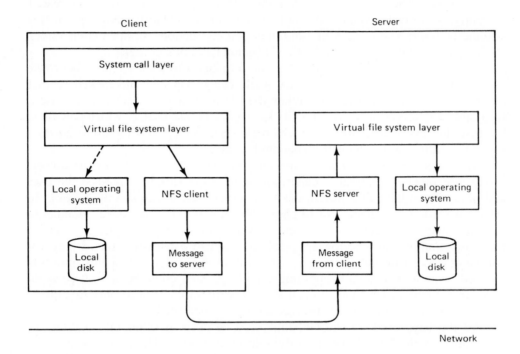

Fig. 5-14. NFS layer structure.

The task of the VFS layer is to maintain a table with one entry for each open file, analogous to the table of i-nodes for open files in UNIX. In ordinary UNIX, an i-node is indicated uniquely by a (device, i-node number) pair. Instead, the VFS layer has an entry, called a **v-node** (**virtual i-node**), for every open file. V-nodes are used to tell whether the file is local or remote. For remote files, enough information is provided to be able to access them.

To see how v-nodes are used, let us trace a sequence of MOUNT, OPEN, and READ system calls. To mount a remote file system, the system administrator calls the *mount* program specifying the remote directory, the local directory on which it is to be mounted, and other information. The *mount* program parses the name of the remote directory to be mounted and discovers the name of the machine on which the remote directory is located. It then contacts that machine asking for a file handle for the remote directory. If the directory exists and is available for remote mounting, the server returns a file handle for the directory. Finally, it makes a MOUNT system call, passing the handle to the kernel.

The kernel then constructs a v-node for the remote directory and asks the

NFS client code in Fig. 5-14 to create an **r-node** (**remote i-node**) in its internal tables to hold the file handle. The v-node points to the r-node. Each v-node in the VFS layer will ultimately contain either a pointer to an r-node in the NFS client code, or a pointer to an i-node in the local operating system (see Fig. 5-14). Thus from the v-node it is possible to see if a file or directory is local or remote, and if it is remote, to find its file handle.

When a remote file is opened, at some point during the parsing of the path name, the kernel hits the directory on which the remote file system is mounted. It sees that this directory is remote and in the directory's v-node finds the pointer to the r-node. It then asks the NFS client code to open the file. The NFS client code looks up the remaining portion of the path name on the remote server associated with the mounted directory and gets back a file handle for it. It makes an r-node for the remote file in its tables and reports back to the VFS layer, which puts in its tables a v-node for the file that points to the r-node. Again here we see that every open file or directory has a v-node that points to either an r-node or an i-node.

The caller is given a file descriptor for the remote file. This file descriptor is mapped onto the v-node by tables in the VFS layer. Note that no table entries are made on the server side. Although the server is prepared to provide file handles upon request, it does not keep track of which files happen to have file handles outstanding and which do not. When a file handle is sent to it for file access, it checks the handle, and if it is valid, uses it. Validation can include verifying an authentication key contained in the RPC headers, if security is enabled.

When the file descriptor is used in a subsequent system call, for example, READ, the VFS layer locates the corresponding v-node, and from that determines whether it is local or remote and also which i-node or r-node describes it.

For efficiency reasons, transfers between client and server are done in large chunks, normally 8192 bytes, even if fewer bytes are requested. After the client's VFS layer has gotten the 8K chunk it needs, it automatically issues a request for the next chunk, so it will have it should it be needed shortly. This feature, known as **read ahead**, improves performance considerably.

For writes an analogous policy is followed. If a WRITE system call supplies fewer than 8192 bytes of data, the data are just accumulated locally. Only when the entire 8K chunk is full is it sent to the server. However, when a file is closed, all of its data are sent to the server immediately.

Another technique used to improve performance is caching, as in ordinary UNIX. Servers cache data to avoid disk accesses, but this is invisible to the clients. Clients maintain two caches, one for file attributes (i-nodes) and one for file data. When either an i-node or a file block is needed, a check is made to see if it can be satisfied out of the cache. If so, network traffic can be avoided.

While client caching helps performance enormously, it also introduces some nasty problems. Suppose that two clients are both caching the same file block and that one of them modifies it. When the other one reads the block, it gets the old (stale) value. The cache is not coherent. We saw the same problem with multiprocessors earlier. However, there it was solved by having the caches snoop on the bus to detect all writes and invalidate or update cache entries accordingly. With a file cache that is not possible, because a write to a file that results in a cache hit on one client does not generate any network traffic. Even if it did, snooping on the network is nearly impossible with current hardware.

Given the potential severity of this problem, the NFS implementation does several things to mitigate it. For one, associated with each cache block is a timer. When the timer expires, the entry is discarded. Normally, the timer is 3 sec for data blocks and 30 sec for directory blocks. Doing this reduces the risk somewhat. In addition, whenever a cached file is opened, a message is sent to the server to find out when the file was last modified. If the last modification occurred after the local copy was cached, the cache copy is discarded and the new copy fetched from the server. Finally, once every 30 sec a cache timer expires, and all the dirty (i.e., modified) blocks in the cache are sent to the server.

Still, NFS has been widely criticized for not implementing the proper UNIX semantics. A write to a file on one client may or may not be seen when another client reads the file, depending on the timing. Furthermore, when a file is created, it may not be visible to the outside world for as much as 30 sec. Similar problems exist as well.

From this example we see that although NFS provides a shared file system, because the resulting system is kind of a patched-up UNIX, the semantics of file access are not entirely well defined, and running a set of cooperating programs again may give different results, depending on the timing. Furthermore, the only issue NFS deals with is the file system. Other issues, such as process execution, are not addressed at all. Nevertheless, NFS is popular and widely used.

5.2.6. Lessons Learned

Based on his experience with various distributed file systems, Satyanarayanan (1990b) has stated some general principles that he believes distributed file system designers should follow. We have summarized these in Fig. 5-15. The first principle says that workstations have enough CPU power that it is wise to use them wherever possible. In particular, given a choice of doing something on a workstation or on a server, choose the workstation because server cycles are precious and workstation cycles are not.

The second principle says to use caches. They can frequently save a large amount of computing time and network bandwidth.

The third principle says to exploit usage properties. For example, in a

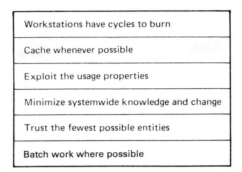

Fig. 5-15. Distributed file system design principles.

typical UNIX system, about a third of all file references are to temporary files, which have short lifetimes and are never shared. By treating these specially, considerable performance gains are possible. In all fairness, there is another school of thought that says: "Pick a single mechanism and stick to it. Do not have five ways of doing the same thing." Which view one takes depends on whether one prefers efficiency or simplicity.

Minimizing systemwide knowledge and change is important for making the system scale. Hierarchical designs help in this respect.

Trusting the fewest possible entities is a long-established principle in the security world. If the correct functioning of the system depends on 10,000 workstations all doing what they are supposed to, the system has a big problem.

Finally, batching can lead to major performance gains. Transmitting a 50K file in one blast is much more efficient than sending it as 50 1K blocks.

5.3. TRENDS IN DISTRIBUTED FILE SYSTEMS

Although rapid change has been a part of the computer industry since its inception, new developments seem to be coming faster than ever in recent years, both in the hardware and software areas. Many of these hardware changes are likely to have major impact on the distributed file systems of the future. In addition to all the improvements in the technology, changing user expectations and applications are also likely to have a major impact. In this section, we will survey some of the changes that can be expected in the foreseeable future and discuss some of the implications these changes may have for file systems. This section will raise more questions than it will answer, but it will suggest some interesting directions for future research.

5.3.1. New Hardware

Before looking at new hardware, let us look at old hardware with new prices. As memory continues to get cheaper and cheaper, we may see a revolution in the way file servers are organized. Currently, all file servers use magnetic disks for storage. Main memory is often used for server caching, but this is merely an optimization for better performance. It is not essential.

Within a few years, memory may become so cheap that even small organizations can afford to equip all their file servers with gigabytes of physical memory. As a consequence, the file system may permanently reside in memory, and no disks will be needed. Such a step will give a large gain in performance and will greatly simplify file system structure.

Most current file systems organize files as a collection of blocks, either as a tree (e.g., UNIX) or as a linked list (e.g., MS-DOS). With an in-core file system, it may be much simpler to store each file contiguously in memory, rather than breaking it up into blocks. Contiguously stored files are easier to keep track of and can be shipped over the network faster. The reason that contiguous files are not used on disk is that if a file grows, moving it to an area of the disk with more room is too expensive. In contrast, moving a file to another area of memory is feasible.

Main memory file servers introduce a serious problem, however. If the power fails, all the files are lost. Unlike disks, which do not lose information in a power failure, main memory is erased when the electricity is removed. The solution may be to make continuous or at least incremental backups onto videotape. With current technology, it is possible to store about 5 gigabytes on a single 8mm videotape that costs less than 10 dollars. While access time is long, if access is needed only once or twice a year to recover from power failures, this scheme may prove irresistible.

A hardware development that may affect file systems is the optical disk. Originally, these devices had the property that they could be written once (by burning holes in the surface with a laser), but not changed thereafter. They were sometimes referred to as **WORM** (**Write Once Read Many**) devices. Some current optical disks use lasers to affect the crystal structure of the disk, but do not damage them, so they can be erased.

Optical disks have three important properties:

1. They are slow.

2. They have huge storage capacities.

3. They have random access.

They are also relatively cheap, although more expensive than videotape. The first two properties are the same as videotape, but the third opens the following possibility. Imagine a file server with an n-gigabyte file system in main memory, and an n-gigabyte optical disk as backup. When a file is created, it is stored in main memory and marked as not yet backed up. All accesses are done using main memory. When the workload is low, files that are not yet backed up are transferred to the optical disk in the background, with byte k in memory going to byte k on the disk. Like the first scheme, what we have here is a main memory file server, but with a more convenient backup device having a one-to-one mapping with the memory.

Another interesting hardware development is very fast fiber optic networks. As we discussed earlier, the reason for doing client caching, with all its inherent complications, is to avoid the slow transfer from the server to the client. But suppose that we could equip the system with a main memory file server and a fast fiber optic network. It might well become feasible to get rid of the client's cache and the server's disk and just operate out of the server's memory, backed up by optical disk. This would certainly simplify the software.

When studying client caching, we saw that a large fraction of the trouble is caused by the fact that if two clients are caching the same file and one of them modifies it, the other does not discover this, which leads to inconsistencies. A little thought will reveal that this situation is highly analogous to memory caches in a multiprocessor. Only there, when one processor modifies a shared word, a hardware signal is sent over the memory bus to the other caches to allow them to invalidate or update that word. With distributed file systems, this is not done.

Why not, actually? The reason is that current network interfaces do not support such signals. Nevertheless, it should be possible to build network interfaces that do. As a very simple example, consider the system of Fig. 5-16 in which each network interface has a bit map, one bit per cached file. To modify a file, a processor sets the corresponding bit in the interface, which is 0 if no processor is currently updating the file. Setting a bit causes the interface to create and send a packet around the ring that checks and sets the corresponding bit in all interfaces. If the packet makes it all the way around without finding any other machines trying to use the file, some other register in the interface is set to 1. Otherwise, it is set to 0. In effect, this mechanism provides a way to globally lock the file on all machines in a few microseconds.

After the lock has been set, the processor updates the file. Each block of the file that is changed is noted (e.g., using bits in the page table). When the update is complete, the processor clears the bit in the bit map, which causes the network interface to locate the file using a table in memory and automatically deposit all the modified blocks in their proper locations on the other machines. When the file has been updated everywhere, the bit in the bit map is cleared on all machines.

Clearly, this is a simple solution that can be improved in many ways, but it

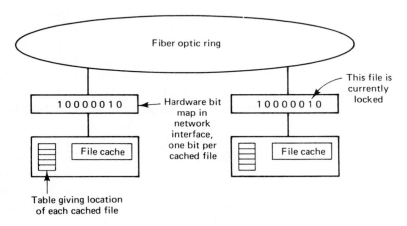

Fig. 5-16. A hardware scheme to updating shared files.

shows how a small amount of well-designed hardware can solve problems that are difficult to handle in software. It is likely that future distributed systems will be assisted by specialized hardware of various kinds.

5.3.2. Scalability

A definite trend in distributed systems is toward larger and larger systems. This observation has implications for distributed file system design. Algorithms that work well for systems with 100 machines may work poorly for systems with 1000 machines and not at all for systems with 10,000 machines. For starters, centralized algorithms do not scale well. If opening a file requires contacting a single centralized server to record the fact that the file is open, that server will eventually become a bottleneck as the system grows.

A general way to deal with this problem is to partition the system into smaller units and try to make each one relatively independent of the others. Having one server per unit scales much better than a single server. Even having the servers record all the opens may be acceptable under these circumstances.

Broadcasts are another problem area. If each machine issues one broadcast per second, with n machines, a total of n broadcasts per second appear on the network, generating a total of n^2 interrupts total. Obviously, as n grows, this will eventually be a problem.

Resources and algorithms should not be linear in the number of users, so having a server maintain a linear list of users for protection or other purposes is not a good idea. In contrast, hash tables are acceptable, since the access time is more or less constant, almost independent of the number of entries.

In general, strict semantics, such as UNIX semantics, get harder to implement as systems get bigger. Weaker guarantees are much easier to implement. Clearly, there is a trade-off here, since programmers prefer easily well-defined semantics, but these are precisely the ones that do not scale well.

In a very large system, the concept of a single UNIX-like file tree may have to be reexamined. It is inevitable that as the system grows, the length of path names will grow too, adding more overhead. At some point it may be necessary to partition the tree into smaller trees.

5.3.3. Wide Area Networking

Most current work on distributed systems focuses on LAN-based systems. In the future, many LAN-based distributed systems will be interconnected to form transparent distributed systems covering countries and continents. As an example, the French PTT is currently putting a small computer in every apartment and house in France. Although the initial goal is to eliminate the need for information operators and telephone books, at some point in time someone is going to ask if it is possible to connect 10 million or more computers spread over all of France into a single transparent system, for applications as yet undreamed of. What kind of file system would be needed to serve all of France? All of Europe? The entire world? At present, no one knows.

Although the French machines are all identical, in most wide-area networks, a large variety of equipment is encountered. This diversity is inevitable when multiple buyers with different-sized budgets and goals are involved, and the purchasing is spread over many years in an era of rapid technological change. Thus a wide-area distributed system must of necessity deal with heterogeneity. This raises issues such as how should you store a character file if not everyone uses ASCII, or what format one should use for files containing floating-point numbers if multiple representations are in use.

Also important is the expected change in applications. Most experimental distributed systems being built at universities focus on programming in a UNIX-like environment as the canonical application, because that is what the researchers themselves do all day (at least when they are not in committee meetings or writing grant proposals). Initial data suggest that not all 50 million French citizens are going to list C programming as their primary activity. As distributed systems become more widespread, we are likely to see a shift to electronic mail, electronic banking, accessing data bases, and recreational activities, which will change file usage, access patterns, and a great deal more in ways we as yet do not know.

An inherent problem with massive distributed systems is that the network bandwidth is extremely low. If the telephone line is the main connection, getting more than 64 Kbps out of it seems unlikely. Bringing fiber optics into everyone's house will take decades and cost billions. On the other hand, vast amounts of data can be stored cheaply on compact disks and videotapes. Instead of logging into the telephone company's computer to look up a telephone number, it may be cheaper for them to send everyone a disk or tape containing the entire data base. We may have to develop file systems in which a distinction is made between static, read-only information (e.g., the phone book), and dynamic information (e.g., electronic mail). This distinction may have to become the basis of the entire file system.

5.3.4. Mobile Users

Portable computers are the fastest-growing segment of the computer business. Laptop computers, notebook computers, and pocket computers can be found everywhere these days, and they are multiplying like rabbits. Although computing while driving is hard, computing while flying is not. Telephones are now common in airplanes, so can flying FAXes and mobile modems be far behind? Nevertheless, the total bandwidth available from an airplane to the ground is quite low, and many places users want to go have no online connection at all.

The inevitable conclusion is that a large fraction of the time, the user will be off-line, disconnected from the file system. Few current systems were designed for such use, although Satyanarayanan (1990b) has reported some initial work in this direction.

Any solution is probably going to have to be based on caching. While connected, the user downloads to the portable those files expected to be needed later. These are used while disconnected. When reconnect occurs, the files in the cache will have to be merged with those in the file tree. Since disconnect can last for hours or days, the problems of maintaining cache consistency are much more severe than in online systems.

Another problem is that when reconnection does occur, the user may be in a city far away from his home base. Placing a phone call to the home machine is one way to get resynchronized, but the telephone bandwidth is low. Besides, in a truly distributed system contacting the local file server should be enough. The design of a worldwide, fully transparent distributed file system for simultaneous use by millions of mobile and frequently disconnected users is left as an exercise for the reader.

5.3.5. Fault Tolerance

Current computer systems, except for very specialized ones like air traffic control, are not fault tolerant. When the computer goes down, the users are expected to accept this as a fact of life. Unfortunately, the general population expects things to work. If a television channel, the phone system, or the electric power company goes down for half an hour, there are many unhappy people the next day. As distributed systems become more and more widespread, the demand for systems that essentially never fail will grow. Current systems cannot meet this need.

Obviously, such systems will need considerable redundancy in hardware and the communication infrastructure, but they will also need it in software and especially data. File replication, often an afterthought in current distributed systems, will become an essential requirement in future ones. Systems will also have to be designed that manage to function when only partial data are available, since insisting that all the data be available all the time does not lead to fault tolerance. Down times that are now considered acceptable by programmers and other sophisticated users, will be increasingly unacceptable as computer use spreads to nonspecialists.

5.3.6. Multimedia

New applications, especially those involving real-time video or multimedia will have a large impact on future distributed file systems. Text files are rarely more than a few megabytes long, but video files can easily exceed a gigabyte. To handle applications such as video-on-demand, completely different file systems will be needed.

5.4. SUMMARY

The heart of any distributed system is the distributed file system. The design of such a file system begins with the interface: What is the model of a file, and what functionality is provided? As a rule, the nature of a file is no different for the distributed case than for the single-processor case. As usual, an important part of the interface is file naming and the directory system. Naming quickly brings up the issue of transparency. To what extent is the name of a file related to its location? Can the system move a single file on its own without the file name being affected? Different systems have different answers to these questions.

File sharing in a distributed system is a complex but important topic. Various semantic models have been proposed, including UNIX semantics, session semantics, immutable files, and transaction semantics. Each has its own strengths and weaknesses. UNIX semantics is intuitive and familiar to most programmers (even non-UNIX programmers), but it is expensive to implement. Session semantics is less deterministic, but more efficient. Immutable files are unfamiliar to most people, and make updating files difficult. Transactions are frequently overkill.

Implementing a distributed file system involves making many decisions. These include whether the system should be stateless or stateful, if and how caching should be done, and how file replication can be managed. Each of these has far-ranging consequences for the designers and the users. NFS illustrates one way of building a distributed file system.

Future distributed file systems will probably have to deal with changes in hardware technology, scalability, wide-area systems, mobile users, and fault tolerance, as well as the introduction of multimedia. Many exciting challenges await us.

PROBLEMS

1. What is the difference between a file service using the upload/download model and one using the remote access model?

2. A file system allows links from one directory to another. In this way, a directory can "include" a subdirectory. In this context, what is the essential criterion that distinguishes a tree-structured directory system from a general graph-structured system?

3. In the text it was pointed out that shared file pointers cannot be implemented reasonably with session semantics. Can they be implemented when there is a single file server that provides UNIX semantics?

4. Name two useful properties that immutable files have.

5. Why do some distributed systems use two-level naming?

6. Why do stateless servers have to include a file offset in each request? Is this also needed for stateful servers?

7. One of the arguments given in the text in favor of stateful file servers is that i-nodes can be kept in memory for open files, thus reducing the number of disk operations. Propose an implementation for a stateless server that achieves almost the same performance gain. In what ways, if any, is your proposal better or worse than the stateful one?

8. When session semantics are used, it is always true that changes to a file are immediately visible to the process making the change and never visible to processes on other machines. However, it is an open question as to whether or not they should be immediately visible to other processes on the same machine. Give an argument each way.

9. Why can file caches use LRU whereas virtual memory paging algorithms cannot? Back up your arguments with approximate figures.

10. In the section on cache consistency, we discussed the problem of how a client cache manager knows if a file in its cache is still up-to-date. The method suggested was to contact the server and have the server compare the client and server times. Does this method fail if the client and server clocks are very different?

11. Consider a system that does client caching using the write-through algorithm. Individual blocks, rather than entire files, are cached. Suppose that a client is about to read an entire file sequentially, and some of the blocks are in the cache and others are not. What problem may occur, and what can be done about it?

12. Imagine that a distributed file uses client caching with a delayed write back policy. One machine opens, modifies, and closes a file. About half a minute later, another machine reads the file from the server. Which version does it get?

13. Some distributed file systems use client caching with delayed writes back to the server or write-on-close. In addition to the problems with the semantics, these systems introduce another problem. What is it? (*Hint*: Think about reliability.)

14. Measurements have shown that many files have an extremely short lifetime. What implication does this observation have for client caching policy?

15. Some distributed file systems use two-level names, ASCII and binary, as we have discussed throughout this chapter; others do not, and use ASCII names throughout. Similarly some file servers are stateless and some are stateful, giving four combinations of these two features. One of these combinations is somewhat less desirable than its alternatives. Which one, and why is it less desirable?

16. When file systems replicate files, they do not normally replicate all files. Give an example of a kind of file that is not worth replicating.

17. A file is replicated on 10 servers. List all the combinations of read quorum and write quorum that are permitted by the voting algorithm.

18. With a main memory file server that stores files contiguously, when a file grows beyond its current allocation unit, it will have to be copied. Suppose that the average file is 20K bytes and it takes 200 nsec to copy a 32-bit word. How many files can be copied per second? Can you suggest a way to do this copying without tying up the file server's CPU the entire time?

19. In NFS, when a file is opened, a file handle is returned, analogous to a file descriptor being returned in UNIX. Suppose that an NFS server crashes after a file handle has been given to a user. When the server reboots, will the file handle still be valid? If so, how does it work? If not, does this violate the principle of statelessness?

20. In the bit-map scheme of Fig. 5-16, is it necessary that all machines caching a given file use the same table entry for it? If so, how can this be arranged?

6

Distributed Shared Memory

In Chap. 1 we saw that two kinds of multiple-processor systems exist: multiprocessors and multicomputers. In a multiprocessor, two or more CPUs share a common main memory. Any process, on any processor, can read or write any word in the shared memory simply by moving data to or from the desired location. In a multicomputer, in contrast, each CPU has its own private memory. Nothing is shared.

To make an agricultural analogy, a multiprocessor is a system with a herd of pigs (processes) eating from a single feeding trough (shared memory). A multicomputer is a design in which each pig has its own private feeding trough. To make an educational analogy, a multiprocessor is a blackboard in the front of the room which all the students are looking at, whereas a multicomputer is each student looking at his or her own notebook. Although this difference may seem minor, it has far-reaching consequences.

The consequences affect both hardware and software. Let us first look at the implications for the hardware. Designing a machine in which many processors use the same memory simultaneously is surprisingly difficult. Bus-based multiprocessors, as described in Sec. 1.3.1, cannot be used with more than a few dozen processors because the bus tends to become a bottleneck. Switched multiprocessors, as described in Sec. 1.3.2, can be made to scale to large systems, but they are relatively expensive, slow, complex, and difficult to maintain.

In contrast, large multicomputers are easier to build. One can take an almost unlimited number of single-board computers, each containing a CPU, memory, and a network interface, and connect them together. Multicomputers with thousands of processors are commercially available from various manufacturers. (Please note that throughout this chapter we use the terms "CPU" and "processor" interchangeably.) From a hardware designer's perspective, multicomputers are generally preferable to multiprocessors.

Now let us consider the software. Many techniques are known for programming multiprocessors. For communication, one process just writes data to memory, to be read by all the others. For synchronization, critical regions can be used, with semaphores or monitors providing the necessary mutual exclusion. There is an enormous body of literature available on interprocess communication and synchronization on shared-memory machines. Every operating systems textbook written in the past twenty years devotes one or more chapters to the subject. In short, a large amount of theoretical and practical knowledge exists about how to program a multiprocessor.

With multicomputers, the reverse is true. Communication generally has to use message passing, making input/output the central abstraction. Message passing brings with it many complicating issues, among them flow control, lost messages, buffering, and blocking. Although various solutions have been proposed, programming with message passing remains tricky.

To hide some of the difficulties associated with message passing, Birrell and Nelson (1984) proposed using remote procedure calls. In their scheme, now widely used, the actual communication is hidden away in library procedures. To use a remote service, a process just calls the appropriate library procedure, which packs the operation code and parameters into a message, sends it over the network, and waits for the reply. While this frequently works, it cannot easily be used to pass graphs and other complex data structures containing pointers. It also fails for programs that use global variables, and it makes passing large arrays expensive, since they must be passed by value rather than by reference.

In short, from a software designer's perspective, multiprocessors are definitely preferable to multicomputers. Herein lies the dilemma. Multicomputers are easier to build but harder to program. Multiprocessors are the opposite: harder to build but easier to program. What we need are systems that are both easy to build and easy to program. Attempts to build such systems form the subject of this chapter.

6.1. INTRODUCTION

In the early days of distributed computing, everyone implicitly assumed that programs on machines with no physically shared memory (i.e., multicomputers) obviously ran in different address spaces. Given this mindset, communication was naturally viewed in terms of message passing between disjoint address spaces, as described above. In 1986, Li proposed a different scheme, now known under the name **distributed shared memory (DSM)** (Li, 1986; and Li and Hudak, 1989). Briefly summarized, Li and Hudak proposed having a collection of workstations connected by a LAN share a single paged, virtual address space. In the simplest variant, each page is present on exactly one machine. A reference to a *local* pages is done in hardware, at full memory speed. An attempt to reference a page on a different machine causes a hardware page fault, which traps to the operating system. The operating system then sends a message to the remote machine, which finds the needed page and sends it to the requesting processor. The faulting instruction is then restarted and can now complete.

In essence, this design is similar to traditional virtual memory systems: when a process touches a nonresident page, a trap occurs and the operating system fetches the page and maps it in. The difference here is that instead of getting the page from the disk, the operating system gets it from another processor over the network. To the user processes, however, the system looks very much like a traditional multiprocessor, with multiple processes free to read and write the shared memory at will. All communication and synchronization can be done via the memory, with no communication visible to the user processes. In effect, Li and Hudak devised a system that is both easy to program (logically shared memory) and easy to build (no physically shared memory).

Unfortunately, there is no such thing as a free lunch. While this system is indeed easy to program and easy to build, for many applications it exhibits poor performance, as pages are hurled back and forth across the network. This behavior is analogous to thrashing in single-processor virtual memory systems. In recent years, making these distributed shared memory systems more efficient has been an area of intense research, with numerous new techniques discovered. All of these have the goal of minimizing the network traffic and reducing the latency between the moment a memory request is made and the moment it is satisfied.

One approach is not to share the entire address space, only a selected portion of it, namely just those variables or data structures that need to be used by more than one process. In this model, one does not think of each machine as having direct access to an ordinary memory but rather, to a collection of shared variables, giving a higher level of abstraction. Not only does this strategy greatly reduce the amount of data that must be shared, but in most cases, considerable information about the shared data is available, such as their types, which can help optimize the implementation.

One possible optimization is to replicate the shared variables on multiple machines. By sharing replicated variables instead of entire pages, the problem of simulating a multiprocessor has been reduced to that of how to keep multiple copies of a set of typed data structures consistent. Potentially, reads can be done locally without any network traffic, and writes can be done using a multicopy update protocol. Such protocols are widely used in distributed data base systems, so ideas from that field may be of use.

Going still further in the direction of structuring the address space, instead of just sharing variables we could share encapsulated data types, often called **objects**. These differ from shared variables in that each object has not only some data, but also procedures, called **methods**, that act on the data. Programs may only manipulate an object's data by invoking its methods. Direct access to the data is not permitted. By restricting access in this way, various new optimizations become possible.

Doing everything in software has a different set of advantages and disadvantages from using the paging hardware. In general, it tends to put more restrictions on the programmer but may achieve better performance. Many of these restrictions (e.g., working with objects) are considered good software engineering practice and are desirable in their own right. We will come back to this subject later.

Before getting into distributed shared memory in more detail, we must first take a few steps backward to see what shared memory really is and how shared-memory multiprocessors actually work. After that we will examine the semantics of sharing, since they are surprisingly subtle. Finally, we will come back to the design of distributed shared memory systems. Because distributed shared memory can be intimately related to computer architecture, operating systems, runtime systems, and even programming languages, all of these topics will come into play in this chapter.

6.2. WHAT IS SHARED MEMORY?

In this section we will examine several kinds of shared memory multiprocessors, ranging from simple ones that operate over a single bus, to advanced ones with highly sophisticated caching schemes. These machines are important for an understanding of distributed shared memory because much of the DSM work is being inspired by advances in multiprocessor architecture. Furthermore, many of the algorithms are so similar that it is sometimes difficult to tell whether an advanced machine is a multiprocessor or a multicomputer using a hardware implementation of distributed shared memory. We will conclude by comparing the various multiprocessor architectures to some distributed shared memory systems and discover that there is a spectrum of possible designs, from those entirely in hardware to those entirely in software. By examing the entire spectrum, we can get a better feel for where DSM fits in.

6.2.1. On-Chip Memory

Although most computers have an external memory, self-contained chips containing a CPU and all the memory also exist. Such chips are produced by the millions, and are widely used in cars, appliances, and even toys. In this design, the CPU portion of the chip has address and data lines that directly connect to the memory portion. Figure 6-1(a) shows a simplified diagram of such a chip.

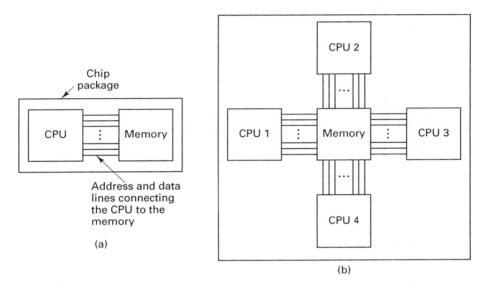

Fig. 6-1. (a) A single-chip computer. (b) A hypothetical shared-memory multiprocessor.

One could imagine a simple extension of this chip to have multiple CPUs directly sharing the same memory, as shown in Fig. 6-1(b). While it is possible to construct a chip like this, it would be complicated, expensive, and highly unusual. An attempt to construct a one-chip multiprocessor this way, with, say, 100 CPUs directly accessing the same memory would be impossible for engineering reasons. A different approach to sharing memory is needed.

6.2.2. Bus-Based Multiprocessors

If we look closely at Fig. 6-1(a), we see that the connection between the CPU and the memory is a collection of parallel wires, some holding the address the CPU wants to read or write, some for sending or receiving data, and the rest for controlling the transfers. Such a collection of wires is called a **bus**. This bus is on-chip, but in most systems, buses are external and are used to connect printed circuit boards containing CPUs, memories, and I/O controllers. On a desktop computer, the bus is typically etched onto the main board (the parent-board), which holds the CPU and some of the memory, and into which I/O cards are plugged. On minicomputers the bus is sometimes a flat cable that wends its way among the processors, memories, and I/O controllers.

A simple but practical way to build a multiprocessor is to base it on a bus to which more than one CPU is connected. Fig. 6-2(a) illustrates a system with three CPUs and a memory shared among all of them. When any of the CPUs wants to read a word from the memory, it puts the address of the word it wants on the bus and asserts (puts a signal on) a bus control line indicating that it wants to do a read. When the memory has fetched the requested word, it puts the word on the bus and asserts another control line to announce that it is ready. The CPU then reads in the word. Writes work in an analogous way.

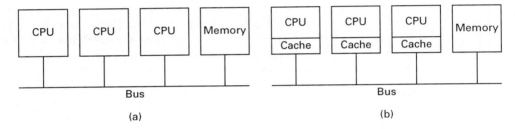

Fig. 6-2. (a) A multiprocessor. (b) A multiprocessor with caching.

To prevent two or more CPUs from trying to access the memory at the same time, some kind of bus arbitration is needed. Various schemes are in use. For example, to acquire the bus, a CPU might first have to request it by asserting a special request line. Only after receiving permission would it be allowed to use the bus. The granting of this permission can be done in a centralized way, using a bus arbitration device, or in a decentralized way, with the first requesting CPU along the bus winning any conflict.

The disadvantage of having a single bus is that with as few as three or four CPUs the bus is likely to become overloaded. The usual approach taken to reduce the bus load is to equip each CPU with a **snooping cache** (sometimes called a **snoopy cache),** so called because it "snoops" on the bus. Caches are shown in Fig. 6-2(b). They have been the subject of a large amount of research over the years (Agarwal et al., 1988; Agarwal and Cherian, 1989; Archibald and Baer, 1986; Cheong and Veidenbaum, 1988; Dahlgren et al., 1994; Eggers and Katz, 1989a, 1989b; Nayfeh and Olukotun, 1994; Przybylski et al., 1988; Scheurich and Dubois, 1987; Thekkath and Eggers, 1994; Vernon et al., 1988; and Weber and Gupta, 1989). All of these papers present slightly different **cache consistency protocols,** that is, rules for making sure that different caches do not contain different values for the same memory location.

One particularly simple and common protocol is called **write through**. When a CPU first reads a word from memory, that word is fetched over the bus and is stored in the cache of the CPU making the request. If that word is needed again later, the CPU can take it from the cache without making a memory request, thus reducing bus traffic. These two cases, read miss (word not cached) and read hit (word cached) are shown in Fig. 6-3 as the first two lines in the table. In simple systems, only the word requested is cached, but in most, a block of words of say, 16 or 32 words, is transferred and cached on the initial access and kept for possible future use.

Event	Action taken by a cache in response to its own CPU's operation	Action taken by a cache in response to a remote CPU's operation
Read miss	Fetch data from memory and store in cache	(No action)
Read hit	Fetch data from local cache	(No action)
Write miss	Update data in memory and store in cache	(No action)
Write hit	Update memory and cache	Invalidate cache entry

Fig. 6-3. The *write-through* cache consistency protocol. The entries for *hit* in the third column mean that the snooping CPU has the word in its cache, not that the requesting CPU has it.

Each CPU does its caching independent of the others. Consequently, it is possible for a particular word to be cached at two or more CPUs at the same time. Now let us consider what happens when a write is done. If no CPU has the word being written in its cache, the memory is just updated, as if caching were not being used. This operation requires a normal bus cycle. If the CPU doing the write has the only copy of the word, its cache is updated and memory is updated over the bus as well.

So far, so good. The trouble arises when a CPU wants to write a word that two or more CPUs have in their caches. If the word is currently in the cache of the CPU doing the write, the cache entry is updated. Whether it is or not, it is also written to the bus to update memory. All the other caches see the write (because they are snooping on the bus) and check to see if they are also holding the word being modified. If so, they invalidate their cache entries, so that after the write completes, memory is up-to-date and only one machine has the word in its cache.

An alternative to invalidating other cache entries is to update all of them. Updating is slower than invalidating in most cases, however. Invalidating requires supplying just the address to be invalidated, whereas updating needs to provide the new cache entry as well. If these two items must be presented on the bus consecutively, extra cycles will be required. Even if it is possible to put an address and a data word on the bus simultaneously, if the cache block size is more than one word, multiple bus cycles will be needed to update the entire block. The issue of invalidate vs. update occurs in all cache protocols and also in DSM systems.

The complete protocol is summarized in Fig. 6-3. The first column lists the four basic events that can happen. The second one tells what a cache does in response to its *own* CPU's actions. The third one tells what happens when a cache sees (by snooping) that a *different* CPU has had a hit or miss. The only time cache S (the snooper) must do something is when it sees that another CPU has written a word that S has cached (a write hit from S's point of view). The action is for S to delete the word from its cache.

The *write-through* protocol is simple to understand and implement but has the serious disadvantage that all writes use the bus. While the protocol certainly reduces bus traffic to some extent, the number of CPUs that can be attached to a single bus is still too small to permit large-scale multiprocessors to be built using it.

Fortunately, for many actual programs, once a CPU has written a word, that CPU is likely to need the word again, and it is unlikely that another CPU will use the word quickly. This situation suggests that if the CPU using the word could somehow be given temporary "ownership" of the word, it could avoid having to update memory on subsequent writes until a different CPU exhibited interest in the word. Such cache protocols exist. Goodman (1983) devised the first one, called **write once**. However, this protocol was designed to work with an existing bus and was therefore more complicated than is strictly necessary. Below we will describe a simplified version of it, which is typical of all ownership protocols. Other protocols are described and compared by Archibald and Baer (1986).

Our protocol manages cache blocks, each of which can be in one of the following three states:

1. INVALID — This cache block does not contain valid data.

2. CLEAN — Memory is up-to-date; the block may be in other caches.

3. DIRTY — Memory is incorrect; no other cache holds the block.

The basic idea is that a word that is being read by multiple CPUs is allowed to be present in all their caches. A word that is being heavily written by only one machine is kept in its cache and not written back to memory on every write to reduce bus traffic.

The operation of the protocol can best be illustrated by an example. For simplicity in this example, we will assume that each cache block consists of a single word. Initially, B has a cached copy of the word at address W, as illustrated in Fig. 6-4(a). The value is W_1. The memory also has a valid copy. In

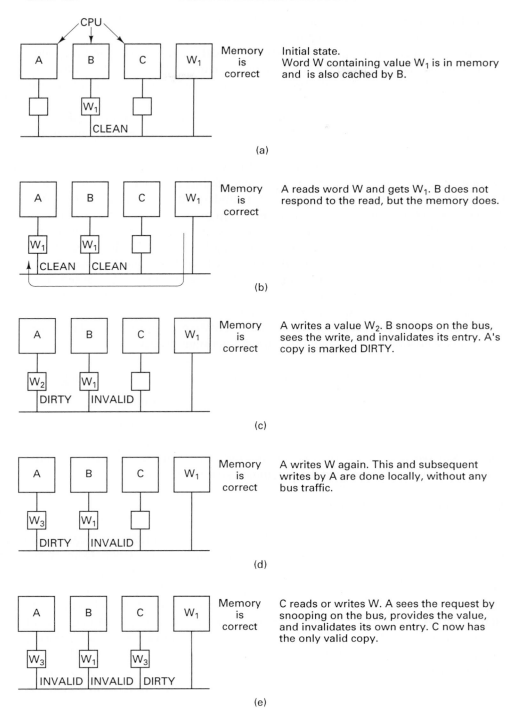

Fig. **6-4.** An example of how a cache ownership protocol works.

Fig. 6-4(b), A requests and gets a copy of W from the memory. Although B sees the read request go by, it does not respond to it.

Now A writes a new value, W_2 to W. B sees the write request and responds by invalidating its cache entry. A's state is changed to DIRTY, as shown in Fig. 6-4(c). The DIRTY state means that A has the only cached copy of W and that memory is out-of-date for W.

At this point, A overwrites the word again, as shown in Fig. 6-4(d). The write is done locally, in the cache, with no bus traffic. All subsequent writes also avoid updating memory.

Sooner or later, some other CPU, C in Fig. 6-4(e), accesses the word. A sees the request on the bus and asserts a signal that inhibits memory from responding. Instead, A provides the needed word and invalidates its own entry. C sees that the word is coming from another cache, not from memory, and that it is in DIRTY state, so it marks the entry accordingly. C is now the owner, which means that it can now read and write the word without making bus requests. However, it also has the responsibility of watching out for other CPUs that request the word, and servicing them itself. The word remains in DIRTY state until it is purged from the cache it is currently residing in for lack of space. At that time it disappears from all caches and is written back to memory.

Many small multiprocessors use a cache consistency protocol similar to this one, often with small variations. It has three important properties:

1. Consistency is achieved by having all the caches do bus snooping.

2. The protocol is built into the memory management unit.

3. The entire algorithm is performed in well under a memory cycle.

As we will see later, some of these do not hold for larger (switched) multiprocessors, and none of them hold for distributed shared memory.

6.2.3. Ring-Based Multiprocessors

The next step along the path toward distributed shared memory systems are ring-based multiprocessors, exemplified by **Memnet** (Delp, 1988; Delp et al., 1991; and Tam et al., 1990). In Memnet, a single address space is divided into a private part and a shared part. The private part is divided up into regions so that each machine has a piece for its stacks and other unshared data and code. The shared part is common to all machines (and distributed over them) and is kept consistent by a hardware protocol roughly similar to those used on bus-based multiprocessors. Shared memory is divided into 32-byte blocks, which is the unit in which transfers between machines take place.

All the machines in Memnet are connected together in a modified token-passing ring. The ring consists of 20 parallel wires, which together allow 16 data bits and 4 control bits to be sent every 100 nsec, for a data rate of 160 Mbps. The ring is illustrated in Fig. 6-5(a). The ring interface, MMU (Memory Management Unit), cache, and part of the memory are integrated together in the **Memnet device**, which is shown in the top third of Fig. 6-5(b).

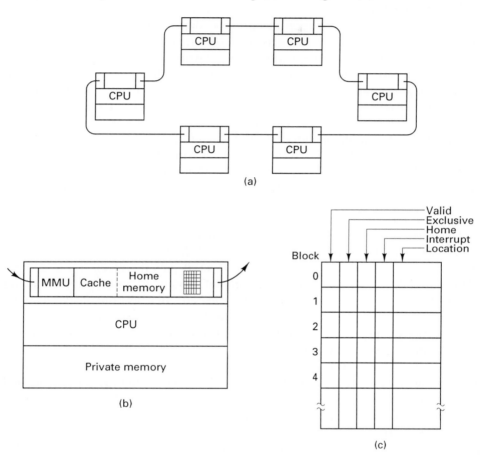

Fig. 6-5. (a) The Memnet ring. (b) A single machine. (c) The block table.

Unlike the bus-based multiprocessors of Fig. 6-2, in Memnet there is no centralized global memory. Instead, each 32-byte block in the shared address space has a home machine on which physical memory is always reserved for it, in the *Home memory* field of Fig. 6-5(b). A block may be cached on a machine other than its home machine. (The cache and home memory areas share the same buffer pool, but since they are used slightly differently, we treat them here as separate entities.) A read-only block may be present on multiple machines; a read-write block may be present on only one machine. In both cases, a block need not be present on its home machine. All the home machine does is provide a guaranteed place to store the block if no other machine wants to cache it. This feature is needed because there is no global memory. In effect, the global memory has been spread out over all the machines.

The Memnet device on each machine contains a table, shown in Fig. 6-5(c), which contains an entry for each block in the shared address space, indexed by block number. Each entry contains a *Valid* bit telling whether the block is present in the cache and up to date, an *Exclusive* bit, specifying whether the local copy, if any, is the only one, a *Home* bit, which is set only if this is the block's home machine, an *Interrupt* bit, used for forcing interrupts, and a *Location* field that tells where the block is located in the cache if it is present and valid.

Having looked at the architecture of Memnet, let us now examine the protocols it uses. When the CPU wants to read a word from shared memory, the memory address to be read is passed to the Memnet device, which checks the block table to see if the block is present. If so, the request is satisfied immediately. If not, the Memnet device waits until it captures the circulating token, then puts a request packet onto the ring and suspends the CPU. The request packet contains the desired address and a 32-byte dummy field.

As the packet passes around the ring, each Memnet device along the way checks to see if it has the block needed. If so, it puts the block in the dummy field and modifies the packet header to inhibit subsequent machines from doing so. If the block's *Exclusive* bit is set, it is cleared. Because the block has to be somewhere, when the packet comes back to the sender, it is guaranteed to contain the block requested. The CPU sending the request then stores the block, satisfies the request, and releases the CPU.

A problem arises if the requesting machine has no free space in its cache to hold the incoming block. To make space, it picks a cached block at random and sends it home, thus freeing up a cache slot. Blocks whose *Home* bit are set are never chosen since they are already home.

Writes work slightly differently than reads. Three cases have to be distinguished. If the block containing the word to be written is present and is the only copy in the system (i.e., the *Exclusive* bit is set), the word is just written locally.

If the needed block is present but it is not the only copy, an invalidation packet is first sent around the ring to force all other machines to discard their copies of the block about to be written. When the invalidation packet arrives back at the sender, the *Exclusive* bit is set for that block and the write proceeds locally.

If the block is not present, a packet is sent out that combines a read request and an invalidation request. The first machine that has the block copies it into the packet and discards its own copy. All subsequent machines just discard the block from their caches. When the packet comes back to the sender, it is stored there and written.

Memnet is similar to a bus-based multiprocessor in most ways. In both cases, read operations always return the value most recently written. Also, in both designs, a block may be absent from a cache, present in multiple caches for reading, or present in a single cache for writing. The protocols are similar, too; however, Memnet has no centralized global memory.

The biggest difference between bus-based multiprocessors and ring-based multiprocessors such as Memnet is that the former are tightly coupled, with the CPUs normally being in a single rack. In contrast, the machines in a ring-based multiprocessor can be much more loosely coupled, potentially even on desktops spread around a building, like machines on a LAN, although this loose coupling can adversely effect performance. Furthermore, unlike a bus-based multiprocessor, a ring-based multiprocessor like Memnet has no separate global memory. The caches are all there is. In both respects, ring-based multiprocessors are almost a hardware implementation of distributed shared memory.

One is tempted to say that a ring-based multiprocessor is like a duck-billed platypus—theoretically it ought not exist because it combines the properties of two categories said to be mutually exclusive (multiprocessors and distributed shared memory machines; mammals and birds, respectively). Nevertheless, it does exist, and shows that the two categories are not quite so distinct as one might think.

6.2.4. Switched Multiprocessors

Although bus-based multiprocessors and ring-based multiprocessors work fine for small systems (up to around 64 CPUs), they do not scale well to systems with hundreds or thousands of CPUs. As CPUs are added, at some point the bus or ring bandwidth saturates. Adding additional CPUs does not improve the system performance.

Two approaches can be taken to attack the problem of not enough bandwidth:

1. Reduce the amount of communication.

2. Increase the communication capacity.

We have already seen an example of an attempt to reduce the amount of communication by using caching. Additional work in this area might center on improving the caching protocol, optimizing the block size, reorganizing the program to increase locality of memory references, and so on.

Nevertheless, eventually there comes a time when every trick in the book has been used, but the insatiable designers still want to add more CPUs and there is no bus bandwidth left. The only way out is to add more bus bandwidth. One approach is to change the topology, going, for example, from one bus to two buses or to a tree or grid. By changing the topology of the interconnection network, it is possible to add additional communication capacity.

A different method is to build the system as a hierarchy. Continue to put some number of CPUs on a single bus, but now regard this entire unit (CPUs plus bus) as a cluster. Build the system as multiple clusters and connect the clusters using an intercluster bus, as shown in Fig. 6-6(a). As long as most CPUs communicate primarily within their own cluster, there will be relatively little intercluster traffic. If one intercluster bus proves to be inadequate, add a second intercluster bus, or arrange the clusters in a tree or grid. If still more bandwidth is needed, collect a bus, tree, or grid of clusters together into a super-cluster, and break the system into multiple superclusters. The superclusters can be connected by a bus, tree, or grid, and so on. Fig. 6-6(b) shows a system with three levels of buses.

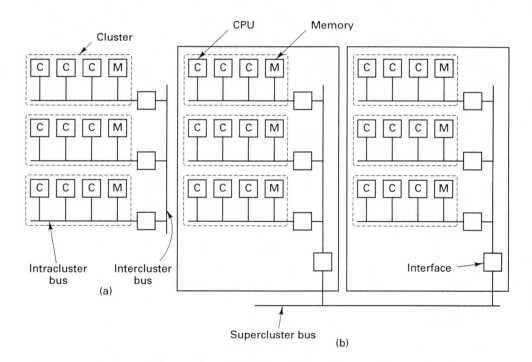

Fig. 6-6. (a) Three clusters connected by an intercluster bus to form one supercluster. (b) Two superclusters connected by a supercluster bus.

In this section we will look at a hierarchical design based on a grid of clusters. The machine, called **Dash**, was built as a research project at Stanford University (Lenoski et al., 1992). Although many other researchers are doing similar work, this one is a typical example. In the remainder of this section we will focus on the 64-CPU prototype that was actually constructed, but the design principles have been chosen carefully so that one could equally well build a much larger version. The description given below has been simplified slightly in a few places to avoid going into unnecessary detail.

A simplified diagram of the Dash prototype is presented in Fig. 6-7(a). It consists of 16 clusters, each cluster containing a bus, four CPUs, 16M of the global memory, and some I/O equipment (disks, etc.). To avoid clutter in the figure, the I/O equipment and two of the CPUs have been omitted from each cluster. Each CPU is able to snoop on its local bus, as in Fig. 6-2(b), but not on other buses.

The total address space available in the prototype is 256M, divided up into 16 regions of 16M each. The global memory of cluster 0 holds addresses 0 to 16M. The global memory of cluster 1 holds addresses 16M to 32M, and so on. Memory is cached and transferred in units of 16-byte blocks, so each cluster has 1M memory blocks within its address space.

Directories

Each cluster has a **directory** that keeps track of which clusters currently have copies of its blocks. Since each cluster owns 1M memory blocks, it has 1M entries in its directory, one per block. Each entry holds a bit map with one bit per cluster telling whether or not that cluster has the block currently cached. The entry also has a 2-bit field telling the state of the block. The directories are essential to the operation of Dash, as we shall see. In fact, the name Dash comes from "Directory Architecture for Shared memory."

Having 1M entries of 18 bits each means that the total size of each directory is over 2M bytes. With 16 clusters, the total directory memory is just over 36M, or about 14 percent of the 256M. If the number of CPUs per cluster is increased, the amount of directory memory is not changed. Thus having more CPUs per cluster allows the directory cost to be amortized over a larger number of CPUs, reducing the cost per CPU. Also, the cost of the directory and bus controllers per CPU are reduced. In theory, the design works fine with one CPU per cluster, but the cost of the directory and bus hardware per CPU then becomes larger.

A bit map is not the only way to keep track of which cluster holds which cache block. An alternative approach is to organize each directory entry as an explicit list telling which clusters hold the corresponding cache block. If there is little sharing, the list approach will require fewer bits, but if there is substantial sharing, it will require more bits. Lists also have the disadvantage of being

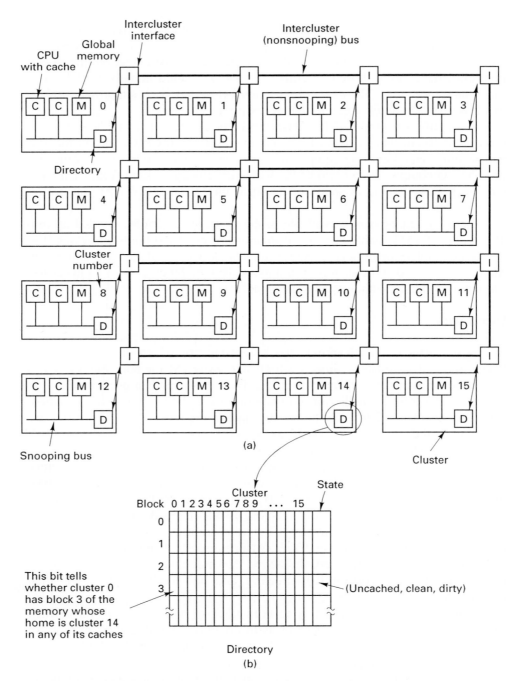

Fig. 6-7. (a) A simplified view of the Dash architecture. Each cluster actually has four CPUs, but only two are shown here. (b) A Dash directory.

variable-length data structures, but these problems can be solved. The M.I.T. Alewife multiprocessor (Agarwal et al., 1991; and Kranz et al., 1993), for example, is similar to Dash in many respects, although it uses lists instead of bit maps in its directories and handles directory overflows in software.

Each cluster in Dash is connected to an interface that allows the cluster to communicate with other clusters. The interfaces are connected by intercluster links (primitive buses) in a rectangular grid, as shown in Fig. 6-7(a). As more clusters are added to the system, more intercluster links are added, too, so the bandwidth increases and the system scales. The intercluster link system uses **wormhole routing**, which means that the first part of a packet can be forwarded even before the entire packet has been received, thus reducing the delay at each hop. Although not shown in the figure, there are actually two sets of intercluster links, one for request packets and one for reply packets. The intercluster links cannot be snooped upon.

Caching

Caching is done on two levels: a first-level cache and a larger second-level cache. The first-level cache is a subset of the second-level cache, so only the latter will concern us here. Each (second-level) cache monitors the local bus using a protocol somewhat similar to the cache ownership protocol of Fig. 6-4.

Each cache block can be in one of the following three states:

1. UNCACHED—The only copy of the block is in this memory.

2. CLEAN   —Memory is up-to-date; the block may be in several caches.

3. DIRTY   —Memory is incorrect; only one cache holds the block.

The state of each cache block is stored in the *State* field of its directory entry, as shown in Fig. 6-7(b).

Protocols

The Dash protocols are based on ownership and invalidation. At every instant, each cache block has a unique owner. For UNCACHED or CLEAN blocks, the block's home cluster is the owner. For DIRTY blocks, the cluster holding the one and only copy is the owner. Writing on a CLEAN block requires first finding and invalidating all existing copies. This is where the directories come in.

To see how this mechanism works, let us first consider how a CPU reads a memory word. It first checks its own caches. If neither cache has the word, a request is issued on the local cluster bus to see if another CPU in the cluster has the block containing it. If one does, a cache-to-cache transfer of the block is executed to place the block in the requesting CPU's cache. If the block is CLEAN, a copy is made; if it is DIRTY, the home directory is informed that the block is now CLEAN and shared. Either way, a hit from one of the caches satisfies the instruction but does not affect any directory's bit map.

If the block is not present in any of the cluster's caches, a request packet is sent to the block's home cluster, which can be determined by examining the upper 4 bits of the memory address. The home cluster might well be the requester's cluster, in which case the message is not sent physically. The directory management hardware at the home cluster examines its tables to see what state the block is in. If it is UNCACHED or CLEAN, the hardware fetches the block from its global memory and sends it back to the requesting cluster. It then updates its directory, marking the block as cached in the requester's cluster (if it was not already so marked).

If, however, the needed block is DIRTY, the directory hardware looks up the identity of the cluster holding the block and forwards the request there. The cluster holding the DIRTY block then sends it to the requesting cluster and marks its own copy as CLEAN because it is now shared. It also sends a copy back to the home cluster so that memory can be updated and the block state changed to CLEAN. All these cases are summarized in Fig. 6-8(a). Where a block is marked as being in a new state, it is the home directory that is changed, as it is the home directory that keeps track of the state.

Writes work differently. Before a write can be done, the CPU doing the write must be sure that it is the owner of the only copy of the cache block in the system. If it already has the block in its on-board cache and the block is DIRTY, the write can proceed immediately. If it has the block but it is CLEAN, a packet is first sent to the home cluster requesting that all other copies be tracked down and invalidated.

If the requesting CPU does not have the cache block, it issues a request on the local bus to see if any of the neighbors have it. If so, a cache-to-cache (or memory-to-cache) transfer is done. If the block is CLEAN, all other copies, if any, must be invalidated by the home cluster.

If the local broadcast fails to turn up a copy and the block is homed elsewhere, a packet is sent to the home cluster. Three cases can be distinguished here. If the block is UNCACHED, it is marked DIRTY and sent to the requester. If it is CLEAN, all copies are invalidated and then the procedure for UNCACHED is followed. If it is DIRTY, the request is forwarded to the remote cluster currently owning the block (if needed). This cluster invalidates its own copy and satisfies the request. The various cases are shown in Fig. 6-8(b).

Obviously, maintaining memory consistency in Dash (or any large multiprocessor) is nothing at all like the simple model of Fig. 6-1(b). A single memory access may require a substantial number of packets to be sent. Furthermore, to keep memory consistent, the access usually cannot be completed until all the

Location where the block was found

Block state	R's cache	Neighbor's cache	Home cluster's memory	Some cluster's cache
UNCACHED			Send block to R; mark as CLEAN and cached only in R's cluster	
CLEAN	Use block	Copy block to R's cache	Copy block from memory to R; mark as also cached in R's cluster	
DIRTY	Use block	Send block to R and to home cluster; tell home to mark it as CLEAN and cached in R's cluster		Send block to R and to home cluster (if cached elsewhere); tell home to mark it as CLEAN and also cached in R's cluster

(a)

Location where the block was found

Block state	R's cache	Neighbor's cache	Home cluster's memory	Some cluster's cache
UNCACHED			Send block to R; mark as DIRTY and cached only in R's cluster	
CLEAN	Send message to home asking for exclusive ownership in DIRTY state; if granted, use block	Copy and invalidate block; send message to home asking for exclusive ownership in DIRTY state	Send block to R; invalidate all cached copies; mark it as DIRTY and cached only in R's cluster	
DIRTY	Use block	Cache-to-cache transfer to R; invalidate neighbor's copy		Send block directly to R; invalidate cached copy; home marks it as DIRTY and cached only in R's cluster

(b)

Fig. 6-8. Dash protocols. The columns show where the block was found. The rows show the state it was in. The contents of the boxes show the action taken. *R* refers to the requesting CPU. An empty box indicates an impossible situation. (a) Reads. (b) Writes.

packets have been acknowledged, which can have a serious effect on performance. To get around these problems, Dash uses a variety of special techniques, such as two sets of intercluster links, pipelined writes, and different memory semantics than one might expect. We will discuss some of these issues later. For the time being, the bottom line is that this implementation of "shared memory" requires a large data base (the directories), a considerable amount of computing power (the directory management hardware), and a potentially large number of packets that must be sent and acknowledged. We will see later that implementing distributed shared memory has precisely the same properties. The difference between the two lies much more in the implementation technique than in the ideas, architecture, or algorithms.

6.2.5. NUMA Multiprocessors

If nothing else, it should be abundantly clear by now that hardware caching in large multiprocessors is not simple. Complex data structures must be maintained by the hardware and intricate protocols, such as those of Fig. 6-8, must be built into the cache controller or MMU. The inevitable consequence is that large multiprocessors are expensive and not in widespread use.

However, researchers have spent a considerable amount of effort looking at alternative designs that do not require elaborate caching schemes. One such architecture is the **NUMA (NonUniform Memory Access)** multiprocessor. Like a traditional **UMA (Uniform Memory Access)** multiprocessor, a NUMA machine has a single virtual address space that is visible to all CPUs. When any CPU writes a value to location a, a subsequent read of a by a different processor will return the value just written.

The difference between UMA and NUMA machines lies not in the semantics but in the performance. On a NUMA machine, access to a remote memory is much slower than access to a local memory, and no attempt is made to hide this fact by hardware caching. The ratio of a remote access to a local access is typically 10:1, with a factor of two variation either way not being unusual. Thus a CPU can directly execute a program that resides in a remote memory, but the program may run an order of magnitude slower than it would have had it been in local memory.

Examples of NUMA Multiprocessors

To make the concept of a NUMA machine clearer, consider the example of Fig. 6-9(a), Cm*, the first NUMA machine (Jones et al., 1977). The machine consisted of a number of clusters, each consisting of a CPU, a microprogrammable MMU, a memory module, and possibly some I/O devices, all connected by a bus. No caches were present, and no bus snooping occurred. The clusters were connected by intercluster buses, one of which is shown in the figure.

When a CPU made a memory reference, the request went to the CPU's MMU, which then examined the upper bits of the address to see which memory was needed. If the address was local, the MMU just issued a request on the local bus. If it was to a distant memory, the MMU built a request packet containing the address (and for a write, the data word to be written), and sent it to the destination cluster over an intercluster bus. Upon receiving the packet, the destination MMU carried out the operation and returned the word (for a read) or an acknowledgement (for a write). Although it was possible for a CPU to run entirely from a remote memory, sending a packet for each word read and each word written slowed down operation by an order of magnitude.

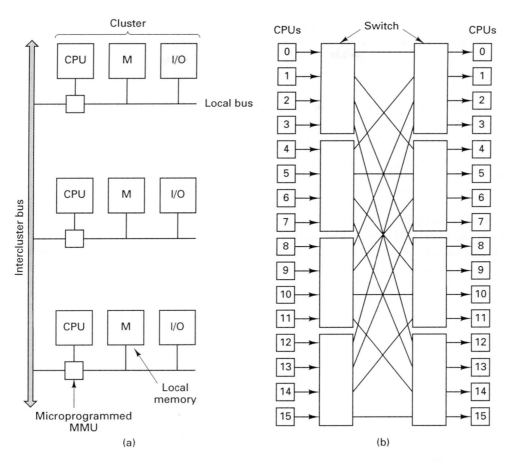

Fig. 6-9. (a) A simplified view of the Cm* system. (b) The BBN Butterfly. The CPUs on the right are the same as those on the left (i.e., the architecture is really a cylinder).

Figure 6-9(b) shows another NUMA machine, the BBN Butterfly. In this design, each CPU is coupled directly to one memory. Each of the small squares in Fig. 6-9(b) represents a CPU plus memory pair. The CPUs on the right-hand side of the figure are the same as those on the left. The CPUs are wired up via eight switches, each having four input ports and four output ports. Local memory requests are handled directly; remote requests are turned into request packets and sent to the appropriate memory via the switching network. Here, too, programs can run remotely, but at a tremendous penalty in performance.

Although neither of these examples has any global memory, NUMA machines can be equipped with memory that is not attached to any CPU.

Bolosky et al. (1989), for example, describe a bus-based NUMA machine that has a global memory that does not belong to any CPU but can be accessed by all of them (in addition to the local memories).

Properties of NUMA Multiprocessors

NUMA machines have three key properties that are of concern to us:

1. Access to remote memory is possible.

2. Accessing remote memory is slower than accessing local memory.

3. Remote access times are not hidden by caching.

The first two points are self explanatory. The third may require some clarification. In Dash and most other modern UMA multiprocessors, remote access is slower than local access as well. What makes this property bearable is the presence of caching. When a remote word is touched, a block of memory around it is fetched to the requesting processor's cache, so that subsequent references go at full speed. Although there is a slight delay to handle the cache fault, running out of remote memory can be only fractionally more expensive than running out of local memory. The consequence of this observation is that it does not matter so much which pages live in which memory: code and data are automatically moved by the hardware to wherever they are needed (although a bad choice of the home cluster for each page in Dash adds extra overhead).

NUMA machines do not have this property, so it matters a great deal which page is located in which memory (i.e., on which machine). The key issue in NUMA software is the decision of where to place each page to maximize performance. Below we will briefly summarize some ideas due to LaRowe and Ellis (1991). Other work is described in (Cox and Fowler, 1989; LaRowe et al., 1991; and Ramanathan and Ni, 1991).

When a program on a NUMA machine starts up, pages may or may not be manually prepositioned on certain processors' machines (their home processors). In either case, when a CPU tries to access a page that is not currently mapped into its address space, it causes a page fault. The operating system catches the fault and has to make a decision. If the page is read-only, the choice is to replicate the page (i.e., make a local copy without disturbing the original) or to map the virtual page onto the remote memory, thus forcing a remote access for all addresses on that page. If the page is read-write, the choice is to migrate the page to the faulting processor (invalidating the original page) or to map the virtual page onto the remote memory.

The trade-offs involved here are simple. If a local copy is made (replication or migration) and the page is not reused much, considerable time will have been wasted fetching it for nothing. On the other hand, if no copy is made, the page is mapped remote, and many accesses follow, they will all be slow. In essence, the operating system has to guess if the page will be heavily used in the future. If it guesses wrong, a performance penalty will be extracted.

Whichever decision is made, the page is mapped in, either local or remote, and the faulting instruction restarted. Subsequent references to that page are done in hardware, with no software intervention. If no other action were taken, then a wrong decision once made could never be reversed.

NUMA Algorithms

To allow mistakes to be corrected and to allow the system to adapt to changes in reference patterns, NUMA systems usually have a daemon process, called the **page scanner**, running in the background. Periodically (e.g., every 4 sec), the page scanner gathers usage statistics about local and remote references, which are maintained with help from the hardware. Every n times it runs, the page scanner reevaluates earlier decisions to copy pages or map them to remote memories. If the usage statistics indicate that a page is in the wrong place, the page scanner unmaps the page so that the next reference causes a page fault, allowing a new placement decision to be made. If a page is moved too often within a short interval, the page scanner can mark the page as **frozen**, which inhibits further movement until some specified event happens (e.g., some number of seconds have elapsed).

Numerous strategies have been proposed for NUMA machines, differing in the algorithm used by the scanner to invalidate pages and the algorithm used to make placement decisions after a page fault. One possible scanner algorithm is to invalidate any page for which there have been more remote references than local ones. A stronger test is to invalidate a page only if the remote reference count has been greater than the local one the last k times the scanner has run. Other possibilities are to defrost frozen pages after t seconds have elapsed or if the remote references exceed the local ones by some amount or for some time interval.

When a page fault occurs, various algorithms are possible, always including replicate/migrate and never including replicate/migrate. A more sophisticated one is to replicate or migrate unless the page is frozen. Recent usage patterns can also be taken into account, as can the fact that the page is or is not on its "home" machine.

LaRowe and Ellis (1991) have compared a large number of algorithms and concluded that no single policy is best. The machine architecture, the size of the penalty for a remote access, and the reference pattern of the program in question all play a large role in determining which algorithm is best.

6.2.6. Comparison of Shared Memory Systems

Shared memory systems cover a broad spectrum, from systems that maintain consistency entirely in hardware to those that do it entirely in software. We have studied the hardware end of the spectrum in some detail and have given a brief summary of the software end (page-based distributed shared memory and object-based distributed shared memory). In Fig. 6-10 the spectrum is shown explicitly.

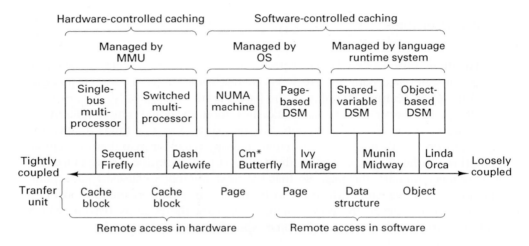

Fig. 6-10. The spectrum of shared memory machines.

On the left-hand side of Fig. 6-10 we have the single-bus multiprocessors that have hardware caches and keep them consistent by snooping on the bus. These are the simplest shared-memory machines and operate entirely in hardware. Various machines made by Sequent and other vendors and the experimental DEC Firefly workstation (five VAXes on a common bus) fall into this category. This design works fine for a small or medium number of CPUs, but degrades rapidly when the bus saturates.

Next come the switched multiprocessors, such as the Stanford Dash machine and the M.I.T. Alewife machine. These also have hardware caching but use directories and other data structures to keep track of which CPUs or clusters have which cache blocks. Complex algorithms are used to maintain consistency, but since they are stored primarily in MMU microcode (with exceptions potentially handled in software), they count as mostly "hardware" implementations.

Next come the NUMA machines. These are hybrids between hardware and software control. As in a multiprocessor, each NUMA CPU can access each word of the common virtual address space just by reading or writing it. Unlike in a multiprocessor, however, caching (i.e., page placement and migration) is controlled by software (the operating system), not by hardware (the MMUs). Cm* (Jones et al., 1977) and the BBN Butterfly are examples of NUMA machines.

Continuing along the spectrum, we come to the machines running a page-based distributed shared memory system such as IVY (Li, 1986) and Mirage (Fleisch and Popek, 1989). Each of the CPUs in such a system has its own private memory and, unlike the NUMA machines and UMA multiprocessors, cannot reference remote memory directly. When a CPU addresses a word in the address space that is backed by a page currently located on a different machine, a trap to the operating system occurs and the required page must be fetched by software. The operating system acquires the necessary page by sending a message to the machine where the page is currently residing and asking for it. Thus both placement and access are done in software here.

Then we come to machines that share only a selected portion of their address spaces, namely shared variables and other data structures. The Munin (Bennett et al., 1990) and Midway (Bershad et al., 1990) systems work this way. User-supplied information is required to determine which variables are shared and which are not. In these systems, the focus changes from trying to pretend that there is a single common memory to how to maintain a set of replicated distributed data structures consistent in the face of updates, potentially from all the machines using the shared data. In some cases the paging hardware detects writes, which may help maintain consistency efficiently. In other cases, the paging hardware is not used for consistency management.

Finally, we have systems running object-based distributed shared memory. Unlike all the others, programs here cannot just access the shared data. They have to go through protected methods, which means that the runtime system can always get control on every access to help maintain consistency. Everything is done in software here, with no hardware support at all. Orca (Bal, 1991) is an example of this design, and Linda (Carriero and Gelernter, 1989) is similar to it in some important ways.

The differences between these six types of systems are summarized in Fig. 6-11, which shows them from tightly coupled hardware on the left to loosely coupled software on the right. The first four types offer a memory model consisting of a standard, paged, linear virtual address space. The first two are regular multiprocessors and the next two do their best to simulate them. Since the first four types act like multiprocessors, the only operations possible are reading and writing memory words. In the fifth column, the shared variables are special, but they are still accessed only by normal reads and writes. The object-based systems, with their encapsulated data and methods, can offer more general operations and represent a higher level of abstraction than raw memory.

| | Multiprocessors | | | DSM | | |
Item	Single bus	Switched	NUMA	Page based	Shared variable	Object based
Linear, shared virtual address space?	Yes	Yes	Yes	Yes	No	No
Possible operations	R/W	R/W	R/W	R/W	R/W	General
Encapsulation and methods?	No	No	No	No	No	Yes
Is remote access possible in hardware?	Yes	Yes	Yes	No	No	No
Is unattached memory possible?	Yes	Yes	Yes	No	No	No
Who converts remote memory accesses to messages?	MMU	MMU	MMU	OS	Runtime system	Runtime system
Transfer medium	Bus	Bus	Bus	Network	Network	Network
Data migration done by	Hardware	Hardware	Software	Software	Software	Software
Transfer unit	Block	Block	Page	Page	Shared variable	Object

Fig. 6-11. Comparison of six kinds of shared memory systems.

The real difference between the multiprocessors and the DSM systems is whether or not remote data can be accessed just by referring to their addresses. On all the multiprocessors the answer is yes. On the DSM systems it is no: software intervention is always needed. Similarly, unattached global memory, that is, memory not associated with any particular CPU, is possible on the multiprocessors but not on the DSM systems (because the latter are collections of separate computers connected by a network).

In the multiprocessors, when a remote access is detected, a message is sent to the remote memory by the cache controller or MMU. In the DSM systems it is sent by the operating system or runtime system. The medium used is also different, being a high-speed bus (or collection of buses) for the multiprocessors and a conventional LAN (usually) for the DSM systems (although sometimes the difference between a "bus" and a "network" is arguable, having mainly to do with the number of wires).

The next point relates to who does data migration when it is needed. Here the NUMA machines are like the DSM systems: in both cases it is the software, not the hardware, which is responsible for moving data around from machine to machine. Finally, the unit of data transfer differs for the six systems, being a cache block for the UMA multiprocessors, a page for the NUMA machines and page-based DSM systems, and a variable or object for the last two.

6.3. CONSISTENCY MODELS

Although modern multiprocessors have a great deal in common with distributed shared memory systems, it is time to leave the subject of multiprocessors and move on. In our brief introduction to DSM systems at the start of this chapter, we said that they have one or more copies of each read-only page and one copy of each writable page. In the simplest implementation, when a writable page is referenced by a remote machine, a trap occurs and the page is fetched. However, if some writable pages are heavily shared, having only a single copy of each one can be a serious performance bottleneck.

Allowing multiple copies eases the performance problem, since it is then sufficient to update any copy, but doing so introduces a new problem: how to keep all the copies consistent. Maintaining perfect consistency is especially painful when the various copies are on different machines that can only communicate by sending messages over a slow (compared to memory speeds) network. In some DSM (and multiprocessor) systems, the solution is to accept less than perfect consistency as the price for better performance. Precisely what consistency means and how it can be relaxed without making programming unbearable is a major issue among DSM researchers.

A **consistency model** is essentially a contract between the software and the memory (Adve and Hill, 1990). It says that if the software agrees to obey certain rules, the memory promises to work correctly. If the software violates these rules, all bets are off and correctness of memory operation is no longer guaranteed. A wide spectrum of contracts have been devised, ranging from contracts that place only minor restrictions on the software to those that make normal programming nearly impossible. As you probably already guessed, the ones with minor restrictions do not perform nearly as well as the ones with major restrictions. Such is life. In this section we will study a variety of consistency models used in DSM systems. For additional information, see the paper by Mosberger (1993).

6.3.1. Strict Consistency

The most stringent consistency model is called **strict consistency**. It is defined by the following condition:

Any read to a memory location x *returns the value stored by the most recent write operation to* x.

This definition is natural and obvious, although it implicitly assumes the existence of absolute global time (as in Newtonian physics) so that the determination of "most recent" is unambiguous. Uniprocessors have traditionally observed strict consistency and uniprocessor programmers have come to expect such behavior as a matter of course. A system on which the program

```
a = 1; a = 2; print(a);
```

printed 1 or any value other than 2 would quickly lead to a lot of very agitated programmers (in this chapter, *print* is a procedure that prints its parameter or parameters).

In a DSM system, the matter is more complicated. Suppose x is a variable stored only on machine B. Imagine that a process on machine A reads x at time T_1, which means that a message is then sent to B to get x. Slightly later, at T_2, a process on B does a write to x. If strict consistency holds, the read should always return the old value regardless of where the machines are and how close T_2 is to T_1. However, if $T_2 - T_1$ is, say, 1 nanosecond, and the machines are 3 meters apart, in order to propagate the read request from A to B to get there before the write, the signal would have to travel at 10 times the speed of light, something forbidden by Einstein's special theory of relativity. Is it reasonable for programmers to demand that the system be strictly consistent, even if this requires violating the laws of physics?

This brings us to the matter of the contract between the software and the memory. If the contract implicitly or explicitly promises strict consistency, then the memory had better deliver it. On the other hand, a programmer who really expects strict consistency, and whose program fails if it is not present, is living dangerously. Even on a small multiprocessor, if one processor starts to write memory location a, and a nanosecond later another processor starts to read a the reader will probably get the old value from its local cache. Anyone who writes programs that fail under these circumstances should be made to stay after school and write a program to print 100 times: "I will avoid race conditions."

As a more realistic example, one could imagine a system to provide sports fans with up-to-the-minute (but perhaps not up-to-the-nanosecond) scores for sporting events worldwide. Answering a query as if it had been made 2 nanoseconds earlier or later might well be acceptable in this case, especially if it gave much better performance by allowing multiple copies of the data to be stored. In this case strict consistency is not promised, delivered, or needed.

To study consistency in detail, we will give numerous examples. To make these examples precise, we need a special notation. In this notation, several processes, P_1, P_2, and so on can be shown at different heights in the figure. The operations done by each process are shown horizontally, with time increasing to the right. Straight lines separate the processes. The symbols

$$W(x)a \text{ and } R(y)b$$

mean that a write to x with the value a and a read from y returning b have been done, respectively. The initial value of all variables in these diagrams throughout this chapter is assumed to be 0. As an example, in Fig. 6-12(a) P_1 does a write to location x, storing the value 1. Later, P_2 reads x and sees the 1. This behavior is correct for a strictly consistent memory.

P_1:   W(x)1 P_1:   W(x)1

P_2:   R(x)1 P_2:   R(x)0   R(x)1

           (a)   (b)

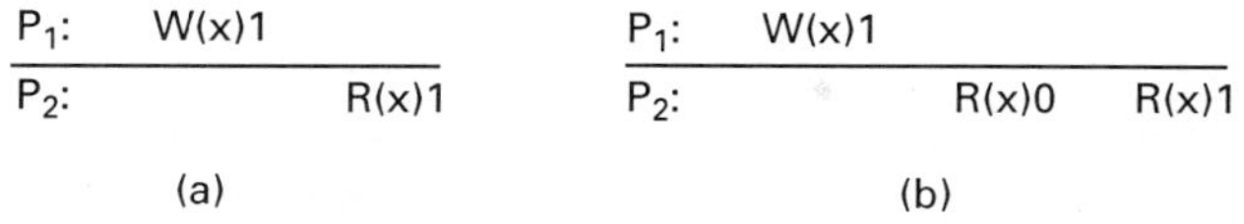

Fig. 6-12. Behavior of two processes. The horizontal axis is time. (a) Strictly consistent memory. (b) Memory that is not strictly consistent.

In contrast, in Fig. 6-12(b), P_2 does a read after the write (possibly only a nanosecond after it, but still after it), and gets 0. A subsequent read gives 1. Such behavior is incorrect for a strictly consistent memory.

In summary, when memory is strictly consistent, all writes are instantaneously visible to all processes and an absolute global time order is maintained. If a memory location is changed, all subsequent reads from that location see the new value, no matter how soon after the change the reads are done and no matter which processes are doing the reading and where they are located. Similarly, if a read is done, it gets the then-current value, no matter how quickly the next write is done.

6.3.2. Sequential Consistency

While strict consistency is the ideal programming model, it is nearly impossible to implement in a distributed system. Furthermore, experience shows that programmers can often manage quite well with weaker models. For example, all textbooks on operating systems discuss critical sections and the mutual exclusion problem. This discussion always includes the caveat that properly-written parallel programs (such as the producer-consumer problem) should not make any assumptions about the relative speeds of the processes or how their statements will interleave in time. Counting on two events within one process to happen so quickly that the other process will not be able to do something in between is looking for trouble. Instead, the reader is taught to program in such a way that the exact order of statement execution (in fact, memory references) does not matter. When the order of events is essential, semaphores or other synchronization operations should be used. Accepting this argument in fact means learning to live with a weaker memory model. With some practice, most parallel programmers are able to adapt to it.

Sequential consistency is a slightly weaker memory model than strict consistency. It was first defined by Lamport (1979), who said that a sequentially consistent memory is one that satisfies the following condition:

> *The result of any execution is the same as if the operations of all processors were executed in some sequential order, and the operations of each individual processor appear in this sequence in the order specified by its program.*

What this definition means is that when processes run in parallel on different machines (or even in pseudoparallel on a timesharing system), any valid interleaving is acceptable behavior, but *all processes must see the same sequence of memory references*. A memory in which one process (or processor) sees one interleaving and another process sees a different one is not a sequentially consistent memory. Note that nothing is said about time; that is, there is no reference to the "most recent" store. Note that in this context, a process "sees" writes from all processes but only its own reads.

That time does not play a role can be seen from Fig. 6-13. A memory behaving as shown in Fig. 6-13(a) is sequentially consistent even though the first read done by P_2 returns the initial value of 0 instead of the new value of 1.

Fig. 6-13. Two possible results of running the same program.

Sequentially consistent memory does not guarantee that a read returns the value written by another process a nanosecond earlier, or a microsecond earlier, or even a minute earlier. It merely guarantees that all processes see all memory references in the same order. If the program that generated Fig. 6-13(a) is run again, it might give the result of Fig. 6-13(b). The results are not deterministic. Running a program again may not give the same result in the absence of explicit synchronization operations.

```
a = 1;          b = 1;          c = 1;
print (b, c);   print (a, c);   print (a, b);

   (a)             (b)             (c)
```

Fig. 6-14. Three parallel processes.

To make this point more explicit, let us consider the example of Fig. 6-14 (Dubois et al., 1988). Here we see the code for three processes that run in parallel on three different processors. All three processes share the same sequentially consistent distributed shared memory, and all have access to the variables *a*, *b*, and c. From a memory reference point of view, an assignment should be seen as a write, and a print statement should be seen as a simultaneous read of its two parameters. All statements are assumed to be atomic.

Various interleaved execution sequences are possible. With six independent statements, there are potentially 720 (6!) possible execution sequences, although some of these violate program order. Consider the 120 (5!) sequences that begin with $a = 1$. Half of these have $print(a, c)$ before $b = 1$ and thus violate program order. Half also have $print(a, b)$ before $c = 1$ and also violate program order. Only 1/4 of the 120 sequences or 30 are valid. Another 30 valid sequences are possible starting with $b = 1$ and another 30 can begin with $c = 1$, for a total of 90 valid execution sequences. Four of these are shown in Fig. 6-15.

a = 1;	a = 1;	b = 1;	b = 1;
print (b, c);	b = 1;	c = 1;	a = 1;
b = 1;	print (a, c);	print (a, b);	c = 1;
print (a, c);	print (b, c);	print (a, c);	print (a, c);
c = 1;	c = 1;	a = 1;	print (b, c);
print (a, c);1	print (a, b);	print (b, c);	print (a, b);
Prints: 001011	Prints: 101011	Prints: 010111	Prints: 111111
Signature: 00101	Signature: 101011	Signature: 110101	Signature: 111111
(a)	(b)	(c)	(d)

Fig. 6-15. Four valid execution sequences for the program of Fig. 6-14. The vertical axis is time, increasing downward.

In Fig. 6-15(a), the three processes are run in order, first P_1, then P_2, then P_3. The other three examples demonstrate different, but equally valid, interleavings of the statements in time. Each of the three processes prints two variables. Since the only values each variable can take on are the initial value (0), or the assigned value (1), each process produces a 2-bit string. The numbers after *Prints* are the actual outputs that appear on the output device.

If we concatenate the output of P_1, P_2, and P_3 in that order, we get a 6-bit string that characterizes a particular interleaving of statements (and thus memory references). This is the string listed as the *Signature* in Fig. 6-15. Below we will characterize each ordering by its signature rather than by its printout.

Not all 64 signature patterns are allowed. As a trivial example, 000000 is not permitted, because that would imply that the print statements ran before the assignment statements, violating Lamport's requirement that statements are executed in program order. A more subtle example is 001001. The first two bits, 00, mean that b and c were both 0 when P_1 did its printing. This situation occurs only when P_1 executes both statements before P_2 or P_3 starts. The next two bits, 10, mean that P_2 must run after P_1 has started but before P_3 has started. The last two bits, 01, mean that P_3 must complete before P_1 starts, but we have already seen that P_1 must go first. Therefore, 001001 is not allowed.

In short, the 90 different valid statement orderings produce a variety of different program results (less than 64, though) that are allowed under the assumption of sequential consistency. The contract between the software and memory here is that the software must accept all of these as valid results. In other words, the software must accept the four results shown in Fig. 6-15 and all the other valid results as proper answers, and must work correctly if any of them occurs. A program that works for some of these results and not for others violates the contract with the memory and is incorrect.

A sequentially consistent memory can be implemented on a DSM or multi-processor system that replicates writable pages by ensuring that no memory operation is started until all the previous ones have been completed. In a system with an efficient, totally-ordered reliable broadcast mechanism, for example, all shared variables could be grouped together on one or more pages, and operations to the shared pages could be broadcast. The exact order in which the operations are interleaved does not matter as long as all processes agree on the order of all operations on the shared memory.

Various formal systems have been proposed for expressing sequential consistency (and other models). Let us briefly consider the system of Ahamad et al. (1993). In their method, the sequence of read and write operations of process i is designated by H_i (the history of P_i). Figure 6-12(b) shows two such sequences, H_1 and H_2 for P_1 and P_2, respectively, as follows:

$H_1 = W(x)1$

$H_2 = R(x)0 \ R(x)1$

The set of all such sequences is called H.

To get the relative order in which the operations appear to be executed, we must merge the operation strings in H into a single string, S, in which each operation appearing in H appears in S once. Intuitively, S gives the order that the operations would have been carried out had there been a single centralized memory. All legal values for S must obey two constraints:

    1. Program order must be maintained.

    2. Memory coherence must be respected.

The first constraint means that if a read or write access, A, appears before another access, B, in one of the strings in H, A must also appear before B in S. If this constraint is true for all pairs of operations, the resulting S will not show any operations in an order that violates any of the programs.

The second constraint, called **memory coherence**, means that a read to some location, x, must always return the value most recently written to x; that is, the value v written by the most recent $W(x)v$ before the $R(x)$. Memory coherence examines in isolation each location and the sequence of operations on it, without regard to other locations. Consistency, in contrast, deals with writes to *different* locations and their ordering.

For Fig. 6-12(b) there is only one legal value of S:

$$S = R(x)0 \ W(x)1 \ R(x)1,$$

For more complicated examples there might be several legal values of S. The behavior of a program is said to be correct if its operation sequence corresponds to some legal value of S.

Although sequential consistency is a programmer-friendly model, it has a serious performance problem. Lipton and Sandberg (1988) proved that if the read time is r, the write time is w, and the minimal packet transfer time between nodes is t, then it is always true that $r + w \geq t$. In other words, for any sequentially consistent memory, changing the protocol to improve the read performance makes the write performance worse, and vice versa. For this reason, researchers have investigated other (weaker) models. In the following sections we will discuss some of them.

6.3.3. Causal Consistency

The **causal consistency** model (Hutto and Ahamad, 1990) represents a weakening of sequential consistency in that it makes a distinction between events that are potentially causally related and those that are not.

To see what causality is all about, consider an example from daily life (of a computer scientist). During a discussion on the relative merits of different programming languages in one of the USENET newsgroups, some hothead posts the message: "Anybody caught programming in FORTRAN should be shot." Very shortly thereafter, a cooler individual writes: "I am against capital punishment, even for major offenses against good taste." Due to varying delays along the message propagation paths, a third subscriber may get the reply first and become quite confused upon seeing it. The problem here is that causality has been violated. If event B is caused or influenced by an earlier event, A, causality requires that everyone else first see A, then see B.

Now consider a memory example. Suppose that process P_1 writes a variable x. Then P_2 reads x and writes y. Here the reading of x and the writing of y are potentially causally related because the computation of y may have depended on the value of x read by P_2 (i.e., the value written by P_1). On the other hand, if two processes spontaneously and simultaneously write two variables, these are not causally related. When there is a read followed later by a write, the two events are potentially causally related. Similarly, a read is causally related to the write that provided the data the read got. Operations that are not causally related are said to be **concurrent**.

For a memory to be considered causally consistent, it is necessary that the memory obey the following condition:

> *Writes that are potentially causally related must be seen by all processes in the same order. Concurrent writes may be seen in a different order on different machines.*

As an example of causal consistency, consider Fig. 6-16. Here we have an event sequence that is allowed with a causally consistent memory, but which is forbidden with a sequentially consistent memory or a strictly consistent memory. The thing to note is that the writes $W(x)2$ and $W(x)3$ are concurrent, so it is not required that all processes see them in the same order. If the software fails when different processes see concurrent events in a different order, it has violated the memory contract offered by causal memory.

P_1:	W(x)1			W(x)3		
P_2:		R(x)1	W(x)2			
P_3:		R(x)1			R(x)3	R(x)2
P_4:		R(x)1			R(x)2	R(x)3

Fig. 6-16. This sequence is allowed with causally consistent memory, but not with sequentially consistent memory or strictly consistent memory.

Now consider a second example. In Fig. 6-17(a) we have $W(x)2$ potentially depending on $W(x)1$ because the 2 may be a result of a computation involving the value read by $R(x)1$. The two writes are causally related, so all processes must see them in the same order. Therefore, Fig. 6-17(a) is incorrect. On the other hand, in Fig. 6-17(b) the read has been removed, so $W(x)1$ and $W(x)2$ are now concurrent writes. Causal memory does not require concurrent writes to be globally ordered, so Fig. 6-17(b) is correct.

Implementing causal consistency requires keeping track of which processes have seen which writes. It effectively means that a dependency graph of which operation is dependent on which other operations must be constructed and maintained. Doing so involves some overhead.

6.3.4. PRAM Consistency and Processor Consistency

In causal consistency, it is permitted that concurrent writes be seen in a different order on different machines, although causally-related ones must be seen in the same order by all machines. The next step in relaxing memory is to drop

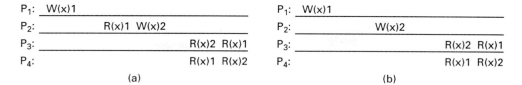

Fig. 6-17. (a) A violation of causal memory. (b) A correct sequence of events in causal memory.

the latter requirement. Doing so gives **PRAM consistency** (Pipelined RAM), which is subject to the condition:

> *Writes done by a single process are received by all other processes in the order in which they were issued, but writes from different processes may be seen in a different order by different processes.*

PRAM consistency is due to Lipton and Sandberg (1988). PRAM stands for Pipelined RAM, because writes by a single process can be pipelined, that is, the process does not have to stall waiting for each one to complete before starting the next one. PRAM consistency is contrasted with causal consistency in Fig. 6-18. The sequence of events shown here is allowed with PRAM consistent memory but not with any of the stronger models we have studied so far.

```
P₁:  W(x)1 _____
P₂:  _____ R(x)1  W(x)2 _____
P₃:  _____ R(x)1  R(x)2 ____
P₄:  _____ R(x)2  R(x)1 ____
```

Fig. 6-18. A valid sequence of events for PRAM consistency.

PRAM consistency is interesting because it is easy to implement. In effect it says that there are no guarantees about the order in which different processes see writes, except that two or more writes from a single source must arrive in order, as though they were in a pipeline. Put in other terms, in this model all writes generated by different processes are concurrent.

Let us now reconsider the three processes of Fig. 6-14, but this time using PRAM consistency instead of sequential consistency. Under PRAM consistency, different processes may see the statements executed in a different order. For example, Fig. 6-19(a) shows how P_1 might see the events, whereas Fig. 6-19(b) shows how P_2 might see them and Fig. 6-19(c) shows P_3's view. For a sequentially consistent memory, three different views would not be allowed.

If we concatenate the output of the three processes, we get a result of

```
a = 1;                  a = 1;                  b = 1;
* print (b, c);         b = 1;                  print (a, c);
b = 1;                  * print (a, c);         c = 1;
print (a, c);           print (b, c);           * print (a, b);
c = 1;                  c = 1;                  a = 1;
print (a, b);           print (a, b);           print (b, c);


Prints: 00              Prints: 10              Prints: 01

   (a)                     (b)                     (b)
```

Fig. 6-19. Statement execution as seen by three processes. The statements marked with asterisks are the ones that actually generate output.

001001, which, as we saw earlier, is impossible with sequential consistency. The key difference between sequential consistency and PRAM consistency is that with the former, although the order of statement execution (and memory references) is nondeterministic, at least all processes agree what it is. With the latter, they do not agree. Different processes can see the operations in a different order.

Sometimes PRAM consistency can lead to results that may be counterintuitive. The following example, due to Goodman (1989), was devised for a slightly different memory model (discussed below), but also holds for PRAM consistency. In Fig. 6-20 one might naively expect one of three possible outcomes: P_1 is killed, P_2 is killed, or neither is killed (if the two assignments go first). With PRAM consistency, however, both processes can be killed. This result can occur if P_1 reads b before it sees P_2's store into b, and P_2 reads a before it sees P_1's store into a. With a sequentially consistent memory, there are six possible statement interleavings, and none of them results in both processes being killed.

```
a = 1;                          b = 1;
if (b == 0) kill (P2);          if (a == 0) kill (P1);

       (a)                             (b)
```

Fig. 6-20. Two parallel processes. (a) P_1. (b) P_2.

Goodman's (1989) model, called **processor consistency**, is close enough to PRAM consistency that some authors have regarded them as being effectively the same (e.g., Attiya and Friedman, 1992; and Bitar, 1990). However, Goodman gave an example that suggests he intended that there be an additional condition imposed on processor consistent memory, namely memory coherence, as described above: in other words, for every memory location, x, there be global agreement about the order of writes to x. Writes to different locations need not be viewed in the same order by different processes. Gharachorloo et al. (1990) describe using processor consistency in the Dash multiprocessor, but use a slightly different definition than Goodman. The differences between PRAM and the two processor consistency models are subtle, and are discussed by Ahamad et al. (1993).

6.3.5. Weak Consistency

Although PRAM consistency and processor consistency can give better performance than the stronger models, they are still unnecessarily restrictive for many applications because they require that writes originating in a single process be seen everywhere in order. Not all applications require even seeing all writes, let alone seeing them in order. Consider the case of a process inside a critical section reading and writing some variables in a tight loop. Even though other processes are not supposed to touch the variables until the first process has left its critical section, the memory has no way of knowing when a process is in a critical section and when it is not, so it has to propagate all writes to all memories in the usual way.

A better solution would be to let the process finish its critical section and then make sure that the final results were sent everywhere, not worrying too much whether all intermediate results had also been propagated to all memories in order, or even at all. This can be done by introducing a new kind of variable, a **synchronization variable**, that is used for synchronization purposes. The operations on it are used to synchronize memory. When a synchronization completes, all writes done on that machine are propagated outward and all writes done on other machines are brought in. In other words, all of (shared) memory is synchronized.

Dubois et al. (1986) define this model, called **weak consistency**, by saying that it has three properties:

1. *Accesses to synchronization variables are sequentially consistent.*

2. *No access to a synchronization variable is allowed to be performed until all previous writes have completed everywhere.*

3. *No data access (read or write) is allowed to be performed until all previous accesses to synchronization variables have been performed.*

Point 1 says that all processes see all accesses to synchronization variables in the same order. Effectively, when a synchronization variable is accessed, this fact is broadcast to the world, and no other synchronization variable can be accessed in any other process until this one is finished everywhere.

Point 2 says that accessing a synchronization variable "flushes the pipeline." It forces all writes that are in progress or partially completed or completed at some memories but not others to complete everywhere. When the synchronization access is done, all previous writes are guaranteed to be done as well. By doing a synchronization after updating shared data, a process can force the new values out to all other memories.

Point 3 says that when ordinary (i.e., not synchronization) variables are accessed, either for reading or writing, all previous synchronizations have been performed. By doing a synchronization before reading shared data, a process can be sure of getting the most recent values.

It is worth mentioning that quite a bit of complexity lurks behind the word "performed" here and elsewhere in the context of DSM. A read is said to have been performed when no subsequent write can affect the value returned. A write is said to have performed at the instant when all subsequent reads return the value written by the write. A synchronization is said to have performed when all shared variables have been updated. One can also distinguish between operations that have performed locally and globally. Dubois et al. (1988) go into this point in detail.

From an implementation standpoint, when the contract between the software and the memory says that memory only has to be brought up to date when a synchronization variable is accessed, a new write can be started before the previous ones have been completed, and in some cases writes can be avoided altogether. Of course, this contract puts a greater burden on the programmer, but the potential gain is better performance. Unlike the previous memory models, it enforces consistency on a group of operations, not on individual reads and writes. This model is most useful when isolated accesses to shared variables are rare, with most coming in clusters (many accesses in a short period, then none for a long time).

```
int a, b, c, d, e, x, y;          /* variables */
int *p, *q;                       /* pointers */
int f(int *p, int *q);            /* function prototype */

a = x * x;                        /* a is stored in a register */
b = y * y;                        /* b too */
c = a * a * a + b * b + a * b;    /* used later */
d = a * a * c;                    /* used later */
p = &a;                           /* p gets the address of a */
q = &b;                           /* q gets the address of b */
e = f(p, q);                      /* function call */
```

Fig. 6-21. A program fragment in which some variables may be kept in registers.

The idea of having memory be wrong is nothing new. Many compilers cheat too. For example, consider the program fragment of Fig. 6-21, with all the variables initialized to appropriate values. An optimizing compiler may decide to compute *a* and *b* in registers and keep the values there for a while, not updating their memory locations. Only when the function *f* is called does the compiler have to put the current values of *a* and *b* back in memory, because *f* might try to access them.

Having memory be wrong is acceptable here because the compiler knows what it is doing (i.e., because the software does not insist that memory be up-to-date). Clearly, if a second process existed that could read memory in an unconstrained way, this scheme would not work. For example, if during the assignment to *d*, the second process read *a*, *b*, and *c*, it would get inconsistent values (the old values of *a* and *b*, but the new value of *c*). One could imagine a special way to prevent chaos by having the compiler first write a special flag bit saying that memory was out-of-date. If another process wanted to access *a*, it would busy wait on the flag bit. In this way one can live with less than perfect consistency, provided that synchronization is done in software and all parties obey the rules.

Now let us consider a somewhat less far-fetched situation. In Fig. 6-22(a) we see that process P_1 does two writes to an ordinary variable, and then synchronizes (indicated by the letter *S*). If P_2 and P_3 have not yet been synchronized, no guarantees are given about what they see, so this sequence of events is valid.

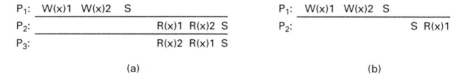

Fig. 6-22. (a) A valid sequence of events for weak consistency. (b) An invalid sequence for weak consistency.

Figure 6-22(b) is different. Here P_2 has been synchronized, which means that its memory is brought up to date. When it reads *x*, it must get the value 2. Getting 1, as shown in the figure, is not permitted with weak consistency.

6.3.6. Release Consistency

Weak consistency has the problem that when a synchronization variable is accessed, the memory does not know whether this is being done because the process is finished writing the shared variables or about to start reading them. Consequently, it must take the actions required in both cases, namely making sure that all locally initiated writes have been completed (i.e., propagated to all other machines), as well as gathering in all writes from other machines. If the memory could tell the difference between entering a critical region and leaving one, a more efficient implementation might be possible. To provide this information, two kinds of synchronization variables or operations are needed instead of one.

Release consistency (Gharachorloo et al., 1990) provides these two kinds. **Acquire** accesses are used to tell the memory system that a critical region is about to be entered. **Release** accesses say that a critical region has just been exited. These accesses can be implemented either as ordinary operations on special variables or as special operations. In either case, the programmer is responsible for putting explicit code in the program telling when to do them, for example, by calling library procedures such as *acquire* and *release* or procedures such as *enter_critical_region* and *leave_critical_region*.

It is also possible to use barriers instead of critical regions with release consistency. A **barrier** is a synchronization mechanism that prevents any process from starting phase $n + 1$ of a program until all processes have finished phase n. When a process arrives at a barrier, it must wait until all other processes get there too. When the last one arrives, all shared variables are synchronized and then all processes are resumed. Departure from the barrier is acquire and arrival is release.

In addition to these synchronizing accesses, reading and writing shared variables is also possible. Acquire and release do not have to apply to all of memory. Instead, they may only guard specific shared variables, in which case only those variables are kept consistent. The shared variables that are kept consistent are said to be **protected**.

The contract between the memory and the software says that when the software does an acquire, the memory will make sure that all the local copies of the protected variables are brought up to date to be consistent with the remote ones if need be. When a release is done, protected variables that have been changed are propagated out to other machines. Doing an acquire does not guarantee that locally made changes will be sent to other machines immediately. Similarly, doing a release does not necessarily import changes from other machines.

P_1:	Acq(L) W(x)1 W(x)2 Rel(L)		
P_2:		Acq(L) R(x)2 Rel(L)	
P_3:			R(x)1

Fig. 6-23. A valid event sequence for release consistency.

Fig. 6-23 depicts a valid sequence of events for release consistency. Process P_1 does an acquire, changes a shared variable twice, and then does a release. Process P_2 does an acquire, and reads x. It is guaranteed to get the value x had at the time of the release, namely 2 (unless P_2's acquire performs before P_1's acquire). If the acquire had been done before P_1 did the release, the acquire would have been be delayed until the release had occurred. Since P_3 does not do an acquire before reading a shared variable, the memory has no obligation to give it the current value of x, so returning 1 is allowed.

To make release consistency clearer, let us briefly describe a possible simple-minded implementation in the context of distributed shared memory (release consistency was actually invented for the Dash multiprocessor, but the idea is the same, even though the implementation is not). To do an acquire, a process sends a message to a synchronization manager requesting an acquire on a particular lock. In the absence of any competition, the request is granted and the acquire completes. Then an arbitrary sequence of reads and writes to the shared data can take place locally. None of these are propagated to other machines. When the release is done, the modified data are sent to the other machines that use them. After each machine has acknowledged receipt of the data, the synchronization manager is informed of the release. In this way, an arbitrary number of reads and writes on shared variables can be done with a fixed amount of overhead. Acquires and releases on different locks occur independently of one another.

While the centralized algorithm described above will do the job, it is by no means the only approach. In general, a distributed shared memory is release consistent if it obeys the following rules:

1. *Before an ordinary access to a shared variable is performed, all previous acquires done by the process must have completed successfully.*

2. *Before a release is allowed to be performed, all previous reads and writes done by the process must have completed.*

3. *The acquire and release accesses must be processor consistent (sequential consistency is not required).*

If all these conditions are met and processes use acquire and release properly (i.e., in acquire-release pairs), the results of any execution will be no different than they would have been on a sequentially consistent memory. In effect, blocks of accesses to shared variables are made atomic by the acquire and release primitives to prevent interleaving.

A different implementation of release consistency is **lazy release consistency** (Keleher et al., 1992). In normal release consistency, which we will henceforth call **eager release consistency**, to distinguish it from the lazy variant, when a release is done, the processor doing the release pushes out all the modified data to all other processors that already have a cached copy and thus might potentially need it. There is no way to tell if they actually will need it, so to be safe, all of them get everything that has changed.

Although pushing all the data out this way is straightforward, it is generally inefficient. In lazy release consistency, at the time of a release, nothing is sent anywhere. Instead, when an acquire is done, the processor trying to do the acquire has to get the most recent values of the variables from the machine or machines holding them. A timestamp protocol can be used to determine which variables have to be transmitted.

In many programs, a critical region is located inside a loop. With eager release consistency, on every pass through the loop a release is done, and all the modified data have to be pushed out to all the processors maintaining copies of them. This algorithm wastes bandwidth and introduces needless delay. With lazy release consistency, at the release nothing is done. At the next acquire, the processor determines that it already has all the data it needs, so no messages are generated here either. The net result is that with lazy release consistency no network traffic is generated at all until another processor does an acquire. Repeated acquire-release pairs done by the same processor in the absence of competition from the outside are free.

6.3.7. Entry Consistency

Another consistency model that has been designed to be used with critical sections is **entry consistency** (Bershad et al., 1993). Like both variants of release consistency, it requires the programmer (or compiler) to use acquire and release at the start and end of each critical section, respectively. However, unlike release consistency, entry consistency requires each ordinary shared variable to be associated with some synchronization variable such as a lock or barrier. If it is desired that elements of an array be accessed independently in parallel, then different array elements must be associated with different locks. When an acquire is done on a synchronization variable, only those ordinary shared variables guarded by that synchronization variable are made consistent. Entry consistency differs from lazy release consistency in that the latter does not associate shared variables with locks or barriers and at acquire time has to determine empirically which variables it needs.

Associating with each synchronization variable a list of shared variables reduces the overhead associated with acquiring and releasing a synchronization variable, since only a few shared variables have to be synchronized. It also allows multiple critical sections involving disjoint shared variables to execute simultaneously, increasing the amount of parallelism. The price paid is the extra overhead and complexity of associating every shared data variable with some synchronization variable. Programming this way is also more complicated and error prone.

Synchronization variables are used as follows. Each synchronization variable has a current owner, namely, the process that last acquired it. The owner may enter and exit critical regions repeatedly without having to send any messages on the network. A process not currently owning a synchronization variable but wanting to acquire it has to send a message to the current owner asking for ownership and the current values of the associated variables. It is also possible for several processes simultaneously to own a synchronization variable in nonexclusive mode, meaning that they can read, but not write, the associated data variables.

Formally, a memory exhibits entry consistency if it meets all the following conditions (Bershad and Zekauskas, 1991):

1. *An acquire access of a synchronization variable is not allowed to perform with respect to a process until all updates to the guarded shared data have been performed with respect to that process.*

2. *Before an exclusive mode access to a synchronization variable by a process is allowed to perform with respect to that process, no other process may hold the synchronization variable, not even in nonexclusive mode.*

3. *After an exclusive mode access to a synchronization variable has been performed, any other process' next nonexclusive mode access to that synchronization variable may not be performed until it has performed with respect to that variable's owner.*

The first condition says that when a process does an acquire, the acquire may not complete (i.e., return control to the next statement) until all the guarded shared variables have been brought up to date. In other words, at an acquire, all remote changes to the guarded data must be made visible.

The second condition says that before updating a shared variable, a process must enter a critical region in exclusive mode to make sure that no other process is trying to update it at the same time.

The third condition says that if a process wants to enter a critical region in nonexclusive mode, it must first check with the owner of the synchronization variable guarding the critical region to fetch the most recent copies of the guarded shared variables.

6.3.8. Summary of Consistency Models

Although other consistency models have been proposed, the main ones are discussed above. They differ in how restrictive they are, how complex their implementations are, their ease of programming, and their performance. Strict consistency is the most restrictive, but because its implementation in a DSM system is essentially impossible, it is never used.

Sequential consistency is feasible, popular with programmers, and widely used. It has the problem of poor performance, however. The way to get around this result is to relax the consistency model. Some of the possibilities are shown in Fig. 6-24(a), roughly in order of decreasing restrictiveness.

Consistency	Description
Strict	Absolute time ordering of all shared accesses matters
Sequential	All processes see all shared accesses in the same order
Causal	All processes see all casually-related shared accesses in the same order
Processor	PRAM consistency + memory coherence
PRAM	All processes see writes from each processor in the order they were issued. Writes from different processors may not always be seen in the same order

(a)

Weak	Shared data can only be counted on to be consistent after a synchronization is done
Release	Shared data are made consistent when a critical region is exited
Entry	Shared data pertaining to a critical region are made consistent when a critical region is entered

(b)

Fig. 6-24. (a) Consistency models not using synchronization operations. (b) Models with synchronization operations.

Causal consistency, processor consistency, and PRAM consistency all represent weakenings in which there is no longer a globally agreed upon view of which operations appeared in which order. Different processes may see different sequences of operations. These three differ in terms of which sequences are allowed and which are not, but in all cases, it is up to the programmer to avoid doing things that work only if the memory is sequentially consistent.

A different approach is to introduce explicit synchronization variables, as weak consistency, release consistency, and entry consistency do. These three are summarized in Fig. 6-24(b). When a process performs an operation on an ordinary shared data variable, no guarantees are given about when they will be visible to other processes. Only when a synchronization variable is accessed are changes propagated. The three models differ in how synchronization works, but in all cases a process can perform multiple reads and writes in a critical section without invoking any data transport. When the critical section has been completed, the final result is either propagated to the other processes or made ready for propagation should anyone else express interest.

In short, weak consistency, release consistency, and entry consistency require additional programming constructs that, when used as directed, allow programmers to pretend that memory is sequentially consistent, when, in fact, it is not. In principle, these three models using explicit synchronization should be able to offer the best performance, but it is likely that different applications will give quite different results. More research is needed before we can draw any firm conclusions here.

6.4. PAGE-BASED DISTRIBUTED SHARED MEMORY

Having studied the principles behind distributed shared memory systems, let us now turn to these systems themselves. In this section we will study "classical" distributed shared memory, the first of which was IVY (Li 1986; and Li and Hudak 1989). These systems are built on top of multicomputers, that is, processors connected by a specialized message-passing network, workstations on a LAN, or similar designs. The essential element here is that no processor can directly access any other processor's memory. Such systems are sometimes called **NORMA** (**NO Remote Memory Access**) systems to contrast them with NUMA systems.

The big difference between NUMA and NORMA is that in the former, every processor can directly reference every word in the global address space just by reading or writing it. Pages can be randomly distributed among memories without affecting the results that programs give. When a processor references a remote page, the system has the option of fetching it or using it remotely. The decision affects the performance, but not the correctness. NUMA machines are true multiprocessors—the hardware allows every processor to reference every word in the address space without software intervention.

Workstations on a LAN are fundamentally different from a multiprocessor. Processors can only reference their own local memory. There is no concept of a global shared memory, as there is with a NUMA or UMA multiprocessor. The goal of the DSM work, however, is to add software to the system to allow a multicomputer to run multiprocessor programs. Consequently, when a processor references a remote page, that page *must* be fetched. There is no choice as there is in the NUMA case.

Much of the early research on DSM systems was devoted to the question of how to run existing multiprocessor programs on multicomputers. Sometimes this is referred to as the "dusty deck" problem. The idea is to breathe new life into old programs just by running them on new (DSM) systems. The concept is especially attractive for applications that need all the CPU cycles they can get and whose authors are thus interested in using large-scale multicomputers rather than small-scale multiprocessors.

Since programs written for multiprocessors normally assume that memory is sequentially consistent, the initial work on DSM was carefully done to provide sequentially consistent memory, so that old multiprocessor programs could work without modification. Subsequent experience has shown that major performance gains can be had by relaxing the memory model, at the cost of reprogramming existing applications and writing new ones in a different style. We will come back to this point later, but first we will look at the major design issues in classical DSM systems of the IVY type.

6.4.1. Basic Design

The idea behind DSM is simple: try to emulate the cache of a multiprocessor using the MMU and operating system software. In a DSM system, the address space is divided up into chunks, with the chunks being spread over all the processors in the system. When a processor references an address that is not local, a trap occurs, and the DSM software fetches the chunk containing the address and restarts the faulting instruction, which now completes successfully. This concept is illustrated in Fig. 6-25(a) for an address space with 16 chunks and four processors, each capable of holding four chunks.

In this example, if processor 1 references instructions or data in chunks 0, 2, 5, or 9, the references are done locally. References to other chunks cause traps. For example, a reference to an address in chunk 10 will cause a trap to the DSM software, which then moves chunk 10 from machine 2 to machine 1, as shown in Fig. 6-25(b).

6.4.2. Replication

One improvement to the basic system that can improve performance considerably is to replicate chunks that are read only, for example, program text, read-only constants, or other read-only data structures. For example, if chunk 10 in Fig. 6-25 is a section of program text, its use by processor 1 can result in a copy being sent to processor 1, without the original in processor 2's memory being disturbed, as shown in Fig. 6-25(c). In this way, processors 1 and 2 can both reference chunk 10 as often as needed without causing traps to fetch missing memory.

Another possibility is to replicate not only read-only chunks, but all chunks. As long as reads are being done, there is effectively no difference between

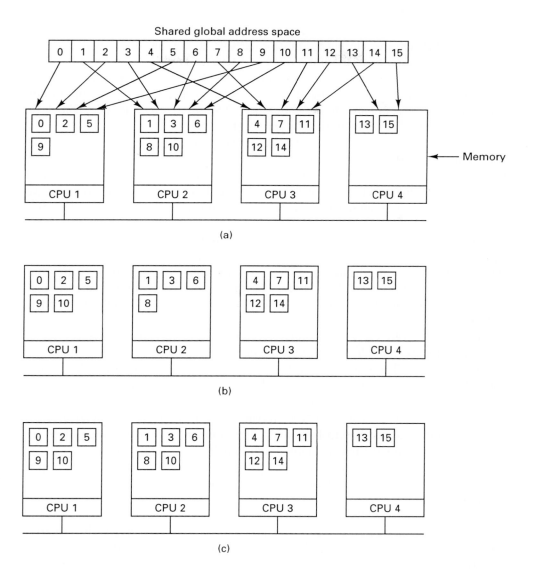

Fig. 6-25. (a) Chunks of address space distributed among four machines. (b) Situation after CPU 1 references chunk 10. (c) Situation if chunk 10 is read only and replication is used.

replicating a read-only chunk and replicating a read-write chunk. However, if a replicated chunk is suddenly modified, special action has to be taken to prevent having multiple, inconsistent copies in existence. How inconsistency is prevented will be discussed in the following sections.

6.4.3. Granularity

DSM systems are similar to multiprocessors in certain key ways. In both systems, when a nonlocal memory word is referenced, a chunk of memory containing the word is fetched from its current location and put on the machine making the reference (main memory or cache, respectively). An important design issue is how big should the chunk be? Possibilities are the word, block (a few words), page, or segment (multiple pages).

With a multiprocessor, fetching a single word or a few dozen bytes is feasible because the MMU knows exactly which address was referenced and the time to set up a bus transfer is measured in nanoseconds. Memnet, although not strictly a multiprocessor, also uses a small chunk size (32 bytes). With DSM systems, such fine granularity is difficult or impossible, due to the way the MMU works.

When a process references a word that is absent, it causes a page fault. An obvious choice is to bring in the entire page that is needed. Furthermore, integrating DSM with virtual memory makes the total design simpler, since the same unit, the page, is used for both. On a page fault, the missing page is just brought in from another machine instead of from the disk, so much of the page fault handling code is the same as in the traditional case.

However, another possible choice is to bring in a larger unit, say a region of 2, 4, or 8 pages, including the needed page. In effect, doing this simulates a larger page size. There are advantages and disadvantages to a larger chunk size for DSM. The biggest advantage is that because the startup time for a network transfer is substantial, it does not take much longer to transfer 1024 bytes than it does to transfer 512 bytes. By transferring data in large units, when a large piece of address space has to be moved, the number of transfers may often be reduced. This property is especially important because many programs exhibit locality of reference, meaning that if a program has referenced one word on a page, it is likely to reference other words on the same page in the immediate future.

On the other hand, the network will be tied up longer with a larger transfer, blocking other faults caused by other processes. Also, too large an effective page size introduces a new problem, called **false sharing**, illustrated in Fig. 6-26. Here we have a page containing two unrelated shared variables, A and B. Processor 1 makes heavy use of A, reading and writing it. Similarly, process 2 uses B. Under these circumstances, the page containing both variables will constantly be traveling back and forth between the two machines.

The problem here is that although the variables are unrelated, since they appear by accident on the same page, when a process uses one of them, it also gets the other. The larger the effective page size, the more often false sharing will occur, and conversely, the smaller the effective page size, the less often it

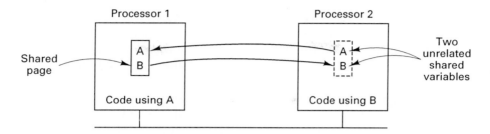

Fig. 6-26. False sharing of a page containing two unrelated variables.

will occur. Nothing analogous to this phenomenon is present in ordinary virtual memory systems.

Clever compilers that understand the problem and place variables in the address space accordingly can help reduce false sharing and improve performance. However, saying this is easier than doing it. Furthermore, if the false sharing consists of processor 1 using one element of an array and processor 2 using a different element of the same array, there is little that even a clever compiler can do to eliminate the problem.

6.4.4. Achieving Sequential Consistency

If pages are not replicated, achieving consistency is not an issue. There is exactly one copy of each page, and it is moved back and forth dynamically as needed. With only one copy of each page, there is no danger that different copies will have different values.

If read-only pages are replicated, there is also no problem. The read-only pages are never changed, so all the copies are always identical. Only a single copy is kept of each read-write page, so inconsistencies are impossible here, too.

The interesting case is that of replicated read-write pages. In many DSM systems, when a process tries to read a remote page, a local copy is made because the system does not know what is on the page or whether it is writable. Both the local copy (in fact, all copies) and the original page are set up in their respective MMUs as read only. As long as all references are reads, everything is fine.

However, if any process attempts to write on a replicated page, a potential consistency problem arises because changing one copy and leaving the others alone is unacceptable. This situation is analogous to what happens in a multiprocessor when one processor attempts to modify a word that is present in multiple caches, so let us review what multiprocessors do under these circumstances.

In general, multiprocessors take one of two approaches: update or invalidation. With update, the write is allowed to take place locally, but the address of the modified word and its new value are broadcast on the bus simultaneously to all the other caches. Each of the caches holding the word being updated sees that an address it is caching is being modified, so it copies the new value from the bus to its cache, overwriting the old value. The final result is that all caches that held the word before the update also hold it afterward, and all acquire the new value.

The other approach multiprocessors can take is invalidation. When this strategy is used, the address of the word being updated is broadcast on the bus, but the new value is not. When a cache sees that one of its words is being updated, it invalidates the cache block containing the word, effectively removing it from the cache. The final result with invalidation is that only one cache now holds the modified word, so consistency problems are avoided. If one of the processors that now holds an invalid copy of the cache block tries to use it, it will get a cache miss and fetch the block from the one processor holding a valid copy.

Whereas these two strategies are approximately equally easy to implement in a multiprocessor, they differ radically in a DSM system. Unlike in a multiprocessor, where the MMU knows which word is to be written and what the new value is, in a DSM system the software does not know which word is to be written or what the new value will be. To find out, it could make a secret copy of the page about to be changed (the page number is known), make the page writable, set the hardware trap bit, which forces a trap after every instruction, and restart the faulting process. One instruction later, it catches the trap and compares the current page with the secret copy it just made, to see which word has been changed. It could then broadcast a short packet giving the address and new value on the network. The processors receiving this packet could then check to see if they have the page in question, and if so, update it.

The amount of work here is enormous, but worse yet, the scheme is not foolproof. If several updates, originating on different processors, take place simultaneously, different processors may see them in a different order, so the memory will not be sequentially consistent. In a multiprocessor this problem does not occur because broadcasts on the bus are totally reliable (no lost messages), and the order is unambiguous.

Another issue is that a process may make thousands of consecutive writes to the same page because many programs exhibit locality of reference. Having to catch all these updates and pass them to remote machines is horrendously expensive in the absence of multiprocessor-type snooping.

For these reasons, page-based DSM systems typically use an invalidation protocol instead of an update protocol. Various protocols are possible. Below we will describe a typical example, in which all pages are potentially writable (i.e., the DSM software does not know what is on which page).

In this protocol, at any instant of time, each page is either in R (readable) or W (readable and writable) state. The state a page is in may change as execution progresses. Each page has an owner, namely the process that most recently wrote on the page. When a page is in *W* state, only one copy exists, mapped into the owner's address space in read-write mode. When a page is in *R* state, the owner has a copy (mapped read only), but other processes may have copies, too.

Six cases can be distinguished, as shown in Fig. 6-27. In all the examples in the figure, process *P* on processor 1 wants to read or write a page. The cases differ in terms of whether *P* is the owner, whether *P* has a copy, whether other processes have copies, and what the state of the page is, as shown.

Let us now consider the actions taken in each of the cases. In the first four cases of Fig. 6-27(a), *P* just does the read. In all four cases the page is mapped into its address space, so the read is done in hardware. No trap occurs. In the fifth and sixth cases, the page is not mapped in, so a page fault occurs and the DSM software gets control. It sends a message to the owner asking for a copy. When the copy comes back, the page is mapped in and the faulting instruction is restarted. If the owner had the page in *W* state, it must degrade to *R* state, but may keep the page. In this protocol, the other process keeps ownership, but in a slightly different protocol that could be transferred as well.

Writes are handled differently, as depicted in Fig. 6-27(b). In the first case, the write just happens, without a trap, since the page is mapped in read-write mode. In the second case (no other copies), the page is changed to *W* state and written. In the third case there are other copies, so they must first be invalidated before the write can take place.

In the next three cases, some other process is the owner at the time *P* does the write. In all three cases, *P* must ask the current owner to invalidate any existing copies, pass ownership to *P*, and send a copy of the page unless *P* already has a copy. Only then may the write take place. In all three cases, *P* ends up with the only copy of the page, which is in *W* state.

In all six cases, before a write is performed the protocol guarantees that only one copy of the page exists, namely in the address space of the process about to do the write. In this way, consistency is maintained.

6.4.5. Finding the Owner

We glossed over a few points in the description above. One of them is how to find the owner of the page. The simplest solution is by doing a broadcast, asking for the owner of the specified page to respond. Once the owner has been located this way, the protocol can proceed as above.

An obvious optimization is not just to ask who the owner is, but also to tell whether the sender wants to read or write and say whether it needs a copy of the page. The owner can then send a single message transferring ownership and the page as well, if needed.

Broadcasting has the disadvantage of interrupting each processor, forcing it

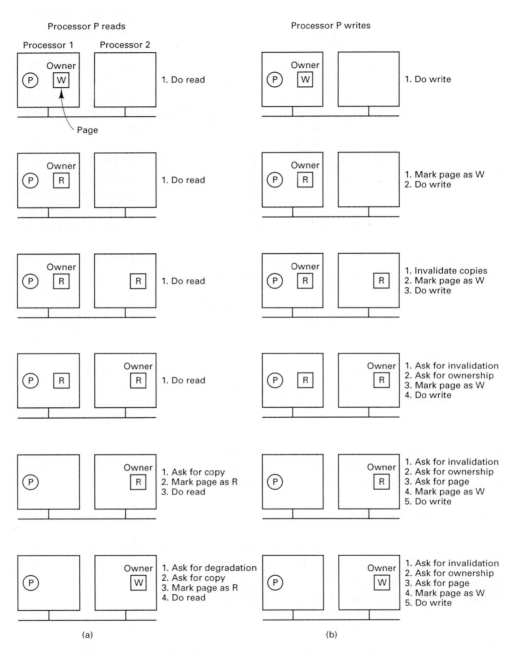

Fig. 6-27. (a) Process *P* wants to read a page. (b) Process *P* wants to write a page.

to inspect the request packet. For all the processors except the owner's, handling the interrupt is essentially wasted time. Broadcasting may use up considerable network bandwidth, depending on the hardware.

Li and Hudak (1989) describe several other possibilities as well. In the first of these, one process is designated as the page manager. It is the job of the manager to keep track of who owns each page. When a process, P, wants to read a page it does not have or wants to write a page it does not own, it sends a message to the page manager telling which operation it wants to perform and on which page. The manager then sends back a message telling who the owner is. P now contacts the owner to get the page and/or the ownership, as required. Four messages are needed for this protocol, as illustrated in Fig. 6-28(a).

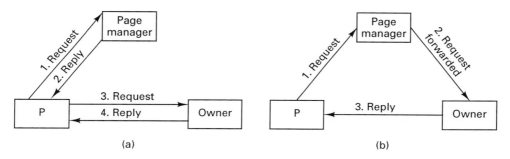

Fig. 6-28. Ownership location using a central manager. (a) Four-message protocol. (b) Three-message protocol.

An optimization of this ownership location protocol is shown in Fig. 6-28(b). Here the page manager forwards the request directly to the owner, which then replies directly back to P, saving one message.

A problem with this protocol is the potentially heavy load on the page manager, handling all the incoming requests. This problem can be reduced by having multiple page managers instead of just one. Splitting the work over multiple managers introduces a new problem, however—finding the right manager. A simple solution is to use the low-order bits of the page number as an index into a table of managers. Thus with eight page managers, all pages that end with 000 are handled by manager 0, all pages that end with 001 are handled by manager 1, and so on. A different mapping, for example by using a hash function, is also possible. The page manager uses the incoming requests not only to provide replies but also to keep track of changes in ownership. When a process says that it wants to write on a page, the manager records that process as the new owner.

Still another possible algorithm is having each process (or more likely, each processor) keep track of the probable owner of each page. Requests for ownership are sent to the probable owner, which forwards them if ownership has changed. If ownership has changed several times, the request message will also have to be forwarded several times. At the start of execution and every *n* times ownership changes, the location of the new owner should be broadcast, to allow all processors to update their tables of probable owners.

The problem of locating the manager also is present in multiprocessors, such as Dash, and also in Memnet. In both of these systems it is solved by dividing the address space into regions and assigning each region to a fixed manager, essentially the same technique as the multiple-manager solution discussed above, but using the high-order bits of the page number as the manager number.

6.4.6. Finding the Copies

Another important detail is how all the copies are found when they must be invalidated. Again, two possibilities present themselves. The first is to broadcast a message giving the page number and ask all processors holding the page to invalidate it. This approach works only if broadcast messages are totally reliable and can never be lost.

The second possibility is to have the owner or page manager maintain a list or **copyset** telling which processors hold which pages, as depicted in Fig. 6-29. Here page 4, for example, is owned by a process on CPU 1, as indicated by the double box around the 4. The copyset consists of 2 and 4, because copies of page 4 can be found on those machines.

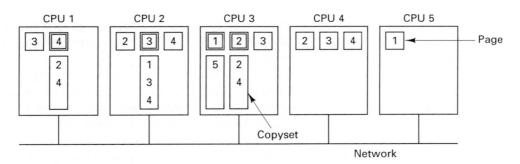

Fig. 6-29. The owner of each page maintains a copyset telling which other CPUs are sharing that page. Page ownership is indicated by the double boxes.

When a page must be invalidated, the old owner, new owner, or page manager sends a message to each processor holding the page and waits for an acknowledgement. When each message has been acknowledged, the invalidation is complete.

Dash and Memnet also need to invalidate pages when a new writer suddenly appears, but they do it differently. Dash uses directories. The writing process sends a packet to the directory (the page manager in our terminology), which then finds all the copies from its bit map, sends each one an invalidation packet, and collects all the acknowledgements. Memnet fetches the needed page and invalidates all copies by broadcasting an invalidation packet on the ring. The first processor having a copy puts it in the packet and sets a header bit saying it is there. Subsequent processors just invalidate their copies. When the packet comes around the ring and arrives back at the sender, the needed data are present and all other copies are gone. In effect, Memnet implements DSM in hardware.

6.4.7. Page Replacement

In a DSM system, as in any system using virtual memory, it can happen that a page is needed but that there is no free page frame in memory to hold it. When this situation occurs, a page must be evicted from memory to make room for the needed page. Two subproblems immediately arise: which page to evict and where to put it.

To a large extent, the choice of which page to evict can be made using traditional virtual memory algorithms, such as some approximation to the least recently used (LRU) algorithm. One complication that occurs with DSM is that pages can be invalidated spontaneously (due to the activities of other processes), which affects the possible choices. However, by maintaining the estimated LRU order of only those pages that are currently valid, any of the traditional algorithms can be used.

As with conventional algorithms, it is worth keeping track of which pages are "clean" and which are "dirty." In the context of DSM, a replicated page that another process owns is always a prime candidate to evict because it is known that another copy exists. Consequently, the page does not have to be saved anywhere. If a directory scheme is being used to keep track of copies, the owner or page manager must be informed of this decision, however. If pages are located by broadcasting, the page can just be discarded.

The second best choice is a replicated page that the evicting process owns. It is sufficient to pass ownership to one of the other copies by informing that process, the page manager, or both, depending on the implementation. The page itself need not be transferred, which results in a smaller message.

If no replicated pages are suitable candidates, a nonreplicated page must be chosen, for example, the least recently used valid page. There are two possibilities for getting rid of it. The first is to write it to a disk, if present. The other is to hand it off to another processor.

Choosing a processor to hand a page off to can be done in several ways. For example, each page could be assigned a home machine, which must accept it, although this probably implies reserving a large amount of normally wasted space to hold pages that might be sent home some day. Alternatively, the number of free page frames could be piggybacked on each message sent, with each processor building up an idea of how free memory was distributed around the network. An occasional broadcast message giving the exact count of free page frames could help keep these numbers up to date.

As an aside, note that a conflict may exist between choosing a replicated page (which may just be discarded) and choosing a page that has not been referenced in a long time (which may be the only copy). The same problem exists in traditional virtual memory systems, however, so the same compromises and heuristics apply.

One problem that is unique to DSM systems is the network traffic generated when processes on different machines are actively sharing a writable page, either through false sharing or true sharing. An ad hoc way to reduce this traffic is to enforce a rule that once a page has arrived at any processor, it must remain there for some time ΔT. If requests for it come in from other machines, these requests are simply queued until the timer expires, thus allowing the local process to make many memory references without interference.

As usual, it is instructive to see how page replacement is handled in multiprocessors. In Dash, when a cache fills up, the option always exists of writing the block back to main memory. In DSM systems, that possibility does not exist, although using a disk as the ultimate repository for pages nobody wants is often feasible. In Memnet, every cache block has a home machine, which is required to reserve storage for it. This design is also possible in a DSM system, although it is wasteful in both Memnet and DSM.

6.4.8. Synchronization

In a DSM system, as in a multiprocessor, processes often need to synchronize their actions. A common example is mutual exclusion, in which only one process at a time may execute a certain part of the code. In a multiprocessor, the TEST-AND-SET-LOCK (TSL) instruction is often used to implement mutual exclusion. In normal use, a variable is set to 0 when no process is in the critical section and to 1 when one process is. The TSL instruction reads out the variable and sets it to 1 in a single, atomic operation. If the value read is 1, the process just keeps repeating the TSL instruction until the process in the critical region has exited and set the variable to 0.

In a DSM system, this code is still correct, but is a potential performance disaster. If one process, A, is inside the critical region and another process, B, (on a different machine) wants to enter it, B will sit in a tight loop testing the variable, waiting for it to go to zero. The page containing the variable will remain on B's machine. When A exits the critical region and tries to write 0 to the variable, it will get a page fault and pull in the page containing the variable.

Immediately thereafter, *B* will also get a page fault, pulling the page back. This performance is acceptable.

The problem occurs when several other processes are also trying to enter the critical region. Remember that the TSL instruction modifies memory (by writing a 1 to the synchronization variable) every time it is executed. Thus every time one process executes a TSL instruction, it must fetch the entire page containing the synchronization variable from whoever has it. With multiple processes each issuing a TSL instruction every few hundred nanoseconds, the network traffic can become intolerable.

For this reason, an additional mechanism is often needed for synchronization. One possibility is a synchronization manager (or managers) that accept messages asking to enter and leave critical regions, lock and unlock variables, and so on, sending back replies when the work is done. When a region cannot be entered or a variable cannot be locked, no reply is sent back immediately, causing the sender to block. When the region becomes available or the variable can be locked, a message is sent back. In this way, synchronization can be done with a minimum of network traffic, but at the expense of centralizing control per lock.

6.5. SHARED-VARIABLE DISTRIBUTED SHARED MEMORY

Page-based DSM takes a normal linear address space and allows the pages to migrate dynamically over the network on demand. Processes can access all of memory using normal read and write instructions and are not aware of when page faults or network transfers occur. Accesses to remote data are detected and protected by the MMU.

A more structured approach is to share only certain variables and data structures that are needed by more than one process. In this way, the problem changes from how to do paging over the network to how to maintain a potentially replicated, distributed data base consisting of the shared variables. Different techniques are applicable here, and these often lead to major performance improvements.

The first question that must be addressed is whether or not shared variables will be replicated, and if so, whether fully or partially. If they are replicated, there is more potential for using an update algorithm rather than on a page-based DSM system, provided that writes to individual shared variables can be isolated.

Using shared variables that are individually managed also provides considerable opportunity to eliminate false sharing. If it is possible to update one variable without affecting other variables, then the physical layout of the variables on the pages is less important. Two of the most interesting examples of such systems are Munin and Midway, which are described below.

6.5.1. Munin

Munin is a DSM system that is fundamentally based on software objects, but which can place each object on a separate page so the hardware MMU can be used for detecting accesses to shared objects (Bennett et al., 1990; and Carter et al., 1991, 1993). The basic model used by Munin is that of multiple processors, each with a paged linear address space in which one or more threads are running a slightly modified multiprocessor program. The goal of the Munin project is to take existing multiprocessor programs, make minor changes to them, and have them run efficiently on multicomputer systems using a form of DSM. Good performance is achieved by a variety of techniques to be described below, including the use of release consistency instead of sequential consistency.

The changes consist of annotating the declarations of the shared variables with the keyword *shared*, so that the compiler can recognize them. Information about the expected usage pattern can also be supplied, to permit certain important special cases to be recognized and optimized. By default, the compiler puts each shared variable on a separate page, although large shared variables, such as arrays, may occupy multiple pages. It is also possible for the programmer to specify that multiple shared variables of the same Munin type be put in the same page. Mixing types does not work since the consistency protocol used for a page depends on the type of variables on it.

To run the compiled program, a root process is started up on one of the processors. This process may generate new processes on other processors, which then run in parallel with the main one and communicate with it and with each other by using the shared variables, as normal multiprocessor programs do. Once started on a particular processor, a process does not move.

Accesses to shared variables are done using the CPU's normal read and write instructions. No special protected methods are used. If an attempt is made to use a shared variable that is not present, a page fault occurs, and the Munin system gets control.

Synchronization for mutual exclusion is handled in a special way and is closely related to the memory consistency model. Lock variables may be declared, and library procedures are provided for locking and unlocking them. Barriers, condition variables, and other synchronization variables are also supported.

Release Consistency

Munin is based on a software implementation of (eager) release consistency. For the theoretical baggage, see the paper by Gharachorloo et al. (1990). What Munin does is to provide the tools for users to structure their programs around critical regions, defined dynamically by acquire (entry) and release (exit) calls.

Writes to shared variables must occur inside critical regions; reads can occur inside or outside. While a process is active inside a critical region, the system gives no guarantees about the consistency of shared variables, but when a critical region is exited, the shared variables modified since the last release are brought up to date on all machines. For programs that obey this programming model, the distributed shared memory acts like it is sequentially consistent.

Munin distinguishes three classes of variables:

1. Ordinary variables.

2. Shared data variables.

3. Synchronization variables.

Ordinary variables are not shared and can be read and written only by the process that created them. Shared data variables are visible to multiple processes and appear sequentially consistent, provided that all processes use them only in critical regions. They must be declared as such, but are accessed using normal read and write instructions. Synchronization variables, such as locks and barriers, are special, and are only accessible via system-supplied access procedures, such as *lock* and *unlock* for locks and *increment* and *wait* for barriers. It is these procedures that make the distributed shared memory work.

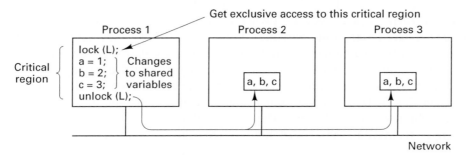

Fig. 6-30. Release consistency in Munin.

The basic operation of Munin's release consistency is illustrated in Fig. 6-30 for three cooperating processes, each running on a different machine. At a certain moment, process 1 wants to enter a critical region of code protected by the lock *L* (all critical regions must be protected by some synchronization variable). The *lock* statement makes sure that no other well-behaved process is currently executing this critical region. Then the three shared variables, *a*, *b*, and *c*, are accessed using normal machine instructions. Finally, *unlock* is called and the results are propagated to all other machines which maintain copies of *a*, *b*, or *c*. These changes are packed into a minimal number of messages. Accesses to these variables on other machines while process 1 is still inside its critical region produce undefined results.

Multiple Protocols

In addition to using release consistency, Munin also uses other techniques for improving performance. Chief among these is allowing the programmer to annotate shared variable declarations by classifying each one into one of four categories, as follows:

1. Read-only.

2. Migratory.

3. Write-shared

4. Conventional.

Originally, Munin supported some other categories as well, but experience showed them to be of only marginal value, so they were dropped. Each machine maintains a directory listing each variable, telling, among other things, which category it belongs to. For each category, a different protocol is used.

Read-only variables are easiest. When a reference to a read-only variable causes a page fault, Munin looks up the variable in the variable directory, finds out who owns it, and asks the owner for a copy of the required page. Since pages containing read-only variables do not change (after they have been initialized), consistency problems do not arise. Read-only variables are protected by the MMU hardware. An attempt to write to one causes a fatal error.

Migratory shared variables use the acquire/release protocol illustrated with locks in Fig. 6-30. They are used inside critical regions and must be protected by synchronization variables. The idea is that these variables migrate from machine to machine as critical regions are entered and exited. They are not replicated.

To use a migratory shared variable, its lock must first be acquired. When the variable is read, a copy of its page is made on the machine referencing it and the original copy is deleted. As an optimization, a migratory shared variable can be associated with a lock, so when the lock is sent, the data are sent along with it, eliminating extra messages.

A write-shared variable is used when the programmer has indicated that it is safe for two or more processes to write on it at the same time, for example, an array in which different processes can concurrently access different subarrays. Initially, pages holding write-shared variables are marked as being read only, potentially on several machines at the same time. When a write occurs, the fault handler makes a copy of the page, called the **twin**, marks the page as dirty, and sets the MMU to allow subsequent writes. These steps are illustrated in Fig. 6-31 for a word that is initially 6 and then changed to 8.

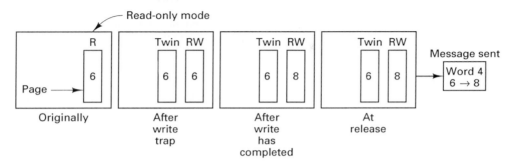

Fig. 6-31. Use of twin pages in Munin.

When the release is done, Munin runs a word-by-word comparison of each dirty write-shared page with its twin, and sends the differences (along with all the migratory pages) to all processes needing them. It then resets the page protection to read only.

When a list of differences comes into a process, the receiver checks each page to see if it has modified the page, too. If a page has not been modified, the incoming changes are accepted. If, however, a page has been modified locally, the local copy, its twin, and the corresponding incoming page are compared word by word. If the local word has been modified but the incoming one has not been, the incoming word overwrites the local one. If both the local and incoming words have been modified, a runtime error is signaled. If no such conflicts exist, the merged page replaces the local one and execution continues.

Shared variables that are not annotated as belonging to one of the above categories are treated as in conventional page-based DSM systems: only one copy of each writable page is permitted, and it is moved from process to process on demand. Read-only pages are replicated as needed.

Let us now look at an example of how the multiwriter protocol is used. Consider the programs of Fig. 6-32(a) and (b). Here, two processes are each incrementing the elements of the same array. Process 1 increments the even elements using function f and process 2 increments the odd elements using function g. Before starting this phase, each process blocks at a barrier until the other one gets there, too. After finishing this phase, they block at another barrier until both are done. Then they both continue with the rest of the program. Parallel programs for quicksort and fast Fourier transforms exhibit this kind of behavior.

With pure sequentially consistent memory both processes pause at the barrier as shown in Fig. 6-32(c). The barrier can be implemented by having each

Process 1

/* Wait for process 2 */
wait_at_barrier(b);

for (i = 0; i < n; i +=2)
    a[i] = a[i] + f(i);

/* Wait until proc 2 is done */
wait_at_barrier(b);

(a)

Process 2

/* Wait for process 1 */
wait_at_barrier(b);

for (i = 1; i < n; i +=2)
    a[i] = a[i] + g(i);

/* Wait until proc 1 is done */
wait_at_barrier(b);

(b)

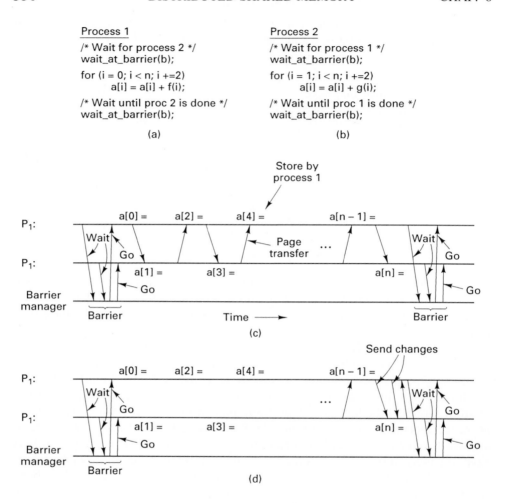

Fig. 6-32. (a) A program using a. (b) Another program using a. (c) Messages sent for sequentially consistent memory. (d) Messages sent for release consistent memory.

process send a message to a barrier manager and block until the reply arrived. The barrier manager does not send any replies until all processes have arrived at the barrier.

After passing the barrier, process 1 might start off, storing into $a[0]$. Then process 2 might try to store into $a[1]$, causing a page fault to fetch the page containing the array. After that, process 1 might try to store into $a[2]$, causing another fault, and so on. With a little bad luck, each of the stores might require a full page to be transferred, generating a great deal of traffic.

With release consistency, the situation is illustrated in Fig. 6-32(d). Again, both processes first pass the barrier. The first store into $a[0]$ forces a twin page to be created for process 1. Similarly, the first store into $a[1]$ forces a twin page to be created for process 2. No page transfers between machines are required at this point. Thereafter, each process can store into its private copy of a at will, without causing any page faults.

When each process arrives at the second barrier statement, the differences between its current values of a and the original values (stored on the twin pages) are computed. These are sent to all the other processes known to be interested in the pages affected. These processes, in turn, may pass them on to other interested processes unknown to the source of the changes. Each receiving process merges the changes with its own version. Conflicts result in a runtime error.

After a process has reported the changes in this way, it sends a message to the barrier manager and waits for a reply. When all processes have sent out their updates and arrived at the barrier, the barrier manager sends out the replies, and everyone can continue. In this manner, page traffic is needed only when arriving at a barrier.

Directories

Munin uses directories to locate pages containing shared variables. When a fault occurs on a reference to a shared variable, Munin hashes the virtual address that caused the fault to find the variable's entry in the shared variable directory. From the entry, it sees which category the variable is, whether a local copy is present, and who the probable owner is. Write-shared pages do not necessarily have a single owner. For a conventional shared variable, it is the last process to acquire write access. For a migratory shared variable, the owner is the process currently holding it.

The location of the probable owner is kept track of using the following algorithm. When a Munin process starts up, the root process owns all the shared variables. When process P_1 later references a shared variable it gets a fault, which generates a message to the root asking for it. The root gives it the page it wants, and notes that P_1 is now the owner. If P_2 asks for the page, the root tells it that P_1 is probably the owner. When P_2 asks P_1 for the variable, it gets it. If P_2 wants to write or the page is migratory, P_2 becomes the new owner and P_1 records this fact. The state of the probable owners at this point in time is shown in Fig. 6-33(a) for a writable or migratory variable.

Now suppose that P_3 and P_4 successively ask for the page. They, too, each follow the chain, resulting in Fig. 6-33(b). Now P_1 needs the variable again. Since it thinks P_2 has it, it sends P_2 a message, only to learn that P_2 thinks that

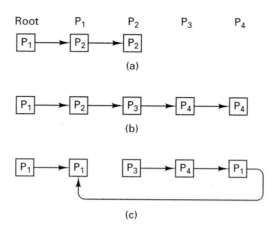

Fig. 6-33. At each point in time, a process can think another process is the probable owner of some page.

P_3 is the owner. After following the chain, P_1 gets the page and the chain looks like Fig. 6-33(c). In this way, every process eventually has an idea of who the probable owner might be, and can follow the chain all the way to find the actual owner.

The directories are also used to keep track of the copysets. However, the copysets need not be perfectly consistent. For example, suppose that P_1 and P_2 are each holding some write-shared variable and each of them knows about the other one. Then P_3 asks the owner, P_1, for a copy and gets it. P_3 records P_1 as having a copy, but does not tell P_2. Later, P_4, which thinks P_2 is the owner, acquires a copy, which updates P_2's copyset to include P_4. At this point no one process has a complete list of who has the page.

Nevertheless, it is possible to maintain consistency. Imagine that P_4 now releases a lock, so it sends the updates to P_2. The acknowledgement message from P_2 to P_4 contains a note saying that P_1 also has a copy. When P_4 contacts P_1 it hears about P_3. In this way, it eventually discovers the entire copyset, so all copies can be updated and it can update its own copyset.

To reduce the overhead of having to send updates to processes that are no longer interested in particular write-shared pages, a timer-based algorithm is used. If a process holds a page, does not reference it within a certain time interval and receives an update, it drops the page. The next time it receives an update for the dropped page, the process tells the updating process that it no longer has a copy, so the updater can reduce the size of its copyset. The probable owner chain is used to denote the copy of last resort, which cannot be dropped without finding a new owner or writing it to disk. This mechanism ensures that a page cannot be dropped by all processes and thus lost.

Synchronization

Munin maintains a second directory for synchronization variables. These are located in a way analogous to the way ordinary shared variables are located. Conceptually, locks act like they are centralized, but in fact a distributed implementation is used to avoid sending too much traffic to any one machine.

When a process wants to acquire a lock, it first checks to see if it owns the lock itself. If it does and the lock is free, the request is granted. If the lock is not local, it is located using the synchronization directory, which keeps track of the probable owner. If the lock is free, it is granted. If it is not free, the requester is added to the tail of the queue. In this way, each process knows the identity of the process following it in the queue. When a lock is released, the owner passes it to the next process on the list.

Barriers are implemented by a central server. When a barrier is created, it is given a count of the number of processes that must be waiting on it before they can all be released. When a process has finished a certain phase in its computation it can send a message to the barrier server asking to wait. When the requisite number of processes are waiting, all of them are sent a message freeing them.

6.5.2. Midway

Midway is a distributed shared memory system that is based on sharing individual data structures. It is similar to Munin in some ways, but has some interesting new features of its own. Its goal was to allow existing and new multiprocessor programs to run efficiently on multicomputers with only small changes to the code. For more information about Midway, see (Bershad and Zekauskas, 1991; and Bershad et al., 1993).

Programs in Midway are basically conventional programs written in C, C++, or ML, with certain additional information provided by the programmer. Midway programs use the Mach C-threads package for expressing parallelism. A thread may fork off one or more other threads. The children run in parallel with the parent thread and with each other, potentially with each thread on a different machine (i.e., each thread as a separate process). All threads share the same linear address space, which contains both private data and shared data. The job of Midway is to keep the shared variables consistent in an efficient way.

Entry Consistency

Consistency is maintained by requiring all accesses to shared variables and data structures to be done inside a specific kind of critical section known to the Midway runtime system. Each of these critical sections is guarded by a special synchronization variable, generally a lock, but possibly also a barrier. Each shared variable accessed in a critical section must be explicitly associated with that critical section's lock (or barrier) by a procedure call. In this way, when a critical section is entered or exited, Midway knows precisely which shared variables potentially will be accessed or have been accessed.

Midway supports entry consistency, which works as follows. To access shared data, a process normally enters a critical region by calling a library procedure, *lock*, with a lock variable as parameter. The call also specifies whether an exclusive lock or a nonexclusive lock is required. An exclusive lock is needed when one or more shared variables are to be updated. If shared variables are only to be read, but not modified, a nonexclusive lock is sufficient, which allows multiple processes to enter the same critical region at the same time. No harm can arise because none of the shared variables can be changed.

When *lock* is called, the Midway runtime system acquires the lock, and at the same time, brings all the shared variables associated with that lock up to date. Doing so may require sending messages to other processes to get the most recent values. When all the replies have been received, the lock is granted (assuming that there are no conflicts) and the process starts executing the critical region. When the process has completed the critical section, it releases the lock. Unlike release consistency, no communication takes place at release time, that is, modified shared variables are *not* pushed out to the other machines that use the shared variables. Only when one of their processes subsequently acquires a lock and asks for the current values are data transferred.

To make the entry consistency work, Midway requires that programs have three characteristics that multiprocessor programs do not have:

1. Shared variables must be declared using the new keyword *shared*.

2. Each shared variable must be associated with a lock or barrier.

3. Shared variables may only be accessed inside critical sections.

Doing these things requires extra effort from the programmer. If these rules are not completely adhered to, no error message is generated and the program may yield incorrect results. Because programming in this way is somewhat error prone, especially when running old multiprocessor programs that no one really understands any more, Midway also supports sequential consistency and release consistency. These models require less detailed information for correct operation.

The extra information required by Midway should be thought of as part of the contract between the software and the memory that we studied earlier under consistency. In effect, if the program agrees to abide by certain rules known in advance, the memory promises to work. Otherwise, all bets are off.

Implementation

When a critical section is entered, the Midway runtime system must first acquire the corresponding lock. To get an exclusive lock, it is necessary to locate the lock's owner, which is the last process to acquire it exclusively. Each process keeps track of the probable owner, the same way that IVY and Munin do, and follows the distributed chain of successive owners until the current one is found. If this process is not currently using the lock, ownership is transferred. If the lock is in use, the requesting process is made to wait until the lock is free. To acquire a lock in nonexclusive mode, it is sufficient to contact any process currently holding it. Barriers are handled by a centralized barrier manager.

At the same time the lock is acquired, the acquiring process brings its copy of all the shared variables up to date. In the simplest protocol, the old owner would just send them all. However, Midway uses an optimization to reduce the amount of data that must be transferred. Suppose that this acquire is being done at time T_1 and the previous acquire done by the same process was done at T_0. Only those variables that have been modified since T_0 are transferred, since the acquirer already has the rest.

This strategy brings up the issue of how the system keeps track of what has been modified and when. To keep track of which shared variables have been changed, a special compiler can be used that generates code to maintain a run-time table with an entry in it for each shared variable in the program. Whenever a shared variable is updated, the change is noted in the table. If this special compiler is not available, the MMU hardware is used to detect writes to shared data, as in Munin.

The time of each change is kept track of using a timestamp protocol based on Lamport's (1978) "happens before" relation. Each machine maintains a logical clock, which is incremented whenever a message is sent and included in the message. When a message arrives, the receiver sets its logical clock to the larger of the sender's clock and its own current value. Using these clocks, time is effectively partitioned into intervals defined by message transmissions. When an acquire is done, the acquiring processor specifies the time of its previous acquire and asks for all the relevant shared variables that have changed since then.

The use of entry consistency implemented in this way potentially has excellent performance because communication occurs only when a process does an acquire. Furthermore, only those shared variables that are out of date need to be transferred. In particular, if a process enters a critical region, leaves it, and enters it again, no communication is needed. This pattern is common in parallel programming, so the potential gain here is substantial. The price paid for this performance is a programmer interface that is more complex and error prone than that used by the other consistency models.

6.6. OBJECT-BASED DISTRIBUTED SHARED MEMORY

The page-based DSM systems that we studied use the MMU hardware to trap accesses to missing pages. While this approach has some advantages, it also has some disadvantages. In particular, in many programming languages, data are organized into objects, packages, modules, or other data structures, each of which has an existence independent of the others. If a process references part of an object, in many cases the entire object will be needed, so it makes sense to transport data over the network in units of objects, not in units of pages.

The shared-variable approach, as taken by Munin and Midway, is a step in the direction of organizing the shared memory in a more structured way, but it is only a first step. In both systems, the programmer must supply information about which variables are shared and which are not, and must also provide protocol information in Munin and association information in Midway. Errors in these annotations can have serious consequences.

By going further in the direction of a high-level programming model, DSM systems can be made easier and less error prone to program. Access to shared variables and synchronization using them can also be integrated more cleanly. In some cases, certain optimizations can also be introduced that are more difficult to perform in a less abstract programming model.

6.6.1. Objects

An **object** is a programmer-defined encapsulated data structure, as depicted in Fig. 6-34. It consists of internal data, the **object state**, and procedures, called **methods** or **operations**, that operate on the object state. To access or operate on the internal state, the program must invoke one of the methods. The method can change the internal state, return (part of) the state, or something else. Direct access to the internal state is not allowed. This property, called **information hiding** (Parnas, 1972). Forcing all references to an object's data to go through the methods helps structure the program in a modular way.

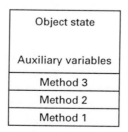

Fig. 6-34. An object.

In an object-based distributed shared memory, processes on multiple machines share an abstract space filled with shared objects, as shown in Fig. 6-35. The location and management of the objects is handled automatically by the runtime system. This model is in contrast to page-based DSM systems such as IVY, which just provide a raw linear memory of bytes from 0 to some maximum.

Any process can invoke any object's methods, regardless of where the process and object are located. It is the job of the operating system and runtime system to make the act of invoking a method work no matter where the process and object are located. Because processes cannot directly access the internal state of any of the shared objects, various optimizations are possible here that are not possible (or at least are more difficult) with page-based DSM. For example, since access to the internal state is strictly controlled, it may be possible to relax the memory consistency protocol without the programmer even knowing it.

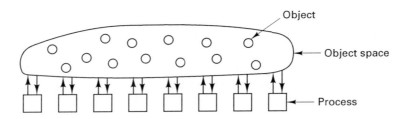

Fig. 6-35. In an object-based distributed shared memory, processes communicate by invoking methods on shared objects.

Once a decision has been made to structure a shared memory as a collection of separate objects instead of as a linear address space, there are many other choices to be made. Probably the most important issue is whether objects should be replicated or not. If replication is not used, all accesses to an object go through the one and only copy, which is simple, but may lead to poor performance. By allowing objects to migrate from machine to machine, as needed, it may be possible to reduce the performance loss by moving objects to where they are needed.

On the other hand, if objects are replicated, what should be done when one copy is updated? One approach is to invalidate all the other copies, so that only the up-to-date copy remains. Additional copies can be created later, on demand, as needed. An alternative choice is not to invalidate the copies, but to update them. Shared-variable DSM also has this choice, but for page-based DSM, invalidation is the only feasible choice. Similarly, object-based DSM, like shared-variable DSM, eliminates most false sharing.

To summarize, object-based distributed shared memory offers three advantages over the other methods:

1. It is more modular than the other techniques.

2. The implementation is more flexible because accesses are controlled.

3. Synchronization and access can be integrated together cleanly.

Object-based DSM also has disadvantages. For one thing, it cannot be used to run old "dusty deck" multiprocessor programs that assume the existence of a shared linear address space that every process can read and write at random. However, since multiprocessors are relatively new, the existing stock of multiprocessor programs that anyone cares about is small.

A second potential disadvantage is that since all accesses to shared objects must be done by invoking the objects' methods, extra overhead is incurred that is not present with shared pages that can be accessed directly. On the other hand, many experts in software engineering recommend objects as a structuring tool, even on single machines, and accept the overhead as well worth the price paid.

Below we will study two quite different examples of object-based DSM: Linda and Orca. Other distributed object-based systems also exist, including Amber (Chase et al., 1989), Emerald (Jul et al., 1988), and COOL (Lea et al., 1993).

6.6.2. Linda

Linda provides processes on multiple machines with a highly structured distributed shared memory. This memory is accessed through a small set of primitive operations that can be added to existing languages, such as C and FORTRAN to form parallel languages, in this case, C-Linda and FORTRAN-Linda. In the description below, we will focus on C-Linda, but conceptually the differences between the variants are small. More information about Linda can be found in (Carriero and Gelernter, 1986, 1989; and Gelernter, 1985).

This approach has several advantages over a new language. A major advantage is that users do not have to learn a new language. This advantage should not be underestimated. A second one is simplicity: turning a language, X, into X-Linda can be done by adding a few primitives to the library and adapting the Linda preprocessor that feeds Linda programs to the compiler. Finally, the Linda system is highly portable across operating systems and machine architectures and has been implemented on many distributed and parallel systems.

Tuple Space

The unifying concept behind Linda is that of an abstract **tuple space**. The tuple space is global to the entire system, and processes on any machine can insert tuples into the tuple space or remove tuples from the tuple space without regard to how or where they are stored. To the user, the tuple space looks like a big, global shared memory, as we saw in Fig. 6-35. The actual implementation may involve multiple servers on multiple machines, and will be described later.

A **tuple** is like a structure in C or a record in Pascal. It consists of one or more fields, each of which is a value of some type supported by the base language. For C-Linda, field types include integers, long integers, and floating-point numbers, as well as composite types such as arrays (including strings) and structures, (but not other tuples). Figure 6-36 shows three tuples as examples.

```
("abc", 2, 5)
("matrix–1", 1, 6, 3.14)
("family", "is-sister", "Carolyn", "Elinor")
```

Fig. 6-36. Three Linda tuples.

Operations on Tuples

Linda is not a fully general object-based system since it provides only a fixed number of built-in operations and no way to define new ones. Four operations are provided on tuples. The first one, *out*, puts a tuple into the tuple space. For example,

out("abc", 2, 5);

puts the tuple ("abc", 2, 5) into the tuple space. The fields of *out* are normally constants, variables, or expressions, as in

out("matrix−1", i, j, 3.14);

which outputs a tuple with four fields, the second and third of which are determined by the current values of the variables i and j.

Tuples are retrieved from the tuple space by the *in* primitive. They are addressed by content rather than by name or address. The fields of *in* can be expressions or formal parameters. Consider, for example,

in("abc", 2, ? i);

This operation "searches" the tuple space for a tuple consisting of the string "abc", the integer, 2, and a third field containing any integer (assuming that i is an integer). If found, the tuple is removed from the tuple space and the variable *i* is assigned the value of the third field. The matching and removal are atomic, so if two processes execute the same *in* operation simultaneously, only one of them will succeed, unless two or more matching tuples are present. The tuple space may even contain multiple copies of the same tuple.

The matching algorithm used by *in* is straightforward. The fields of the *in* primitive, called the **template**, are (conceptually) compared to the corresponding fields of every tuple in the tuple space. A match occurs if the following three conditions are all met:

1. The template and the tuple have the same number of fields.

2. The types of the corresponding fields are equal.

3. Each constant or variable in the template matches its tuple field.

Formal parameters, indicated by a question mark followed by a variable name or type, do not participate in the matching (except for type checking), although those containing a variable name are assigned after a successful match.

If no matching tuple is present, the calling process is suspended until another process inserts the needed tuple, at which time the caller is automatically revived and given the new tuple. The fact that processes block and unblock automatically means that if one process is about to output a tuple and another is about to input it, it does not matter which goes first. The only difference is that if the *in* is done before the *out*, there will be a slight delay until the tuple is available for removal.

The fact that processes block when a needed tuple is not present can be put to many uses. For example, it can be used to implement semaphores. To create or do an *UP* (*V*) on semaphore *S*, a process can execute

out("semaphore S");

To do a *DOWN* (*P*), it does

in("semaphore S");

The state of semaphore *S* is determined by the number of ("semaphore S") tuples in the tuple space. If none exist, any attempt to get one will block until some other process supplies one.

In addition to *out* and *in*, Linda also has a primitive *read*, which is the same as *in* except that it does not remove the tuple from the tuple space. There is also a primitive *eval*, which causes its parameters to be evaluated in parallel and the resulting tuple to be deposited in the tuple space. This mechanism can be used to perform an arbitrary computation. This is how parallel processes are created in Linda.

A common programming paradigm in Linda is the **replicated worker**

model. This model is based on the idea of a **task bag** full of jobs to be done. The main process starts out by executing a loop containing

out("task-bag", job);

in which a different job description is output to the tuple space on each iteration. Each worker starts out by getting a job description tuple using

in("task-bag", ?job);

which it then carries out. When it is done, it gets another. New work may also be put into the task bag during execution. In this simple way, work is dynamically divided among the workers, and each worker is kept busy all the time, all with little overhead.

In certain ways, Linda is similar to Prolog, on which it is loosely based. Both support an abstract space that functions as a kind of data base. In Prolog, the space holds facts and rules; in Linda it holds tuples. In both cases, processes can provide templates to be matched against the contents of the data base.

Despite these similarities, the two systems also differ in significant ways. Prolog was intended for programming artificial intelligence applications on a single processor, whereas Linda was intended for general programming on multicomputers. Prolog has a complex pattern-matching scheme involving unification and backtracking; Linda's matching algorithm is much simpler. In Linda, a successful match removes the matching tuple from the tuple space; in Prolog it does not. Finally, a Linda process unable to locate a needed tuple blocks, which forms the basis for interprocess synchronization. In Prolog, there are no processes and programs never block.

Implementation of Linda

Efficient implementations of Linda are possible on various kinds of hardware. Below we will discuss some of the more interesting ones. For all implementations, a preprocessor scans the Linda program, extracting useful information and converting it to the base language where need be (e.g., the string "? int" is not allowed as a parameter in C or FORTRAN). The actual work of inserting and removing tuples from the tuple space is done during execution by the Linda runtime system.

An efficient Linda implementation has to solve two problems:

1. How to simulate associative addressing without massive searching.

2. How to distribute tuples among machines and locate them later.

The key to both problems is to observe that each tuple has a **type signature**, consisting of the (ordered) list of the types of its fields. Furthermore, by

convention, the first field of each tuple is normally a string that effectively partitions the tuple space into disjoint subspaces named by the string. Splitting the
tuple space into subspaces, each of whose tuples has the same type signature and
same first field, simplifies programming and makes certain optimizations possible.

For example, if the first parameter to an *in* or *out* call is a literal string, it is
possible to determine at compile time which subspace the call operates on. If
the first parameter is a variable, the determination is made at run time. In both
cases, this partitioning means that only a fraction of the tuple space has to be
searched. Figure 6-37 shows four tuples and four templates. Together they
form four subspaces. For each *out* or *in*, it is possible to determine at compile
time which subspace and tuple server are needed. If the initial string was a variable, the determination of the correct subspace would have to be delayed until
run time.

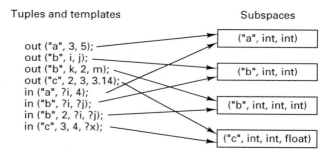

Fig. 6-37. Tuples and templates can be associated with subspaces.

In addition, each subspace can be organized as a hash table using its *i*th
tuple field as the hash key. If field *i* is a constant or variable (but not a formal
parameter), an *in* or *out* can be executed by computing the hash function of the
*i*th field to find the position in the table where the tuple belongs. Knowing the
subspace and table position eliminates all searching. If the *i*th field of a certain
in is a formal parameter, hashing is not possible, so a complete search of the
subspace is needed except in some special cases. By carefully choosing the
field to hash on, however, the preprocessor can usually avoid searching most of
the time. Other subspace organizations beside hashing are also possible for special cases (e.g., a queue when there is one writer and one reader).

Additional optimizations are also used. For example, the hashing scheme
described above distributes the tuples of a given subspace into bins, to restrict
searching to a single bin. It is possible to place different bins on different
machines, both to spread the load more widely and to take advantage of locality.
If the hashing function is the key modulo the number of machines, the number
of bins scales linearly with the system size.

Now let us examine various implementation techniques for different kinds of hardware. On a multiprocessor, the tuple subspaces can be implemented as hash tables in global memory, one for each subspace. When an *in* or an *out* is performed, the corresponding subspace is locked, the tuple entered or removed, and the subspace unlocked.

On a multicomputer, the best choice depends on the communication architecture. If reliable broadcasting is available, a serious candidate is to replicate all the subspaces in full on all machines, as shown in Fig. 6-38. When an *out* is done, the new tuple is broadcast and entered into the appropriate subspace on each machine. To do an *in*, the local subspace is searched. However, since successful completion of an *in* requires removing the tuple from the tuple space, a delete protocol is required to remove it from all machines. To prevent races and deadlocks, a two-phase commit protocol can be used.

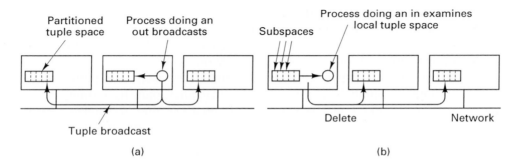

Fig. 6-38. Tuple space can be replicated on all machines. The dotted lines show the partitioning of the tuple space into subspaces. (a) Tuples are broadcast on *out*. (b). *In*s are local, but the deletes must be broadcast.

This design is straightforward, but may not scale well as the system grows in size, since every tuple must be stored on every machine. On the other hand, the total size of the tuple space is often quite modest, so problems may not arise except in huge systems. The S/Net Linda system uses this approach because S/Net has a fast, reliable, word-parallel bus broadcast (Carriero and Gelernter, 1986).

The inverse design is to do *out*s locally, storing the tuple only on the machine that generated it, as shown in Fig. 6-39. To do an *in*, a process must broadcast the template. Each recipient then checks to see if it has a match, sending back a reply if it does.

If the tuple is not present, or if the broadcast is not received at the machine holding the tuple, the requesting machine retransmits the broadcast request ad infinitem, increasing the interval between broadcasts until a suitable tuple materializes and the request can be satisfied. If two or more tuples are sent, they

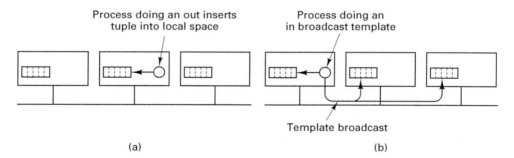

Fig. 6-39. Unreplicated tuple space. (a) An *out* is done locally. (b) An *in* requires the template to be broadcast in order to find a tuple.

are treated like local *out*s and the tuples are effectively moved from the machines that had them to the one doing the request. In fact, the runtime system can even move tuples around on its own to balance the load. Carriero et al. (1986) used this method for implementing Linda on a LAN.

These two methods can be combined to produce a system with partial replication. A simple example is to imagine all the machines logically forming a rectangle, as shown in Fig. 6-40. When a process on a machine, *A*, wants to do an *out*, it broadcasts (or sends by point-to-point message) the tuple to all machines in its row of the matrix. When a process on a machine, *B*, wants to do an *in* it broadcasts the template to all machines in its column. Due to the geometry, there will always be exactly one machine that sees both the tuple and the template (*C* in this example), and that machine makes the match and sends the tuple to the process asking for it. Krishnaswamy (1991) used this method for a hardware Linda coprocessor.

Finally, let us consider the implementation of Linda on systems that have no broadcast capability at all (Bjornson, 1993). The basic idea is to partition the tuple space into disjoint subspaces, first by creating a partition for each type signature, then by dividing each of these partitions again based on the first field. Potentially, each of the resulting partitions can go on a different machine, handled by its own tuple server, to spread the load around. When either an *out* or an *in* is done, the required partition is determined, and a single message is sent to that machine either to deposit a tuple there or to retrieve one.

Experience with Linda shows that distributed shared memory can be handled in a radically different way than moving whole pages around, as in the page-based systems we studied above. It is also quite different from sharing variables with release or entry consistency. As future systems become larger and more powerful, novel approaches such as this may lead to new insights into how to program these systems in an easier way.

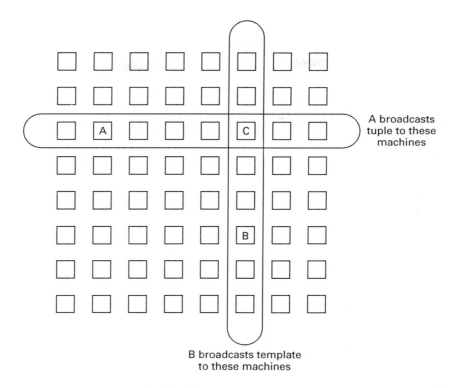

Fig. 6-40. Partial broadcasting of tuples and templates.

6.6.3. Orca

Orca is a parallel programming system that allows processes on different machines to have controlled access to a distributed shared memory consisting of protected objects (Bal, 1991; and Bal et al., 1990, 1992). These objects can be thought of as a more powerful (and more complicated) form of the Linda tuples, supporting arbitrary operations instead of just *in* and *out*. Another difference is that Linda tuples are created on-the-fly during execution in large volume, whereas Orca objects are not. The Linda tuples are used primarily for communication, whereas the Orca objects are also used for computation and are generally more heavyweight.

The Orca system consists of the language, compiler, and runtime system, which actually manages the shared objects during execution. Although language, compiler, and runtime system were designed to work together, the runtime system is independent of the compiler and could be used for other languages as well. After an introduction to the Orca language, we will describe how the runtime system implements an object-based distributed shared memory.

The Orca Language

In some respects, Orca is a traditional language whose sequential statements are based roughly on Modula-2. However, it is a type secure language with no pointers and no aliasing. Array bounds are checked at runtime (except when the checking can be done at compile time). These and similar features eliminate or detect many common programming errors such as wild stores, into memory. The language features have been chosen carefully to make a variety of optimizations easier.

Two features of Orca important for distributed programming are shared data-objects (or just **objects**) and the **fork** statement. An object is an abstract data type, somewhat analogous to a package in Ada®. It encapsulates internal data structures and user-written procedures, called **operations** (or **methods**) for operating on the internal data structures. Objects are passive, that is, they do not contain threads to which messages can be sent. Instead, processes access an object's internal data by invoking its operations. Objects do not inherit properties from other objects, so Orca is considered an object-based language rather than an object-oriented language.

Each operation consists of a list of (guard, block-of-statements) pairs. A guard is a Boolean expression that does not contain any side effects, or the empty guard, which is the same as the value *true*. When an operation is invoked, all of its guards are evaluated in an unspecified order. If all of them are *false*, the invoking process is delayed until one becomes *true*. When a guard is found that evaluates to *true*, the block of statements following it is executed. Figure 6-41 depicts a *stack* object with two operations, *push* and *pop*.

```
Object implementation stack;                # variable indicating the top
    top: integer;                           # storage for the stack
    stack: array [integer 0..N–1] of integer;

    operation push (item: integer);         # function returning nothing
    begin
        stack [top] := item;                # push item onto the stack
        top := top + 1;                     # increment the stack pointer
    end;

    operation pop(): integer;               # function returning an integer
    begin
        guard top > 0 do                    # suspend if the stack is empty
            top := top – 1;                 # decrement the stack pointer
            return stack [top];             # return the top item
        od;
    end;
begin
    top := 0;                               # initialization
end;
```

Fig. 6-41. A simplified stack object, with internal data and two operations.

Once a *stack* has been defined, variables of this type can be declared, as in

s, t: stack;

which creates two stack objects and initializes the *top* variable in each to 0. The integer variable *k* can be pushed onto the stack *s* by the statement

s$push(k);

and so forth. The *pop* operation has a guard, so an attempt to pop a variable from an empty stack will suspend the caller until another process has pushed something on the stack.

Orca has a **fork** statement to create a new process on a user-specified processor. The new process runs the procedure named in the **fork** statement. Parameters, including objects, may be passed to the new process, which is how objects become distributed among machines. For example, the statement

for i **in** 1 .. n **do fork** foobar(s) **on** i; **od**;

generates one new process on each of machines 1 through *n*, running the process **foobar** in each of them. As these *n* new processes (and the parent) execute in parallel, they can all push and pop items onto the shared stack *s* as though they were all running on a shared-memory multiprocessor. It is the job of the runtime system to sustain the illusion of shared memory where it really does not exist.

Operations on shared objects are atomic and sequentially consistent. The system guarantees that if multiple processes perform operations on the same shared object nearly simultaneously, the net effect is that it looks like the operations took place strictly sequentially, with no operation beginning until the previous one finished.

Furthermore, the operations appear in the same order to all processes. For example, suppose that we were to augment the *stack* object with a new operation, *peek*, to inspect the top item on the stack. Then if two independent processes push 3 and 4 simultaneously, and all processes later use *peek* to examine the top of the stack, the system guarantees that either every process will see 3 or every process will see 4. A situation in which some processes see 3 and other processes see 4 cannot occur in a multiprocessor or a paged-based distributed shared memory, and it cannot occur in Orca either. If only one copy of the stack is maintained, this effect is trivial to achieve, but if the stack is replicated on all machines, more effort is required, as described below.

Although we have not emphasized it, Orca integrates shared data and synchronization in a way not present in page-based DSM systems. Two kinds of synchronization are needed in parallel programs. The first kind is mutual exclusion synchronization, to keep two processes from executing the same critical region at the same time. In Orca, each operation on a shared object is effectively like a critical region because the system guarantees that the final result is the same as if all the critical regions were executed one at a time (i.e., sequentially). In this respect, an Orca object is like a distributed form of a monitor (Hoare, 1975).

The other kind of synchronization is condition synchronization, in which a process blocks waiting for some condition to hold. In Orca, condition synchronization is done with guards. In the example of Fig. 6-41, a process trying to pop an item from an empty stack will be suspended until the stack is no longer empty.

Management of Shared Objects in Orca

Object management in Orca is handled by the runtime system. It works on both broadcast (or multicast) networks and point-to-point networks. The runtime system handles object replication, migration, consistency, and operation invocation.

Each object can be in one of two states: single copy or replicated. An object in single-copy state exists on only one machine. A replicated object is present on all machines containing a process using it. It is not required that all objects be in the same state, so some of the objects used by a process may be replicated while others are single copy. Objects can change from single-copy state to replicated state and back during execution.

The big advantage of replicating an object on every machine is that reads can be done locally, without any network traffic or delay. When an object is not replicated, all operations must be sent to the object, and the caller must block waiting for the reply. A second advantage of replication is increased parallelism: multiple read operations can take place at the same time. With a single copy, only one operation at a time can take place, slowing down execution. The principal disadvantage of replication is the overhead of keeping all the copies consistent.

When a program performs an operation on an object, the compiler calls a runtime system procedure, *invoke_op*, specifying the object, the operation, the parameters, and a flag telling whether the object will be modified (called a write) or not modified (called a read). The action taken by *invoke_op* depends on whether the object is replicated, whether a copy is available locally, whether it is being read or written, and whether the underlying system supports reliable, totally-ordered broadcasting. Four cases have to be distinguished, as illustrated in Fig. 6-42.

In Fig. 6-42(a), a process wants to perform an operation on a nonreplicated object that happens to be on its own machine. It just locks the object, invokes the operation, and unlocks the object. The point of locking it is to inhibit any remote invocations temporarily while the local operation is in progress.

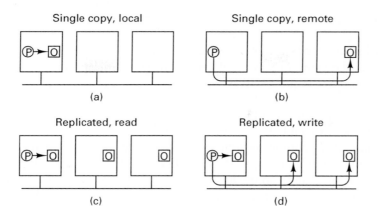

Fig. 6-42. Four cases of performing an operation on an object, O.

In Fig. 6-42(b) we still have a single-copy object, but now it is somewhere else. The runtime system does an RPC with the remote machine asking it to perform the operation, which it does, possibly with a slight delay if the object was locked when the request came in. In neither of these two cases is a distinction made between reads and writes (except that writes can awaken blocked processes).

If the object is replicated, as in Fig. 6-42(c) and (d), a copy will always be available locally, but now it matters if the operation is a read or a write. Reads are just done locally, with no network traffic and thus no overhead.

Writes on replicated objects are trickier. If the underlying system provides *reliable*, totally-ordered broadcasting, the runtime system broadcasts the name of the object, the operation, and the parameters and blocks until the broadcast has completed. All the machines, including itself, then compute the new value.

Note that the broadcasting primitive must be reliable, meaning that lower layers automatically detect and recover from lost messages. The Amoeba system, on which Orca was developed, has such a feature. Although the algorithm will be described in detail in Chap. 7, we will summarize it here very briefly. Each message to be broadcast is sent to a special process called the **sequencer**, which assigns it a sequence number and then broadcasts it using the unreliable hardware broadcast. Whenever a process notices a gap in the sequence numbers, it knows that it has missed a message and takes action to recover.

If the system does not have reliable broadcasting (or does not have any broadcasting at all), the update is done using a two-phase, primary copy algorithm. The process doing the update first sends a message to the primary copy of the object, locking and updating it. The primary copy then sends individual messages to all other machines holding the object, asking them to lock their copies. When all of them have acknowledged setting the lock, the originating process enters the second phase and sends another message telling them to perform the update and unlock the object.

Deadlocks are impossible because even if two processes try to update the same object at the same time, one of them will get to the primary copy first to lock it, and the other request will be queued until the object is free again. Also note that during the update process, all copies of the object are locked, so no other processes can read the old value. This locking guarantees that all operations are executed in a globally unique sequential order.

Notice that this runtime system uses an update algorithm rather than an invalidation algorithm as most page-based DSM systems do. Most objects are relatively small, so sending an update message (the new value or the parameters) is often no more expensive than an invalidate message. Updating has the great advantage of allowing subsequent remote reads to occur without having to refetch the object or perform the operation remotely.

Now let us briefly look at the algorithm for deciding whether an object should be in single-copy state or replicated. Initially, an Orca program consists of one process, which has all the objects. When it forks, all other machines are told of this event and given current copies of all the child's shared parameters. Each runtime system then calculates the expected cost of having each object replicated versus having it not replicated.

To make this calculation, it needs to know the expected ratio of reads to writes. The compiler estimates this information by examining the program, taking into account that accesses inside loops count more and accesses inside if-statements count less than other accesses. Communication costs are also factored into the equation. For example, an object with a read/write ratio of 10 on a broadcast network will be replicated, whereas an object with a read/write ratio of 1 on a point-to-point network will be put in single-copy state, with the single copy going on the machine doing the most writes. For a more detailed description, see (Bal and Kaashoek, 1993).

Since all runtime systems make the same calculation, they come to the same conclusion. If an object currently is present on only one machine and needs to be on all, it is disseminated. If it is currently replicated and that is no longer the best choice, all machines but one discard their copy. Objects can migrate via this mechanism.

Let us see how sequential consistency is achieved. For objects in single-copy state, all operations genuinely are serialized, so sequential consistency is achieved for free. For replicated objects, writes are totally ordered either by the reliable, totally-ordered broadcast or by the primary copy algorithm. Either way, there is global agreement on the order of the writes. The reads are local and can be interleaved with the writes in an arbitrary way without affecting sequential consistency.

Assuming that a reliable, totally-ordered broadcast can be done in two (plus epsilon) messages, as in Amoeba, the Orca scheme is highly efficient. Only after an operation is finished are the results sent out, no matter how many local variables were changed by the operation. If one regards each operation as a critical region, the efficiency is the same as for release consistency—one broadcast at the end of each critical region.

Various optimizations are possible. For example, instead of synchronizing *after* an operation, it could be done when an operation is started, as in entry consistency or lazy release consistency. The advantage here is that if a process executes an operation on a shared object repeatedly (e.g., in a loop), no broadcasts at all are sent until some other process exhibits interest in the object.

Another optimization is not to suspend the caller while doing the broadcast after a write that does not return a value (e.g., *push* in our stack example). Of course, this optimization must be done in such a transparent way. Information supplied by the compiler makes other optimizations possible.

In summary, the Orca model of distributed shared memory integrates good software engineering practice (encapsulated objects), shared data, simple semantics, and synchronization in a natural way. Also, in many cases an implementation as efficient as release consistency is possible. It works best when the underlying hardware and operating system must provide efficient, reliable, totally-ordered broadcasting, and the application must has an inherently high ratio of reads to writes for accesses to shared objects.

6.7. COMPARISON

Let us now briefly compare the various systems we have examined. IVY just tries to mimic a multiprocessor by doing paging over the network instead of to a disk. It offers a familiar memory model—sequential consistency, and can run existing multiprocessor programs without modification. The only problem is the performance.

Munin and Midway try to improve the performance by requiring the programmer to mark those variables that are shared and by using weaker consistency models. Munin is based on release consistency, and on every release transmits all modified pages (as deltas) to other processes sharing those pages. Midway, in contrast, does communication only when a lock changes ownership.

Midway supports only one kind of shared data variable, whereas Munin has four kinds (read only, migratory, write-shared, and conventional). On the other hand, Midway supports three different consistency protocols (entry, release, and processor), whereas Munin only supports release consistency. Whether it is better to have multiple types of shared data or multiple protocols is open to discussion. More research will be needed before we understand this subject fully.

Finally, the way writes to shared variables are detected is different. Munin uses the MMU hardware to trap writes, whereas Midway offers a choice between a special compiler that records writes and doing it the way Munin does, with the MMU. Not having to take a stream of page faults, especially inside critical regions, is definitely an advantage for Midway.

Now let us compare Munin and Midway to object-based shared memory of the Linda-Orca variety. Synchronization and data access in Munin and Midway are up to the programmer, whereas they are tightly integrated in Linda and Orca. In Linda there is less danger that a programmer will make a synchronization error, since *in* and *out* handle their own synchronization internally. Similarly, when an operation on a shared object is invoked in Orca, the locking is handled completely by the runtime system, with the programmer not even being aware of it. Condition synchronization (as opposed to mutual exclusion synchronization) is not part of the Munin or Midway model, so it is up to the programmer to do all the work explicitly. In contrast, it is an integral part of the Linda model (blocking when a tuple is not present) and the Orca model (blocking on a guard).

In short, the Munin and Midway programmers must do more work in the area of synchronization and consistency, with little support, and must get it all right. There is no encapsulation and there are no methods to protect shared data, as Linda and Orca have. On the other hand, Munin and Midway allow programming in only slightly modified C or C++, whereas Linda's communication is unusual and Orca is a whole new language. In terms of efficiency, Midway is best in terms of the number and size of messages transmitted, although the use of fundamentally different programming models (open C code, objects, and tuples) may lead to substantially different algorithms in the three cases, which also can affect efficiency.

6.8. SUMMARY

Multiple CPU computer systems fall into two categories: those that have shared memory and those that do not. The shared memory machines (multiprocessors) are easier to program but harder to build, whereas the machines without shared memory (multicomputers) are harder to program but easier to build. Distributed shared memory is a technique for making multicomputers easier to program by simulating shared memory on them.

Small multiprocessors are often bus based, but large ones are switched. The protocols the large ones use require complex data structures and algorithms to keep the caches consistent. NUMA multiprocessors avoid this complexity by forcing the software to make all the decisions about which pages to place on which machine.

A straightforward implementation of DSM, as done in IVY, is possible, but often has substantially lower performance than a multiprocessor. For this reason, researchers have looked at various memory models in an attempt to obtain better performance. The standard against which all models are measured is sequential consistency, which means that all processes see all memory references in the same order. Causal consistency, PRAM consistency, and processor consistency all weaken the concept that processes see *all* memory references in the same order.

Another approach is that of weak consistency, release consistency, and entry consistency, in which memory is not consistent all the time, but the programmer can force it to become consistent by certain actions, such as entering or leaving a critical region.

Three general techniques have been used to provide DSM. The first simulates the multiprocessor memory model, giving each process a linear, paged memory. Pages are moved back and forth between machines as needed. The second uses ordinary programming languages with annotated shared variables. The third is based on higher-level programming models such as tuples and objects.

In this chapter we studied five different approaches to DSM. IVY operates essentially like a virtual memory, with pages moved from machine to machine when page faults occur. Munin uses multiple protocols and release consistency to allow individual variables to be shared. Midway is similar to Munin, except that it uses entry consistency instead of release consistency as the normal case. Linda represents the other end of the spectrum, with an abstract tuple space far removed from the details of paging. Orca supports a model in which data objects are replicated on multiple machines and accessed through protected methods that make the objects look sequentially consistent to the programmer.

PROBLEMS

1. A Dash system has b bytes of memory divided over n clusters. Each cluster has p processors in it. The cache block size is c bytes. Give a formula for the total amount of memory devoted to directories (excluding the two state bits per directory entry).

2. Is it really essential that Dash make a distinction between the CLEAN and UNCACHED states? Would it have been possible to dispense with one of them? After all, in both cases memory has an up-to-date copy of the block.

3. In the text it is stated that many minor variations of the cache ownership protocol of Fig. 6-6 are possible. Describe one such variation and give one advantage yours has over the one in the text.

4. Why is the concept of "home memory" needed in Memnet but not in Dash?

5. In a NUMA multiprocessor, local memory references take 100 nsec and remote references take 800 nsec. A certain program makes a total of N memory references during its execution, of which 1 percent are to a page P. That page is initially remote, and it takes C nsec to copy it locally. Under what conditions should the page be copied locally in the absence of significant use by other processors?

6. During the discussion of memory consistency models, we often referred to the contract between the software and memory. Why is such a contract needed?

7. A multiprocessor has a single bus. Is it possible to implement strictly consistent memory?

8. In Fig. 6-13(a) an example of a sequentially consistent memory is shown. Make a minimal change to P_2 that violates sequential consistency.

9. In Fig. 6-14, is 001110 a legal output for a sequentially consistent memory? Explain your answer.

10. At the end of Sec. 6-2.2, we discussed a formal model that said every set of operations on a sequentially consistent memory can be modeled by a string, S, from which all the individual process sequences can be derived. For processes P_1 and P_2 in Fig. 6-16, give all the possible values of S. Ignore processes P_3 and P_4 and do not include their memory references in S.

11. In Fig. 6-20, a sequentially consistent memory allows six possible statement interleavings. List them all.

12. Why is $W(x)1 \ R(x)0 \ R(x)1$ not legal for Fig. 6-12(b)?

13. In Fig. 6-14, is 000000 a legal output for a memory that is only PRAM consistent? Explain your answer.

14. In most implementations of (eager) release consistency in DSM systems, shared variables are synchronized on a release, but not on an acquire. Why is acquire needed at all then?

15. In Fig. 6-27, suppose that the page owner is located by broadcasting. In which of the cases should the page be sent for a read?

16. In Fig. 6-28 a process may contact the owner of a page via the page manager. It may want ownership or the page itself, which are independent quantities. Do all four cases exist (excepting, of course, the case where the requester does not want the page and does not want ownership)?

17. Suppose that two variables, *A* and *B* are both located, by accident, on the same page of a page-based DSM system. However, both of them are unshared variables. Is false sharing possible?

18. Why does IVY use an invalidation scheme for consistency instead of an update scheme?

19. Some machines have a single instruction that, in one atomic action, exchanges a register with a word in memory. Using this instruction, it is possible to implement semaphores for protecting critical regions. Will programs using this instruction work on a page-based DSM system? If so, under what circumstances will they work efficiently?

20. What happens if a Munin process modifies a shared variable outside a critical region?

21. Give an example of an *in* operation in Linda that does not require any searching or hashing to find a match.

22. When Linda is implemented by replicating tuples on multiple machines, a protocol is needed for deleting tuples. Give an example of a protocol that does not yield races when two processes try to delete the same tuple at the same time.

23. Consider an Orca system running on a network with hardware broadcasting. Why does the ratio of read operations to write operations affect the performance?

7

Case Study 1: Amoeba

In this chapter we will give our first example of a distributed operating system: Amoeba. In the following one we will look at a second example: Mach. Amoeba is a distributed operating system: it makes a collection of CPUs and I/O equipment act like a single computer. It also provides facilities for parallel programming where that is desired. This chapter describes the goals, design, and implementation of Amoeba. For more information about Amoeba, see (Mullender et al., 1990; and Tanenbaum et al., 1990).

7.1. INTRODUCTION TO AMOEBA

In this section we will give an introduction to Amoeba, starting with a brief history and its current research goals. Then we will look at the architecture of a typical Amoeba system. Finally, we will begin our study of the Amoeba software, both the kernel and the servers.

7.1.1. History of Amoeba

Amoeba originated at the Vrije Universiteit, Amsterdam, The Netherlands in 1981 as a research project in distributed and parallel computing. It was designed primarily by Andrew S. Tanenbaum and three of his Ph.D. students, Frans

Kaashoek, Sape J. Mullender, and Robbert van Renesse, although many other people also contributed to the design and implementation. By 1983, an initial prototype, Amoeba 1.0, was operational.

Starting in 1984, the Amoeba fissioned, and a second group was set up at the Centre for Mathematics and Computer Science, also in Amsterdam, under Mullender's leadership. In the succeeding years, this cooperation was extended to sites in England and Norway in a wide-area distributed system project sponsored by the European Community. This work used Amoeba 3.0, which unlike the earlier versions, was based on RPC. Using Amoeba 3.0, it was possible for clients in Tromso to access servers in Amsterdam transparently, and vice versa.

The system evolved for several years, acquiring such features as partial UNIX emulation, group communications and a new low-level protocol. The version described in this chapter is Amoeba 5.2.

7.1.2. Research Goals

Many research projects in distributed operating systems have started with an existing system (e.g., UNIX) and added new features, such as networking and a shared file system, to make it more distributed. The Amoeba project took a different approach. It started with a clean slate and developed a new system from scratch. The idea was to make a fresh start and experiment with new ideas without having to worry about backward compatibility with any existing system. To avoid the chore of having to rewrite a huge amount of application software from scratch as well, a UNIX emulation package was added later.

The primary goal of the project was to build a transparent distributed operating system. To the average user, using Amoeba is like using a traditional timesharing system like UNIX. One logs in, edits and compiles programs, moves files around, and so on. The difference is that each of these actions makes use of multiple machines over the network. These include process servers, file servers, directory servers, compute servers, and other machines, but the user is not aware of any of this. At the terminal, it just looks like a timesharing system.

An important distinction between Amoeba and most other distributed systems is that Amoeba has no concept of a "home machine." When a user logs in, it is to the system as a whole, not to a specific machine. Machines do not have owners. The initial shell, started upon login, runs on some arbitrary machine, but as commands are started up, in general they do not run on the same machine as the shell. Instead, the system automatically looks around for the most lightly loaded machine to run each new command on. During the course of a long terminal session, the processes that run on behalf of any one user will be spread more-or-less uniformly spread over all the machines in the system, depending on the load, of course. In this respect, Amoeba is higly location transparent.

In other words, all resources belong to the system as a whole and are managed by it. They are not dedicated to specific users, except for short periods of time to run individual processes. This model attempts to provide the transparency that is the holy grail of all distributed systems designers.

A simple example is *amake*, the Amoeba replacement for the UNIX *make* program. When the user types *amake*, all the necessary compilations happen, as expected, except that the system (and not the user) determines whether they happen sequentially or in parallel, and on which machine or machines this occurs. None of this is visible to the user.

A secondary goal of Amoeba is to provide a testbed for doing distributed and parallel programming. While some users just use Amoeba the same way they would use any other timesharing system most users are specifically interested in experimenting with distributed and parallel algorithms, languages, tools, and applications. Amoeba supports these users by making the underlying parallelism available to people who want to take advantage of it. In practice, most of Amoeba's current user base consists of people who are specifically interested in distributed and parallel computing in its various forms. A language, Orca, has been specifically designed and implemented on Amoeba for this purpose. Orca and its applications are described in (Bal, 1991; Bal et al., 1990; and Tanenbaum et al., 1992). Amoeba itself, however, is written in C.

7.1.3. The Amoeba System Architecture

Before describing how Amoeba is structured, it is useful first to outline the kind of hardware configuration for which Amoeba was designed, since it differs somewhat from what most organizations presently have. Amoeba was designed with two assumptions about the hardware in mind:

1. Systems will have a very large number of CPUs.

2. Each CPU will have tens of megabytes of memory.

These assumptions are already true at some installations, and will probably become true at almost all corporate, academic, and governmental sites within a few years.

The driving force behind the system architecture is the need to incorporate large numbers of CPUs in a straightforward way. In other words, what do you do when you can afford 10 or 100 CPUs per user? One solution is to give each user a personal 10-node or 100-node multiprocessor.

Although giving everyone a personal multiprocessor is certainly a possibility, doing so is not an effective way to spend the available budget. Most of the time, nearly all the processors will be idle, but some users will want to run massively parallel programs and will not be able to harness all the idle CPU cycles because they are in other users' personal machines.

Instead of this personal multiprocessor approach, Amoeba is based on the model shown in Fig. 7-1. In this model, all the computing power is located in one or more **processor pools**. A processor pool consists of a substantial number of CPUs, each with its own local memory and network connection. Shared memory is not required, or even expected, but if it is present it could be used to optimize message passing by doing memory-to-memory copying instead of sending messages over the network.

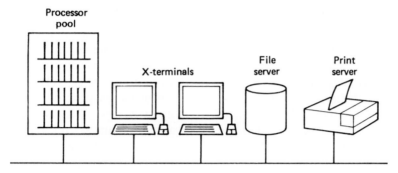

Fig. 7-1. The Amoeba system architecture.

The CPUs in a pool can be of different architectures, for example, a mixture of 680x0, 386, and SPARC machines. Amoeba has been designed to deal with multiple architectures and heterogeneous systems. It is even possible for the children of a single process to run on different architectures.

Pool processors are not "owned" by any one user. When a user types a command, the operating system dynamically chooses one or more processors on which to run that command. When the command completes, the processes are terminated and the resources held go back into the pool, waiting for the next command, very likely from a different user. If there is a shortage of pool processors, individual processors are timeshared, with new processes being assigned to the most lightly loaded CPUs. The important point to note here is that this model is quite different from current systems in which each user has exactly one personal workstation for all his computing activities.

The expected presence of large memories in future systems has influenced the design in many ways. Many time-space trade-offs have been made to provide high performance at the cost of using more memory. We will see examples later.

The second element of the Amoeba architecture is the terminal. It is through the terminal that the user accesses the system. A typical Amoeba terminal is an X terminal, with a large bit-mapped screen and a mouse. Alternatively, a personal computer or workstation running X windows can also be used as a terminal. Although Amoeba does not forbid running user programs on the terminal, the idea behind this model is to give the users relatively cheap terminals and concentrate the computing cycles into a common pool so that they can be used more efficiently.

Pool processors are inherently cheaper than workstations because they consist of just a single board with a network connection. There is no keyboard, monitor, or mouse, and the power supply can be shared by many boards. Thus, instead of buying 100 high-performance workstations for 100 users, one might buy 50 high-performance pool processors and 100 X terminals for the same price (depending on the economics, obviously). Since the pool processors are allocated only when needed, an idle user only ties up an inexpensive X terminal instead of an expensive workstation. The trade-offs inherent in the pool processor model versus the workstation model were discussed in Chap. 4.

To avoid any confusion, the pool processors do not *have* to be single-board computers. If these are not available, a subset of the existing personal computers or workstations can be designated as pool processors. They also do not need to be located in one room. The physical location is actually irrelevant. The pool processors can even be in different countries, as we will discuss later.

Another important component of the Amoeba configuration consists of specialized servers, such as file servers, which for hardware or software reasons need to run on a separate processor. In some cases a server is able to run on a pool processor, being started up as needed, but for performance reasons it is better to have it running all the time.

Servers provide services. A **service** is an abstract definition of what the server is prepared to do for its clients. This definition defines what the client can ask for and what the results will be, but it does not specify how many servers are working together to provide the service. In this way, the system has a mechanism for providing fault-tolerant services by having multiple servers doing the work.

An example is the directory server. There is nothing inherent about the directory server or the system design that would prevent a user from starting up a new directory server on a pool processor every time he wanted to look up a file name. However, doing so would be horrendously inefficient, so one or more directory servers are kept running all the time, generally on dedicated machines to enhance their performance. The decision to have some servers always running and others to be started explicitly when needed is up to the system administrator.

7.1.4. The Amoeba Microkernel

Having looked at the Amoeba hardware model, let us now turn to the software model. Amoeba consists of two basic pieces: a microkernel, which runs on every processor, and a collection of servers that provide most of the traditional operating system functionality. The overall structure is shown in Fig. 7-2.

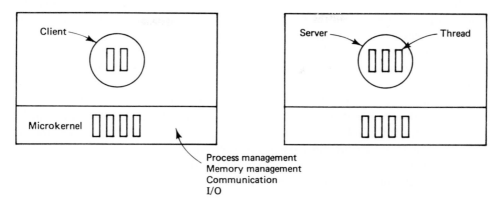

Fig. 7-2. Amoeba software structure.

The Amoeba microkernel runs on all machines in the system. The same kernel can be used on the pool processors, the terminals (assuming that they are computers, rather than X terminals), and the specialized servers. The microkernel has four primary functions:

1. Manage processes and threads.

2. Provide low-level memory management support.

3. Support communication.

4. Handle low-level I/O.

Let us consider each of these in turn.

Like most operating systems, Amoeba supports the concept of a process. In addition, Amoeba also supports multiple threads of control within a single address space. A process with one thread is essentially the same as a process in UNIX. Such a process has a single address space, a set of registers, a program counter, and a stack.

In contrast, although a process with multiple threads still has a single address space shared by all threads, each thread logically has its own registers, its own program counter, and its own stack. In effect, a collection of threads in a process is similar to a collection of independent processes in UNIX, with the one exception that they all share a single common address space.

A typical use for multiple threads might be in a file server, in which every incoming request is assigned to a separate thread to work on. That thread might begin processing the request, then block waiting for the disk, then continue work. By splitting the server up into multiple threads, each thread can be purely sequential, even if it has to block waiting for I/O. Nevertheless, all the threads can, for example, have access to a single shared software cache. Threads can synchronize using semaphores or mutexes to prevent two threads from accessing the shared cache simultaneously.

The second task of the kernel is to provide low-level memory management. Threads can allocate and deallocate blocks of memory, called **segments**. These segments can be read and written, and can be mapped into and out of the address space of the process to which the calling thread belongs. A process must have at least one segment, but it may also have many more of them. Segments can be used for text, data, stack, or any other purpose the process desires. The operating system does not enforce any particular pattern on segment usage.

The third job of the kernel is to handle interprocess communication. Two forms of communication are provided: point-to-point communication and group communication. These are closely integrated to make them similar.

Point-to-point communication is based on the model of a client sending a message to a server, then blocking until the server has sent a reply back. This request/reply exchange is the basis on which almost everything else is built.

The other form of communication is group communication. It allows a message to be sent from one source to multiple destinations. Software protocols provide reliable, fault-tolerant group communication to user processes in the presence of lost messages and other errors.

The fourth function of the kernel is to manage low-level I/O. For each I/O device attached to a machine, there is a device driver in the kernel. The driver manages all I/O for the device. Drivers are linked with the kernel and cannot be loaded dynamically.

Device drivers communicate with the rest of the system by the standard request and reply messages. A process, such as a file server, that needs to communicate with the disk driver, sends it request messages and gets back replies. In general, the client does not have to know that it is talking to a driver. As far as it is concerned, it is just communicating with a thread somewhere.

Both the point-to-point message system and the group communication make use of a specialized protocol called FLIP. This protocol is a network layer protocol and has been designed specifically to meet the needs of distributed computing. It deals with both unicasting and multicasting on complex internetworks. It will be discussed later.

7.1.5. The Amoeba Servers

Everything that is not done by the kernel is done by server processes. The idea behind this design is to minimize kernel size and enhance flexibility. By not building the file system and other standard services into the kernel, they can be changed easily, and multiple versions can run simultaneously for different user populations.

Amoeba is based on the client-server model. Clients are typically written by the users and servers are typically written by the system programmers, but users are free to write their own servers if they wish. Central to the entire software design is the concept of an object, which is like an abstract data type. Each object consists of some encapsulated data with certain operations defined on it. File objects have a READ operation, for example, among others.

Objects are managed by servers. When a process creates an object, the server that manages the object returns to the client a cryptographically protected capability for the object. To use the object later, the proper capability must be presented. All objects in the system, both hardware and software, are named, protected, and managed by capabilities. Among the objects supported this way are files, directories, memory segments, screen windows, processors, disks, and tape drives. This uniform interface to all objects provides generality and simplicity.

All the standard servers have stub procedures in the library. To use a server, a client normally just calls the stub, which marshals the parameters, sends the message, and blocks until the reply comes back. This mechanism hides all the details of the implementation from the user. A stub compiler is available for users who wish to produce stub procedures for their own servers.

Probably the most important server is the file server, known as the **bullet server**. It provides primitives to manage files, creating them, reading them, deleting them, and so on. Unlike most file servers, the files it creates are immutable. Once created, a file cannot be modified, but it can be deleted. Immutable files make automatic replication easier since they avoid many of the race conditions inherent in replicating files that are subject to being changed during the replication process.

Another important server is the **directory server**, for obscure historical reasons also known as the **soap server**. It is the directory server that manages directories and path names and maps them onto capabilities. To read a file, a process asks the directory server to look up the path name. On a successful lookup, the directory server returns the capability for the file (or other object). Subsequent operations on the file do not use the directory server, but go straight to the file server. Splitting the file system into these two components increases flexibility and makes each one simpler, since it only has to manage one type of object (directories or files), not two.

Other standard servers are present for handling object replication, starting processes, monitoring servers for failures, and communicating with the outside world. User servers perform a wide variety of application-specific tasks.

The rest of this chapter is structured as follows. First we will describe objects and capabilities, since these are the heart of the entire system. Then we will look at the kernel, focusing on process management, memory management, and communication. Finally, we will examine some of the main servers, including the bullet server, the directory server, the replication server, and the run server.

7.2. OBJECTS AND CAPABILITIES IN AMOEBA

The basic unifying concept underlying all the Amoeba servers and the services they provide is the **object**. An object is an encapsulated piece of data upon which certain well-defined operations may be performed. It is, in essence, an abstract data type. Objects are passive. They do not contain processes or methods or other active entities that "do" things. Instead, each object is managed by a server process.

To perform an operation on an object, a client does an RPC with the server, specifying the object, the operation to be performed, and optionally, any parameters needed. The server does the work and returns the answer. Operations are performed synchronously, that is, after initiating an RPC with a server to get some work done, the client thread is blocked until the server replies. Other threads in the same process are still runnable, however.

Clients are unaware of the locations of the objects they use and the servers that manage these objects. A server might be running on the same machine as the client, on a different machine on the same LAN, or even on a machine thousands of kilometers away. Furthermore, although most servers run as user processes, a few low-level ones, such as the segment (i.e., memory) server and process server, run as threads in the kernel. This distinction, too, is invisible to clients. The RPC protocol for talking to user servers or kernel servers, whether local or remote, is identical in all cases. Thus a client is concerned entirely with what it wants to do, not where objects are stored and where servers run. A certain directory contains the capabilities for all the accessible file servers along with a specification of the default choice, so a user can override the default in cases where it matters. Usually, the system administrator sets up the default to be the local one.

7.2.1. Capabilities

Objects are named and protected in a uniform way, by special tickets called **capabilities**. To create an object, a client does an RPC with the appropriate server specifying what it wants. The server then creates the object and returns a capability to the client. On subsequent operations, the client must present the capability to identify the object. A capability is just a long binary number. The Amoeba 5.2 format is shown in Fig. 7-3.

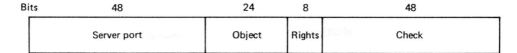

Fig. 7-3. A capability in Amoeba.

When a client wants to perform an operation on an object, it calls a stub procedure that builds a message containing the object's capability and then traps to the kernel. The kernel extracts the *Server port* field from the capability and looks it up in its cache to locate the machine on which the server resides. If the port is not in the cache, it is located by broadcasting, as will be described later. The port is effectively a logical address at which the server can be reached. Server ports are thus associated with a particular server (or a set of servers), not with a specific machine. If a server moves to a new machine, it takes its server port with it. Many server ports, like that of the file server, are publicly known and stable for years. The only way a server can be addressed is via its port, which it initially chose itself.

The rest of the information in the capability is ignored by the kernels and passed to the server for its own use. The *Object* field is used by the server to identify the specific object in question. For example, a file server might manage thousands of files, with the object number being used to tell it which one is being operated on. In a sense, the *Object* field in a file capability is analogous to a UNIX i-node number.

The *Rights* field is a bit map telling which of the allowed operations the holder of a capability may perform. For example, although a particular object may support reading and writing, a specific capability may be constructed with all the rights bits except READ turned off.

The *Check* field is used for validating the capability. Capabilities are manipulated directly by user processes. Without some form of protection, there would be no way to prevent user processes from forging capabilities.

7.2.2. Object Protection

The basic algorithm used to protect objects is as follows. When an object is created, the server picks a random *Check* field and stores it both in the new capability and inside its own tables. All the rights bits in a new capability are initially on, and it is this **owner capability** that is returned to the client. When the capability is sent back to the server in a request to perform an operation, the *Check* field is verified.

To create a restricted capability, a client can pass a capability back to the server, along with a bit mask for the new rights. The server takes the original

Check field from its tables, EXCLUSIVE ORs it with the new rights (which must be a subset of the rights in the capability), and then runs the result through a one-way function. Such a function, $y = f(x)$, has the property that given x it is easy to find y, but given only y, finding x requires an exhaustive search of all possible x values (Evans et al., 1974).

The server then creates a new capability, with the same value in the *Object* field, but the new rights bits in the *Rights* field and the output of the one-way function in the *Check* field. The new capability is then returned to the caller. The client may send this new capability to another process, if it wishes, as capabilities are managed entirely in user space.

The method of generating restricted capabilities is illustrated in Fig. 7-4. In this example, the owner has turned off all the rights except one. For example, the restricted capability might allow the object to be read, but nothing else. The meaning of the *Rights* field is different for each object type since the legal operations themselves also vary from object type to object type.

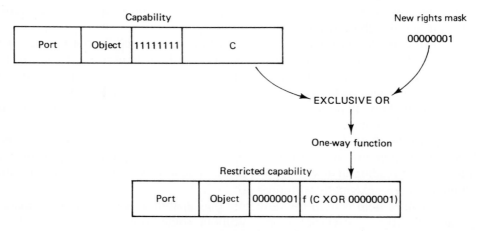

Fig. 7-4. Generation of a restricted capability from an owner capability.

When the restricted capability comes back to the server, the server sees from the *Rights* field that it is not an *owner capability* because at least one bit is turned off. The server then fetches the original random number from its tables, EXCLUSIVE ORs it with the *Rights* field from the capability, and runs the result through the one-way function. If the result agrees with the *Check* field, the capability is accepted as valid.

It should be obvious from this algorithm that a user who tries to add rights that he does not have will simply invalidate the capability. Inverting the *Check* field in a restricted capability to get the argument (C XOR 00000001 in Fig. 7-4) is impossible because the function f is a one-way function (that is what "one-way" means—no algorithm exists for inverting it). It is through this crypto-graphic technique that capabilities are protected from tampering.

Capabilities are used throughout Amoeba for both naming of all objects and for protecting them. This single mechanism leads to a uniform naming and pro-tection scheme. It also is fully location transparent. To perform an operation on an object, it is not necessary to know where the object resides. In fact, even if this knowledge were available, there would be no way to use it.

Note that Amoeba does not use access control lists for authentication. The protection scheme used requires almost no administrative overhead. However, in an insecure environment, additional cryptography (e.g., link encryption) may be required to keep capabilities from being disclosed accidentally to wiretappers on the network.

7.2.3. Standard Operations

Although many operations on objects depend on the object type, there are some operations that apply to most objects. These are listed in Fig. 7-5. Some of these require certain rights bits to be set, but others can be done by anyone who can present a server with a valid capability for one of its objects.

Call	Description
Age	Perform a garbage collection cycle
Copy	Duplicate the object and return a capability for the copy
Destroy	Destroy the object and reclaim its storage
Getparams	Get parameters associated with the server
Info	Get an ASCII string briefly describing the object
Restrict	Produce a new, restricted capability for the object
Setparams	Set parameters associated with the server
Status	Get current status information from the server
Touch	Pretend the object was just used

Fig. 7-5. The standard operations valid on most objects.

It is possible to create an object in Amoeba and then lose the capability, so some mechanism is needed to get rid of old objects that are no longer accessible. The way that has been chosen is to have servers run a garbage collector periodically, removing all objects that have not been used in n garbage collection cycles. The AGE call starts a new garbage collection cycle. The TOUCH call tells the server that the object touched is still in use. When objects are entered into the directory server, they are touched periodically, to keep the garbage collector at bay. Rights for some of the standard operations, such as AGE, are normally present only in capabilities owned by the system administrator.

The COPY operation is a shortcut that makes it possible to duplicate an object without actually transferring it. Without this operation, copying a file would require sending it over the network twice: from the server to the client and then back again. COPY can also fetch remote objects or send objects to remote machines.

The DESTROY operation deletes the object. It always needs the appropriate right, for obvious reasons.

The GETPARAMS and SETPARAMS calls normally deal with the server as a whole rather than with a particular object. They allow the system administrator to read and write parameters that control server operation. For example, the algorithm used to choose processors can be selected using this mechanism.

The INFO and STATUS calls return status information. The former returns a short ASCII string describing the object briefly. The information in the string is server dependent, but in general, it indicates the type of object and tells something useful about it (e.g., for files, it tells the size). The latter gets information about the server as a whole, for example, how much free memory it has. This information helps the system administrator monitor the system better.

The RESTRICT call generates a new capability for the object, with a subset of the current rights, as described above.

7.3. PROCESS MANAGEMENT IN AMOEBA

A process in Amoeba is basically an address space and a collection of threads that run in it. A process with one thread is roughly analogous to a UNIX or MS-DOS process in terms of how it behaves and what it can do. In this section we will explain how processes and threads work, and how they are implemented.

7.3.1. Processes

A process is an object in Amoeba. When a process is created, the parent process is given a capability for the child process, just as with any other newly created object. Using this capability, the child can be suspended, restarted, signaled, or destroyed.

Process creation in Amoeba is different from UNIX. The UNIX model of creating a child process by cloning the parent is inappropriate in a distributed system due to the considerable overhead of first creating a copy somewhere (FORK) and almost immediately afterward replacing the copy with a new program (EXEC). Instead, in Amoeba it is possible to create a new process on a specific processor with the intended memory image starting right at the beginning. In this one respect, process creation in Amoeba is similar to MS-DOS. However, in contrast to MS-DOS, a process can continue executing in parallel with its child, and thus can create an arbitrary number of additional children. The children can create their own children, leading to a tree of processes.

Process management is handled at three different levels in Amoeba. At the lowest level are the process servers, which are kernel threads running on every machine. To create a process on a given machine, another process does an RPC with that machine's process server, providing it with the necessary information.

At the next level up we have a set of library procedures that provide a more convenient interface for user programs. Several flavors are provided. They do their job by calling the low-level interface procedures.

Finally, the simplest way to create a process is to use the run server, which does most of the work of determining where to run the new process. We will discuss the run server later in this chapter.

Some of the process management calls use a data structure called a **process descriptor** to provide information about the process to be run. One field in the process descriptor (see Fig. 7-6) tells which CPU architecture the process can run on. In heterogeneous systems, this field is essential to make sure that 386 binaries are not run on SPARCs, and so on.

Another field contains the process' owner's capability. When the process terminates or is stunned (see below), RPCs will be done using this capability to report the event. It also contains descriptors for all the process' segments, which collectively define its address space, as well as descriptors for all its threads.

Finally, the process descriptor also contains a descriptor for each thread in the process. The content of a thread descriptor is architecture dependent, but as a bare minimum, it contains the thread's program counter and stack pointer. It may also contain additional information necessary to run the thread, including other registers, the thread's state, and various flags. Brand new processes contain only one thread in their process descriptors, but stunned processes may have created additional threads before being stunned.

The low-level process interface consists of about a half-dozen library procedures. Only three of these will concern us here. The first, *exec*, is the most important. It has two input parameters, the capability for a process server and a process descriptor. Its function is to do an RPC with the specified process server asking it to run the process. If the call is successful, a capability for the new process is returned to the caller for use in controlling the process later.

A second important library procedure is *getload*. It returns information

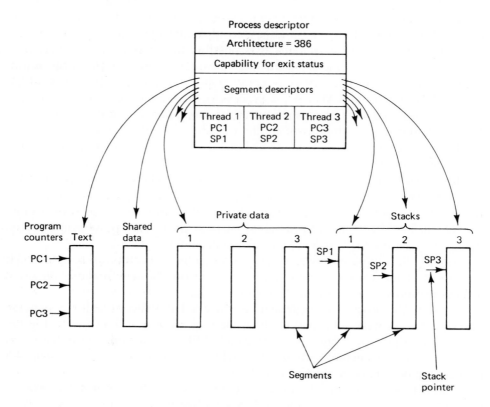

Fig. 7-6. A process descriptor.

about the CPU speed, current load, and amount of memory free at the moment. It is used by the run server to determine the best place to execute a new process.

A third major library procedure is *stun*. A process' parent can suspend it by **stunning** it. More commonly, the parent can give the process' capability to a debugger, which can stun it and later restart it for interactive debugging purposes. Two kinds of stuns are supported: normal and emergency. They differ with respect to what happens if the process is blocked on one or more RPCs at the time it is stunned. With a normal stun, the process sends a message to the server it is currently waiting for, saying, in effect: "I have been stunned. Finish your work instantly and send me a reply." If the server is also blocked, waiting for another server, the message is propagated further, all the way down the line to the end. The server at the end of the line is expected to reply immediately with a special error message. In this way, all the pending RPCs are terminated almost immediately in a clean way, with all of the servers finishing properly. The nesting structure is not violated, and no "long jumps" are needed.

An emergency stun stops the process instantly and does not send any messages to servers that are currently working for the stunned process. The computations being done by the servers become orphans. When the servers finally finish and send replies, these replies are ultimately discarded.

The high-level process interface does not require a fully formed process descriptor. One of the calls, *newproc*, takes as its first three parameters, the name of the binary file and pointers to the argument and environment arrays, similar to UNIX. Additional parameters provide more detailed control of the initial state.

7.3.2. Threads

Amoeba supports a simple threads model. When a process starts up, it has one thread. During execution, the process can create additional threads, and existing threads can terminate. The number of threads is therefore completely dynamic. When a new thread is created, the parameters to the call specify the procedure to run and the size of the initial stack.

Although all threads in a process share the same program text and global data, each thread has its own stack, its own stack pointer, and its own copy of the machine registers. In addition, if a thread wants to create and use variables that are global to all its procedures but invisible to other threads, library procedures are provided for that purpose. Such variables are called **glocal**. One library procedure allocates a block of glocal memory of whatever size is requested, and returns a pointer to it. Blocks of glocal memory are referred to by integers. A system call is available for a thread to acquire its glocal pointer.

Three methods are provided for threads to synchronize: signals, mutexes, and semaphores. Signals are asynchronous interrupts sent from one thread to another thread in the same process. They are conceptually similar to UNIX signals, except that they are between threads rather than between processes. Signals can be raised, caught, or ignored. Asynchronous interrupts between processes use the stun mechanism.

The second form of interthread communication is the mutex. A **mutex** is like a binary semaphore. It can be in one of two states, locked or unlocked. Trying to lock an unlocked mutex causes it to become locked. The calling thread continues. Trying to lock a mutex that is already locked causes the calling thread to block until another thread unlocks the mutex. If more than one thread is waiting on a mutex, when the mutex is unlocked, exactly one thread is released. In addition to the calls to lock and unlock mutexes, there is also one that tries to lock a mutex, but if it is unable to do so within a specified interval, times out and returns an error code. Mutexes are fair and respect thread priorities.

The third way that threads can communicate is by counting semaphores.

These are slower than mutexes, but there are times when they are needed. They work in the usual way, except that here too an additional call is provided to allow a DOWN operation to time out if it is unable to succeed within a specified interval.

All threads are managed by the kernel. The advantage of this design is that when a thread does an RPC, the kernel can block that thread and schedule another one in the same process if one is ready. Thread scheduling is done using priorities, with kernel threads getting higher priority than user threads. Thread scheduling can be set up to be either pre-emptive or run-to-completion (i.e., threads continue to run until they block), as the process wishes.

7.4. MEMORY MANAGEMENT IN AMOEBA

Amoeba has an extremely simple memory model. A process can have any number of segments it wants to have, and they can be located wherever it wants in the process' virtual address space. Segments are not swapped or paged, so a process must be entirely memory resident to run. Furthermore, although the hardware MMU is used, each segment is stored contiguously in memory.

Although this design is perhaps somewhat unusual these days, it was done for three reasons: performance, simplicity, and economics. Having a process entirely in memory all the time makes RPC go faster. When a large block of data must be sent, the system knows that all of the data are contiguous not only in virtual memory, but also in physical memory. This knowledge saves having to check if all the pages containing the buffer happen to be around at the moment, and eliminates having to wait for them if they are not. Similarly, on input, the buffer is always in memory, so the incoming data can be placed there simply and without page faults. This design has allowed Amoeba to achieve extremely high transfer rates for large RPCs.

The second reason for the design is simplicity. Not having paging or swapping makes the system considerably simpler and makes the kernel smaller and more manageable. However, it is the third reason that makes the first two feasible. Memory is becoming so cheap that within a few years, all Amoeba machines will probably have tens of megabytes of it. Such large memories will substantially reduce the need for paging and swapping, namely, to fit large programs into small machines.

7.4.1. Segments

Processes have several calls available to them for managing segments. Most important among these is the ability to create, destroy, read, and write segments. When a segment is created, the caller gets back a capability for it. This capability is used for reading and writing the segment and for all the other calls involving the segment.

When a segment is created it is given an initial size. This size may change during process execution. The segment may also be given an initial value, either from another segment or from a file.

Because segments can be read and written, it is possible to use them to construct a main memory file server. To start, the server creates a segment as large as it can. It can determine the maximum size by asking the kernel. This segment will be used as a simulated disk. The server then formats the segment as a file system, putting in whatever data structures it needs to keep track of files. After that, it is open for business, accepting requests from clients.

7.4.2. Mapped Segments

Virtual address spaces in Amoeba are constructed from segments. When a process is started, it must have at least one segment. However, once it is running, a process can create additional segments and map them into its address space at any unused virtual address. Figure 7-7 shows a process with three memory segments currently mapped in.

A process can also unmap segments. Furthermore, a process can specify a range of virtual addresses and request that the range be unmapped, after which those addresses are no longer legal. When a segment or a range of addresses is unmapped, a capability is returned so the segment may still be accessed, or even mapped back in again later, possibly at a different virtual address.

A segment may be mapped into the address space of two or more processes at the same time. This allows processes to operate on shared memory. However, usually it is better to create a single process with multiple threads when shared memory is needed. The main reason for having distinct processes is better protection, but if the two processes are sharing memory, protection is generally not desired.

7.5. COMMUNICATION IN AMOEBA

Amoeba supports two forms of communication: RPC, using point-to-point message passing, and group communication. At the lowest level, an RPC consists of a request message followed by a reply message. Group communication uses hardware broadcasting or multicasting if it is available; otherwise, the kernel transparently simulates it with individual messages. In this section we will describe both Amoeba RPC and Amoeba group communication and then discuss the underlying FLIP protocol that is used to support them.

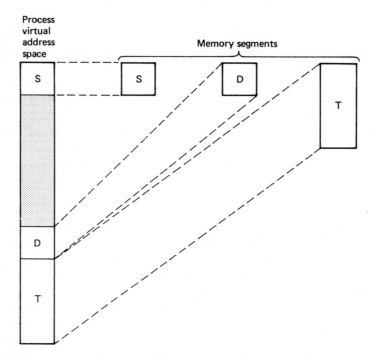

Fig. 7-7. A process with three segments mapped into its virtual address space.

7.5.1. Remote Procedure Call

Normal point-to-point communication in Amoeba consists of a client sending a message to a server followed by the server sending a reply back to the client. It is not possible for a client just to send a message and then go do something else except by bypassing the RPC interface, which is done only under very special circumstances. The RPC primitive that sends the request automatically blocks the caller until the reply comes back, thus forcing a certain amount of structure on programs. Separate *send* and *receive* primitives can be thought of as the distributed system's answer to the *goto* statement: parallel spaghetti programming. They should be avoided by user programs and used only by language runtime systems that have unusual communication requirements.

Each standard server defines a procedural interface that clients can call. These library routines are stubs that pack the parameters into messages and invoke the kernel primitives to send the message. During message transmission, the stub, and hence the calling thread, are blocked. When the reply comes back, the stub returns the status and results to the client. Although the kernel-level primitives are actually related to the message passing, the use of stubs makes this mechanism look like RPC to the programmer, so we will refer to the basic communication primitives as RPC, rather than the slightly more precise "request/reply message exchange."

In order for a client thread to do an RPC with a server thread, the client must know the server's address. Addressing is done by allowing any thread to choose a random 48-bit number, called a **port**, to be used as the address for messages sent to it. Different threads in a process may use different ports if they so desire. All messages are addressed from a sender to a destination port. A port is nothing more than a kind of logical thread address. There is no data structure and no storage associated with a port. It is similar to an IP address or an Ethernet address in that respect, except that it is not tied to any particular physical location. The first field in each capability gives the port of the server that manages the object (see Fig. 7-3).

RPC Primitives

The RPC mechanism makes use of three principal kernel primitives:

1. get_request — indicates a server's willingness to listen on a port.

2. put_reply — done by a server when it has a reply to send.

3. trans — send a message from client to server and wait for the reply.

The first two are used by servers. The third is used by clients to *transmit* a message and wait for a reply. All three are true system calls, that is, they do not work by sending a message to a communication server thread. (If processes are able to send messages, why should they have to contact a server for the purpose of sending a message?) Users access the calls through library procedures, as usual, however.

When a server wants to go to sleep waiting for an incoming request, it calls *get_request*. This procedure has three parameters, as follows:

```
get_request(&header, buffer, bytes)
```

The first parameter points to a message header, the second points to a data buffer, and the third tells how big the data buffer is. This call is analogous to

```
read(fd, buffer, bytes)
```

in UNIX or MS-DOS in that the first parameter identifies what is being read, the second provides a buffer in which to put the data, and the third tells how big the buffer is.

When a message is transmitted over the network, it contains a header and (optionally) a data buffer. The header is a fixed 32-byte structure and is shown in Fig. 7-8. What the first parameter of the *get_request* call does is tell the kernel where to put the incoming header. In addition, prior to making the *get_request* call, the server must initialize the header's *Port* field to contain the port it is listening to. This is how the kernel knows which server is listening to which port. The incoming header overwrites the one initialized by the server.

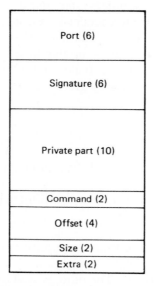

Fig. 7-8. The header used on all Amoeba request and reply messages. The numbers in parentheses give the field sizes in bytes.

When a message arrives, the server is unblocked. It normally first inspects the header to find out more about the request. The *Signature* field has been reserved for authentication purposes, but is not currently used.

The remaining fields are not specified by the RPC protocol, so a server and client can agree to use them any way they want. The normal conventions are as follows. Most requests to servers contain a capability, to specify the object being operated on. Many replies also have a capability as a return value. The *Private part* is normally used to hold the rightmost three fields of the capability.

Most servers support multiple operations on their objects, such as reading, writing, and destroying. The *Command* field is conventionally used on requests to indicate which operation is needed. On replies it tells whether the operation was successful or not, and if not, it gives the reason for failure.

The last three fields hold parameters, if any. For example, when reading a segment or file, they can be used to indicate the offset within the object to begin reading at, and the number of bytes to read.

Note that for many operations, no buffer is needed or used. In the case of reading again, the object capability, the offset, and the size all fit in the header. When writing, the buffer contains the data to be written. On the other hand, the reply to a READ contains a buffer, whereas the reply to a WRITE does not.

After the server has completed its work, it makes a call

```
put_reply(&header, buffer, bytes)
```

to send back the reply. The first parameter provides the header and the second provides the buffer. The third tells how big the buffer is. If a server does a *put_reply* without having previously done an unmatched *get_request*, the *put_reply* fails with an error. Similarly, two consecutive *get_request* calls fail. The two calls must be paired in the correct way.

Now let us turn from the server to the client. To do an RPC, the client calls a stub which makes the following call:

```
trans(&header1, buffer1, bytes1, &header2, buffer2, bytes2)
```

The first three parameters provide information about the header and buffer of the outgoing request. The last three provide the same information for the incoming reply. The *trans* call sends the request and blocks the client until the reply has come in. This design forces processes to stick closely to the client-server RPC communication paradigm, analogous to the way structured programming techniques prevent programmers from doing things that generally lead to poorly structured programs (such as using unconstrained GOTO statements).

If Amoeba actually worked as described above, it would be possible for an intruder to impersonate a server just by doing a *get_request* on the server's port. These ports are public after all, since clients must know them to contact the servers. Amoeba solves this problem cryptographically. Each port is actually a pair of ports: the **get-port**, which is private, known only to the server, and the **put-port**, which is known to the whole world. The two are related through a one-way function, F, according to the relation

$$\text{put-port} = F\,(\text{get-port})$$

The one-way function is in fact the same one as used for protecting capabilities, but need not be since the two concepts are unrelated.

When a server does a *get_request*, the corresponding put-port is computed by the kernel and stored in a table of ports being listened to. All *trans* requests use put-ports, so when a packet arrives at a machine, the kernel compares the put-port in the header to the put-ports in its table to see if any match. Since get-ports never appear on the network and cannot be derived from the publicly known put-ports, the scheme is secure. It is illustrated in Fig. 7-9 and described in more detail in (Tanenbaum et al., 1986).

Amoeba RPC supports at-most-once semantics. In other words, when an

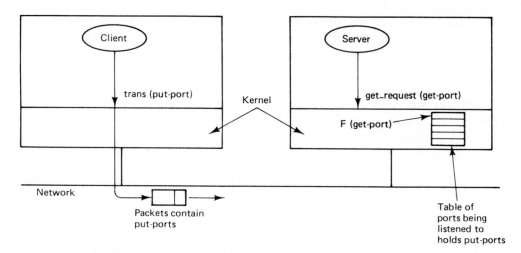

Fig. 7-9. Relationship between get-ports and put-ports.

RPC is done, the system guarantees that an RPC will never be carried out more than one time, even in the face of server crashes and rapid reboots.

7.5.2. Group Communication in Amoeba

RPC is not the only form of communication supported by Amoeba. It also supports group communication. A group in Amoeba consists of one or more processes that are cooperating to carry out some task or provide some service. Processes can be members of several groups at the same time. Groups are closed, meaning that only members can broadcast to the group. The usual way for a client to access a service provided by a group is to do an RPC with one of its members. That member then uses group communication within the group, if necessary, to determine who will do what.

This design was chosen to provide a greater degree of transparency than an open group structure would have. The idea behind it is that clients normally use RPC to talk to individual servers, so they should use RPC to talk to groups as well. The alternative—open groups and using RPC to talk to single servers but using group communication to talk to group servers—is much less transparent. (Using group communication for everything would eliminate the many advantages of RPC that we have discussed earlier.) Once it has been determined that clients outside a group will use RPC to talk to the group (actually, to talk to one process in the group), the need for open groups vanishes, so closed groups, which are easier to implement, are adequate.

Group Communication Primitives

The operations available for group communication in Amoeba are listed in Fig. 7-10. *CreateGroup* creates a new group and returns a group identifier used in the other calls to identify which group is meant. The parameters specify various sizes and how much fault tolerance is required (how many dead members the group must be able to withstand and continue to function correctly).

Call	Description
CreateGroup	Create a new group and set its parameters
JoinGroup	Make the caller a member of a group
LeaveGroup	Remove the caller from a group
SendToGroup	Reliably send a message to all members of a group
ReceiveFromGroup	Block until a message arrives from a group
ResetGroup	Initiate recovery after a process crash

Fig. 7-10. Amoeba group communication primitives.

JoinGroup and *LeaveGroup* allow processes to enter and exit from existing groups. One of the parameters of *JoinGroup* is a small message that is sent to all group members to announce the presence of a newcomer. Similarly, one of the parameters of *LeaveGroup* is another small message sent to all members to say goodbye and wish them good luck in their future activities. The point of the little messages is to make it possible for all members to know who their comrades are, in case they are interested, for example, to reconstruct the group if some members crash. When the last member of a group calls *LeaveGroup*, it turns out the lights and the group is destroyed.

SendToGroup atomically broadcasts a message to all members of a specified group, in spite of lost messages, finite buffers, and processor crashes. Amoeba supports global time ordering, so if two processes call *SendToGroup* simultaneously, the system ensures that all group members will receive the messages in the same order. This is guaranteed; programmers can count on it. If the two calls are exactly simultaneous, the first one to get its packet onto the LAN successfully is declared to be first. In terms of the semantics discussed in Chap. 6, this model corresponds to sequential consistency, not strict consistency.

ReceiveFromGroup tries to get a message from a group specified by one of its parameter. If no message is available (that is, currently buffered by the kernel), the caller blocks until one is available. If a message has already arrived, the caller gets the message with no delay. The protocol ensures that in the absence of processor crashes, no messages are irretrievably lost. The protocol can also be made to tolerate crashes, at the cost of additional overhead, as discussed later.

The final call, *ResetGroup*, is used to recover from crashes. It specifies how many members the new group must have as a minimum. If the kernel is able to establish contact with the requisite number of processes and rebuild the group, it returns the size of the new group. Otherwise, it fails. In this case, recovery is up to the user program.

The Amoeba Reliable Broadcast Protocol

Let us now look at how Amoeba implements group communication. Amoeba works best on LANs that support either multicasting or broadcasting (or like Ethernet, both). For simplicity, we will just refer to broadcasting, although in fact the implementation uses multicasting when it can to avoid disturbing machines that are not interested in the message being sent. It is assumed that the hardware broadcast is good, but not perfect. In practice, lost packets are rare, but receiver overruns do happen occasionally. Since these errors can occur they cannot simply be ignored, so the protocol has been designed to deal with them.

The key idea that forms the basis of the implementation of group communication is **reliable broadcasting**. By this we mean that when a user process broadcasts a message (e.g., with *SendToGroup*) the user-supplied message is delivered correctly to all members of the group, even though the hardware may lose packets. For simplicity, we will assume that each message fits into a single packet. For the moment, we will assume that processors do not crash. We will consider the case of unreliable processors afterward. The description given below is just an outline. For more details, see (Kaashoek and Tanenbaum, 1991; and Kaashoek et al., 1989). Other reliable broadcast protocols are discussed in (Birman and Joseph, 1987a; Chang and Maxemchuk, 1984; Garcia-Molina and Spauster, 1991; Luan and Gligor, 1990; Melliar-Smith et al., 1990; and Tseung, 1989).

The hardware/software configuration required for reliable broadcasting in Amoeba is shown in Fig. 7-11. The hardware of all the machines is normally identical, and they all run exactly the same kernel. However, when the application starts up, one of the machines is elected as sequencer (like a committee electing a chairman). If the sequencer machine subsequently crashes, the remaining members elect a new one. Many election algorithms are known, such as choosing the process with the highest network address. We will discuss fault tolerance later in this chapter.

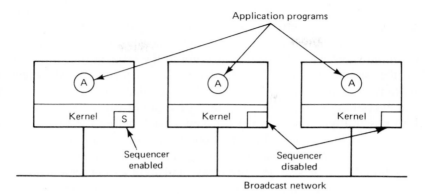

Fig. 7-11. System structure for group communication in Amoeba.

One sequence of events that can be used to achieve reliable broadcasting can be summarized as follows.

1. The user process traps to the kernel, passing it the message.

2. The kernel accepts the message and blocks the user process.

3. The kernel sends a point-to-point message to the sequencer.

4. When the sequencer gets the message, it allocates the next available sequence number, puts the sequence number in a header field reserved for it, and broadcasts the message (and sequence number).

5. When the sending kernel sees the broadcast message, it unblocks the calling process to let it continue execution.

Let us now consider these steps in more detail. When an application process executes a broadcasting primitive, such as *SendToGroup*, a trap to its kernel occurs. The kernel then blocks the caller and builds a message containing a kernel-supplied header and the application-supplied data. The header contains the message type (*Request for Broadcast* in this case), a unique message identifier (used to detect duplicates), the number of the last broadcast received by the kernel (usually called a **piggybacked acknowledgement**), and some other information.

The kernel sends the message to the sequencer using a normal point-to-point message, and simultaneously starts a timer. If the broadcast comes back before the timer runs out (normal case), the sending kernel stops the timer and returns control to the caller. In practice, this case happens well over 99 percent of the time, because modern LANs are highly reliable.

On the other hand, if the broadcast has not come back before the timer expires, the kernel assumes that either the message or the broadcast has been lost. Either way, it retransmits the message. If the original message was lost, no harm has been done, and the second (or subsequent) attempt will trigger the broadcast in the usual way. If the message got to the sequencer and was broadcast, but the sender missed the broadcast, the sequencer will detect the retransmission as a duplicate (from the message identifier) and just tell the sender that everything is all right. The message is not broadcast a second time.

A third possibility is that a broadcast comes back before the timer runs out, but it is the wrong broadcast. This situation arises when two processes attempt to broadcast simultaneously. One of them, *A*, gets to the sequencer first, and its message is broadcast. *A* sees the broadcast and unblocks its application program. However its competitor, *B*, sees *A*'s broadcast and realizes that it has failed to go first. Nevertheless, *B* knows that its message probably got to the sequencer (since lost messages are rare), where it will be queued and broadcast next. Thus *B* accepts *A*'s broadcast and continues to wait for its own broadcast to come back or its timer to expire.

Now consider what happens at the sequencer when a *Request for Broadcast* arrives there. First a check is made to see if the message is a retransmission, and if so, the sender is informed that the broadcast has already been done, as mentioned above. If the message is new (normal case), the next sequence number is assigned to it, and the sequencer counter incremented by 1 for next time. The message and its identifier are then stored in a **history buffer**, and the message is then broadcast. The message is also passed to the application running on the sequencer's machine (because the broadcast does not cause an interrupt on the machine that issued the broadcast).

Finally, let us consider what happens when a kernel receives a broadcast. First, the sequence number is compared to the sequence number of the broadcast received most recently. If the new one is 1 higher (normal case), no broadcasts have been missed, so the message is passed up to the application program, assuming that it is waiting. If it is not waiting, it is buffered until the program calls *ReceiveFromGroup*.

Suppose that the newly received broadcast has sequence number 25, while the previous one had number 23. The kernel is immediately alerted to the fact that it has missed number 24, so it sends a point-to-point message to the sequencer asking for a private retransmission of the missing message. The sequencer fetches the missing message from its history buffer and sends it. When it arrives, the receiving kernel processes 24 and 25, passing them to the application program in numerical order. Thus the only effect of a lost message is a (normally) minor time delay. All application programs see all broadcasts in the same order, even if some messages are lost.

The reliable broadcast protocol is illustrated in Fig. 7-12. Here the application program running on machine *A* passes a message, *M*, to its kernel for broadcasting. The kernel sends the message to the sequencer, where it is assigned sequence number 25. The message (containing the sequence number 25) is now broadcast to all machines and also passed to the application program running on the sequencer itself. This broadcast message is denoted by *M25* in the figure.

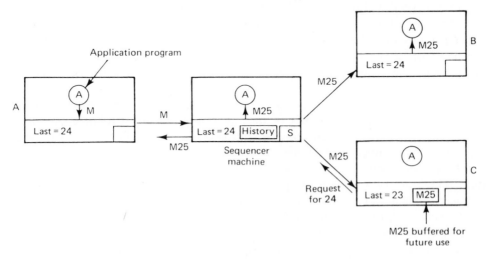

Fig. 7-12. The application of machine *A* sends a message to the sequencer, which then adds a sequence number (25) and broadcasts it. At *B* it is accepted, but at *C* it is buffered until 24, which was missed, can be retrieved from the sequencer.

The *M25* message arrives at machines *B* and *C*. At machine B the kernel sees that it has already processed all broadcasts up to and including 24, so it immediately passes *M25* up to the application program. At *C*, however, the last message to arrive was 23 (24 must have been lost), so *M25* is buffered in the kernel, and a point-to-point message requesting 24 is sent to the sequencer. Only after the reply has come back and been given to the application program will *M25* be passed upward as well.

Now let us look at the management of the history buffer. Unless something is done to prevent it, the history buffer will quickly fill up. However, if the sequencer knows that all machines have received broadcasts, say, 0 through 23, correctly, it can delete these from its history buffer.

Several mechanisms are provided to allow the sequencer to discover this information. The basic one is that each *Request for Broadcast* message sent to the sequencer carries a piggybacked acknowledgement, *k*, meaning that all broadcasts up to and including *k* have been correctly received. This way, the sequencer can maintain a piggyback table, indexed by machine number, telling for each machine which broadcast was the last one received. Whenever the history buffer begins to fill up, the sequencer can make a pass through this table to find the smallest value. It can then safely discard all messages up to and including this value.

If one machine happens to be silent for an unusually long period of time, the sequencer will not know what its status is. To inform the sequencer, it is required to send a short acknowledgement message when it has sent no broadcast messages for a certain period of time. Furthermore, the sequencer can broadcast a *Request for Status* message, which directs all other machines to send it a message giving the number of the highest broadcast received in sequence. In this way, the sequencer can update its piggyback table and then truncate its history buffer.

Although in practice *Request for Status* messages are rare, they do occur, and thus raise the mean number of messages required for a reliable broadcast slightly above 2, even when there are no lost messages. The effect increases slightly as the number of machines grows.

There is a subtle design point concerning this protocol that should be clarified. There are two ways to do the broadcast. In method 1 (described above), the user sends a point-to-point message to the sequencer, which then broadcasts it. In method 2, the user broadcasts the message, including a unique identifier. When the sequencer sees this, it broadcasts a special *Accept* message containing the unique identifier and its newly assigned sequence number. A broadcast is "official" only when the *Accept* message has been sent. The two methods are compared in Fig. 7-13.

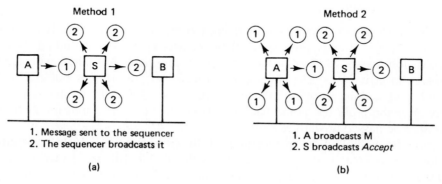

Fig. 7-13. Two methods for doing reliable broadcasting.

These protocols are logically equivalent, but they have different performance characteristics. In method 1, each message appears in full on the network twice: once to the sequencer and once from the sequencer. Thus a message of length m bytes consumes $2m$ bytes worth of network bandwidth. However, only the second of these is broadcast, so each user machine is interrupted only once (for the second message).

In method 2, the full message appears only once on the network, plus a very short *Accept* message from the sequencer, so only half the bandwidth is consumed. On the other hand, every machine is interrupted twice, once for the message and once for the *Accept*. Thus method 1 wastes bandwidth to reduce interrupts compared to method 2. Depending on the average message size, one may be preferable to the other.

In summary, this protocol allows reliable broadcasting to be done on an unreliable network in just over two messages per reliable broadcast. Each broadcast is indivisible, and all applications receive all messages in the same order, no matter how many are lost. The worst that can happen is that some delay is introduced when a message is lost, which rarely happens. If two processes attempt to broadcast at the same time, one of them will get to the sequencer first and win. The other will see a broadcast from its competitor coming back from the sequencer, and will realize that its request has been queued and will appear shortly, so it simply waits.

Fault-Tolerant Group Communication

So far we have assumed that no processors crash. In fact, this protocol has been designed to withstand the loss of an arbitrary collection of k processors (including the sequencer), where k (the resilience degree) is selected when the group is created. The larger k is, the more redundancy is required, and the slower the operation is in the normal case, so the user must choose k with care. We will sketch the recovery algorithm below. For more details, see (Kaashoek and Tanenbaum, 1991).

When a processor crashes, initially no one detects this event. Sooner or later, however, some kernel notices that messages sent to the crashed machine are not being acknowledged, so the kernel marks the crashed processor as dead and the group as unusable. All subsequent group communication primitives on that machine fail (return an error status) until the group has been reconstructed.

Shortly after noticing a problem, the user process getting the error return calls *ResetGroup* to initiate recovery. The recovery is done in two phases (Garcia-Molina, 1982). In phase one, one process is elected as coordinator. In phase two, the coordinator rebuilds the group and brings all the other processes up to date. At that point, normal operation continues.

In Fig. 7-14(a) we see a group of six machines, of which machine 5, the sequencer, has just crashed. The numbers in the boxes indicate the last message correctly received by each machine. Two machines, 0 and 1, detect the sequencer failure simultaneously, and both call *ResetGroup* to start recovery.

This call results in the kernel sending a message to all other members inviting them to participate in the recovery and asking them to report back the sequence number of the highest message they have seen. At this point it is discovered that two processes have declared themselves coordinator. The one that has seen the message with the highest sequence number wins. In case of a tie, the one with the highest network address wins. This leads to a single coordinator, as shown in Fig. 7-14(b).

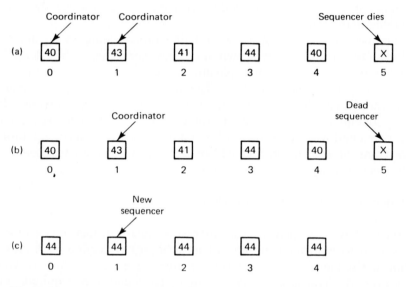

Fig. 7-14. (a) The sequencer crashes. (b) A coordinator is selected. (c) Recovery.

Once the coordinator has been voted into office, it collects from the other members any messages it may have missed. Now it is up to date and is able to become the new sequencer. It builds a *Results* message announcing itself as sequencer and telling the others what the highest sequence number is. Each member can now ask for any messages that it missed. When a member is up to date, it sends an acknowledgement back to the new sequencer. When the new sequencer has an acknowledgement from all the surviving members, it knows that all messages have been correctly delivered to the application programs in order, so it discards its history buffer, and normal operation can resume.

Another problem remains: How does the coordinator get any messages it has missed if the sequencer has crashed? The solution lies in the value of k, the resilience degree, chosen at group creation time. When k is 0 (non-fault tolerant case), only the sequencer maintains a history buffer. However, when k is greater than 0, $k + 1$ machines continuously maintain an up-to-date history buffer. Thus if an arbitrary collection of k machines fail, it is guaranteed that at least one history buffer survives, and it is this one that supplies the coordinator with any messages it needs. The extra machines can maintain their history buffers simply by watching the network.

There is one additional problem that must be solved. Normally, a *SendTo-Group* terminates successfully when the sequencer has received and broadcast or approved the message. If $k > 0$, this protocol is insufficient to survive k arbitrary crashes. Instead, a slightly modified version of method 2 is used. When the sequencer sees a message, M, that was just broadcast, it does not immediately broadcast an *Accept* message, as it does when $k = 0$. Instead, it waits until the k lowest-numbered kernels have acknowledged that they have seen and stored it. Only then does the sequencer broadcast the *Accept* message. Since $k + 1$ machines (including the sequencer) now are known to have stored M in their history buffers, even if k machines crash, M will not be lost.

As in the usual case, no kernel may pass M up to its application program until it has seen the *Accept* message. Because the *Accept* message is not generated until it is certain that $k + 1$ machines have stored M, it is guaranteed that if one machine gets M, they all will eventually. In this way, recovery from the loss of any k machines is always possible. As an aside, to speed up operation for $k > 0$, whenever an entry is made in a history buffer, a short control packet is broadcast to announce this event to the world.

To summarize, the Amoeba group communication scheme guarantees atomic broadcasting with global time ordering even in the face of k arbitrary crashes, where k is chosen by the user when the group is created. This mechanism provides an easy-to-understand basis for doing distributed programming. It is used in Amoeba to support object-based distributed shared memory for the Orca programming language and for other facilities. It can also be implemented efficiently. Measurements with 68030 CPUs on a 10-Mbps Ethernet show that it is possible to handle 800 reliable broadcasts per second continuously (Tanenbaum et al., 1992).

7.5.3. The Fast Local Internet Protocol

Amoeba uses a custom protocol called **FLIP** (**Fast Local Internet Protocol**) for actual message transmission. This protocol handles both RPC and group communication and is below them in the protocol hierarchy. In OSI terms, FLIP is a network layer protocol, whereas RPC is more of a connectionless transport or session protocol (the exact location is arguable, since OSI was designed for connection-oriented networks). Conceptually, FLIP can be replaced by another network layer protocol, such as IP, although doing so would cause some of Amoeba's transparency to be lost. Although FLIP were designed in the context of Amoeba, it is intended to be useful in other operating systems as well. In this section we will describe its design and implementation.

Protocol Requirements for Distributed Systems

Before getting into the details of FLIP, it is useful to understand something about why it was designed. After all, there are plenty of existing protocols, so the invention of a new one clearly has to be justified. In Fig. 7-15 we list the principal requirements that a protocol for a distributed system should meet. First, the protocol must support both RPC and group communication efficiently. If the underlying network has hardware multicast or broadcast, as Ethernet does, for example, the protocol should use it for group communication. On the other hand, if the network does not have either of these features, group communication must still work exactly the same way, even though the implementation will have to be different.

Item	Description
RPC	The protocol should support RPC
Group communication	The protocol should support group communication
Process migration	Processes should be able to take their addresses with them
Security	Processes should not be able to impersonate other processes
Network management	Support is needed for automatic reconfiguration
Wide-area networks	The protocol should also work on wide area networks

Fig. 7-15. Desirable characteristics for a distributed system protocol.

A characteristic that is increasingly important is support for process migration. A process should be able to move from one machine to another, even to one in a different network, with nobody noticing. Protocols such as OSI, X.25, and TCP/IP that use machine addresses to identify processes make migration difficult, because a process cannot take its address with it when it moves.

Security is also an issue. Although the get-ports and put-ports provide security for Amoeba, a security mechanism should also be present in the packet protocol so it can be used with operating systems that do not have cryptographically secure addresses.

Another point on which most existing protocols score badly is network management. It should not be necessary to have elaborate configuration tables telling which network is connected to which other network. Furthermore, if the configuration changes, due to gateways going down or coming back up, the protocol should adapt to the new configuration automatically.

Finally, the protocol should work on both local and wide-area networks. In particular, the same protocol should be usable on both.

The FLIP Interface

The FLIP protocol and its associated architecture was designed to meet all these requirements. A typical FLIP configuration is shown in Fig. 7-16. Here we see five machines, two on an Ethernet and four on a token ring. Each machine has one user process, *A* through *E*. One of the machines is connected to both networks, and as such, functions automatically as a gateway. Gateways may also run clients and servers, just like other nodes.

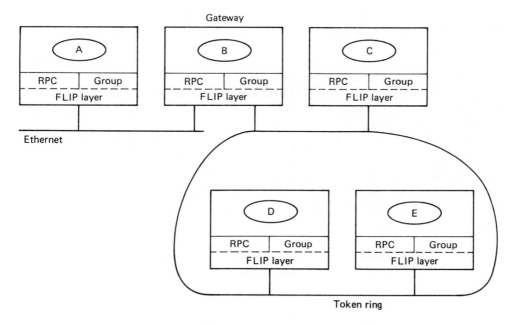

Fig. 7-16. A FLIP system with five machines and two networks.

The software is structured as shown in Fig. 7-16. The kernel contains two layers. The top layer handles calls from user processes for RPC or group communication services. The bottom layer handles the FLIP protocol. For example, when a client calls *trans*, it traps to the kernel. The RPC layer examines the header and buffer, builds a message from them, and passes the message down to the FLIP layer for transmission.

All low-level communication in Amoeba is based on **FLIP addresses**. Each process has exactly one FLIP address: a 64-bit random number chosen by the system when the process is created. If the process ever migrates, it takes its FLIP address with it. If the network is ever reconfigured, so that all machines are assigned new (hardware) network numbers or network addresses, the FLIP addresses still remain unchanged. It is the fact that a FLIP address uniquely identifies a process, not a machine, that makes communication in Amoeba insensitive to changes in network topology and network addressing.

A FLIP address is really two addresses, a public-address and a private-address, related by

$$\text{Public-address} = \text{DES}(\text{private-address})$$

where DES is the Data Encryption Standard. To compute the public-address from the private one, the private-address is used as a DES key to encrypt a 64-bit block of 0s. Given a public-address, finding the corresponding private address is computationally infeasible. Servers listen to private-addresses, but clients send to public-addresses, analogous to the way put-ports and get-ports work, but at a lower level.

FLIP has been designed to work not only with Amoeba, but also with other operating systems. A version for UNIX also exists, and there is no reason one could not be made for MS-DOS. The security provided by the private-address, public-address scheme also works for UNIX to UNIX communication using FLIP, independent of Amoeba.

Furthermore, FLIP has been designed so that it can be built in hardware, for example, as part of the network interface chip. For this reason, a precise interface with the layer above it has been specified. The interface between the FLIP layer and the layer above it (which we will call the RPC layer) has nine primitives, seven for outgoing traffic and two for incoming traffic. Each one has a library procedure that invokes it. The nine calls are listed in Fig. 7-17.

	Description	Direction
Init	Allocate a table slot	↓
End	Return a table slot	↓
Register	Listen to a FLIP address	↓
Unregister	Stop listening	↓
Unicast	Send a point-to-point message	↓
Multicost	Send a multicost message	↓
Broadcast	Send a broadcast message	↓
Receive	Packet received	↑
Notdeliver	Undeliverable packet received	↑

Fig. 7-17. The calls supported by the FLIP layer.

The first one, *init*, allows the RPC layer to allocate a table slot and initialize it with pointers to two procedures (or in a hardware implementation, two interrupt vectors). These procedures are the ones called when normal and undeliverable packets arrive, respectively. *End* deallocates the slot when the machine is being shut down.

Register is invoked to announce a process' FLIP address to the FLIP layer. It is called when the process starts up (or at least, on the first attempt at getting or sending a message). The FLIP layer immediately runs the private-address offered to it through the DES function and stores the public-address in its tables. If an incoming packet is addressed to the public FLIP address, it will be passed to the RPC layer for delivery. The *unregister* call removes an entry from the FLIP layer's tables.

The next three calls are for sending point-to-point messages, multicast messages, and broadcast messages, respectively. None of these guarantee delivery. To make RPC reliable, acknowledgements are used. To make group communication reliable, even in the face of lost packets, the sequencer protocol discussed above is used.

The last two calls are for incoming traffic. The first is for messages originating elsewhere and directed to this machine. The second is for messages sent by this machine but sent back as undeliverable.

Although the FLIP interface is intended primarily for use by the RPC and broadcast layers within the kernel, it is also visible to user processes, in case they have a special need for raw communication.

Operation of the FLIP Layer

Packets passed by the RPC layer or the group communication layer (see Fig. 7-16) to the FLIP layer are addressed by FLIP addresses, so the FLIP layer must be able to convert these addresses to network addresses for actual transmission. In order to perform this function, the FLIP layer maintains the routing table shown in Fig. 7-18. Currently this table is maintained in software, but chip designers could implement it in hardware in the future.

Whenever an incoming packet arrives at any machine, it is first handled by the FLIP layer, which extracts from it the FLIP address and network address of the sender. The number of hops the packet has made is also recorded. Since the hop count is incremented only when a packet is forwarded by a gateway, the hop count tells how many gateways the packet has passed through. The hop count is therefore a crude attempt to measure how far away the source is. (Actually, things are slightly better than this, as slow networks can be made to count for multiple hops.) If the FLIP address is not presently in the routing table, it is entered. This entry can later be used to send packets *to* that FLIP address, since its network number and address are now known.

FLIP address	Network address	Hop count	Trusted bit	Age

Fig. 7-18. The FLIP routing table.

An additional bit present in each packet tells whether the path the packet has followed so far is entirely over trusted networks. It is managed by the gateways. If the packet has gone through one or more untrusted networks, packets to the source address should be encrypted if absolute security is desired. With trusted networks, encryption is not needed.

The last field of each routing table entry gives the age of the routing table entry. It is reset to 0 whenever a packet is received from the corresponding FLIP address. Periodically, all the ages are incremented. This field allows the FLIP layer to find a suitable table entry to purge if the table fills up (large numbers indicate that there has been no traffic for a long time).

Locating Put-Ports

To see how FLIP works in the context of Amoeba, let us consider a simple example using the configuration of Fig. 7-16. *A* is a client and *B* is a server. With FLIP, any machine having connections to two or more networks is automatically a gateway, so the fact that *B* happens to be running on a gateway machine is irrelevant.

When *B* is created, the kernel picks a new random FLIP address for it and registers it with the FLIP layer. After starting, *B* initializes itself and then does a *get_request* on its get-port, which causes a trap to the kernel. The RPC layer looks up the put-port in its get-port to put-port cache (or computes it if no entry is found) and makes a note that a process is listening to that port. It then blocks until a request comes in.

Later, *A* does a *trans* on the put-port. Its RPC layer looks in its tables to see if it knows the FLIP address of the server process that listens to the put-port. Since it does not, the RPC layer sends a special broadcast packet to find it. This packet has a maximum hop count set to make sure that the broadcast is confined to its own network. (When a gateway sees a packet whose current hop count is already equal to its maximum hop count, the packet is discarded instead of being forwarded.) If the broadcast fails, the sending RPC layer times out and tries again with a maximum hop count one larger, and so on, until it locates the server.

When the broadcast packet arrives at B's machine, the RPC layer there sends back a reply announcing its FLIP address. Like all incoming packets, this packet causes A's FLIP layer to make an entry for that FLIP address before passing the reply packet up to the RPC layer. The RPC layer now makes an entry in its own tables mapping the put-port onto the FLIP address. Then it sends the request to the server. Since the FLIP layer now has an entry for the server's FLIP address, it can build a packet containing the proper network address and send it without further ado. Subsequent requests to the server's put-port use the RPC layer's cache to find the FLIP address and the FLIP layer's routing table to find the network address. Thus broadcasting is used only the very first time a server is contacted. After that, the kernel tables provide the necessary information.

To summarize, locating a put-port requires two mappings:

1. From the put-port to the FLIP address (done by the RPC layer).

2. From the FLIP address to the network address (done by the FLIP layer).

The reason for this two-stage process is twofold. First, FLIP has been designed as a general-purpose protocol for use in distributed systems, including non-Amoeba systems. Since these systems generally do not use Amoeba-style ports, the mapping of put-ports to FLIP addresses has not been built into the FLIP layer. Other users of FLIP may just use FLIP addresses directly.

Second, a put-port really identifies a *service* rather than a *server*. A service may be provided by multiple servers to enhance performance and reliability. Although all the servers listen to the same put-port, each one has its own private FLIP address. When a client's RPC layer issues a broadcast to find the FLIP address corresponding to a put-port, any or all of the servers may respond. Since each server has a different FLIP address, each response creates a different routing table entry. All the responses are passed to the RPC layer, which chooses one to use.

The advantage of this scheme over having just a single (port, network address) cache is that it permits servers to migrate to new machines or have their machines be wheeled over to new networks and plugged in without requiring any manual reconfiguration, as, say, TCP/IP does. There is a strong analogy here with a person moving and being assigned the same telephone number at the new residence as he had at the old one. (For the record, Amoeba does not currently support process migration, but this feature could be added in the future.)

The advantage over having clients and servers use FLIP addresses directly is the protection offered by the one-way function used to derive put-ports from get-ports. In addition, if a server crashes, it will pick a new FLIP address when it reboots. Attempts to use the old FLIP address will time out, allowing the RPC layer to indicate failure to the client. This mechanism is how at-most-once semantics are guaranteed. The client, however, can just try again with the same put-port if it wishes, since that is not necessarily invalidated by server crashes.

FLIP over Wide-Area Networks

FLIP also works transparently over wide-area networks. In Fig. 7-19 we have three local-area networks connected by a wide-area network. Suppose that the client A wants to do an RPC with the server E. A's RPC layer first tries to locate the put-port using a maximum hop count of 1. When that fails, it tries again with a maximum hop count of 2. This time, C forwards the broadcast packet to all the gateways that are connected to the wide-area network, namely, D and G. Effectively, C simulates broadcast over the wide-area network by sending individual messages to all the other gateways. When this broadcast fails to turn up the server, a third broadcast is sent, this time with a maximum hop count of 3. This one succeeds. The reply contains E's network address and FLIP address, which are then entered into A's routing table. From this point on, communication between A and E happens using normal point-to-point communication. No more broadcasts are needed.

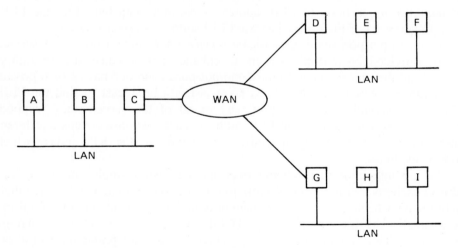

Fig. 7-19. Three LANs connected by a WAN.

Communication over the wide-area network is encapsulated in whatever protocol the wide-area network requires. For example, on a TCP/IP network, C

might have open connections to *D* and *G* all the time. Alternatively, the implementation might decide to close any connection not used for a certain length of time.

Although this method does not scale well to thousands of LANs, for modest numbers it works quite well. In practice, few servers move, so that once a server has been located by broadcasting, subsequent requests will use the cached entries. Using this method, a substantial number of machines all over the world can work together in a totally transparent way. An RPC to a thread in the caller's address space and an RPC to a thread halfway around the world are done in exactly the same way.

Group communication also uses FLIP. When a message is sent to multiple destinations, FLIP uses the hardware multicast or broadcast on those networks where it is available. On those that do not have it, broadcast is simulated by sending individual messages, just as we saw on the wide-area network. The choice of mechanism is done by the FLIP layer, with the same user semantics in all cases.

7.6. THE AMOEBA SERVERS

Most of the traditional operating system services (such as the file server) are implemented in Amoeba as server processes. Although it would have been possible to put together a random collection of servers, each with its own model of the world, it was decided early on to provide a single model of what a server does to achieve uniformity and simplicity. Although voluntary, most servers follow it. The model, and some examples of key Amoeba servers, are described in this section.

All standard servers in Amoeba are defined by a set of stub procedures. The newer stubs are defined in **AIL**, the **Amoeba Interface Language**, although the older ones are handwritten in C. The stub procedures are generated by the AIL compiler from the stub definitions and then placed in the library so that clients can use them. In effect, the stubs define precisely what services the server provides and what their parameters are. In our discussion below, we will refer to the stubs frequently.

7.6.1. The Bullet Server

Like all operating systems, Amoeba has a file system. However, unlike most other ones, the choice of file system is not dictated by the operating system. The file system runs as a collection of server processes. Users who do not like the standard ones are free to write their own. The kernel does not know, or care, which is the "real" file system. In fact, different users may use different and incompatible file systems at the same time if they desire.

The standard file system consists of three servers, the **bullet server**, which handles file storage, the **directory server**, which takes care of file naming and directory management, and the **replication server**, which handles file replication. The file system has been split into these separate components to achieve increased flexibility and make each of the servers straightforward to implement. We will discuss the bullet server in this section and the other two in the following ones.

Very briefly, a client process can create a file using the *create* call. The bullet server responds by sending back a capability that can be used in subsequent calls to *read* to retrieve all or part of the file. In most cases, the user will then give the file an ASCII name, and the (ASCII name, capability) pair will be given to the directory server for storage in a directory, but this operation has nothing to do with the bullet server.

The bullet server was designed to be very fast (hence the name). It was also designed to run on machines having large primary memories and huge disks, rather than on low-end machines, where memory is always scarce. The organization is quite different from that of most conventional file servers. In particular, files are **immutable**. Once a file has been created, it cannot subsequently be changed. It can be deleted and a new file created in its place, but the new file has a different capability from the old one. This fact simplifies automatic replication, as will be seen. It is also well suited for use on large-capacity, write-once optical disks.

Because files cannot be modified after their creation, the size of a file is always known at creation time. This property allows files to be stored contiguously on the disk and also in the main memory cache. By storing files contiguously, they can be read into memory in a single disk operation, and they can be sent to users in a single RPC reply message. These simplifications lead to the high performance.

The conceptual model behind the file system is thus that a client creates an entire file in its own memory, and then transmits it in a single RPC to the bullet server, which stores it and returns a capability for accessing it later. To modify this file (e.g., to edit a program or document), the client sends back the capability and asks for the file, which is then (ideally) sent in one RPC to the client's memory. The client can then modify the file locally any way it wants to. When it is done, it sends the file to the server (ideally) in one RPC, thus causing a new file to be created and a new capability to be returned. At this point the client can ask the server to destroy the original file, or it can keep the old file as a backup.

As a concession to reality, the bullet server also supports clients that have too little memory to receive or send entire files in a single RPC. When reading, it is possible to ask for a section of a file, specified by an offset and a byte count.

This feature allows clients to read files in whatever size unit they find convenient.

Writing a file in several operations is complicated by the fact that bullet server files are guaranteed to be immutable. This problem is dealt with by introducing two kinds of files, **uncommitted files**, which are in the process of being created, and **committed files**, which are permanent. Uncommitted files can be changed; committed files cannot be. An RPC doing a *create* must specify whether the file is to be committed immediately or not.

In both cases, a copy of the file is made at the server and a capability for the file is returned. If the file is not committed, it can be modified by subsequent RPCs; in particular, it can be appended to. When all the appends and other changes have been completed, the file can be committed, at which point it becomes immutable. To emphasize the transient nature of uncommitted files, they cannot be read. Only committed files can be read.

The Bullet Server Interface

The bullet server supports the six operations listed in Fig. 7-20, plus an additional three that are reserved for the system administrator. In addition, the relevant standard operations listed in Fig. 7-5 are also valid. All these operations are accessed by calling stub procedures from the library.

Call	Description
Create	Create a new file; optionally commit it as well
Read	Read all or part of a specified file
Size	Return the size of a specified file
Modify	Overwrite n bytes of an uncommitted file
Insert	Insert or append n bytes to an uncommitted file
Delete	Delete n bytes from an uncommitted file

Fig. 7-20. Bullet server calls.

The *create* procedure supplies some data, which are put into a new file whose capability is returned in the reply. If the file is committed (determined by a parameter), it can be read but not changed. If it is not committed, it cannot be read until it is committed, but it can be changed or appended to.

The *read* call can read all or part of any committed file. It specifies the file to be read by providing a capability for it. Presentation of the capability is proof that the operation is allowed. The bullet server does not make any checks based on the client's identity: it does not even know the client's identity. The *size* call takes a capability as parameter and tells how big the corresponding file is.

The last three calls all work on uncommitted files. They allow the file to be changed by overwriting, inserting, or deleting bytes. Multiple calls can be made in succession. The last call can indicate via a parameter that it wants to commit the file.

The bullet server also supports three special calls for the system administrator, who must present a special super-capability. These calls flush the main memory cache to disk, allow the disk to be compacted, and repair damaged file systems.

The capabilities generated and used by the bullet server use the *Rights* field to protect the operations. In this way, a capability can be made that allows a file to be read but not to be destroyed, for example.

Implementation of the Bullet Server

The bullet server maintains a file table with one entry per file, analogous to the UNIX i-node table and shown in Fig. 7-21. The entire table is read into memory when the bullet server is booted and is kept there as long as the bullet server is running.

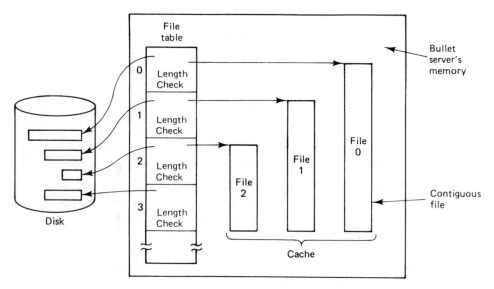

Fig. 7-21. Implementation of the bullet server.

Roughly speaking, each table entry contains two pointers and a length, plus some additional information. One pointer gives the disk address of the file and the other gives the main memory address if the file happens to be in the main memory cache at the moment. All files are stored contiguously, both on disk and in the cache, so a pointer and a length is enough. Unlike UNIX, no direct or indirect blocks are needed.

Although this strategy wastes space due to external fragmentation, both in memory and on disk, it has the advantage of extreme simplicity and high performance. A file on disk can be read into memory in a single operation, at the maximum speed of the disk, and it can be transmitted over the network at the maximum speed of the network. As memories and disks get larger and cheaper, it is likely that the cost of the wasted memory will be acceptable in return for the speed provided.

When a client process wants to read a file, it sends the capability for the file to the bullet server. The server extracts the object number from the capability and uses it as an index into the file table to locate the entry for the file. The entry contains the random number used in the capability's *Check* field, which is then used to verify that the capability is valid. If it is invalid, the operation is terminated with an error code. If it is valid, the entire file is fetched from the disk into the cache, unless it is already there. Cache space is managed using LRU, but the implicit assumption is that the cache is usually large enough to hold the set of files currently in use.

If a file is created and the capability lost, the file can never be accessed but will remain forever. To prevent this situation, timeouts are used. An uncommitted file that has not been accessed in 10 minutes is simply deleted and its table entry freed. If the entry is subsequently reused for another file, but the old capability is presented 15 minutes later, the *Check* field will detect the fact that the file has changed and the operation on the old file will be rejected. This approach is acceptable because files normally exist in the uncommitted state for only a few seconds.

For committed files, a less draconian method is used. Associated with every file (in the file table entry) is a counter, initialized to *MAX_LIFETIME*. Periodically, a daemon does an RPC with the bullet server, asking it to perform the standard *age* operation (see Fig. 7-5). This operation causes the bullet server to run through the file table, decrementing each counter by 1. Any file whose counter goes to 0 is destroyed and its disk, table, and cache space reclaimed.

To prevent this mechanism from removing files that are in use, another operation, *touch*, is provided. Unlike *age*, which applies to all files, *touch* is for a specific file. Its function is to reset the counter to *MAX_LIFETIME*. *Touch* is called periodically for all files listed in any directory, to keep them from timing out. Typically, every file is touched once an hour, and a file is deleted if it has not been touched in 24 hours. This mechanism removes lost files (i.e., files not in any directory).

The bullet server can run in user space as an ordinary process. However, if it is running on a dedicated machine, with no other processes on that machine, a small performance gain can be achieved by putting it in the kernel. The semantics are unchanged by this move. Clients cannot even tell where it is located.

7.6.2. The Directory Server

The bullet server, as we have seen, just handles file storage. The naming of files and other objects is handled by the **directory server**. Its primary function is to provide a mapping from human-readable (ASCII) names to capabilities. Processes can create one or more directories, each of which can contain multiple rows. Each row describes one object and contains both the object's name and its capability. Operations are provided to create and delete directories, add and delete rows, and look up names in directories. Unlike bullet files, directories are *not* immutable. Entries can be added to existing directories and entries can be deleted from existing directories.

Directories themselves are objects and are protected by capabilities, just as other objects. The operations on a directory, such as looking up names and adding new entries, are protected by bits in the *Rights* field, in the usual way. Directory capabilities may be stored in other directories, permitting hierarchical directory trees and more general structures.

Although the directory server can be used simply to store (file-name, capability) pairs, it can also support a more general model. First, a directory entry can name any kind of object that is described by a capability, not just a bullet file or directory. The directory server neither knows nor cares what kind of objects its capabilities control. The entries in a single directory may be for a variety of different kinds of objects, and these objects may be scattered randomly all over the world. There is no requirement that objects in a directory all be the same kind or all be managed by the same server. When a capability is fetched, its server is located by broadcasting, as described earlier.

ASCII string	Capability set	Owner	Group	Others
Mail	▭ ▭ ▭	1111	0000	0000
Games	▭ ▭ ▭	1111	1110	1110
Exams	▭ ▭ ▭	1111	0000	0000
Papers	▭ ▭ ▭	1111	1100	1000
Committees	▭ ▭ ▭	1111	1010	0010

Fig. 7-22. A typical directory managed by the directory server.

Second, a row may contain not just one capability, but a whole set of capabilities, as shown in Fig. 7-22. Generally, these capabilities are for identical copies of the object, and are managed by different servers. When a process looks up a name, it is given the entire set of capabilities. To see how this feature might be of use, consider the library procedure *open* for opening a file. It looks up a file and gets a capability set in return. It then tries each of the capabilities in turn until it finds one whose server is alive. In this way, if one object is unavailable, another one can be used in its place. It should be clear that this mechanism works best when the files are immutable, so there is no danger that any of them will have changed since they were created.

Third, a row may contain multiple columns, each forming a different protection domain and having different rights. For example, a directory may have one column for the owner, one for the owner's group, and one for everyone else, to simulate the UNIX protection scheme. A capability for a directory is really a capability for a specific column in a directory, making it possible for the owner, group, and others to have different permissions. Since the underlying capability set is the same for all columns of a row, it is only necessary to store the rights bits for each column. The actual capabilities can be computed as needed.

The layout of an example directory with five entries is shown in Fig. 7-22. This directory has one row for each of the five file names stored in it. The directory has three columns, each one representing a different protection domain, in this case for the owner, the owner's group, and everyone else. When the directory owner gives away a capability for, say, the last column, the recipient has no access to the more powerful capabilities in the first two columns.

As we mentioned above, directories may contain capabilities for other directories. This ability allows us to build not only trees but also directory graphs in their full generality. One obvious use of this power is to place the capability for a file in two or more directories, thus creating multiple links to it. These capabilities may also have different rights, making it possible for people sharing a file to have different access permissions, something impossible in UNIX.

In any distributed system, especially one intended for use on wide-area networks, it is difficult to have any concept of a single, global root directory. In Amoeba, every user has his own root directory, as shown in Fig. 7-23. It contains capabilities for not only the user's private subdirectories, but also for various public directories containing system programs and other shared files.

Some of the directories in each user's root are similar to those in UNIX, such as *bin*, *dev*, and *etc*. However, others are fundamentally different. One of these is *home*, which is the user's home directory.

Another is *public*, which contains the start of the shared public tree. Here we find *cap*, *hosts*, and *pool*, among others. When a process wants to contact the bullet server, the directory server, or any other server, for example, to create a new object, it must have a generic capability for talking to that server. These capabilities are kept in */public/cap*.

Another directory in *public* is *hosts*, which contains a directory for each

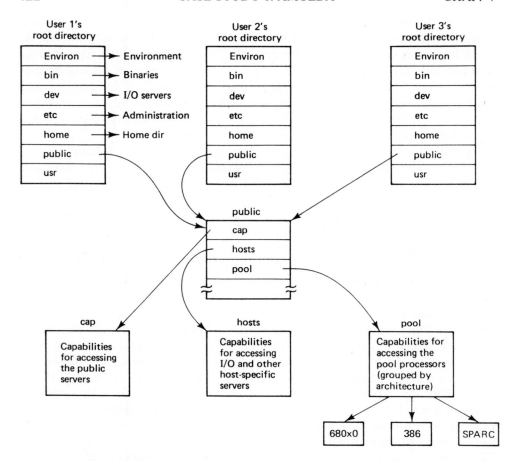

Fig. 7-23. A simplified version of the Amoeba directory hierarchy.

machine in the system. This directory contains capabilities for various servers that can be found on a host, such as a disk server, a terminal server, a process server, a random number server, and so on. Finally, *pool* contains capabilities for the pool processors, grouped by CPU architecture. A mechanism is present to restrict each user to a specific set of pool processors.

The Directory Server Interface

The principal directory server calls are listed in Fig. 7-24. The first two, *create* and *delete*, are used to make and remove directories, respectively. When a directory is created, its capability is returned, just as with making any object. This capability can subsequently be inserted into another directory to build a hierarchy. This low-level interface gives maximum control over the shape of the naming graph. Since many programs are content to work with conventional directory trees, a library package is available to make this easier.

Call	Description
Create	Create a new directory
Delete	Delete a directory or an entry in a directory
Append	Add a new directory entry to a specified directory
Replace	Replace a single directory entry
Lookup	Return the capability set corresponding to a specified name
Getmasks	Return the rights masks for the specified entry
Chmod	Change the rights bits in an existing directory entry

Fig. 7-24. The principal directory server calls.

It is worth noting that deleting a directory entry is not the same as destroying the object itself. If a capability is removed from a directory, the object itself continues to exist. The capability can be put into another directory, for example. To get rid of the object, it must explicitly be destroyed or garbage collected.

To add a new entry to a directory, be it a file, a directory, or another kind of object, the *append* call is used. Like most of the directory server calls, it specifies the capability of the directory to be used (added to), as well as the capability to put in the directory and the rights bits for all the columns. An existing entry can be overwritten with *replace*, for example, when a file has been edited and the new version is to be used instead of the old one.

The most common directory operation is *lookup*. Its parameters are a capability for a directory (column) and an ASCII string. It returns the corresponding capability set. Opening a file for reading requires first looking up its capabilities.

The last two operations listed are for reading and writing the rights masks for all the columns in a row specified by its string.

A few other directory operations also exist. These are mostly concerned with looking up or replacing multiple files at the same time. They can be useful for implementing atomic transactions involving multiple files.

Implementation of the Directory Server

The directory server is a critical component in the Amoeba system, so it has been implemented in a fault-tolerant way. The basic data structure is an array of capability pairs stored on a raw disk partition. This array does not use the bullet server because it must be updated frequently and the overhead was thought to be too much.

When a directory is created, the object number put into its capability is an index into this array. When a directory capability is presented, the server inspects the object number contained in it and uses it to fetch the corresponding capability pair from the array. These capabilities are for identical files, stored on different bullet servers, each of which contains the directory and the *Check* field used to verify the authenticity of the directory capability.

When a directory is changed, a new bullet file is created for it, and the arrays on the raw disk partition are overwritten. The second copy is created later by a background thread. The old directories are then destroyed. Although this mechanism has some extra overhead, it provides a much higher degree of reliability than traditional file systems. In addition, normally, directory servers come in pairs, each with its own array of capability pairs (on different disks), to prevent disaster if one of the raw disk partitions is damaged. The two servers communicate to keep synchronized. It is also possible to run with only one. The two-server mode is shown in Fig. 7-25.

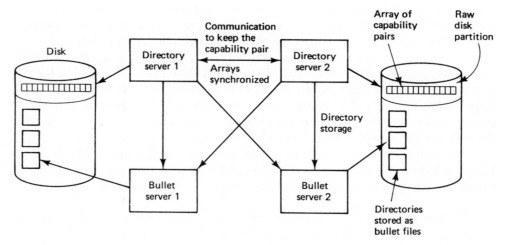

Fig. 7-25. A pair of directory servers. All data are stored twice, on different bullet servers.

In Fig. 7-22 the capability set is shown as being stored only once per row, even though there are multiple columns. This organization is actually used. In most cases, the *owner* column contains rights bits that are all 1s, so the capabilities in the set are true owner capabilities (i.e., the *Check* field has not been run through the one-way function). When a name in another column is looked up, the directory server itself computes the restricted capability by XORing the *rights* field taken from the directory entry with the *Check* field taken from the owner capability. This result is then run through the one-way function and returned to the caller.

This method eliminates the need to store large numbers of capabilities. Furthermore, the directory server caches heavily used capabilities to avoid unnecessary use of the one-way function. If the capability set does not contain owner capabilities, the server has to be invoked to compute the restricted capabilities because the directory server then does not have access to the original *Check* field.

7.6.3. The Replication Server

Objects managed by the directory server can be replicated automatically by using the replication server. It practices what is called **lazy replication**. What this means is that when a file or other object is created, initially only one copy is made. Then the replication server can be invoked to produce identical replicas, when it has time. Instead of making direct calls to it, the replication server is kept running in the background all the time, scanning specified parts of the directory system periodically. Whenever it finds a directory entry that is supposed to contain *n* capabilities but contains fewer, it contacts the relevant servers and arranges for additional copies to be made. Although the replication server can be used to replicate any kind of object, it works best for immutable objects, such as bullet files. The advantage is that immutable objects cannot change during the replication process, so it can safely go in the background, even if it takes a substantial time. Mutable objects might change during the replication process, adding additional complexity to avoid inconsistency.

In addition, the replication server runs the aging and garbage collection mechanism used by the bullet server and other servers. Periodically, it touches every object under the directory server's control, to prevent them from timing out. It also sends the *age* messages to the servers to cause them to decrement all the object counters and garbage collect any that have reached zero.

7.6.4. The Run Server

When the user types a command (e.g., *sort*) at the terminal, two decisions must be made:

1. On what architecture type should the process be run?

2. Which processor should be chosen?

The first question relates to whether the process should run on a 386, SPARC, 680x0, and so on. The second relates to the choice of the specific CPU and depends on the load and memory availability of the candidate processors. The **run server** helps make these decisions.

Each run server manages one or more processor pools. A processor pool is represented by a directory called a **pooldir**, which contains subdirectories for each of the CPU architectures supported. The subdirectories contain capabilities for accessing the process servers on each of the machines in the pool. An example arrangement is shown in Fig. 7-26. Other arrangements are also possible, including mixed and overlapping pools, and dividing pools into subpools.

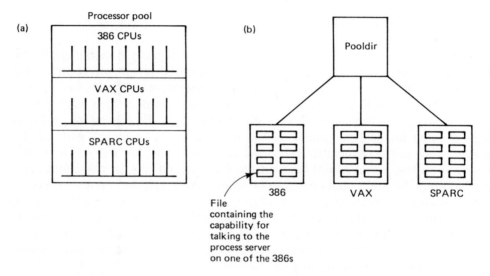

Fig. 7-26. (a) A processor pool. (b) The corresponding pooldir.

When the shell wants to run a program, it looks in /*bin* to find, say, *sort*. If *sort* is available for multiple architectures, *sort* will not be a single file, but a directory containing executable programs for each available architecture. The shell then does an RPC with the run server sending it all the available process descriptors and asking it to pick both an architecture and a specific CPU.

The run server then looks in its pooldir to see what it has to offer. The selection is made approximately as follows. First, the intersection of the process descriptors and pool processors is computed. If there are process descriptors (i.e., binary programs) for the 386, SPARC, and 680x0, and this run server manages 386, SPARC, and VAX pool processors, only the 386 is a possibility, so the other machines are eliminated as candidates.

Second, the run server checks to see which of the candidate machines have enough memory to run the program. Those that do not are also eliminated. The run server keeps track of the memory and CPU usage of each of its pool processors by making *getload* calls to each one regularly to request these values, so the numbers in the run server's tables are continuously refreshed.

Third, and last, for each of the remaining machines, an estimate is obtained of the computing power that can be devoted to the new program. Each CPU makes its own estimate. The heuristic used takes as input the known total computing power of the CPU and the number of currently active threads running on it. For example, if a 20-MIPS machine currently has four active threads, the addition of a fifth one means that each one, including the new one, will get 4 MIPS on the average. If another processor has 10 MIPS and one thread, on this machine the new program can expect 5 MIPS. The run server chooses the processor that can deliver the most MIPS and returns the capability for talking to its process server to the caller. The caller then uses this capability to create the process, as described in Sec. 7.3.

7.6.5. The Boot Server

As another example of an Amoeba server, let us consider the *boot server*. The boot server is used to provide a degree of fault tolerance to Amoeba by checking that all servers that are supposed to be running are in fact running, and taking corrective action when they are not. A server that is interested in surviving crashes can be included in the boot server's configuration file. Each entry tells how often the boot server should poll and how it should poll. As long as the server responds correctly, the boot server takes no further action.

However, if the server should fail to respond after a specified number of attempts, the boot server declares it dead, and attempts to restart it. If that fails, it arranges to allocate a new pool processor on which a new copy is started. In this manner, critical services are rebooted automatically if they should ever fail. The boot server can itself be replicated, to guard against its own failure.

7.6.6. The TCP/IP Server

Although Amoeba uses the FLIP protocol internally to achieve high performance, sometimes it is necessary to speak TCP/IP, for example, to communicate with X terminals, to send and receive mail to non-Amoeba machines and to interact with other Amoeba systems via the Internet. To permit Amoeba to do these things, a TCP/IP server has been provided.

To establish a connection, an Amoeba process does an RPC with the TCP/IP server giving it a TCP/IP address. The caller is then blocked until the connection has been established or refused. In the reply, the TCP/IP server provides a capability for using the connection. Subsequent RPCs can send and receive packets from the remote machine without the Amoeba process having to know that TCP/IP is being used. This mechanism is less efficient than FLIP, so it is used only when it is not possible to use FLIP.

7.6.7. Other Servers

Amoeba supports various other servers. These include a disk server (used by the directory server for storing its arrays of capability pairs), various other I/O servers, a time-of-day server, and a random number server (useful for generating ports, capabilities, and FLIP addresses). The so-called Swiss Army Knife server deals with many activities that have to be done later by starting up processes at a specified time in the future. Mail servers deal with incoming and outgoing electronic mail.

7.7. SUMMARY

Amoeba is a new operating system designed to make a collection of independent computers appear to its users as a single timesharing system. In general, the users are not aware of where their processes are running (or even on what type of CPU), and are not aware of where their files are stored or how many copies are being maintained for reasons of availability and performance. However, users who are explicitly interested in parallel programming can exploit the existence of multiple CPUs for splitting a single job over many machines.

Amoeba is based on a microkernel that handles low-level process and memory management, communication, and I/O. The file system and the rest of the operating system can run as user processes. This division of labor keeps the kernel small and simple.

Amoeba has a single mechanism for naming and protecting all objects— capabilities. Each capability contains rights telling which operations may be performed using it. Capabilities are protected cryptographically using one-way functions. Each one contains a checksum field that assures the security of the capability.

Three communication mechanisms are supported: RPC and raw FLIP for point-to-point communication, and reliable group communication for multiparty communication. The RPC guarantees at-most-once semantics. The group communication is based on reliable broadcasting as provided by the sequencer algorithm. Both mechanisms are supported on top of the FLIP protocol and are closely integrated. Raw FLIP is only used under special circumstances.

The Amoeba file system consists of three servers: the bullet server for file storage, the directory server for file naming, and the replication server for file replication. The bullet server maintains immutable files that are stored contiguously on disk and in the cache. The directory server is a fault-tolerant server that maps ASCII strings to capabilities. The replication server handles lazy replication.

PROBLEMS

1. The Amoeba designers assumed that memory would soon be available in large amounts for low prices. What impact did this assumption have on the design?

2. State an advantage and a disadvantage of the processor pool model compared to the personal multiprocessor model.

3. List three functions of the Amoeba microkernel.

4. Some Amoeba servers can be run in the kernel as well as in user space. Their clients cannot tell the difference (except by timing them). What is it about Amoeba that makes it impossible for clients to tell the difference?

5. A malicious user is trying to guess the bullet server's get-port by picking a random 48-bit number, running it through the well-known one-way function, and seeing if the put-port comes out. It takes 1 msec per trial. How long will it take to guess the get-port, on the average?

6. How does a server tell that a capability is an owner capability, as opposed to a restricted capability? How are owner capabilities verified?

7. If a capability is not an owner capability, how do servers check it for validity?

8. Explain what a glocal variable is.

9. Why does the *trans* call have parameters for both sending and receiving? Would it not have been better and simpler to have two calls, *send_request* and *get_reply*, one for sending and one for receiving?

10. Amoeba claims to guarantee at-most-once semantics on RPCs. Suppose that three file servers offer the same service. A client does an RPC with one of them, which carries out the request and then crashes. Then the RPC is repeated with another server, resulting in the work being done twice. Is this possible? If so, what does the guarantee mean? If not, how is it prevented?

11. Why does the sequencer need a history buffer?

12. Two algorithms for broadcasting in Amoeba were presented in the text. In method 1, the sender sends a point-to-point message to the sequencer, which then broadcasts it. In method 2, the sender does the broadcast, with the sequencer then broadcasting a small acknowledgement packet. Consider a 10-Mbps network on which processing a packet-arrived interrupt takes 500 microsec, independent of the packet size. If all data packets are 1K bytes, and acknowledgement packets are 100 bytes, how much bandwidth and how much CPU time are consumed per 1000 broadcasts by the two methods?

13. What property of FLIP addressing makes it possible to handle process migration and automatic network reconfiguration in a straightforward way?

14. The bullet server supports immutable files for its users. Are the bullet server's own tables also immutable?

15. Why does the bullet server have uncommitted and committed files?

16. In Amoeba, links to a file can be created by putting capabilities with different rights in different directories. These give different users different permissions. This feature is not present in UNIX. Why?

8

Case Study 2: Mach

Our second example of a modern, microkernel-based operating system is Mach. We will start out by looking at its history and how it has evolved from earlier systems. Then we will examine in some detail the microkernel itself, focusing on processes and threads, memory management, and communication. Finally, we will discuss UNIX emulation. More information about Mach can be found in (Accetta et al., 1986; Baron et al., 1985; Black et al., 1992; Boykin et al., 1993; Draves et al., 1991; Rashid, 1986a; Rashid, 1986b; and Sansom et al., 1986).

8.1. INTRODUCTION TO MACH

In this section we will give a brief introduction to Mach. We will start with the history and goals. Then we will describe the main concepts of the Mach microkernel and the principal server that runs on the microkernel.

8.1.1. History of Mach

Mach's earliest roots go back to a system called **RIG (Rochester Intelligent Gateway)**, which began at the University of Rochester in 1975 (Ball et al., 1976). RIG was written for a 16-bit Data General minicomputer called the

Eclipse. Its main research goal was to demonstrate that operating systems could be structured in a modular way, as a collection of processes that communicated by message passing, including over a network. The system was designed and built, and indeed showed that such an operating system could be constructed.

When one of its designers, Richard Rashid, left the University of Rochester and moved to Carnegie-Mellon University in 1979, he wanted to continue developing message-passing operating systems but on more modern hardware. Various machines were considered. The machine selected was the PERQ, an early engineering workstation, with a bitmapped screen, mouse, and network connection. It was also microprogrammable. The new operating system for the PERQ was called **Accent**. It improved on RIG by adding protection, the ability to operate transparently over the network, 32-bit virtual memory, and other features. An initial version was up and running in 1981.

By 1984 Accent was being used on 150 PERQs but it was clearly losing out to UNIX. This observation led Rashid to begin a third-generation operating systems project called **Mach**. By making Mach compatible with UNIX, he hoped to be able to use the large volume of UNIX software becoming available. In addition, Mach had many other improvements over Accent, including threads, a better interprocess communication mechanism, multiprocessor support, and a highly imaginative virtual memory system.

Around this time, DARPA, the U.S. Department of Defense's Advanced Research Projects Agency, was hunting around for an operating system that supported multiprocessors as part of its Strategic Computing Initiative. CMU was selected, and with substantial DARPA funding, Mach was developed further. Initially, Mach consisted of a modified version of 4.1 BSD with additional features inserted for communication and memory management. As 4.2 BSD and 4.3 BSD became available, the Mach code was combined with them to give updated versions. Although this approach led to a large kernel, it did guarantee absolute compatibility with Berkeley UNIX, an important goal for DARPA.

The first version of Mach was released in 1986 for the VAX 11/784, a four-CPU multiprocessor. Shortly thereafter, ports to the IBM PC/RT and Sun 3 were done. By 1987, Mach was also running on the Encore and Sequent multiprocessors. Although Mach had networking facilities, at this time it was conceived of primarily as a single machine or multiprocessor system rather than as a transparent distributed operating system for a collection of machines on a LAN.

Shortly thereafter, the Open Software Foundation, a consortium of computer vendors led by IBM, DEC, and Hewlett Packard was formed in an attempt to wrest control of UNIX from its owner, AT&T, which was then working closely with Sun Microsystems to develop System V Release 4. The OSF members feared that this alliance would give Sun a competitive advantage over them. After some missteps, OSF chose Mach 2.5 as the basis for its first operating system, OSF/1. Although Mach 2.5 and OSF/1 contained large amounts of

Berkeley and AT&T code, the hope was that OSF would at least be able to control the direction in which UNIX was going.

As of 1988, the Mach 2.5 kernel was large and monolithic, due to the presence of a large amount of Berkeley UNIX code in the kernel. In 1988, CMU removed all the Berkeley code from the kernel and put it in user space. What remained was a microkernel consisting of pure Mach. In this chapter, we will focus on the Mach 3 microkernel and one user-level operating system emulator, for BSD UNIX. One difficulty, however, is that Mach is under development, so any description is at best a snapshot. Fortunately, most of the basic ideas discussed in this chapter are relatively stable, but some of the details may change in time.

8.1.2. Goals of Mach

Mach has evolved considerably since its first incarnation as RIG. The goals of the project have also changed as time has gone on. The current primary goals can be summarized as follows:

1. Providing a base for building other operating systems (e.g., UNIX).

2. Supporting large sparse address spaces.

3. Allowing transparent access to network resources.

4. Exploiting parallelism in both the system and the applications.

5. Making Mach portable to a larger collection of machines.

These goals encompass both research and development. The idea is to explore multiprocessor and distributed systems while being able to emulate existing systems, such as UNIX, MS-DOS, and the Macintosh operating system.

Much of the initial work on Mach concentrated on single- and multiprocessor systems. At the time Mach was designed, few systems had support for multiprocessors. Even now, few multiprocessor systems other than Mach are machine independent.

8.1.3. The Mach Microkernel

The Mach microkernel has been built as a base upon which UNIX and other operating systems can be emulated. This emulation is done by a software layer that runs outside the kernel, as shown in Fig. 8-1. Each emulator consists of a part that is present in its application programs' address space, as well as one or more servers that run independently from the application programs. It should be noted that multiple emulators can be running simultaneously, so it is possible to run 4.3BSD, System V, and MS-DOS programs on the same machine at the same time.

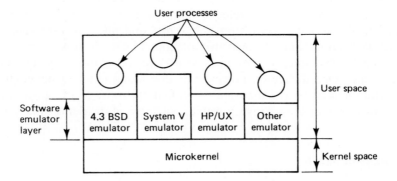

Fig. 8-1. The abstract model for UNIX emulation using Mach.

Like other microkernels, the Mach kernel, provides process management, memory management, communication, and I/O services. Files, directories, and other traditional operating system functions are handled in user space. The idea behind the Mach kernel is to provide the necessary mechanisms for making the system work, but leaving the policy to user-level processes.

The kernel manages five principal abstractions:

1. Processes.

2. Threads.

3. Memory objects.

4. Ports.

5. Messages.

In addition, the kernel manages several other abstractions either related to these or less central to the model.

A process is basically an environment in which execution can take place. It has an address space holding the program text and data, and usually one or more stacks. The process is the basic unit for resource allocation. For example, a communication channel is always "owned" by a single process.

As an aside, for the most part we will stick with the traditional nomenclature throughout this chapter, even though this means deviating from the terminology used in the Mach papers (e.g., Mach, of course, has processes, but they are called "tasks."

A thread in Mach is an executable entity. It has a program counter and a set of registers associated with it. Each thread is part of exactly one process. A process with one thread is similar to a traditional (e.g., UNIX) process.

A concept that is unique to Mach is the **memory object**, a data structure that can be mapped into a process' address space. Memory objects occupy one or more pages and form the basis of the Mach virtual memory system. When a process attempts to reference a memory object that is not presently in physical main memory, it gets a page fault. As in all operating systems, the kernel catches the page fault. However, unlike other systems, the Mach kernel can send a message to a user-level server to fetch the missing page.

Interprocess communication in Mach is based on message passing. To receive messages, a user process asks the kernel to create a kind of protected mailbox, called a **port**, for it. The port is stored inside the kernel, and has the ability to queue an ordered list of messages. Queues are not fixed in size, but for flow control reasons, if more than n messages are queued on a port, a process attempting to send to it is suspended to give the port a chance to be emptied. The parameter n is settable per port.

A process can give the ability to send to (or receive from) one of its ports to another process. This permission takes the form of a **capability**, and includes not only a pointer to the port, but also a list of rights that the other process has with respect to the port (e.g., SEND right). Once this permission has been granted, the other process can send messages to the port, which the first process can then read. All communication in Mach uses this mechanism. Mach does not support a full capability mechanism; ports are the only objects for which capabilities exist.

8.1.4. The Mach BSD UNIX Server

As we described above, the Mach designers have modified Berkeley UNIX to run in user space, as an application program. This structure has a number of significant advantages over a monolithic kernel. First, by breaking the system up into a part that handles the resource management (the kernel) and a part that handles the system calls (the UNIX server), both pieces become simpler and easier to maintain. In a way, this split is somewhat reminiscent of the division of labor in IBM's mainframe operating system VM/370, in which the kernel simulates a collection of bare 370s, each of which runs a single-user operating system.

Second, by putting UNIX in user space, it can be made extremely machine independent, enhancing its portability to a wide variety of computers. All the machine dependencies can be removed from UNIX and hidden away inside the Mach kernel.

Third, as we mentioned earlier, multiple operating systems can run simultaneously. On a 386, for example, Mach can run a UNIX program and an MS-DOS program at the same time. Similarly, it is possible to test a new experimental operating system and run a production operating system at the same time.

Fourth, real-time operation can be added to the system because all the traditional obstacles that UNIX presents to real-time work, such as disabling interrupts in order to update critical tables are either eliminated altogether or moved into user space. The kernel can be carefully structured not to have this type of hindrance to real-time applications.

Finally, this arrangement can be used to provide better security between processes, if need be. If each process has its own version of UNIX, it is very difficult for one process to snoop on the other one's files.

8.2. PROCESS MANAGEMENT IN MACH

Process management in Mach deals with processes, threads, and scheduling. In this section we will look at each of these in turn.

8.2.1. Processes

A process in Mach consists primarily of an address space and a collection of threads that execute in that address space. Processes are passive. Execution is associated with the threads. Processes are used for collecting all the resources related to a group of cooperating threads into convenient containers.

Figure 8-2 illustrates a Mach process. In addition to an address space and threads, it has some ports and other properties. The ports shown in the figure all have special functions. The **process port** is used to communicate with the kernel. Many of the kernel services that a process can request are done by sending a message to the process port, rather than making a system call. This mechanism is used throughout Mach to reduce the actual system calls to a bare minimum. A small number of them will be discussed in this chapter, to give an idea of what they are like.

In general, the programmer is not even aware of whether or not a service requires a system call. All services, including both those accessed by system calls and those accessed by message passing, have stub procedures in the library. It is these procedures that are described in the manuals and called by application programs. The procedures are generated from a service definition by the **MIG (Mach Interface Generator)** compiler.

The **bootstrap port** is used for initialization when a process starts up. The very first process reads the bootstrap port to learn the names of kernel ports that provide essential services. UNIX processes also use it to communicate with the UNIX emulator.

The **exception port** is used to report exceptions caused by the process.

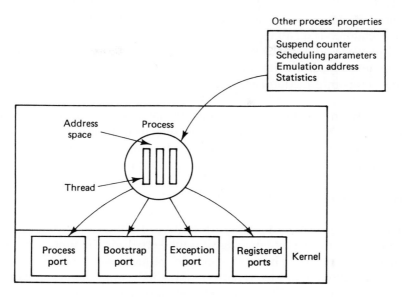

Fig. 8-2. A Mach process.

Typical exceptions are division by zero and illegal instruction executed. The port tells the system where the exception message should be sent. Debuggers also use the exception port.

The **registered ports** are normally used to provide a way for the process to communicate with standard system servers. For example, the name server makes it possible to present a string and get back the corresponding port for certain basic servers.

Processes also have other properties. A process can be runnable or blocked, independent of the state of its threads. If a process is runnable, those threads that are also runnable can be scheduled and run. If a process is blocked, its threads may not run, no matter what state they are in.

The per-process items also include scheduling parameters. These include the ability to specify which processors the process' threads can run on. This feature is most useful on a multiprocessor system. For example, the process can use this power to force each thread to run on a different processor, or to force them all to run on the same processor, or anything in between. In addition, each process has a default priority that is settable. When a thread is created, the new thread is given this priority. It is also possible to change the priority of all the existing threads.

Emulation addresses can be set to tell the kernel where in the process' address space system call handlers are located. The kernel needs to know these addresses to handle UNIX system calls that need to be emulated. These are set once when the UNIX emulator is started up and are inherited by all of the emulator's children (i.e., all the UNIX processes).

Finally, every process has statistics associated with it, including the amount of memory consumed, the run times of the threads, and so on. A process that is interested in this information can acquire it by sending a message to the process port.

It is also worth mentioning what a Mach process does not have. A process does not have a uid, gid, signal mask, root directory, working directory, or file descriptor array, all of which UNIX processes do have. All of this information is managed by the emulation package, so the kernel knows nothing at all about it.

Process Management Primitives

Mach provides a small number of primitives for managing processes. Most of these are done by sending messages to the kernel via the process port, rather than actual system calls. The most important of these calls are shown in Fig. 8-3. These, like all calls in Mach, have prefixes indicating the group they belong to, but we have omitted these here (and in subsequent tables) for the sake of brevity.

Call	Description
Create	Create a new process, inheriting certain properties
Terminate	Kill a specified process
Suspend	Increment suspend counter
Resume	Decrement suspend counter. If it is 0, unblock the process
Priority	Set the priority for current or future threads
Assign	Tell which processor new threads should run on
Info	Return information about execution time, memory usage, etc.
Threads	Return a list of the process' threads

Fig. 8-3. Selected process management calls in Mach.

The first two calls in Fig. 8-3 are for creating and destroying processes, respectively. The process creation call specifies a prototype process, not necessarily the caller. The child is a copy of the prototype, except that the call has a parameter that tells whether or not the child is to inherit the parent's address space. If it does not inherit the parent's address space, objects (e.g., text, initialized data, and a stack) can be mapped in later. Initially, the child has no threads. It does, however, automatically get a process port, a bootstrap port, and an exception port. Other ports are not inherited automatically since each port may have only one reader.

Processes can be suspended and resumed under program control. Each process has a counter, incremented by the *suspend* call and decremented by the *resume* call, that can block or unblock it. When the counter is 0, the process is able to run. When it is positive, it is suspended. Having a counter is more general than just having a bit, and helps avoid race conditions.

The *priority* and *assign* calls give the programmer control over how and where its threads run on multiprocessor systems. CPU scheduling is done using priorities, so the programmer has fine-grain control over which threads are most important and which are least important. The *assign* call makes it possible to control which thread runs on which CPU or group of CPUs.

The last two calls of Fig. 8-3 return information about the process. The former gives statistical information and the latter returns a list of all the threads.

8.2.2. Threads

The active entities in Mach are the threads. They execute instructions and manipulate their registers and address spaces. Each thread belongs to exactly one process. A process cannot do anything unless it has one or more threads.

All the threads in a process share the address space and all the process-wide resources shown in Fig. 8-2. Nevertheless, threads also have private per-thread resources. One of these is the **thread port**, which is analogous to the process port. Each thread has its own thread port, which it uses to invoke thread-specific kernel services, such as exiting when the thread is finished. Since ports are process-wide resources, each thread has access to its siblings' ports, so each thread can control the others if need be.

Mach threads are managed by the kernel, that is, they are what are sometimes called heavyweight threads rather than lightweight threads (pure user space threads). Thread creation and destruction are done by the kernel and involve updating kernel data structures. They provide the basic mechanisms for handling multiple activities within a single address space. What the user does with these mechanisms is up to the user.

On a single CPU system, threads are timeshared, first one running, then another. On a multiprocessor, several threads can be active at the same time. This parallelism makes mutual exclusion, synchronization, and scheduling more important than they normally are, because performance now becomes a major issue, along with correctness. Since Mach is intended to run on multiprocessors, these issues have received special attention.

Like a process, a thread can be runnable or blocked. The mechanism is similar, too: a counter per thread that can be incremented and decremented. When it is zero, the thread is runnable. When it is positive, the thread must wait until another thread lowers it to zero. This mechanism allows threads to control each other's behavior.

A variety of primitives is provided. The basic kernel interface provides about two dozen thread primitives, many of them concerned with controlling scheduling in detail. On top of these primitives one can build various thread packages.

Mach's approach is the **C threads** package. This package is intended to make the kernel thread primitives available to users in a simple and convenient form. It does not have the full power that the kernel interface offers, but it is enough for the average garden-variety programmer. It has also been designed to be portable to a wide variety of operating systems and architectures.

The C threads package provides sixteen calls for direct thread manipulation. The most important ones are listed in Fig. 8-4. The first one, *fork*, creates a new thread in the same address space as the calling thread. It runs the procedure specified by a parameter rather than the parent's code. After the call, the parent thread continues to run in parallel with the child. The thread is started with a priority and on a processor determined by the process' scheduling parameters, as discussed above.

Call	Description
Fork	Create a new thread running the same code as the parent thread
Exit	Terminate the calling thread
Join	Suspend the caller until a specified thread exits
Detach	Announce that the thread will never be jointed (waited for)
Yield	Give up the CPU voluntarily
Self	Return the calling thread's identity to it

Fig. 8-4. The principal C threads calls for direct thread management.

When a thread has done its work, it calls *exit*. If the parent is interested in waiting for the thread to finish, it can call *join* to block itself until a specific child thread terminates. If the thread has already terminated, the parent continues immediately. These three calls are roughly analogous to the FORK, EXIT, and WAITPID system calls in UNIX.

The fourth call, *detach*, does not exist in UNIX. It provides a way to announce that a particular thread will never be waited for. If that thread ever exits, its stack and other state information will be deleted immediately. Normally, this cleanup happens only after the parent has done a successful *join*. In a server, it might be desirable to start up a new thread to service each incoming request. When it has finished, the thread exits. Since there is no need for the initial thread to wait for it, the server thread should be detached.

The *yield* call is a hint to the scheduler that the thread has nothing useful to do at the moment, and is waiting for some event to happen before it can continue. An intelligent scheduler will take the hint and run another thread. In Mach, which normally schedules its threads preemptively, *yield* is only optimization. In systems that have nonpreemptive scheduling, it is essential that a thread that has no work to do release the CPU, to give other threads a chance to run.

Finally, *self* returns the caller's identity, analogous to GETPID in UNIX.

The remaining calls (not shown in the figure), allow threads to be named, allow the program to control the number of threads and the sizes of their stacks, and provide interfaces to the kernel threads and message-passing mechanism.

Synchronization is done using mutexes and condition variables. The mutex primitives are *lock*, *trylock*, and *unlock*. Primitives are also provided to allocate and free mutexes. Mutexes work like binary semaphores, providing mutual exclusion, but not conveying information.

The operations on condition variables are *signal*, *wait*, and *broadcast*, which are used to allow threads to block on a condition and later be awakened when another thread has caused that condition to occur.

Implementation of C Threads in Mach

Various implementations of C threads are available on Mach. The original one did everything in user space inside a single process. This approach timeshared all the C threads over one kernel thread, as shown in Fig. 8-5(a). This approach can also be used on UNIX or any other system that provides no kernel support. The threads were run as coroutines, which means that they were scheduled nonpreemptively. A thread could keep the CPU as long as it wanted or was able to. For the producer-consumer problem, the producer would eventually fill the buffer and then block, giving the consumer a chance to run. For other applications, however, threads had to call *yield* from time to time to give other threads a chance.

The original implementation package suffers from a problem inherent to most user-space threads packages that have no kernel support. If one thread makes a blocking system call, such as reading from the terminal, the whole process is blocked. To avoid this situation, the programmer must avoid blocking system calls. In Berkeley UNIX, there is a call SELECT that can be used to tell whether any characters are pending, but the whole situation is quite messy.

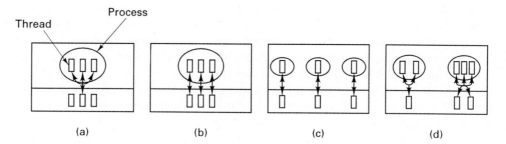

Fig. 8-5. (a) All C threads use one kernel thread. (b) Each C thread has its own kernel thread. (c) Each C thread has its own single-threaded process. (d) Arbitrary mapping of user threads to kernel threads.

A second implementation is to use one Mach thread per C thread, as shown in Fig. 8-5(b). These threads are scheduled preemptively. Furthermore, on a multiprocessor, they may actually run in parallel, on different CPUs. In fact, it is also possible to multiplex m user threads on n kernel threads, although the most common case is $m = n$.

A third implementation package has one thread per process, as shown in Fig. 8-5(c). The processes are set up so that their address spaces all map onto the same physical memory, allowing sharing in the same way as in the previous implementations. This implementation is only used when specialized virtual memory usage is required. The method has the drawback that ports, UNIX files, and other per-process resources cannot be shared, limiting its value appreciably.

The fourth package allows an arbitrary number of user threads to be mapped onto an arbitrary number of kernel threads, as shown in Fig. 8-5(d).

The main practical value of the first approach is that because there is no true parallelism, successive runs give reproducible results, allowing easier debugging. The second approach has the advantage of simplicity and was used for a long time. The third one is not normally used. The fourth one, although the most complicated, gives the greatest flexibility and is the one normally used at present.

8.2.3. Scheduling

Mach scheduling has been heavily influenced by its goal of running on multiprocessors. Since a single-processor system is effectively a special case of a multiprocessor (with only one CPU), our discussion will focus on scheduling in multiprocessor systems. For more information, see (Black, 1990).

The CPUs in a multiprocessor can be assigned to **processor sets** by software. Each CPU belongs to exactly one processor set. Threads can also be assigned to processor sets by software. Thus each processor set has a collection of CPUs at its disposal and a collection of threads that need computing power. The job of the scheduling algorithm is to assign threads to CPUs in a fair and efficient way. For purposes of scheduling, each processor set is a closed world, with its own resources and its own customers, independent of all the other processor sets.

This mechanism gives processes a large amount of control over their threads. A process can assign an important thread to a processor set with one CPU and no other threads, thus ensuring that the thread runs all the time. It can also dynamically reassign threads to processor sets as the work proceeds, keeping the load balanced. While the average compiler is not likely to use this facility, a data base management system or a real-time system might well use it.

Thread scheduling in Mach is based on priorities. Priorities are integers from 0 to some maximum (usually 31 or 127), with 0 being the highest priority and 31 or 127 being the lowest priority. This priority reversal comes from UNIX. Each thread has three priorities assigned to it. The first priority is a base priority, which the thread can set itself, within certain limits. The second priority is the lowest numerical value that the thread may set its base priority to. Since using a higher value gives worse service, a thread will normally set its value to the lowest value it is permitted, unless it is trying intentionally to defer to other threads. The third priority is the current priority, used for scheduling purposes. It is computed by the kernel by adding to the base priority a function based on the thread's recent CPU usage.

Mach threads are visible to the kernel, at least when the model of Fig. 8-5(b) is used. Each thread competes for CPU cycles with all other threads, without regard to which thread is in which process. When making scheduling decisions, the kernel does not take into account which thread belongs to which process.

Associated with each processor set is an array of run queues, as shown in Fig. 8-6. The array has 32 queues, corresponding to threads currently at priorities 0 through 31. When a thread at priority n becomes runnable, it is put at the end of queue n. A thread that is not runnable is not present on any run queue.

Each run queue has three variables attached to it. The first is a mutex that is used to lock the data structure. It is used to make sure that only one CPU at a time is manipulating the queues. The second variable is the count of the number of threads on all the queues combined. If this count becomes 0, there is no work to do. The third variable is a hint as to where to find the highest-priority thread. It is guaranteed that no thread is at a higher priority, but the highest may be at a lower priority. This hint allows the search for the highest-priority thread to avoid the empty queues at the top.

In addition to the global run queues shown in Fig. 8-6, each CPU has its own local run queue. Each local run queue holds those threads that are permanently bound to that CPU, for example, because they are device drivers for I/O devices

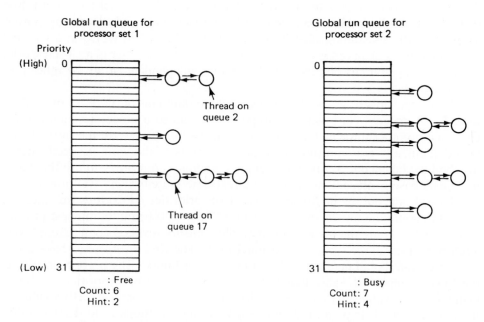

Fig. 8-6. The global run queues for a system with two processor sets.

attached to that CPU. These threads can run on only one CPU, so putting them on the global run queue is incorrect (because the "wrong" CPU might choose them).

We can now describe the basic scheduling algorithm. When a thread blocks, exits, or uses up its quantum, the CPU it is running on first looks on its local run queue to see if there are any active threads. This check merely requires inspecting the count variable associated with the local run queue. If it is nonzero, the CPU begins searching the queue for the highest-priority thread, starting at the queue specified by the hint. If the local run queue is empty, the same algorithm is applied to the global run queue, the only difference being that the global run queue must be locked before it can be searched. If there are no threads to run on either queue, a special idle thread is run until some thread becomes ready.

If a runnable thread is found, it is scheduled and run for one quantum. At the end of the quantum, both the local and global run queues are checked to see if any other threads at its priority or higher are runnable, with the understanding that all threads on the local run queue have higher priority than all threads on the global run queue. If a suitable candidate is found, a thread switch occurs. If not, the thread is run for another quantum. Threads may also be preempted. On multiprocessors, the length of the quantum is variable, depending on the number of threads that are runnable. The more runnable threads and the fewer CPUs there are, the shorter the quantum. This algorithm gives good response time to short requests, even on heavily loaded systems, but provides high efficiency (i.e., long quanta) on lightly loaded systems.

On every clock tick, the CPU increments the priority counter of the currently running thread by a small amount. As the value goes up, the priority goes down and the thread will eventually move to a higher-numbered (i.e., lower-priority) queue. The priority counters are lowered by the passage of time.

For some applications, a large number of threads may be working together to solve a single problem, and it may be important to control the scheduling in detail. Mach provides a hook to give threads some additional control over their scheduling (in addition to the processor sets and priorities). The hook is a system call that allows a thread to lower its priority to the absolute minimum for a specified number of seconds. Doing so gives other threads a chance to run. When the time interval is over, the priority is restored to its previous value.

This system call has another interesting property: it can name its successor if it wants to. For example, after sending a message to another thread, the sending thread can give up the CPU and request that the receiving thread be allowed to run next. This mechanism, called **handoff scheduling**, bypasses the run queues entirely. Used wisely, it can enhance performance. The kernel also uses it in some circumstances, as an optimization.

Mach can be configured to do affinity scheduling, but generally this option is off. When it is on, the kernel schedules a thread on the CPU it last ran on, in hopes that part of its address space is still in that CPU's cache. Affinity scheduling is only applicable to multiprocessors.

Finally, several other scheduling algorithms are supported in some versions, including algorithms useful for real-time applications.

8.3. MEMORY MANAGEMENT IN MACH

Mach has a powerful, elaborate, and highly flexible memory management system based on paging, including features found in few other operating systems. In particular, it separates the machine-independent parts of the memory management system from the machine-dependent parts in an extremely clear and unusual way. This separation makes the memory management far more portable than in other systems. In addition, the memory management system interacts closely with the communication system, which we will discuss in the following section.

The aspect of Mach's memory management that sets it apart from all others is that the code is split into three parts. The first part is the *pmap* module, which runs in the kernel and is concerned with managing the MMU. It sets up the

MMU registers and hardware page tables, and catches all page faults. This code depends on the MMU architecture and must be rewritten for each new MMU Mach has to support. The second part, the machine-independent kernel code, is concerned with processing page faults, managing address maps, and replacing pages.

The third part of the memory management code runs as a user process called a **memory manager** or sometimes an **external pager**. It handles the logical (as opposed to physical) part of the memory management system, primarily management of the backing store (disk). For example, keeping track of which virtual pages are in use, which are in main memory, and where pages are kept on disk when they are not in main memory are all done by the memory manager.

The kernel and the memory manager communicate through a well-defined protocol, making it possible for users to write their own memory managers. This division of labor gives users the ability to implement special-purpose paging systems in order to write systems with special requirements. It also has the potential for making the kernel smaller and simpler by moving a large section of the code out into user space. On the other hand, it has the potential for making it more complicated, since the kernel must protect itself from buggy or malicious memory managers, and with two active entities involved in handling memory, there is now the danger of race conditions.

8.3.1. Virtual Memory

The conceptual model of memory that Mach user processes see is a large, linear virtual address space. For most 32-bit CPU chips, the user address space runs from address 0 to address $2^{31} - 1$ because the kernel uses the top half for its own purposes. The address space is supported by paging. Since paging was designed to give the illusion of ordinary memory, bt more of it than there really is, in principle there should be nothing else to say about how Mach manages virtual address space.

In reality, there is a great deal more to say. Mach provides a great deal of fine-grained control over how the virtual pages are used (for processes that are interested in that). To start with, the address space can be used in a sparse way. For example, a process might have dozens of sections of the virtual address space in use, each many megabytes from its nearest neighbor, with large holes of unused addresses between the sections.

Theoretically, any virtual address space can be used this way, so the ability to use a number of widely scattered sections is not really a property of the virtual address space architecture. In other words, any 32-bit machine should allow a process to have a 50K section of data spaced every 100 megabytes, from 0 to the 4-gigabyte limit. However, in many implementations, a linear page table from 0 to the highest used page is kept in kernel memory. On a machine with a

1K page size, this configuration requires 4 million page table entries, making it expensive, if not impossible. Even with a multilevel page table, such sparse usage is inconvenient at best. With Mach, the intention is to fully support sparse address spaces.

To determine which virtual addresses are in use and which are not, Mach provides a way to allocate and deallocate sections of virtual address space, called **regions**. The allocation call can specify a base address and a size, in which case the indicated region is allocated, or it can just specify a size, in which case the system finds a suitable address range and returns its base address. A virtual address is valid only if it falls in an allocated region. An attempt to use an address between allocated regions results in a trap, which, however, can be caught by the process if it so desires.

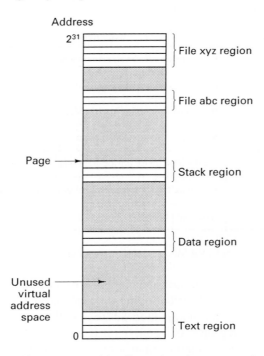

Fig. 8-7. An address space with allocated regions, mapped objects, and unused addresses.

A key concept relating to the use of virtual address space is the **memory object**. A memory object can be a page or a set of pages, but it can also be a file or other, more specialized data structure. A memory object can be mapped into an unused portion of the virtual address space, forming a new region, as shown in Fig. 8-7. When a file is mapped into the virtual address space, it can be read and written by normal machine instructions. Mapped files are paged in the usual way. When a process terminates, its mapped files automatically appear back in the file system, complete with all the changes that were made to them when they were mapped in. It is also possible to unmap files or other memory objects explicitly, freeing their virtual addresses and making them available for subsequent allocation or mapping.

As an aside, file mapping is not the only way to access files. They can also be read the conventional way. However, even then, the library may map the files behind the user's back rather than reading them using the I/O system. Doing so allows the file pages to use the virtual memory system, rather than using dedicated buffers elsewhere in the system.

Mach supports a number of calls for manipulating virtual address spaces. The main ones are listed in Fig. 8-8. None are true system calls. Instead, they all write messages to the caller's process port.

Call	Description
Allocate	Make a region of virtual address space usable
Deallocate	Invalidate a region of virtual address space
Map	Map a memory object into the virtual address space
Copy	Make a copy of a region at another virtual address
Inherit	Set the inheritance attribute for a region
Read	Read data from another process' virtual address space
Write	Write data to another process' virtual address space

Fig. 8-8. Selected Mach calls for managing virtual memory.

The first call, *allocate*, makes a region of virtual address space usable. A process may inherit allocated virtual address space and it may allocate more, but any attempt to reference an unallocated address will fail. The second call, *deallocate*, invalidates a region (i.e., removes it from the memory map), thus making it possible to allocate it again or map something into it, using the *map* call.

The *copy* call copies a memory object onto a new region. The original remains unchanged. In this way, a single memory object can appear multiple times in the address space. Conceptually, calling *copy* is no different than having the object copied by a programmed loop. However *copy* is implemented in an optimized way, using shared pages, to avoid physical copying.

The *inherit* call affects the way that regions are inherited when new processes are created. The address space can be set up so that some regions are inherited and others are not. It will be discussed in the next section.

The *read* and *write* calls allow a thread to access virtual memory belonging to another process. These calls require the caller to have possession of the process port belonging to the remote process, something that process can pass to its friends if it wants to.

In addition to the calls listed in Fig. 8-8, a few other calls also exist. These calls are concerned primarily with getting and setting attributes, protection modes, and various kinds of statistical information.

8.3.2. Memory Sharing

Sharing plays an important role in Mach. No special mechanism is needed for the threads in a process to share objects: they all see the same address space automatically. If one of them has access to a piece of data, they all do. More interesting is the possibility of two or more processes sharing the same memory objects, or just sharing data pages, for that matter. Sometimes sharing is important on single CPU systems. For example, in the classical producer-consumer problem, it may be desirable to have the producer and consumer be different processes, yet share a common buffer so that the producer can put data into the buffer and the consumer can take data out of it.

On multiprocessor systems, sharing of objects between two or more processes is frequently even more important. In many cases, a single problem is being solved by a collection of cooperating processes running in parallel on different CPUs (as opposed to being timeshared on a single CPU). These processes may need access to buffers, tables, or other data structures continuously, in order to do their work. It is essential that the operating system allow this sharing to take place. Early versions of UNIX did not have this ability, for example, although it was added later.

Consider, for example, a system that analyzes digitized satellite images of the earth in real time, as they are transmitted to the ground. Such analysis is time consuming, and the same picture has to be examined for use in weather forecasting, predicting crop harvests, and tracking pollution. As each picture is received, it is stored as a file.

A multiprocessor is available to do the analysis. Since the meteorological, agricultural, and environmental programs are all quite different, and were written by different people, it is not reasonable to make them threads of the same process. Instead, each is a separate process, and each maps the current photograph into its address space, as shown in Fig. 8-9. Note that the file containing the photograph may be mapped in at a different virtual address in each process. Although each page is present in memory only once, it may appear in each process' page map at a different place. In this manner, all three processes can work on the same file at the same time in a convenient way.

Another important use of sharing is process creation. As in UNIX, in Mach

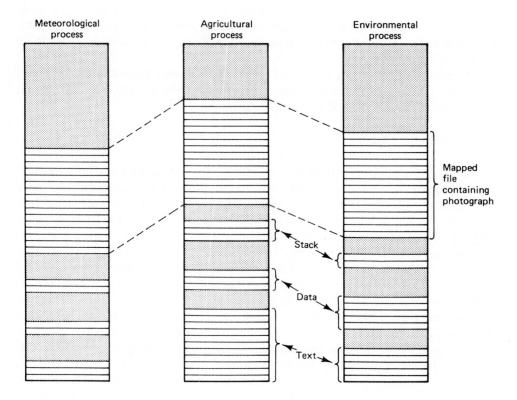

Fig. 8-9. Three processes sharing a mapped file.

the basic way for a new process to be created is as a copy of an existing process. In UNIX, a copy is always a clone of the process executing the FORK system call, whereas in Mach the child can be a clone of a different process (the prototype). Either way, the child is a copy of some other process.

One way to create the child is to copy all the pages needed and map the copies into the child's address space. Although this method is valid, it is unnecessarily expensive. The program text is normally read-only, so it cannot change, and parts of the data may also be read-only. There is no reason to copy read-only pages, since mapping them into both processes will do the job. Writable pages cannot always be shared because the semantics of process creation (at least in UNIX) say that although at the moment of creation the parent and child are identical, subsequent changes to either one are not visible in the other's address space.

In addition, some regions (e.g., certain mapped files) may not be needed in the child. Why go to a lot of trouble to arrange for them to be present in the child if they are not needed there?

To achieve these various goals, Mach allows processes to assign an **inheritance attribute** to each region in its address space. Different regions may have different attributes. Three values are provided:

1. The region is unused in the child process.

2. The region is shared between the prototype process and the child.

3. The region in the child process is a copy of the prototype.

If a region has the first value, the corresponding region in the child is unallocated. References to it are treated as references to any other unallocated memory—they generate traps. The child is free to allocate the region for its own purposes or to map a memory object there.

The second option is true sharing. The pages of the region are present in both the prototype's address space and the child's. Changes made by either one are visible to the other. This choice is not used for implementing the FORK system call in UNIX, but is frequently useful for other purposes.

The third possibility is to copy all the pages in the region and map the copies into the child's address space. FORK uses this option. Actually, Mach does not really copy the pages but uses a clever trick called **copy-on-write** instead. It places all the necessary pages in the child's virtual memory map, but marks them all read-only, as illustrated in Fig. 8-10. As long as the child makes only read references to these pages, everything works fine.

However, if the child attempts to write on any page, a protection fault occurs. The operating system then makes a copy of the page and maps the copy into the child's address space, replacing the read-only page that was there. The new page is marked read-write. In Fig. 8-10(b), the child has attempted to write to page 7. This action has resulted in page 7 being copied to page 8, and page 8 being mapped into the address space in place of page 7. Page 8 is marked read-write, so subsequent writes do not trap.

Copy-on-write has several advantages over doing all the copying at the time the new process is created. First, some pages are read-only, so there is no need to copy them. Second, other pages may never be referenced, so even if they are potentially writable, they do not have to be copied. Third, still other pages may be writable, but the child may deallocate them rather than using them. Here too, avoiding a copy is worthwhile. In this manner, only those pages that the child actually writes on have to be copied.

Copy-on-write also has some disadvantages. For one thing, the administration is more complicated, since the system must keep track of the fact that some pages are genuinely read-only, with a write being a programming error, whereas other pages are to be copied if written. For another, copy-on-write requires multiple kernel traps, one for each page that is ultimately written. Depending on the

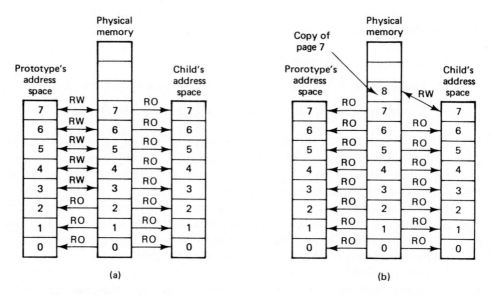

Fig. 8-10. Operation of copy-on-write. (a) After the FORK, all the child's pages are marked read-only. (b) When the child writes page 7, a copy is made.

hardware, one kernel trap followed by a multipage copy may not be that much more expensive than multiple kernel traps, each followed by a one-page copy. Finally, copy-on-write does not work over a network. Physical transport is always needed.

8.3.3. External Memory Managers

At the start of our discussion on memory management in Mach we briefly mentioned the existence of user-level memory managers. Let us now take a deeper look at them. Each memory object that is mapped in a process' address space must have an external memory manager that controls it. Different classes of memory objects are handled by different memory managers. Each of these can implement its own semantics, can determine where to store pages that are not in memory, and can provide its own rules about what becomes of objects after they are mapped out.

To map an object into a process' address space, the process sends a message to a memory manager asking it to do the mapping. Three ports are needed to do the job. The first, the **object port**, is created by the memory manager and will later be used by the kernel to inform the memory manager about page faults and other events relating to the object. The second, the **control port**, is created by the kernel itself so that the memory manager can respond to these events (many require some action on the memory manager's part). The use of distinct ports is due to the fact that ports are unidirectional. The object port is written by the kernel and read by the memory manager; the control port works the other way around. The third port, the **name port**, is used as a kind of name to identify the object. For example, a thread can give the kernel a virtual address and ask which region it belongs to. The answer is a pointer to the name port. If addresses belong to the same region, they will be identified by the same name port.

When the memory manager maps in an object, it provides the capability for the object port as one of the parameters. The kernel then creates the other two ports and sends an initial message to the object port telling it about the control and name ports. The memory manager then sends back a reply telling the kernel what the object's attributes are, and informing it whether or not to keep the object in its cache after it is unmapped. Initially, all the object's pages are marked as unreadable/unwritable, to force a trap on the first use.

At this point the memory manager does a read on the object port and blocks. The memory manager remains idle until the kernel requests it to do something by writing a message to the object port. The thread that mapped the object in is now unblocked and allowed to execute.

Sooner or later, the thread will undoubtedly attempt to read or write a page belonging to the memory object. This operation will cause a page fault and a trap to the kernel. The kernel will then send a message to the memory manager via the object port, telling it which page has been referenced and asking it to please provide the page. This message is asynchronous because the kernel does not dare to block any of its threads waiting for a user process that may not reply. While waiting for a reply, the kernel suspends the faulting thread and looks for another thread to run.

When the memory manager hears about the page fault, it checks to see if the reference is legal. If not, it sends the kernel an error message. If it is legal, the memory manager gets the page by whatever method is appropriate for the object in question. If the object is a file, the memory manager seeks to the correct address and reads the page into its own address space. It then sends a reply back to the kernel providing a pointer to the page. The kernel maps the page into the faulting thread's address space, The thread can now be unblocked. This process is repeated as often as necessary to load all the pages needed.

To make sure that there is a steady supply of free page frames, a paging daemon thread in the kernel wakes up from time to time and checks the state of memory. If there are not enough free page frames, it picks a page to free using the second-chance algorithm. If the page is clean, it is normally just discarded. If the page is dirty, the daemon sends it to the memory manager in charge of the page's object. The memory manager is expected to write the page to disk and tell when it is done. If the page belongs to a file, the memory manager will first seek to the page's offset in the file, then write it there.

Pages can be marked as **precious**, in which cases they will never be just discarded, even if they are clean. They will always be returned to their memory manager. Precious pages can be used, for example, for pages shared over the network for which there is only one copy which must never be discarded. Communication can also be initiated by the memory manager, for example, when a SYNC system call is done to flush the cache back to disk.

It is worth noting that the paging daemon is part of the kernel. Although the page replacement algorithm is completely machine independent, with a memory full of pages owned by different memory managers, there is no suitable way to let one of them decide which page to evict. The only method that might be possible is to statically partition the page frames among the various managers and let each one do page replacement on its set. However, since global algorithms are generally more efficient than local ones, this approach was not taken. Subsequent work has investigated this subject (Harty and Cheriton, 1992; and Subramian, 1991).

In addition to the memory managers for mapped files and other specialized objects, there is also a default memory manager for "ordinary" paged memory. When a process allocates a region of virtual address space using the *allocate* call, it is in fact mapping an object managed by the default manager. This manager provides zero-filled pages as needed. It uses a temporary file for swap space, rather than a separate swap area as UNIX does.

To make the idea of an external memory manager work, a strict protocol must be used for communication between the kernel and the memory managers. This protocol consists of a small number of messages that the kernel can send to a memory manager, and a small number of replies the memory manager can send back to the kernel. All communication is initiated by the kernel in the form of an asynchronous message on an object port for some memory object. Later, the memory manager sends an asynchronous reply on the control port.

Figure 8-11 lists the principal message types that the kernel sends to memory managers. When an object is mapped in using the *map* call of Fig. 8-8, the kernel sends an *init* message to the appropriate memory manager to let it initialize itself. The message specifies the ports to be used for discussing the object later. Requests from the kernel to ask for a page and deliver a page use *data_request* and *data_write* respectively. These handle the page traffic in both directions, and as such are the most important calls.

Data_unlock is a request from the kernel for the memory manager to unlock a locked page so that the kernel can use it for another process. *Lock_completed* signals the end of a *lock_request* sequence, and will be described below. Finally, *terminate* tells the memory manager that the object named in the message is no longer in use and can be removed from memory. Some calls that are

Call	Description
Init	Initialize a newly mapped-in memory object
Data_request	Give kernel a specific page to handle a page fault
Data_write	Take a page from memory and write it out
Data_unlock	Unlock a page so kernel can use it
Lock_completed	Previous Lock_request has been completed
Terminate	Be informed that this object is no longer in use

Fig. 8-11. Selected message types from the kernel to the external memory managers.

specific to the default memory manager also exist, as well as a few managing attributes and error handling.

The messages in Fig. 8-11 go from the kernel to the memory manager. The replies listed in Fig. 8-12 go the other way, from the memory manager back to the kernel. They are replies that the memory manager can use to respond to the above requests.

Call	Description
Set_attributes	Reply to Init
Data_provided	Here is the requested page (Reply to Data_request)
Data_unavailable	No page is available (Reply to Data_request)
Lock_request	Ask kernel to clean, flush, or lock pages
Destroy	Destroy an object that is no longer needed

Fig. 8-12. Selected message types from the external memory managers to the kernel.

The first one, *set_attributes*, is a reply to *init*. It tells the kernel that it is ready to handle a newly mapped-in object. The reply also provides mode bits for the object and tells the kernel whether or not to cache the object, even if no process currently has it mapped in. The next two are replies to *data_request*. That call asks the memory manager to provide a page. Which reply it gives depends on whether or not it can provide the page. The former supplies the page; the latter does not.

Lock_request allows the memory manager to ask the kernel to make certain pages clean, that is, send it the pages so that they can be written to disk. This call can also be used to change the protection mode on pages (read, write, execute). Finally, *destroy* is used to tell the kernel that a certain object is no longer needed.

It is worth noting that when the kernel sends a message to a memory manager, it is effectively making an upcall. Although flexibility is gained this way, some system designers consider it inelegant for the kernel to call user programs to perform services for it. These people usually believe in hierarchical systems, with the lower layers providing services to the upper layers, not vice versa.

8.3.4. Distributed Shared Memory in Mach

The Mach external memory manager concept lends itself well to implementing a page-based distributed shared memory. In this section we will briefly describe some of the work done in this area. For more details, see (Forin et al., 1989). To review the basic concept, the idea is to have a single, linear, virtual address space that is shared among processes running on computers that do not have any physical shared memory. When a thread references a page that it does not have, it causes a page fault. Eventually, the page is located and shipped to the faulting machine, where it is installed so that the thread can continue executing.

Since Mach already has memory managers for different classes of objects, it is natural to introduce a new memory object, the shared page. Shared pages are managed by one or more special memory managers. One possibility is to have a single memory manager that handles all shared pages. Another is to have a different one for each shared page or collection of shared pages, to spread the load around.

Still another possibility is to have different memory managers for pages with different semantics. For example, one memory manager could guarantee complete memory coherence, meaning that any read following a write always sees the most recent data. Another memory manager could offer weaker semantics, for example, that a read never returns data that are more than 30 seconds out of date.

Let us consider the most basic case: one shared page, centralized control, and complete memory coherence. All other pages are local to a single machine. To implement this model, we need one memory manager that serves all the machines in the system. Let us call it the DSM (Distributed Shared Memory) server. The DSM server handles references to the shared page. Conventional memory managers handle the other pages. Up until now we have tacitly assumed that the memory manager or managers that service a machine must be local to that machine. In fact, because communication is transparent in Mach, a memory manager need not reside on the machine whose memory it is managing.

The shared page is always either readable or writable. If it is readable, it may be replicated on multiple machines. If it is writable, there is only one copy. The DSM server always knows the state of the shared page as well as which machine or machines it is currently on. If the page is readable, DSM has a valid copy itself.

Suppose that the page is readable and a thread somewhere tries to read it. The DSM server just sends that machine a copy, updates its tables to indicate one more reader, and is finished. The page will be mapped in on the new machine for reading.

Now suppose that one of the readers tries to write the page. The DSM server sends a message to the kernel or kernels that have the page asking for it back. The page itself need not be transferred, because the DSM server has a valid copy itself. All that is needed is an acknowledgement that the page is no longer in use. When all the kernels have released the page, the writer is given a copy along with exclusive permission to use it (for writing).

If somebody else now wants the page (when it is writable), the DSM server tells the current owner to stop using it and to send it back. When the page arrives, it can be given to one or more readers or one writer. Many variations on this centralized algorithm are possible, such as not asking for a page back until the machine currently using it has had it for some minimum time. A distributed solution is also possible.

8.4. COMMUNICATION IN MACH

The goal of communication in Mach is to support a variety of styles of communication in a reliable and flexible way (Draves, 1990). It can handle asynchronous message passing, RPC, byte streams, and other forms as well. Mach's interprocess communication mechanism is based on that of its ancestors, RIG and Accent. Due to this evolution, the mechanism used has been optimized for the local case (one node) rather than the remote case (distributed system).

We will first explain the single-node case in considerable detail, and then come back to how it has been extended for networking. It should be noted that in these terms, a multiprocessor is a single node, so communication between processes on different CPUs within the same multiprocessor uses the local case.

8.4.1. Ports

The basis of all communication in Mach is a kernel data structure called a **port**. A port is essentially a protected mailbox. When a thread in one process wants to communicate with a thread in another process, the sending thread writes the message to the port and the receiving thread takes it out. Each port is protected to ensure that only authorized processes can send to it and receive from it.

Ports support unidirectional communication, like pipes in UNIX. A port that can be used to send a request from a client to a server cannot also be used to send the reply back from the server to the client. A second port is needed for the reply.

Ports support reliable, sequenced, message streams. If a thread sends a message to a port, the system guarantees that it will be delivered. Messages are never lost due to errors, overflow, or other causes (at least if there are no crashes). Messages sent by a single thread are also guaranteed to be delivered in the order sent. If two threads write to the same port in an interleaved fashion, taking turns, the system does not provide any guarantee about message sequencing, since some buffering may take place in the kernel due to locking and other factors.

Unlike pipes, ports support message streams, not byte streams. Messages are never concatenated. If a thread writes five 100-byte messages to a port, the receiver will always see them as five distinct messages, never as a single 500-byte message. Of course, higher-level software can ignore the message boundaries if they are not important to it.

A port is shown in Fig. 8-13. When a port is created, 64 bytes of kernel storage space are allocated and maintained until the port is destroyed, either explicitly, or implicitly under certain conditions, for example, when all the processes that are using it have exited. The port contains the fields shown in Fig. 8-13 and a few others.

Messages are not actually stored in the port itself but in another kernel data structure, the **message queue**. The port contains a count of the number of messages currently present in the message queue and the maximum permitted. If the port belongs to a port set, a pointer to the port set data structure is present in the port. As we mentioned briefly above, a process can give other processes capabilities to use its ports. For various reasons, the kernel has to know how many capabilities of each type are outstanding, so the port stores the counts.

If certain errors occur when using the port, they are reported by sending messages to other ports whose capabilities are stored there. Threads can block when reading from a port, so a pointer to the list of blocked threads is included. It is also important to be able to find the capability for reading from the port (there can only be one), so that information is present too. If the port is a process port, the next field holds a pointer to the process it belongs to. If it is a thread port, the field holds a pointer to the kernel's data structure for the thread, and so on. A few miscellaneous fields not described here are also needed.

When a thread creates a port, it gets back an integer identifying the port, analogous to a file descriptor in UNIX. This integer is used in subsequent calls

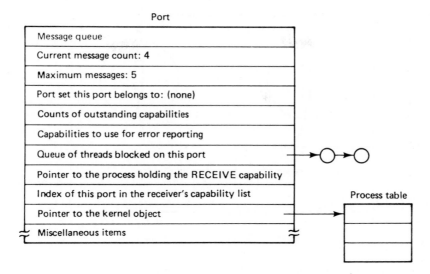

Fig. 8-13. A Mach port.

that send messages to the port or receive messages from it in order to identify which port is to be used. Ports are kept track of per process, not per thread, so if one thread creates a port and gets back the integer 3 to identify it, another thread in the same process will never get 3 to identify its new port. The kernel, in fact, does not even maintain a record of which thread created which port.

A thread can pass port access to another thread in a different process. Clearly, it cannot do so merely by putting the appropriate integer in a message, any more than a UNIX process can pass a file descriptor for standard output through a pipe by writing the integer 1 to the pipe. The exact mechanism used is protected by the kernel and will be discussed later. For the moment, it is sufficient to know that it can be done.

In Fig. 8-14 we see a situation in which two processes, A and B, each have access to the same port. A has just sent a message to the port, and B has just read the message. The header and body of the message are physically copied from A to the port and later from the port to B.

Ports may be grouped into **port sets** for convenience. A port may belong to at most one port set. It is possible to read from a port set (but not write to one). A server, for example, can use this mechanism to read from a large number of ports at the same time. The kernel returns one message from one of the ports in the set. No promises are made about which port will be selected. If all the ports are empty, the server is blocked. In this way a server can maintain a different port for each of the many objects that it supports, and get messages for any of

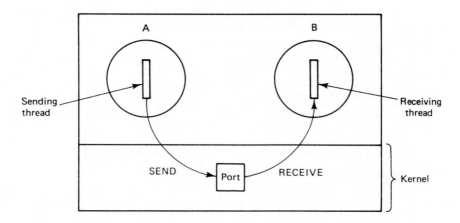

Fig. 8-14. Message passing goes via a port.

them without having to dedicate a thread to each one. The current implementation queues all the messages for the port set onto a single chain. In practice, the only difference between receiving from a port and receiving from a port set is that in the latter, the actual port sent to is identified to the receiver and in the former it is not.

Some ports are used in special ways. Every process has a special **process port** that it needs to communicate with the kernel. Most of the "system calls" associated with processes (see Fig. 8-3) are done by writing messages to this port. Similarly, each thread also has its own port for doing the "system calls" related to threads. Communication with I/O drivers also uses the port mechanism.

Capabilities

To a first approximation, for each process, the kernel maintains a table of all ports to which the process has access. This table is kept safely inside the kernel, where user processes cannot get at it. Processes refer to ports by their position in this table, that is, entry 1, entry 2, and so on. These table entries are effectively classical capabilities. We will refer to them as capabilities and will call the table containing the capabilities a **capability list**.

Each process has exactly one capability list. When a thread asks the kernel to create a port for it, the kernel does so and enters a capability for it in the capability list for the process to which the thread belongs. The calling thread and all the other threads in the same process have equal access to the capability. The integer returned to the thread to identify the capability is usually an index into the capability list (but it can also be a large integer, such as a machine address). We will refer to this integer as a **capability name**, (or sometimes just a capability, where the context makes it clear that we mean the index and not the capability itself). It is always a 32-bit integer, never a string.

Each capability consists not only of a pointer to a port, but also a rights field telling what access the holder of the capability has to the port. (All the threads in a process are equally considered holders of the process' capabilities.) Three rights exist: RECEIVE, SEND, and SEND-ONCE. The RECEIVE right gives the holder the ability to read messages from the port. Earlier we mentioned that communication in Mach is unidirectional. What this really means is that at any instant only one process may have the RECEIVE right for a port. A capability with a RECEIVE right may be transferred to another process, but doing so causes it to be removed from the sender's capability list. Thus for each port there is a single potential receiver.

A capability with the SEND right allows the holder to send messages to the specified port. Many processes may hold capabilities to send to a port. This situation is roughly analogous to the banking system in most countries: anyone who knows a bank account number can deposit money to that account, but only the owner can make withdrawals.

The SEND-ONCE right also allows a message to be sent, but only one time. After the send is done, the kernel destroys the capability. This mechanism is used for request-reply protocols. For example, a client wants something from a server, so it creates a port for the reply message. It then sends the server a request message containing a (protected) capability for the reply port with the SEND-ONCE right. After the server sends the reply, the capability is deallocated from its capability list and the name is made available for a new capability in the future.

Capability names have meaning only within a single process. It is possible for two processes to have access to the same port but use different names for it, just as two UNIX processes may have access to the same open file but use different file descriptors to read it. In Fig. 8-15 both processes have a capability to send to port Y, but in A it is capability 3 and in B it is capability 4.

A capability list is tied to a specific process. When that process exits or is killed, its capability list is removed. Ports for which it holds a capability with the RECEIVE right are no longer usable and are therefore also destroyed, even if they contain undelivered (and now undeliverable) messages.

If different threads in a process acquire the same capability multiple times, only one entry is made in the capability list. To keep track of how many times each is present, the kernel maintains a reference count for each port. When a capability is deleted, the reference count is decremented. Only when it gets to zero is the capability actually removed from the capability list. This mechanism

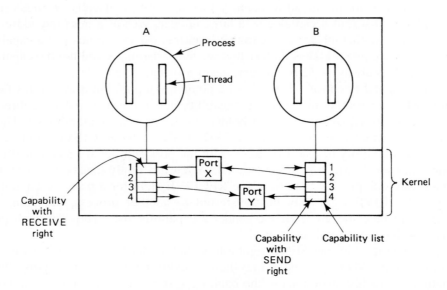

Fig. 8-15. Capability lists.

is important because different threads may acquire and release capabilities without each other's knowledge, for example, the UNIX emulation library and the program being run.

Each capability list entry is one of the following four items:

1. A capability for a port.

2. A capability for a port set.

3. A null entry.

4. A code indicating that the port that was there is now dead.

The first possibility has already been explained in some detail. The second allows a thread to read from a set of ports without even being aware that the capability name is backed up by a set rather than by a single port. The third is a place holder that indicates that the corresponding entry is not currently in use. If an entry is allocated for a port that is later destroyed, the capability is replaced by a null entry to mark it as unused.

Finally, the fourth option marks ports that no longer exist but for which capabilities with SEND rights still exist. When a port is deleted, for example, because the process holding the RECEIVE capability for it has exited, the kernel tracks down all the SEND capabilities and marks them as dead. Attempts to send to null and dead capabilities fail with an appropriate error code. When all the SEND capabilities for a port are gone, for whatever reasons, the kernel (optionally) sends a message notifying the receiver that there are no senders left and no messages will be forthcoming.

Primitives for Managing Ports

Mach provides about 20 calls for managing ports. All of these are invoked by sending a message to a process port. A sampling of the most important ones is given in Fig. 8-16.

Call	Description
Allocate	Create a port and insert its capability in the capability list
Destroy	Destroy a port and remove its capability from the list
Deallocate	Remove a capability from the capability list
Extract_right	Extract the n-th capability from another process
Insert_right	Insert a capability in another process' capability list
Move_member	Move a capability into a capability set
Set_qlimit	Set the number of messages a port can hold

Fig. 8-16. Selected port management calls in Mach.

The first one, *allocate*, creates a new port and enters its capability into the caller's capability list. The capability is for reading from the port. A capability name is returned so that the port can be used.

The next two undo the work of the first. *Destroy* removes a capability. If it is a RECEIVE capability, the port is destroyed and all other capabilities for it in all processes are marked as dead. *Deallocate* decrements the reference count associated with a capability. If it is zero, the capability is removed but the port remains intact. *Deallocate* can only be used to remove SEND or SEND-ONCE capabilities or dead capabilities.

Extract_right allows a thread to select out a capability from another process' capability list and insert the capability in its own list. Of course, the calling thread needs access to the process port controlling the other process (e.g., its own child). *Insert_right* goes the other way. It allows a process to take one of its own capabilities and add it to (for example) a child's capability list.

The *move_member* call is used for managing port sets. It can add a port to a port set or remove one. Finally, *set_qlimit* determines the number of messages a port can hold. When a port is created, the default is five messages, but with this call that number can be increased or decreased. The messages can be of any size since they are not physically stored in the port itself.

8.4.2. Sending and Receiving Messages

The purpose of having ports is to send messages to them. In this section we will look at how messages are sent, how they are received, and what they contain. Mach has a single system call for sending and receiving messages. The call is wrapped in a library procedure called *mach_msg*. It has seven parameters and a large number of options. To give an idea of its complexity, there are 35 different error messages that it can return. Below we will give a simplified sketch of some of its possibilities. Fortunately, it is used primarily in procedures generated by the stub compiler, rather than being written by hand.

The *mach_msg* call is used for both sending and receiving. It can send a message to a port and then return control to the caller immediately, at which time the caller can modify the message buffer without affecting the data sent. It can also try to receive a message from a port, blocking if the port is empty, or giving up after a certain interval. Finally, it can combine these two operations, first sending a message and then blocking until a reply comes back. In the latter mode, *mach_msg* can be used for RPC.

A typical call to *mach_msg* looks like this:

```
mach_msg(&hdr,options,send_size,rcv_size,rcv_port,timeout,notify_port);
```

The first parameter, *hdr*, is a pointer to the message to be sent or to the place where the incoming message is put, or both. The message begins with a fixed header and is followed directly by the message body. This layout is shown in Fig. 8-17. We will explain the details of the message format later, but for the moment just note that the header contains a capability name for the destination port. This information is needed so that the kernel can tell where to send the message. When doing a pure RECEIVE, the header is not filled in, since it will be overwritten entirely by the incoming message.

The second parameter of the *mach_msg* call, *options*, contains a bit specifying that a message is to be sent, and another one specifying that a message is to be received. If both are on, an RPC is done. Another bit enables a timeout, given by the *timeout* parameter, in milliseconds. If the requested operation cannot be performed within the timeout interval, the call returns with an error code. If the SEND portion of an RPC times out (e.g., due to the destination port being full too long), the RECEIVE is not even attempted.

Other bits in *options* allow a SEND that cannot complete immediately to return control anyway, with a status report being sent to *notify_port* later. All kinds of errors can occur here if the capability for *notify_port* is unsuitable or

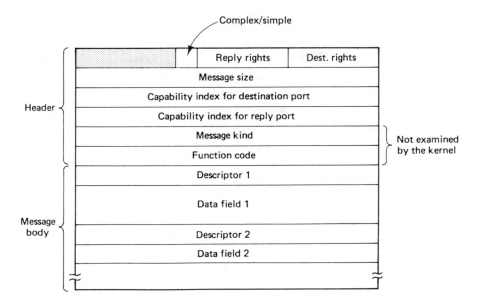

Fig. 8-17. The Mach message format.

changed before the notification can occur. It is even possible for the call to ruin *notify_port* itself (calls can have complex side effects, as we will see later).

The *mach_msg* call can be aborted part-way through by a software interrupt. Another *options* bit tells whether to give up or try again.

The *send_size* and *rcv_size* parameters tell how large the outgoing message is and how many bytes are available for storing the incoming message, respectively. *Rcv_port* is used for receiving messages. It is the capability name of the port or port set being listened to.

Now let us turn to the message format of Fig. 8-17. The first word contains a bit telling whether the message is simple or complex. The difference is that simple messages cannot carry capabilities or protected pointers, whereas complex ones can. Simple messages require less work on the part of the kernel and are therefore more efficient. Both message types have a system-defined structure, described below. The *message size* field tells how big the combined header plus body is. This information is needed both for transmission and by the receiver.

Next come two capability names (i.e., indices into the sender's capability list). The first specifies the destination port; the second can give a reply port. In client-server RPC, for example, the destination field designates the server and the reply field tells the server which port to send the response to.

The last two header fields are not used by the kernel. Higher levels of software can use them as desired. By convention, they are used to specify the kind of message and give a function code or operation code (e.g., to a server, is this request for reading or for writing?). This usage is subject to change in the future.

When a message is sent and successfully received, it is copied into the destination's address space. It can happen, however, that the destination port is already full. What happens then depends on the various options and the rights associated with the destination port. One possibility is that the sender is blocked and simply waits until space becomes available in the port. Another is that the sender times out. In some cases, it can exceed the port limit and send anyway.

A few issues concerning receiving messages are worth mentioning. For one, if an incoming message is larger than the buffer, what should be done with it? Two options are provided: throw it away or have the *mach_msg* call fail but return the size, thus allowing the caller to try again with a bigger size.

If multiple threads are blocked trying to read from the same port and a message arrives, one of them is chosen by the system to get the message. The rest remain blocked. If the port being read from is actually a port set, it is possible for the composition of the set to change while one or more threads are blocked on it. This is probably not the place to go into all the details, but suffice it to say that there are precise rules governing this and similar situations.

Message Formats

A message body can be either simple or complex, controlled by a header bit, as mentioned above. Complex messages are structured as shown in Fig. 8-17. A complex message body consists of a sequence of (descriptor, data field) pairs. Each descriptor tells what is in the data field immediately following it. Descriptors come in two formats, differing only in how many bits each of the fields contains. The normal descriptor format is illustrated in Fig. 8-18. It specifies the type of the item that follows, how large an item is, and how many of them there are (a data field may contain multiple items of the same type). The available types include raw bits and bytes, integers of various sizes, unstructured machine words, collections of Booleans, floating-point numbers, strings, and capabilities. Armed with this information, the system can attempt to do conversions between machines when the source and destination machines have different internal representations. This conversion is not done by the kernel but by the network message server (described below). It is also done for internode transport even for simple messages (also by the network message server).

One of the more interesting items that can be contained in a data field is a capability. Using complex messages it is possible to copy or transfer a capability from one process to another. Because capabilities are protected kernel objects in Mach, a protected mechanism is needed to move them about.

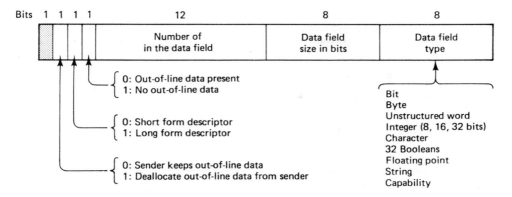

Fig. 8-18. A complex message field descriptor.

This mechanism is as follows. A descriptor can specify that the word directly after it in the message contains the name for one of the sender's capabilities, and that this capability is to be passed to the receiving process and inserted in the receiver's capability list. The descriptor also specifies whether the capability is to be copied (the original is not touched) or moved (the original is deleted).

Furthermore, certain values of the *Data field type* ask the kernel to modify the capability's rights while doing the copy or move. A RECEIVE capability, for example, can be mutated into a SEND or SEND-ONCE capability, so that the receiver will have the power to send a reply to a port for which the sender has only a RECEIVE capability. In fact, the normal way to establish communication between two processes is to have one of them create a port and then send the port's RECEIVE capability to the other one, turning it into a SEND capability in flight.

To see how capability transport works, consider Fig. 8-19(a). Here we see two processes, *A* and *B*, with 3 capabilities and 1 capability, respectively. All are RECEIVE capabilities. Numbering starts at 1 since entry 0 is the null port. One of the threads in *A* is sending a message to *B* containing capability 3.

When the message arrives, the kernel inspects the header and sees that it is a complex message. It then begins processing the descriptors in the message body, one by one. In this example there is only one descriptor, for a capability, with instructions to turn it into a SEND (or maybe SEND-ONCE) capability. The kernel allocates a free slot in the receiver's capability list, slot 2 in this example, and modifies the message so that the word following the descriptor is now 2 instead of 3. When the receiver gets the message, it sees that it has a new capability, with name (index) 2. It can use this capability immediately (e.g., for sending a reply message).

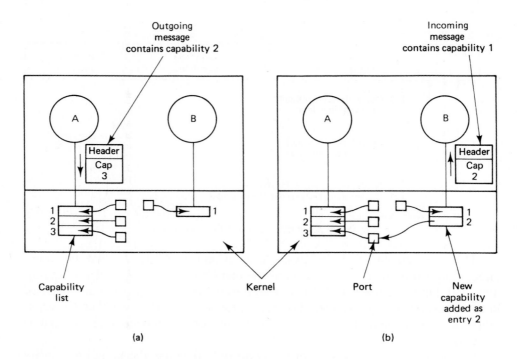

Fig. 8-19. (a) Situation just before the capability is sent. (b) Situation after it has arrived.

There is one last aspect of Fig. 8-18 that we have not yet discussed: **out-of-line data**. Mach provides a way to transfer bulk data from a sender to a receiver without doing any copying (on a single machine or multiprocessor). If the out-of-line data bit is set in the descriptor, the word following the descriptor contains an address, and the size and number fields of the descriptor give a 20-bit byte count. Together these specify a region of the sender's virtual address space. For larger regions, the long form of the descriptor is used.

When the message arrives at the receiver, the kernel chooses an unallocated piece of virtual address space the same size as the out-of-line data, and maps the sender's pages into the receiver's address space, marking them copy-on-write. The address word following the descriptor is changed to reflect the address at which the region is located in the receiver's address space. This mechanism provides a way to move blocks of data at extremely high speed, because no copying is required except for the message header and the two-word body (the descriptor and the address). Depending on a bit in the descriptor, the region is either removed from the sender's address space or kept there.

Although this method is highly efficient for copies between processes on a single machine (or between CPUs in a multiprocessor), it is not as useful for communication over a network because the pages must be copied if they are used, even if they are only read. Thus the ability to transmit data logically without moving physically them is lost. Copy-on-write also requires that messages be aligned on page boundaries and be an integral number of pages in length for best results. Fractional pages allow the receiver to see data before or after the out-of-line data that it should not see.

8.4.3. The Network Message Server

Everything we have said so far about communication in Mach is limited to communication within a single node, either one CPU or a multiprocessor node. Communication over the network is handled by user-level servers called **network message servers**, which are vaguely analogous to the external memory managers we studied earlier. Every machine in a Mach distributed system runs a network message server. The network message servers work together to handle intermachine messages, trying to simulate intramachine messages as best they can.

A network message server is a multithreaded process that performs a variety of functions. These include interfacing with local threads, forwarding messages over the network, translating data types from one machine's representation to another's, managing capabilities in a secure way, doing remote notification, providing a simple network-wide name lookup service, and handling authentication of other network message servers. Network message servers can speak a variety of protocols, depending on the networks to which they are attached.

The basic method by which messages are sent over the network is illustrated in Fig. 8-20. Here we have a client on machine *A* and a server on machine *B*. Before the client can contact the server, a port must be created on *A* to function as a proxy for the server. The network message server has the RECEIVE capability for this port. A thread inside it is constantly listening to this port (and other remote ports, which together form a port set). This port is shown as the small box in *A*'s kernel.

Message transport from the client to the server requires five steps, numbered 1 to 5 in Fig. 8-20. First, the client sends a message to the server's proxy port. Second, the network message server gets this message. Since this message is strictly local, out-of-line data may be sent to it and copy-on-write works in the usual way. Third, the network message server looks up the local port, 4 in this example, in a table that maps proxy ports onto **network ports**. Once the network port is known, the network message server looks up its location in other tables. It then constructs a network message containing the local message, plus any out-of-line data and sends it over the LAN to the network message server on the server's machine. In some cases, traffic between the network message servers has to be encrypted for security. The transport module takes care of

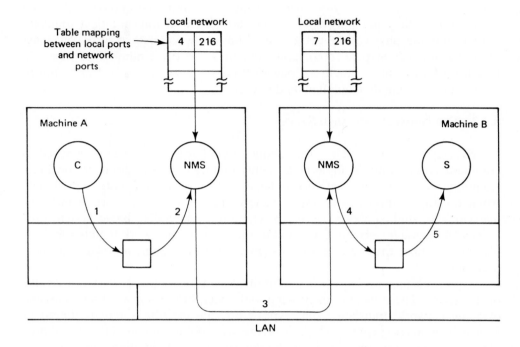

Fig. 8-20. Intermachine communication in Mach proceeds in five steps.

breaking the message into packets and encapsulating them in the appropriate protocol wrappers.

When the remote network message server gets the message, it looks up the network port number contained in it and maps it onto a local port number. In step 4, it writes the message to the local port just looked up. Finally, the server reads the message from the local port and carries out the request. The reply follows the same path in the reverse direction.

Complex messages require a bit more work. For ordinary data fields, the network message server on the server's machine must perform conversion, if necessary, for example, taking account of different byte ordering on the two machines. Capabilities must also be processed. When a capability is sent over the network, it must be assigned a network port number, and both the source and destination network message servers must make entries for it in their mapping tables. If these machines do not trust each other, elaborate authentication procedures will be necessary to convince each machine of the other's true identity.

Although the idea of relaying messages from one machine to another via a user-level server offers some flexibility, a substantial price is paid in performance as compared to a pure kernel implementation, which most other distributed systems use. To solve this problem, a new version of the network communication package is being developed (the NORMA code), which runs inside the kernel and achieves faster communication. It will eventually replace the network message server.

8.5. UNIX EMULATION IN MACH

Mach has various servers that run on top of it. Probably the most important one is a program that contains a large amount of Berkeley UNIX (e.g., essentially the entire file system code) inside itself. This server is the main UNIX emulator (Golub et al., 1990). This design is a legacy of Mach's history as a modified version of Berkeley UNIX.

The implementation of UNIX emulation on Mach consists of two pieces, the UNIX server and a system call emulation library, as shown in Fig. 8-21. When the system starts up, the UNIX server instructs the kernel to catch all system call traps and vector them to addresses inside the emulation library of the UNIX process making the system call. From that moment on, any system call made by a UNIX process will result in control passing temporarily to the kernel and immediately thereafter passing to its emulation library. At the moment control is given to the emulation library, all the machine registers have the values they had at the time of the trap. This method of bouncing off the kernel back into user space is sometimes called the **trampoline mechanism**.

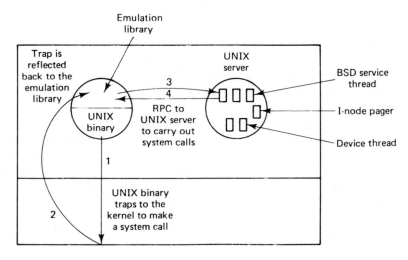

Fig. 8-21. UNIX emulation in Mach uses the trampoline mechanism.

Once the emulation library gets control, it examines the registers to determine which system call was invoked. It then makes an RPC to another process, the UNIX server, to do the work. When it is finished, the user program is given control again. This transfer of control need not go through the kernel.

When the *init* process forks off children, they automatically inherit both the emulation library and the trampoline mechanism, so they, too, can make UNIX system calls. The EXEC system call has been changed so that it does not replace the emulation library but just the UNIX program part of the address space.

The UNIX server is implemented as a collection of C threads. Although some threads handle timers, networking, and other I/O devices, most threads handle BSD system calls, carrying out requests on behalf of the emulators inside the UNIX processes. The emulation library communicates with these threads using the usual Mach interprocess communication.

When a message comes in to the UNIX server, an idle thread accepts it, determines which process it came from, extracts the system call number and parameters from it, carries it out, and finally, sends back the reply. Most messages correspond exactly to one BSD system call.

One set of system calls that work differently are the file I/O calls. They *could* have been implemented like this, but for performance reasons, a different approach was taken. When a file is opened, it is mapped directly into the caller's address space, so the emulation library can get at it directly, without having to do an RPC to the UNIX server. To satisfy a READ system call, for example, the emulation library locates the bytes to be read in the mapped file, locates the user buffer, and copies from the former to the latter as fast as it can.

Page faults will occur during the copy loop if the file's pages are not in memory. Each fault will cause Mach to send a message to the external memory manager backing up the mapped UNIX file. This memory manager is a thread inside the UNIX server called the **i-node pager**. It gets the file page from the disk and arranges for it to be mapped into the application program's address space. It also synchronizes operations on files that are open by several UNIX processes simultaneously.

Although this method of running UNIX programs looks cumbersome, measurements have shown that it compares favorably with traditional monolithic kernel implementations (Golub et al., 1990). Future work will focus on splitting the UNIX server into multiple servers with more specific functions. Eventually, the single UNIX server may be eliminated, although this depends on how the work with multiple servers develops during the course of time.

8.6. SUMMARY

Mach is a microkernel-based operating system. It was designed as a base for building new operating systems and emulating existing ones. It also provides a flexible way to extend UNIX to multiprocessors and distributed systems.

Mach is based on the concepts of processes, threads, ports, and messages. A Mach process is an address space and a collection of threads that run in it. The active entities are the threads. The process is merely a container for them. Each process and thread has a port to which it can write to have kernel calls carried out, eliminating the need for direct system calls.

Mach has an elaborate virtual memory system, featuring memory objects that can be mapped and unmapped into address spaces, and backed up by external, user-level memory managers. Files can be made directly readable and writable in this way, for example. Memory objects can be shared in various ways, including copy-on-write. Inheritance attributes determine which parts of a process' address space will be passed to its children.

Communication in Mach is based on ports, which are kernel objects that hold messages. All messages are directed to ports. Ports are accessed using capabilities, which are stored inside the kernel and referred to by 32-bit integers that are usually indices into capability lists. Ports can be passed from one process to another by including them in complex messages.

BSD UNIX emulation is done by an emulation library that lives in the address space of each UNIX process. Its job is to catch system calls reflected back to it by the kernel, and pass them on to the UNIX server to have them carried out. A few calls are handled locally, within the process' address space. Other UNIX emulators are also being developed.

Amoeba and Mach have many aspects in common, but also various differences. Both have processes and threads and are based on message passing. Amoeba has reliable broadcasting as a primitive, which Mach does not, but Mach has demand paging, which Amoeba does not. In general, Amoeba is more oriented toward making a collection of distributed machines act like a single computer, whereas Mach is more oriented toward making efficient use of multiprocessors. Both are undergoing constant development and will no doubt change as time goes on.

PROBLEMS

1. Name one difference between a process with two threads and two processes each with one thread that share the same address space, that is, the same set of pages.

2. What happens if you *join* on yourself?

3. A Mach thread creates two new threads as its children, A and B. Thread A does a *detach* call; B does not. Both threads exit and the parent does a *join*. What happens?

4. The global run queues of Fig. 8-6 must be locked before being searched. Do the local run queues (not shown in the figure) also have to be locked before being searched? Why or why not?

5. Each of the global run queues has a single mutex for locking it. Suppose that a particular multiprocessor has a global clock that causes clock interrupts on all the CPUs simultaneously. What implications does this have for the Mach scheduler?

6. Mach supports the concept of a processor set. On what class of machines does this concept make the most sense? What is it used for?

7. Mach supports three inheritance attributes for regions of virtual address space. Which ones are needed to make UNIX FORK work correctly?

8. A small process has all its pages in memory. There is enough free memory available for ten more copies of the process. It forks off a child. Is it possible for the child to get a page or protection fault?

9. Why do you think there is a call to copy a region of virtual memory (see Fig. 8-8)? After all, any thread can just copy it by sitting in a tight copy loop.

10. Why is the page replacement algorithm run in the kernel instead of in an external memory manager?

11. Give an example when it is desirable for a thread to deallocate an object in its virtual address space.

12. Can two processes simultaneously have RECEIVE capabilities for the same port? How about SEND capabilities?

13. Does a process know that a port it is reading from is actually a port set? Does it matter?

14. Mach supports two types of messages: simple and complex. Are the complex messages actually required, or is this merely an optimization?

15. Now answer the previous question about SEND-ONCE capabilities and out-of-line messages. Are either of these essential to the correct functioning of Mach?

16. In Fig. 8-15 the same port has a different name in different processes. What problems might this cause?

17. Mach has a system call that allows a process to request that non-Mach traps be given to a special handler, rather than causing the process to be killed. What is this system call good for?

9

Case Study 3: Chorus

Our third example of a modern, microkernel-based operating system is Chorus. The structure of this chapter is similar to that of the previous two: first a brief history, then an overview of the microkernel, followed by a more detailed look at process management, memory management, and communication. After that, we will study how Chorus tackles UNIX emulation. Next comes a section on distributed object-oriented programming in Chorus. We will conclude with a short comparison of Amoeba, Mach, and Chorus. More information about Chorus can be found in (Abrossimov et al., 1989, 1992; Armand and Dean, 1992; Batlivala, et al., 1992; Bricker et al., 1991; Gien and Grob, 1992; and Rozier et al., 1988).

9.1. INTRODUCTION TO CHORUS

In this section we will summarize how Chorus has evolved over the years, discuss its goals briefly, and then give a technical introduction to its microkernel and two of its subsystems. In subsequent sections we will describe the kernel and subsystems in more detail. The Chorus documentation uses a somewhat nonstandard terminology. In this chapter we will use the standard names but give the Chorus terms in parentheses.

9.1.1. History of Chorus

Chorus started out at the French research institute INRIA in 1980, as a research project in distributed systems. It has since gone through four versions, numbered from 0 through 3. The idea behind Version 0 was to model distributed applications as a collection of **actors**, essentially structured processes, each of which alternated between performing an atomic transaction and executing a communication step. In effect, each actor was a macroscopic finite-state automaton. Each machine in the system ran the same kernel, which managed the actors, communication, files, and I/O devices. Version 0 was written in interpreted UCSD Pascal and ran on a collection of 8086s connected by a ring network. It was operational by mid-1982.

Version 1, which lasted from 1982 to 1984, focused on multiprocessor research. It was written for the French SM90 multiprocessor, which consisted of eight Motorola 68020 CPUs on a common bus. One of the CPUs ran UNIX; the other seven ran Chorus and used the UNIX CPU for system services and I/O. Multiple SM90s were connected by an Ethernet. The software was similar to Version 0, with the addition of structured messages and some support for fault tolerance. Version 1 was written in compiled, rather than interpreted, Pascal and was distributed to about a dozen universities and companies for experimental use.

Version 2 (1984-1986) was a major rewrite of the system, in C. It was designed to be system call compatible with UNIX at the source code level, meaning that it was possible to recompile existing UNIX programs on Chorus and have them run on it. The Version 2 kernel was completely redesigned, moving as much functionality as possible from it to user code, and turning the kernel into what is now regarded as a microkernel. The UNIX emulation was done by several processes, for handling process management, file management, and device management, respectively. Support was added for distributed applications, including remote execution and protocols for distributed naming and location.

Version 3 was started in 1987. This version marked the transition from a research system to a commercial product, as the Chorus designers left INRIA and formed a company, Chorus Systèmes, to further develop and market Chorus. Numerous technical changes were made in Version 3, including further refinement of the microkernel and its relation to the rest of the system. The last vestiges of the actor model, with its atomic transactions, disappeared, and RPC (Remote Procedure Call) was introduced as the usual communication model. Kernel mode processes also appeared.

To make Chorus a viable commercial product, the ability to emulate UNIX was beefed up. Binary compatibility was added, so existing UNIX programs could be run without being recompiled. Part of the UNIX emulation, which had been in the microkernel, was moved to the emulation subsystem, which was simultaneously made more modular. Exception handling was changed to be able to handle UNIX signals correctly.

Its performance was improved. Also, the system was partially rewritten in C++. Furthermore, it was made more portable and implemented on a number of different architectures. Version 3 also borrowed many ideas from other distributed system microkernels, notably the interprocess communication system, virtual memory design, and external pagers from Mach, and the use of sparse capabilities for global naming and protection from Amoeba.

9.1.2. Goals of Chorus

The goals of the Chorus project have evolved along with the system itself. Initially, it was pure academic research, designed to explore new ideas in distributed computing based on the actor model. As time went on, it became more commercial, and the emphasis shifted. The current goals can be roughly summarized as follows:

1. High-performance UNIX emulation.

2. Use on distributed systems.

3. Real-time applications.

4. Integrating object-oriented programming into Chorus.

As a commercial system, much work focuses on tracking evolving UNIX standards, porting the system to new CPU chips, and improving performance. The company wants Chorus to be seen as an alternative to AT&T UNIX, re-engineered, easier to maintain, and oriented to future user requirements.

A second major theme is the need for distribution. Chorus is intended to allow UNIX programs to run on a collection of machines connected by a network. To support distributed applications, various extensions have been added to the programming model. Some of these, such as message-based communication, fit easily in the existing model. Others, such as the introduction of threads, required a rethinking of existing features, such as UNIX signal handling.

A third direction is the introduction of support for real-time applications. The approach taken is to allow real-time programs to run (partly) in kernel mode and have direct access to the microkernel, without any software in the way. User control over interrupts and the scheduling algorithm are also important here.

Finally, another goal is the introduction of object-oriented programming into Chorus in a clean way, without disturbing existing subsystems and applications. How this is being done will be described in detail later in this chapter.

9.1.3. System Structure

Chorus is structured in layers, as illustrated in Fig. 9-1. At the bottom is the microkernel (called the **nucleus** in the Chorus documentation). It provides minimal management of names, processes, threads, memory, and communication. These services are accessed by calls to the microkernel. Over 100 calls exist. Processes in higher layers provide the rest of the operating system. Every machine in a distributed system based on Chorus runs an identical copy of the Chorus microkernel.

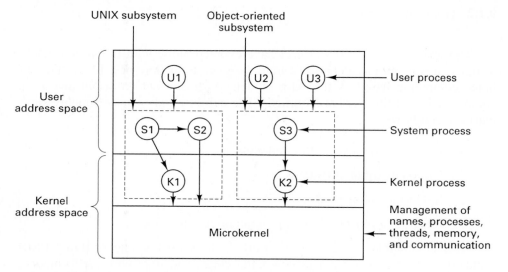

Fig. 9-1. Chorus is structured in layers, with a microkernel, subsystems, and user processes.

On top of the microkernel, but also operating in kernel mode, are the **kernel processes**. These processes can be dynamically loaded and removed during system execution and provide a way to extend the functionality of the microkernel without permanently increasing its size and complexity. Since these processes share the kernel space with the microkernel and with each other, they must be relocated after being loaded. They can invoke the microkernel to obtain services, and can call one another as well.

For example, interrupt handlers are written as kernel processes. On a machine with a disk drive, at system initialization time, the disk interrupt handler process will be loaded. When disk interrupts occur, they will be handled by this process. On diskless workstations, the disk interrupt handler is not needed and will not be loaded. The ability to dynamically load and unload kernel processes makes it possible to configure the system software to match the hardware, without having to recompile or relink the microkernel.

The next layer contains the **system processes**. These run in user mode, but can send messages to kernel processes (and each other) and can make calls to the microkernel, as shown by the arrows in Fig. 9-1. A collection of kernel and system processes can work together to form a **subsystem**. In Fig. 9-1, processes *S1*, *S2*, and *K1* form one subsystem and processes *S3* and *K2* form a second one. A subsystem presents a well-defined interface to its users, such as the UNIX system call interface. One process in each subsystem is the manager and controls the operation of the subsystem.

On top of the subsystems are the **user processes**. For example, system calls made by a user process *U1* might be caught by *K1* and passed on to *S1* or *S2* for processing. These, in turn, could use microkernel services, where appropriate. Subsystems make it possible to build new (or old) operating systems on top of the microkernel in a modular way, and to allow multiple operating system interfaces to exist on the same machine at the same time.

The microkernel knows which subsystem (if any) each user process is using, and ensures that it is restricted to making the system calls offered by that subsystem. Direct calls from user processes to the microkernel are not permitted, except for those calls that the subsystem defines as legal. Real-time processes can run as system processes, rather than as user processes, and thus make full use of the microkernel without intervention or overhead.

9.1.4. Kernel Abstractions

The kernel (by which we mean the microkernel) provides and manages six key abstractions that together form the basis for Chorus. These concepts are processes, threads, regions, messages, ports, port groups, and unique identifiers. They are illustrated in Fig. 9-2. Chorus **processes** (still called **actors** in the Chorus documentation) are essentially the same as processes in other operating systems. They are containers that encapsulate resources. A process owns certain resources, and when the process disappears, so do its resources.

Within a process, one or more **threads** can exist. Each thread is similar to a process in that it has its own stack, stack pointer, program counter, and registers. However, all threads in a process share the same address space and other process-wide resources. In principle, the threads of a process are independent of one another. On a multiprocessor, several threads may be running at the same time, on different CPUs. All three kinds of processes can have multiple threads.

Each process has an address space, normally going from 0 to some maximum address, such as $2^{32} - 1$. All the threads in a process have access to this address space. A consecutive range of addresses is called a **region**. Each region is associated with some piece of data, such as a program or a file. In systems that support virtual memory and paging, regions may be paged. Regions play a major role in memory management in Chorus.

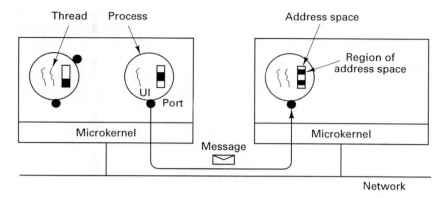

Fig. 9-2. Processes, threads, regions, messages, and, ports are identified by UIs.

Threads in different processes (potentially on different machines) communicate by passing **messages**. Messages can have a fixed part and a variable-sized body, both of which are optional. The body is untyped and may contain whatever information the sender puts into it. A message is addressed not to a thread, but to an intermediate structure called a **port**. A port is a buffer for incoming messages and holds those messages received by a process but not yet read. Like a thread, region, or other resource, at any instant, each port belongs to a single process. Only that process can read its messages. Ports can be put together to form port groups. These groups will be discussed below.

The last kernel abstraction relates to naming. Most kernel resources (e.g., processes and ports) are named by a 64-bit **unique identifier** or **UI**. Once a UI has been assigned to a resource, it is guaranteed never to be reused for another resource, not even on a different machine a year later. This uniqueness is guaranteed by encoding in each UI the site (machine or multiprocessor) where the UI was created plus an epoch number and a counter valid in that epoch. The epoch number is incremented each time the system is rebooted.

UIs are just binary numbers and are themselves not protected. Processes can send UIs to other processes in messages or store them in files. When a UI is transferred across the network and the receiver tries to access the corresponding object, the location information in the UI is used as a hint for where the object might be.

Because UIs are long and expensive to use, **local identifiers** or **LI**s are used within a single process to identify resources, similar to the use of small integers as file descriptors to identify open files in UNIX.

The kernel abstractions are not the only ones used by Chorus. Three other abstractions that are jointly managed by the kernel and subsystems also are important. These are capabilities, protection identifiers, and segments. A

capability is a name for a resource managed by a subsystem (or, in a few cases, by the kernel). It consists of the 64-bit UI of a port belonging to that subsystem and a 64-bit key assigned by the subsystem, as shown in Fig. 9-3.

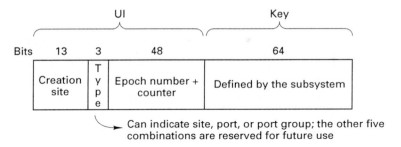

Fig. 9-3. A capability in Chorus.

When a subsystem creates an object, such as a file, it returns to the caller the capability for the object. From the capability, that process, or any subsequent process acquiring the capability, can find the UI of a port to which messages can be sent to request operations on the object. The 64-bit key must be included in such messages to tell the subsystem which of its many objects is being referenced. Included in the 64 bits is an index into the subsystem's tables, to identify the object. Other bits are randomly chosen to make it difficult to guess valid capabilities. Like UIs, capabilities may be freely passed in messages and files. This naming scheme was taken from Amoeba (Tanenbaum et al., 1986).

Memory management in Chorus is based on two concepts, regions, which were described above, and segments. A **segment** is a linear sequence of bytes identified by a capability. When a segment is mapped onto a region, the bytes of the segment are accessible to the threads of the region's process just by reading and writing addresses in the region. Programs, files, and other forms of data are stored as segments in Chorus and can be mapped onto regions. A segment can also be read and written by system calls, even when it is not mapped onto a region. An example address space is shown in Fig. 9-4.

9.1.5. Kernel Structure

Having described the main abstractions provided by the Chorus kernel, let us now briefly examine how the kernel is structured internally. The kernel consists of four pieces, as illustrated in Fig. 9-5. At the bottom is the **supervisor**, which manages the raw hardware and catches traps, exceptions, interrupts, and other hardware details, and handles context switching. It is written partly in assembler and has to be redone when Chorus is ported to new hardware.

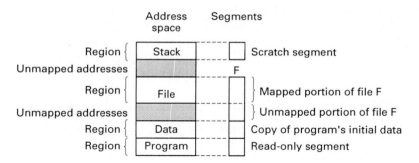

Fig. 9-4. An address space with four mapped regions.

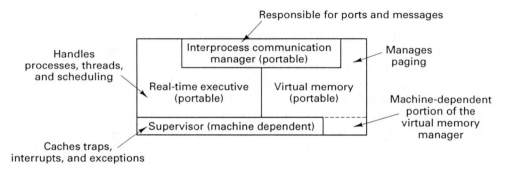

Fig. 9-5. Structure of the Chorus kernel.

Next comes the **virtual memory manager**, which handles the low-level part of the paging system. The largest piece of it deals with managing page caches and other logical concepts, and is machine independent. A small part, however, has to know how to load and store the MMU registers. This part is machine dependent and has to be modified when Chorus is ported to a new computer.

The two parts of the virtual memory manager together do not do all the work of managing the paging system. A third part, the mapper, is outside the kernel and does the high-level part. The communication protocol between the virtual memory manager and the mapper is well defined, so users can provide their own specialized mappers.

The third part of the kernel is the **real-time executive**. It is responsible for managing processes, threads, and scheduling. It also takes care of arranging for synchronization between threads for mutual exclusion and other purposes.

Finally, we have the **interprocess communication manager**, which handles UIs, ports, and the sending of messages in a transparent way. It makes use of the services of the real-time executive and virtual memory manager to do its work. It is completely portable and does not have to be changed at all when Chorus is moved to a new platform. The four parts of the kernel are constructed in a modular way, so changes to one usually do not affect any of the others.

9.1.6. The UNIX Subsystem

Since Chorus is now a commercial product, it must give the masses what they want, and what they want (at least in the high-end workstation world) is compatibility with UNIX. Chorus accomplishes this goal by providing a standard subsystem, called **MiX**, that is compatible with System V. The compatibility is both at the source level (i.e., UNIX source programs can be compiled and run on Chorus) and at the binary level (i.e., executable programs compiled on a true UNIX system for the same architecture run without modification on Chorus). An earlier version of MiX (3.2) was compatible with 4.2 BSD, but we will not discuss that version further in this chapter.

MiX is also compatible with UNIX in other ways. For example, the file system is compatible, so Chorus can read a UNIX disk. Furthermore, the Chorus device drivers are interface compatible with the UNIX ones, so if UNIX device drivers exist for a device machine, they can be ported to Chorus with relatively little work.

The implementation of the MiX subsystem is more modular than UNIX. It consists of four processes, one for process management, one for file management, one for device management, and one for streams and interprocess communication. These processes do not share any variables or other memory, and communicate exclusively by remote procedure call. Later in this chapter we will describe in detail how they work.

9.1.7. The Object-Oriented Subsystem

As a research experiment, a second subsystem has been implemented, this one for object-oriented programming. It consists of three layers. The bottom layer does object management in a generic way and is effectively a microkernel for object-oriented systems. The middle layer provides a general runtime system. The top layer is the language runtime system. This subsystem, called COOL, will also be discussed later in this chapter.

9.2. PROCESS MANAGEMENT IN CHORUS

In this section we will describe how processes and threads work in Chorus, how exceptions are handled, and how scheduling is done. We will conclude by describing briefly some of the major process management kernel calls available.

9.2.1. Processes

A process in Chorus is a collection of active and passive elements that work together to perform some computation. The active elements are the threads. The passive elements are an address space (containing some regions) and a collection of ports (for sending and receiving messages). A process with one thread is like a traditional UNIX process. A process with no threads cannot do anything useful, and normally exists only for a very short interval while a process is being created.

Three kinds of processes exist, differing in the amount of privilege and trust they have, as listed in Fig. 9-6. Privilege refers to the ability to execute I/O and other protected instructions. Trust means that the process is allowed to call the kernel directly.

Type	Trust	Privilege	Mode	Space
User	Untrusted	Unprivileged	User	User
System	Trusted	Unprivileged	User	User
Kernel	Trusted	Privileged	Kernel	Kernel

Fig. 9-6. The three kinds of processes in Chorus.

Kernel processes are the most powerful. They run in kernel mode and all share the same address space with each other and with the microkernel. They can be loaded and unloaded during execution, but other than that, can be thought of as extensions to the microkernel itself. Kernel processes can communicate with each other using a special lightweight RPC that is not available to other processes.

Each system process runs in its own address space. System processes are unprivileged (i.e., run in user mode), and thus cannot execute I/O and other protected instructions directly. However, the kernel trusts them to make kernel calls, so system processes can obtain kernel services directly, without any intermediary.

User processes are untrusted and unprivileged. They cannot perform I/O directly, and cannot even call the kernel, except for those calls that their subsystem has decided to make on their behalf. Each user process has two parts: the regular user part and a system part that is invoked after a trap. This arrangement is similar to the way that UNIX works.

Every process (and port) has a **protection identifier** associated with it. If the process forks, its children inherit the same protection identifier. This identifier is just a bit string, and does not have any semantics associated with it that the kernel knows about. Protection identifiers provide a mechanism which can be used for authentication. For example, the UNIX subsystem could assign a

UID (user identifier) with each process and use the Chorus protection identifiers to implement the UIDs.

9.2.2. Threads

Every active process in Chorus has one or more threads that execute code. Each thread has its own private context (i.e., stack, program counter, and registers), which is saved when the thread blocks waiting for some event and is restored when the thread is later resumed. A thread is tied to the process in which it was created, and cannot be moved to another process.

Chorus threads are known to the kernel and scheduled by the kernel, so creating and destroying them requires making kernel calls. An advantage of having kernel threads (as opposed to a threads package that runs entirely in user space, without kernel knowledge), is that when one thread blocks waiting for some event (e.g., a message arrival), the kernel can schedule other threads. Another advantage is the ability to run different threads on different CPUs when a multiprocessor is available. The disadvantage of kernel threads is the extra overhead required to manage them. Of course, users are still free to implement a user-level threads package inside a single kernel thread.

Threads communicate with one another by sending and receiving messages. It does not matter if the sender and receiver are in the same process or are on different machines. The semantics of communication are identical in all cases. If two threads are in the same process, they can also communicate using shared memory, but then the system cannot later be reconfigured to run with threads in different processes.

The following states are distinguished, but they are not mutually exclusive:

1. ACTIVE   — The thread is logically able to run.

2. SUSPENDED — The thread has been intentionally suspended.

3. STOPPED   — The thread's process has been suspended.

4. WAITING   — The thread is waiting for some event to happen.

A thread in the ACTIVE state is either currently running or waiting its turn for a free CPU. In both cases it is logically unblocked and able to run. A thread in the SUSPENDED state has been suspended by another thread (or itself) that issued a kernel call asking the kernel to suspend the thread. Similarly, when a kernel call is made to stop a process, all the threads in the ACTIVE state are put in the STOPPED state until the process is released. Finally, when a thread performs a blocking operation that cannot be completed immediately, the thread is put in WAITING state until the event occurs.

A thread can be in more than one state at the same time. For example, a thread in SUSPENDED state can later also enter the STOPPED state as well if its process is suspended. Conceptually, each thread has three independent bits associated with it, one each for SUSPENDED, STOPPED, and WAITING. Only when all three bits are zero can the thread run.

Threads run in the mode and address space corresponding to their process. In other words, the threads of a kernel process run in kernel mode, and the threads of a user process run in user.

The kernel provides two synchronization mechanisms that threads can use. The first is the traditional (counting) semaphore, with operations UP (or V) and DOWN (or P). These operations are always implemented by kernel calls, so they are expensive. The second mechanism is the mutex, which is essentially a semaphore whose values are restricted to 0 and 1. Mutexes are used only for mutual exclusion. They have the advantage that operations that do not cause the caller to block can be carried out entirely in the caller's space, saving the overhead of a kernel call.

A problem that occurs in every thread-based system is how to manage the data private to each thread, such as its stack. Chorus solves this problem by assigning two special **software registers** to each thread. One of them holds a pointer to the thread's private data when it is in user mode. The other holds a pointer to the private data when the thread has trapped to the kernel and is executing a kernel call. Both registers are part of the thread's state, and are saved and restored along with the hardware registers when a thread is stopped or started. By indexing off these registers, a thread can access data that (by convention) are not available to other threads in the same process.

9.2.3. Scheduling

CPU scheduling is done using priorities on a per-thread basis. Each process has a priority and each thread has a relative priority within its process. The absolute priority of a thread is the sum of its process' priority and its own relative priority. The kernel keeps track of the priority of each thread in ACTIVE state and runs the one with the highest absolute priority. On a multiprocessor with k CPUs, the k highest-priority threads are run.

However, to accommodate real-time processes, an additional feature has been added to the algorithm. A distinction is made between threads whose priority is above a certain level and threads whose priority is below it. High-priority threads, such as A and B in Fig. 9-7(a), are not timesliced. Once such a thread starts running, it continues to run until either it voluntarily releases its CPU (e.g., by blocking on a semaphore), or an even higher priority thread moves into the ACTIVE state as a result of I/O completing or some other event happening. In particular, it is not stopped just because it has run for a long time.

In contrast, in Fig. 9-7(b), thread C will be run, but after it has consumed

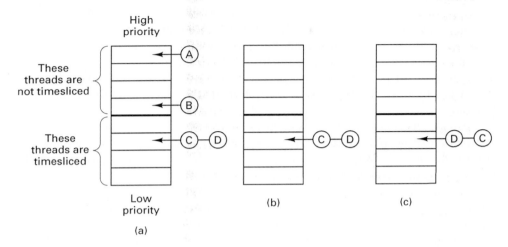

Fig. 9-7. (a) Thread *A* will be run until it is finished or it blocks. (b)–(c) Threads *C* and *D* will alternate, in round robin mode.

one quantum of CPU time, it will be put on the end of the queue for its priority, and thread *D* will be given one quantum. In the absence of competition for the CPU, they will alternate indefinitely.

This mechanism provides enough generality for most real-time applications. System calls are available for changing process and thread priorities, so applications can tell the system which threads are most important and which are least important. Additional scheduling algorithms are available to support System V real-time and system processes.

9.2.4. Traps, Exceptions, and Interrupts

The Chorus software distinguishes between three kinds of entries into the kernel. **Traps** are intentional calls to the kernel or a subsystem to invoke services. Programs cause traps by calling a system call library procedure. The system supports two ways of handling traps. In the first way, all traps for a particular trap vector go to a single kernel thread that has previously announced its willingness to handle that vector. In the second way, each trap vector is tied to an array of kernel threads, with the Chorus supervisor using the contents of a certain register to index into the array to pick a thread. The latter mechanism allows all system calls to use the same trap vector, with the system call number going into the register used to select a handler.

Exceptions are unexpected events that are caused by accident, such as the divide-by-zero exception, floating-point overflow, or a page fault. It is possible to arrange for a kernel thread to be invoked to handle the exception. If the handler can complete the processing, it returns a special code and the exception handling is finished. Otherwise (or if no kernel handler is assigned), the kernel suspends the thread that caused the exception and sends a message to a special exception-handling port associated with the thread's process. Normally, some other thread will be waiting for a message on this port and will take whatever action the process requires. If no exception port exists, the faulting thread is killed.

Interrupts are caused by asynchronous events, such as clock ticks or the completion of an I/O request. They are not necessarily related to anything the current thread is doing, so it is not possible to let that thread's process handle them. Instead, it is possible to arrange in advance that when an interrupt occurs on a certain interrupt vector (i.e., a specific device), a new kernel thread will be created spontaneously to process it. If a second interrupt occurs on the same vector before the first one has terminated, a second thread is created, and so on. All I/O interrupts except the clock are handled this way. The clock is fielded by the supervisor itself, but it can be set up to notify a user thread if desired. Interrupt threads can invoke only a limited set of kernel services because the system is in an unknown state when they are started. All they can do are operations on semaphores and mutexes, or send minimessages to special miniports.

9.2.5. Kernel Calls for Process Management

The best way to find out what a kernel or operating system really does is to examine its interface, that is, the system calls it provides to its users. In this section we will look at the most important Chorus kernel calls available to system processes. Calls of less importance and protected calls available only to kernel threads will be omitted.

Call	Description
actorCreate	Create a new process
actorDelete	Remove a process
actorStop	Stop a process, put its threads in STOPPED state
actorStart	Restart a process from STOPPED state
actorPriority	Get or set a process' priority
actorExcept	Get or set the port used for exeception handling

Fig. 9-8. Selected process calls supported by the Chorus kernel.

Let us start with the process calls, listed in Fig. 9-8. *ActorCreate* creates a new process and returns that process' capability to the caller. The new process inherits the priority, protection identifier, and exception port of the parent process. Parameters specify whether the new process is to be a user, system, or kernel process, and tell what state it is to start in. Just after creation, the new process is empty, with no threads and no regions and only one port, the default port. Note that *actorCreate* represents a major orthographic advance over UNIX: "Create" is spelled with an "e" at the end.

The *actorDelete* call kills a process. The process to be killed is specified by a capability passed as a parameter. *ActorStop* freezes a process, putting all of its threads into STOPPED state. The threads can only run again when an *actorStart* call is made. A process may stop itself. These calls are typically used for debugging. For example, if a thread hits a breakpoint, the debugger can use *actorStop* to stop the process' other threads.

The *actorPriority* call allows a process to read the priority of another process, and optionally, to reset it to a new value. Although Chorus is generally location transparent, it is not perfect. Some calls, including this one, work only when the target process is on the caller's machine. In other words, it is not possible to get or reset the priority of a distant process.

ActorExcept is used to get or change the exception port for the caller or some other process for which the caller has a capability. It can also be used to remove the exception port, in which case if an exception has to be sent to the process, the process is killed instead.

The next group of kernel calls relate to threads, and are shown in Fig. 9-9. *ThreadCreate* and *threadDelete* create and delete threads in some process (not necessarily the caller's), respectively. Parameters to *threadCreate* specify the privilege level, initial status, priority, entry point, and stack pointer.

Call	Description
threadCreate	Create a new thread
threadDelete	Delete a thread
threadSuspend	Suspend a thread
threadResume	Restart a suspended thread
threadPriority	Get or set a thread's priority
threadLoad	Get a thread's context pointer
threadStore	Set a thread's context pointer
threadContext	Get or set a thread's execution context

Fig. 9-9. Selected thread calls supported by the Chorus kernel.

ThreadSuspend and *threadResume* stop and then restart threads in the target process. *ThreadPriority* returns the target thread's current relative priority, and optionally resets it to a value given as a parameter.

Our last three calls are used to manage a thread's private context. The *threadLoad* and *threadStore* calls load and set the current software context register, respectively. This register points to the thread's context, including its private variables. The *threadContext* call optionally copies the thread's old context to a buffer, and optionally sets the new context from another buffer.

The synchronization operations are given in Fig. 9-10. Calls are provided for initializing, acquiring, and releasing both mutexes and semaphores. These all work in the usual way.

Call	Description
mutexInit	Initialize a mutex
mutexGet	Try to acquire a mutex
mutexRel	Release a mutex
semInit	Initialize a semaphore
semP	Do a DOWN on a semaphore
semV	Do an UP on a semaphore

Fig. 9-10. Selected synchronization calls supported by the Chorus kernel.

9.3. MEMORY MANAGEMENT IN CHORUS

Memory management in Chorus borrows many ideas from Mach. However, it also contains some ideas not present in Mach. In this section we will describe the basic concepts and how they are used.

9.3.1. Regions and Segments

The main concepts behind memory management in Chorus are regions and segments. A **region** is a contiguous range of virtual address, for example, 1024 to 6143. In theory, a region can begin at any virtual address and end at any virtual address, but to do anything useful, a region should be page aligned and have a length equal to some whole number of pages. All bytes in a region must have the same protection characteristics (e.g., read-only). Regions are a property of processes, and all the threads in a process see the same regions. Two regions in the same process may not overlap.

A **segment** is a contiguous collection of bytes named and protected by a capability. Files and swap areas on disk are the most common kinds of segments. Segments can be read and written using system calls that provide the segment's capability, the offset, the number of bytes, the buffer, and the transfer direction. These calls are used for doing traditional I/O operations on files.

However, another possibility is mapping segments onto regions, as shown in Fig. 9-4. It is not necessary that a segment be exactly the size of its region. If the segment is larger than the region, only a portion of the segment will be visible in the address space, although which portion is visible can be changed by remapping it. If the segment is smaller than the region, the result of reading an unmapped address is up to the mapper. For example, it can raise an exception, return 0, or extend the segment, as it wishes.

Mapped segments are usually demand paged (unless this feature is disabled, for example, for real-time programs). When a process first references a newly mapped segment, a page fault occurs and the segment page corresponding to the address referenced is brought in and the faulting instruction restarted. In this way, ordinary virtual memory can be implemented, and in addition, a process can make one or more files visible in its virtual address space, so it can access them directly instead of having to read or write them using system calls.

The kernel supports special I/O segments for accessing the machine's I/O registers on machines with memory-mapped device registers. Using these segments, kernel threads can perform I/O by reading and writing memory directly.

9.3.2. Mappers

Chorus supports Mach-style external pagers, which are called **mappers**. Each mapper controls one or more segments that are mapped onto regions. A segment can be mapped into multiple regions, even in different address spaces at the same time, as shown in Fig. 9-11. Here segments *S1* and *S2* are both mapped into processes *A* and *B*, on the same machine but at different addresses. If process *A* writes address *A1* it changes the first word of *S1*. If process *B* later reads *B1* it also gets the value *A* wrote. Furthermore, if *S1* is a file, when both processes terminate, the change will be made in the file on disk.

The virtual memory manager in each kernel maintains a page cache and keeps track of which page belongs to which segment. Pages in the local cache can belong to named segments, such as files, or to nameless segments, such as swap areas. The kernel keeps track of which pages are clean and which are dirty. It may discard clean pages at will, but must return dirty pages to the appropriate mappers to reclaim their space.

A protocol between the kernel and mapper determines the flow of pages in both directions. When a page fault occurs, the kernel checks to see if the needed page is cached. If it is not, the kernel sends a message to the mapper controlling the page's segment asking for the page (and possibly adjacent pages as well). The faulting thread is then suspended until the page arrives.

When the mapper gets the request, it checks to see if the needed page is in its own cache (in its own address space). If not, it sends a message to the thread managing the disk to perform I/O and fetch the page. When the page arrives (or if it was already present), the mapper notifies the kernel, which then accepts the page, adjusts the MMU page tables, and resumes the faulting thread.

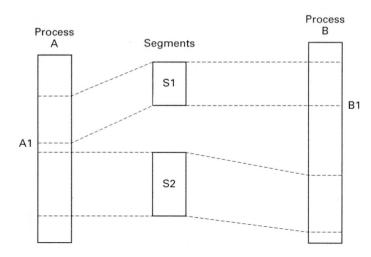

Fig. 9-11. Segments can be mapped into multiple address spaces at the same time.

The mapper can also take the initiative and ask the kernel to return dirty pages to it. When the kernel returns them, the mapper can keep some of them in its own cache and write others to disk. Various calls are provided to allow the mapper to specify which pages it wants back. Most mappers do not keep track of how many page frames their segments are occupying since the kernel is free to discard clean pages and will return dirty pages to their mappers when space gets tight.

The same caching and management mechanism is used for pages that are part of mapped segments as for pages that are read and written using explicit segment I/O commands. This approach guarantees that if one process modifies a mapped page by writing on it, and immediately thereafter another process tries to read the file it is part of, the second process will get the new data, since only one copy of the page exists in memory.

9.3.3. Distributed Shared Memory

Chorus supports paged distributed shared memory in the style of IVY, as discussed in Chap. 6. It uses a dynamic decentralized algorithm, meaning that different managers keep track of different pages, and the manager for a page changes as the page moves around the system (for writable pages).

The unit of sharing between multiple machines is the segment. Segments are split up into fragments of one or more pages. At any instant, each fragment is either read-only, and potentially present on multiple machines, or read/write, and present only on one machine.

9.3.4. Kernel Calls for Memory Management

Memory management in Chorus supports 26 different system calls plus several upcalls from the kernel to the mappers. In this section we will briefly describe just the more important ones. The calls we will describe relate to region management (*rgn* prefix), segment management (*sg* prefix), and upcalls to the mappers (*Mp* prefix—not *mp*, which is used for miniport calls, described later). The calls not described here relate to managing local caches (*lc* prefix) and virtual memory (*vm* prefix).

A selection of the region management calls is given in Fig. 9-12. *RgnAllocate* specifies a region by giving the capability for a process, a starting address, a size, and various options. If there are no conflicts with other regions and no other problems, the region is created. The options include initializing the region to zero bytes, setting its read/write/executable bits, and wiring it down so it is not paged. *RgnFree* returns a previously allocated region so its portion of the address space is free for allocation to another region or regions.

Call	Description
rgnAllocate	Allocate a memory region and set its properties
rgnFree	Release a previously allocated region
rgnInit	Allocate a region and fill it from a given segment
rgnSetInherit	Set the inheritance properties of a region
rgnSetPaging	Set the paging properties of a region
rgnSetProtect	Set the protection options of a region
rgnStat	Get the statistics associated with a region

Fig. 9-12. Selected calls supported by the Chorus kernel for managing regions.

RgnInit is similar to *rgnAllocate* except that after the region is allocated, it is also filled in from a segment whose capability is a parameter to the call. Several other calls that are similar to *rgnInit* are also present, filling the region in different ways.

The next three calls change the properties of an existing region in various ways. *RgnSetInherit* relates to the possibility that a region might later be copied, and specifies whether the copy is to get its own pages or to share the original region's pages. *RgnSetPaging* is used primarily by processes that are interested in providing real-time response and cannot tolerate page faults or being swapped out. It also tells what to do if the process is trying to allocate a nonswappable nonpageable region that is wired down, but there is insufficient memory available. *RgnSetProtect* changes the read/write/execute bits associated with a region and can also make a region accessible only to the kernel. Finally, *rgnStat* returns to the caller the size of a region and other information.

The segment I/O calls are shown in Fig. 9-13. *sgRead* and *sgWrite* are the basic I/O calls that allows a process to read and write a segment. The segment is specified by a descriptor. The offset and number of bytes are also provided, as is the buffer address to copy to or from. *SgStat* allows the caller, typically a mapper, to ask for statistical information about a page cache. *SgFlush* (and several related calls) allow mappers to ask the kernel to send them pages so they can be cached in the mapper's address space or written back to their segments on disk. This mechanism is needed, for example, to ensure that a group of mappers collectively supporting distributed shared memory can remove writable pages from all machines but one. Other calls in this group relate to locking and unlocking individual pages in memory and getting various sizes and other information about the paging system.

Call	Description
sgRead	Read data from a segment
sgWrite	Write data to a segment
sgStat	Request information about a page cache
sgFlush	Request from a mapper to the kernel asking for dirty pages

Fig. 9-13. Selected calls relating to segments.

The calls in Fig. 9-14 are calls to a mapper, either from the kernel or from an application program asking the mapper to do something for the caller. The first one, *MpCreate* is used when the kernel or a program wants to swap out a segment and needs to allocate disk space for it. The mapper responds by allocating a new segment on disk and returning a capability for it.

Call	Description
MpCreate	Request to create a dummy segment for swapping
MpRelease	Request asking to release a previously created segment
MpPullIn	Request asking for one or more pages
MpPushOut	Request asking mapper to accept one or more pages

Fig. 9-14. Mapper calls.

The *MpRelease* call returns a segment created using *MpCreate*. *MpPullIn* is used by the kernel to acquire data from a newly created or existing segment. The mapper is required to respond to it by sending a message containing the pages needed. By using clever MMU programming, the pages need not be copied physically.

The *MpPushOut* call is for transfers the other way, from kernel to mapper, either in response to a *sgFlush* (or similar) call, or when the kernel wants to swap out a segment on its own. Although the list of calls described above is not complete, it does give a reasonable picture of how memory management works in Chorus.

9.4. COMMUNICATON IN CHORUS

The basic communication paradigm in Chorus is message passing. During the Version 1 era, when the research was focused on multiprocessors, using shared memory as the communication paradigm was considered, but rejected as not being general enough. In this section we will discuss messages, ports, and the communication operations, concluding with a summary of the kernel calls available for communication.

9.4.1. Messages

Each message contains a header (for the microkernel's internal use only), an optional fixed part and an optional body. The header identifies the source and destination and contains various protection identifiers and flags. The fixed part, if present, is always 64 bytes long and is entirely under user control. The body is variable sized, with a maximum of 64K bytes, and also entirely under user control. From the kernel's point of view, both the fixed part and the body are untyped byte arrays in the sense that the kernel does not care what is in them.

When a message is sent to a thread on a different machine, it is always copied. However, when it is sent to a thread on the same machine, there is a choice between actually copying it and just mapping it into the receiver's address space. In the latter case, if the receiver writes onto a mapped page, a genuine copy is made on the spot (i.e., Mach's copy-on-write mechanism). When a message is not an integral number of pages but the message is mapped, some data just beyond the buffer (or before it) will be lost when the final (or first) page is mapped in.

Another form of message is the **minimessage**, which is only used between kernel processes for short synchronization messages, typically to signal the occurrence of an interrupt. The minimessages are sent to special low-overhead **miniports**.

9.4.2. Ports

Messages are addressed to ports, each of which contains storage for a certain number of messages. If a message is sent to a port that is full, the sender is suspended until sufficient space is available. When a port is created, both a unique identifier and a local identifier are returned to the caller. The former can be sent to other processes so they can send messages to the port. The latter is used within the process to reference the port directly. Only threads in the process currently holding the port can read from the port (ports can migrate).

When a process is created, it automatically gets a default port that the kernel uses to send it exception messages. It can also create as many additional ports as it needs. These additional ports (but not the default port) can be moved to other processes, even on other machines. When a port is moved, all the messages currently in it can be moved with it. Port movement is useful, for example, when a server on a machine that is going down for maintenance wants to let another server on a different machine take over its work. In this way, services can be maintained in a transparent way, even as server machines go down and come back up again later.

Chorus provides a way to collect several ports together into a **port group**. To do so, a process first creates an empty port group and gets back a capability for it. Using this capability, it can add ports to the group, and later it can use the capability to delete ports from the group. A port may be present in multiple port groups, as illustrated in Fig. 9-15.

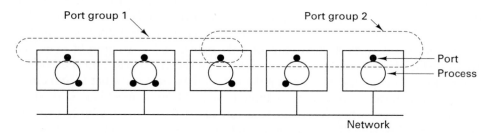

Fig. 9-15. A port may be a member of multiple port groups.

Groups are commonly used to provide reconfigurable services. Initially some set of servers belongs to the group, which provides some service. Clients can send messages to the group without having to know which servers are available to do the work. Later, new servers can join the group and old ones can leave without disrupting the services and without the clients even being aware that the system has been reconfigured.

9.4.3. Communication Operations

Two kinds of communication operations are provided by Chorus: asynchronous send and RPC. Asynchronous send allows a thread simply to send a message to a port. There is no guarantee that the message arrives and no notification if something goes wrong. This is the purest form of datagram and allows users to build arbitrary communication patterns on top of it.

The other communication operation is RPC. When a process performs an RPC operation, it is blocked automatically until either the reply comes in or the RPC timer expires, at which time the sender is unblocked. The message that unblocks the sender is guaranteed to be the response to the request. Any message that does not bear the RPC's transaction identifier will be stored in the port for future consumption but will not awaken the sender.

RPCs use at-most-once semantics, meaning that in the event of an unrecoverable communication or processing failure, the system guarantees that an RPC will return an error code rather than take a chance on having an operation executed more than once.

It is also possible to send a message to a port group. Various options are available, as shown in Fig. 9-16. These options determine how many messages are sent and to which ports.

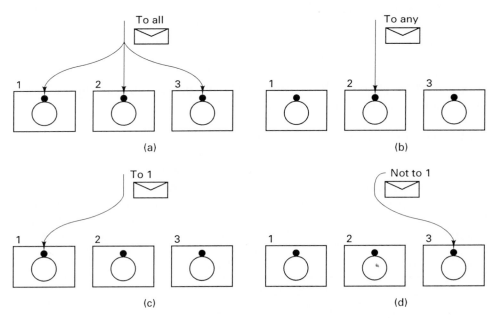

Fig. 9-16. Options for sending to a port group. (a) Send to all members. (b) Send to any member. (c) Send to port at the same site as a given port. (d) Send to a port not at a specific site.

Option (a) in Fig. 9-16 sends the message to all ports in the group. For highly reliable storage, a process might want to have every file server store certain data. Option (b) sends it to just one, but lets the system choose which one. When a process just wants some service, such as the current date, but does not care where it comes from, this option is the best choice, as the system can then select the most efficient way to provide the service.

The other two options also send to just one port, but limit the choice the system may make. In (c), the caller can specify that the port must be on a specific site, for example, to balance the system load. Option (d) says that any port *not* on the specified site may be used. A use for this option might be to force a backup copy of a file onto a different machine than the primary copy.

Sends to port groups use the asynchronous send. Broadcast sends (i.e., to all members) are not flow controlled. If flow control is required, it must be supplied by the user.

To receive a message, a thread makes a kernel call telling which port it wants to receive on. If a message is available, the fixed part of the message is copied to the caller's address space, and the body, if any, is either copied or mapped in, depending on the options. If no message is available, the calling thread is suspended until a message arrives or a user-specified timer expires.

Furthermore, a process can specify that it wants to receive from one of the ports it owns, but it does not care which one. This option can be further refined by disabling some of the ports, in which case only enabled ports are eligible to satisfy the request. Finally, ports can be assigned priorities, which means that if more than one enabled port has a message, the enabled port with the highest priority will be selected. Ports can be enabled and disabled dynamically, and their priorities can be changed at will.

9.4.4. Kernel Calls for Communication

The port management calls are shown in Fig. 9-17. The first four are straightforward, allowing ports to be created, destroyed, enabled, and disabled. The last one specifies a port and a process. After the call completes, the port no longer belongs to its original owner (which need not be the caller) but instead belongs to the target process. It alone can now read messages from the port.

Call	Description
portCreate	Create a port and return its capability
portDelete	Destroy a port
portEnable	Enable a port so its messages count on a receive from all ports
portDisable	Disable a port
portMigrate	Move a port to a different process

Fig. 9-17. Selected port management calls.

Three calls are present for managing port groups. They are listed in Fig. 9-18. The first, *grpAllocate*, creates a new port group and returns a capability for it to the caller. Using this capability, the caller or any other process that subsequently acquires the capability can add or delete ports from the group.

Call	Description
grpAllocate	Create a port group
grpPortInsert	Add a new port to an existing port group
grpPortRemove	Delete a port from a port group

Fig. 9-18. Calls relating to port groups.

Our last group of kernel calls handles the actual sending and receiving of messages. These are listed in Fig. 9-19. *IpcSend* sends a message asynchronously to a specified port or port group. *IpcReceive* blocks until a message arrives from a specified port. This message may have been sent directly to the port, to a port group of which the specified port is a member, or to all enabled ports (assuming that the specified port is enabled). An address into which the fixed part is to be copied must be supplied, but an address for the body is optional, because the size is not always known in advance. If no buffer is provided for the body the *ipcGetData* call can be executed to acquire the body from the kernel (the size is now known since it is returned by the *IpcReceive* call). A reply message can be sent using *ipcReply*. Finally, *ipcCall* performs a remote procedure call.

Call	Description
ipcSend	Send a message asynchronously
ipcReceive	Block until a message arrives
ipcGetData	Get the current message's body
ipcReply	Send a reply to the current message
ipcCall	Perform a remote procedure call

Fig. 9-19. Selected communication calls.

9.5. UNIX EMULATION IN CHORUS

Although being UNIX-like was not even one of the original goals of Chorus at all (it had a totally different interface and was written in interpreted UCSD Pascal), with the advent of Version 3, UNIX compatibility became a major goal. The approach taken is to have the kernel be operating system neutral, but to have a subsystem that allows existing UNIX binary programs to run on it without modification. This subsystem consists partly of new code written by the Chorus implementers, and partly of the System V UNIX code itself, licensed from UNIX System Laboratories. In this section we will describe what Chorus UNIX is like

and how it is implemented. The UNIX subsystem is called **MiX**, which stands
for **Modular UNIX**.

9.5.1. Structure of a UNIX Process

A UNIX process runs as a Chorus user process, on top of the UNIX subsystem.
As such, it has all the features of a Chorus process, although existing UNIX programs will not use all of them. The standard text, data, and stack segments are
implemented by three mapped Chorus segments.

On the whole, the way Chorus works is not hidden from the UNIX runtime
system and library (although it is hidden from the *program*). For example, when
the program wants to open a file, the library procedure *open* invokes the subsystem, which ultimately gets a file capability. It stores the file capability internal
to itself and uses it when the user process calls *read*, *write*, and other procedures
that deal with the open file.

Open files are not the only UNIX concepts that are mapped onto Chorus
resources. Open directories (including the working directory and root directory), open devices, pipes, and in-use segments are all represented internally as
capabilities for the corresponding Chorus resources. Operations on all of these
are done by the UNIX subsystem by passing the capability to the appropriate
server. To remain binary compatible with UNIX, the user process must never see
the capabilities.

9.5.2. Extensions to UNIX

Chorus provides UNIX processes with many extensions to make distributed
programming easier. Most of these are just standard Chorus properties that are
made visible. For example, UNIX processes can create and destroy new threads
using the Chorus threads package. These threads run in quasiparallel (on a multiprocessor, actually in parallel).

Since Chorus threads are managed by the kernel, when one thread blocks,
for example on a system call, the kernel is able to schedule and run another
thread in the same process. However, it is not usually possible for two threads
in the same process to execute most system calls simultaneously because the
ancient UNIX code that handles the system calls is not reentrant. In most cases,
the second thread is suspended transparently before starting the system call until
the first one has completed.

The addition of threads has necessitated rethinking how signals are handled.
Instead of all signal handlers being common to the entire process, the synchronous ones (the ones caused by a thread action) are associated with specific
threads whereas the asynchronous ones (like the user hitting the DEL key) are
process wide. For example, the ALARM system call arranges for the calling

thread to be interrupted after the indicated number of seconds. Other threads are not affected.

Similarly, one thread can arrange to catch floating-point overflows and similar exceptions, while another ignores them, and a third thread does not catch them (meaning that it will be killed if one occurs).

Other signals are, by nature, not specific to one thread. A KILL signal sent by another process, or a SIGINT or SIGQUIT from the keyboard are sent to all threads. Each one can catch or ignore it as it wishes. If no thread catches or ignores a signal, the entire process is killed.

Signals are handled by the process itself. Associated with every UNIX process is a control thread within the UNIX subsystem that spends its day listening to the exception port. When a signal is triggered, this normally dormant thread is awakened. The thread then gets the message sent to the control port, examines its internal tables, and performs the required action, namely interrupting the appropriate thread or threads.

A third area in which UNIX has been extended is in making it distributed. It is possible for a process to make a system call to indicate that new processes are not to be created on the local machine, but on a specific remote machine. When a new process is forked off, it starts on the same machine as the parent process, but when it does an EXEC system call, the new process is started on the remote machine.

User processes using the UNIX subsystem can create ports and port groups and send and receive messages, like any other Chorus processes. They can also create regions and map segments onto them. In general, all the Chorus facilities related to process management, memory management, and interprocess communication are available to UNIX processes as well.

9.5.3. Implementation of UNIX on Chorus

The implementation of the UNIX subsystem is constructed from four principal components: the **process manager**, the **object manager**, the **streams manager**, and the **interprocess communication manager**, as depicted in Fig. 9-20. Each of these has a specific function in the emulation. The process manager catches system calls and does process management. The object manager handles the file system calls and also paging activity. The streams manager takes care of I/O. The interprocess communication manager does System V IPC. The process manager is new code. The others are largely taken from UNIX itself to minimize the designer's work and maximize compatibility. These four managers can each handle multiple sessions, so only one of each is present on a given site, no matter how many users are logged into it.

In the original design, the four processes should have been able to run either in kernel mode or in user mode. However, as more privileged code was added,

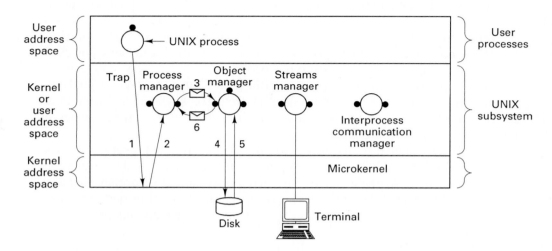

Fig. 9-20. The structure of the Chorus UNIX subsystem. The numbers show the sequence of steps involved in a typical file operation.

this became more difficult to do. In practice now, they normally all run in kernel mode, which also is needed to give acceptable performance.

To see how the pieces relate, we will examine how system calls are processed. At system initialization time, the process manager tells the kernel that it wants to handle the trap numbers standard AT&T UNIX uses for making system calls (to achieve binary compatibility). When a UNIX process later issues a system call by trapping to the kernel, as indicated by (1) in Fig. 9-21, a thread in the process manager gets control. This thread acts as though it is the same as the calling thread, analogous to the way system calls are made in traditional UNIX systems. Depending on the system call, the process manager may perform the requested system call itself, or as shown in Fig. 9-20, send a message to the object manager asking it to do the work. For I/O calls, the streams manager is invoked. For IPC calls, the communication manager is used.

In this example, the object manager does a disk operation and then sends a reply back to the process manager, which sets up the proper return value and restarts the blocked UNIX process.

The Process Manager

The process manager is the central player in the emulation. It catches all system calls and decides what to do with them. It also handles process management (including creating and terminating processes), signals (both generating them and receiving them), and naming. When a system call that it does not handle comes in, the process manager does an RPC to either the object manager or streams manager. It can also make kernel calls to do its job; for example, when forking off a new process, the kernel does most of the work.

If the new process is to be created on a remote machine, a more complicated mechanism is required, as shown in Fig. 9-21. Here the process manager catches the system call, but instead of asking the local kernel to create a new Chorus process, it does an RPC to the process manager on the target machine, step (3) in Fig. 9-21. The remote process manager then asks its kernel to create the process, as shown in step 4. Each process manager has a dedicated port to which RPCs from other process managers are directed.

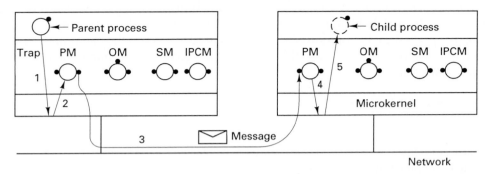

Fig. 9-21. Creating a process on a remote machine. The reply message is not shown.

The process manager has multiple threads. For example, when a user thread sets an alarm, a process manager thread goes to sleep until the timer goes off. Then it sends a message to the exception port belonging to the thread's process.

The process manager also manages the unique identifiers. It maintains tables that map the UIs onto the corresponding resources.

The Object Manager

The object manager handles files, swap space, and other forms of tangible information. It may also contain the disk driver. In addition to its exception port, the object manager has a port for receiving paging requests and a port for receiving requests from local or remote process managers. When a request comes in, a thread is dispatched to handle it. Several object manager threads may be active at once.

The object manager acts as a mapper for the files it controls. It accepts page fault requests on a dedicated port, does the necessary disk I/O, and sends appropriate replies.

The object manager works in terms of segments named by capabilities, in other words, in the Chorus way. When a UNIX process references a file descriptor, its runtime system invokes the process manager, which uses the file descriptor as an index into a table to locate the capability corresponding to the file's segment.

Logically, when a process reads from a file, that request should be caught by the process manager and then forwarded to the object manager using the normal RPC mechanism. However, since reads and writes are so important, an optimized strategy is used to improve their performance. The process manager maintains a table with the segment capabilities for all the open files. It makes an *sgRead* call to the kernel to get the required data. If the data are available, the kernel copies them directly to the user's buffer. If they are not, the kernel makes an *MpPullIn* upcall to the appropriate mapper (usually, the object manager). The mapper issues one or more disk reads, as needed. When the pages are available, the mapper gives them to the kernel, which copies the required data to the user's buffer and completes the system call.

The Streams Manager

The streams manager handles all the System V streams, including the keyboard, display, mouse, and tape devices. During system initialization, the streams manager sends a message to the object manager, announcing its port and telling which devices it is prepared to handle. Subsequent requests for I/O on these devices can then be sent to the streams manager.

The streams manager also handles Berkeley sockets and networking. In this way, a process on Chorus can communicate using TCP/IP as well as other network protocols. Pipes and named pipes are also handled here.

The Interprocess Communication Manager

This process handles those system calls relating to System V messages (not Chorus messages), System V semaphores (not Chorus semaphores), and System V shared memory (not Chorus shared memory). The system calls are unpleasant and the code is taken mostly from System V itself. The less said about them, the better.

Configurability

The division of labor within the UNIX subsystem makes it relatively straightforward to configure a collection of machines in different ways so that each one only has to run the software it needs. The nodes of a multiprocessor can also be configured differently. All machines need the process manager, but the other managers are optional. Which managers are needed depends on the application.

Let us now briefly discuss several different configurations that can be built using Chorus. Figure 9-22(a) shows the full configuration, which might be used on a workstation (with a hard disk) connected to a network. All four of the UNIX subsystem processes are required and present.

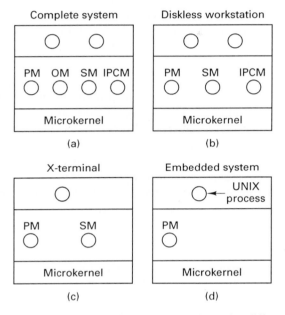

Fig. 9-22. Different applications may best be handled using different configurations.

The object manager is needed only on machines containing a disk, so on a diskless workstation the configuration of Fig. 9-22(b) would be most appropriate. When a process reads or writes a file on this machine, the process manager forwards the request to the object manager on the user's file server. In principle, either the user's machine or the file server can do caching, but not both, except for segments that have been opened or mapped in read-only mode.

For dedicated applications, such as an X-terminal, it is known in advance which system call the program may do and which it may not do. If no local file system and no System V IPC are needed, the object manager and interprocess communication manager can be omitted, as in Fig. 9-23(c).

Finally, for a disconnected embedded system, such as the controller for a car, television set, or talking teddy bear, only the process manager is needed. The others can be left out to reduce the amount of ROM needed. It is even possible for a dedicated application program to run directly on top of the microkernel.

The configuration can be done dynamically. When the system is booted it can inspect its environment and determine which of the managers are needed. If the machine has a disk, the object manager is loaded; otherwise, it is not, and so on. Alternatively, configuration files can be used. Also, each manager can be created with one thread. As requests come in, additional threads can be created on-the-fly. Table space, for example, the process table, is allocated dynamically from a pool, so it is not necessary to have a different kernel binary for small systems, with only a few processes, and large ones, with thousands of processes.

Real-Time Applications

Chorus has been designed to handle real-time applications, with or without UNIX. The Chorus scheduler, in particular, reflects this goal. Priorities range from 1 to 255. The lower the number, the higher the priority, as in UNIX.

Ordinary UNIX application processes run at priorities 128 to 255, as shown in Fig. 9-23. At these priority levels, when a process uses up its CPU quantum, it is put on the end of the queue for its priority level. The processes that make up the UNIX subsystem run at priorities 64 through 68. Thus a large number of priorities are available both higher and lower than the ones used by the UNIX subsystem for real-time processes.

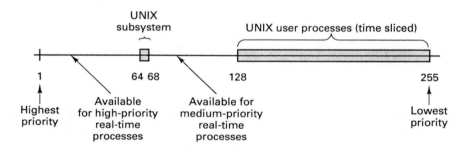

Fig. 9-23. Priorities and real-time processes.

Another facility that is important for real-time work is the ability to reduce the amount of time the CPU is disabled after an interrupt. Normally, when an interrupt occurs, an object manager or streams manager thread does the required processing immediately. However, an option is available to have the interrupt thread arrange for another, lower-priority thread to do the real work, so the interrupt can terminate almost immediately. Doing this reduces the amount of dead time after an interrupt, but it also increases the overhead of interrupt processing, so this feature must be used with care.

These facilities merge well with UNIX, so it is possible to debug a program under UNIX in the usual way, but have it run as a real-time process when it goes into production just by configuring the system differently.

9.6. COOL: AN OBJECT-ORIENTED SUBSYSTEM

The UNIX subsystem is really nothing more than a collection of Chorus processes that are marked as a subsystem. Consequently, it is possible to have other subsystems running at the same time. A second subsystem that has been developed for Chorus is **COOL** (**Chorus Object-Oriented Layer**). It was designed for research on object-oriented programming and to bridge the gap between coarse-grained system objects, such as files, and fine-grained language objects, such as structures (records). We will describe COOL in this section. For more information, see (Lea et al., 1991, 1993).

Work on the first version, COOL-1, began in 1988. The goal was to provide system-level support for fine-grained object-oriented languages and applications, and do so in such a way that new COOL programs and old UNIX programs could run side by side on the same machine without interfering.

Each Object in COOL-1 consisted of two Chorus segments, one for the data and one for the code. Programs did not access the data segments directly. Instead they invoked procedures, called **methods**, located in the objects' code segments. In this way, the objects' internal representation was hidden from the user, allowing object writers the freedom to use whatever representation seemed best (for example, an array or a linked list). This representation could even be changed later, without programs using the objects even knowing. Multiple objects of the same class shared the same code segment, to save memory.

To make a long story short, the resulting system was disappointing in terms of performance, resource usage, and so on, and the gap between coarse-grained system objects and fine-grained language objects was not bridged. In 1990, the designers started over and designed COOL-2. This system was running a year later. Below we will describe its architecture and implementation.

9.6.1. The COOL Architecture

Conceptually COOL provides a **COOL base layer** that spans machine boundaries. This layer provides a form of address space that is visible to all COOL processes without regard to where they are running, much like a distributed file system provides a global file space. On top of this layer is the **generic runtime system**, which is also system wide. Above that are the language runtime systems and then the user programs, as illustrated in Fig. 9-24.

9.6.2. The COOL Base Layer

The COOL base provides a set of services for COOL user processes, specifically for the COOL generic library that is linked with each COOL process. The most important service is a memory abstraction, roughly analogous to

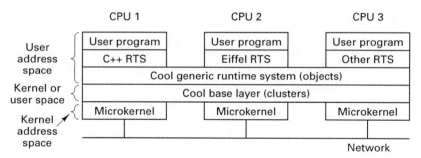

Fig. 9-24. The COOL architecture.

distributed shared memory, but more tuned to object-oriented programming. This abstraction is based on the **cluster**, which is a set of Chorus regions backed by segments. Each cluster normally holds a group of related objects, for example, objects belonging to the same class. It is up to the upper layers of software to determine which objects go in which cluster.

A cluster can be mapped into the address spaces of multiple processes, possibly on different machines. A cluster always begins on a page boundary, and occupies the same addresses in all processes that are currently using it. The regions in a cluster need not be contiguous in virtual address space, so a cluster may, for example, occupy addresses 1024-2047, 4096-8191, and 14336-16535 (assuming a 1K page size).

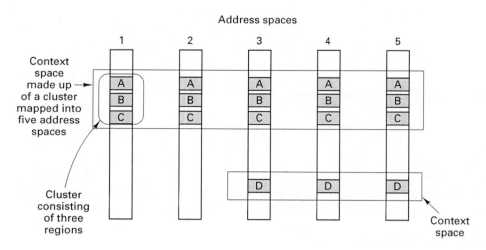

Fig. 9-25. Context spaces and clusters.

A second concept supported by the COOL base is the **context space**, which is a collection of address spaces, again, possibly on multiple machines. Figure

9-25 shows a system with five address spaces (on up to five machines) and two context spaces. The first context space spans all the machines and contains a cluster with three regions. The threads living in these address spaces can all access the objects in this cluster as though they were in a shared memory. The second context space spans only three machines and has a cluster with one region. Threads in address spaces 1 and 2 cannot access the objects in this cluster. The corresponding clusters in different address spaces must be mapped in at the same virtual addresses. Internal pointers are relocated at the time the mapping occurs.

Clusters are not replicated. This means that although a cluster may appear in multiple address spaces at the same time, there is only one physical copy of each cluster. When a user thread tries to invoke a method on an object that is in its address space but physically not present on its machine, a trap occurs to the COOL base. The base then either forwards the request to the machine holding the cluster for remote invocation or arranges for the cluster to migrate to its machine for local invocation.

9.6.3. The COOL Generic Runtime System

The COOL generic runtime uses clusters and context spaces to manage objects. Objects are persistent and exist on disk when no process has them mapped in. Operations are provided to the language runtime system to create and delete objects, map them into and out of address spaces, and invoke their methods. When an object invokes a method of another object that is located in its own cluster, the invocation is done by a local procedure call. When the invoked object is in a different cluster, the generic runtime system is used to ask the COOL base to arrange for the remote invocation. Because the overhead of intracluster invocations is so much smaller than that of intercluster invocations, putting objects that invoke each other a lot together in one cluster greatly reduces system overhead. In COOL-1, all invocations were effectively intercluster operations, which proved to be expensive.

The generic runtime system has a standard interface to the language-dependent runtime systems that use it. The interface is based on **up calls**, in which the generic runtime system calls the language runtime system to find out properties of objects, for example, to find internal pointers for relocation purposes when an object is mapped in.

9.6.4. The Language Runtime System

Normally, when programmers define objects, they define them in a special interface definition language. These definitions then are compiled into objects that can be called at run time to invoke the objects. These interface objects then decide whether invocations on remote objects will be done remotely, or the object will be migrated locally. Methods in the interface objects allow the program to control the policy used.

9.6.5. Implementation of COOL

The COOL subsystem runs on top of the Chorus microkernel, just like the UNIX one. It consists of a process that implements the COOL base and a COOL generic runtime system that is linked with every COOL program (along with the language library), as shown in Fig. 9-26. This design allows COOL processes to make calls to the COOL subsystem, while at the same time UNIX processes make calls to the UNIX subsystem, without the two interfering. This modularity is a direct result of the microkernel design, and holds for Amoeba and Mach as well, of course.

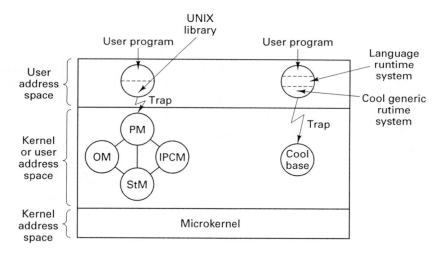

Fig. 9-26. Implementation of COOL.

9.7. COMPARISON OF AMOEBA, MACH, AND CHORUS

In this and the preceding two chapters we have looked at three microkernel-based distributed operating systems, Amoeba, Mach, and Chorus, in considerable detail. While they have some points in common, Amoeba and Mach differ in many of the technical details. Chorus has borrowed many ideas from both Amoeba and Mach, and thus often takes an intermediate position between the two. In this section we will look at all three systems side-by-side to illustrate the various choices that designers can make.

9.7.1. Philosophy

Amoeba, Mach and Chorus have different histories and different philosophies. Amoeba was designed from scratch as a distributed system for use on a collection of CPUs connected by a LAN. Later, multiprocessors and WANs were added. Mach (actually RIG) started out as an operating system for a single processor, with multiprocessors and LANs being added afterward. Chorus began as a distributed operating systems research project quite far from the UNIX world, and went through three major revisions, getting closer and closer to UNIX each time. The consequences of these differing backgrounds are still visible in the systems.

Amoeba is based on the processor pool model. A user does not log into a particular machine, but into the system as a whole. The operating system decides where to run each command, based on the current load. It is normal for requests to use multiple processors; rarely will two consecutive commands run on the same processor. There is no concept of a home machine.

In contrast, Mach and Chorus (UNIX) were designed with the idea that a user definitely logs into a specific machine and runs all his programs there by default. There is no attempt to spread each user's work over as many machines as possible (although on a multiprocessor, the work will be spread automatically over all the multiprocessor's CPUs). While it is possible to run remotely, the philosophical difference is that each user has a home machine (e.g., a workstation) where most of his work is carried out. However, this distinction was later blurred when Mach was ported to the Intel Paragon, a machine consisting of a pool of processors.

Another philosophical difference relates to what a "microkernel" is. The Amoeba view follows the famous dictum expounded by the French aviator and writer Antoine de St. Exupéry: Perfection is not achieved when there is nothing left to add, but when there is nothing left to take away. Whenever a proposal was made to add a new feature to the kernel, the deciding question was: Can we live without it? This philosophy led to a minimal kernel, with most of the code in user-level servers.

The Mach designers, in contrast, wanted to provide enough functionality in the kernel to handle the widest possible range of applications. In many areas, Amoeba contains one way to do something and Mach contains two or three, each more convenient or efficient under different circumstances. Consequently, the Mach kernel is much larger and has five times as many system calls (including calls to kernel threads) as Amoeba. Chorus occupies an intermediate position between Amoeba and Mach, but it still has more system calls than 4.2 BSD UNIX, which is hardly a microkernel. A comparison is given in Fig. 9-27.

System	Kernel calls
Amoeba	30
Version 7 UNIX	45
4.2 BSD	84
Chorus	112
Mach	153
SunOS	165

Fig. 9-27. Number of system calls and calls to kernel threads in selected systems.

Another philosophical difference between Amoeba and Mach is that Amoeba has been optimized for the remote case (communication over the network) and Mach for the local case (communication via memory). Amoeba has extremely fast RPC over the network, while Mach's copy-on-write mechanism provides high-speed communication on a single node, for example. Chorus has primarily emphasized single CPU and multiprocessor systems, but since the communication management is done in the kernel (as in Amoeba) and not in a user process (as in Mach), it potentially can have good RPC performance, too.

9.7.2. Objects

Objects are the central concept in Amoeba. A few are built in, like threads and processes, but most are user defined (e.g., files) and can have arbitrary operations on them. About a dozen generic operations (e.g., get status) are defined on nearly all objects, with various object-specific operations defined on each one as well.

In contrast, the only objects supported directly by Mach are threads, processes, ports, and memory objects, each with a fixed set of operations. Higher level software can use these concepts to build other objects, but they are qualitatively different than the built-in objects like memory objects.

In all three systems, objects are named, addressed, and protected by capabilities. In Amoeba, capabilities are managed in user space and protected by one-way functions. Capabilities for system-defined objects (e.g., processes) and for user-defined objects (e.g., directories) are treated in a uniform way and appear in user-level directories for naming and addressing all objects. Amoeba capabilities are in principle worldwide, that is, a directory can hold capabilities for files and other objects that are located anywhere. Objects are located by broadcasting, with the results cached for future use.

Mach also has capabilities, but only for ports. These are managed by the kernel in capability lists, one per process. Unlike Amoeba, there are no capabilities for processes or other system or user-defined objects, and they are not generally used directly by application programs. Port capabilities are passed between processes in a controlled way, so Mach can find them by looking them up in kernel tables.

Chorus supports about the same built-in objects as Mach, but also uses Amoeba's capability system for allowing subsystems to define new protected objects. Unlike Amoeba, Chorus capabilities do not have an explicit (cryptographically protected) field giving the allowed rights. Like Amoeba's capabilities and unlike Mach's, Chorus' capabilities can be passed from one process to another simply by including them in a message or writing them to a shared file.

9.7.3. Processes

All three systems support processes with multiple threads per process. Again in all three cases, the threads are managed and scheduled by the kernel, although a user-level threads packages can be built on top of them. Amoeba does not provide user control over thread scheduling, whereas Mach and Chorus allows processes to set the priorities and policies of their threads in software. Mach provides more elaborate multiprocessor support than the other two.

In Amoeba and Chorus, synchronization between threads is done by mutexes and semaphores. In Mach it is done by mutexes and condition variables. Amoeba and Mach support some form of glocal variables. Chorus uses software registers to define each thread's private context.

Amoeba, Mach, and Chorus all work on multiprocessors, but they differ on how they deal with threads on these machines. In Amoeba, all the threads of a process run on the same CPU, in pseudoparallel, timeshared by the kernel. In Mach processes have fine-grained control over which threads run on which CPUs (using the processor set concept). Consequently, the threads of the same process can run in parallel on different CPUs.

In Amoeba, a similar effect can be achieved by having several single-threaded processes run on different CPUs and share a common address space. Nevertheless, it is clear that the Mach designers have devoted more attention to multiprocessors than have the Amoeba designers.

Chorus supports having multiple threads within a single process running on different CPUs at the same time, but this is handled entirely by the operating system. There are no user-visible primitives for managing thread-to-processor allocation, but there will be in the future.

However, the Amoeba designers have put more work into supporting load balancing and heterogeneity. When the Amoeba shell starts a process, it asks the run server to find it the CPU with the lightest workload. Unless the user has specified a specific architecture, the process may be started on any architecture for which a binary is available, with the user not even being aware which kind has been selected. This scheme is designed to spread the workload over as many machines as possible all the time.

In Mach, processes are normally started on the user's home machine. Only when explicitly requested to do so by the user are processes run remotely on idle workstations, and even then they have to be evicted quickly if the workstation's owner touches the keyboard. This difference relates to the fundamental difference between the processor pool model and the workstation model.

Chorus allows a process to be started on any machine. The UNIX emulation provides a way to set the default site.

9.7.4. Memory Model

Amoeba's memory model is based on variable-length segments. A virtual address space consists of some number of segments mapped in at specific addresses. Segments can be mapped in and out at will. Each segment is controlled by a capability. A remote process that has the capabilities for another process' segments (e.g., a debugger) can read and write them from any other Amoeba machine. Amoeba does not support paging. When a process is running, all of its segments are in memory. The ideas behind this decision are simplicity of design and high performance, coupled with the fact that extremely large memories are becoming common on even the smallest machines.

Mach's memory model is based on memory objects and is implemented in terms of fixed-size pages. Memory objects can be mapped and unmapped at will. A memory object need not be entirely in main memory to be used. When an absent page is referenced, a page fault occurs and a message is sent to an external memory manager to find the page and map it in. Together with the default memory manager, this mechanism supports paged virtual memory.

Pages can be shared between multiple processes in various ways. One common configuration is the copy-on-write sharing used to attach a child process to its parent. Although this mechanism is a highly efficient way of sharing on a single node, it loses its advantages in a distributed system because physical transport is always required (assuming that the receiver needs to read the data). In such an environment, the extra code and complexity are wasted. This is a clear example of where Mach has been optimized for single-CPU and multiprocessor systems, rather than for distributed systems.

Chorus' memory management model is taken largely from Mach. It too has memory objects (segments) that can be mapped in. These are demand paged under the control of an external pager (mapper), as in Mach.

Amoeba, Mach, and Chorus all support distributed shared memory, but they do it in different ways. Amoeba supports shared objects that are replicated on all machines using them. Objects can be of any size and can support any operations. Reads are done locally, and writes are done using the Amoeba reliable broadcast protocol.

Mach and Chorus, in contrast, support a page-based distributed shared memory. When a thread references a page that is not present on its machine, the page is fetched from its current machine and brought in. If two machines heavily access the same writable page, thrashing can occur. The trade-off here is the more expensive update on Amoeba (due to the replication of writable objects), versus the potential for thrashing on Mach and Chorus (only one copy of writable pages).

9.7.5. Communication

Amoeba supports both RPC and group communication as fundamental primitives. RPCs are addressed to put-ports, which are service addresses. They are protected cryptographically using one-way functions. The sending and receiving machines can be anywhere. The RPC interface is very simple: only three system calls, none with any options.

Group communication provides reliable broadcasting as a user primitive. Messages can be sent to any group with a guarantee of reliable delivery. In addition, all group members see all messages arrive in exactly the same order.

Low-level communication uses the FLIP protocol, which provides process addressing (as opposed to machine addressing). This feature allows process migration and (inter)network reconfiguration automatically, without the software even being aware of it. It also supports other facilities useful in distributed systems.

In contrast, Mach's communication is from process to port, rather than from process to process. Furthermore, the sender and port must be on the same node. Using a network message server or the NORMA code as a proxy, communication can be extended over a network, but this indirection extracts a performance penalty. Mach does not support group communication or reliable broadcasting as basic kernel primitives.

Communication is done using the *mach_msg* system call, which has seven parameters, ten options, and 35 potential error messages. It supports both synchronous and asynchronous message passing. This approach is the antithesis of the Amoeba strategy of "Keep it simple and make it fast." The idea here is to provide the maximum flexibility and the widest range of support for present and future applications.

Mach messages can be either simple or complex. Simple messages are just bits and are not processed in any special way by the kernel. Complex messages may contain capabilities. They may also pass out-of-line data using copy-on-write, something Amoeba does not have. On the other hand, this facility is of little value in a distributed system because the out-of-line data must be fetched by the network message server, combined with the message header and in-line data, and sent over the network. This optimization is for the local case and wins nothing when the sender and receiver are on different machines.

On the network, Mach uses conventional protocols such as TCP/IP. These have the advantage of being stable and widely available. FLIP, in contrast, is new, but is faster for typical RPC usage and has been specifically designed for the needs of distributed computing.

Communication in Chorus is philosophically similar to Mach, but simpler. Messages are directed to ports and can either be sent asynchronously or by using RPC. All Chorus communication is handled by the kernel, as in Amoeba. There is nothing like the network message server in Chorus. Like Amoeba and unlike Mach, a Chorus message has a fixed header containing source and destination information, and an untyped body that is just an array of bytes as far as the system is concerned. As in Amoeba, capabilities in messages are not treated in any special way.

Chorus supports broadcasting at the kernel level but in a way more like Mach (which does not support it) than like Amoeba (which does). Ports can be grouped together in port groups, and messages sent to all the members of a port group (or to just one). There is no guarantee that all processes see all messages in the same order, as in Amoeba.

9.7.6. Servers

Amoeba has a variety of servers for specific functions, including file management, directory management, object replication, and load balancing. All are based on objects and capabilities. Amoeba supports replicated objects via directories that contain capability sets. UNIX emulation is provided at the source code level, is based on POSIX, but is not 100 percent complete. The emulation is done by mapping UNIX concepts onto Amoeba ones and calling on the native Amoeba servers to do the work. For example, when a file is opened, the capability for the file is acquired and stored in the file descriptor table.

Mach has a single server that runs BSD UNIX as an application program. It provides 100 percent binary-compatible emulation, a great boon for running existing software for which the source code is not available. General object replication is not supported. Other servers also exist.

Chorus provides full binary compatibility with System V UNIX. The emulation is done by a collection of processes (like Amoeba) rather than by running UNIX as an application program (like Mach). However, some of these processes contain actual UNIX code, like Mach and unlike Amoeba. Like Amoeba, the native servers were designed from scratch with distributed computing in mind, so the emulation translates the UNIX constructs onto the native ones. Just as in

Amoeba, for example, when a file is opened, a capability for it is fetched and stored in the file descriptor table.

A brief summary of some of the points discussed above is given in Fig. 9-28.

Item	Amoeba	Mach	Chorus
Designed for:	Distributed system	1 CPU, multiprocessor	1 CPU, multiprocessor
Execution model	Pool processor	Workstation	Workstation
Microkernel?	Yes	Yes	Yes
Number of kernel calls	30	153	112
Automatic load balancing?	Yes	No	No
Capabilities	General	Only ports	General
Capabilities in:	User space	Kernel	User space
Threads managed by:	Kernel	Kernel	Kernel
Transparent heterogenity?	Yes	No	No
User-settable priorities?	No	Yes	Yes
Multiprocessor support	Minimal	Extensive	Moderate
Mapped object	Segment	Memory object	Segment
Demand paging?	No	Yes	Yes
Copy on write?	No	Yes	Yes
External pagers?	No	Yes	Yes
Distributed shared memory	Object based	Page based	Page based
RPC?	Yes	Yes	Yes
Group communication	Reliable, ordered	None	Unreliable
Asynchronous communication?	No	Yes	Yes
Intermachine messages	Kernel	User space/ kernel	Kernel
Messages address to:	Process	Port	Port
UNIX emulation	Source	Binary	Binary
UNIX compatibility	POSIX (partial)	BSD	System V
Single-server UNIX?	No	Yes	No
Multiserver UNIX?	Yes	No	Yes
Optimized for:	Remote case	Local case	Local case
Automatic file replication?	Yes	No	No

Fig. 9-28. A comparison of Amoeba, Mach, and Chorus.

9.8. SUMMARY

Like Amoeba and Mach, Chorus is a microkernel-based operating system for use in distributed systems. It provides binary compatibility with System V UNIX, support for real-time applications, and object-oriented programming.

Chorus consists of three conceptual layers: the kernel layer, the subsystems, and the user processes. The kernel layer contains the microkernel proper, as well as some kernel processes that run in kernel mode and share the microkernel's address space. The middle layer contains the subsystems, which are used to build provide operating system support to user programs, which reside in the top layer.

The microkernel provides six key abstractions: processes, threads, regions, messages, ports, port groups, and unique identifiers. Processes provide a way to collect and manage resources. Threads are the active entities in the system, and are scheduled by the kernel using a priority-based scheduler. Regions are areas of virtual address space that can have segments mapped into them. Ports are buffers used to hold incoming messages not yet read. Unique identifiers are binary names used to identifying resources.

The microkernel and subsystems together provide three additional constructs: capabilities, protection identifiers, and segments. The first two are used to name and protect subsystem resources. The third is the basis of memory allocation, both within a running process and on disk.

Two subsystems were described in this chapter. The UNIX subsystem consists of the process, object, streams, and interprocess communication managers, which work together to provide binary compatible UNIX emulation. The COOL subsystem provides support for object-oriented programming.

PROBLEMS

1. Capabilities in Chorus use epoch numbers in their UIs. Why?

2. What is the difference between a region and a segment?

3. The Chorus supervisor is machine dependent, whereas the real-time executive is machine independent. Explain.

4. Why does Chorus need system processes in addition to user processes and kernel processes?

5. What is the difference between a thread being SUSPENDED and it being STOPPED? After all, in both cases it cannot run.

6. Briefly describe how exceptions and interrupts are handled in Chorus, and tell why they are handled differently.

7. Chorus supports both semaphores and mutexes. Is this strictly necessary? Would it not be sufficient to support only semaphores?

8. What is the function of a mapper?

9. Briefly describe what *MpPullIn* and *MpPushOut* are used for.

10. Chorus supports both RPC and an asynchronous send. What is the essential difference between these two?

11. Give a possible use of port migration in Chorus.

12. It is possible to send a message to a port group in Chorus. Does the message go to all the ports in the group, or to a randomly selected port?

13. Chorus has explicit calls to create and delete ports, but only a call for creating port groups (*grpAllocate*). Make an educated guess as to why there is no *grpDelete*.

14. Why were miniports introduced? Do they do anything that regular ports do not do?

15. Why does Chorus support both preemptive and nonpreemptive scheduling?

16. Name one way in which Chorus is like Amoeba. Name one way in which it is like Mach.

17. How does Chorus' use of port groups differ from group communication in Amoeba?

18. Why did Chorus extend the semantics of UNIX signals?

10

Case Study 4: DCE

In the preceding three chapters we have looked at microkernel-based distributed systems in some detail. In this chapter we will examine a completely different approach, the Open System Foundation's **Distributed Computing Environment**, or **DCE** for short. Unlike the microkernel-based approaches, which are revolutionary in nature—throwing out current operating systems and starting all over—DCE takes an evolutionary approach, building a distributed computing environment on top of existing operating systems. In the next section we will introduce the ideas behind DCE, and in those following it, we will look at each of the principal components of DCE in some detail.

10.1. INTRODUCTION TO DCE

In this section we will give an overview of the history, goals, models, and components of DCE, as well as an introduction to the cell concept, which plays an important role in DCE.

10.1.1. History of DCE

OSF was set up by a group of major computer vendors, including IBM, DEC, and Hewlett Packard, as a response to AT&T and Sun Microsystems signing an agreement to further develop and market the UNIX operating system. The other companies were afraid that this arrangement would give Sun a competitive advantage over them. The initial goal of OSF was to develop and market a new version of UNIX, over which they, and not AT&T/Sun, had control. This goal was accomplished with the release of OSF/1.

From the beginning it was apparent that many the OSF consortium's customers wanted to build distributed applications on top of OSF/1 and other UNIX systems. OSF responded to this need by issuing a "Request for Technology" in which they asked companies to supply tools and other software needed to put together a distributed system. Many companies made bids, which were carefully evaluated. OSF then selected a number of these offerings, and developed them further to produce a single integrated package—DCE— that could run on OSF/1 and also on other systems. DCE is now one of OSF's major products. A complementary product, **DME (Distributed Management Environment)**, for managing distributed systems was planned but never made it.

10.1.2. Goals of DCE

The primary goal of DCE is to provide a coherent, seamless environment that can serve as a platform for running distributed applications. Unlike Amoeba, Mach, and Chorus, this environment is built on top of existing operating systems, initially UNIX, but later it was ported to VMS, WINDOWS, and OS/2. The idea is that the customer can take a collection of existing machines, add the DCE software, and then be able to run distributed applications, all without disturbing existing (nondistributed) applications. Although most of the DCE package runs in user space, in some configurations a piece (part of the distributed file system) must be added to the kernel. OSF itself only sells source code, which vendors integrate into their systems. For simplicity, in this chapter we will concentrate primarily on DEC on top of UNIX.

The environment offered by DCE consists of a large number of tools and services, plus an infrastructure for them to operate in. The tools and services have been chosen so that they work together in an integrated way and make it easier to develop distributed applications. For example, DCE provides tools that make it easier to write applications that have high availability. As another example, DCE provides a mechanism for synchronizing clocks on different machines, to yield a global notion of time.

DCE runs on many different kinds of computers, operating systems, and networks. Consequently, application developers can easily produce portable software that runs on a variety of platforms, amortizing development costs and increasing the potential market size.

The distributed system on which a DCE application runs can be a heterogeneous system, consisting of computers from multiple vendors, each of which has its own local operating system. The layer of DCE software on top of the operating system hides the differences, automatically doing conversions between data types when necessary. All of this is transparent to the application programmer.

As a consequence of all of the above, DCE makes it easier to write applications in which multiple users at multiple sites work together, collaborating on some project by sharing hardware and software resources. Security is an important part of any such arrangement, so DCE provides extensive tools for authentication and protection.

Finally, DCE has been designed to interwork with existing standards in a number of areas. For example, a group of DCE machines can communicate with each other and with the outside world using either TCP/IP or the OSI protocols, and resources can be located either using the DNS or X.500 naming systems. The POSIX standards are also used.

10.1.3. DCE Components

The programming model underlying all of DCE is the client/server model. User processes act as clients to access remote services provided by server processes. Some of these services are part of DCE itself, but others belong to the applications and are written by the applications programmers. In this section we will give a quick introduction to those distributed services that are provided by the DCE package itself, mainly the time, directory, security, and file system services.

In most DCE applications, client programs are more-or-less normal C programs that have been linked with a special library. The client binary programs then contain a small number of library procedures that provide the interfaces to the services, hiding the details from the programmers. Servers, in contrast, are normally large daemon programs. They run all the time, waiting for requests for work to arrive. When requests come in, they are processed and replies are sent back.

In addition to offering distributed services, DCE also furnishes two facilities for distributed programming that are not organized as services: threads and RPC (Remote Procedure Call). The threads facility allows multiple threads of control to exist in the same process at the same time. Some versions of UNIX provide threads themselves, but using DCE provides a standard thread interface across systems. Where possible, DCE can use the native threads to implement DCE threads, but where there are no native threads, DCE provides a threads package from scratch.

The other DCE facility is RPC, which is the basis for all communication in DCE. To access a service, the client process does an RPC to a remote server process. The server carries out the request and (optionally) sends back a reply.

DCE handles the complete mechanism, including locating the server, binding to it, and performing the call.

Figure 10-1 gives an approximate idea of how the various parts of DCE fit together. At the lowest level is the computer hardware, on top of which the native operating system (with DCE additions) runs. To support a full-blown DCE server, the operating system must either be UNIX or be another system with essentially the functionality of UNIX, including multiprogramming, local interprocess communication, memory management, timers, and security. To support only a DCE client, less functionality is required, and even MS-DOS is sufficient.

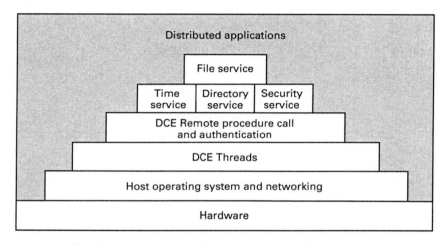

Fig. 10-1. Rough sketch of how the parts of DCE fit together.

On top of the operating system is the DCE threads package. If the operating system has a suitable threads package itself, the DCE threads library just serves to convert the interface to the DCE standard. If there is no native threads package, DCE supplies a threads package that runs almost entirely in user space, except for a few hundred lines of assembly code in the kernel for managing thread stacks. Next comes the RPC package, which, like the threads code is a collection of library procedures. A portion of the security is logically also in this layer, since it is required for performing authenticated RPC.

On top of the RPC layer come the various DCE services. Not every service runs on every machine. The system administrator determines which service to run where. The standard services are the time, directory, and security, with the distributed file service on top of them, as shown. In a typical configuration, these services run only on "system server" machines and not on client workstations. A short introduction to each of these follows.

The general function of the threads and RPC packages should be clear, but a short explanation of the services may be helpful now. Detailed discussions of all the facilities and services will be presented later. The **distributed time service** is needed because each machine in the system normally has its own clock, so the concept of what time it is is more complicated than in a single system. For example, the UNIX *make* program examines the creation times of the source and binary files of a large program to determine which sources have changed since the binary was last made. Only these sources need to be recompiled. Consider, however, what happens if the sources and binaries are stored on different machines, and the clocks are not synchronized. The fact that the creation time for a binary file is later than the creation time for the corresponding source file does not mean than recompilation can be skipped. The difference might be a consequence of the two clocks being different. The DCE time service attempts to solve this problem by keeping the clocks synchronized in order to provide a global notion of time.

The **directory service** is used to keep track of the location of all resources in the system. These resources include machines, printers, servers, data, and much more, and they may be distributed geographically over the entire world. The directory service allows a process to ask for a resource and not have to be concerned about where it is, unless the process cares.

The **security service** allows resources of all kinds to be protected, so access can be restricted to authorized persons. For example, in a hospital information system, it might be the policy that a doctor could see all the medical information about her own patients, but not about other doctors' patients. People working in the billing department might be allowed to see all patients' records, but only the financial aspects. If a blood test is performed, the doctor can see what the medical results are and the bookkeeper can see how much it cost (but not the medical results). The security service provides tools that aid the construction of applications like this.

Finally, the **distributed file service** is a worldwide file system that provides a transparent way of accessing any file in the system in the same way. It can either be built on top of the hosts' native file systems or be used instead of them.

At the top of the DCE food chain are the distributed applications. These can use (or bypass) any of the DCE facilities and services. Simple applications may implicitly use RPC (via the library, and without realizing it) and little else, whereas more complex applications may make many explicit calls to all the services.

The picture given in Fig. 10-1 is not completely accurate, but it is hard to depict the dependencies between the parts because they are recursive. For example, the directory service uses RPC for internal communication among its various servers, but the RPC package uses the directory service to locate the destination. Thus it is not strictly true that the directory service layer is on top of RPC, as shown. As a second example, illustrating horizontal dependencies, the time service uses the security service to see who may set the clock, but the security service uses the time service to issue permission tickets with short life-times. Nevertheless, to a first approximation, Fig. 10-1 gives an indication of the gross structure, so we will use it as our model henceforth.

10.1.4. Cells

Users, machines, and other resources in a DCE system are grouped together to form **cells**. Naming, security, administration, and other aspects of DCE are based upon these cells. Cell boundaries usually mirror organizational units, for example, a small company or a department of a large company might be one cell.

When determining how to group machines into cells, four factors should be taken into consideration:

1. Purpose.

2. Security.

3. Overhead.

4. Administration.

The first factor, purpose, means that the machines in a cell (and their users) should all be working toward a common goal or on a common long-term project (probably measured in years). The users should know each other and have more contact with each other than with people outside the cell. Departments in companies are often structured this way. Cells can also be organized around a common service offered, such as online banking, with all the automated teller machines and the central computer belonging to a single cell.

The second factor, security, has to do with the fact that DCE works better when the users in a cell trust each other more than they trust people outside the cell. The reason for this is that cell boundaries act like firewalls—getting at internal resources is straightforward, but accessing anything in another cell requires the two cells to perform an arms' length negotiation to make sure that they trust one another.

The third factor, overhead, is important because some DCE functions are optimized for intracell operation (e.g., security). Geography can play a role here because putting distant users in the same cell means that they will often have to go over a wide-area network to communicate. If the wide-area network is slow and unreliable, extra overhead will be incurred to deal with these problems and compensate for them where possible.

Finally, every cell needs an administrator. If all the people and machines in a cell belong to the same department or project, there should be no problem appointing an administrator. However, if they belong to two widely separated departments, each with its own czar, it may be harder to agree upon one person to administer the cell and make cell-wide decisions.

Subject to these constraints, it is desirable to have as few cells as possible to minimize the number of operations that cross cell boundaries. Also, if an intruder ever breaks into a cell and steals the security data base, new passwords will have to be established with every other cell. The more of them there are, the more work is involved.

To make the idea of cells clearer, let us consider two examples. The first is a large manufacturer of electrical equipment whose products range from aircraft engines to toasters. The second is a publisher whose books cover everything from art to zoos. Since the electrical manufacturer's products are so diverse, it may organize its cells around products, as shown in Fig. 10-2(a), with different cells for the toaster group and the jet engine group. Each cell would contain the design, manufacturing, and marketing people, on the grounds that people marketing jet engines need more contact with people manufacturing jet engines than they do with people marketing toasters.

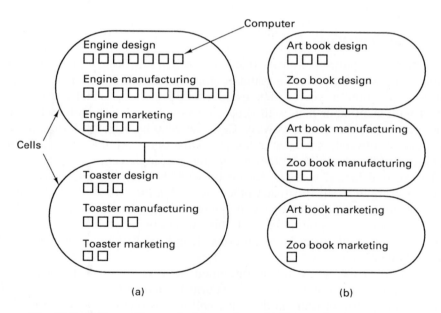

Fig. 10-2. (a) Two cells organized by product. (b) Three cells organized by function.

In contrast, the publisher would probably organize the cells as in Fig. 10-2(b) because manufacturing (i.e., printing and binding) a book on art is pretty much like manufacturing a book on zoos, so the differences between the departments are probably more significant than the differences between the products.

On the other hand, if the publisher has separate, autonomous divisions for childrens' books, trade books, and textbooks, all of which were originally separate companies with their own management structures and corporate cultures, arranging the cells by division rather than function may be best.

The point of these examples is that the determination of cell boundaries tends to be driven by business considerations, not technical properties of DCE.

Cell size can vary considerably, but all cells must contain a time server, a directory server, and a security server. It is possible for the time server, directory server, and security server all to run on the same machine. In addition, most cells will either contain one or more application clients (for doing work) or one or more application servers (for delivering a service). In a large cell, there might be multiple instances of the time, directory, and security servers, as well as hundreds of applications client and servers.

10.2. THREADS

The threads package, along with the RPC package, is one of the fundamental building blocks of DCE. In this section we will discuss the DCE threads package, focusing on scheduling, synchronization, and the calls available.

10.2.1. Introduction to DCE Threads

The DCE threads package is based on the P1003.4a POSIX standard. It is a collection of user-level library procedures that allow processes to create, delete, and manipulate threads. However, if the host system comes with a (kernel) threads package, the vendor can set up DCE to use it. The basic calls are for creating and deleting threads, waiting for a thread, and synchronizing computation between threads. Many other calls are provided for handling all the details and other functions.

A thread can be in one of four states, as shown in Fig. 10-3. A **running** thread is one that is actively using the CPU to do computation. A **ready** thread is willing and able to run, but cannot run because the CPU is currently busy running another thread. In contrast, a **waiting** thread is one that logically cannot run because it is waiting for some event to happen (e.g., a mutex to be unlocked). Finally, a **terminated** thread is one that has exited but has not yet been deleted and whose memory (i.e., stack space) has not yet been recovered. Only when another thread explicitly deletes it does a thread vanish.

On a machine with one CPU, only one thread can be actually running at a given instant. On a multiprocessor, several threads within a single process can be running at once, on different CPUs (true parallelism).

The threads package has been designed to minimize the impact on existing

State	Description
Running	The thread is actively using the CPU
Ready	The thread wants to run
Waiting	The thread is blocked waiting for some event
Terminated	The thread has exited but not yet been destroyed

Fig. 10-3. A thread can be in one of four states.

software, so programs designed for a single-threaded environment can be converted to multithreaded processes with a minimum of work. Ideally, a single-threaded program can be converted into a multithreaded one just by setting a parameter indicating that more threads should be used. However, problems can arise in three areas.

The first problem relates to signals. Signals can be left in their default state, ignored, or caught. Some signals are synchronous, caused specifically by the running thread. These include floating-point exception, causing a memory protection violation, and having your own timer go off. Others are asynchronous, caused by some external agency, such as the user hitting the DEL key to interrupt the running process.

When a synchronous signal occurs, it is handled by the current thread, except that if it is neither ignored nor caught, the entire process is killed. When an asynchronous signal occurs, the threads package checks to see if any threads are waiting for it. If so, it is passed to all the threads that want to handle it.

The second problem relates to the standard library, most of whose procedures are not reentrant. It can happen that a thread is busy allocating memory when a clock interrupt forces a thread switch. At the moment of the switch, the memory allocator's internal data structures may be inconsistent, which will cause problems if the newly scheduled thread tries to allocate some memory.

This problem is solved by providing jackets around some of the library procedures (mostly I/O procedures) that provide mutual exclusion for the individual calls. For the other procedures, a single global mutex makes sure that only one thread at a time is active in the library. The library procedures, such as *read* and *fork* are all jacketed procedures that handle the mutual exclusion and then call another (hidden) procedure to do the work. This solution is something of a quick hack. A better solution would be to provide a proper reentrant library.

The third problem has to do with the fact that UNIX system calls return their error status in a global variable, *errno*. If one thread makes a system call but just after the call completes, another thread is scheduled and it, too, makes a system call, the original value of *errno* will be lost. A solution is provided by providing an alternative error handling interface. It consists of a macro that allows the programmer to inspect a thread-specific version of *errno* that is saved and restored upon thread switches. This solution avoids the need to examine the global version of *errno*. In addition, it is also possible to have system calls indicate errors by raising exceptions, thus bypassing the problem altogether.

10.2.2. Scheduling

Thread scheduling is similar to process scheduling, except that it is visible to the application. The scheduling algorithm determines how long a thread may run, and which thread runs next. Just as with process scheduling, many thread scheduling algorithms are possible.

Threads in DCE have priorities and these are respected by the scheduling algorithm. High-priority threads are assumed to be more important than low-priority threads, and therefore should get better treatment, meaning they run first and get a larger portion of the CPU.

DCE supports the three thread scheduling algorithms illustrated in Fig. 10-4. The first, FIFO, searches the priority queues from highest to lowest, to locate the highest priority queue with one or more threads on it. The first thread on this queue is then run until it finishes, either by blocking or exiting. In principle, the selected thread can run as long as it needs to. When it has finished, it is removed from the queue of runnable threads. Then the scheduler once again searches the queues from high to low and takes the first thread it finds.

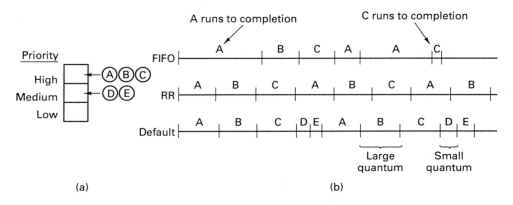

Fig. 10-4. (a) A system with five threads and three priority levels. (b) Three thread scheduling algorithms.

The second algorithm is round robin. Here the scheduler locates the highest populated queue and runs each thread for a fixed quantum. If a thread blocks or

exits before its quantum is up, it is (temporarily) removed from the queue system. If it uses up its entire quantum, it is suspended and placed at the end of its
queue. In the middle example of Fig. 10-4(b), the threads *A*, *B*, and *C* will run
alternately forever if they want to. The medium-priority threads *D* and *E* will
never get a chance as long as one of the high-priority threads wants to run.

The third algorithm is the default algorithm. It runs the threads on all the
queues using a time-sliced round-robin algorithm, but the higher the priority, the
larger the quantum a thread gets. In this manner, all threads get to run and there
is no starvation as in the second algorithm.

There is also a fourth algorithm that has variable-sized quanta, but with starvation. However, this one is not defined by POSIX, so it is not portable and
should be avoided.

10.2.3. Synchronization

DCE provides two ways for threads to synchronize: mutexes and condition
variables. Mutexes are used when it is essential to prevent multiple threads
from accessing the same resource at the same time. For example, when moving
items around on a linked list, partway through the move, the list will be in an
inconsistent state. To prevent disaster, when one thread is manipulating the list,
all other threads must be kept away. By requiring a thread to first successfully
lock the mutex associated with the list before touching the list (and unlock it
afterward), correct operation can be ensured.

Three kinds of mutexes are available, as shown in Fig. 10-5. They differ in
the way they deal with nested locks. A **fast mutex** is analogous to a lock in a
data base system. If a process tries to lock an unlocked record, it will succeed.
However, if it tries to acquire the same lock a second time, it will block, waiting
for the lock to be released, something that will never happen. Deadlock will
occur.

Mutex type	Properties
Fast	Locking it a second time causes a deadlock
Recursive	Locking it a second time is allowed
Nonrecursive	Locking it a second time gives an error

Fig. 10-5. Three kinds of mutexes supported by DCE.

A **recursive mutex** allows a thread to lock a mutex that it has already
locked. The idea is this. Suppose that the main program of a thread locks a
mutex, then calls a procedure that also locks the mutex. To avoid deadlock, the

second lock is accepted. As long as the mutex is ultimately unlocked as many times as it is locked, the nesting can be arbitrarily deep. Although recursive mutexes are more user friendly, they are also considerably slower, so the programmer has to make a choice. As a compromise, DCE provides a third kind of mutex, one in which an attempt to lock a mutex that is already locked does not deadlock, but returns an error instead.

Condition variables provide a second synchronization mechanism. These are used in conjunction with mutexes. Typically, when a thread needs some resource, it uses a mutex to gain exclusive access to a data structure that keeps track of the status of the resource. If the resource is not available, the thread waits on a condition variable, which atomically suspends the thread and releases the mutex. Later, when another thread signals the condition variable, the waiting thread is restarted.

10.2.4. Thread Calls

The DCE threads package has a total of 54 primitives (library procedures). Many of these are not strictly necessary but are provided for convenience only. This approach is somewhat analogous to a four-function pocket calculator that has keys not only for +, −, ×, and /, but also has keys for +1, −1, × 2, × 10, × π, /2, and /10, on the grounds that these save the user time and effort. Due to the large number of calls, we will discuss only the most important ones (about half the total). Nevertheless, our treatment should give a reasonable impression of the available functionality.

Call	Description
Create	Create a new thread
Exit	Called by a thread when it is finished
Join	Like the WAIT system call in UNIX
Detach	Make it unnecessary for parent thread to wait when caller exits

Fig. 10-6. Selected DCE thread calls for managing threads. All the calls in this section are actually prefixed by *pthread_* (i.e., *pthread_create*, not *create*), which we have omitted to save space.

For our discussion, it is convenient to group the calls into seven categories, each dealing with a different aspect of threads and their use. The first category, listed in Fig. 10-6, deals with thread management. These calls allow threads to be created and for them to exit when done. A parent thread can wait for a child using *join*, which is similar to the WAIT system call in UNIX. If a parent has no interest in a child and does not plan to wait for it, the parent can disown the child by calling *detach*. In this case, when the child thread exits, its storage is reclaimed immediately instead of having it wait for the parent to call *join*.

The DCE package allows the user to create, destroy, and manage **templates** for threads, mutexes, and condition variables. The templates can be set up to have appropriate initial values. When an object is created, one of the parameters to the create call is a pointer to a template. For example, a thread template can be created and given the attribute (property) that the stack size is 4K. Whenever a thread is created with that template as parameter, it will get an 4K stack. The point of having templates is to eliminate the need for specifying all the options as separate parameters. As the package evolves, the create calls can remain the same. Instead, new attributes can be added to the templates. Some of the template calls are listed in Fig. 10-7.

Call	Description
Attr_create	Create template for setting thread parameters
Attr_delete	Delete template for threads
Attr_setprio	Set the default scheduling priority in the template
Attr_getprio	Read the default scheduling priority from the template
Attr_setstacksize	Set the default stack size in the template
Attr_getstacksize	Read the default stack size from the template
Attr_mutexattr_create	Create template for mutex parameters
Attr_mutexattr_delete	Delete template for mutexes
Attr_mutexattr_setkind_np	Set the default mutex type in the template
Attr_mutexattr_getkind_np	Read the default mutex type from the template
Attr_condattr_create	Create template for condition variable parameters
Attr_condattr_delete	Delete template for condition variables

Fig. 10-7. Selected template calls.

The *attr_create* and *attr_delete* calls create and delete thread templates, respectively. Other calls allow programs to read and write the template's attributes, such as the stack size and scheduling parameters to be used for threads created with the template. Similarly, calls are provided to create and delete templates for mutexes and condition variables. The need for the latter is not entirely obvious, since they have no attributes and no operations. Perhaps, the designers were hoping that someone would one day think of an attribute.

The third group deals with mutexes, which can be created and destroyed dynamically. Three operations are defined on mutexes, as shown in Fig. 10-8. The operations are for locking, unlocking mutexes, and for trying but accepting failure if locking cannot be done.

Call	Description
Mutex_init	Create a mutex
Mutex_destroy	Delete a mutex
Mutex_lock	Try to lock a mutex; if it is already locked, block
Mutex_trylock	Try to lock a mutex; fail if it is already locked
Mutex_unlock	Unlock a mutex

Fig. 10-8. Selected mutex calls.

Next come the calls relating to condition variables, listed in Fig. 10-9. Condition variables, too, can be created and destroyed dynamically. Threads can sleep on condition variables pending the availability of some needed resource. Two wakeup operations are provided: signaling, which wakes up exactly one waiting thread, and broadcasting, which wakes them all up.

Call	Description
Cond_init	Create a condition variable
Cond_destroy	Delete a condition variable
Cond_wait	Wait on a condition variable until a signal or broadcast arrives
Cond_signal	Wake up at most one thread waiting on the condition variable
Cond_broadcast	Wake up all the threads waiting on the condition variable

Fig. 10-9. Selected condition variable calls.

Figure 10-10 lists the three calls for manipulating per-thread global variables. These are variables that may be used by any procedure in the thread that created them, but which are invisible to other threads. The concept of a per-thread global variable is not supported by any of the popular programming languages, so they have to be managed at run time. The first call creates an identifier and allocates storage, the second assigns a pointer to a per-thread global variable, and the third allows the thread to read back a per-thread global variable value. Many computer scientists consider global variables to be in the same league as that all-time great pariah, the GOTO statement, so they would no doubt rejoice at the idea of making them cumbersome to use. (The author once tried to design a programming language with a

IKNOWTHISISASTUPIDTHINGTODOBUTNEVERTHELESSGOTO LABEL;

statement, but was forcibly restrained from doing so by his colleagues.) It can be argued that having per-thread global variables use procedure calls instead of language scoping rules, like locals and globals, is an emergency measure introduced simply because most programming languages do not allow the concept to be expressed syntactically.

Call	Description
Keycreate	Create a global variable for this thread
Setspecific	Assign a pointer value to a per–thred global variable
Getspecific	Read a pointer value from a per–thread global variable

Fig. 10-10. Selected per-thread global variable calls.

The next group of calls (see Fig. 10-11) deals with killing threads and the threads' ability to resist. The *cancel* call tries to kill a thread, but sometimes killing a thread can have devastating effects, for example, if the thread has a mutex locked at the time. For this reason, threads can arrange for attempts to kill them to be enabled or disabled in various ways, very roughly analogous to the ability of UNIX processes to catch or ignore signals instead of being terminated by them.

Call	Description
Cancel	Try to kill another thread
Setcancel	Enable or disable ability of other threads to kill this thread

Fig. 10-11. Selected calls relating to killing threads.

Finally, our last group (see Fig. 10-12) is concerned with scheduling. The package allows the threads in a process to be scheduled according to FIFO, round robin, preemptive, nonpreemptive, and other algorithms. By using these calls, the algorithm and priorities can be set. The system works best if threads do not elect to be scheduled with conflicting algorithms.

Call	Description
Setscheduler	Set the scheduling algorithm
Getscheduler	Read the current scheduling algorithm
Setprio	Set the scheduliing priority
Getprio	Get the current scheduling priority

Fig. 10-12. Selected scheduling calls.

10.3. REMOTE PROCEDURE CALL

DCE is based on the client/server model. Clients request services by making remote procedure calls to distant servers. In this section we will describe how this mechanism appears to both sides and how it is implemented.

10.3.1. Goals of DCE RPC

The goals of the DCE RPC system are relatively traditional. First and foremost, the RPC system makes it possible for a client to access a remote service by simply calling a local procedure. This interface makes it possible for client (i.e., application) programs to be written in a simple way, familiar to most programmers. It also makes it easy to have large volumes of existing code run in a distributed environment with few, if any, changes.

It is up to the RPC system to hide all the details from the clients, and, to some extent, from the servers as well. To start with, the RPC system can automatically locate the correct server and bind to it, without the client having to be aware that this is occurring. It can also handle the message transport in both directions, fragmenting and reassembling them as needed (e.g., if one of the parameters is a large array). Finally, the RPC system can automatically handle data type conversions between the client and the server, even if they run on different architectures and have a different byte ordering.

As a consequence of the RPC system's ability to hide the details, clients and servers are highly independent of one another. A client can be written in C and a server in FORTRAN, or vice versa. A client and server can run on different hardware platforms and use different operating systems. A variety of network protocols and data representations are also supported, all without any intervention from the client or server.

10.3.2. Writing a Client and a Server

The DCE RPC system consists of a number of components, including languages, libraries, daemons and utility programs, among others. Together these make it possible to write clients and servers. In this section we will describe the pieces and how they fit together. The entire process of writing and using an RPC client and server is summarized in Fig. 10-13.

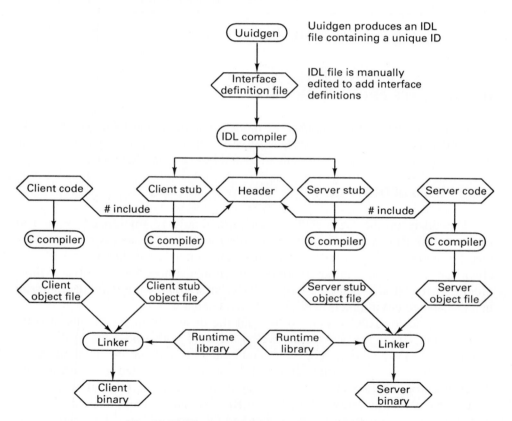

Fig. 10-13. The steps in writing a client and a server.

In a client/server system, the glue that holds everything together is the interface definition. This is effectively a contract between the server and its clients, specifying the services that the server is offering to the clients.

The concrete representation of this contract is a file, the interface definition file, which lists all the procedures that the server allows its clients to invoke remotely. Each procedure has a list of the names and types of its parameters and of its result. Ideally, the interface definition should also contain a formal definition of what the procedures do, but such a definition is beyond the current state of the art, so the interface definition just defines the syntax of the calls, not their semantics. At best the writer can add a few comments describing what he hopes the procedures will do.

Interface definitions are written in a language brilliantly named the **Interface Definition Language**, or **IDL**. It permits procedure declarations in a form closely resembling function prototypes in ANSI C. IDL files can also contain type definitions, constant declarations, and other information needed to correctly marshal parameters and unmarshal results.

A crucial element in every IDL file is an identifier that uniquely identifies the interface. The client sends this identifier in the first RPC message and the server verifies that it is correct. In this way, if a client inadvertently tries to bind to the wrong server, or even to an older version of the right server, the server will detect the error and the binding will not take place.

Interface definitions and unique identifiers are closely related in DCE. As illustrated in Fig. 10-13, the first step in writing a client/server application is usually calling the *uuidgen* program, asking it to generate a prototype IDL file containing an interface identifier guaranteed never to be used again in any interface generated anywhere by *uuidgen*. Uniqueness is ensured by encoding in it the location and time of creation. It consists of a 128-bit binary number represented in the IDL file as an ASCII string in hexadecimal.

The next step is editing the IDL file, filling in the names of the remote procedures and their parameters. It is worth noting that RPC is not totally transparent—for example, the client and server cannot share global variables—but the IDL rules make it impossible to express constructs that are not supported.

When the IDL file is complete, the IDL compiler is called to process it. The output of the IDL compiler consists of three files:

1. A header file (e.g., *interface.h*, in C terms).

2. The client stub.

3. The server stub.

The header file contains the unique identifier, type definitions, constant definitions, and function prototypes. It should be included (using *#include*) in both the client and server code.

The client stub contains the actual procedures that the client program will call. These procedures are responsible for collecting and packing the parameters into the outgoing message and then calling the runtime system to send it. The client stub also handles unpacking the reply and returning values to the client.

The server stub contains the procedures called by the runtime system on the server machine when an incoming message arrives. These, in turn, call the actual server procedures that do the work.

The next step is for the application writer to write the client and server code. Both of these are then compiled, as are the two stub procedures. The resulting client code and client stub object files are then linked with the runtime library to produce the executable binary for the client. Similarly, the server code and server stub are compiled and linked to produce the server's binary. At runtime, the client and server are started to make the application run.

10.3.3. Binding a Client to a Server

Before a client can call a server, it has to locate the server and bind to it. Naive users can ignore the binding process and let the stubs take care of it automatically, but binding happens nevertheless. Sophisticated users can control it in detail, for example, to select a specific server in a particular distant cell. In this section we will describe how binding works in DCE.

The main problem in binding is how the client locates the correct server. In theory, broadcasting a message containing the unique identifier to every process in every cell and asking all servers for it to please raise their hands might work (security considerations aside), but this approach is so slow and wasteful that it is not practical. Besides, not all networks support broadcasting.

Instead, server location is done in two steps:

1. Locate the server's machine.

2. Locate the correct process on that machine.

Different mechanisms are used for each of these steps. The need to locate the server's machine is obvious, but the problem with locating the server once the machine is known is more subtle. Basically, what it comes down to is that for a client to communicate reliably and securely with a server, a network connection is generally required. Such a connection needs an **endpoint**, a numerical address on the server's machine to which network connections can be attached and messages sent. Having the server choose a permanent numerical address is risky, since another server on the same machine might accidentally choose the same one. For this reason, endpoints can be dynamically assigned, and a database of (server, endpoint) entries is maintained on each server machine by a process called the **RPC daemon**, as described below.

The steps involved in binding are shown in Fig. 10-14. Before it becomes available for incoming requests, the server must ask the operating system for an endpoint. It then registers this endpoint with the RPC daemon. The RPC dae-mon records this information (including which protocols the server speaks) in the endpoint table for future use. The server also registers with some cell direc-tory server, passing it the number of its host.

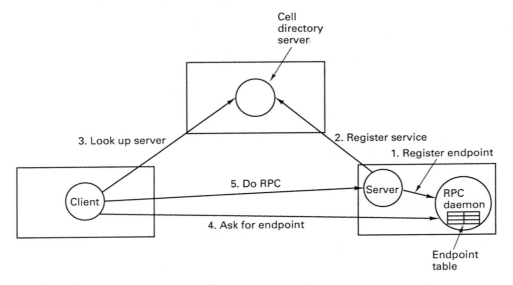

Fig. 10-14. Client-to-server binding in DCE.

Now let us look at the client side. In the simplest case, at the time of the first RPC, the client stub asks the cell directory server to find it a host running an instance of the server. The client then goes to the RPC daemon, which has a well-known endpoint, and asks it to look up the endpoint (e.g., TCP port) in its endpoint table. Armed with this information, the RPC can now take place. On subsequent RPCs this lookup is not needed. DCE also gives clients the ability to do more sophisticated searches for a suitable server when that is needed. Authenticated RPC is also an option. We will discuss authentication and protec-tion later in this chapter.

10.3.4. Performing an RPC

The actual RPC is carried out transparently and in the usual way. The client stub marshals the parameters and passes the resulting buffer (possibly in chunks) to the runtime library for transmission using the protocol chosen at binding time. When a message arrives at the server side, it is routed to the correct server based on the endpoint contained in the incoming message. The runtime library passes the message to the server stub, which unmarshals the parameters and calls the server. The reply goes back by the reverse route.

DCE provides several semantic options. The default is at-most-once operation, in which case no call is ever carried out more than once, even in the face of system crashes. In practice, what this means is that if a server crashes during an RPC and then recovers quickly, the client does not repeat the operation, for fear that it might already have been carried out once.

Alternatively, it is possible to mark a remote procedure as idempotent (in the IDL file), in which case it can be repeated multiple times without harm. For example, reading a specified block from a file can be tried over and over until it succeeds. When an idempotent RPC fails due to a server crash, the client can wait until the server reboots and then try again. Other semantics are also theoretically available (but rarely used), including broadcasting the RPC to all the machines on the local network.

10.4. TIME SERVICE

Time is an important concept in most distributed systems. To see why, consider a research program in radio astronomy. A number of radio telescopes spread all over the world observe the same celestial radio source simultaneously, accurately recording the data and the observation time. The data are sent over a network to a central computer for processing. For some kinds of experiments (e.g., long-baseline interferometry), it is essential for the analysis that the various data streams be synchronized exactly. Thus the experiment succeeds or fails with the ability to synchronize remote clocks accurately.

As another example, in a computerized stock trading system, it might matter who bid first on a block of stock offered for sale. If the bidders were located in New York, San Francisco, London, and Tokyo, timestamping the bids might be one way to achieve fairness. However, if the clocks at all these locations were not properly synchronized, the whole scheme would collapse and result in numerous lawsuits featuring expert witnesses trying to explain the concept of the speed of light to bewildered juries.

To try to prevent problems like these, DCE has a service called **DTS** (**Distributed Time Service**). The goal of DTS is to keep clocks on separate machines synchronized. Getting them synchronized once is not enough, because the crystals in different clocks tick at a slightly different rates, so the clocks gradually drift apart. For example, a clock might be rated to have a relative error of one part in a million. This means that even if it is set perfectly, after 1 hour, the clock could be off by as much as 3.6 msec either way. After 1 day it could be off by as much as 86 msec either way. After a month, two clocks that were synchronized precisely might now differ by 5 seconds.

DTS manages the clocks in DCE. It consists of time servers that keep asking each other: "What time is it?" as well as other components. If DTS knows the maximum drift rate of each clock (which it does because it measures the drift rate), it can run the time calculations often enough to achieve the desired synchronization. For example, with clocks that are accurate to one part in a million, if no clock is to ever to be off by more than 10 msec, resynchronization must take place at least every three hours.

Actually, DTS must deal with two separate issues:

1. Keeping the clocks mutually consistent.

2. Keeping the clocks in touch with reality.

The first point has to do with making sure that all clocks return the same value when queried about the time (corrected for time zones, of course). The second has to do with ensuring that even if all the clocks return the same time, this time agrees with clocks in the real world. Having all the clocks agree that it is 12:04:00.000 is little consolation if it is actually 12:05:30.000. How DTS achieves these goals will be described below, but first we will explain what the DTS time model is and how programs interface to it.

10.4.1. DTS Time Model

Unlike most systems, in which the current time is simply a binary number, in DTS all times are recorded as intervals. When asked what the time is, instead of saying that it is 9:52, DTS might say it is somewhere between 9:51 and 9:53 (grossly exaggerated). Using intervals instead of values allows DTS to provide the user with a precise specification of how far off the clock might be.

Internally, DTS keeps track of time as a 64-bit binary number starting at the beginning of time. Unlike UNIX, in which time begins at 0000 on January 1, 1970, or TAI, which starts at 0000 on January 1, 1958, the beginning of time in DTS is 0000 on October 15, 1582, the date that the Gregorian calendar was introduced in Italy. (You never know when an old FORTRAN program from the 17th Century might turn up.)

People are not expected to deal with the binary representation of time. It is just used for storing times and comparing them. When displayed, times are shown in the format of Fig. 10-15. This representation is based on International Standard 8601 which solves the problem of whether to write dates as month/day/year (as in the United States) or day/month/year (everywhere else) by doing neither. It uses a 24-hour clock and records seconds accurately to 0.001 sec. It also effectively includes the time zone by giving the time difference from Greenwich Mean Time. Finally, and most important, the inaccuracy is given after the "I" in seconds. In this example, the inaccuracy is 5.000 seconds, meaning that the true time might be anywhere from 3:29:55 P.M. to 3:30:05 P.M. In addition to absolute times, DTS also manages time differences, including the inaccuracy aspect.

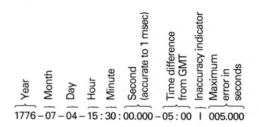

Fig. 10-15. Displaying time in DTS.

Recording times as intervals introduces a problem not present in other systems: it is not always possible to tell if one time is earlier than another. For example, consider the UNIX *make* program. Suppose that a source file has time interval 10:35:10 to 10:35:15 and the corresponding binary file has time interval 10:35:14 to 10:35:19. Is the binary file more recent? Probably, but not definitely. The only safe course of action for *make* is to recompile the source.

In general, when a program asks DTS to compare two times, there are three possible answers:

1. The first time is older.

2. The second time is older.

3. DTS cannot tell which is older.

Software using DTS has to be prepared to deal with all three possibilities. To provide backward compatibility with older software, DTS also supports a conventional interface with time represented as a single value, but using this value blindly may lead to errors.

DTS supports 33 calls (library procedures) relating to time. These calls are divided into the six groups listed in Fig. 10-16. We will now briefly mention these in turn. The first group gets the current time from DTS and returns it. The two procedures differ in how the time zone is handled. The second group handles time conversion between binary values, structured values, and ASCII values. The third group makes it possible to present two times as input and get back a time whose inaccuracy spans the full range of possible times. The fourth group compares two times, with or without using the inaccuracy part. The fifth group provides a way to add two times, subtract two times, multiply a relative time by a constant, and so on. The last group manages time zones.

Group	# Calls	Description
Retreiving times	2	Get the time
Converting times	18	Binary-ASCII conversion
Manipulating times	3	Interval arithmetic
Comparing times	2	Compare two times
Calculating times	5	Arithmetic operations on times
Using time zones	3	Time zone management

Fig. 10-16. Groups of time-related calls in DTS.

10.4.2. DTS Implementation

The DTS service consists (conceptually) of several components. The **time clerk** is a daemon process that runs on client machines and keeps the local clock synchronized with the remote clocks. The clerk also keeps track of the linearly growing uncertainty of the local clock. For example, a clock with a relative error of one part in a million might gain or lose as much as 3.6 msec per hour, as discussed above. When the time clerk calculates that the possible error has passed the bound of what is allowed, it resynchronizes.

A time clerk resynchronizes by contacting all the **time servers** on its LAN. These are daemons whose job it is to keep the time consistent and accurate within known bounds. For example, in Fig. 10-17 a time clerk has asked for and received the time from four time servers. Each one provides an interval in which it believes that UTC falls. The clerk computes its new value of time as follows. First, values that do not overlap with any over values (such as source 4) are discarded as being untrustworthy. Then the largest intersection falling within the remaining intervals is computed. The clerk then sets its value of UTC to the midpoint of this interval.

After resynchronizing, a clerk has a new UTC that is usually either ahead or behind its current one. It could just set the clock to the new value, but generally doing so is unwise. First of all, this might require setting the clock backward, which means that files created after the resynchronization might appear to be older than files created just before it. Programs such as *make* will behave incorrectly under these circumstances.

Even if the clock has to be set forward, it is better not to do it abruptly because some programs display information and then give the user a certain number of seconds to react. Having this interval sharply reduced could, for

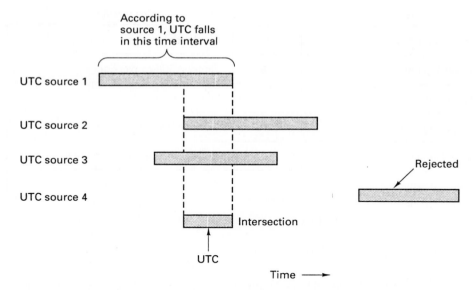

Fig. 10-17. Computation of the new UTC from four time sources.

example, cause an automated test system to display a question on the screen for a student, and then immediately time out, telling the student that he had taken too long to answer it.

Consequently, DTS can make the correction gradually. For example, if the clock is 5 sec behind, instead of adding 10 msec to it 100 times a second, 11 msec could be added at each tick for the next 50 seconds.

Time servers come in two varieties, local and global. The local ones participate in timekeeping within their cells. The global ones keep local time servers in different cells synchronized. The time servers communicate among themselves periodically to keep their clocks consistent. They also use the algorithm of Fig. 10-17 for choosing the new UTC.

Although it is not required, best results are obtained if one or more global servers are directly connected to a UTC source via a satellite, radio, or telephone connection. DTS defines a special interface, the **time provider interface**, which defines how DTS acquires and distributes UTC from external sources.

10.5. DIRECTORY SERVICE

A major goal of DCE is to make all resources accessible to any process in the system, without regard to the relative location of the resource user (client) and the resource provider (server). These resources include users, machines, cells, servers, services, files, security data, and many others. To accomplish this goal, it is necessary for DCE to maintain a directory service that keeps track of where all resources are located and to provide people-friendly names for them. In this section we will describe this service and how it operates.

The DCE directory service is organized per cell. Each cell has a **Cell Directory Service (CDS)**, which stores the names and properties of the cell's resources. This service is organized as a replicated, distributed data base system to provide good performance and high availability, even in the face of server crashes. To operate, every cell must have at least one running CDS server.

Each resource has a unique name, consisting of the name of its cell followed by the name used within its cell. To locate a resource, the directory service needs a way to locate cells. Two such mechanisms are supported, the **Global Directory Service (GDS)** and the **Domain Name System (DNS)**. GDS is the "native" DCE service for locating cells. It uses the X.500 standard. However, since many DCE users use the Internet, the standard Internet naming system, DNS, is also supported. It would have been better to have had a single mechanism for locating cells (and a single syntax for naming them), but political considerations made this impossible.

The relationship between these components is illustrated in Fig. 10-18. Here we see another component of the directory service, the **Global Directory Agent (GDA)**, which CDS uses to interact with GDS and DNS. When CDS needs to look up a remote name, it asks its GDA to do the work for it. This design makes CDS independent of the protocols used by GDS and DNS. Like CDS and GDS, GDA is implemented as a daemon process that accept queries using RPC and returns replies.

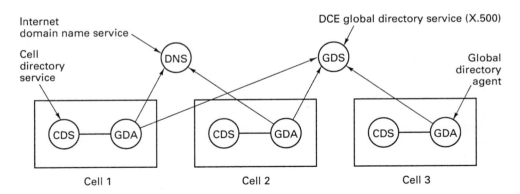

Fig. 10-18. Relation between CDS, GDS, GDA, and DNS.

In the following section we will describe how names are formed in DCE. After that, we will examine CDS and GDS.

10.5.1. Names

Every resource in DCE has a unique name. The set of all names forms the DCE namespace. Each name can have up to five parts, some of which are optional. The five parts are shown in Fig. 10-19.

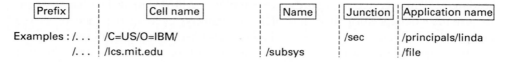

Fig. 10-19. DCE names can have up to five parts.

The first part is the **prefix**, which tells whether the name is global to the entire DCE namespace or local to the current cell. The prefix /... indicates a global name, whereas the prefix /.: denotes a local name. A global name must contain the name of the cell needed; a local name must not. When a request comes in to CDS, it can tell from the prefix whether it can handle the request itself or whether it must pass it to the GDA for remote lookup by GDS.

Cell names can be specified either in X.500 notation or in DNS notation. Both systems are highly elaborate, but for our purposes the following brief introduction will suffice. X.500 is an international standard for naming. It was developed within the world of telephone companies to provide future telephone customers with an electronic phonebook. It can be used for naming people, computers, services, cells, or anything else needing a unique name.

Every named entity has a collection of attributes that describe it. These can include its country (e.g., US, GB, DE), its organization (e.g., IBM, HARVARD, DOD), its department (e.g., CS, SALES, TAX), as well as more detailed items such as employee number, supervisor, office number, telephone number, and name. Each attribute has a value. An X.500 name is a list of *attribute=value* items separated by slashes. For example,

/C=US/O=YALE/OU=CS/TITLE=PROF/TELEPHONE=3141/OFFICE=210/SURNAME=LIN/

might describe Professor Lin in the Yale Computer Science Department. The attributes C, O, and OU are present in most names and refer to country, organization, and organization unit (department), respectively.

The idea behind X.500 is that a query must supply enough attributes that the target is uniquely specified. In the example above, C, O, OU, and SURNAME might do the job, but C, O, OU, and OFFICE might work, too, if the requester had forgotten the name but remembered the office number. Providing all the attributes except the country and expecting the server to search the entire world for a match is not sporting.

DNS is the Internet's scheme for naming hosts and other resources. It divides the world up into top-level domains consisting of countries and in the United States, EDU (educational institutions), COM (companies), GOV (government), MIL (military sites), plus a few others. These, in turn, have sub-domains such as *harvard.edu*, *princeton.edu*, and *stanford.edu*, and subsub-domains such as *cs.cmu.edu*. Both X.500 and DNS can be used to specify cell names. In Fig. 10-19 the two example cells might be the tax department at IBM and the Laboratory for Computer Science at M.I.T.

The next level of name is usually the name of a standard resource or a junction, which is analogous to a mount point in UNIX, causing the search to switch over to a different naming system, such as the file system or the security system. Finally, comes the resource name itself.

10.5.2. The Cell Directory Service

The CDS manages the names for one cell. These are arranged as a hierarchy, although as in UNIX, symbolic links (called **soft links**) also exist. An example of the top of the tree for a simple cell is shown in Fig. 10-20.

The top level directory contains two profile files containing RPC binding information, one of them topology independent and one of them reflecting the network topology for applications where it is important to select a server on the client's LAN. It also contains an entry telling where the CDS data base is. The *hosts* directory lists all the machines in the cell, and each subdirectory there has an entry for the host's RPC daemon (*self*) and default profile (*profile*), as well as various parts of the CDS system and the other machines. The junctions provide the connections to the file system and security data base, as mentioned above, and the *subsys* directory contains all the user applications plus DCE's own administrative information.

The most primitive unit in the directory system is the **CDS directory entry**, which consists of a name and a set of attributes. The entry for a service contains the name of the service, the interface supported, and the location of the server.

It is important to realize that CDS only holds information about resources. It does not provide access to the resources themselves. For example, a CDS entry for *printer23* might say that it is a 20-page/min, 600-dot/inch color laser printer located on the second floor of Toad Hall with network address 192.30.14.52. This information can be used by the RPC system for binding, but to actually use the printer, the client must do an RPC with it.

Associated with each entry is a list of who may access the entry and in what way (e.g., who may delete the entry from the CDS directory). This protection information is managed by CDS itself. Getting access to the CDS entry does not ensure that the client may access the resource itself. It is up to the server that manages the resource to decide who may use the resource and how.

A group of related entries can be collected together into a **CDS directory**.

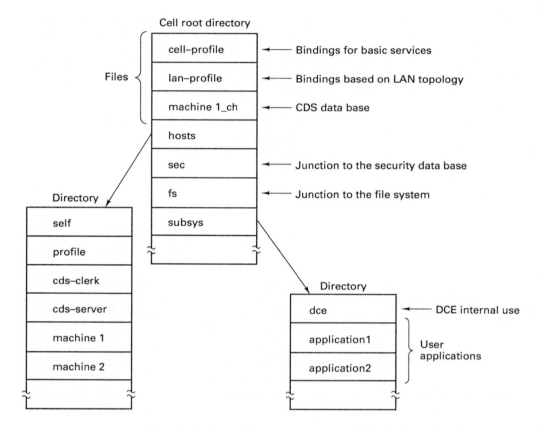

Fig. 10-20. The namespace of a simple DCE cell.

For example, all the printers might be grouped for convenience into a directory *printers*, with each entry describing a different printer or group of printers.

CDS permits entries to be replicated to provide higher availability and better fault tolerance. The directory is the unit of replication, with an entire directory either being replicated or not. For this reason, directories are a heavier weight concept than in say, UNIX. CDS directories cannot be created and deleted from the usual programmer's interface. Special administrative programs are used.

A collection of directories forms a **clearinghouse**, which is a physical data base. A cell may have multiple clearinghouses. When a directory is replicated, it appears in two or more clearinghouses.

The CDS for a cell may be spread over many servers, but the system has been designed so that a search for any name can begin by any server. From the prefix it is possible to see if the name is local or global. If it is global, the request is passed on to the GDA for further processing. If it is local, the root directory of the cell is searched for the first component. For this reason, every CDS server has a copy of the root directory. The directories pointed to by the root can either be local to that server or on a different server, but in any event, it is always possible to continue the search and locate the name.

With multiple copies of directories within a cell, a problem occurs: How are updates done without causing inconsistency? DCE takes the easy way out here. One copy of each directory is designated as the master; the rest are slaves. Both read and update operations may be done on the master, but only reads may be done on the slaves. When the master is updated, it tells the slaves.

Two options are provided for this propagation. For data that must be kept consistent all the time, the changes are sent out to all slaves immediately. For less critical data, the slaves are updated later. This scheme, called **skulking**, allows many updates to be sent together in larger and more efficient messages.

CDS is implemented primarily by two major components. The first one, the **CDS server**, is a daemon process that runs on a server machine. It accepts queries, looks them up in its local clearinghouse, and sends back replies.

The second one, the **CDS clerk**, is a daemon process that runs on the client machine. Its primary function is to do client caching. Client requests to look up data in the directory go through the clerk, which then caches the results for future use. Clerks learn about the existence of CDS servers because the latter broadcast their location periodically.

As a simple example of the interaction between client, clerk, and server, consider the situation of Fig. 10-21(a). To look up a name, the client does an RPC with its local CDS clerk. The clerk then looks in its cache. If it finds the answer, it responds immediately. If not, as shown in the figure, it does an RPC over the network to the CDS server. In this case the server finds the requested name in its clearinghouse and sends it back to the clerk, which caches it for future use before returning it to the client.

In Fig. 10-21(b), there are two CDS servers in the cell, but the clerk only knows about one of them—the wrong one, as it turns out. When the CDS server sees that it does not have the directory entry needed, it looks in the root directory (remember that all CDS servers have the full root directory), to find the soft link to the correct CDS server. Armed with this information, the clerk tries again (message 4). As before, the clerk caches the results before replying.

10.5.3. The Global Directory Service

In addition to CDS, DCE has a second directory service, GDS, which is used to locate remote cells, but can also be used to store other arbitrary directory information. GDS is important because it is the DCE implementation of X.500, and as such, can interwork with other (non-DCE) X.500 directory services. X.500 is defined in International Standard ISO 9594.

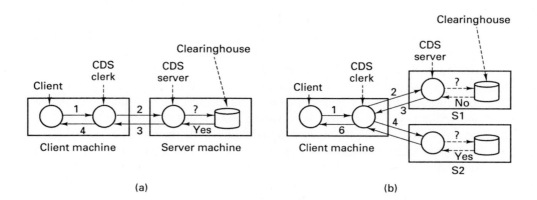

Fig. 10-21. Two examples of a client looking up a name. (a) The CDS server first contacted has the name. (b) The CDS server first contacted does not have the name.

X.500 uses an object-oriented information model. Every item stored in an X.500 directory is an object. An object can be a country, a company, a city, a person, a cell, or a server, for example.

Every object has one or more attributes. An attribute consists of a type and a value (or sometimes multiple values). In written form, the type and value are separated by an equal sign, as in *C=US* to indicate that the type is *country* and the value is *United States*.

Objects are grouped into classes, with all the objects of a given class referring to the same "kind" of object. A class can have mandatory attributes, such as a zipcode for a post office object, and optional attributes, such as a FAX number for a company object. The object class attribute is always mandatory.

The X.500 naming structure is hierarchical. A simple example is given in Fig. 10-22. Here we have shown just two of the entries below the root, a country (US) and an organization (IBM). The decision of which object to put where in the tree is not part of X.500, but is up to the relevant registration authority. For example, if a newly-formed company, say, Invisible Graphics, wishes to register to be just below *C=US* in the worldwide tree, it must contact ANSI to see if that name is already in use, and if not, claim it and pay a registration fee.

Paths through the naming tree are given by a sequence of attributes separated by slashes, as we saw earlier. In our current example, Joe of Joe's Deli in San Francisco would be

/C=US/STATE=CA/LOC=SF/O=JOE'S-DELI/CN=JOE/

where *LOC* indicates a location and *CN* is the (common) name of the object. In X.500 jargon, each component of the path is called the **RDN (Relative**

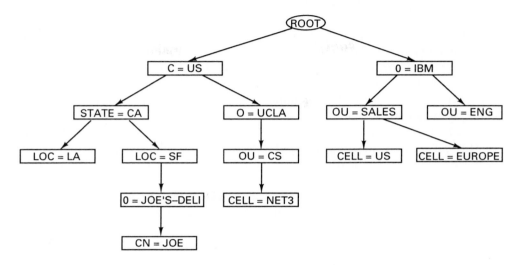

Fig. 10-22. An X.500 directory information tree.

Distinguished Name) and the full path is called the **DN (Distinguished Name)**. All the RDNs originating at any given object must be distinct, but RDNs originating at different objects may be the same.

In addition to normal objects, the X.500 tree can contain **aliases**, which name other objects. Aliases are similar to symbolic links in a file system.

The structure and properties of an X.500 directory information tree are defined by its **schema**, which consists of three tables:

1. Structure Rule Table—Where each object belongs in the tree.

2. Object Class Table —Inheritance relationships among the classes.

3. Attribute Table   —Specifies the size and type of each attribute.

The Structure Rule Table is basically a description of the tree in table form and primarily tells which object is a child of which other object. The Object Class Table describes the inheritance hierarchy of the objects. For example, there might conceivably be a class telephone number, with subclasses voice and FAX.

Note that the example of Fig. 10-22 contains no information at all about the object inheritance hierarchy since organizations there occur under country, location, and the root. The structure depicted in this figure would be reflected in the Structure Rule Table. The Object Class Table might be set up with organizational unit as a subclass of an organization, and cell as a subclass of organizational unit, but this information cannot be derived from the figure. In addition to telling which class a given class is derived from, the Object Class Table lists its unique object identifier, and its mandatory and optional attributes.

The Attribute Table tells how many values each attribute may have, how much memory they may occupy, and what their types are (e.g., integers, Booleans, or reals). Attributes are described in the OSI ASN.1 notation. DCE provides a compiler from ASN.1 to C (MAVROS), which is analogous to its IDL compiler for RPC stubs. This compiler is really for use in building DCE; normally, users do not encounter it.

Each attribute can be marked as PUBLIC, STANDARD, or SENSITIVE. It is possible to associate with each object access control lists specifying which users may read and which users may modify attributes in each of these three categories.

The standard interface to X.500, called **XOM (X/Open Object Management)**, is supported. However, the usual way for programs to access the GDS system is via the **XDS (X/Open Directory Server)** library. When a call is made to one of the XDS procedures, it checks to see if the entry being manipulated is a CDS entry or a GDS entry. If it is CDS, it just does the work directly. If it is GDS, it makes the necessary XOM calls to get the job done.

The XDS interface is amazingly small, only 13 calls (versus 101 calls and a 409-page manual for DCE RPC). Of these, five set up and initialize the connection between the client and the directory server. The eight calls that actually use directory objects are listed in Fig. 10-23.

Call	Description
Add_entry	Add an object or alias to the directory
Remove_entry	Remove an object or alias from the directory
List	List all the objects directly below a specified object
Read	Read the attributes of a specified object
Modify_entry	Atomically change the attributes of a specified object
Compare	Compare a certain attribute value with a given one
Modify_rdn	Rename an object
Search	Search a portion of the tree for an object

Fig. 10-23. The XDS calls for manipulating directory objects.

The first two calls add and delete objects from the directory tree, respectively. Each call specifies a full path so there is never any ambiguity about which object is being added or deleted. The *list* call lists all the objects directly under the object specified. *Read* and *modify_entry* read and write the attributes of the specified object, copying them from the tree to the caller, or vice versa. *Compare* examines a particular attribute of a specified object, compares it to a given value, and tells whether the two match or not. *Modify_rdn* changes one relative distinguished name, for example, changing the path *a/b/c* to *a/x/c*. Finally, *search* starts at a given object and searches the object tree below it (or a portion of it) looking for objects that meet a given criterion.

All of these calls operate by first determining whether CDS or GDS is needed. X.500 names are handled by GDS; DNS or mixed names are handled by CDS, as illustrated in Fig. 10-24. First let us trace the lookup of a name in X.500 format. The XDS library sees that it needs to look up an X.500 name, so it calls the **DUA (Directory User Agent)**, a library linked into the client code. This handles GDS caching, analogous to the CDS clerk, which handles CDS caching. Users have more control over GDS caching than they do over CDS caching and can, for example, specify which items are to be cached. They can even bypass the DUA if it is absolutely essential to get the latest data.

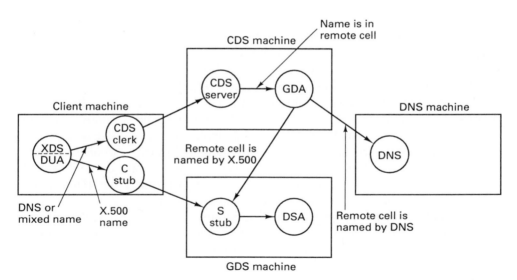

Fig. 10-24. How the servers involved in name lookup invoke one another.

Analogous to the CDS server, there is a **DSA (Directory Server Agent)** that handles incoming requests from DUAs, from both its own cell and from remote ones. If a request cannot be handled because the information is not available, the DSA either forwards the request to the proper cell or tells the DUA to do so.

In addition to the DUA and DSA processes, there are also separate stub processes that handle the wide-area communication using the OSI ASCE and ROSE protocols on top of the OSI transport protocols.

Now let us trace the lookup of a DNS or mixed name. XDS does an RPC with the CDS clerk to see if it is cached. If it is not, the CDS server is asked. If the CDS server sees that the name is local, it looks it up. If, however, it belongs to a remote cell, it asks the GDA to work on it. The GDA examines the name of the remote cell to see whether it is specified as a DNS name or an X.500 name. In the former case it asks the DNS server to find a CDS server in the cell; in the latter case it uses the DSA. All in all, name lookup is a complex business.

10.6. SECURITY SERVICE

In most distributed systems, security is a major concern. The system administrator may have definite ideas about who can use which resource (e.g., no lowly undergraduates using the fancy color laser printer), and many users may want their files and mailboxes protected from prying eyes. These issues arise in traditional timesharing systems too, but there they are solved simply by having the kernel manage all the resources. In a distributed system consisting of potentially untrustworthy machines communicating over an insecure network, this solution does not work. Nevertheless, DCE provides excellent security. In this section we will examine how that is accomplished.

Let us begin our study by introducing a few important terms. In DCE, a **principal** is a user or process that needs to communicate securely. Human beings, DCE servers (such as CDS), and application servers (such as the software in a automated teller machine in a banking system) can all be principals. For convenience, principals with the same access rights can be collected together in groups. Each principal has a **UUID (Unique User IDentifier)**, which is a binary number associated with it and no other principal.

Authentication is the process of determining if a principal really is who he/she/it claims to be. In a timesharing system, a user logs in by typing his login name and password. A simple check of the local password file tells whether the user is lying or not. After a user logs in successfully, the kernel keeps track of the user's identity and allows or refuses access to files and other resources based on it.

In DCE a different authentication procedure is necessary. When a user logs in, the login program verifies the user's identity using an authentication server. The protocol will be described later, but for the moment it is sufficient to say that it does *not* involve sending the password over the network. The DCE authentication procedure uses the Kerberos system developed at M.I.T. (Kohl, 1991; and Steiner et al., 1988). Kerberos, in turn, is based on the ideas of Needham and Schroeder (1978). For other approaches to authentication, see (Lampson et al., 1992; Wobber et al., 1994; and Woo and Lam, 1992).

Once a user has been authenticated, the question of which resources that user may access, and how, comes up. This issue is called **authorization**. In DCE, authorization is handled by associating an **ACL** (**Access Control List**) with each resource. The ACL tells which users, groups, and organizations may access the resource and what they may do with it. Resources may be as coarse as files or as fine as data base entries.

Protection in DCE is closely tied to the cell structure. Each cell has one **security service** that the local principals have to trust. The security service, of which the authentication server is part, maintains keys, passwords and other security-related information in a secure data base called the **registry**. Since different cells can be owned by different companies, communicating securely from one cell to another requires a complex protocol, and can be done only if the two cells have set up a shared secret key in advance. For simplicity, we will restrict our subsequent discussion to the case of a single cell.

10.6.1. Security Model

In this section we will review briefly some of the basic principles of **cryptography**, the science of sending secret messages, and the DCE requirements and assumptions in this area. Let us assume that two parties, say a client and a server, wish to communicate securely over an insecure network. What this means is that even if an intruder (e.g., a wiretapper) manages to steal messages, he will not be able to understand them. Stronger yet, if the intruder tries to impersonate the client or if the intruder records legitimate messages from the client and plays them back for the server later, the server will be able to see this and reject these messages.

The traditional cryptographic model is shown in Fig. 10-25. The client has an unencrypted message, P, called the **plaintext**, which is transformed by an encryption algorithm parametrized by a key, K. The encryption can be done by the client, the operating system, or by special hardware. The resulting message, C, called the **ciphertext** is unintelligible to anyone not possessing the key. When the ciphertext arrives at the server, it is decrypted using K, which results in the original plaintext. The notation generally used to indicate encryption is

Ciphertext = {Plaintext} Key

that is, the string inside the curly brackets is the plaintext, and the key used is written afterward.

Cryptographic systems in which the client and server use different keys (e.g., public key cryptography) also exist, but since they are not used in DCE, we will not discuss them further.

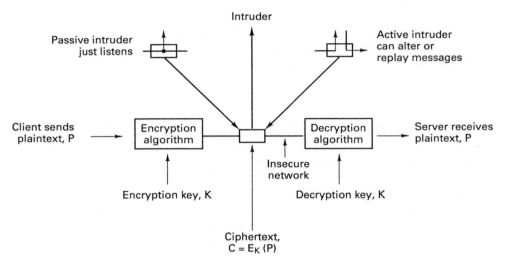

Fig. 10-25. A client sending an encrypted message to a server.

It is probably worthwhile to make some of the assumptions underlying this model explicit, to avoid any confusion. We assume that the network is totally insecure, and that a determined intruder can capture any message sent on it, possibly removing it as well. The intruder can also inject arbitrary new messages and replay old ones to his heart's content.

Although we assume that most of the major servers are moderately secure, we explicitly assume that the security server (including its disks) can be placed in a tightly locked room guarded by a nasty three-headed dog (Kerberos of Greek mythology) and that no intruder can tamper with it. Consequently, it is permitted for the security server to know each user's password, even though the passwords cannot be sent over the network. It is also assumed that users do not forget their passwords or accidentally leave them lying around the terminal room on bits of paper. Finally, we assume that clocks in the system are roughly synchronized, for example, using DTS.

As a consequence of this hostile environment, a number of requirements were placed on the design from its inception. The most important of these are as follows. First, at no time may user passwords appear in plaintext (i.e., unencrypted) on the network or be stored on normal servers. This requirement precludes doing authentication just by sending user passwords to an authentication server for approval.

Second, user passwords may not even be stored on client machines for more than a few microseconds, for fear that they might be exposed in a core dump should the machine crash.

Third, authentication must work both ways. That is, not only must the server be convinced who the client is, but the client must also be convinced who the server is. This requirement is necessary to prevent an intruder from capturing messages from the client and pretending that it is, say, the file server.

Finally, the system must have firewalls built into it. If a key is somehow compromised (disclosed), the damage done must be limited. This requirement can be met, for example, by creating temporary keys for specific purposes and with short lifetimes, and using these for most work. If one of these keys is ever compromised, the potential for damage is restricted.

10.6.2. Security Components

The DCE security system consists of several servers and programs, the most important of which are shown in Fig. 10-26. The **registry server** manages the security data base, the registry, which contains the names of all the principals, groups, and organizations. For each principal, it gives account information, groups and organizations the principal belongs to, whether the principal is a client or a server, and other information. The registry also contains policy information per cell, including the length, format, and lifetime for passwords and related information. The registry can be thought of as the successor to the password file in UNIX (/etc/passwd). It can be edited by the system administrator using the registry editor. These can add and delete principals, change keys, and so on.

The **authentication server** is used when a user logs in or a server is booted. It verifies the claimed identity of the principal and issues a kind of ticket (described below) that allows the principal to do subsequent authentication without having to use the password again. The authentication server is also known as the **ticket granting server** when it is granting tickets rather than authenticating users, but these two functions reside in the same server.

The **privilege server** issues documents called **PACs** (**Privilege Attribute Certificates**) to authenticated users. PACs are encrypted messages that contain the principal's identity, group membership, and organizational membership in such a way that servers are instantly convinced without need for presenting any additional information. All three of these servers run on the security server machine in the locked room with the mutant dog outside.

The **login facility** is a program that asks users their names and passwords during the login sequence. It uses the authentication and privilege servers to do its job, which is to get the user logged in and to collect the necessary tickets and PACs for them.

Once a user is logged in, he can start a client process that can communicate

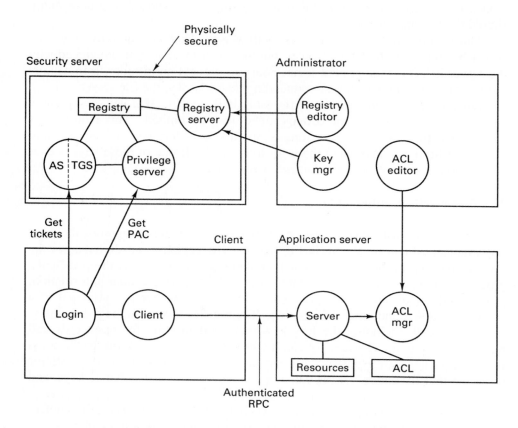

Fig. 10-26. Major components of the DCE security system for a single cell.

securely with a server process using authenticated RPC. When an authenticated RPC request comes in, the server uses the PAC to determine the user's identity, and then checks its ACL to see if the requested access is permitted. Each server has its own ACL manager for guarding its own objects. Users can be added or removed from an ACL, permissions granted or removed, and so on, using an ACL editor program.

10.6.3. Tickets and Authenticators

In this section we will describe how the authentication and privilege servers work and how they allow users to log into DCE in a secure way over an insecure network. The description covers only the barest essentials, and ignores most of the variants and options available.

Each user has a secret key known only to himself and to the registry. It is computed by passing the user's password through a one-way (i.e., noninvertible) function. Servers also have secret keys. To enhance their security, these keys are used only briefly, when a user logs in or a server is booted. After that authentication is done with tickets and PACs.

A **ticket** is an encrypted data structure issued by the authentication server or ticket-granting server to prove to a specific server that the bearer is a client with a specific identity. Tickets have many options, but mostly we will discuss tickets that look like this:

ticket = S, {session-key, client, expiration-time, message-id}K_S

where S is the server for whom the ticket is intended. The information within curly braces is encrypted using the server's private key, K_S. The fields encrypted include a temporary session key, the client's identity, the time at which the ticket ceases to be valid, and a message identifier or **nonce** that is used to relate requests and replies. When the server decrypts the ticket with its private key, it obtains the session key to use when talking to the client. In our descriptions below, we will omit all encrypted ticket fields except the session-key and client name.

In some situations tickets and PACs are used together. Tickets establish the identity of the sender (as an ASCII string), whereas PACs give the numerical values of user-id and group-ids that a particular principal is associated with. Tickets are generated by the authentication server or ticket-granting server (one and the same server), whereas PACs are generated by the privilege server.

In many situations, it is not essential that messages be secret, only that intruders not be able to forge or modify them. For this purpose, authenticators can be attached to plaintext messages to prevent active intruders from changing them. An **authenticator** is an encrypted data structure containing at least the following information:

authenticator = {sender, MD5-checksum, timestamp} K

where the checksum algorithm, **MD5** (**Message Digest 5**), has the property that given a 128-bit MD5 checksum it is computationally infeasible to modify the message so that it still matches the checksum (which is protected by encryption). The timestamp is needed to make it possible for the receiver to detect the replay of an old authenticator.

10.6.4. Authenticated RPC

The sequence from logging in to the point where the first authenticated RPC is possible typically requires five steps. Each step consists of a message from the client to some server, followed by a reply back from the server to the client. The steps are summarized in Fig. 10-27 and are described below. For simplicity, most of the fields, including the cells, message IDs, lifetimes, and identifiers have been omitted. The emphasis is on the security fundamentals: keys, tickets, authenticators, and PACs.

Principals
    A: Authentication server (handles authentication)
    C: Client (user)
    P: Privilege server (issues PAC's)
    S: Application server (does the real work)
    T: Ticket–granting server (issues tickets)

Step 1: Client gets a ticket for the ticket–granting server using a password
    $C \rightarrow A$: C (just the client's name, in plaintext)
    $C \leftarrow A$: $\{K_1, \{K_1, C\}K_A \}K_C$

Step 2: Client uses the previous ticket to get a ticket for the privilege server
    $C \rightarrow T$: $\{K_1, C\}K_A$, $\{C, \text{MD–5 checksum, Timestamp}\}K_1$
    $C \leftarrow T$: $\{K_2, \{C, K_2\}K_p\}K_1$

Step 3: Client asks the privilege server for the initial PAC
    $C \rightarrow P$: $\{C, K_2\}K_p$, $\{C, \text{MD–5 checksum, Timestamp}\}K_2$
    $C \leftarrow P$: $\{K_3, \{PAC, K_3\}K_A\}K_2$

Step 4: Client asks the ticket–granting server for a PAC usable by S
    $C \rightarrow T$: $\{K_3, \{PAC, K_3\}K_A\}K_3$, $\{C, \text{MD–5 checksum, Timestamp}\}K_3$
    $C \leftarrow T$: $\{K_4, \{PAC, K_4\}K_S\}K_3$

Step 5: Client establishes a key with the application server
    $C \rightarrow S$: $\{PAC, K_4\}K_S$, $\{C, \text{MD–5checksum, Timestamp}\}K_4$
    $C \leftarrow S$: $\{K_5, \text{Timestamp}\}K_4$

Fig. 10-27. From login to authenticated RPC in five easy steps.

When a user sits down at a DCE terminal, the login program asks for his login name. The program then sends this login name to the authentication server in plaintext. The authentication server looks it up in the registry and finds the user's secret key. It then generates a random number for use as a session key and sends back a message encrypted by the user's secret key, K_C, containing the first session key, K_1, and a ticket good for later use with the ticket-granting server. These messages are shown in Fig. 10-27 in step 1. Note that this figure shows 10 messages, and for each the source and destination are given before the message, with the arrow pointing from the source to the destination.

When the encrypted message arrives at the login program, the user is prompted for his password. The password is immediately run through the one-way function that generates secret keys from passwords. As soon as the secret key, K_C has been generated from the password, the password is removed from memory. This procedure minimizes the chance of password disclosure in the event of a client crash. Then the message from the authentication server is decrypted to get the session key and the ticket. When that has been done, the client's secret key can also be erased from memory.

Note that if an intruder intercepts the reply message, it will be unable to decrypt it and thus unable to obtain the session key and ticket inside it. If it spends enough time, the intruder might eventually be able to break the message, but even then the damage will be limited because session keys and tickets are valid only for relatively short periods of time.

In step 2 of Fig. 10-27, the client sends the ticket to the ticket-granting server (in fact, the authentication server under a different name) and asks for a ticket to talk to the privilege server. Except for the initial authentication in step 1, talking to a server in an authenticated way always requires a ticket encrypted with that server's private key. These tickets can be obtained from the ticket-granting server as in step 2.

When the ticket-granting server gets the message, it uses its own private key, K_A to decrypt the message. When it finds the session key, K_1, it looks in the registry and verifies that it recently assigned this key to client C. Since only C knows K_C, the ticket-granting server knows that only C was able to decrypt the reply sent in step 1, and this request must have come from C.

The request also contains an authenticator, basically, a timestamped cryptographically strong checksum of the rest of the message, including the cell name, request, and other fields not shown in the figure. This scheme makes it impossible for an intruder to modify the message without detection, yet does not require the client to encrypt the entire message, which would be expensive for a long message. (In this case the message is not so long, but authenticators are used all the time, for simplicity.) The timestamp in the authenticator guards against an intruder capturing the message and playing in back later because the authentication server will process a request only if it is accompanied by a fresh authenticator.

In this example, we generate and use a new session key at each step. This much paranoia is not required, but the protocol allows it and doing so allows very short lifetimes for each key if the clocks are well synchronized.

Armed with a ticket for the privilege server, the client now asks for a PAC. Unlike a ticket, which contains only the user's login name (in ASCII), a PAC contains the user's identity (in binary as a UUID) plus a list of all the groups to which he belongs. These are important because resources (e.g., a certain printer) are often available to all the members of certain groups (e.g., the marketing department). A PAC is proof that the user named in it belongs to the groups listed in it.

The PAC obtained in step 3 is encrypted with the authentication server/ticket-granting server's secret key. The importance of this choice is that throughout the session, the client may need PACs for several application servers. To get a PAC for use with an application server, the client executes step 4. Here the PAC is sent to the ticket-granting server, which first decrypts it. Since the decryption works, the ticket-granting server is immediately convinced that the PAC is legitimate, and then it reencrypts it for the client's choice of server, in this case, S.

Note that the ticket-granting server does not have to understand the format of a PAC. All it is doing in step 4 is decrypting something encrypted with its own key and then reencrypting it with another key it gets from the registry. While it is at it, the ticket-granting server throws in a new session key, but this action is optional. If the client needs PACs for other servers later, it repeats step 4 with the original PAC as often as needed, specifying the desired server each time.

In step 5, the client sends the new PAC to the application server, which decrypts it, exposing key K_4 used to encrypt the authenticator as well as the client's ID and groups. The server responds with the last key, known only to the client and server. Using this key, the client and server can now communicate securely.

This protocol is complicated, but the complexity is due to the fact that it has been designed to be resistant to a large variety of possible attacks (Bellovin and Merritt, 1991). It also has many features and options that we have not discussed. For example, it can be used to establish secure communication with a server in a distant cell, possibly transiting several potentially untrustworthy cells on every RPC, and can verify the server to the client to prevent **spoofing** (an intruder masquerading as a trusted server).

Once authenticated RPC has been established, it is up to the client and server to determine how much protection is desired. In some cases client authentication or mutual authentication is enough. In others, every packet is authenticated against tampering. Finally, when industrial-strength security is required, all traffic in both directions can be encrypted.

10.6.5. ACLs

Every resource in DCE can be protected by an ACL, modeled after the one in the POSIX 1003.6 standard. The ACL tells who may access the resource and how. ACLs are managed by **ACL managers**, which are library procedures incorporated into every server. When a request comes in to the server that controls the ACL, it decrypts the client's PAC to see what his ID and groups are, and based on these, the ACL, and the operation desired, the ACL manager is called to make a decision about whether to grant or deny access. Up to 32 operations per resource are supported.

Most servers use a standard, but less mathematically inclined, ACL manager, however. This one divides the resources into two categories: simple resources, such as files and data base entries, and containers, such as directories and data base tables, that hold simple resources. It distinguishes between users who live in the cell and foreign users, and for each category further subdivides them as owner, group, and other. Thus it is possible to specify that the owner can do anything, the local members of the owner's group can do almost anything, unknown users from other cells can do nothing, and so on.

Seven standard rights are supported: read, write, execute, change-ACL, container-insert, container-delete, and test. The first three are as in UNIX. The change-ACL right grants permission to modify the ACL itself. The two container rights are useful to control who may add or delete files from a directory, for example. Finally, test allows a given value to be compared to the resource without disclosing the resource itself. For example, a password file entry might allow users to ask if a given password matched, but would not expose the password file entry itself. An example ACL is shown in Fig. 10-28.

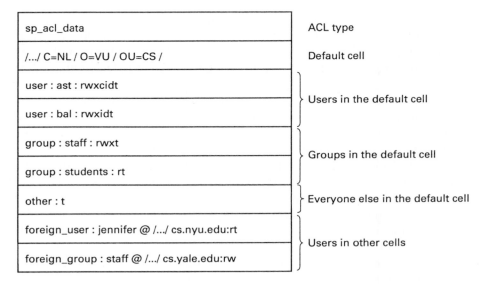

Fig. 10-28. A sample ACL.

In this example, as in all ACLs, the ACL type is specified. This type effectively partitions ACLs into classes based on the type. The default cell is specified next. After that come permissions for two specific users in the default cell, two specific groups in the default cell, and a specification of what all the other users in that cell may do. Finally, the rights of users and groups in other cells can be specified. If a user who does not fit any of the listed categories attempts an access, it will be denied.

To add new users, delete users, or add, delete, or change permissions, an ACL editor program is supplied. To use this program on an access control list, the user must have permission to change the access control list, indicated by the code c in the example of Fig. 10-28.

10.7. DISTRIBUTED FILE SYSTEM

The last component of DCE that we will study is **DFS (Distributed File System)** (Kazar et al., 1990). It is a worldwide distributed file system that allows processes anywhere within a DCE system to access all files they are authorized to use, even if the processes and files are in distant cells.

DFS has two main parts: the local part and the wide-area part. The local part is a single-node file system called **Episode**, which is analogous to a standard UNIX file system on a stand-alone computer. One DCE configuration would have each machine running Episode instead of (or in addition to) the normal UNIX file system.

The wide-area part of DFS is the glue that puts all these individual file systems together to form a seamless wide-area file system spanning many cells. It is derived from the CMU AFS system, but has evolved considerably since then. For more information about AFS, see (Howard et al. 1988; Morris et al., 1986, and Satyanarayanan et al., 1985). For Episode itself, see (Chutani et al., 1992).

DFS is a DCE application, and as such can use all the other facilities of DCE. In particular, it uses threads to allow multiple file access requests to be served simultaneously, RPC for communication between clients and servers, DTS to synchronize server clocks, the directory system to allow file servers to be located, and the authentication and privilege servers to protect files.

From DFS' viewpoint, every DCE node is either a file client, a file server, or both. A file client is a machine that uses other machines' file systems. A file client has a cache for storing pieces of recently used files, to improve performance. A file server is a machine with a disk that offers file service to processes on that machine and possibly to processes on other machines as well.

DFS has a number of features that are worth mentioning. To start with, it has uniform naming, integrated with CDS, so file names are location independent. Administrators can move files from one file server to another one within the same cell without requiring any changes to user programs. Files can also be replicated to spread the load more evenly and maintain availability in the event of file server crashes. There is also a facility to automatically distribute new versions of binary programs and other heavily used read-only files to servers (including user workstations).

Episode is a rewrite of the UNIX file system and can replace it on any DCE machine with a disk. It supports the proper UNIX single-system file semantics in the sense that when a write to a file is done and immediately thereafter a read is done, unlike in NFS, the read will see the value just written. It is conformant to the POSIX 1003.1 system-call standard, and also supports POSIX-conformant access control using ACLs, which give flexible protection in large systems. It has also been designed to support fast recovery after a crash by eliminating the need to run the UNIX *fsck* program to repair the file system.

Since many sites may not want to tinker with their existing file system just to run DCE, DFS has been designed to provide seamless integration over machines running 4.3 BSD, System V, NFS, Episode, and other file systems. However, some features of DFS, such as protection by ACLs, will not be available on those parts of the file system supported by non-Episode servers.

10.7.1. DFS Interface

The basic interface to DFS is (intentionally) very similar to UNIX. Files can be opened, read, and written in the usual way, and most existing software can simply be recompiled with the DFS libraries and will work immediately. Mounting of remote file systems is also possible.

The / directory is still the local root, and directories such as /*bin*, /*lib*, and /*usr* still refer to local binary, library, and user directories, as they did in the absence of DFS. A new entry in the root directory is /..., which is the global root. Every file in a DFS system (potentially worldwide), has a unique path from the global root consisting of its cell name concatenated with its name within that cell. In Fig. 10-29(a) we see how a file, *january*, would be addressed globally using an Internet cell name. In Fig. 10-29(b) we see the name of the same file using an X.500 cell name. These names are valid everywhere in the system, no matter what cell the process using the file is in.

(a) Global file name (Internet format)
    /.../cs.ucla.edu/fs/usr/ann/exams/january

(b) Global file name (X.500 format)
    /.../C=US/O=UCLA/OU=CS/fs/usr/ann/exams/january

(c) Global file name (Cell relative)
    /.:/fs/usr/ann/exams/january

(d) Global file name (File system relative)
    /:/usr/ann/exams/january

Fig. 10-29. Four ways to refer to the same file.

Using global names everywhere is rather longwinded, so some shortcuts are available. A name starting with /.:/*fs* means a name in the current cell starting from the *fs* junction (the place where the local file system is mounted on the global DFS tree), as shown in Fig. 10-29(c). This usage can be shortened even further as given in Fig. 10-29(d)

Unlike in UNIX, protection in DFS uses ACLs instead of the three groups of RWX bits, at least for those files managed by Episode. Each file has an ACL telling who can access it and how. In addition, each directory has three ACLs These ACLs give access permissions for the directory itself, the files in the directory, and the directories in the directory, respectively.

ACLs in DFS are managed by DFS itself because the directories are DFS objects. An ACL for a file or directory consists of a list of entries. Each entry describes either the owner, the owner's group, other local users, foreign (i.e., out-of-cell) users or groups, or some other category, such as unauthenticated users. For each entry, the allowed operations are specified from the set: read, write, execute, insert, delete, and control. The first three are the same as in UNIX. Insert and delete make sense on directories, and control makes sense for I/O devices subject to the IOCTL system call.

DFS supports four levels of aggregation. At the bottom level are individual files. These can be collected into directories in the usual way. Groups of directories can be put together into **filesets**. Finally, a collection of filesets forms a disk partition (an **aggregate** in DCE jargon).

A fileset is normally a subtree in the file system. For example, it may be all the files owned by one user, or all the files owned by the people in a certain department or project. A fileset is a generalization of the concept of the file system in UNIX (i.e., the unit created by the *mkfs* program). In UNIX, each disk partition holds exactly one file system, whereas in DFS it may hold many filesets.

The value of the fileset concept can be seen in Fig. 10-30. In Fig. 10-30(a), we see two disks (or two disk partitions) each with three empty directories. In the course of time, files are created in these directories. As it turns out, disk 1 fills up much faster than disk 2, as shown in Fig. 10-30(b). If disk 1 becomes full while disk 2 still has plenty of space, we have a problem.

The DFS solution is to make each of the directories *A*, *B*, and *C* (and their subdirectories) a separate fileset. DFS allows filesets to be moved, so the system administrator can rebalance the disk space simply by moving directory *A* to disk 2, as shown in Fig. 10-30(c). As long as both disks are in the same cell, no global names change, so everything continues to work after the move as it did before.

In addition to moving filesets, it is also possible to replicate them. One replica is designated as the master, and is read/write. The others are slaves and are read only. Filesets, rather than disk partitions, are the units that are manipulated for motion, replication, backup, and so on. For UNIX systems, each disk partition is considered to be an aggregate with one fileset. Various commands are available to system administrators for managing filesets.

10.7.2. DFS Components in the Server Kernel

DFS consists of additions to both the client and server kernels, as well as various user processes. In this section and the following ones, we will describe this software and what it does. An overview of the parts is presented in Fig. 10-31.

On the server we have shown two file systems, the native UNIX file system and, alongside it, the DFS local file system, Episode. On top of both of them is

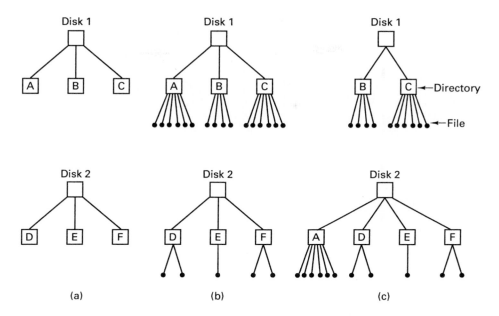

Fig. 10-30. (a) Two empty disks. (b) Disk 1 fills up faster than disk 2. (c) Configuration after moving one fileset.

the token manager, which handles consistency. Further up are the file exporter, which manages interaction with the outside world, and the system call interface, which manages interaction with local processes. On the client side, the major new addition is the cache manager, which caches file fragments to improve performance.

Let us now examine Episode. As mentioned above, it is not necessary to run Episode, but it offers some advantages over conventional file systems. These include ACL-base protection, fileset replication, fast recovery, and files of up to 2^{42} bytes. When the UNIX file system is used, the software marked "Extensions" in Fig. 10-31(b) handles matching the UNIX file system interface to Episode, for example, converting PACs and ACLs into the UNIX protection model.

An interesting feature of Episode is its ability to clone a fileset. When this is done, a virtual copy of the fileset is made in another partition and the original is marked "read only." For example, it might be cell policy to make a read-only snapshot of the entire file system every day at 4 A.M. so that even if someone deleted a file inadvertently, he could always go back to yesterday's version.

Episode does cloning by copying all the file system data structures (i-nodes in UNIX terms) to the new partition, simultaneously marking the old ones as read only. Both sets of data structures point to the same data blocks, which are not

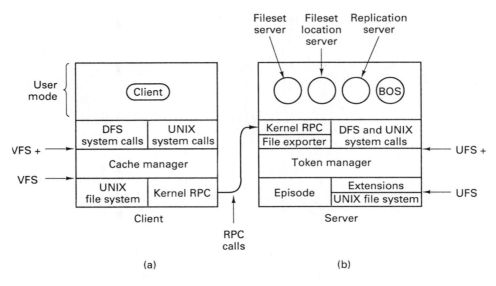

Fig. 10-31. Parts of DFS. (a) File client machine. (b) File server machine.

copied. As a result, cloning can be done extremely quickly. An attempt to write on the original file system is refused with an error message. An attempt to write on the new file system succeeds, with copies made of the new blocks.

Episode was designed for highly concurrent access. It avoids having threads take out long-term locks on critical data structures to minimize conflicts between threads needing access to the same tables. It also has been designed to work with asynchronous I/O, providing an event notification system when I/O completes.

Traditional UNIX systems allow files to be any size, but limit most internal data structures to fixed-size tables. Episode, in contrast, uses a general storage abstraction called an **a-node** internally. There are a-nodes for files, filesets, ACLs, bit maps, logs, and other items. Above the a-node layer, Episode does not have to worry about physical storage (e.g., a very long ACL is no more of a problem than a very long file). An a-node is a 252-byte data structure, this number being chosen so that four a-nodes and 16 bytes of administrative data fit in a 1K disk block.

When an a-node is used for a small amount of data (up to 204 bytes) the data are stored directly in the a-node itself. Small objects, such as symbolic links and many ACLs often fit. When an a-node is used for a larger data structure, such as a file, the a-node holds the addresses of eight blocks full of data and four indirect blocks that point to disk blocks containing yet more addresses.

Another noteworthy aspect of Episode is how it deals with crash recovery.

Traditional UNIX systems tend to write changes to bit maps, i-nodes, and directories back to the disk quickly to avoid leaving the file system in an inconsistent state in the event of a crash. Episode, in contrast, writes a log of these changes to disk instead. Each partition has its own log. Each log entry contains the old value and the new value. In the event of a crash, the log is read to see which changes have been made and which have not been. The ones that have not been made (i.e., were lost on account of the crash) are then made. It is possible that some recent changes to the file system are still lost (if their log entries were not written to disk before the crash), but the file system will always be correct after recovery.

The primary advantage of this scheme is that using it the recovery time is proportional to the length of the log rather than proportional to the size of the disk, as it is when the UNIX *fsck* program is run to repair a potentially sick disk in traditional systems.

Getting back to Fig. 10-31, the layer on top of the file systems is the token manager. Since the use of tokens is intimately tied to caching, we will discuss tokens when we come to caching in the next section. At the top of the token layer, an interface is supported that is an extension of the Sun NFS VFS interface. VFS supports file system operations, such as mounting and unmounting, as well as per file operations such as reading, writing, and renaming files. These and other operations are supported in VFS+. The main difference between VFS and VFS+ is the token management.

Above the token manager is the file exporter. It consists of several threads whose job it is to accept and process incoming RPCs that want file access. The file exporter handles requests not only for Episode files, but also for all the other file systems present in the kernel. It maintains tables keeping track of the various file systems and disk partitions available. It also handles client authentication, PAC collection, and establishment of secure channels. In effect, it is the application server described in step 5 of Fig. 10-27.

10.7.3. DFS Components in the Client Kernel

The main addition to the kernel of each client machine in DCE is the DFS cache manager. The goal of the cache manager is to improve file system performance by caching parts of files in memory or on disk, while at the same time maintaining true UNIX single-system file semantics. To make it clear what the nature of the problem is, let us briefly look at UNIX semantics and why this is an issue.

In UNIX (and all uniprocessor operating systems, for that matter), when one process writes on a file, and then signals a second process to read the file, the value read *must* be the value just written. Getting any other value violates the semantics of the file system.

This semantic model is achieved by having a single buffer cache inside the operating system. When the first process writes on the file, the modified block goes into the cache. If the cache fills up, the block may be written back to disk. When the second process tries to read the modified block, the operating system first searches the cache. Failing to find it there, it tries the disk. Because there is only one cache, under all conditions, the correct block is returned.

Now consider how caching works in NFS. Several machines may have the same file open at the same time. Suppose that process 1 reads part of a file and caches it. Later, process 2 writes that part of the file. The write does not affect the cache on the machine where process 1 is running. If process 1 now rereads that part of the file, it will get an obsolete value, thus violating the UNIX semantics. This is the problem thar DFS was designed to solve.

Actually, the problem is even worse than just described, because directories can also be cached. It is possible for one process to read a directory and delete a file from it. Nevertheless, another process on a different machine may subsequently read its previously cached copy of the directory and still see the now-deleted file. While NFS tries to minimize this problem by rechecking for validity frequently, errors can still occur.

DFS solves this problem using tokens. To perform any file operation, a client makes a request to the cache manager, which first checks to see if it has the necessary token and data. If it has both the token and the data, the operation may proceed immediately, without contacting the file server. If the token is not present, the cache manager does an RPC with the file server asking for it (and for the data). Once it has acquired the token, it may perform the operation.

Tokens exist for opening files, reading and writing files, locking files, and reading and writing file status information (e.g., the owner). Files can be opened for reading, writing, both, executing, or exclusive access. Open and status tokens apply to the entire file. Read, write, and lock tokens, in contrast, refer only to some specific byte range. Tokens are granted by the token manager in Fig. 10-31(b).

Figure 10-32 gives an example of token usage. In message 1, client 1 asks for a token to open some file for reading, and also asks for a token (and the data) for the first chunk of the file. In message 2, the server grants both tokens and provides the data. At this point, client 1 may cache the data it has just received and read it as often as it likes. The normal transfer unit in DFS is 64K bytes.

A little later, client 2 asks for a token to open the same file for reading and writing, and also asks for the initial 64K of data to selectively overwrite part of it. The server cannot just grant these tokens, since it no longer has them. It must send message 4 to client 1 asking for them back.

As soon as is reasonably convenient, client 1 must return the revoked tokens to the server. After it gets the tokens back, the server gives them to client 2, which can now read and write the data to its hearts' content without notifying

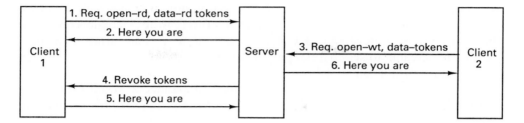

Fig. 10-32. An example of token revocation.

the server. If client 1 asks for the tokens back, the server will instruction client 2 to return the tokens along with the updated data, so these data can be sent to client 1. In this way, single-system file semantics are maintained.

To maximize performance, the server understands about token compatibility. It will not simultaneously issue two write tokens for the same data, but it will issue two read tokens for the same data, provided that both clients have the file open only for reading.

Tokens are not valid forever. Each token has an expiration time, usually two minutes. If a machine crashes and is unable (or unwilling) to return its tokens when asks, the file server can just wait two minutes and then act like they have been returned.

On the whole, caching is transparent to user processes. However, calls are available for certain cache management functions, such as prefetching a file before it is used, flushing the cache, disk quota management, and so on. The average user does not need these, however.

Two differences between DFS and its predecessor, AFS, are worth mentioning. In AFS, entire files were transferred, instead of 64K chunks. This strategy made a local disk essential, since files were often too large to cache in memory. With a 64K transfer unit, local disks are no longer required.

A second difference is that in AFS part of the file system code was in the kernel and part was in user space. Unfortunately, the performance left much to be desired, so in DFS it is all in the kernel.

10.7.4. DFS Components in User Space

We have now finished discussing those parts of DFS that run in the server and client kernels. Let us now briefly discuss those parts of it that run in user space (see Fig. 10-31). The **fileset server** manages entire filesets. Each fileset contains one or more directories and their files and must be located entirely with one partition. Filesets can be mounted to form a hierarchy. Each fileset has a disk quota to which it is restricted.

The fileset server allows the system administrator to create, delete, move, duplicate, clone, backup, or restore an entire fileset with a single command. Each of these operations locks the fileset, does the work, and releases the lock. A fileset is created to set up a new administrative unit for future use. When it is no longer needed, it can be deleted.

A fileset can be moved from one machine to another to balance the load, both in terms of disk storage and in terms of number of requests per second that must be handled. When a fileset is copied but the original is not deleted, a duplicate is created. Duplicates are supported, and provide both load balancing and fault tolerance. Only one copy is writable.

Cloning, as described above, just copies the status information (a-nodes) but does not copy the data. Duplication makes a new copy of the data as well. A clone must be in the same disk partition as the original. A duplicate can be anywhere (even if a different cell).

Backup and restore are functions that allow a fileset to be linearized and copied to or from tape for archival storage. These tapes can be stored in a different building to make it possible to survive not only disk crashes, but also fires, floods and other disasters.

The fileset server also can provide information about filesets, manipulate fileset quotas, and perform other management functions.

The **fileset location server** manages a cell-wide replicated data base that maps fileset names onto the names of the servers that hold the filesets. If a fileset is replicated, all the servers having a copy can be found.

The fileset location server is used by cache managers to locate filesets. When a user program accesses a file for the first time, its cache manager asks the fileset location server where it can find the fileset. This information is cached for future use.

Each entry in the data base contains the name of the fileset, the type (read/write, read-only, or backup), the number of servers holding it, the addresses of these servers, the fileset's owner and group information, information about clones, cache timeout information, token timeout information, and other administrative information.

The **replication server** keeps replicas of filesets up to date. Each fileset has one master (i.e., read/write) copy and possibly one or more slave (i.e., read-only) copies. The replication server runs periodically, scanning each replica to see which files have been changed since the replica was last updated. These files are replaced from the current files in the master copy. After the replication server has finished, all the replicas are up to date.

The **Basic Overseer Server** runs on every server machine. Its job is to make sure that the other servers are alive and well. If it discovers that some servers have crashed, it brings up new versions. It also provides an interface for system administrators to stop and start servers manually.

10.8. SUMMARY

DCE is a different approach to building a distributed system than that taken by Amoeba, Mach, and Chorus. Instead of starting from scratch with a new operating system running on the bare metal, DCE provides a layer on top of the native operating system that hides the differences among the individual machines, and provides common services and facilities that unify a collection of machines into a single system that is transparent in some (but not all) respects. DCE runs on top of UNIX and other operating systems.

DCE supports two facilities that are used heavily, both within DCE itself and by user programs—threads and RPC. Threads allow multiple control streams to exist within one process. Each has its own program counter, stack, and registers, but all the threads in a process share the same address space, file descriptors, and other process resources.

RPC is the basic communication mechanism used throughout DCE. It allows a client process to call a procedure on a remote machine. DCE provides a variety of options for a client to select and bind to a server.

DCE supports four major services (and several minor ones) that can be accessed by clients. These are the time, directory, security, and file services. The time service attempts to keep all the clocks with a DCE system synchronized within known limits. An interesting feature of the time service is that it represents times not as single values, but as intervals. As a result, it is possible that when comparing two times it is not possible to say unambiguously which came first.

The directory service stores the names and locations of all kinds of resources and allows clients to look them up. The CDS holds local names (within the cell). The GDS holds global (out-of-cell) names. Both the DNS and X.500 naming systems are supported. Names form a hierarchy. The directory service is, in fact, a replicated, distributed data base system.

The security service allows clients and servers to authenticate each other and perform authenticated RPC. The heart of the security system is a way for clients to be authenticated and receive PACs without having their passwords appear on the network, not even in encrypted form. PACs allow clients to prove who they are in a convenient and foolproof way.

Finally, the distributed file system provides a single, system-wide name space for all files. A global file name consists of a cell name followed by a local name. The DCE file system consists (optionally) of the DCE local file system, Episode, plus the file exporter, which makes all the local file systems visible throughout the system. Files are cached using a token scheme that maintains the traditional single-system file semantics.

Although DCE provides many facilities and tools, it is not complete and probably never will be. Some areas in which more work is needed are specification and design techniques and tools, debugging aids, runtime management, object orientation, atomic transactions, and multimedia support.

PROBLEMS

1. A university is installing DCE on all computers on campus. Suggest at least two ways of dividing the machines into cells.

2. DCE threads can be in one of four states, as described in the text. In two if these states, ready and waiting, the thread is not running. What is the difference between these states?

3. In DCE, some data structures are process wide, and others are per thread. Do you think that the UNIX environment variables should be process wide, or should every thread have its own environment? Defend your viewpoint.

4. A condition variable in DCE is always associated with a mutex. Why?

5. A programmer has just written a piece of multithreaded code that uses a private data structure. The data structure may not be accessed by more than one thread at a time. Which kind of mutex should be used to protect it?

6. Name two plausible attributes that the template for a thread might contain.

7. Each IDL file contains a unique number (e.g., produced by the *uuidgen* program). What is the value of having this number?

8. Why does IDL require the programmer to specify which parameters are input and which are output?

9. Why are RPC endpoints assigned dynamically by the RPC daemon instead of statically? A static assignment would surely be simpler.

10. A DCE programmer needs to time a benchmark program. It calls the local clock time procedure (on its own machine) and learns that the time is 15:30:00.0000. Then it starts the benchmark immediately. When the benchmark finishes, it calls the time procedure again and learns that the time is now 15:35:00.0000. Since it used the same clock, on the same machine, for both measurements, is it safe to conclude that the benchmark ran for 5 minutes ($\pm$ 0.1 msec)? Defend your answer.

11. In a DCE system, the uncertainty in the clock is $\pm$ 5 sec. If source file has time interval 14:20:30 to 14:20:40 and its binary file has time 14:20:32 to 14:20:42, what should *make* do if called at 14:20:38? Suppose that *make* takes 1 sec to do its job. What happens if *make* is called a second time a few minutes later?

12. A time clerk asks four time servers for the current time. The responses are

    16:00:10.075 ± 0.003,
    16:00:10.085 ± 0.003,
    16:00:10.069 ± 0.007,
    16:00:10.070 ± 0.010,

    What time does the clerk set its clock to?

13. Can DTS run without a UTC source connected to any of the machines in the system? What are the consequences of doing this?

14. Why do distinguished names have to be unique, but not RDNs?

15. Give the X.500 name for the sales department at Kodak in Rochester, NY.

16. What is the function of the CDS clerk? Would it have been possible to have designed DCE without the CDS clerks? What would the consequences have been?

17. CDS is a replicated data base system. What happens if two processes try simultaneously to change the same item in different replicas to different values?

18. If DCE did not support the Internet naming system, which parts of Fig. 10-24 could be dispensed with?

19. During the authentication sequence, a client first acquires a ticket and later a PAC. Since both of them contain the user's ID, why go to the trouble of acquiring a PAC once the necessary ticket has been obtained?

20. What is the difference, if any, between the following messages:

    $\{\{\text{message}\}K_A\}K_C$ and
    $\{\{\text{message}\}K_C\}K_A$.

21. The authentication protocol described in the text allows an intruder to send arbitrarily many messages to the authentication server in an attempt to get a reply containing an initial session key. What weakness does this observation introduce into the system? (*Hint*: You may assume that all messages contain a timestamp and other information, so it is easy to tell a valid message from random junk.)

22. The text discussed only the case of security within a single cell. Propose a way to do authentication for RPC when the client is in the local cell and server is in a remote cell.

23. Tokens can expire in DFS. Does this require synchronized clocks using DFS?

24. An advantage of DFS over NFS is that DFS preserves single-system file semantics. Name a disadvantage.

25. Why must a clone of a fileset be in the same disk partition?

11

Reading List and Bibliography

In the previous ten chapters we have touched upon a variety of topics. This appendix is intended as an aid to readers interested in pursuing their study of operating systems further. Section A.1 is a list of suggested readings. Section A.2 is an alphabetical bibliography of all books and articles cited in this book.

In addition to the references given below, the *Proceedings of the* n-*th ACM Symposium on Operating Systems Principles* (SOSP) held every other year and the *Proceedings of the* n-*th International Conf. on Distributed Computing Systems* (DCS) held every year are good places to look for recent papers on distributed operating systems. Furthermore, *ACM Transactions on Computer Systems* and *Operating Systems Review* are two journals that often have interesting articles on distributed operating systems.

11.1. SUGGESTIONS FOR FURTHER READING

11.1.1. Introduction and General Works

Andrews, *Concurrent Programming—Principles and Practice*
   A comprehensive introduction to programming concurrent systems.

Byte Magazine, June 1994

A special report on distributed computing gives a user-oriented perspective on the subject. The five articles deal with DCE, distributed data management, security, executive information systems, and remote clients.

Champine et al., "Project Athena as a Distributed Computer System"

Athena is a network operating system at M.I.T. consisting of over 1000 UNIX-based workstations connected together. The project has developed several software packages that have become de facto standards, such as X (window management) and Kerberos (authentication). This paper gives an overview of the whole system.

Coulouris et al. *Distributed Systems Concepts and Design,* 2nd ed.

A good general text on distributed systems. It covers network protocols, RPC, distributed operating systems, file systems, name servers, time, replication, transactions, concurrency control, fault tolerance, security, and DSM. Four short case studies are given: Mach, Chorus, Amoeba, and Clouds.

Mullender, *Distributed Systems*, 2nd ed.

A summer school proceedings containing 21 papers by leading authorities on distributed systems. The topics cover modeling, specification, fault tolerance, real time, communication, naming, file systems, scheduling, and security, among others.

11.1.2. Communication in Distributed Systems

Ballart and Ching, "SONET: Now It's the Standard Optical Network"

Understanding SONET is not for neophytes, but this tutorial highlights the main features of SONET in a relatively painless way. It also covers part of the history of the standardization process.

Bershad et al., "Lightweight Remote Procedure Call"

A method for doing fast RPC on a single processor or multiprocessor is described. It involves having the client run a preselected procedure in the server's address space, thus avoiding a context switch.

Birman and van Renesse, "Reliable Distr. Computing with the ISIS Toolkit"

A collection of papers about numerous aspects of ISIS. About one third of the papers contain overview material, one third describe the theoretical basis of ISIS, and one third cover applications of ISIS.

Birrell and Nelson, "Implementing Remote Procedure Calls"
   Remote procedure calls are commonly used in distributed systems for interprocess communication. This paper describes the design and implementation of the original remote procedure call system.

Clark et al., "The Aurora Gigabit Testbed"
   Aurora is one of several experimental gigabit networks designed for future distributed systems. This paper describes the network, host adaptors, protocols, applications, and network management.

De Prycker, *Asynchronous Transfer Mode*
   An entire book on ATM. If you want the entire story, look here.

Hutchinson et al., "RPC in the x-Kernel: Evaluating New Design Techniques"
   The x-kernel uses a technique similar to UNIX streams to allow protocol stacks to be assembled for handling RPC-based layered protocols. The mechanism is lightweight, using procedure calls between the layers.

Le Boudec, "The Asynchronous Transfer Mode"
   A simple introduction to ATM. This paper covers the physical, ATM, and adaptation layers, discusses future services based on ATM, and gives some background on the history of ATM.

Mullender, "Interprocess Communication"
   Networks, protocols, and RPC are all examined in detail in this tutorial on interprocess communication. A number of system issues are also covered.

Tay and Ananda, "A Survey of Remote Procedure Calls"
   Despite certain fundamental similarities, RPC systems differ in various ways. This paper surveys eight different RPC systems, ranging from academic research projects to commercial systems, and compares them in various ways.

11.1.3. Synchronization in Distributed Systems

Fidge, "Logical Time in Distributed Computing Systems"
   An approach to dealing with event ordering in distributed systems that is based on causality and partial time ordering, rather than total time ordering.

Ramanathan et al., "Fault-Tolerant Clock Synchronization in Distr. Systems,"
   An overview of clock synchronization algorithms for use in distributed systems. Hardware, software, and hybrid methods are covered.

Raynal, "A Simple Taxonomy for Distributed Mutual Exclusion Algorithms"
    A taxonomy and bibliography of distributed mutual exclusion algorithms. The major categories defined are permission-based and token-based, with centralized algorithms occurring at the intersection of the two.

Silberschatz and Galvin, *Operating System Concepts*
    Chapter 18 of this textbook deals with synchronization in distributed systems, including event ordering, mutual exclusion, agreement protocols, and election algorithms.

Singhal, "Deadlock Detection in Distributed Systems"
    A tutorial on distributed deadlock detection. First it looks at the issue involved. Then it goes on to discuss centralized, decentralized, and hierarchical algorithms in distributed systems.

Weihl, "Transaction-Processing Techniques"
    An introduction to atomic transactions including nested transactions. The chapter contains an extensive discussion of recovery methods, for both single-site and distributed failures.

11.1.4. Processes and Processors in Distributed Systems

Anderson et al., "Scheduler Activations: Effective Kernel Support for the User-Level Management of Parallelism"
    A new abstraction is presented for combining the best properties of user-level and kernel-level thread management. The abstraction is to give each process a virtual multiprocessor and use upcalls to inform users about relevant scheduling events.

Burns and Wellings, *Real-Time Systems and Their Programming Languages*
    An introductory text on how to design and program real-time systems in Ada, Modula 2, and occam 2. Topics covered include fault tolerance, exception handling, synchronization, atomic actions, resource control, and low-level programming issues. The book contains many code fragments to illustrate the ideas.

Cristian, "Understanding Fault-Tolerant Distributed Systems"
    An introduction to fault tolerance in distributed systems, including failure classification, semantics, and masking. Both hardware and software issues are treated. Hardware examples include Tandem, Sequoia, VAX cluster, and IBM XRF. Software issues group communication and global agreement.

Marsh et al., "First-Class, User-Level Threads"
A set of mechanisms and conventions are presented to allow threads to be managed in user space but still take advantage of kernel knowledge. The idea is based on upcalls.

Natarajan and Zhao, "Issues in Building Dynamic Real-Time Systems"
A short tutorial on real-time systems that looks at issues such as requirements, availability, guarantees, and resource management.

Nichols, "Using Idle Workstations in a Shared Computing Environment"
A description of the Butler system for finding and using idle UNIX workstations. A registry keeps track of machines and allocates them.

Shivarati et al., "Load Distributing for Locally Distributed Systems"
In a distributed system, the workload can easily get out of balance, with some machines idle and others overloaded. A number of algorithms for balancing the load are discussed in this tutorial.

Verissimo, "Real-Time Communication"
Fault-tolerant real-time distributed systems have specific communication needs not present in most other systems. This paper discusses some of them and how they can be achieved.

11.1.5. Distributed File Systems

Levy and Silberschatz, "Distributed File Systems: Concepts and Examples"
The first half of this paper covers principles of distributed file systems. The second half is on examples: UNIX United, Locus, NFS, Sprite, and Andrew.

Satyanarayanan, "A Survey of Distributed File Systems"
Some basic design issues for distributed file systems are examined in this survey. Case studies of NFS, Apollo Domain, Andrew, AIX, RFS, and Sprite are also presented.

Satyanarayanan, "Distributed File Systems"
Both principles and practice are treated in this introduction to distributed file systems. Commonly used mechanisms, such as caching, bulk transfer, and hints are covered, as are several existing systems, AFS, Coda, and NFS.

Svobodova, "File Servers for Network-Based Distributed Systems"
A survey of file servers used in distributed systems. The emphasis is on file servers that provide atomic actions and transactions.

11.1.6. Distributed Shared Memory

Li and Hudak, "Memory Coherence in Shared Virtual Memory Systems"
    The work of Li and Hudak created the field of DSM. This paper describes
page-based DSM systems using both centralized and decentralized managers.

Nitzberg and Lo, "Distr. Shared Memory: A Survey of Issues and Algorithms"
    A tutorial on the design and implementation of DSM systems focusing on
consistency models. Nine different examples are compared and another eight
are cited.

Stumm and Zhou, "Algorithms Implementing Distributed Shared Memory"
    A tutorial on distributed shared memory.

Tanenbaum et al., "Parallel Progr. Using Shared Objects and Broadcasting,"
    In contrast to the above references, all of which deal with page-based DSM,
this one shows how shared objects can be implemented on a network of
machines with local memories.

11.1.7. Case Study 1: Amoeba

Douglis et al., "A Comparison of Two Distr. Systems: Amoeba and Sprite,"
    A comparison of two distributed systems: Amoeba, which has a microkernel
and uses the processor pool model, and Sprite, which has a monolithic kernel
and uses the workstation model.

Kaashoek and Tanenbaum, "Group Communication in the Amoeba Distributed
Operating System"
    An introduction to group communication in Amoeba, especially the reliable
broadcast protocol used and its implementation. This paper also discusses fault
tolerance in the protocol, and how the reliable broadcast protocol recovers from
sequencer and other crashes.

Mullender et al., "Amoeba: A Distributed Operating System for the 1990s"
    An overview of Amoeba, emphasizing the communication mechanism,
objects, security, the file system, and process management.

Tanenbaum et al., "Experiences with the Amoeba Distr. Operating System"
    Another introduction to Amoeba. This one emphasizes objects, RPC,
servers, wide-area Amoeba, applications, and performance. It concludes with an
evaluation of the design based on actual experience—what was done right but
even more important, what was done wrong.

11.1.8. Case Study 2: Mach

Accetta et al., "Mach: A New Kernel Foundation for UNIX Development"
   One of the first published papers on the Mach system. It describes the goals of the system, the basic ideas, such as threads, ports, and messages, and the implementation.

Black, "Scheduling Support for Concurrency and Parallelism in the Mach Sys."
   The Mach scheduling algorithm for multiprocessors is described here. Various optimizations, such as handoff scheduling, are discussed, and performance measurements are given.

Boykin et al., *Programming under Mach*
   An entire book about how to write programs that run on Mach and use its many facilities. The emphasis is on how to use Mach, rather than on how it works inside.

Boykin and Langerman, "Mach/4.3BSD: A Conservative Approach to Parallelization,"
   The trials and tribulations of making the Mach UNIX emulator run efficiently on a multiprocessor, something for which it was never intended. The problems encountered with I/O and the file system are described, as are some solutions.

Rashid, "From RIG to Accent to Mach: The Evolution of a Network Op. Sys."
   A brief history of RIG, Accent, and Mach written by their author. The evolution of the system is described, emphasizing the changes that occurred as a result of new technology and new goals.

Young et al., "The Duality of Memory and Communication in the Implementation of a Multiprocessor Operating System"
   The goals, design, and implementation of the Mach memory management system, and how it interacts with the communication system. The use of external memory managers is described.

11.1.9. Case Study 3: Chorus

Gien, "Micro-kernel Architecture: Key to Modern Operating Systems Design"
   An introduction to the philosophy and aims of Chorus by one of the designers.

Gien and Grob, "Microkernel Based Operating Systems"
   A discussion of how Chorus can be used to emulate UNIX.

Rozier et al., "Chorus Distributed Operating Systems"
Although slightly dated, this is still the best general introduction to the architecture of the Chorus microkernel.

11.1.10. Case Study 4: DCE

Bever et al., "Distributed Systems, OSF DCE and Beyond"
A useful introduction to DCE emphasizing the architecture and RPC interface. This paper also points out a number of features that DCE does not have (e.g. advanced tools, object orientation, distributed transactions, multimedia support) and shows how they could be made to fit the DCE model.

Kazar et al., "DEcorum File System Architectural Overview"
DEcorum is the distributed file system component of DCE and the successor to AFS. An overview is given here, along with a discussion of token, caching, replication, deadlocks, and other issues.

OSF, *Introduction to OSF DCE*
The most accessible tutorial to DCE, covering the same topics as those treated in this book.

Rosenberry et al., *Understanding DCE*
A general introduction to DCE covering all the basic ideas in 14 chapters and 4 appendices.

Shirley, *Guide to Writing DCE Applications*
A tutorial telling how to write programs that run on DCE, both servers and clients. Numerous code fragments are given as illustrations.

11.2. ALPHABETICAL BIBLIOGRAPHY

ABROSSIMOV, A., ARMAND, F., and ORTEGA, M.: "A Distributed Consistency Server for the CHORUS System," *Proc. SEDMS III, Symp. on Experience with Distributed and Multiprocessor Systems*, USENIX, pp. 129-148, 1992.

ABROSSIMOV, A., ROZIER, M., and SHAPIRO, M.: "Generic Virtual Memory Management in Operating Systems Kernels," *Proc. 12th Symp. on Operating Systems Principles*, ACM, pp. 123-136, 1989.

ACCETTA, M., BARON, R., GOLUB, D., RASHID, R., TEVANIAN, A., and YOUNG, M.: "Mach: A New Kernel Foundation for UNIX Development," *Proc. Summer 1986 USENIX Conf.*, USENIX, pp. 93-112, 1986.

ADVE, S., and HILL, M.: "Weak Ordering: A New Definition," *Proc. 17th Ann. Int'l Symp. on Computer Architecture*, ACM, pp. 2-14, 1990.

AGARWAL, A., CHAIKEN, D., D'SOUZA, G., JOHNSON, K., KRANZ, D., KUBIA-TOWICZ, J., KURIHARA, K., LIM, B., MAA, G., NUSSBAUM, D., PARKIN, M., and YEUNG, D.: "The MIT Alewife Machine: A Large-Scale Distributed-Memory Multiprocessor," *Proc. Workshop on Scalable Shared Memory Multiprocessors*, Kluwer, 1991.

AGARWAL, A., and CHERIAN, M.: "Adaptive Backoff Synchronization Techniques," *Proc. 16th Ann. Int'l Symp. on Computer Architecture*, ACM, pp. 396-406, 1989.

AGARWAL, A., SIMONI, R., HENNESSY, J., and HOROWITZ, M.: "An Evaluation of Directory Schemes for Cache Coherence," *Proc. 15th Ann. Int'l Symp. on Computer Architecture*, ACM, pp. 280-289, 1988.

AGRAWAL, D., and EL ABBADI, A: "An Efficient and Fault-Tolerant Solution of Distributed Mutual Exclusion," *ACM Trans. on Computer Systems*, vol. 9, pp. 1-20, Feb. 1991.

AHAMAD, M., BAZZI, R.A., JOHN, R., KOHLI, P., and NEIGER, G.: "The Power of Processor Consistency," Tech. Rep. GIT-CC-92/34, College of Computing, Georgia Inst. of Technology, March 1993.

AHMADI, H., and DENZEL, W.: "A Survey of Modern High-Performance Switching Techniques," *IEEE Journal of Selected Areas in Communication*, vol. 7, pp. 1091-1103, Sept. 1989.

ANDERSON, T.E., BERSHAD, B.N., LAZOWSKA, E.D., and LEVY, H.M.: "Scheduler Activations: Effective Kernel Support for the User-Level Management of Parallelism," *Proc. 13th Symp. on Operating Systems Principles*, ACM, pp. 95-109, 1991.

ANDERSON, T.E., OWICKI, S.S., SAXE, J.B., and THACKER, C.P.: "High-Speed Switch Scheduling for Local-Area Networks," *ACM Trans. on Computer Systems*, vol. 11, pp. 319-352, Nov. 1993.

ANDREWS, G.R.: *Concurrent Programming—Principles and Practice*, Redwood City, CA: Benjamin/Cummings, 1991.

ARCHIBALD, J., and BAER, J.-L.: "Cache Coherence Protocols: Evaluation Using a Multiprocessor Simulation Model," *ACM Trans. on Computer Systems*, vol. 4, pp. 273-298, Nov. 1986.

ARMAND, F., and DEAN, R: "Data Movement in Kernelized Systems," *Proc. USENIX Workshop on Microkernels and Other Kernel Architectures*, USENIX, pp. 243-261, 1992.

ARTSY, Y., and FINKEL, R.: "Designing a Process Migration Facility," *IEEE Computer*, vol. 22, pp. 47-56, Sept. 1989.

ATTIYA, H., and FRIEDMAN, R.: "A Correctness Condition for High Performance Multiprocessors," *Proc. 24th ACM Symp. on Theory of Computing*, ACM, pp. 679-690, 1992.

BAL, H.E.: *Programming Distributed Systems*, Hemel Hempstead, England: Prentice Hall Int'l, 1991.

BAL, H.E., and KAASHOEK, M.F.: "Object Distribution in Orca using Compile-Time and Run-Time Techniques," *Proc. Conf. on Object-Oriented Programming Systems, Languages and Applications (OOPSLA '93)*, ACM, pp. 162-177, Sept. 1993.

BAL, H.E., KAASHOEK, M.F., and TANENBAUM, A.S.: "Experience with Distributed Programming in Orca," *Proc. Int'l Conf. on Computer Languages '90*, IEEE, pp. 79-89, 1990.

BAL, H.E., KAASHOEK, M.F., and TANENBAUM, A.S.: "Orca: A Language for Parallel Programming of Distributed Systems," *IEEE Trans. on Software Engineering*, vol. 18, pp. 190-205, March 1992.

BALL, J.E., FELDMAN, J.A., LOW, J.R., RASHID, R.F., and ROVNER, P.D.: "RIG, Rochester's Intelligent Gateway: System Overview," *IEEE Trans. on Software Engineering*, vol. SE-2, pp. 321-328, Dec. 1976.

BALLART, R., and CHING, Y.-Y.: "SONET: Now It's the Standard Optical Network," *IEEE Communications Magazine*, vol. 29, pp. 8-15, March 1989.

BARBORAK, M., MALEK, M., and DAHBURA, A.: "The Consensus Problem in Fault-Tolerant Computing," *ACM Computing Surveys*, vol. 25, pp. 171-220, June 1993.

BARON, R.; RASHID, R.; SIEGEL, E.; TEVANIAN, A., and YOUNG, M.: "Mach-1: An Operating Environment for Large-Scale Multiprocessor Applications," *IEEE Software*, vol. 2, pp. 65-67, July 1985.

BATLIVALA, N., GLEESON, B., HAMRICK, J., LURNDAL, S., PRICE, D., SODDY, J., and ABROSSIMOV, V.: "Experience with SVR4 Over CHORUS," *Proc. USENIX Workshop on Microkernels and Other Kernel Architectures*, USENIX, pp. 223-241, 1992.

BELLOVIN, S.M., and MERRITT, M.: "Limitations of the Kerberos Authentication System," *Proc. Winter 1991 USENIX Conf.*, USENIX, Jan. 1991.

BENNETT, J.K., CARTER, J.K., and ZWAENEPOEL, W.: "Munin: Distributed Shared Memory Based on Type-Specific Memory Coherence," *Proc. Second ACM Symp. on Principles and Practice of Parallel Programming*, ACM, pp. 168-176, 1990.

BERNSTEIN, P.A., and GOODMAN, N.: "An Algorithm for Concurrency Control and Recovery in Replicated Distributed Databases," *ACM Trans. on Database Systems*, vol. 9, pp. 596-615, Dec. 1984.

BERSHAD, B.N., ANDERSON, T.E., LAZOWSKA, E.D., and LEVY, H.M.: "Lightweight Remote Procedure Call," *ACM Trans. on Computer Systems*, vol. 8, pp. 37-55, Feb. 1990.

BERSHAD, B.N., and ZEKAUSKAS, M.J.: "Midway: Shared Memory Parallel Programming with Entry Consistency for Distributed Memory Multiprocessors," CMU Report CMU-CS-91-170, Sept. 1991.

BERSHAD, B.N., ZEKAUSKAS, M.J., and SAWDON, W.A.: "The Midway Distributed Shared Memory System," *Proc. IEEE COMPCON Conf.*, IEEE, pp. 528-537, 1993.

BEVER, M., GEIHS, K., HEUSER, L., MUHLHAUSER, M., and SCHILL, A.: "Distributed Systems, OSF DCE, and Beyond," in *DCE—The OSF Distributed Computing Environment*, A. Schill (ed.), Berlin: Springer-Verlag, pp. 1-20, 1993.

BIRMAN, K.P.: "The Process Group Approach to Reliable Distributed Computing," *Commun. of the ACM*, vol. 36, pp. 36-53, Dec. 1993.

BIRMAN, K.P., and JOSEPH, T.: "Reliable Communication in the Presence of Failures," *ACM Trans. on Computer Systems*, vol. 5, pp. 47-76, Feb. 1987a.

BIRMAN, K.P., and JOSEPH, T.: "Exploiting Virtual Synchrony in Distributed Systems," *Proc. 11th Symp. on Operating Systems Principles*, ACM, pp. 123-138, Nov. 1987b.

BIRMAN, K.P., SCHIPER, A., and STEPHENSON, P.: "Lightweight Causal and Atomic Group Multicast," *ACM Trans. on Computer Systems*, vol. 9, pp. 272-314, Aug. 1991.

BIRMAN, K.P., and VAN RENESSE, R.: *Reliable Distributed Computing with the ISIS Toolkit*, Los Alamitos, CA: IEEE Computer Society Press, 1994.

BIRRELL, A.D., and NELSON, B.J.: "Implementing Remote Procedure Calls," *ACM Trans. on Computer Systems*, vol. 2, pp. 39-59, Feb. 1984.

BITAR, P.: "MIMD Synchronization and Coherence," Tech. Rep. 90/605, Univ. of Calif. at Berkeley, Nov. 1990.

BJORNSON, R.D.: "Linda on Distributed Memory Multiprocessors," Ph.D. Thesis, Yale Univ., 1993.

BLACK, D.: "Scheduling Support for Concurrency and Parallelism in the Mach Operating System," *IEEE Computer*, vol. 23, pp. 35-43, May 1990.

BLACK, D.L., GOLUB, D.B., JULIN, D.P., RASHID, R.F., DRAVES, R.P., DEAN, R.W., FORIN, A., BARRERA, J., TOKUDA, H., MALAN, G., and BOHMAN, D.: "Microkernel Operating System Architecture and Mach," *Proc. USENIX Workshop on Microkernels and Other Kernel Architectures*, USENIX, pp. 11-30, 1992.

BOLOSKY, W.J., FITZGERALD, R.P., and SCOTT, M.L.: "Simple but Effective Techniques for NUMA Memory Management," *Proc. 12th Symp. on Operating Systems Principles*, ACM, pp. 19-31, 1989.

BOYKIN, J., KIRSCHEN, D., LANGERMAN, A., and LoVERSO, S.: *Programming Under Mach*, Reading, MA: Addison-Wesley, 1993.

BOYKIN, J., and LANGERMAN, A.: "Mach/4.3BSD: A Conservative Approach to Parallelization," *Computing Systems*, vol. 3., pp. 69-99, Winter 1990.

BRERETON, O.P.: "Management of Replicated Files in a UNIX Environment," *Software—Practice and Experience*, vol. 16, pp. 771-780, Aug. 1986.

BRICKER, A., GIEN, M., GUILLEMONT, M., LIPKIS, J., ORR, D., and ROZIER, M.: "A New Look at Microkernel-based UNIX operating systems: Lessons in performance and compatibility," *Proc. EurOpen Spring'91 Conf.*, EurOpen, pp. 13-32, 1991.

BUDHIRAJA, N., MARZULLO, K., SCHNEIDER, F.B., and TOUEG, S.: "The Primary—Backup Approach," in *Distributed Systems*, 2nd ed., S. Mullender (ed.), New York, NY: ACM Press, pp. 199-216, 1993.

BURNS, A., and WELLINGS, A.: *Real-Time Systems and Their Programming Languages*, Reading, MA: Addison-Wesley, 1990.

CARRIERO, N., and GELERNTER, D.: "The S/Net's Linda Kernel," *ACM Trans. on Computer Systems*, vol. 4, pp. 110-129, May 1986.

CARRIERO, N., and GELERNTER, D.: "Linda in Context," *Commun. of the ACM*, vol. 32, pp. 444-458, April 1989.

CARRIERO, N., GELERNTER, D., and LEICHTER, J.: "Distributed Data Structures in Linda," *Proc. ACM Symposium on Principles of Programming Languages*, ACM, 1986.

CARTER, J.B., BENNETT, J.K., and ZWAENEPOEL, W.: "Implementation and Performance of Munin," *Proc. 13th Symp. on Operating Systems Principles*, ACM, pp. 152-164, 1991.

CARTER, J.B., BENNETT, J.K., and ZWAENEPOEL, W.: "Techniques for Reducing Consistency-Related Communication in Distributed Shared memory Systems," *ACM Trans. on Computer Systems*, vol. 12, 1994.

CATLETT, C.E.: "In Search of Gigabit Applications," *IEEE Communications Magazine*, vol. 30, pp. 42-51, April 1992.

CHAMPINE, G.A., GEER, D.E., Jr., and RUH, W.N.: "Project Athena as a Distributed Computer System," *IEEE Computer*, vol. 23, pp. 40-51, Sept. 1990.

CHANDY, K.M., MISRA, J., and HAAS, L.M.: "Distributed Deadlock Detection," *ACM Trans. on Computer Systems*, vol. 1, pp. 144-156, May 1983.

CHANG, J., and MAXEMCHUK, N.F.: "Reliable Broadcast Protocols," *ACM Trans. on Computer Systems*, vol. 2, pp. 39-59, Feb. 1984.

CHASE, J.S., AMADOR, F.G., LAZOWSKA, E.D., LEVY, H.M., and LITTLEFIELD, R.J.: "The Amber System: Parallel Programming on a Network of Multiprocessors," *Proc. 12th Symp. on Operating Systems Principles*, ACM, pp. 147-158, 1989.

CHEONG, H., and VEIDENBAUM, A.V.: "A Cache Coherence Scheme with Fast Selective Invalidation," *Proc. 15th Ann. Int'l Symp. on Computer Architecture*, ACM, pp. 299-307, 1988.

CHEUNG, N.K.: "The Infrastructure of Gigabit Computer Networks," *IEEE Communications Magazine*, vol. 30, pp. 60-68, April 1992.

CHOW, T.C.K., and ABRAHAM, J.A.: "Load Balancing in Distributed Systems," *IEEE Trans. on Software Engineering*, vol. SE-8, pp. 401-412, July 1982.

CHUTANI, S., ANDERSON, O.T., KAZAR, M.L., LEVERETT, B.W., MASON, W.A., and SIDEBOTHAM, R.N.: "The Episode File System," *Proc. Winter 1992 USENIX Conf.*, USENIX, pp. 43-60, 1992.

CLARK, D.D., DAVIE, B.S., FARBER, D.J., GOPAL, I.S., KADABA, B.K., SINCOSKIE, W.D., SMITH, J.M., and TENNENHOUSE, D.L.: "The Aurora Gigabit Testbed," *Computer Networks and ISDN Systems*, vol. 25, pp. 599-621, June 1993.

COHEN, D.: "On Holy Wars and a Plea for Peace," *IEEE Computer*, vol. 14, pp. 48-54, Oct. 1981.

COMER, D.E.: *Internetworking with TCP/IP*. Vol. 1: Principles, Protocols and Architectures, 2nd ed., Englewood Cliffs, NJ: Prentice Hall, 1991

COULOURIS, G.F., DOLLIMORE, J., and KINDBERG, T.: *Distributed Systems Concepts and Design*, 2nd ed. Reading, MA: Addison-Wesley, 1994.

COX, A.L., and FOWLER, R.J.: "The Implementation of a Coherent Memory Abstraction of a NUMA Multiprocessor: Experiences with PLATINUM," *12th Symp. on Operating Systems Principles*, ACM, pp. 32-43, 1989.

CRISTIAN, F.: "Probabilistic Clock Synchronization," *Distributed Computing*, vol. 3, pp. 146-158, 1989.

CRISTIAN, F.: "Understanding Fault-Tolerant Distributed Systems," *Commun. of the ACM*, vol. 34, pp. 56-78, Feb. 1991.

DAHLGREN, F., DUBOIS, M., and STENSTROM, P.: "Combined Performance Gains of Simple Cache Protocol Extensions," *Proc. 21st Ann. Int'l Symp. on Computer Architecture*, ACM, pp. 187-195.

DAY, J.D., and ZIMMERMAN, H.: "The OSI Reference Model," *Proc. IEEE*, vol. 71, pp. 1334-1340, Dec. 1983.

DE PRYCKER, M.: *Asynchronous Transfer Mode*, Chichester, England: Ellis Horwood, 1991.

DELP, G.S.: *The Architecture and Implementation of MemNet: An Experiment on High-Speed Memory Mapped Network Interface*, Ph.D. Thesis, Univ. of Delaware, 1988.

DELP, G.S., FARBER, D.J., MINNICH, R.G., SMITH, J.M., and TAM, M.-C.: "Memory as a Network Abstraction," *IEEE Network*, vol. 5, pp. 34-41, July 1991.

DOUGLIS, F., and OUSTERHOUT, J.: "Transparent Process Migration: Design Alternatives and the Sprite Implementation," *Software—Practice and Experience*, vol. 21, pp. 757-785, Aug. 1991.

DOUGLIS, F., OUSTERHOUT, J.K., KAASHOEK, M.F., and TANENBAUM, A.S.: "A Comparison of Two Distributed Systems: Amoeba and Sprite," *Computing Systems*, vol. 4, pp. 353-384, Fall 1991.

DRAVES, R.P.: "The Revised IPC Interface," *Proc. First USENIX Mach Symp.*, USENIX, pp. 101-121, 1990.

DRAVES, R.P., BERSHAD, B.N., RASHID, R.F., and DEAN, R.W.: "Using Continuations to Implement Thread Management and Communication in Operating Systems," *Proc. 13th Symp. on Operating Systems Principles*, ACM, pp. 122-136, 1991.

DRUMMOND, R., and BABAOGLU, O.: "Low-Cost Clock Synchronization," *Distributed Computing*, vol. 6, pp. 193-203, 1993.

DUBOIS, M., SCHEURICH, C., and BRIGGS, F.A.: "Memory Access Buffering in Multiprocessors," *Proc. 13th Ann. Int'l Symp. on Computer Architecture*, ACM, pp. 434-442, 1986.

DUBOIS, M., SCHEURICH, C., and BRIGGS, F.A.: "Synchronization, Coherence, and Event Ordering in Multiprocessors," *IEEE Computer*, vol. 21, pp. 9-21, Feb. 1988.

EAGER, D.L., LAZOWSKA, E.D., and ZAHORJAN, J.: "Adaptive Load Sharing in Homogeneous Distributed Systems," *IEEE Trans. on Software Engineering*, vol. SE-12, pp. 662-675, May 1986.

ECKBERG, A.E. "B-ISDN/ATM Traffic Control and Congestion," *IEEE Network*, vol. 5, pp. 28-37, Sept. 1992.

EDLER, J., LIPKIS, J., and SCHONBERG, E.: "Process Management for Highly Parallel UNIX Systems," *Proc. USENIX Workshop on UNIX and Supercomputers*, USENIX, pp. 1-17, Sept. 1988.

EGGERS, S.J., and KATZ, R.H.: "The Effect of Sharing on the Cache and Bus Performance of Parallel Programs," *Proc. Second ASPLOS Conf.*, ACM, pp. 257-271, 1989a.

EGGERS, S.J., and KATZ, R.H.: "Evaluating the Performance of Four Snooping Cache Coherency Protocols," *Proc. 16th Ann. Int'l Symp. on Computer Architecture*, ACM, pp. 2-15, 1989b.

ESWARAN, K.P., GRAY, J.N., LORIE, J.N., and TRAIGER, I.L.: "The Notions of Consistency and Predicate Locks in a Database System," *Commun. of the ACM*, vol. 19, pp. 624-633, Nov. 1976.

EVANS, A., KANTROWITZ, W., and WEISS, E.: "A User Authentication Scheme Not Requiring Secrecy in the Computer," *Commun. of the ACM*, vol 17., pp. 437-442, Aug. 1974.

FERGUSON, D., YEMINI, Y., and NIKOLAOU, C.: "Microeconomic Algorithms for Load Balancing in Distributed Computer Systems," *Proc. Eighth Int'l Conf. on Distributed Computing Systems*, IEEE, pp. 491-499, 1988.

FIDGE, C.: "Logical Time in Distributed Computing Systems," *IEEE Computer*, vol. 24, pp. 28-33, Aug. 1991.

FISCHER, M., LYNCH, N., and PATERSON, M.: "Impossibility of Distributed Consensus with One Faulty Process," *Journal of the ACM*, vol. 32, pp. 374-382, April 1985.

FLEISCH, B., and POPEK, G.: "Mirage: A Coherent Distributed Shared Memory Design," *Proc. 12th Symp. on Operating Systems Principles*, ACM, pp. 211-223, 1989.

FLYNN, M.J.: "Some Computer Organizations and Their Effectiveness," *IEEE Trans. on Computers*, vol. C-21, pp. 948-960, Sept. 1972.

FORIN, A., BARRERA, J., YOUNG, M., and RASHID, R.: "Design, Implementation, and Performance Evaluation of a Distributed Shared Memory Server for Mach," *Proc. Winter 1989 USENIX Conf.*, USENIX, Jan. 1989.

FREDRICKSON, N, and LYNCH, N.: "Electing a Leader in a Synchronous Ring," *Journal of the ACM*, vol. 34, pp. 98-115, Jan. 1987.

GANTENBEIN, R.E.: "An Annotated Bibliography of Dependable Distributed Computing," *Operating Systems Review*, vol. 20, pp. 60-81, April 1992.

GARCIA-MOLINA, H.: "Elections in a Distributed Computing System," *IEEE Trans. on Computers*, vol. 31, pp. 48-59, Jan. 1982.

GARCIA-MOLINA, H., and SPAUSTER, A: "Ordered and Reliable Multicast Communication," *ACM Trans. on Comp. Syst.*, vol. 9, pp. 242-271, Aug. 1991.

GELERNTER, D.: "Generative Communication in Linda," *ACM Trans. on Programming Languages and Systems*, vol. 7, pp. 80-112, Jan. 1985.

GHARACHORLOO, K., LENOSKI, D., LAUDON, J., GIBBONS, P., GUPTA, A., and HENNESSY, J.: "Memory Consistency and Event Ordering in Salable Shared-Memory Multiprocessors," *Proc. 17th Ann. Int'l Symp. on Computer Architecture*, ACM, pp. 15-26, 1990.

GIEN, M.: "Micro-Kernel Architecture: Key to Modern Operating Systems Design," *UNIX Review*, pp. 10, Nov. 1990

GIEN, M., and GROB, L.: "Microkernel Based Operating Systems: Moving UNIX onto Modern System Architectures," *Proc. UniForum'92 Conf.*, USENIX, pp. 43-55, 1992.

GIFFORD, D.K.: "Weighted Voting for Replicated Data," *Proc. Seventh Symp. on Operating Systems Principles*, ACM, pp. 150-162, 1979.

GOLUB, D., DEAN, R., FORIN, A., and RASHID, R.: "UNIX as an Application Program," *Proc. Summer 1990 USENIX Conf.*, USENIX, pp. 87-95, June 1990.

GOODMAN, J.R.: "Using Cache Memory to Reduce Processor Memory Traffic," *10th Ann. Int'l Symp. on Computer Architecture*, ACM, pp. 124-131, 1983.

GOODMAN, J.R.: "Cache Consistency and Sequential Consistency," Tech. Rep. 61, IEEE Scalable Coherent Interface Working Group, IEEE, 1989.

GOPAL, I., GUERIN, R., JANNIELLO, J., and THEOHARAKIS, V.: "ATM Support in a Transparent Network," *IEEE Network*, vol. 6, pp. 62-68, Nov. 1992.

GRAY, J.: "Notes on Database Operating Systems," in *Operating Systems: An Advanced Course*, R. Bayer, R.M. Graham, and G. Seegmuller (eds.), Berlin: Springer-Verlag, pp. 394-481, 1978.

GRAY, C., and CHERITON, D.: "Leases: An Efficient Fault-Tolerant Mechanism for Distributed File System Consistency," *Proc. 11th Symp. on Operating Systems Principles*, ACM, pp. 202-210, 1989.

GRAY, J.N., HOMAN, P., KORTH, H.F., and OBERMARCK, R.L.: "A Straw Man Analysis of the Probability of Waiting and Deadlock in a Database System," Report RJ 3066, IBM Research Laboratory, San Jose CA, 1981.

GUSELLA, R., and ZATTI, S.: "The Accuracy of the Clock Synchronization Achieved by TEMPO in Berkeley UNIX 4.3BSD," *IEEE Trans. on Software Engineering*, vol. 15, pp. 847-853, July 1989.

HARTY, K., and CHERITON, D.: "Application-Controlled Physical Memory Using External Page-Cache Management," *Proc. Fifth ASPLOS Conf.*, ACM, pp. 187-199, 1992.

HOARE, C.A.R.: "Monitors, An Operating System Structuring Concept," *Commun. of the ACM*, vol. 17, pp. 549-557, Oct. 1974; Erratum in *Commun. of the ACM*, vol. 18, p. 95, Feb. 1975.

HONG, D., and SUDA., T: "Congestion Control and Prevention in ATM Networks," *IEEE Network*, vol. 5, pp. 10-16, July 1991.

HOWARD, J.H., KAZAR, M.J., MENEES, S.G., NICHOLS, D.A., SATYANARAYANAN, M., SIDEBOTHAM, R.N., and WEST, M.J.: "Scale and Performance in a Distributed File System," *ACM Trans. on Computer Systems*, vol. 6, pp. 55-81, Feb. 1988.

HUTCHINSON, N.C., PETERSON, L.L., ABBOTT, M.B., and O'MALLEY, S.: "RPC in the *x*-Kernel: Evaluating New Design Techniques," *Proc. 12th Symp. on Operating Systems Principles*, ACM, pp. 911-101, 1989.

HUTTO, P.W., and AHAMAD, M.: "Slow Memory: Weakening Consistency to Enhance Concurrency in Distributed Shared Memories," *Proc. 10th Int'l Conf. on Distributed Computing Systems*, IEEE, pp. 302-311, 1990.

JONES, A.K., CHANSLER, R.J., Jr., DURHAM, I., FEILER, P., and SCHWANS, K.: "Software Manaagement of CM*—A Distributed Multiprocessor," *Proc. NCC*, AFIPS, pp. 657-663, 1977.

JUL, E., LEVY, H., HUTCHINSON, N., and BLACK, A.: "Fine-Grained Mobility in the Emerald System," *ACM Trans. on Computer Systems*, vol. 6, pp. 109-133, Feb. 1988.

KAASHOEK, M.F., and TANENBAUM, A.S.: "Group Communication in the Amoeba Distributed Operating System," *Proc. 11th Int'l Conf. on Distributed Computing Systems*, IEEE, pp. 222-230, 1991.

KAASHOEK, M.F., TANENBAUM, A.S., HUMMEL, S., and BAL, H.E.: "An Efficient Reliable Broadcast Protocol," *Operating Systems Review*, vol. 23, pp. 5-19, Oct. 1989.

KARLIN, A.R., LI, K., MANASSE, M.S., and OWICKI, S: "Empirical Studies of Competitive Spinning for a Shared-Memory Multiprocessor," *Proc. 13th Symp. on Operating Systems Principles*, ACM, pp. 41-55, 1991.

KAZAR, M.L., LEVERETT, B.W., ANDERSON, O.T., APOSTOLIDES, V., BOTTOS, B.A., CHUTANI, S., EVERHART, C.F., MASON, W.A., TU, S.-T., and ZAYAS, E.R.: "DEcorum File System Architectural Overview," *Proc. Summer 1990 USENIX Conf.*, USENIX, pp. 151-163, Summer 1990.

KELEHER, P., COX, A.L., and ZWAENEPOEL, W.: "Lazy Release Consistency," *Proc. 19th Ann. Int'l Symp. on Computer Architecture*, ACM, pp. 13-21, 1992.

KLEIN, M.H., LEHOCZKY, J.P., and RAJKUMAR, R.: "Rate-Monotonic Analysis for Real-Time Industrial Computing," *IEEE Computer*, vol. 27, pp. 24-33, Jan. 1994.

KLEINROCK, L.: *Queueing Systems.* Vol. 1, New York: John Wiley, 1974.

KLEINROCK, L.: "The Latency/Bandwidth Tradeoff in Gigabit Networks," *IEEE Communications Magazine*, vol. 30, pp. 36-40, April 1992.

KNAPP, E.: "Deadlock Detection in Distributed Databases," *ACM Computing Surveys*, vol. 19, pp. 303-328, Dec. 1987.

KOHL, J.T.: "The Evolution of the *Kerberos* Authentication Service," *Proc. EurOpen Spring'91 Conf.*, EurOpen, pp. 295-313, 1991.

KOPETZ, H., DAMM, A., KOZA, C., MULAZZANI, M., SCHWABL, W., SENFT, C., and ZAINLINGER, R.: "Distributed Fault-Tolerant Real-Time Systems: The MARS Approach," *IEEE Micro*, vol. 9, pp. 25-40, Feb. 1989.

KOPETZ, H., and GRUNSTEIDL, G.: "TTP—A Protocol for Fault-Tolerant Real-Time Systems," *IEEE Computer*, vol. 27, pp. 14-23, Jan 1994.

KOPETZ, H., and OCHSENREITER, W.: "Clock Synchronization in Distributed Real-Time Systems," *IEEE Trans. on Computers*, vol. C-36, pp. 933-940, Aug. 1987.

KRANZ, D., JOHNSON, K., AGARWAL, A., KUBIATOWICZ, J.J., and LIM, B.: "Integrating Message Passing and Shared Memory: Early Experiences," *Proc. Fourth Symp. on Principles and Practice of Parallel Programming*, ACM, pp. 54-63, May 1993.

KRISHNASWAMY, V.: "A Language Based Architecture for Parallel Computing," Ph.D. Thesis, Yale Univ., 1991.

KUNG, H.T., and ROBINSON, J.T.: "On Optimistic Methods for Concurrency Control," *ACM Trans. on Database Systems*, vol. 6, pp. 213-226, June 1981.

LAMPORT, L.: "Time, Clocks, and the Ordering of Events in a Distributed System," *Commun. of the ACM*, vol. 21, pp. 558-564, July 1978.

LAMPORT, L.: "How to Make a Multiprocessor Computer That Correctly Executes Multiprocess Programs," *IEEE Trans. on Computers*, vol. C-28, pp. 690-691, Sept. 1979.

LAMPORT, L.: "Concurrent Reading and Writing of Clocks," *ACM Trans. on Computer Systems*, vol. 8, pp. 305-310, Nov. 1990.

LAMPORT, L., SHOSTAK, R., and PEASE, M.: "The Byzantine Generals Problem," *ACM Trans. on Programming Languages and Systems*, vol. 4, pp. 382-401, July 1982.

LAMPSON, B.W., ABADI, M., BURROWS, M., and WOBBER, E.: "Authentication in Distributed Systems: Theory and Practice," *ACM Trans. on Computer Systems*, vol. 10, pp. 265-310, Nov. 1992.

LaROWE, R.P., and ELLIS, C.S.: "Experimental Comparison of Memory Management Policies for NUMA Multiprocessors," *ACM Trans. on Computer Systems*, vol. 9, pp. 319-363, Nov. 1991.

LaROWE, R.P., ELLIS, C.S., and KAPLAN, L.S.: "The Robustness of NUMA Memory Management," *Proc. 13th Symp. on Operating Systems Principles*, ACM, pp. 137-151, 1991.

LE BOUDEC, J.-Y.: "The Asynchronous Transfer Mode: A Tutorial" *Computer Networks and ISDN Systems*, vol. 24, pp. 279-309, April 1992.

LEA, R., AMARAL, P., and JACQUEMOT, C.: "COOL-2: An Object-Orient Support Platform Built above the Chorus Microkernel," *Proc. Int'l Workshop on Object-Oriented Systems*, pp. 51-55, 1991.

LEA, R., JACQUEMOT, C., and PILLEVESSE, E.: "COOL: System Support for Distributed Programming," *Commun. of the ACM*, vol. 36, pp. 37-46, Sept. 1993.

LENOSKI, D., LAUDON, J., GHARACHORLOO, K., WEBER, W.-D., GUPTA, A., HENNESSY, J., HOROWITZ, M., and LAM, M.: "The Stanford Dash Multiprocessor," *IEEE Computer*, vol. 25, pp. 63-79, March 1992.

LEVY, E., and SILBERSCHATZ, A.: "Distributed File Systems: Concepts and Examples" *Computing Surveys*, vol. 22, pp. 321-374, Dec. 1990.

LI, K.: "Shared Virtual Memory on Loosely Coupled Multiprocessors," Ph.D. Thesis, Yale Univ., 1986.

LI, K., and HUDAK, P.: "Memory Coherence in Shared Virtual Memory Systems," *ACM Trans. on Computer Systems*, vol. 7, pp. 321-359, Nov. 1989.

LILJA, D.J.: "Cache Coherence in Large-Scale Shared-Memory Multiprocessors: Issues and Comparisons," *ACM Computing Surveys*, vol. 25, pp. 303-338, Sept. 1993.

LIPTON, R.J., and SANDBERG, J.S.: "Pram: A Scalable Shared Memory," Tech. Rep. CS-TR-180-88, Princeton Univ., Sept. 1988.

LISKOV, B.: "Practical Uses of Synchronized Clocks in Distributed Systems," *Distributed Computing*, vol. 6, pp. 211-219, 1993.

LITZKOW, M.J., LIVNY, M., and MUTKA, M.W.: "Condor—A Hunter of Idle Workstations," *Proc. Eighth Int'l Conf. on Distributed Computing Systems*, IEEE, pp. 104-111, 1988.

LIU, C.L., and LAYLAND, J.W.: "Scheduling Algorithms for Multiprogramming in a Hard Real-Time Environment," *Journal of the ACM*, vol. 20, pp. 46-61, Jan. 1973.

LO, V.M.: "Heuristic Algorithms for Task Assignment in Distributed Systems," *Proc. Fourth Int'l Conf. on Distributed Computing Systems*, IEEE, pp. 30-39, 1984.

LUAN, S.-W., and GLIGOR, V.D.: "A Fault-Tolerant Protocol for Atomic Broadcast," *IEEE Trans. on Parallel and Distributed Systems*, vol. 1, pp. 271-285, July 1990.

LUNDELIUS-WELCH, J., and LYNCH, N.: "A New Fault-Tolerant Algorithm for Clock Synchronization," *Information and Computation*, vol. 77, pp. 1-36, Jan. 1988.

LYLES, J.B., and SWINEHART, D.C.: "The Emerging Gigabit Environment and the Role of Local ATM," *IEEE Communications Magazine*, vol. 30, pp. 52-58, April 1992.

MAEKAWA, M., OLDEHOEFT, A.E., and OLDEHOEFT, R.R.: *Operating Systems: Advanced Concepts*, Menlo Park, CA: Benjamin/Cummings, 1987.

MALCOLM, N., and ZHAO, W.: "The Timed-Token Protocol for Real-Time Communication," *IEEE Computer*, vol. 27, pp. 35-41, Jan 1994.

MARSH, B.D., SCOTT, M.L., LeBLANC, T.J., and MARKATOS, E.P.: "First-Class User-Level Threads," *Proc. 13th Symp. on Operating Systems Principles*, ACM, pp. 110-121, 1991.

MELIAR-SMITH, P.M., MOSER, L.E., and AGRAWALA, V.: "Broadcast Protocols for Distributed Systems," *IEEE Trans. on Parallel and Distributed Systems*, vol. 1, pp. 17-25, Jan. 1990.

MINZER, S.E.: "Broadband ISDN and Asynchronous Transfer Mode (ATM)," *IEEE Communications Magazine*, vol. 29, pp. 17-24, Sept. 1989.

MORRIS, J.H., SATYANARAYANAN, M., CONNER, M.H., HOWARD, J.H., ROSENTHAL, D.S., and SMITH, F.D.: "Andrew: A Distributed Personal Computing Environment," *Commun. of the ACM*, vol. 29, pp. 184-201, March 1986.

MOSBERGER, D.: "Memory Consistency Models," Tech,. Report TR 93/11, Dept. of Computer Science, Univ. of Arizona, 1993.

MULLENDER, S.J. (ed.): *Distributed Systems*, 2nd ed., New York, NY: ACM Press, 1993.

MULLENDER, S.J.: "Interprocess Communication," in *Distributed Systems*, 2nd ed., S. Mullender (ed.), New York, NY: ACM Press, pp. 217-250, 1993.

MULLENDER, S.J., ROSSUM, G. VAN, TANENBAUM, A.S., RENESSE, R. VAN, and STAVEREN, H. VAN: "Amoeba: A Distributed Operating System for the 1990s," *IEEE Computer*, vol. 23, pp. 44-53, May 1990.

MULLENDER, S.J., and TANENBAUM, A.S.: "Immediate Files," *Software—Practice and Experience*, vol. 14, pp. 365-368, April 1984.

MUTKA, M.W., and LIVNY, M.: "Scheduling Remote Processor Capacity in a Workstation-Processor Bank Network," *Proc. Seventh Int'l Conf. on Distributed Computing Systems*, IEEE, pp. 2-9, 1987.

NATARAJAN, S., and ZHAO, W.: "Issues in Building Dynamic Real-Time Systems," *IEEE Software*, vol. 9, pp. 16-21, Sept. 1992.

NAYFEH, B.A., and OLUKOTUN, K.: "Exploring the Design Space for a Shared-Cache Multiprocessor," *Proc. 21st Ann. Int'l Symp. on Computer Architecture*, ACM, pp. 166-175, 1994.

NEEDHAM, R.M., and SCHROEDER, M.D.: "Using Encryption for Authentication in Large Networks of Computers," *Commun. of the ACM*, vol. 21, pp. 993-999, Dec. 1978.

NELSON, B.J.: *Remote Procedure Call*, Ph.D. Thesis, Carnegie-Mellon Univ., 1981.

NELSON, V.P.: "Fault-Tolerant Computing: Fundamental Concepts," *IEEE Computer*, vol. 23, pp. 19-25, July 1990.

NEWMAN, P: "ATM Local Area Networks," *IEEE Communications Magazine*, vol. 32, pp. 86-98, March 1994.

NICHOLS, D.A.: "Using Idle Workstations in a Shared Computing Environment," *Proc. 11th Symp. on Operating Systems Principles*, ACM, pp. 5-12, 1987.

NIKOLAIDIS, I., and ONVURAL, R.O.: "A Bibliography on Performance Issues in ATM Networks," *Computer Communication Review*, vol. 22, pp. 8-23, Oct. 1992.

NITZBERG, B., and LO, V.: "Distributed Shared Memory: A Survey of Issues and Algorithms," *IEEE Computer*, vol. 24, pp. 52-60, Aug. 1991.

OSF: *Introduction to OSF DCE*, Englewood Cliffs, NJ: Prentice Hall, 1992.

OUSTERHOUT, J.K.: "Scheduling Techniques for Concurrent Systems," *Proc. Third Int'l Conf. on Distributed Computing Systems*, IEEE, pp. 22-30, 1982.

PANZIERI, F., and SHRIVASTAVA, S.K.: "Rajdoot: a remote procedure call mechanism with orphan detection and killing," *IEEE Trans. on Software Engineering*, vol. 14, pp. 30-37, Jan. 1988.

PARNAS, D.: "On the Criteria to Be Used in Decomposing Systems into Modules," *Commun. of the ACM*, vol. 15, pp. 1053-1058, Dec. 1972.

PARTRIDGE, C.: "Protocols for High-Speed Networks: Some Questions and a Few Answers," *Computer Networks and ISDN Systems*, vol. 25, pp. 1019-1028, Sept. 1993.

PARTRIDGE, C.: *Gigabit Networking*, Reading, MA: Addison-Wesley, 1994.

PATTAVINA, A.: "Nonblocking Architectures for ATM Switching," *IEEE Communications Magazine*, vol. 31, pp. 38-48, Feb. 1993.

PEASE, M., SHOSTAK, R., and LAMPORT, L,: "Reaching Agreement in the Presence of Faults," *Journal of the ACM*, vol. 27, pp. 228-234, April 1980.

PRZYBYLSKI, M., HOROWITZ, J., and HENNESSY, J.: "Performance Tradeoffs in Cache Design," *Proc. 15th Ann. Int'l Symp. on Computer Architecture*, ACM, pp. 290-298, 1988.

PU, C., NOE, J.D., and PROUDFOOT, A.: "Regeneration of Replicated Objects: A Technique and its Eden Implementation," *Proc. Second Int'l Conf. on Data Engineering*, pp. 175-187, Feb 1986.

PURDIN, T.D., SCHLICHTING, R.D., and ANDREWS, G.R.: "A File Replication Facility for Berkeley UNIX," *Software—Practice and Experience*, vol. 17, pp. 923-940, Dec. 1987.

RAMAMRITHAM, K., STANKOVIC, J.A., and SHIAH, P.-F.: "Efficient Scheduling Algorithms and Real-Time Multiprocessor Systems," *IEEE Trans. on Parallel and Distributed Systems*, vol. 1, pp. 184-194, April 1990.

RAMANATHAN, J., and NI, L.M.: "Critical Factors in NUMA Memory Management," *Proc. 11th Int'l Conf. on Distributed Computing Systems*, IEEE, pp. 500-507, 1991.

RAMANATHAN, P., KANDLUR, D.D., and SHIN, K.G.: "Hardware-Assisted Software Clock Synchronization for Homogeneous Distributed Systems," *IEEE Trans. on Computers*, vol. C-39, pp. 514-524, April 1990a.

RAMANATHAN, P., and SHIN, K.G.: "Delivery of Time-Critical Messages Using a Multiple Copy Approach," *ACM Trans. on Computer Systems*, vol. 10, pp. 144-166, May 1992.

RAMANATHAN, P., SHIN, K.G., and BUTLER, R.W.: "Fault-Tolerant Clock Synchronization in Distributed Systems," *IEEE Computer*, vol. 23, pp. 33-42, Oct. 1990b.

RASHID, R.F.: "Threads of a New System," *Unix Review*, vol. 4, pp. 37-49, Aug. 1986a.

RASHID, R.F.: "From RIG to Accent to Mach: The Evolution of a Network Operating System," *Fall Joint Computer Conf.*, AFIPS, pp. 1128-1137, 1986b.

RAYNAL, M.: "A Simple Taxonomy for Distributed Mutual Exclusion Algorithms," *Operating Systems Review*, vol. 25, pp. 47-50, April 1991.

REED, D.P.: "Implementing Atomic Actions on Decentralized Data," *ACM Trans. on Computer Systems*, vol. 1, pp. 3-23, Feb. 1983.

RICART, G., and AGRAWALA, A.K.: "An Optimal Algorithm for Mutual Exclusion in Computer Networks," *Commun. of the ACM*, vol. 24, pp. 9-17, Jan. 1981.

ROOHOLAMINI, R., CHERKASSKY, V., and GARVER, M.: "Finding the Right ATM Switch for the Market," *IEEE Computer*, vol. 27, pp. 16-28, April 1994.

ROSENBERRY, W., KENNEY, D., and FISHER, G.: *Understanding DCE*, Sebastopol, CA: O'Reilly, 1992.

ROZIER, M., ABROSSIMOV, V., ARMAND, F., BOULE, I., GIEN, M., GUILLEMONT. M., HERRMANN, F., KAISER, C., LEONARD, P., LANGLOIS, S., and NEUHAUSER, W.: "Chorus Distributed Operating Systems," *Computing Systems*, vol. 1, pp. 305-379, Oct. 1988.

SANDERS, B.A.: "The Information Structure of Distributed Mutual Exclusion," *ACM Trans. on Computer Systems*, vol. 5, pp. 284-299, Aug. 1987.

SANSOM, R.D., JULIN, D.P., and RASHID, R.F.: "Extending a Capability Based System into a Network Environment," *Proc. SIGCOMM '86*, ACM, pp. 265-274, 1986.

SATYANARAYANAN, M.: "A Study of File Sizes and Functional Lifetimes," *Proc. Eighth Symp. on Operating Systems Principles*, ACM, pp. 96-108, 1981.

SATYANARAYANAN, M.: "A Survey of Distributed File Systems," *Annual Review of Computer Science*, vol. 4, pp. 73-104, 1990a.

SATYANARAYANAN, M.: "Scalable, Secure, and Highly Available Distributed File Access," *IEEE Computer*, vol. 23, pp. 9-21, May 1990b.

SATYANARAYANAN, M.: "Distributed File Systems," in *Distributed Systems*, 2nd ed., S. Mullender (ed.), New York, NY: ACM Press, pp. 353-383, 1993.

SCHEURICH, C., and DUBOIS, M.: "Correct Memory Operation of Cache-Based Multiprocessors," *Proc. Fourth Ann. Int'l Symp. on Computer Architecture*, ACM, pp. 234-24, 1987.

SCHNEIDER, F.B.: "Implementing Fault-Tolerant Services Using the State Machine Approach," *ACM Computing Surveys*, vol. 22, pp. 299-319, Dec. 1990.

SCHROEDER, M.D., and BURROWS, M.: "Performance of Firefly RPC," *ACM Trans. on Computer Systems*, vol. 8, pp. 1-17, Feb. 1990.

SCHWAN, K., and ZHOU, H.: "Dynamic Scheduling of Hard Real-Time Tasks and Real-Time Threads," *IEEE Trans. on Software Engineering*, vol. 18, pp. 736-747, Aug. 1992.

SCOTT, M., LeBLANC, T., and MARSH, B.: "Multi-model Parallel Programming in Psyche," *Proc. Second ACM Symp. on Principles and Practice of Parallel Programming*, ACM, pp. 70-78, 1990.

SHIN, K.: "HARTS: A Distributed Real-Time Architecture," *IEEE Computer*, vol. 24, pp. 25-35, May 1991.

SHIRLEY, J.: *Guide to Writing DCE Applications*, Sebastopol, CA: O'Reilly, 1992.

SHIVARATI, N.G., KRUEGER, P., and SINGHAL, M.: "Load Distributing for Locally Distributed Systems," *IEEE Computer*, vol. 25, pp. 33-44, Dec 1992.

SILBERSCHATZ, A., and GALVIN, P.: *Operating System Concepts*, Reading, MA: Addison-Wesley, 1994.

SINGH, S., and KUROSE, J.: "Electing 'Good' Leaders," *Journal of Parallel and Distributed Computing*, vol. 21, pp. 184-201, May 1994.

SINGHAL, M.: "Deadlock Detection in Distributed Systems," *IEEE Computer*, vol. 22, pp. 37-48, Nov. 1989.

SRIKANTH, T.K., and TOUEG, S.: "Optimal Clock Synchronization," *Journal of the ACM*, vol. 34, pp. 626-645, July 1987.

STANKOVIC, J.A.: "Misconceptions about Real-Time Computing: A Serious Problem for Next-Generation Systems," *IEEE Computer*, vol. 21, pp. 10-19, Oct. 1988.

STEINER, J.G., NEUMAN, B.C., and SCHILLER, J.I.: "Kerberos: An Authentication Service for Open Network Systems," *Proc. Winter 1988 USENIX Conf.*, USENIX, pp. 191-202, Feb 1988.

STONE, H.S., and BOKHARI, S.H.: "Control of Distributed Processes," *IEEE Computer*, vol. 11, pp. 97-106, July 1978.

STUMM, M., and ZHOU, S.: "Algorithms Implementing Distributed Shared Memory," *IEEE Computer*, vol. 23, pp. 54-64, May 1990.

SUBRAMANIAN, I.: "Managing Discardable Pages with an External Pager," *Proc. Second USENIX Mach Symp.*, USENIX, pp. 77-86, 1991.

SUZUKI, T.: "ATM Adaptation Layer Protocol," *IEEE Communications Magazine*, vol. 32, pp. 80-83, April 1994.

SVOBODOVA, L.: "File Servers for Network-Based Distributed Systems," *ACM Computing Surveys*, vol. 16, pp. 353-398, Dec. 1984.

TAM, M.-C., SMITH, J.M., and FARBER, D.J.: "A Taxonomy-Based Comparison of Several Distributed Shared Memory Systems," *Operating Systems Review*, vol. 24, pp. 40-67, July 1990.

TANENBAUM, A.S.: *Computer Networks*, 2nd ed., Englewood Cliffs, NJ: Prentice Hall, 1988.

TANENBAUM, A.S., KAASHOEK, M.F., and BAL, H.E.: "Parallel Programming Using Shared Objects and Broadcasting," *IEEE Computer*, vol. 25, 1992.

TANENBAUM, A.S., MULLENDER, S.J., and VAN RENESSE, R.: "Using Sparse Capabilities in a Distributed Operating System," *Proc. Sixth Int'l Conf. on Distributed Computing Systems*, IEEE, pp. 558-563, 1986.

TANENBAUM, A.S., VAN RENESSE, R., STAVEREN, H. VAN, SHARP, G.J., MUL-LENDER, S.J., JANSEN, J., and ROSSUM, G. VAN: "Experiences with the Amoeba Distributed Operating System," *Commun. of the ACM*, vol. 33, pp. 46-63, Dec. 1990.

TAY, B.H., and ANANDA, A.L.: "A Survey of Remote Procedure Calls," *Operating Systems Review*, vol. 24, pp. 68-79, July 1990.

THEIMER, M.M., LANTZ, K.A., and CHERITON, D.A.: "Preemptable Remote Execution Facilities in the V System," *Proc. 10th Symp. on Operating Systems Principles*, ACM, pp. 2-12, 1985.

THEKKATH, R., and EGGERS, S.J.: "Impactof Sharing-Based Thread Placement on Multithreaded Architectures," *Proc. 21st Ann. Int'l Symp. on Computer Architecture*, ACM, pp. 176-186, 1994.

TRAJKOVIC, L., and GOLESTANI, S.J.: "Congestion Control for Multimedia Services," *IEEE Network*, vol. 6, pp. 20-26, Sept. 1992.

TSEUNG, L.N.: "Guaranteed, Reliable, Secure Broadcast Networks," *IEEE Network*, vol. 3, pp. 33-37. Nov. 1989.

TUREK, J., and SHASHA, D.: "The Many Faces of Consensus in Distributed Systems," *IEEE Computer*, vol. 25, pp. 8-17, June 1992.

ULLMAN, J.: "Complexity of Sequence Problems," in *Computers and Job/Shop Scheduling Theory*, E.G. Coffman (ed.), New York: Wiley, 1976.

VAN RENESSE, R., and TANENBAUM, A.S.: "Voting with Ghosts," *Proc. Eighth Int'l Conf. on Distributed Computer Systems*, IEEE, 1988.

VAN TILBORG, A.M., and WITTIE, L.D.: "Wave Scheduling: Distributed Allocation of Task Forces in Network Computers," *Proc. Sixth Int'l Conf. on Distributed Computing Systems*, IEEE, pp. 337-347, 1981.

VASWANI, R., and ZAHORJAN, J.: "The Implications of Cache Affinity on Processor Scheduling for Multiprogrammed Shared Memory Multiprocessors," *Proc. 13th Symp. on Operating Systems Principles*, ACM, pp. 26-40, 1991.

VERISSIMO, P.: "Real-Time Communication," in *Distributed Systems*, 2nd ed., S. Mullender (ed.), New York, NY: ACM Press, pp. 447-490, 1993.

VERNON, M.K., LAZOWSKA, E.D., and ZAHORJAN, J.: "Snooping Cache-Consistency Protocols," *Proc. 15th Ann. Int'l Symp. on Computer Architecture*, ACM, pp. 308-317, 1988.

WEBER, W., and GUPTA, A.: "Analysis of Cache Invalidation Patterns in Multiprocessors," *Proc. Third ASPLOS Conf.*, ACM, pp. 243-256, 1989.

WEIHL, W.: "Transaction-Processing Techniques," in *Distributed Systems*, 2nd ed., S. Mullender (ed.), New York, NY: ACM Press, pp. 329-352, 1993.

WITTIE, L.D., and VAN TILBORG, A.M.: "MICROS, a Distributed Operating System for MICRONET, A Reconfigurable Network Computer," *IEEE Trans. on Computers*, vol. C-29, pp. 1133-1144, Dec. 1980.

WOBBER, E., ABADI, M., BURROWS, M., and LAMPSON, B.: "Authentication in the Taos Operating System," *ACM Trans. on Computer Systems*, vol. 12, pp. 3-32, Feb. 1994.

WOO, T.Y.C., and LAM, S.S.: "Authentication for Distributed Systems," *IEEE Computer*, vol. 25, pp. 39-52, Jan. 1992.

YOUNG, M., TEVANIAN, A. Jr., RASHID, R., GOLUB, D., EPPINGER, J., CHEW, J., BOLOSKY, W., BLACK, D., and BARON, R.: "The Duality of Memory and Communication in the Implementation of a Multiprocessor Operating System," *Proc. 11th Symp. on Operating Systems Principles*, ACM, pp. 63-76, Nov. 1987.

ZAYAS, E.R.: "Attacking the Process Migration Bottleneck," *Proc. 11th Symp. on Operating Systems Principles*, ACM, pp. 13-24, 1987.

ZEGURA, E.W.: "Architectures for ATM Switching Systems," *IEEE Communications Magazine*, vol. 31, pp. 28-37, Feb. 1993.

Index

A

A-node, 568
ABCAST, 112
Accent, 432
Access control list, 247, 555, 562-563
ACID properties, 148
Acknowledgement, 86-88
ACL (*see* Access control list)
ACL manager, 562
Active Replication, 215-217
Actor, Chorus, 479
Actuator, 224
Addressing, predicate, 105
Aggregate, DCE, 566
Agreement in faulty systems, 217-222
AIL (*see* Amoeba interface language)
Algorithm
    Berkeley clock synchronization 130
    bidding, 209-210
    bully, 141-142
    clock synchronization, 124-132
    Cristian's, 128-130
    earliest deadline first, 236
    election, 140-143
    graph-theoretic, 204
    hierarchical allocation, 206-208

Algorithm (*continued*)
    least laxity, 237
    migratory allocation, 198
    nonmigratory allocation, 198
    NUMA, 311
    primary copy, 270
    processor allocation, 203-210
    rate monotonic, 236
    real-time scheduling, 237-241
    receiver-initiated, 208-209
    ring, 143
    sender-initiated, 208
    up-down, 205
    voting, 270-271
    wait-die, 164
    wound-wait, 165
Alias, 551
Allocation algorithm, processor, 203-210
Allocation model, processor, 197-199
Amoeba, 376-429
    boot server, 427
    broadcast protocol, 400-407
    bullet server, 383, 415-420
    capability, 384-388
    communication, 393-415
    comparison with Mach and Chorus, 510-517
    directory server, 383, 420-425

Amoeba (*continued*)
    fault tolerance, 405-407
    FLIP protocol, 407-415
    get-port, 397
    glocal variable, 391
    goals, 377-378
    group communication, 398-407
    history buffer, 402
    history, 376-377
    memory management, 392-393
    microkernel, 380-382
    mutex, 391-392
    objects, 384-388
    port, 395
    process management, 388-392
    processor pool, 379-380
    put-port, 397, 412-414
    replication server, 425
    RPC, 394-398
    run server, 425-427
    segment, 382, 392-393
    servers, 415-428
    service, 380
    soap server, 383
    system architecture, 378-380
    TCP/IP server, 427-428
    thread, 391-392
    wide-area networks, 414-415
Amoeba directory server, 383
Amoeba interface language, 415
Aperiodic event, 224
Application layer, 42
ARPANET, 42
Asynchronous system, 214
Asynchronous transfer mode, 42-50
At least once semantics, 83
At most once semantics, 83, 132-133
AT&T, 432-433
ATM (*see* Asynchronous transfer mode)
ATM adaptation layer, 46-47
ATM layer, 45-46
ATM physical layer, 44-45
ATM switching, 47-49
ATM switching fabric, 47
Atomic broadcast, 106-107, 217
Atomic transaction, 144-158
Atomicity, 106-107
Attributes, file, 246
Authenticated RPC, 559-562
Authentication, 554
Authentication server, 557
Authenticator, 558-559

Authorization, 555
Automounting, NFS, 274
Availability, 27

B

Barrier, 328
Basic overseer server, 572
BBN Butterfly, 309
Berkeley clock synchronization algorithm, 130
Big endian machine, 74
Binary names, 252
Binder, 78
Binding, 538-539
Boot server, Amoeba, 427
Bootstrap port, Mach, 436
Broadcast protocol, Amoeba, 400-407
Broadcasting, 100
Bullet server
    Amoeba, 383, 415-420
    implementation, 418-420
Bully algorithm, 141-142
Bus, 293-294
Busy waiting, 180
Byzantine empire, 214
Byzantine fault, 214
Byzantine generals problem, 220-222

C

C threads, 440-442
Cache
    multiprocessor, 305
    snooping, 294
Cache consistency algorithm, 265-268
Cache consistency protocol, 294
    write once, 296
    write through, 295
Caching, file, 262-268
    write-on-close algorithm, 266
    write-through algorithm, 265-266
Call-by-copy/restore, 70
Call-by-reference parameter, 69
Call-by-value parameter, 69
Canonical form, 75
Capability, 247
    Amoeba, 384-388
    Chorus, 481
    Mach, 435, 460-463
Capability list, Mach, 460-462

Capability name, Mach, 461
Cascaded aborts, 155
Causal consistency, 321-322
Causally related events, 112
CBCAST, 112-114
CDS (*see* Cell directory service)
CDS directory, 547-548
CDS server, 549
Cell, 43-44, DCE, 525-527
Cell directory service, 545, 547-549
Centralized system, 2
Cesium clock, 125
Checksum, 38
Chicken, rubber, 36
Chorus, 475-518
  actor, 479
  capability, 481
  communication calls, 498-499
  communication, 495-499
  comparison with Amoeba and Mach, 510-517
  configurability, 504-506
  exception handling, 487-488
  goals, 477
  history, 476-477
  interprocess communication, 482
  IPC manager, 504
  kernel abstraction, 479-481
  kernel process, 478
  kernel structure, 481-483
  mapper, 491-492
  memory management calls, 493-495
  memory management, 490-495
  message, 495
  microkernel, 478
  minimessage, 495
  miniport, 495
  nucleus, 478
  object manager, 503-504
  object orientation, 483
  port, 480
  process management calls, 488-490
  process management, 483-490
  process manager, 502-503
  protection identifier, 484
  real time, 506
  real-time executive, Chorus,482
  region, 479, 490
  scheduling, 486-487
  segment, 481, 490
  software register, 486
  streams manager, 504
  subsystem, 479

Chorus (*continued*)
  supervisor, 481-483
  system process, 479
  system structure, 478-479
  thread, 479, 485,486
  UNIX emulation, 483, 499-506
  UNIX extensions, 500-501
  UNIX implementation, 501-506
  user process, 479
  virtual memory manager, 482
Chorus object-oriented layer, 507-510
  base layer, 507-509
  cluster, 508
  context space, 508-509
  context space, implementation, 510
  context space, runtime system, 509-510
Ciphertext, 555
Clearinghouse, DCE, 548
Client, 17, 51
  DCE, 536-538
Client crashes, 83-84
Client/server binding, 538-539
Client/server model, 50-68
  addressing, 56-58
  example, 52-55
  implementing, 65-68
Client stub, 70
Clock
  logical, 120-124
  physical, 124-127
Clock skew, 121
Clock synchronization, 119-133, 226
Clock tick, 121
Clocks, synchronized, 132-133
Closed group, 101-102
Co-scheduling, 211-212
Coarse-grained parallelism, 29
Coherent memory, 11
Committed file, 417
Communication, 515-516
  Amoeba, 393-415
  Chorus, 495-499
  Mach, 457-471
  one-to-many, 99
  point-to-point, 99
  real-time, 230-234
Communication primitives, 58-65
  asynchronous, 59-61
  blocking, 58-59
  buffered, 61-63
  group, 105-106
  mailbox, 63

Communication primitives (*continued*)
  nonblocking, 59-61
  reliable, 63-65
  synchronous, 58-59
  unbuffered, 61-63
  unreliable, 63-65
Comparison of Amoeba, Mach, Chorus, 510-517
Component fault, 212-213
Computer supported cooperative work, 4-5
Concurrency control, 154-158
  optimistic, 156
Concurrent events, 112, 122
Concurrent operations, 322
Condition variable, 175-176, 530
Consistency
  causal, 321-322
  eager release, 329
  entry, 330-331, 353-354
  lazy release, 329
  PRAM, 322-325
  processor, 324-325
  release, 327-330, 346-348
  sequential, 317-321
  strict, 315-317
  summary of models, 331-333
Consistency models, 315-333
COOL (*see* Chorus object-oriented layer)
Copy-on-write, Mach, 451
Crashes
  client, 83-84
  server, 82-83
Cristian's algorithm, 128-130
Critical path, RPC, 88-92
Crossbar switch, 12
Cryptography, 555

D

DARPA, 432
Dash, 303-307
Data link layer, 38-40
DCE (*see* Distributed computing environment)
Deadlock, 158-165
Deadlock detection, 159-163
Deadlock prevention, 163-165
DFS (*see* DCE, distributed file system)
Directory, multiprocessor, 303-305
Directory server
  Amoeba, 383, Amoeba, 420-425
  implementation, 423-425
Directory server agent, 553

Directory user agent, 553
Disk, optical, 280-281
Diskless workstation, 186-187
Dispatcher, 172
Distinguished name, 551
Distributed computing environment, 520-574
  access control list, 562-563
  authenticated RPC, 559-562
  basic overseer server, 572-573
  CDS, 545, 547-549
  cell, 525-527
  cell directory service, 545, 547-549
  clearinghouse, 548
  clerk, 549
  client, 536-538
  components, 522-525
  DFS, 524, 564-573
  directory service, 524, 544-554
  distributed file service, 524, 564-573
  distributed time service, 524, 540-544
  DTS, 524, 540-544
  Episode, 564
  fileset location server, 572
  fileset server, 571-572
  GDA, 545
  GDS, 545, 549-554
  global directory service, 545, 549-554
  goals, 521-522
  history, 520-521
  Kerberos, 555
  mutex, 530-531
  names, 546-547
  replication server, 572
  RPC, 535-540
  security, 554-563
  security registry
  security service, 524
  server, 536-538
  template, 532
  thread, 527-535
  thread calls, 531-535
  time clerk, 543
  time provider, 544
  time server, 543
  time service, 540-544
Distributed file system (*see* File system)
Distributed shared memory, 289-373
  Chorus, 492
  comparison of approaches, 371-372
  design, 334
  false sharing, 336-337
  finding the page owner, 339-342

Distributed shared memory (*continued*)
   finding the pages, 342-343
   granularity, 336-337
   Mach, 456-457
   Munin, 346-353
   object-based, 356-371
   page replacement, 343-344
   page-based, 333-345
   replication, 334-335
   sequentially consistent, 337-339
   shared variable, 345-355
   synchronization, 344-345
Distributed system
   advantages, 3-6
   Amoeba, 376-429
   Chorus, 475-518
   DCE, 520-574
   definition, 2
   design issues, 22-31
   disadvantages, 6-8
   goals, 3-8
   Mach, 430-473
   software, 15-22
DN (*see* Distinguished name)
DNS (*see* Domain name system)
Domain name system, 545
Drift rate, clock, 128
DSA (*see* Directory server agent)
DSM (*see* Distributed shared memory)
DTS (*see* DCE, distributed time service)
DUA (*see* Directory user agent)
Dynamic binding, 77-80
Dynamic real-time scheduling, 236-237, 240-241

E

Eager release consistency, 329
Earliest deadline first algorithm, 236
Einstein's theory of relativity, 316
Election algorithm, 140-143
Endpoint, DCE, 538
Entry consistency, 330-331, 353-354
Episode, 564
Errno, 176
Ethernet, 230
Event-triggered system, 226
Exactly once semantics, 83
Exception, 81
Exception handling, Chorus, 487-488
Exception port, Mach, 436
Extermination, orphan, 84

External memory manager
   Mach, 452-457
External pager
   Chorus, 491
   Mach, 446

F

Fail-safe system, 229
Fail-silent fault, 213-214
Fail-stop fault, 214
Failures, RPC, 80-84
False deadlock, 161
False sharing, 336-337
Fast local internet protocol, 407-415
   interface, 409-411
Fault
   Byzantine, 214
   intermittent, 212
   permanent, 212
   transient, 212
Fault tolerance, 28, 212-222
   Amoeba, 405-407
   file system, 284-285
   primary-backup, 217-219
Fault-tolerant system, real-time, 228-229
File, immutable, 247, 255, 416
File attribute, 246
File extension, 248
File handle, NFS, 273-274
File server, 17, 245
   bullet, 415-420
File service, 245
   interface, 246-248
File sharing semantics, 253-256
File system, 245-286
   caching, 262-268
   design, 246-256
   fault tolerance, 284-285
   hierarchical, 248
   implementation, 256-279
   lessons learned, 278-279
   NFS, 272-278
   replicated, 268-270
   replication algorithms, 270-272
   stateful, 260-262
   stateless, 260-262
   structure, 258-262
   trends, 279-285
File usage, 256-258
Fileset, DCE, 566

Fileset location server, 572
Fileset server, 571-572
Fine-grained parallelism, 29
Firefly multiprocessor, 90
FLIP (*see* Fast local internet protocol)
FLIP address, 409
FLIP layer, 411-412
Flow control, 87
Frame, 38
Frozen page, 311

G

GBCAST, 112
GDA (*see* Global directory agent)
GDS (*see* Global directory service)
Get-port, Amoeba, 397
Ghosts, 271
Global directory agent, 545
Global directory service, 545, 549-554
Glocal variable, 391
Grain size, 29
Gregorian calendar, 541
Group
    closed, 101-102
    hierarchical, 102-103
    open, 101-102
    overlapping, 109
    peer, 102-103
Group addressing, 104-105
Group communication, 99-114
    Amoeba, 398-407
    Chorus, 496
    design issues, 101-109
    ISIS, 110-114
Group membership, 103-104
Group server, 103

H

Handle, RPC, 78
Happens-before relation, 122
Head-of-line blocking, 48
Header, 36
Heuristics, allocation, 200
Hierarchical group, 102-103
History buffer, 402
Hypercube, 14

I

IDL (*see* Interface definition language)
Idle workstations, 189-193
Immutable file, 247, 255, 416
Implicit receive, 185
Information hiding, 356
Intentions list, 152
Interface, 36
Interface definition language, 537
Intermittent fault, 212
International atomic time, 125
Internet protocol, 40
Interrupt handling, Chorus, 488
IP (*see* Internet protocol)
ISIS, 110-114

J

Jacket, 180

K

Kerberos (*see* Security, DCE)

L

LAN (*see* Local area network)
Layered protocols, 35-42
Lazy release consistency, 329
Lazy replication, 269, 425
Leap second, 126
Lease, 133
Least laxity algorithm, 237
Lessons learned, 278-279
LI (*see* Local identifier, Chorus)
Lightweight process (*see* Thread)
Linda, 358-365
    implementation, 361-365
    replicated worker model, 360-361
    template, 360
    tuple space, 359-361
Little endian machine, 73-74
Local area network, 1
Local identifier, Chorus, 480
Locate packet, 57
Location independence, 251
Location policy, 201
Location transparency, 251

Locking, 154-156
Log, writeahead, 152-153
Logical clock, 120-124
Login facility, 557
Loosely synchronous system, 111
Loosely-coupled system, 9-10
Lost messages, 81-82

M

Mach, 430-473
  C threads, 440-442
  capability, 435, 460-463
  capability list, 460-462
  capability name, 461
  communication, 457-471
  comparison with Amoeba and Chorus, 510-517
  control port, 452-453
  copy-on-write, 451
  distributed shared memory, 456-457
  external memory manager, 452-457
  external pager, 446
  goals, 433
  handoff scheduling, 445
  history, 431-433
  memory management, 445-457
  memory object, 435, 447
  memory sharing, 449-452
  message formats, 466-469
  message primitives, 464-466
  message queue, 458
  name port, 453
  network message server, 469-471
  network port, 469
  object port, 452
  out-of-line data, 468
  port, 435, 457-460, 463-464
  port set, 459-460
  process management, 436-445
  process port, 460
  processor set, 442
  region, 447
  thread, 439-442
  thread scheduling, 442-445
  trampoline mechanism, 471
  UNIX emulation, 471-472
  UNIX server, 435-436
  virtual memory, 446-449
Mach interface generator, 436
Mailbox, 63
Mapper, Chorus, 491-492

MARS, 232
Marshaling, parameter, 72
MD5 (*see* Message digest 5)
Mean solar second, 125
Mean time to failure, 213
Memnet, 298-301
Memory coherence, 321
Memory management
  Amoeba, 392-393
  Chorus, 490-495
  Mach, 445-457
Memory model, 514-515
Message, Chorus, 495
Message digest 5, 559
Message ordering, 107-108
Method, 292, 356, 366
Microkernel
  Amoeba, 380-382
  Chorus, 478
  Mach, 433-435
MICROS, 206-208
Midway, 353-355
  entry consistency, 353-354
  implementation, 355
MIG (*see* Mach interface generator)
Migratory allocation algorithms, 198
Minimessage, Chorus, 495
Miniport, Chorus, 495
Minitel, 29
MiX, Chorus, 483
Mobile users, 284
MSF, 127
Multicasting, 100
Multicomputer, 8
  bus-based, 13-14
  Switched, 14-15
Multiprocessor, 8-13
  bus-based, 10-12, 293-298
  directory-based, 303-305
  NUMA, 308-311
  ring-based, 298-301
  switched, 12-13, 301-307
  timesharing, 20-22
  UMA, 308
Munin, 346-353
  directories, 351-352
  protocols, 348-351
  release consistency, 346-348
  synchronization, 353
Mutex, 175, 391-392
  fast, 530
  recursive, 530-531

Mutual exclusion, 134-140
  comparison of methods, 139-140

N

Name
  binary, 252
  DCE, 546-547
  symbolic, 252
Name server, 58
Naming, two-level, 252
Naming transparency, 251
Nested transactions, 149-150
Network file system, 272-278
  architecture, 272-273
  implementation, 275-278
  NIS, 275
  protocol, 273-275
  r-node, 277
  v-node, 276
  yellow pages, 275
Network information service, 275
Network layer, 40,
Network message server, Mach, 469-471
Network operating system, 16-18
NFS (*see* Network file system)
NIS (*see* Network information service)
No remote access system, 333
Nonce, 559
Nonmigratory allocation algorithms, 198
NonUniform Memory Access, 13
NORMA (*see* No remote access system)
Nucleus, Chorus, 478
NUMA (*see* NonUniform Memory Access)
NUMA multiprocessor, 308-311
NUMA multiprocessor, paging algorithm, 311

O

Object, 292, 356, 366, 512-513
  Amoeba, 384-388
  operations, 387-388
  protection, 385-387
Object-based DSM, 356-371
OC-1, 45
Omega network, 12
Open group, 101-102
Open Software Foundation, 432
Open system, 35

Open systems interconnection, 35-42
Operation, 366
Optical disk, 280-281
Optimistic concurrency control, 156
Orca, 365-371
  language, 366-368
  object management, 368-371
Orphan, 83-84
  expiration, 84
  extermination, 84
  gentle reincarnation, 84
  reincarnation, 84
OSF (*see* Open Software Foundation)
OSF DCE (*see* Distributed computing environment)
OSI model (*see* Open systems interconnection)
Overrun error, 87

P

PAC (*see* Privilege attribute certificate)
Page scanner, 311
Peer group, 102-103
Periodic event, 224
Permanent fault, 212
Physical clock, 124-127
Physical layer, 38
Piggybacked acknowledgement, 401
Pipeline model, 173
Pipelined RAM (*see* PRAM consistency)
Plaintext, 555
Point-to-point communication, 99
Pop-up thread, 185
Pope Gregory, 541
Port
  Amoeba, 395
  Chorus, 480, 495-496, 495-496
  Mach, 435, 457-460, 463-464
  Mach bootstrap, 436
  Mach control, 452-453
  Mach exception, 436
  Mach name, 453
  Mach network, 469
  Mach object, 452
  Mach process, 460
  Mach registered, 437
  thread, 439
Port group, Chorus, 496
Port set, Mach, 459-460
PRAM consistency, 322-325
Precious page, 454
Presentation layer, 41-42

Primary copy replication, 270
Primary-backup fault tolerance, 217-219
Primitives (*see* Communication primitives)
Principal, security, 554
Privilege attribute certificate, 557
Privilege server, 557
Probe, 162
Process, 513-514
    Amoeba, 388-391
    Chorus, 484-485
    Mach, 436
Process descriptor, 389
Process management
    Amoeba, 388-392
    Chorus, 483-490
    Mach, 436-445
Processor allocation, 197-210
Processor allocation algorithms
    bidding, 209-210
    centralized, 206
    design issues, 199-201
    graph-theoretic, 204
    hierarchical, 206-208
    implementation, 201-203
    receiver-initiated, 208-209
    sender-initiated, 208
    up-down, 205
Processor consistency, 324-325
Processor pool, 193-197, 379-380
Processor set
    Mach, 442
Protecion identifier
    Chorus, 484
Protected variable, 328
Protocol, 35
    Amoeba broadcast, 400-407
    blast, 86
    cache consistency, 294-298
    connection-oriented, 36
    connectionless, 36
    multiprocessor, 305-307
    NFS, 273-275
    request/reply, 52
    RPC, 85-86
    selective repeat, 87
    stop-and-wait, 86
    TCP/IP, 40-41
    time-triggered, 232-234
    two-phase commit, 153-154
    distributed systems, 408
Protocol stack, 38
Put-port, Amoeba, 397, 412-414

Q

Queueing systems, 194-196
Quorum, 271

R

R-node, 277
Rate monotonic algorithm, 236
RDN (*see* Relative distinguished name)
Read ahead, 277
Read quorum, 271
Read-driven pipeline, 97
Real-time communication, 230-234
Real-time connection, 231
Real-time distributed systems, 223-241
Real-time executive, Chorus, 482
Real-time program, 223
Real-time scheduling, 234-241
    dynamic, 236-237, 240-241
    earliest deadline first, 236
    least laxity, 237
    rate monotonic, 236
    static, 237-241
Real-time system
    Chorus, 506
    design, 226-230
    event-triggered, 226
    fail-safe, 229
    fault-tolerant, 228-229
    hard, 225
    language support, 229-230
    myths, 225-226
    predictable, 227-228
    soft, 225
    time-triggered, 227
Redundancy, 214-215
Region
    Chorus, 479, 490
    Mach, 447
Registered port, Mach, 437
Registry server, 557
Relative distinguished name, 550-551
Release consistency, 327-330, 346-348
Reliability, 27-28
Reliable broadcasting, 400-407
Remote access model, 248
Remote file system, 275
Remote procedure call, 68-98, 88-92
    Amoeba, 394-398
    basic operation, 68-72

Remote procedure call (*continued*)
  binding, 77-80
  Chorus, 47
  copying overhead, 92-94
  critical path, 90-92
  DCE, 535-540
  handle, 78
  implementation, 84-98
  interaction with threads, 184,185
  marshaling, 72
  parameter passing, 72-77
  problem areas, 95-98
  protocols, 85-86
  semantics, 80-84
  sweep algorithm, 95
  timer management, 94-95
Replicated worker model, 360-361
Replication
  active, 215-217
  file system, 268-270
  lazy, 269
Replication server, 416
  Amoeba, 425
  DCE, 572
Replication transparency, 268-269
Request/reply protocol, 52
Response ratio, 199
Response time, 198
RFS (*Remote file system*)
Ring algorithm, 143
Ring-based multiprocessor, 298-301
Rochester intelligent gateway, 431-432
Rollback, 152
Routing, 40
RPC (*see* Remote procedure call)
RPC daemon, 538-539
Run server, Amoeba, 425-427

S

Scalability, 29-31, 109-110, 282-283
Scatter/gather, 93
Schedulable system, 236
Scheduler activations, 182-183
Schedules, 149
Scheduling, 210-212
  Chorus, 486-487
  DCE, 529-530
  dynamic real-time, 236-237, 240-241
  handoff, 445
  Mach, 442-445

Scheduler (*continued*)
    real-time, 234-241
    static real-time, 237-241
Scheduling algorithms, comparison, 240-241
Schema, 551
SDH (*see* Synchronous digital hierarchy)
SEAL (*see* Simple and efficient adaptation layer)
Security
  components, 557-558
  DCE, 554-563
Security model, 555-557
Security service
  DCE, 555
Segment
  Amoeba, 382, 392-393
  Chorus, 481, 490
  mapped, 393
Selective repeat protocol, 87
Semantics
  at least once, 83
  at most once, 83
  exactly once, 83
  file sharing, 253-256
  RPC, 80-84
  session, 253-254
  UNIX, 253-254
Sensor, 224
Sequencer, 369
Sequential consistency, 317-321
Server, 51, 516-517
  Amoeba, 382-384, 415-428
  DCE, 536-538
Server crashes, 82-83
Server stub, 70
Session layer, 41
Session semantics, 253-254
Shadow block, 151
Shared memory, 292-314
Shared memory machines, comparison, 312-314
Simple and efficient adaptation layer, 47
Single-processor system, 2
Single-system image, 19
Skulking, 549
Snooping cache, 11, 294
Snoopy cache (*see* Snooping cache)
SOAP server (*see* Amoeba, directory server)
Solar second, 124
SONET (*see* Synchronous optical network)
SONET frame, 45
Spin lock, 180
Spoofing, 562
Sporadic event, 224

St. Exupéry, Antoine de, 511
Stable storage, 146-147
State machine approach, 215
Stateless file system, 260-262
Stateless server, 274-275
Static real-time scheduling, 237-241
Strict consistency, 315-317
Stub
   client, 70
   server, 70
Stunning, 390
Supervisor, Chorus, 481-483
Sweep algorithm, 95
Switching fabric, 47
Symbolic link, 252
Symbolic names, 252
Synchronization
   clock, 119-133, 124-132
   Distributed shared memory, 344-345
   Munin, 353
Synchronization variable, 325
Synchronous digital hierarchy, 44
Synchronous optical network, 44-45
Synchronous system, 214
System failure, 213-214

T

TAI (*see* International atomic time)
TCP (*see* Transmission control protocol)
TCP/IP server
   Amoeba, 427-428
TDMA (*see* Time division multiple access)
Team model, 183
Template
   DCE, 532
Thread, 169-185
   Amoeba, 391-392
   Chorus, 479, Chorus, 485-486
   DCE, 527-535
   interaction with RPC, 184-185
   kernel, 181-182
   Mach, 439-442
   pop-up, 185
   user space, 178-181
Thread package, 174-178
Thread scheduling, Mach, 442-445
Thread synchronization, DCE, 530-531
Ticket, security, 558-559
Ticket granting server, 557
Tight-coupled system, 9-10

Time clerk, 543
Time division multiple access, 231-234, 238-240
Time ordering
   consistent, 108
   global, 108
Time provider, 544
Time server, 543
Time service, DCE, 540-544
Time-triggered protocol, 232-234
Time-triggered system, 227
Timer, 120
Timer management, 94-95
Timestamps, 156-168
TMR (*see* Triple modular redundancy)
Token ring, 230-231
Token ring mutual exclusion, 138-139
TP0, 41
Trampoline mechanism, Mach, 471
Transaction, 255-256
   atomic, 144-158
   implementation, 150-154
   nested, 149-150
Transfer policy, 200
Transient fault, 212
Transmission control protocol, 41
Transparency, 22-25
   concurrency, 24
   location, 23, 251
   migration, 23
   naming, 251
   parallelism, 24
   replication, 24, 268-269
Transport layer, 40-41
Trends, file system, 279-285
Triple modular redundancy, 215-217
Tuple space, 359-361
Two-army problem, 219-220
Two-level naming, 252
Two-phase commit protocol, 153-154
Two-phase locking, 155
Two-phase locking, strict, 155

U

UDP (*see* Universal datagram protocol)
UI (*see* Unique identifier, Chorus)
UMA multiprocessor, 308
Uncommitted file, 417
Unicasting, 100
Unique identifier, Chorus, 480
Unique user identifier, 554

Universal coordinated time, 126, 543-544
Universal datagram protocol, 41
UNIX emulation
    Chorus, 499-506
    Mach, 471-472
UNIX file semantics, 253-254
Unsolicited message, 267
Upcall, 183
Update protocol, 270-272
Upload/download model, 247
UTC (*see* Universal coordinated time)
UUID (*see* Unique user identifier)

V

V-node, 276
Virtual memory,
    Chorus, 490-495
    Mach, 446-449
Virtual uniprocessor, 19
Virtually synchronous system, 111
Voting algorithm, 270-271
Voting with ghosts, 271

W

Wait-die algorithm, 164
WAN (*see* Wide area network)
Weak consistency, 325-327
Wide area network, 2, 283-284
Workstation
    diskful, 186-188
    diskless, 186-188
    home, 191
    using idle, 189-193
Workstation model, 186-189
WORM device (*see* Write once read many device)
Wormhole routing, 305
Wound-wait algorithm, 165
Write once read many device, 280
Write quorum, 271
Write-on-close caching, 266
Write-once protocol, 296
Write-through cache, 11, 265-266
Write-through protocol, 295
Writeahead log, 152-153
WWV, 126-127

X

X.25, 40
X/Open directory server, 552
X/Open object management, 552
XDS (*see* X/Open directory server)
XOM (*see* X/Open object management)

Y

Yellow pages, 275